W9-CFI-449

2

CRIMINALISTICS
and
SCIENTIFIC
INVESTIGATION

FREDERICK CUNLIFFE
Northeastern University

Peter B. Piazza
Northeastern University

PRENTICE-HALL, INC., Englewood Cliffs, New Jersey 07632

Library of Congress Cataloging in Publication Data

CUNLIFFE, FREDERICK,
 Criminalistics and scientific investigation.

 (Prentice-Hall series in criminal justice)
 Bibliography: p.
 Includes index.
 1. Criminal investigation. 2. Crime laboratories.
3. Chemistry, Forensic. 4. Evidence, Criminal.
I. Piazza, Peter B.,   joint author. II. Title.
HV8073.C78   364.12   79-22196
ISBN 0-13-193284-5

PRENTICE-HALL SERIES IN CRIMINAL JUSTICE
James D. Stinchcomb, *Editor*

Editorial/production supervision by Pamela Wilder
Cover design by Mario Piazza
Manufacturing buyer: John Hall

Printed in the United States of America
10 9 8 7 6 5 4 3 2 1

Prentice-Hall International, Inc., *London*
Prentice-Hall of Australia Pty. Limited, *Sydney*
Prentice-Hall of Canada, Ltd., *Toronto*
Prentice-Hall of India Private Limited, *New Delhi*
Prentice-Hall of Japan, Inc., *Tokyo*
Prentice-Hall of Southeast Asia Pte. Ltd., *Singapore*
Whitehall Books Limited, *Wellington, New Zealand*

CONTENTS

PREFACE

Criminalistics is the use of scientific methods of observation and analysis to detect and interpret physical evidence. It is a field that has often been relegated to a position of secondary importance in the area of criminal investigation partly through the ignorance of many investigators of the capabilities of the crime laboratory, partly through professional jealousy, and partly through the very human reluctance to change traditional habits of mind.

Although many of these attitudes continue to exist, law enforcement agencies have become increasingly aware in recent years of the value of criminalistics and other scientific aids to investigation. Laws passed out of a concern for the constitutional rights of individuals have imposed restrictions on the ways police officers may deal with suspects. Criminals are less likely to confess when apprehended by the police than they used to be; consequently, investigators are being forced to learn how to exploit physical evidence.

This book is designed to serve as an introductory level text to the field of criminalistics and scientific investigation. It is directed primarily at students engaged in college level criminal justice programs. Its aim is to acquaint future investigators with the basic practices and capabilities of the crime laboratory and to instruct them in the proper ways of

collecting and processing physical evidence so that the crime laboratory can take full advantage of its probative value.

The book assumes that most of the students taking the course do
not have a strong scientific background; therefore, the early chapters
are devoted to simple explanations of the fundamental technical concepts necessary for an understanding of the analytical methods of criminalistics. The bulk of the book discusses individual types of evidence
and how they are handled both in the field and in the laboratory. In
addition, there are separate chapters on crime scene investigation, especially as it pertains to the handling of physical evidence, and technical investigative aids such as photography, voice prints, and lie
detection.

The authors wish to express their sincere thanks to the following
people for their time and effort involved in the critical reading of
various parts of the manuscript and for helping to assemble illustrative
materials: Charles J. Porfert, Dr. Samuel J. Golub, Leo Barish, Seth
Bredbury, Geoffrey H. Purdy, Dr. Pierre Smith, Archie Brodsky, LTC
Robert S. Collins, Jr., Michael P. Kradz, David Brody, Garrett M. Shee-
han, Dr. Michael J. Camp, and Marshall K. Robinson.

CHAPTER ONE

— INTRODUCTION —

PHYSICAL EVIDENCE

It is almost impossible for a person to commit a crime without leaving some kind of evidence of the act. In a great number of cases the evidence that brings a criminal to justice is testimonial in nature. That is, the criminal is identified by the victim or some other eyewitness, the criminal is betrayed by an informer, or the criminal is induced to confess. Since so many routine crimes are quickly solved by such human testimony, many investigators have tended to overrely on it. Indeed, the ability to make sense out of the confused recollections of witnesses and elicit the truth from evasive suspects is one of the most valuable assets an investigator can possess.

Often, however, testimonial evidence is simply not available. If the victim is dead or if it is a crime against property and there are no witnesses, the only evidence available to the investigator is physical evidence. Also, as our society has become increasingly conscious of the individual rights of suspects, legal constraints on the kinds of testimony that are admissible in court have led investigators to make more and more use of the silent testimony of physical evidence.

What do we mean then when we talk about physical evidence? No easy narrow definition is possible because under the proper circum-

1

stances almost any object, substance, trace, or impression could constitute physical evidence. It is a matter of things rather than people or words. Anything that proves that a crime has taken place or that serves to identify criminals, trace them, or associate them with their crimes is a form of physical evidence. Evidence which proves that a crime has occurred is *corpus delicti* evidence. *Corpus delicti* is a Latin phrase meaning "the essential elements of the crime." In a homicide the body of the victim would constitute such evidence; in a burglary it might be a rifled cashbox or blown safe.

A person cannot commit a crime without performing some kind of activity. Whether such activity is violent or gentle, there is a good chance that criminals will either leave something at the scene or take something away from it that can help connect them to the crime. Perhaps the best known example of physical evidence is fingerprints, which a person can leave simply by touching something. Tool marks, shoe prints, tire marks, and other impressions found at a crime scene can implicate a suspect if the object that made the impression is found in his or her possession. Similarly, a firearm found in the possession of a suspect can associate the suspect with a murder if the markings on test bullets fired from the firearm match the markings on the bullets taken from the victim's body. Many materials of which the criminal is completely unaware can be transferred between the criminal and the victim or the scene. For example, it is often necessary to break glass to make an illegal entry. If particles of glass are discovered adhering to a suspect's clothing, the glass particles can be compared with the remaining glass of the scene. Chips of paint, splinters of wood, soil, and metallic fragments can be used in the same way. When a person makes physical contact with a victim or an object during the commission of a crime, he or she may pick up hairs, fibers, or traces of blood or other body fluids and take them away from the crime scene. Conversely, criminals may leave similar traces from their own persons at the scene.

The items mentioned above are some typical examples of physical evidence that an investigator may encounter. They can be examined with regard to both their *class* characteristics and their *individual* characteristics. The class characteristics serve to categorize the evidence itself. A tire impression may be identified as having been made by a certain make and model of tire on the basis of the tread pattern. A murder weapon may be identified as a caliber .38 special on the basis of the diameter and weight of the bullet. Neither of these identifies a specific tire or weapon, but it does narrow them down to a limited class within the overall categories of tires and firearms. Individual characteristics are those that identify a specific item or person. Through wear, a tire will develop nicks and irregularities in the tread that will differentiate it from all other tires, and each gun barrel will impart its own unique pattern of striations to the bullets it fires. Although the class characteristics are useful, the greatest value of physical evidence lies in its ability to individualize. The more individual characteristics an item has, the smaller the probability is that it can occur twice in the same form. For example, a bit of white cotton fiber found under a victim's fingernail would be of relatively little value because cotton is present in so many fabrics, whereas a clear fingerprint found on a murder weapon can be of great value because it is unique. The ideal bit of evidence would be one that identifies a specific person as the guilty party. Unfortunately, the ideal case seldom occurs. Even the fingerprint on the murder weapon only proves that a certain individual handled the weapon, not that the individual committed the murder.

Every investigator should understand that physical evidence cannot prove identity with absolute certainty but only within varying degrees of probability. Even fingerprints, which are generally considered to be positive proof of identity when they match, can be accepted as such only because of the high probability that no two fingers will ever have identical prints. To illustrate the point, let us assume for the sake of argument that there is a probability of 1 in 20 that two people will have any one matching identification point in the same location on the same respective finger. Since the probability is 1 in 20 of any single point matching, the chance of any two points matching would be 1 in 400 (20 X 20) and the chances of any three points matching would be 1 in 8,000 (20 X 20 X 20). In most jurisdictions, 8 to 12 matching points of comparison are considered positive identification. So continuing with our assumed probability of 1 in 20 for one matching point, the probability of two people's having eight matching points is 1 in 25,600,000,000; or to look at the situation from a different angle, a person would have to screen approximately six times the population of the world before finding another person having a fingerprint that matched one of his or hers in only eight points. The possibility of two people's having a matching fingerprint or even an entire matching set still exists, but because of the astronomical probabilities against it, it is remote to the point of mathematical absurdity. Experience has so far corroborated the probability calculations. In all the millions of fingerprint examinations that have been carried out throughout the world, no two prints have ever been found to match.

In actual investigations it is very unusual to collect usable fingerprints at a crime scene. In a planned crime the criminal is careful not to leave any fingerprints, and when they are left they tend to be smudged or incomplete. But even if no other single piece of evidence is likely to have the same positive identification value as fingerprints, other forms of evidence can work in combination with each other to narrow down the range of possible suspects. We can illustrate this with a hypothetical case. A crime is committed in a city that has a population of 1 million people. Investigators at the scene find a combination of textile fibers which indicate that the criminal wore a certain type of jacket. If 5,000 jackets of that type had been sold in the city, one person in 200 would be expected to own one. Let us assume that the criminal discarded a cigarette butt at the scene. From the saliva on the butt the crime laboratory determines that the criminal has type B blood. It is known through statistical sampling that 14 percent of the population of the United States has type B blood; therefore, 140,000 people in the city of 1 million, or 1 in 7, will have type B blood. The number of people having a jacket matching the fibers of the jacket found at the crime and having type B blood would be one in 1,400 (7 X 200). Finally, let us say that the criminal broke a window to gain access to the crime scene and that a suspect is found who has glass particles in his pants cuff which have the same physical characteristics as the glass of the broken window. It is impossible to assess the probable number of people who would have glass particles of the same type on their person, but 1 in 1,000 would seem to be a conservative estimate. If the same suspect also has type B blood and a jacket of the type identified, it would be highly probable that he is the culprit, because the chances against finding a second person possessing all these elements (jacket, blood, and glass) would be 1 in 1,400,000 (200 X 7 X 1,000). This results in a probability of 99.99993 percent that the suspect in custody is the only person in that city who fits all the items of evidence (1/1,400,000 = 0.00007%; 100 − 0.00007 = 99.99993). This presents a very convincing case that that person is the criminal.

The problem with using probabilities is that, because of a lack of statistical sampling, it is usually difficult or impossible to assign the precise probability of occurrence of a given item of evidence. As in the example of the glass in the pants cuff in the above hypothetical problem, there is often simply no way of taking a population sampling of the phenomenon in question. For this reason, courts are very reluctant to allow any such explicit reasoning on the basis of probabilities. The way probability works for us in actual practice usually comes down to a matter of common sense and experience. Even when numerical values cannot be assigned, probability does come into play in certain kinds of expert testimony. For example, the fact that a bullet removed from a homicide victim was a Remington .45 ACP would not be very helpful because there are so many of them in existence. The bullet becomes useful as evidence when the microscopic striations made on it by the barrel can be compared with the striations on a test bullet fired from a suspect pistol. The comparison is made visually under a microscope and if there is a clear match, it is immediately obvious that the pistol is the murder weapon. We know from experience that nature tends never to duplicate random phenomena; therefore, our common sense tells us that the probability of there being another pistol that creates the exact same striation pattern is so small as to be virtually impossible.

CRIMINALISTICS

Unlike the evidence of human testimony, physical evidence never lies, evades, or forgets, but for it to be of any use its significance has to be understood and related to the investigation. It is here that criminalistics and the crime laboratory play their role. *Criminalistics* is the use of scientific methods of observation and analysis to detect and interpret physical evidence. The scientists who do this work are called *criminalists*. The qualifications of a criminalist depend largely on the requirements of the individual crime laboratory. Each crime laboratory serves a community, and the laboratory must be tailored to fit that community's needs. For example, if 80 percent of the investigations conducted by a certain police force involve drugs, then it is obvious that the training and expertise of the criminalists in that laboratory must be weighted toward drug analysis.

However, even though there is a natural tendency for crime laboratories to specialize in the areas they are most often called upon to handle, it is a mistake for a laboratory to become overspecialized. Since almost everything can become physical evidence at one time or another, scientific investigation can encompass many different facets of science, including elements of physics, chemistry, biology, geology, and metallurgy. For this reason, it is desirable for the criminalist to be something of a scientific generalist. The criminalist should have a solid background in one of the natural sciences, preferably chemistry or physics, and enough flexibility and natural inquisitiveness to pick up a basic knowledge of the other scientific disciplines, at least to the degree necessary to perform and understand the common evidentiary tests and examinations.

There are many advantages to such generalized knowledge. Very often several different kinds of scientific examinations will have to be conducted in the investigation of a single crime. Frequently in such cases no single item of evidence will have sufficient individuality to identify the criminal, but the accumulated weight of several items can point to the guilt of an individual with a very high degree of probability.

If one person in the crime laboratory can conduct, or at least oversee, the various examinations, he or she will be able to pull all the threads together to construct a coherent case. In addition, this capability makes for a powerful courtroom presentation. If one person can testify on all the diverse scientific elements of a case, he or she can make a jury see how the elements all fit together much more effectively than can several criminalists testifying on isolated aspects. Of course, in larger laboratories in which the case loads are heavy it is inevitable that criminalists will have to specialize, but even then it is essential that each one understands the others' fields.

Perhaps the most important advantage of a general scientific background is the ability that it gives criminalists to adapt their inquiries to meet new and unforeseen circumstances. All of the techniques mentioned in this book were first devised by people who made imaginative use of their scientific knowledge to meet a certain need. Criminalistics is a growing field in which there is still a great need for innovative thinking.

In addition to knowledge, a criminalist must possess scientific integrity. As we pointed out earlier, physical evidence does not lie. It is possible, however, for it to be misinterpreted. Most crime laboratories in the United States work for the law enforcement establishment of their state or community. Unfortunately, under those circumstances criminalists often feel pressured to support the prosecuting attorney's case, and sometimes this pressure causes them to see things in the evidence that are not there. There was one case in which several criminalists employed by the state testified that they had each independently come to the conclusion that the bullets removed from the body of the murder victim came from a rifle owned by the defendant. In the meanwhile, the members of the defense team were quietly laughing because a representative of the firm that made the rifle was present in court with documentary evidence that the rifle in question had not been manufactured at the time of the crime. The prosecuting witnesses were not lying; they really thought the bullets had come from the rifle, but they had become so convinced that the defendant was guilty that they had allowed their bias to interfere with their scientific judgment. The result was detrimental not only to their case but also to their own reputations. Some states have eliminated this problem by creating an independent laboratory which is equally available to both the prosecution and the defense. But regardless of the lines of authority, the criminalist must let the evidence speak for itself. It is just as much the responsibility of the criminalist to exculpate the innocent as it is to incriminate the guilty.

There is no single right or wrong way to set up a crime laboratory. Its size and organization depend on the nature of the community it serves, the amount of funding available, the expected case load, and the space available. It is obvious that a laboratory serving a densely populated industrial state or a large city that has a high crime rate will have very different requirements from one supporting a predominately agricultural state or a small community. The following are some of the general capabilities that crime laboratories should possess. The capabilities of the larger laboratories will naturally be more extensive.

Photography Section

This section should include the camera and illumination equipment for crime scene photography, a studio for in-house photography, and sufficient darkroom facilities to provide for the processing of all the photographic work done by the laboratory.

Evidence Storage Section

This section should provide a secure area for storing the evidence and a receiving procedure for maintaining accountability of all items of evidence and ensuring the continuity of the chain of custody.

Identification Section

This section should provide the capability of recording the fingerprints of individuals both inside and outside the laboratory, searching for and recording fingerprints at crime scenes and on evidence brought into the laboratory, and classifying and filing ten-finger print cards. Larger laboratories may want to maintain single-finger files on known local criminals. The identification section may also include the capability of making and examining casts of tool marks and tire and foot impressions.

Chemistry Section

Although traditional techniques of "wet" chemistry analysis are giving way to instrumental methods, the crime laboratory still needs a chemistry capability for a variety of tests and examinations. The chemistry section might include drug analysis, toxicology, examination of blood and other body fluids, and serial number restoration. The large volume of work in certain areas might justify the larger laboratories having separate sections for drugs, serology, and toxicology.

General Examination Section

This section should be closely allied to the chemistry section and there would be many areas of overlap. The section should contain the capability for the various types of microscopic examinations, for document examinations, and for examinations and comparisons of the physical properties of such items as glass, soil, paint, metal, explosive residues, hairs, and fibers. Again, if there is a large volume of work in any particular area, that area might constitute a separate section on its own. It is often desirable, for example, to have a separate section for the various aspects of document and ink examinations.

Firearms Section

This section should provide the capability to identify firearms, bullets, and shell cases and to associate spent bullets with the weapon that fired them. There should be a shooting room and an examination area for firing test bullets and comparing powder and shot patterns for distance determinations. This section should work in coordination with the chemistry and photography sections.

Instrument Section

This section may be rather limited or very extensive, depending on the degree of instrumental sophistication of the laboratory. The size and layout of this section, of course, depend on the instruments the laboratory has. Following are some of the instruments likely to be found in crime laboratories (only the most sophisticated laboratories would have all of these): gas chromatograph,[1] emission spectrograph, infrared, ultraviolet, and atomic absorption spectrophotometers, X-ray diffraction unit, mass spectrometer, thin-layer chromatography and electrophoresis equipment, polygraph, and sound spectrograph.

Crime Scene Search Section

The matter of who should go to the crime scene and collect the physical evidence is often a source of controversy. Investigating officers tend to feel that anything to do with a crime scene falls under their authority, but, for the most part, investigators do not have sufficient training in the procedures for collecting evidence so that it is preserved uncontaminated for laboratory examination. This is to a large extent so because they do not understand criminalistics. Many police forces are

[1]The instruments and their functions are explained in Chapter 4 or as they arise in the text.

now beginning to develop teams of criminalists or specially trained investigators responsible to the crime laboratory whose job it is to go to crime scenes, detect and collect the evidence in a professional manner, and bring it back to the laboratory. Only big city and state laboratories have sufficient case loads to justify this kind of manpower expenditure. But where such teams exist, the output of the laboratory is so much more effective that it saves manpower in other areas because it reduces the need for much investigative footwork. It is clear that many of these functions of the crime laboratory overlap each other and that in different laboratories these functions will be organized in different combinations. When laboratories do not have certain facilities, they usually have someplace they can go to to get special jobs done. The Federal Bureau of Investigation offers its laboratory services to police forces, but there is normally a long wait for the services. Many laboratories have working relationships with local hospitals, the medical examiner's office, and nearby universities for examinations that are beyond their scope.

Review Questions

1. Which of the following are examples of physical evidence?
   a. Soil adhering to a suspect's shoes
   b. An accusation by a neighbor
   c. Hair found under a victim's fingernails
   d. Broken glass found in a suspect's trouser cuff
   e. All the above
   f. a, c, and d
2. The nicks and irregularities caused by wear in a tire tread
   a. Are class characteristics
   b. Form identical patterns on front and rear tires mounted on the same side
   c. Reveal the make, model, and year of a car
   d. Are individual characteristics
3. (T, F) A fingerprint found at a crime scene constitutes proof that the person who made the print is guilty.
4. (T, F) Investigators rarely find useful fingerprint evidence at a crime scene.
5. Some of the desirable qualifications of a criminalist are
   a. A knowledge of at least two foreign languages
   b. A background in science
   c. An ability to adapt to new situations
   d. Scientific integrity

    e. a, b, and d

    f. b, c, and d

6. (T, F) If some of the evidence points to a suspect's innocence and other evidence points to a suspect's guilt, the criminalist should use only the incriminating evidence.

7. In general, criminalists should
   a. Find out who the prosecuter thinks is guilty so that they can make the evidence support the prosecutor's case
   b. Ignore class characteristics
   c. Let the evidence speak for itself
   d. All the above

CHAPTER TWO

— *BASIC SCIENTIFIC* — *CONCEPTS*

Although students do not need a strong scientific background to use this textbook, there are certain scientific concepts underlying laboratory procedures and instruments that are fundamental to any understanding of criminalistics. Everything that a criminalist deals with is *matter*. Matter is the material of which everything in the universe is made. By definition, matter is anything that has mass and occupies space. It can exist as solids, liquids, or gases. Every form of matter has physical and chemical properties that differentiate it from all other forms. *Chemical properties* are the behavioral characteristics of matter as it changes from one substance to another. For example, hydrogen (H_2) and Oxygen (O_2) are separate substances. When hydrogen burns, it combines with oxygen to form a third substance, water (H_2O). The ability of hydrogen to combine with oxygen is one of its chemical properties. *Physical properties* are the characteristics and behavior of a substance that do not involve chemical changes. They can be affected by outside influences such as temperature and pressure, but the substance remains the same. Some of the physical properties of water are that at normal atmospheric pressure it is a solid at temperatures below 0°C, a liquid from 0°C to 100°C, and a gas at temperatures above 100°C. Regardless of these changes in physical state, it still remains H_2O. It is by observing and quantifying chemical and physical properties that scientists can identify the myriad forms of matter and compare them with each other.

MEASUREMENT

All forms of matter can be measured in some way. The basic units of most concern to us are length, mass, volume, and temperature. While the United States still uses the English system of measurements (feet, pounds, quarts, etc.) in most phases of everyday life, the scientific community here and around the world uses the metric system as the standard of all measurements and calculations. Most of the measurements in this book are given in metric units, except in a few cases in which popular usage of the English units continues to prevail. The major advantage of the metric system is that it operates in units of tens, thereby eliminating the need to convert to similar units (i.e., feet to inches, pounds to ounces, etc.).

Length

The basic metric unit of length is the *meter* (m), which is based on an official standard bar of platinum-iridium kept at the International Bureau of Weights and Measures in Sèvres, France. It is equivalent to 1.094 yards. All other units of length in the metric system are expressed in relation to the meter and are designated according to the series of standard prefixes shown in Table 2–1. Thus, a *kilo*meter is a thousand meters; a *mega*meter is a million meters; a *deci*meter is one-tenth of a meter; a *centi*meter is one-hundredth of a meter; a *milli*meter is one-thousandth of a meter, and so on. These prefixes are constant throughout the metric system and always represent the same relationship to the basic unit.

Mass

The basic unit of mass is the *kilogram* (kg), which is based on a standard block of platinum kept at the International Bureau of Weights and Measures in Sèvres, France. In chemistry most measurements of mass are based on the *gram* (g), which is one-thousandth of a kilogram. One gram equals 0.0022 pound and there are 453.6 grams in 1 pound. Although mass and weight are often used interchangeably, they are not quite the same thing. Mass refers to the amount of matter a substance contains and always remains constant. The weight of a substance is a function of its mass and the force of gravity. If gravity changes, then the

TABLE 2–1. Prefixes Used in the Metric System to Show Relationships to Basic Units

Prefix	Meaning	Example
mega- (M)	1 million times the basic unit	1 megagram (Mg) = 1,000,000 g
kilo- (k)	1 thousand times the basic unit	1 kiloliter (kl) = 1,000 l
deci- (d)	1 tenth the basic unit	1 decimeter (dm) = 0.1 m
centi- (c)	1 hundredth the basic unit	1 centigram (cg) = 0.01 g
milli- (m)	1 thousandth the basic unit	1 milliliter (ml) = 0.001 l
micro- (μ)*	1 millionth the basic unit	1 micrometer (μm) = 0.000001 m
nano- (n)	1 billionth the basic unit	1 nanogram (ng) = 0.000000001 g

*Greek letter mu

weight changes, but the mass remains the same. At mean sea level on earth mass and weight are identical, and for the purpose of this textbook they can be considered virtually the same. The mass of a substance is determined by balancing it against objects of known mass.

Volume

The basic unit of volume is the *liter* (l). One liter is 1.06 quarts. Volume can also be expressed in cubic terms. A cubic meter (m^3) is the volume of a cube measuring 1 meter on each edge. A liter is one-tenth of a cubic meter, or 1 cubic decimeter (dm^3). Small volumes are frequently expressed in terms of cubic centimeters (cm^3 or cc) or milliliters (ml). The two terms mean the same thing and can be used interchangeably.

Temperature

In the metric system temperature is expressed in degrees Celsius, or centigrade (C). The Celsius scale is based on the freezing point and boiling point of water at sea level. The freezing (and melting) point of water is 0°C (or 32° Fahrenheit) and the boiling point is 100°C (212° Fahrenheit). The relationship between the Fahrenheit scale and the Celsius scale is shown by the following equations:

$$°C = \frac{5}{9}(F - 32) \qquad °F = \frac{9}{5}°C + 32$$

The basic unit of heat energy in the metric system is the calorie (cal), which is the amount of heat needed to raise the temperature of 1 cm^3 of water by 1°C.

We have mentioned that matter can take the form of solids, liquids, and gases, but that does not tell what matter is actually made of. The purpose of this section is to give the student who has little scientific background a fundamental understanding of the nature of matter and how different forms of matter interact with each other to produce the world we live in.

Atoms

The basic building block of all substances is the atom. It is the smallest unit of matter that retains a unique and constant chemical identity. Atoms are themselves made up of various subatomic particles, the most important of which for our purposes are *protons, neutrons,* and *electrons.* Almost the entire mass of an atom resides in its nucleus, which is made up of protons and neutrons. Protons and neutrons have identical masses, but each proton bears a positive electrical charge while neutrons have no charge. Electrons are relatively tiny particles of almost negligible mass which fly around the nucleus in series of energy levels called *shells.* Although these shells are usually depicted as two-dimensional orbits similar to those of planets revolving around the sun, electrons actually move so rapidly in all directions that they form three-dimensional clouds around the nucleus. Each electron bears a negative electrical charge which is equal and opposite to the charge of a proton. When an atom has the same number of orbital electrons as protons in the nucleus, the positive and negative charges balance each other and the atom is electrically neutral.

Figure 2–1 illustrates a few common atoms. We can see that they differ from each other in the number of protons, neutrons, and electrons. The neutrons add to the mass of an atom, but they do not affect its chemical properties.

Molecules

The atoms shown in Figure 2–1 are electrically balanced because they have the same number of electrons as protons, but they are chemically unstable. The reason for the chemical instability lies in the arrangement of the electrons in the outermost shell. Each of the electron shells surrounding an atom is capable of holding a certain number of electrons and no more. As the atoms increase in size, each shell fills to capacity and then a new shell forms. The 1 shell, that is, the shell closest to the nucleus, is capable of holding two electrons and is stable only

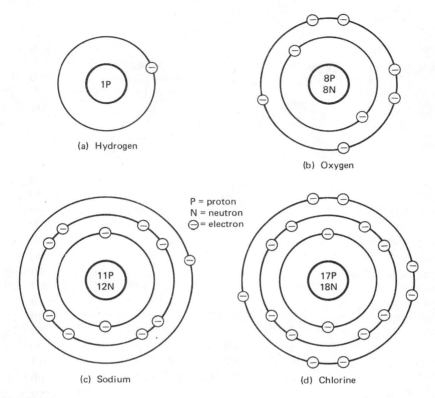

(a) Hydrogen

(b) Oxygen

P = proton
N = neutron
⊖ = electron

(c) Sodium

(d) Chlorine

FIGURE 2–1

when it is filled. The 2 shell can hold a total of eight electrons and it too is most stable when it is filled. Although the 3 shell[1] can hold more than eight electrons in the heavier atoms, in the lighter atoms that we are considering here, eight is the most stable arrangement. When the outer shell contains fewer than its most stable arrangement of electrons, the atom tends to be chemically unstable. Such atoms seek stability by combining with other atoms. When two or more atoms combine with each other, they form a molecule. For example, the hydrogen atom that has only one electron cannot exist alone, but it can combine with another hydrogen atom to form a *diatomic*[2] molecule, hydrogen gas (H_2), as illustrated in Figure 2–2(a), and two atoms of hydrogen can

[1]Electron shells are sometimes designated K, L, M, etc. instead of 1, 2, 3, etc.

[2]Diatomic molecules are those formed by a combination of two atoms of the same kind. Many common gases exist in diatomic form, such as oxygen (O_2) nitrogen (N_2), and chlorine (Cl_2).

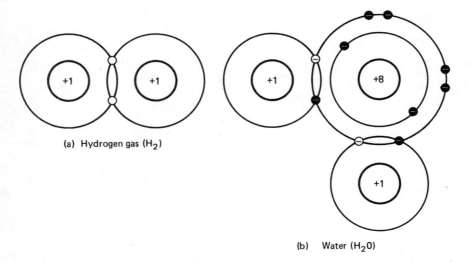

(a) Hydrogen gas (H_2)

(b)   Water (H_2O)

FIGURE 2–2

combine with one atom of oxygen to form a molecule of water (H_2O), as shown in Figure 2–2(b). In both of these cases the atoms have shared electrons with other atoms in order to fill each other's outer shells. This is known as a *covalent bond.* Molecules can also be formed by a transfer of electrons from one atom to another, as in the case of sodium and chlorine. Sodium has one electron in its outer shell; chlorine has seven. When the two atoms combine chemically to form a molecule of sodium chloride (see Figure 2–3), or common salt, the sodium donates its one electron to fill the chlorine 3 shell. When the sodium atom gives up its electron, it becomes positively charged since it now has more protons

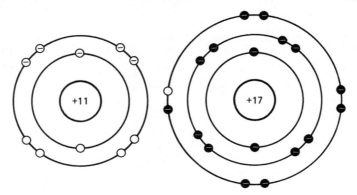

FIGURE 2–3 Sodium chloride.

TABLE 2–2. Some Common Elements and Their Symbols

Element	Symbol	Element	Symbol
hydrogen	H	sulfur	S
carbon	C	chlorine	Cl
nitrogen	N	potassium	K
oxygen	O	iron	Fe
sodium	Na	copper	Cu

than electrons. Similarly, the chlorine atom becomes negatively charged by gaining an extra electron, and the molecule is held together by electrical attraction. When an atom gains or loses electrons and becomes electrically charged, it is called an *ion*. Molecules formed in this manner are held together by *ionic bonds*.

Elements and Compounds

The chemical differences between atoms are a function of the number of protons in their nuclei. The number of protons an atom contains is the *atomic number* of that atom. Hydrogen, with one proton in its nucleus, has an atomic number of 1. Helium, with two protons, has an atomic number of 2, and so on. Any substance that is made up entirely of atoms having the same atomic number is called an *element*. Scientists have identified some 105 different elements, but only a relatively small number of these make up the majority of materials we encounter in everyday life. In chemical notation every element is represented by a chemical symbol of one or two letters. Table 2–2 lists some common elements and their symbols. The symbols which do not seem to be related to the name of the element are usually taken from the Latin or Greek names.

When two or more elements combine with each other chemically, the result is a *compound*. The two elements hydrogen and oxygen can combine to form the compound water; similarly, the elements sodium and chlorine can combine to form the compound salt. The process of chemical combination is called a *reaction*, and scientists express reactions by using the chemical symbols in the form of equations, as:

$$2Na \quad + \quad Cl_2 \quad \rightarrow \quad 2NaCl$$
$$\text{sodium} \quad \quad \text{chlorine} \quad \text{yields} \quad \text{sodium chloride}$$

$$2H_2 \quad + \quad O_2 \quad \rightarrow \quad 2H_2O$$
$$\text{hydrogen} \quad \quad \text{oxygen} \quad \text{yields} \quad \text{water}$$

Note that the total number of atoms must balance on both sides of the equation so that when two molecules of hydrogen react with one molecule of oxygen to form two molecules of water, there are a total of four hydrogen atoms and two oxygen atoms involved.

Chemical reactions can take place between two or more elements, between elements and compounds, and between two or more compounds. Also, compounds can be decomposed to their constituent elements. Whenever a chemical reaction takes place, it is always accompanied by a gain or loss of energy in the form of heat, light, or electricity. Some energy is often needed to initiate a reaction which then releases more energy than it absorbs. Reactions that release more energy than they absorb are said to be *exothermic*. An explosion is a dramatic example of an exothermic reaction. A relatively small amount of energy in the form of heat from a fuse or detonator initiates a reaction which produces a tremendous amount of energy in the form of heat, light, and blast. A reaction that absorbs more energy than it releases is called *endothermic*. Water can be decomposed to hydrogen and oxygen by passing a direct current through it in the presence of an electrolyte. Since this reaction cannot take place without the absorption of electrical energy, it is endothermic.

Organic and Inorganic Compounds

The terms *organic* and *inorganic* occur frequently in this book because they are concepts with which criminalists continuously deal. Broadly speaking, organic chemistry is the chemistry of plant and animal compounds whose principal raw materials are petroleum, coal, wood, and animal matter. Since carbon is the main element in all these materials, organic chemistry is essentially the chemistry of carbon. Inorganic chemistry is everything else. The terms are sometimes used loosely and since inorganic materials form compounds with organic compounds, the distinction between the two is not always clear. Some of the organic compounds that criminalists encounter frequently are drugs, plastics, alcohol, organic solvents like chloroform and ether, petroleum products, most synthetic fibers, botanical material, and physiological material like blood and hair. Metals, minerals, and anything that does not contain carbon are inorganic compounds.

Solids, Liquids, and Gases

Matter can exist in the three states of solids, liquids, and gases. The difference between them is a function of the arrangement of atoms and molecules. Most substances can exist in all three states, depending on conditions of temperature and pressure. For example, water at normal pressure exists as a solid at temperatures below 0°C, as a liquid between 0°C and 100°C, and as a gas above 100°C. Solids are rigid and have a definite shape and volume. These characteristics are due to the fact that their atoms and molecules have a strong attraction for each other which causes them to be closely packed in relatively fixed positions. Many solids are crystalline in nature. That means their atoms are aligned in regular geometrical configurations called *crystal lattices.* Salt is one example of a crystalline solid. Its atoms are so arranged that each sodium atom is surrounded by six chlorine atoms, and each chlorine atom is surrounded by six sodium atoms. This arrangement is illustrated in Figure 2–4(a). All metals are crystalline in their solid state, and their lattices can take varied and sometimes complex forms. Figure 2–4(b) illustrates a lattice structure common to several metals, including chromium, tungsten, and some forms of iron. Some solids, for example glass, wax, and asphalt, are not crystalline in nature. Their atoms are distributed in completely random formation. Solids of this kind are said to be *amorphous,* which means shapeless.

When heat is applied to a solid, its atoms become excited and start moving apart from each other. They break out of their crystal lattices and move around in random directions, causing the material to lose its hardness and rigidity and to become able to flow. It is now a liquid. Liquids have a definite volume but they assume the shape of their container. In the liquid state the arrangement of atoms is always amorphous.

When sufficient heat is applied to convert a liquid to a gas, the atoms become even more excited and the distance between them becomes greater until the atoms are able to fly freely in all directions. Gases have neither shape nor fixed volume, but their volume can expand to fill a container. Unlike solids and liquids, the volume of gases is highly sensitive to changes in temperature and pressure. As the tem-

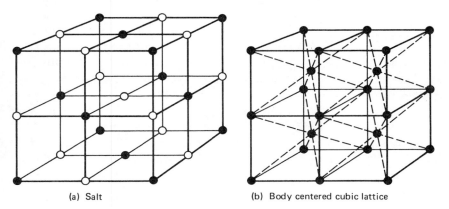

(a) Salt   (b) Body centered cubic lattice

FIGURE 2–4 Crystal lattice structures.

perature increases, the volume increases as long as the pressure remains constant. As the pressure increases, the volume decreases as long as the temperature remains constant.

Solutions and Suspensions

In general terms, a solution is a mixture of two or more substances whose molecules have approximately the same attraction for each other as they have for molecules of their own kind. In such mixtures the *solute* (the substance being dissolved) becomes thoroughly interspersed in equal concentration throughout the *solvent* (the substance in which the solute is dissolved). For example, methanol (wood alcohol) and ethanol (grain alcohol) both form solutions when mixed with water because the molecules of the alcohols and those of water are mutually attracted to each other, whereas gasoline and water separate into two layers because their molecules are mutually repellent. Many kinds of solutions are possible. Alcohol and water is an example of a liquid dissolved in a liquid. Air is a solution of various gases, mainly nitrogen and oxygen. Soda water is a solution of a gas in water. Metal alloys are solutions of metals in metals. Salt and sugar are solids that will dissolve in water.

Suspensions are mixtures which may look like solutions but which are actually dispersions of finely divided particles much larger than molecules throughout a medium. Many suspensions, like clay in water, will eventually settle if allowed to stand, but in some suspensions the particles are so small that they can actually be held in permanent dispersion by the constant bombardment of the molecules of the dispersing medium. Such small particles are called *colloids*. Most inks and paints, for example, are colloidal suspensions of solids in a liquid. Smoke is a colloidal suspension of a solid (carbon) in air.

Acids and Bases

Acids and bases play a large role in a criminalist's life. They are extremely important in drug examinations, and acids especially are used continuously in various aspects of evidence analysis. To understand acids and bases, we must first take another look at the nature of water. While we normally think of water as an aggregation of H_2O molecules, we can also think of it as a mixture of positive *hydrogen ions* (H^+) and negative *hydroxide ions* (OH^-).[3] In pure water there is an equal balance between H^+ and OH^- ions, and it is therefore said to be

---

[3]We learned earlier in this chapter (p. 17) that an ion is an atom that becomes electrically charged by gaining or losing electrons. Groups of atoms, like the OH group, can also carry charges. When they do, they are also referred to as ions.

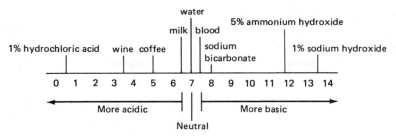

FIGURE 2–5 pH scale, showing approximate pH values for some common solutions.

neutral. Acids are compounds that release H^+ ions when dissolved in water, thereby increasing the concentration of H^+ ions over that of OH^- ions. For example, hydrogen chloride (HCl) is a gas that dissolves readily in water to become hydrochloric acid. In solution, the H^+ ion and the Cl^- ion become dissociated from each other and disperse freely throughout the water, thereby raising the relative H^+ ion concentration. Conversely, a base is a compound that causes the relative concentration of OH^- ions to be increased. Sodium hydroxide (NaOH) is an example of a strong base. When it dissolves in water, the Na^+ ion and the OH^- ion dissociate and raise the OH^- concentration of the mixture. Compounds having strong basic properties are cometimes called *alkalis*.

Acids and bases can be strong or weak; it depends on the extent to which they increase the respective H^+ and OH^- concentrations of a solution. The strength of acids and bases is measured in terms of pH values. The pH values are expressed in a scale ranging usually from 0 to 14, with the lower number being more acidic and the higher numbers being more basic (see Figure 2–5). Water, being neutral, has a pH value of 7.

Density

Mass and volume taken separately cannot be considered properties of matter because they do not help identify the matter. A gram of gold has exactly the same mass as a gram of water, and a cubic centimeter of iron has the same volume as a cubic centimeter of air. But when mass and volume are taken together, they bear a relationship to each other which is unique and constant for every substance at standard temperatures and pressure. This relationship of the mass of a substance to a unit of its volume is called *density* and is expressed by the equation:

$$\text{Density} = \frac{\text{Mass}}{\text{Volume}}$$

Mass is conventionally stated in terms of grams and the unit of volume used is the cubic centimeter. Thus, if 5 cm^3 of gold has a mass of 96.6 g, its density is 19.32.

$$D = \frac{96.6}{5} = 19.32$$

The mass of 1 cm^3 of water at 4°C and normal atmospheric pressure is 1 g. Therefore, the density of water is 1. Density is a physical property that is used frequently in criminalistics to help identify such solid items of evidence as glass, soil, paint, hairs, and fibers. If a solid sample is large enough to displace a measurable amount of water, its density can be determined by measuring its mass on a balance and dividing it by the volume of water displaced. However, criminalists often have to deal with samples whose volumes are too small to be measured by water displacement. In these cases density can be determined by comparison flotation methods. That is, the sample is placed into a test tube containing a heavy (high density) liquid such as bromoform (density 2.890). If the evidence sample is less dense than the liquid, as the items mentioned above normally are, the evidence sample floats on the surface. Then a lighter liquid, such as chlorobenzene (density 1.1066), is gradually mixed in until the evidence sample begins to sink. If it sinks to the bottom, more of the heavy liquid must be added. When the liquid mixture is such that the object being tested is held suspended in the middle, the density of the liquid is the same as that of the object and its density can be determined by immersing calibration beads (objects of known density) in the mixture. The bead that hangs suspended at the same level as the object is of the same density.

Criminalists normally use density to help determine if two similar items are from the same source—for example, a piece of broken glass taken from a suspect's clothing and broken glass remaining at the crime scene. Here, they are not interested in knowing the numerical, or absolute, density of the samples; they are interested only in observing how the samples compare to each other. To make the comparison, the criminalist prepares a liquid mixture of the same density as the known sample (i.e., that taken from the crime scene) and drops any unknown samples into the same mixture. If some of the unknowns float at the same level as the known, they are of the same density and the criminalist is on the way to making an identification. The samples should all be of approximately the same size because variations in surface tension can affect the result. Density alone is not sufficient to prove that two samples are of identical origin because different objects can have densities so close as to be indistinguishable from each other. All density determinations must be made under carefully controlled temperature conditions because the volume of liquids and gases can change significantly at different temperatures.

The Nature of Light

The behavior of light can be explained by two theories: the *quantum theory,* which holds that light is made up of tiny particles each having a measurable amount of energy, and the *wave theory,* which describes light as a continuous wave of energy. Although neither of these theories can explain all the effects of light, the wave theory is applicable to the optical principles used in microscopy and photography.

Like heat, radio waves, X-rays, gamma rays, and cosmic rays, light is part of the electromagnetic spectrum. These are all forms of radiant energy, which travel in a straight line at approximately 300,000,000 meters per second (186,000 miles per second) in a vacuum. This velocity is commonly referred to as the *speed of light.* These electromagnetic radiations differ from each other in frequency and wavelength. Although they travel in a straight line, their motion along that line is wavelike. This motion is depicted by a sine wave as in Figure 2–6. Frequency is the number of complete alternations, or *cycles,* that a wave makes in one second. The motion of the wave from *A* to *B* in Figure 2–6 is one cycle. The wavelength is the distance between the crests of the wave, that is, the distance from *C* to *D* in Figure 2–6. Frequency is inversely proportional to wavelength. The higher the frequency, the smaller the wavelength. The rays having higher frequencies and shorter wavelengths contain more energy than those having lower frequencies and longer wavelengths.

Visible light occupies a very small portion of the total electromagnetic spectrum (see Figure 2–7) between ultraviolet rays and infrared rays.

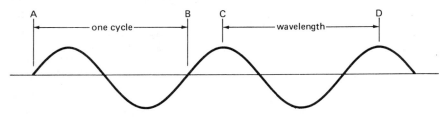

FIGURE 2–6 The wave motion of light.

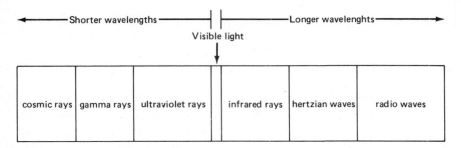

FIGURE 2–7   Electromagnetic spectrum.

Refraction

Light travels in straight lines without being deflected as long as the medium through which it passes is of a constant density. When light passes from a medium of one density into a medium of a heavier density, as from air into glass, the rays are slowed down by the denser medium. If the rays strike the surface of the denser medium obliquely (i.e., at an angle other than 90 degrees), the decrease in velocity causes the rays to be bent. This phenomenon is known as *refraction* (See Figure 2–8).

The degree to which a given medium changes the velocity of light is the *refractive index* of that medium. This is the ratio of the speed of light in a vacuum to the speed of light in the medium. For example, the speed of light in a vacuum is 300,000,000 meters per second and the speed of light in water is 225,000,000 meters per second; therefore, the refractive index of water is

$$\frac{300,000,000}{225,000,000} = 1.333$$

Dispersion

The total visible portion of the electromagnetic spectrum appears to us in the form of white light, that is, the light that comes from the sun

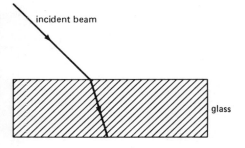

FIGURE 2–8   Refraction of light.

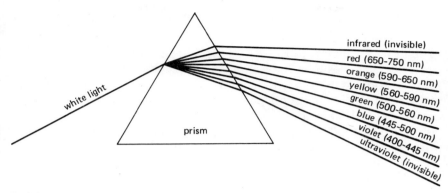

FIGURE 2-9

or from an ordinary light bulb. White light is, itself, a mixture of different wavelengths ranging from 400 nanometers (nm) to 750 nanometers. A nanometer is one-billionth of a meter. These radiations of different wavelengths make up what the eye perceives as colors. Light can be separated into its component colored wavelengths by passing a beam of white light through a prism. This separation of colors is known as *dispersion,* and it occurs because radiations of different wavelengths travel through the prism at different rates and are therefore refracted at different angles (see Figure 2-9). White light also contains invisible radiations which are dispersed at either end of the visible spectrum. The higher energy rays beyond the violet are *ultraviolet,* and the lower energy rays below the red are *infrared.*

Reflection and Absorption

Unless we look directly at the sun or at a light bulb, most of the light that we see is reflected off objects. It is the ability of objects to reflect light that enables us to see them and photograph them, for it is the light bouncing off them that enters the eye or the camera. However, most of the objects we see do not reflect all the wavelengths of visible light. They selectively absorb some wavelengths. When an object absorbs some wavelengths and reflects others, we perceive the object as colored. For example, if an object absorbs violet, blue, green, yellow, and orange and reflects red, we perceive that object as red because only the wavelengths in the red part of the visible spectrum enter our eyes. If an object reflects all the wavelengths of visible light, we see it as white; if it absorbs all the wavelengths, we see it as black. If it partially absorbs and partially reflects all the wavelengths in an equal mixture, we see it as gray. The different hues and shadings of colors that we see are made up of various mixtures of wavelengths.

Refractive Index as a Physical Property

Refractive index, which we have seen to be the ratio of the speed of light in a vacuum to the speed of light in a medium, is a physical property that is used in the crime laboratory in much the same way as density as an aid in the identification and comparison of evidence materials. It is used for the most part in the examination of solid evidence materials like broken glass, textile fibers, and hair. It is applicable to any substance that will transmit light. If hairs and fibers are heavily coated with dye pigments, they may not be susceptible to refractive index examinations.

If a transparent solid like clear glass is immersed in a liquid that has the same refractive index as the solid, the solid becomes invisible because it bends the light at the same angle as the liquid. If the liquid has a higher or lower refractive index, the glass is visible. When making refractive index determinations in the laboratory, the criminalist exploits this phenomenon by observing the optical behavior of the evidence when it is immersed in liquids of known refractive index. All these observations are conducted under a microscope; consequently, they can be used for the tiniest particles of evidence material that can be manipulated onto a microscope slide.

Like density, refractive index is a property that remains the same for a given material under constant conditions. However, it varies with changes in temperature. A rise in temperature lowers the refractive index of a substance and a decrease in temperature raises it. The change is significant in liquids and gases but it is almost negligible in solids. The refractive index of an evidence sample also varies with changes in the wavelength of the light used to illuminate it. When observed through a microscope, evidence samples tend to diffuse white light like a prism and thereby reduce the accuracy of refractive index determinations. To improve accuracy, the criminalist uses a *monochromatic* light source, that is, light transmitted at a single or very narrow wavelength band. Any wavelength can be used, but the one most commonly used is the sodium D band (589.0 nanometers and 589.6 nanometers), which is a very close pair of the wavelengths that sodium emits when it is burned. Sodium D light is used in preference to others because, being in the middle of the yellow portion of the visible spectrum, it appears bright to the human eye. If different wavelengths are used and the temperature remains constant, the refractive index value varies. As the wavelength increases (i.e., moves toward the red end of the spectrum), the refractive index decreases; as the wavelength decreases, the refractive index increases.

Refractive index examinations can be done in two ways: (1) by using a series of liquids of different indexes of refraction or (2) by varying the refractive index of a single liquid through controlled temperature changes.[4]

The first method is more time-consuming and less precise than the second, but it can be done with an ordinary compound microscope that has no special attachments and therefore may be more suitable to a smaller laboratory. A small fragment of the evidence sample is placed onto a microscope slide and immersed in a drop of liquid that has a refractive index somewhere close to that of the sample. There is some guesswork at this point, but most types of glass and fibers have refractive indexes in the range of from 1.47 to 1.65. The microscope is focused on a sharp edge of the sample and if it is of a different refractive index from the liquid, a light halo will be visible around the edge of the sample. This halo is known as the *Becke line*. To test whether the sample is of higher or lower refractive index than the liquid, the microscope focus is raised slightly. When this is done, the Becke line moves. If the sample has a higher index than the liquid, the Becke line moves toward the sample. After this is determined, the drop of liquid is removed by absorbing it with a bit of filter paper and new liquids are tried until one is found that has the same refractive index as the sample. In the last step it may be necessary to mix one liquid of slightly higher index with one of slightly lower index to arrive at one that matches the sample. All of these tests must be made at the same temperature.

As in the case of density determinations, the criminalist is normally not interested in knowing the absolute refractive index of a sample, but only in comparing an unknown with a known standard in order to connect a suspect with a crime scene. Once the appropriate liquid is found for the known standard, evidence samples can be tested in the same liquid and if one is found which matches, there is a good chance that it is from the same source as the standard.

The temperature control method requires the use of a hot-stage microscope (the stage is the platform on the microscope which holds the slide in place under the lens). A hot stage is one in which the temperature of the sample can be precisely controlled and held steady up to 100°C. Since the amount of change in refractive index per degree Celsius is known very exactly for each of the Cargille liquids (approximately 0.004), the precise temperature control makes for a very accurate method. A liquid is chosen that has a refractive index slightly higher than that of the sample at room temperature. This is determined as before by observing the movement of the Becke line when the focus is raised. The halo should move away from the sample. Then the micro-

---

[4]R. P. Cargille Laboratories, Inc., 55 Commerce Road, Cedar Grove, N.J. 07004 produces series of liquid mixtures that have accurately graduated refractive indexes.

scope stage is heated degree by degree until the Becke line disappears. The refractive index of the liquid at the final temperature is the refraction index of the sample. When doing comparison work, two samples, the known and an unknown, can be placed near each other without touching on the slide and observed simultaneously. If their Becke lines disappear at the same time, they have the same refractive index.

Review Questions

1. (T, F)   Matter is anything that has mass and occupies space.
2. Which of the following are examples of physical properties?
   a. Density
   b. Melting point
   c. Temperature
   d. Volume
   e. a and b
   f. a, b, and d
3. Which of the following belong to the metric system?
   a. Deciliters
   b. Photons
   c. cm^3
   d. Quarts
   e. All the above
   f. a and c
4. (T, F)   A cubic meter of lead would have the same mass on the moon that it has on Earth.
5. (T, F)   Protons, neutrons, and electrons have equal and opposite electrical charges.
6. H_2, O_2, and Cl_2 are examples of
   a. Chemically unstable molecules
   b. Diatomic gases
   c. Atoms
   d. Salts
7. When an atom becomes electrically charged by gaining or losing an electron, it is known as
   a. An ion
   b. An element
   c. An isomer
   d. Covalent

8. Name the elements represented by the following symbols: O, Na, H, K, Fe, S, I, and C

9. Reactions that release more energy than they absorb are said to be _____.

10. Which of the following compounds are inorganic?
    a. CO_2
    b. NaCl
    c. H_2SO_4
    d. $C_{12}H_{22}O_{11}$
    e. a, b, and c
    f. b and c

11. Metallic solids are
    a. Salts
    b. Endothermic
    c. Amorphous
    d. Crystalline

12. All liquids are
    a. Unstable
    b. Amorphous
    c. Exothermic
    d. Insoluble

13. (T, F)   Table salt forms a colloidal suspension in water.

14. Pure water is said to be neutral because
    a. It is potable
    b. It is only slightly basic
    c. It has a pH value of 0
    d. It contains an equal balance of H^+ and OH^- ions

15. If light travels through a certain type of glass at 197,000,000 meters per second, the refractive index of the glass is
    a. 1.523
    b. 1.999
    c. 3.404
    d. 1.037

16. (T, F)   A liter of water has the same density on earth as it would have on the moon.

17. If an object partially reflects all the wavelengths of visible light in equal concentrations, we see it as
    a. A Becke line
    b. Endothermic
    c. Ultraviolet
    d. Gray
    e. All the above

CHAPTER THREE

— *THE MICROSCOPE* —

If a crime laboratory were limited to only one scientific instrument, it would surely be some form of microscope. The microscope actually comprises a group of instruments which are designed to project a magnified image of an object into the human eye.

Magnification is caused by an enlargement of the size of the image projected onto the retina. It can be achieved to some extent simply by bringing an object closer to the eye, thereby increasing the acceptance angle, i.e., the angle at which the light is received into the eye (see Figure 3-1). However, the closest distance at which the human eye can comfortably see things is approximately 25 centimeters (approximately 10 inches). As an object is brought in closer than that distance, the eye undergoes increasing strain until it can no longer keep the object in focus.

Microscopes work by interposing between the object and the eye a convex lens which increases the acceptance angle of the light without straining the eye. This projects an enlarged image on the retina which the eye seems to picture at a distance of 25 centimeters. Because this image is not real but only apparent, it is referred to as a *virtual image* (see Figure 3.2).

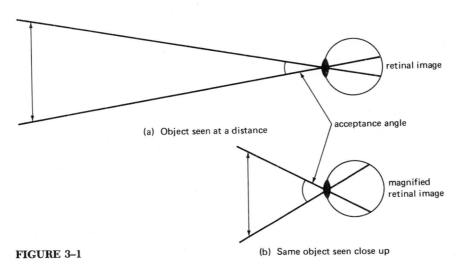

(a) Object seen at a distance

retinal image

acceptance angle

magnified
retinal image

FIGURE 3-1

(b) Same object seen close up

The microscopes that are most useful in scientific investigation are:

Simple	Stereoscopic
Compound	Polarizing
Comparison	Electron

SIMPLE MICROSCOPES

Simple microscopes generally have one or two lenses that work according to the principle illustrated in Figure 3-2. Hand magnifiers and fingerprint magnifiers (see Figure 3-3) are examples of simple microscopes, which are invaluable tools both for the field investigator in searching for evidence and for the criminalist in making rapid preliminary screening examinations. The maximum effective magnification of these types of magnifiers, without incurring undue distortion, is in the neighborhood of 20X. That is, the virtual image is 20 times as large as the object.

COMPOUND MICROSCOPE

The basic compound microscope improves on the simple microscope by magnifying the specimen twice. Two separate sets of lenses are used: the *objective* and the *ocular.* The ocular is also called the *eyepiece.*

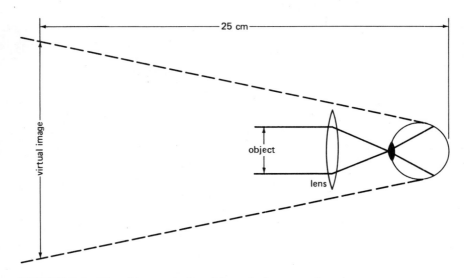

FIGURE 3–2 Virtual image produced by a single convex lens.

FIGURE 3–3 Fingerprint magnifier. (Courtesy of Sirchie Finger Print Laboratories)

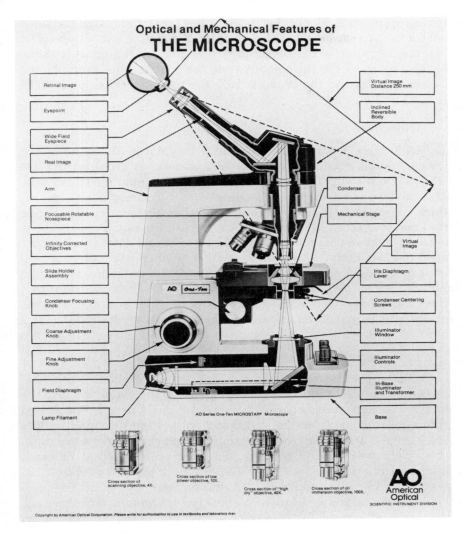

Optical and Mechanical Features of THE MICROSCOPE

Retinal Image

Eyepoint

Wide Field Eyepiece

Real Image

Arm

Focusable Rotatable Nosepiece

Infinity Corrected Objectives

Slide Holder Assembly

Condenser Focusing Knob

Coarse Adjustment Knob

Fine Adjustment Knob

Field Diaphragm

Lamp Filament

Virtual Image Distance 250 mm

Inclined Reversible Body

Condenser

Mechanical Stage

Virtual Image

Iris Diaphragm Lever

Condenser Centering Screws

Illuminator Window

Illuminator Controls

In-Base Illuminator and Transformer

Base

AO *One-Ten*

AO Series One-Ten MICROSTAR® Microscope

Cross section of scanning objective, 4X.

Cross section of low power objective, 10X.

Cross section of "high dry" objective, 40X.

Cross section of oil immersion objective, 100X.

AO American Optical SCIENTIFIC INSTRUMENT DIVISION

Copyright by American Optical Corporation. Please write for authorization to use in textbooks and laboratory man.

FIGURE 3–4 (Courtesy of American Optical Corporation)

Figure 3-4 illustrates the locations of the various parts of the instrument. The objective, positioned directly above the object being examined, projects a magnified image of the object into the microscope tube. This is a real image, and if a piece of ground glass or white paper were inserted into the tube at the focal point of the objective, the image would appear on it. The ocular receives this projected image and magnifies it again according to the principles of a simple microscope. The total magnification of the resulting virtual image is the product of the magnifying powers of the objective and the ocular. If, for example, the objective is 45X and the ocular is 10X, the total magnification is 450X (10 x 45 = 450).

Objectives

Objectives are available in various magnifications. Some of the more common general-purpose objectives used in criminalistics are 10X, 45X, and 100X. The power of the objective is engraved on its side. Most modern microscopes are equipped with rotating nosepieces on which anywhere from two to six objectives may be mounted. To change from one to another, the user has only to turn the nosepiece until the desired objective clicks into place. High-quality objectives are *parcentered* and *parfocal.* Parcentered means that when a specimen is centered in the field of view of one objective, the specimen will remain centered when the next one is clicked into place. Parfocal means that when a specimen has been brought into focus under one objective, the specimen will remain approximately in focus under the other objectives.

Lens Aberrations

The lenses in objectives are subject to two problems: *spherical aberration* and *chromatic aberration.* Spherical aberration refers to the tendency of light passing through the center of a lens to be focused at a different distance from the lens than light passing through its edges [see Figure 3-5(a)]. Chromatic aberration is a related phenomenon in which light waves of different wavelengths are focused at different distances from the lens [See Figure 3-5(b)]. Both of these problems can be corrected by using additional lenses. The degree to which an objective is corrected is a measure of its quality. *Achromatic objectives* are used for most general-purpose microscopy. The chromatic aberration of most of these lenses is corrected for two colors; spherical aberration is corrected for one color. *Fluorite* or *apochromatic* lenses may be used for highly refined work. In fluorite lenses, chromatic and spherical aberrations are each corrected for two colors. In apochromatic lenses, chromatic aberrations are corrected for three colors and spherical aberrations are corrected for two colors.

Numerical Aperture

Numerical aperture (NA) is a measure of the *resolving power* of an objective. Resolving power refers to the ability of a lens to distin-

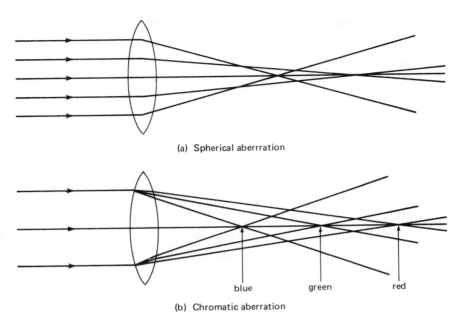

(a) Spherical aberrration

(b) Chromatic aberration

FIGURE 3–5   Lens aberrations.

guish small details. As a rule of thumb, the maximum useful magnification of a given objective is 1,000 times its numerical aperture. Hence, if a lens has a numerical aperture of 0.65, its maximum useful magnification is 650X. Further magnification is called *empty magnification* because there will be no further increase in resolving power. The numerical aperture of an objective is engraved on its side along with its magnification.

Oculars

Oculars also come in a variety of different magnifications, usually from 4X to 30X. The most useful ones for most microscopic work are in the 10X to 20X range. The most common oculars are the *Huygenian* and the *wide-field*. The Huygenian ocular is simple and serviceable for general-purpose use, and it has an *eyepoint* of 7.4 millimeters. The eyepoint is the point above the ocular where the principal light rays intersect. The eye should be positioned at or above this point. The wide-field ocular increases the field of view by approximately 25 percent, and it has an eyepoint of 23.6 millimeters. The higher eyepoint makes the wide-field ocular more convenient for people who wear glasses.

The Condenser

The condenser is a set of lenses under the stage whose function is to collect the light rays from the illumination source and focus them up through the bottom of the slide onto the specimen being examined. Like objectives, condensers are rated as to numerical aperture. On any given microscope the numerical aperture of the condenser should equal that of the most powerful objective. Otherwise, the full resolving power of the objective cannot be realized.

Focus

The microscope is focused on a specimen by changing the distance between the objective and the specimen. When the lower-power objectives are being used, the specimen is brought into approximate focus by turning the *coarse adjustment* knobs. The best focus is achieved by turning the *fine adjustment* knobs. It is always a good practice to focus upward since when focusing downward it is possible to damage the objective by striking it against the specimen preparation. When working with objectives of 40X or higher magnification, all focusing is done with the fine adjustment. At these magnifications the working distance (distance between the bottom of the objective and the top of the specimen preparation) is 0.7 millimeter or less.

Although the beginner often wants to view specimens at the highest magnification, the lower magnifications are often more useful. One of the main advantages of lower magnifications is the greater *depth of focus*, that is, the thickness of the specimen that is in focus at any one time. The more powerful the objective, the narrower the depth of focus is. A good general rule of microscopy is always to begin the examination at low power and work upward to higher powers.

Oil Immersion

When the highest power objectives (90X and higher) are being used, the working distance is 0.2 millimeter or less. At this close distance the angle of light from the illumination source is so great that much of it does not enter the lens. An oil immersion system is generally used to correct this problem. After the sample preparation is put in place on the stage, a drop of oil with a high refractive index is placed on the cover glass and the objective is gently lowered until its front lens comes into contact with the oil. Because it has a higher refractive index than air, the oil bends the light inward, thereby increasing the amount of light entering the lens (see Figure 3-6). To take full advantage of the image-enhancing properties of oil immersion, the condenser should also be oiled to the bottom of the slide.

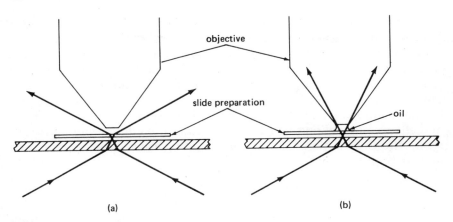

FIGURE 3-6 The oil immersion objective: (a) shows the path of the light rays when no oil is used; (b) shows how the oil drop bends the rays so that they enter the objective.

Illumination

If the fullest advantage of the capabilities of the microscope is to be obtained, there must be adequate illumination. In general, the desired qualities of an illumination system are (1) uniform intensity across the entire field of view, (2) the ability to control the intensity, and (3) the ability to control the size of the field of view and the angle at which the light enters the objective. Two kinds of illumination are used in microscopy: *transmitted* and *reflected*. Transmitted illumination is light that comes up from beneath the stage, passing through the condenser and the specimen preparation and into the objective. For the most part, transmitted light is used to illuminate transparent or translucent objects. Normally, the specimen is mounted in a clear liquid that has a refractive index either higher or lower than that of the object. As the light passes up through the preparation, the difference in refractive index between the specimen and the mounting liquid causes the specimen to stand out in contrast to the liquid.

Reflected illumination, or top lighting, is used for opaque specimens (i.e., specimens that do not transmit light) and for some translucent materials that do not transmit light well. The light is directed down onto the specimen at an angle from above and is reflected up into the objective. The most effective top lighting for most uses is provided by vertical lighting systems which are either built into the microscope or can be attached to the nosepiece. However, a separate light source can be used from the side. Side illumination is especially useful when viewing bullet striations or tool marks because the shadows cast by the ridges and valleys of the striations give a three-dimensional effect.

Illumination can be either *bright-field* or *dark-field*. In bright-field illumination, which is the type most commonly used, the light shines straight up through the condenser and the specimen appears dark in contrast to a bright background. Dark-field illumination is used when the contrast is not marked enough to make the specimen stand out. A circular barrier is mechanically placed in the center of the cone of light coming up from the condenser. This blocks out the direct light and allows only oblique rays coming around the edge of the barrier to strike the preparation. The oblique lighting causes the specimen to appear bright in contrast to a dark background.

COMPARISON MICROSCOPE

Because one of the principal tasks of the criminalist is to compare small samples of evidence materials to determine whether or not they are of common origin, the comparison microscope is one of the most useful tools in the laboratory (see Figure 3-7). In essence, the comparison microscope is two compound microscopes that have been attached by an optical bridge. The optical bridge splits in half the field of view of each of the component microscopes so that one-half of the picture that the user sees comes from one microscope and the other half comes from the other microscope. This feature allows the criminalist to examine two articles of evidence side by side. It is especially useful for comparing

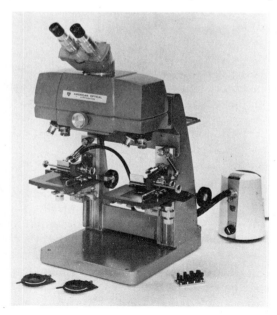

FIGURE 3–7 Comparison microscope. (Courtesy of American Optical Corporation)

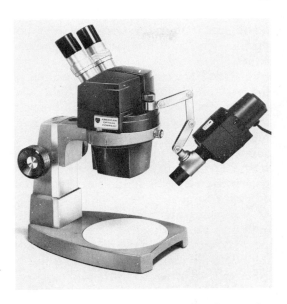

FIGURE 3–8 Binocular stereoscopic microscope. (Courtesy of American Optical Corporation)

bullets and tool marks because one-half of the suspect sample can be lined up with the other half of the known standard and a direct observation made of any matches in the striation patterns (see Figure 15-5).

STEREOSCOPIC MICROSCOPE

The stereoscopic microscope is a low-power instrument that has a wide field of view and a long working distance which allows for the easy manipulation of evidence materials (see Figure 3-8). The stereo microscope uses two objective lenses, which are focused on the sample at slightly different angles of view. The different angles give rise to a stereoscopic effect that gives the specimen a three-dimensional appearance. Stereo microscopes are especially useful for rapidly screening evidence materials, sorting evidence particles out from contaminating materials such as vacuum filter contents, and examining documents for signs of tampering. Most stereoscopic microscope examinations are conducted by using reflected light, but some instruments also come equipped with substage illumination for transmitted light.

POLARIZING MICROSCOPE

In the earlier discussion of the behavior of light, we saw that light travels in a straight line but with a vibratory wave motion. When we attempt to illustrate the wave motion of light, we usually draw a sine wave as shown in Figure 2-6. This depicts the wave as vibrating in one plane, that of the page. Ordinary light, however, actually vibrates in all planes—parallel to the page, perpendicular to it, and all planes in between.

There are certain kinds of crystal prisms which, when placed in the path of a beam or ordinary light, allow only the light vibrating in one plane to pass and filter out all the rest. This process is called *polarization*. Light vibrating in only one plane is said to be *polarized*. A second polarizing prism placed in the path of a beam of polarized light allows the beam to pass if its plane of polarization is the same as that of the first prism. If the second prism is rotated so that its plane of polarization is at 90 degrees to that of the first prism, it does not allow any light to pass.

A polarizing microscope has one such prism, called the *polarizer,* built into the substage optical system between the condenser and the stage. It has a second prism, called the *analyzer,* built into the tube or the ocular. When the analyzer and the polarizer are turned at 90 degrees to each other, they are said to be *crossed.* If there is no specimen in the field of view, no light reaches the viewer's eye.

The polarizing microscope is used predominately in the examination and identification of optically active crystalline and pseudocrystalline substances. Pseudocrystals are materials like hairs and fibers whose cellular and molecular structure is so regular that they exhibit some of the optical properties of crystals. When such optically active materials are examined in a polarizing microscope with crossed polars, these materials turn the light so that they become visible against the dark background, often with characteristic colors that aid in identification.

Most crystalline and pseudocrystalline materials exhibit the property of *double refraction.* This means that they have different refractive indexes when they are viewed in different directions. These differences can be determined by viewing the sample under polarized light. With the polarizer and analyzer parallel to each other, thereby letting light pass in one plane, refractive index readings are taken of the specimen as it is turned in different angles to the plane of light. Some of the more complex crystals have more than two refractive indexes. When the lowest refractive index value is subtracted from the highest, the resulting difference is a constant physical property of the substance known as *birefringence.*

ELECTRON MICROSCOPES

There is a limit to the amount of magnification possible with an optical microscope. This limit is imposed by the wavelength range of visible light (400 nanometers to 750 nanometers). The smaller the particle or area to be examined, the shorter the wavelength of light must be to resolve it. Visible light cannot resolve particles smaller than 250 nanometers; therefore, if one wants to get greater magnifications, an energy beam having a shorter wavelength is required. This can be accomplished by means of a high-energy electron beam, which has a wavelength in the neighborhood of 0.0037 nanometer.

There are two kinds of electron microscopes: the *transmitting electron microscope* (TEM) and the *scanning electron microscope* (SEM). The transmitting electron microscope is similar in principle to the optical microscope using transmitted light in that the electron beam penetrates the sample. The scanning electron microscope is analogous to the optical microscope using reflected illumination. In both types of instruments a cloud of electrons generated by heating a tungsten fila-

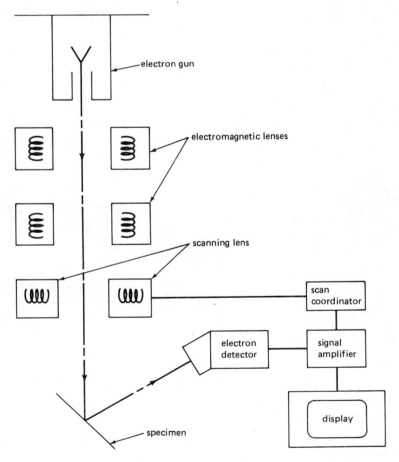

FIGURE 3–9 Schematic diagram of scanning electron microscope.

ment is projected at the specimen in a high-energy beam by means of electrostatic forces. Instead of using glass lenses, electron microscopes use electromagnets to focus the beam. The TEM has magnification values as high as 250,000X and the SEM has a range from 20X to 100,000X.

The scanning electron microscope (see Figure 3-9) is somewhat simpler to use than is the transmitting electron microscope because no elaborate specimen preparation is required, and it is more likely to be the instrument of choice for a crime laboratory. The finely focused beam of electrons is scanned across the surface of the specimen. This causes some of the electrons to scatter back from the surface and dislodge some of the electrons that were part of the atomic structure of the specimen. These scattered electrons are collected by an electron detector. The electron signal is amplified and coordinated with the scanning beam and is displayed on a raster like a television screen. The final image can also be recorded on photographic film.

In addition to superior magnification, electron microscopes have much greater depth of focus than do optical microscopes. The final image looks almost three-dimensional (see Figure 3-10). The SEM provides information on the shape, granularity, and size of minute surface features, both of the material being examined and any contaminants appearing on the surface.

If full analytical value is to be gotten out of an electron micro-

(a)   (b)

FIGURE 3–10   Scanning electron microscopes are not always used at very high magnifications. These two photomicrographs of automobile headlight filaments were both taken at 100X; (a) was taken with an optical microscope and (b) with a SEM. Note the difference in clarity and depth of focus. (M. A. Haas, M. J. Camp. and R. F. Dragen, "A Comparative Study of the Applicability of the Scanning Electron Microscope in the Examination of Vehicle Light Filaments." Reprinted, with permission, from the *Journal of Forensic Sciences,* Jan. 1975. Copyright American Society for Testing and Materials, 1916 Race Street, Philadelphia, Pa 19103).

scope, the microscope should be equipped with an energy dispersive X-ray analyzer (EDXRA). The high-energy electron beam bombarding the specimen can penetrate to the interior of its surface atoms and dislodge electrons from any of the orbital shells. When electrons are dislodged from the lower shells, they are replaced by electrons dropping down from a higher shell. The farther away an electron is from the nucleus, the more energetic the electron has to be to maintain its position. Therefore, when an electron drops from a higher shell to a lower shell, it needs less energy. It can release the excess energy in various forms, one of which is X-rays. X-rays, then, are scattered back from the specimen along with electrons. These X-rays can also be detected, amplified, and converted into electrical signals that can be displayed on an oscilloscope or an oscillogram (a graphic printout of the oscilloscope pattern on chart paper). The strength of the electric signal is proportional to the energy of the X-rays. Every element has a unique X-ray dispersion pattern, and all but a few elements can be detected and recorded by the EDXRA.

Review Questions

1. The human eye perceives a virtual image
   a. On a piece of ground glass or white paper
   b. Anywhere up to 25 meters from the ocular
   c. Only against a dark background
   d. At an apparent distance of 25 centimeters from the eyes

2. (T, F) The ocular and the eyepiece are the same thing.

3. If the objective of a microscope has a power of 95X and if the ocular has a power of 15X, the magnification will be
   a. 1425X
   b. 6.33×10^5
   c. 15.79 percent
   d. Insignificant

4. If a specimen remains in the center of the field of view when different oculars are rotated into place, the microscope is said to be
   a. Stereoscopic
   b. Parfocal
   c. Subject to spherical aberration
   d. Parcentered

5. Numerical aperture refers to
   a. The number of colors for which an objective is corrected

    b. Depth of focus

    c. The number of air holes in the condenser

    d. The resolving power of an objective

6. (T, F) A person who has a steady hand never needs to use the fine adjustment knob.

7. An oil immersion system

    a. Keeps a microscope free of rust

    b. Allows more light to enter the objective

    c. Is used mainly with reflected illumination

    d. Increases working distance

8. A stereoscopic microscope is used for

    a. Comparing tool marks

    b. Separating useful evidence from contaminating materials

    c. Examinations requiring high magnification

    d. All the above

9. Birefringence

    a. Occurs when the polarizer and the analyzer are crossed

    b. Causes light to vibrate in one plane

    c. Is a physical property

    d. Does not occur in pseudocrystals

10. Electron microscopes have higher powers of magnification than optical microscopes do because

    a. The human eye is more sensitive to electrons than to light rays

    b. The electron beam displaces electrons in the specimen

    c. The electron beam is not subject to refraction

    d. The electron beam operates at shorter wavelengths than light does

CHAPTER FOUR

—— *ANALYTICAL* ——
INSTRUMENTS

The examination of physical evidence can often be laborious and time-consuming for the criminalist. Traditional "wet" chemical methods[1] of analysis may require painstaking testing and retesting of an unknown material with different reagents until the composite behavior patterns give a clue to the identity of the material. Although a certain amount of wet chemistry is still necessary, most crime laboratories today provide a variety of sophisticated instruments to assist the criminalist in performing examinations not only more rapidly and more efficiently but also more accurately. In this chapter we will briefly cover the operating principles and uses of the most important analytical instruments used in crime laboratories.

CHROMATOGRAPHY

Different kinds of molecules have varying degrees of surface attraction for each other. When the surface attraction is relatively strong, the molecules of one substance cling to the surface molecules of the other

---

[1]"Wet" chemistry refers to analytical techniques in which various chemical reagents, such as acids, bases, and salts, are applied to a sample, and an identification of the sample is made on the basis of its reactions to the various reagents.

substance without being drawn into the internal chemical structure of the second substance. This surface phenomenon is known as *adsorption*. *Chromatography* is a term used to describe the analytical techniques which separate the various compounds in a mixture according to the relative adsorption potential of their molecules. Chromatographic techniques are widely used in criminalistics, primarily in the analysis of organic substances. The two main systems used in crime laboratories are gas chromatography (GC) and thin-layer chromatography (TLC).

Gas Chromatography

The gas chromatograph is essentially a thermal chamber, or oven, capable of precise temperature control, in which a long, thin spiral tube called a *column* is installed. The interior of the column is packed with a finely divided solid onto which a viscous liquid is coated. This liquid is known as the *stationary phase*. One end of the column is equipped with an injection port, a self-sealing rubber septum, into which a sample of the compound to be analyzed is injected by means of a gas-tight syringe. Once injected, the sample is forced through the column by a pressurized stream of carrier gas known as the *mobile phase*. The carrier gas is usually helium. The sample can be in either gas or liquid form. If it is a liquid, the internal temperature of the injection port must be high enough to vaporize the liquid instantaneously.

As the sample is swept along the column, its molecules tend to be adsorbed by the liquid stationary phase. Molecules of different kinds have different degrees of attraction for the liquid. As fresh carrier gas comes along, it tends to detach, or *desorb*, the molecules which had been adsorbed by the stationary phase. Consequently, the molecules of the sample are continuously being adsorbed and desorbed as they move along the column. During this process the molecules of the sample separate and sort themselves out according to their attraction to the stationary phase. Those that have a lesser tendency to adsorption move ahead of those that have a greater tendency to adsorption because they spend more time in the gas stream and less time clinging to the stationary phase. In general, lighter-weight molecules move through the column faster than heavier-weight molecules do (see Figure 4–1).

When a test sample reaches the end of the column, the sample is separated into bands of like molecules. As they leave the column, these bands pass through a detector. The most commonly used detector is the flame ionization detector. The bands of gas molecules pass through a flame of burning hydrogen gas which ionizes them in an electrical field. The ionized gases cause fluctuations in the resistance of the electrical

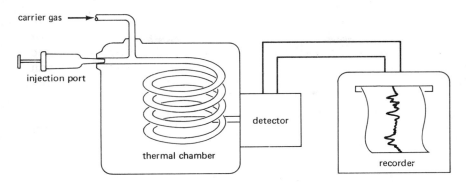

FIGURE 4–1 Schematic diagram of a gas chromatograph.

field, thereby generating an electrical signal. The electrical signal is amplified and used to power a mechanical stylus (pen) which inks the readout, or *chromatogram,* onto a strip of moving chart paper (see Figure 4–2). By comparing this chromatogram with chromatograms of known reference standards made under identical conditions, the criminalist is able to identify the compounds present in the unknown mixture. The position of the peak along the chart paper (peak retention time) identifies the substance. The area of the peak indicates its approximate concentration.

The chromatograph by itself can analyze only liquids and gases, but if a pyrolyzer is attached to the chromatograph, organic solids can also be identified. *Pyrolysis* is the decomposition of solid materials by high heat into simpler volatile (gaseous) components. The pyrolyzer used in conjunction with the gas chromatograph is a small heating chamber that decomposes organic solids into gases in an oxygen-free atmosphere. If oxygen were present, the gases would simply burn. These gases are then injected into the chromatograph and analyzed like any other gaseous sample. This process is generally known as *pyrolysis-gas chromatography.*

Thin-Layer Chromatography

Thin-layer chromatography can be used in the analysis of any mixture of soluble organic compounds. Its most frequent applications in criminalistics are the identification of drugs and inks. Thin-layer chromatography operates on the same principle as gas chromatography, but the method is very different. In TLC the stationary phase is a granular material that is coated on a flat support plate, usually of glass. The most common stationary phase material is silica gel. The mobile phase in thin-layer chromatography can be any one of a number of

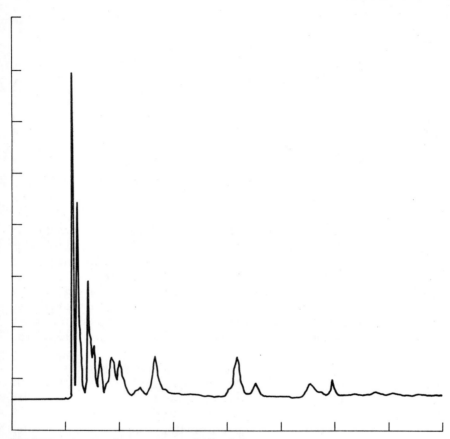

FIGURE 4-2 Gas chromatogram of unleaded gasoline.

liquid solvents. More than one substance at a time can be analyzed by TLC. The samples to be tested are applied in spots along a start line near the bottom of the plate. In a tightly closed developing chamber the bottom edge of the TLC plate is immersed in a small amount of the mobile phase solvent. The solvent begins to migrate up the plate by capillary action, that is, by a progressive surface attraction of the solvent to the silica gel granules. When the solvent front reaches the start line where the test samples are spotted, the solvent dissolves them and carries them along with it as it migrates up the plate. The different molecules contained in the samples now show varying tendencies to become adsorbed to the silica gel and desorbed by the moving solvent phase. After the solvent front has migrated a certain distance up the plate, usually 100 millimeters, the plate is considered to be developed

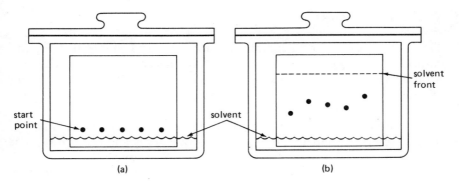

FIGURE 4–3   TLC plates: (a) at the begining of the test; (b) after development.

and is removed from the chamber and dried in the air. During the development the component parts of the samples become separated into individual spots at different distances from the start line (see Figure 4–3).

The distance that each compound travels up the plate during the development period is given a numerical value called the *Rf value*. The Rf value is determined by dividing the distance of the spot center from the start line by the distance of the solvent front from the start line. For example, if the spot of one compound has migrated 25 millimeters and the solvent front has migrated 100 millimeters, the Rf value for that spot is 0.25:

$$Rf = \frac{25}{100} = 0.25$$

Rf values are always between 0.00 and 1.00. As long as the same stationary and mobile phases are used, a given compound will regularly reproduce the same Rf value.

In most cases the spots produced by the developed compound are completely colorless and therefore invisible without some detection aid. The first step in the detection process is usually to view the plate under ultraviolet light. Since many organic compounds fluoresce under ultraviolet light, the position on the plate can be outlined with a pencil. In addition, the plates can be finely sprayed with a variety of chemical reagents that produce different color reactions with different compounds. Since the color reactions are often specific to certain organic compounds, they are considered along with Rf values in the identification of the substance.

The most sensitive and accurate instruments used to identify organic compounds are *mass spectrometers.* To date, because of costs that are prohibitive to the average laboratory, only the most advanced crime laboratories have them, but the technology will probably become more generally available in the future.

Although there are many different types of mass spectrometers, they all operate according to the same physical principle. Each type of instrument has (1) a system for introducing the sample, (2) an ionization system, (3) a system for sorting the ions according to the ratio of their mass to their electric charge, and (4) a detection and readout system.

The sample compound must be introduced in gaseous form at a steady measured rate into the ionization chamber. In the ionization chamber the sample gas is bombarded at right angles by a stream of energized electrons. The stream of energized electrons strikes the molecules of the sample compound, causing these molecules to break up into ionic fragments with electrical charges. Since these fragments bear charges, they can be accelerated by being subjected to electrostatic forces. Positively charged particles fly toward the negative poles, and negatively charged particles fly toward the positive poles. By varying the combinations of electrostatic forces in the path of the accelerated particles, particles of any given mass to charge ratio can be selected out from all other particles. The selected particles are accelerated through the system until they strike a collector, but those that have different mass to charge ratios are drawn off along the way. As the electrostatic fields are progressively changed, particles of different mass to charge ratios are drawn to the collector. The particles striking the collector set up weak electrical signals which are detected and amplified and converted into a visual readout. The readout may be in the form of an oscilloscope, an oscillogram, or a computerized digital printout. A given compound under the same conditions of ionization, temperature, and pressure is always fragmented into the same kinds of particles, and therefore can be very precisely identified by its mass spectra.

Although mass spectrometry has been in existence since the 1930s, it is only in recent years that it has been a suitable technique for criminalistics. The reason is that crime laboratories commonly deal with highly contaminated mixtures of compounds and mass spectrometers can analyze only pure compounds. The development that made their use profitable in crime laboratories was the successful interface between the gas chromatograph and the mass spectrometer. The gas chromatograph, as we saw earlier, is an ideal instrument for separating mixtures into pure bands of their component compounds. The main difficulty that had to be overcome was that the gas chromatograph operates under high pressures and the mass spectrometer operates nearly at a vacuum. Several interfacing systems now exist for collecting a pure sample of gas from the GC, separating it from the carrier gas, and introducing it under appropriate pressure into the mass spectrometer (see Figure 4–4).

SPECTROPHOTOMETERS

We have already seen (p. 25) that our perception of colors depends on the ability of substances to selectively absorb and reflect various wavelengths of the visible light spectrum. Because materials of the same chemical composition always absorb the same wavelength of light, the absorption characteristics of an unknown substance can be used to help identify it or compare it with a known standard. This field of study is called *absorptiometry;* the analytical instruments based on it are *spectrophotometers.*

The principles of absorption cannot be entirely explained by the wave theory of light because they concern the energy present in light. According to the quantum theory, light waves are made up of particles of energy called *photons.* The radiant energy in a given beam of light is a function of the number of photons per second propagated by the beam. The higher frequency wavelengths of light toward the blue end of the spectrum are more energetic than those of lower frequency

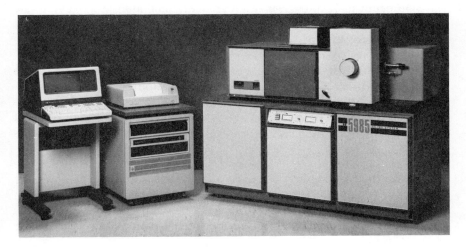

FIGURE 4–4   Gas Chromatograph/Mass Spectrometer. (Courtesy of Hewlett-Packard)

toward the red end of the spectrum. When a substance absorbs light, its atoms and molecules are actually absorbing energy in the form of photons, and each substance can only accept photons that reach it at certain specific wavelengths.

Ultraviolet, Visible Light, and Infrared Spectrophotometers

Almost all the organic materials that criminalists have to deal with absorb light in either the ultraviolet, visible, or infrared range. When a photon is absorbed, it causes the atom that absorbed it to rise from its normal, or *ground,* state to a more highly energized state. With ultraviolet and visible light this is accomplished by the shift of an electron from a lower to a higher energy orbit. In the infrared range the increased energy causes an increase in the vibrational stretching and bending of atoms or groups of atoms that continuously take place within every molecule. The basic operating principles of ultraviolet, visible light, and infrared spectrophotometers, as illustrated in Figure 4–5, are fairly simple.

The energy source of a spectrophotometer is a lamp that radiates a band of wavelengths appropriate to the analytical system. If it is ultraviolet, it must emit wavelengths in the range of 210 nanometers to 380 nanometers. If it is visible light, it must cover the range of approximately 400 nanometers to 750 nanometers. If it is infrared, the range of greatest use is from 2.5 micrometers to 50 micrometers. The radiation is passed through a prism that disperses it into its component wavelengths. The dispersed beam is projected against a barrier that has a slit in it. This slit allows rays of selected wavelengths to pass. The position of the slit can be adjusted so that any wavelength may be chosen. The size of the slit can be adjusted to allow the passage of wider or narrower bands of wavelengths. The selected wavelengths pass through a cell that holds a solution of the sample being analyzed. The sample partially absorbs its characteristic wavelengths and lets other wavelengths pass. The light that passes through the sample strikes a photoelectric cell which sets up a weak electric current. The current

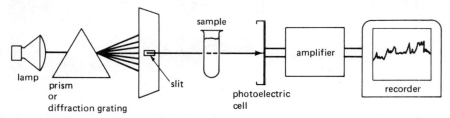

FIGURE 4–5 Schematic diagram of a spectrophotometer.

is amplified and the strength of the signal is measured. A series of such readings is taken at different wavelengths and a curve is constructed of the measure of strengths of the signal. Each substance has its characteristic curve which identifies it (see Figure 4–6). The curve is known as the *absorption spectrum* of the substance. The ultraviolet and visible spectra are not so reliable as the infrared spectrum is because the curves tend to be broad and different materials may produce similar ones. The infrared curves are much more specific, and if the sample is free of contaminants (a very rare circumstance), the infrared spectrum can provide a positive identification.

Ultraviolet, visible light, and infrared spectrophotometry is especially suitable for analyzing organic compounds because it does not just detect single dissociated atoms; it is sensitive to the *groupings* of atoms that are commonly found in organic molecules.

Atomic Absorption Spectrophotometers

While ultraviolet, visible light, and infrared spectrophotometers are used primarily to detect organic compounds, atomic absorption (AA) spectrophotometers are used to give a quantitative analysis of metallic elements. Since atomic absorption is designed to analyze elements instead of compounds, it is necessary to atomize the sample, that is, dissociate the constituent atoms of the compounds being analyzed. This is done by subjecting the sample to an intense heat either in a flame, such as that produced by a nitrous oxide-acetylene burner, or in a heated graphite furnace. The flameless method is a more recent development and is sensitive to extremely minute concentrations of an element.

Instead of using a light source that radiates across a broad range of wavelengths, atomic absorption uses lamps that radiate only in the wavelengths absorbed by the individual elements. This is accomplished by using special hollow cathode lamps whose filaments are constructed from the individual elements. The lamp must be changed every time a different element is to be analyzed. Consequently, atomic absorption is not a good method for determining what elements are present in an unknown sample. Its main value is in determining very precisely the concentrations of elements that are known to be present. A good example of the appropriate use of atomic absorption is in the analysis of gunpowder residues. Almost all gunpowders contain the elements barium and antimony in various concentrations. By comparing the concentrations of these elements in gunpowder residues found on a suspect's hand with residues found on the victim's clothing, it is possible to tell whether the gunpowders were from the same source.

Figure 4–7 illustrates the principles of atomic absorption. A beam

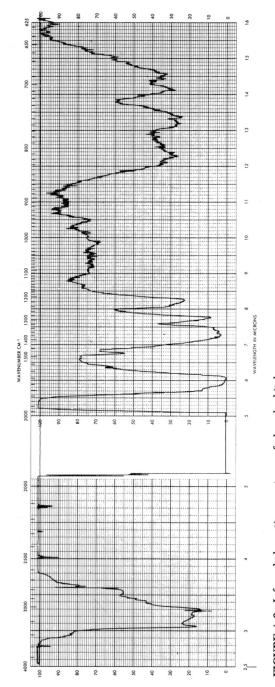

FIGURE 4-6 Infrared absorption spectrum of phenobarbitol.

54

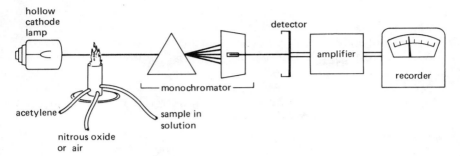

FIGURE 4–7 Schematic diagram of an atomic absorption spectrophotometer.

of light made up of specific wavelengths for the test element is passed through the flame or oven in which the sample is atomized. The test element absorbs a quantity of this light in proportion to its concentration in the sample. The unabsorbed light then passes through a monochromator, which isolates the component wavelengths, and into a detector, which senses the intensity of the light and transmits the signal to an amplifier and readout system. The readout is usually a numerical value, and the exact concentration is determined by plotting the value on a graph against the values of reference standards with known concentrations.

THE SPECTROGRAPH

The spectrophotometers discussed above are based on the selective absorption of light. The *spectrograph* (see Figure 4–8) is based on the selective emission of light. Absorption occurs when the bombardment of a substance by the appropriate wavelength of light causes the atoms of the substance to pass from their ground state to an excited state. Conversely, when an excited atom returns from an excited state to its

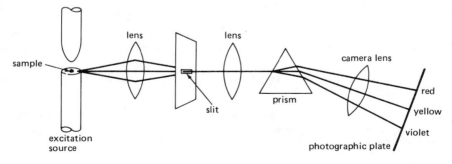

FIGURE 4–8 Schematic diagram of a spectrograph.

ground state, it gives off the absorbed energy that it no longer needs in the form of the same wavelength of light that it absorbed.

In absorptiometry an external light source is used, but in spectrography the test sample itself becomes the light source. The atoms of a sample are dissociated and excited by subjecting them to intense heat in the form of a flame, electric spark, or electric arc. The electric arc is by far the most common. While being subjected to this excitation, the atoms are continuously shifting back and forth between the ground state and the excited state. As they shift from the excited state to the ground state, they emit photons of light at their characteristic wavelengths. This light is beamed against a barrier that has a narrow rectangular slit in it. This slit shapes the beam of light that it allows to pass. The beam is then focused by a collimating lens into a prism that diffuses the beam into its component wavelengths. The now separated wavelengths are in turn focused onto a photographic filmstrip. The filmstrip records the different wavelengths as a series of thin, dark, rectangular lines which take their shape from the slit. These lines, known as *line spectra,* are constant for each element (see Figure 4–9). To determine what elements are present in an unknown sample, the criminalist must compare the line spectra with the known spectra of various elements. The spectrograph is primarily used to detect the presence of metallic elements.

Although it is not sensitive enough to give precise quantitative determinations, it is possible to make a rough estimate of the concentration of each element in a sample by the intensity of the lines. If a precise determination of quantity is needed, the test substance can be examined by atomic absorption spectrophotometry after the elemental composition has been determined by the spectrograph. Both the spectrograph and the atomic absorption spectrophotometer destroy the sample, but since very small amounts of sample material are needed for the tests, it is usually possible to use only a small portion of the available evidence material.

An important refinement of the spectrograph is the *laser microprobe.* In this technique a very tiny sample or spot (as small as 10 micrometers) is atomized by a laser beam which is focused under a

FIGURE 4–9   Line spectra. The top two lines are reference standards of two metals. The two bottom lines are two runs of an unknown sample that are compared to the standards to see whether the unknown contains either of the two metals. (Courtesy of Dr. Michael J. Camp, Northeastern University)

microscope. The cloud of atoms that results from the action of the laser beam passes through an electric arc, which excites the atoms, and the emission spectra are analyzed as with the spectrograph.

X-RAY DIFFRACTION

X-ray diffraction is a method of identifying crystalline materials without regard to their organic or inorganic nature. Any crystalline material can be identified by comparing its X-ray diffraction pattern with known standards. The American Society for Testing and Materials[2] maintains a data file that contains the X-ray powder diffraction data for over 20,000 different compounds.

When an atom is subjected to a beam of X-rays, the atom diffracts (i.e., scatters) the beam in all directions. In noncrystalline materials the diffraction is completely random, but because the atoms of crystals are arranged in regular, repetitive lattice systems, they interfere with the diffracted beam in ways that cause the beam to emerge from the crystal in regular patterns.

The identification principle of X-ray diffraction is photographic. A narrow beam of X-rays is focused on a sample in the interior of a special camera (see Figure 4–10) and the diffracted rays imprint their pattern on a filmstrip which is curved around the interior wall of the camera. The resulting pattern is a "fingerprint" for the compound (see Figure 4–11). X-ray diffraction can identify both single crystalline compounds and the crystalline components of a mixture.

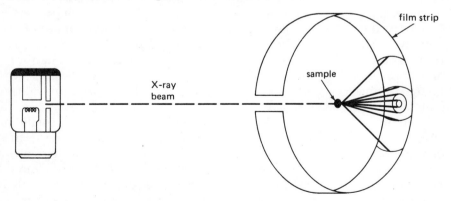

FIGURE 4–10   Schematic diagram of an X-ray diffraction camera.

[2]American Society for Testing and Materials, 1916 Race Street, Philadelphia, Pa. 19103.

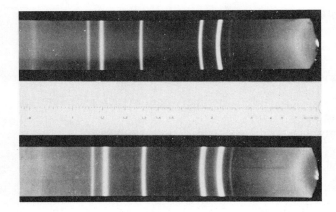

FIGURE 4–11 X-ray diffraction patterns. The top film strip is that of a reference standard; the bottom one is a film strip of an unknown sample. (Courtesy of Wisconsin State Crime Laboratory)

NEUTRON ACTIVATION ANALYSIS

Most of the analytical instruments described so far have relied on changes in the energy levels of the electrons of the materials being analyzed and have not concerned the nucleus of their atoms. *Neutron activation analysis* (NAA) is an analytical technique for identifying metallic elements by measuring energy changes in the nucleus of the atom. Neutron activation analysis is so sensitive that it can detect and analyze some elements in subnanogram concentrations.

As we have already seen, the chemical differences between elements are a function of the number of protons in their atoms. Nuclei of atoms of a given element always contain the same number of protons. However, the number of neutrons in an atom of the same element may vary. Atoms of a single element containing different numbers of neutrons are called *isotopes* of that element. Every element has a number of isotopes, and for the most part they are stable. However, when the neutron imbalance becomes too great, the nucleus becomes unstable and is said to be *radioactive.*

Radioactive atoms seek stability by decomposing into smaller atoms. In the process of decomposition they emit energy in the form of alpha particles, beta particles, and gamma rays. Alpha particles are positively charged particles containing two protons, two neutrons, and no electrons. Beta particles are electrons and positrons (positively charged particles having approximately the same mass as electrons). Gamma rays are highly energetic electromagnetic radiations above X-rays in the electromagnetic spectrum (Figure 2–7).

Neutron activation analysis is a method of artificially creating unstable isotopes of metallic elements. When the specimen being analyzed is subjected to a dense bombardment of neutrons, some neutrons adhere to the nuclei of metallic atoms. These nuclei become radioactive and immediately begin to decompose. During decomposition, each element emits gamma rays at wavelengths uniquely characteristic for that element. Neutron activation analysis identifies an element by detecting and measuring these wavelengths.

The gamma rays pass into a special scintillating crystal that gives off light flashes proportional in intensity to the energy of the gamma rays. These light flashes are converted to electrical impulses and amplified. These signals are either recorded on an oscilloscope or an oscillogram or are stored on computer tape.

Although the potential value of neutron activation analysis for criminalistics is great, its costs are prohibitive for most laboratories. There is also a logistical problem for most crime laboratories because neutron activation analysis requires access to a nuclear reactor. At present only a few of the largest crime laboratories can take advantage of this analytical tool.

Review Questions

1. (T, F) Although the gas chromatograph can be used to analyze liquids and solids, the liquids and solids must be vaporized before they enter the column.

2. Chromatography relies on
   a. The mobility of organic compounds
   b. Surface tension
   c. Chemical reactions between the sample and the stationary phase.
   d. Adsorption of the mobile phase to the stationary phase
   e. All the above
   f. None of the above

3. (T, F) Solids can be analyzed by thin-layer chromatography if they are first pyrolyzed.

4. (T, F) The Rf value of phenobarbitol is 1.35.

5. In thin-layer chromatography the solvent phase
   a. Is the mobile phase
   b. Migrates by capillary action
   c. Is granular
   d. All the above
   e. a and b

6. The operating principle of the mass spectrometer
   a. Is a function of the ionization rate of the sample compound
   b. Is the same as the gas chromatograph but more accurate

    c. Depends on the mass to charge ratio of ionized particles

    d. Was discovered in the 1960s

7. (T, F)   Since infrared, ultraviolet, and visible light spectrophotometers all operate according to the same principles, they are considered interchangeable.

8. A photon
    a. Is larger than an atom
    b. Is a particle of light energy
    c. Has the same mass as a neutron
    d. Is usually red in color

9. An atom that has absorbed light energy is said to be
    a. Energized
    b. Grounded
    c. Ionized
    d. Endothermic

10. When an atom returns from an energized state to its ground state,
    a. It absorbs photons
    b. It is radioactive
    c. It falls to the ground
    d. It emits energy

11. Non-metallic crystalline materials can be identified by
    a. Their line spectra
    b. Their X-ray diffraction patterns
    c. Their characteristic odors
    d. The laser microprobe

12. In neutron activation analysis the sample is bombarded with
    a. Alpha rays
    b. Beta rays
    c. Gamma rays
    d. Neutrons

13. An isotope becomes radioactively unstable when
    a. It is injected into the gas chromatograph
    b. The ratio of protons to electrons is out of balance
    c. There are too many neutrons in the nucleus
    d. It absorbs gamma rays

CHAPTER FIVE

—— *INVESTIGATING* ——
THE CRIME SCENE

When called to a crime scene an investigator usually has numerous lines of inquiry to pursue, from the taking of human testimony to collecting physical evidence. Since this book is about scientific investigation, this chapter will deal with the aspects of crime scene investigation that pertain to physical evidence. Investigators must use their own judgment in deciding where to lay the stress of their investigative efforts. The scientific analysis of physical evidence is one of many tools at the disposal of investigators which they may use or ignore as they deem necessary. However, since human testimony can be subject to unforeseeable changes, investigators should as a matter of common sense try to develop the physical evidence available at a crime scene to the fullest extent possible.

The ability of the criminalist to process physical evidence in a way that is useful to the investigator depends on the condition in which it is received in the laboratory, and this in turn depends on the way the evidence was collected and packaged at the scene. The crime scene search and the laboratory examination are interdependent aspects of a cooperative effort aimed at solving the crime.

This chapter deals in a general way with the procedures of crime scene investigation as they relate to the collection and preservation of physical evidence. Subsequent chapters provide specific investigative guidelines for individual items of evidence.

PROTECTING THE CRIME SCENE

The first responsibility of the police officer or investigator on arriving at a crime scene is to protect the scene from unauthorized intruders. These include not only curious bystanders and members of the press but also police and other officials who have nothing to do with the investigation. People entering a scene after the crime will be likely to contaminate it by disturbing the criminal's traces and leaving traces of their own. Consequently, the purpose of protecting the crime scene from unauthorized intrusion is to reduce such contamination to an absolute minimum. If seriously injured victims are present, providing medical care for them, of course, supersedes all other considerations, and medical attendants must be given access to them and be allowed to remove them. A dead body, however, constitutes evidence in itself and should not be removed from the scene until the investigating officer has examined it.

In an indoor crime scene the main focus of attention is the room in which the crime occurred. This area must absolutely be protected, and normally the protection extends to the whole building during the period of the search. The borderlines of protected areas can be physically delineated by means of ropes stretched in front of all points of access and signs instructing unauthorized persons to keep out. Whether signs and ropes are used or not, police officers should be posted at all access points to enforce the restriction.

In the case of outdoor and vehicular crimes the area surrounding the immediate locus of the crime should be cordoned off with ropes, and officers should be posted to ensure that no one crosses the barriers. The size of the cordoned area must be left up to the judgment of the investigator depending on the circumstances. A crime discovered in an open field would probably require a larger roped off search area than one on a narrow city street. The investigator must estimate how large an area could reasonably be expected to contain evidence.

PROCESSING THE CRIME SCENE

If officers other than the investigating team were the first on the scene, the investigating officer in charge should ascertain from them what steps were taken to preserve the scene and what disturbances if any have occurred. For example, if a patrol officer arriving at the scene moved a body while checking for signs of life, the investigator should be informed.

Before beginning the actual processing, the investigator should take a few minutes to survey the scene and formulate a systematic plan suited to the individual case. There is no one correct approach that is valid for all crime scenes.

The scene must be searched in order to locate items of physical evidence that may connect the culprit with the crime, but the processing of the crime scene entails much more than just finding the evidence. Each item must be recorded as it is found. The place where the item is found must also be recorded. The location of each item must be related to the overall crime scene. This recording process must be carried out in such a way that it can form the basis of the investigator's courtroom testimony, which may take place months or even years after the event—long after the investigator's memory of the search has faded. The scene and the evidence found in it are recorded by means of a combination of photography, sketches, and the investigator's notes. After the evidence is recorded, it must be collected and packaged so that it may be preserved with as little change as possible for laboratory examination and presentation in court.

Conduct of the Search

The search should be conducted in an efficient, systematic manner which covers the entire area without duplication of effort. The method used depends on the nature of the scene and the number of investigators involved. If there is only one investigator, as might be the case in a straightforward case in which there are few complications, the investigator may want to start at the main access point and proceed in either a clockwise or counterclockwise direction around the periphery and work his or her way by decreasing concentric circles to the center of the scene; the investigator may want to divide the area into segments and search segment by segment; or if the obvious items of evidence are concentrated in one area, the investigator may want to process them first and then proceed with a systematic search for possible less obvious items.

If there are several investigators, they may proceed as a team in the same manner or each officer may be assigned a search sector. In outdoor crimes, because of the size of the scene, the search area is usually divided into sectors and one individual is responsible for each sector.

Because having several officers appear to testify to the collection of items found in different sectors of a scene would create confusion in the courtroom, it is a good practice to have the searchers do nothing but search and note the locations of evidence items without touching the items. One officer is then assigned to collect and package all the evidence and that officer alone will be required to testify. If this system is used, the primary collecting officer should have an assistant who aids and observes in the collection of each items so that if one of the officers is unable to testify, the other can take his or her place.

Search and Examination of Dead Bodies

If there is a dead body, or bodies, that may be the starting point of the search, or it may be reserved until the end. Sometimes a separate investigator is assigned to the body while others conduct the evidence search. First the body itself is systematically searched, starting with the head and working down one side and then the other. Then the area immediately surrounding the body is searched. At the completion of the examination the body can be removed and the area under it searched. If the body was the starting point, the evidence search then proceeds outward in widening concentric circles or in sectors.

The examination of a dead body often provides important clues to the investigation. Trace materials from the murderer may be found adhering to the clothing and skin or embedded under the fingernails. In addition, a corpse often provides a means for estimating the time of the crime. Although establishing the time of death is officially the job of the medical examiner, an experienced investigator can often make a fairly close estimate by checking the body for certain changes (see Figure 5–1). Any such estimates are necessarily very rough since the time it takes for these changes to occur can be influenced by various factors.

Body temperature. From the moment of death the body releases heat until it cools down to the temperature of the environment. This may take 24 hours or more, depending on the original temperature of the body, the amount of clothing and body fat, and the condition of the surrounding air. However, a body generally continues to feel warm to the touch up to approximately 8 hours after death; after that it feels cold and clammy.

Rigor mortis. When a person dies, the muscles of the body immediately relax, causing the extremities to become pliable and limp and allowing an evacuation of the bowels and bladder. Somewhere between 3 and 6 hours after death *rigor mortis* begins to set in. This is a general stiffening of the body that is caused by degenerative chemical activity in the muscle tissues. The stiffness begins in the jaw and facial muscles and then the neck and spreads inward from the extremities; the abdominal region is the last affected. It persists for approximately 12 hours and disappears in the same order it appeared. After 24 hours the body muscles are limp again. These time factors can be influenced by the age and physical condition of the victim and by the external temperature. The onset is faster in children than it is in adults and it is slower in heavily muscled people. The higher the air temperature, the faster rigor mortis sets in and the faster it disappears.

A condition similar to *rigor mortis* can occur immediately after death if the victim is clutching something tightly or undergoing some other form of strong muscular tension at the moment of death. This is known as a *cadaveric spasm* and can be differentiated from *rigor mortis* because it occurs only in the tensed area while *rigor mortis* is general.

Livor mortis or *post-mortem lividity.* After death a body stops bleeding and begins to drain. If there are wounds in the lower lying parts of the body, the blood drains out of them until it is stopped by coagulation. Otherwise, the blood, drawn by the force of gravity, drains into the lower parts of the body, settles there, and finally coagulates. This process causes a purplish discoloration known as *livor mortis* or *post-mortem lividity* to appear in the parts of the body where the blood has settled. The condition begins within one-half hour after death and becomes more pronounced until the draining is complete after approximately 4 hours. After settling, the blood begins to coagulate in place. Because of the absence of air, coagulation takes place more slowly inside the body than at the site of an open wound. After approximately 12 hours the coagulation process is so far advanced that no further drainage takes place if the body is moved. Consequently, if a body is found with signs of lividity showing in an upper part, it is proof that the body was moved.

Hours after death	1	2	3	4	5	6	7	8	9	10	11	12	13	14	15	
Body temperature	Steadily decreases after death									Body begins to feel clammy			Body temperature cools to environment			
Rigor mortis	Muscles flaccid			Rigor mortis sets in and lasts up to 36 hours												
Post mortem lividity	Blood starts draining to lower parts of body			After about 4 hours coagulation begins												

FIGURE 5–1 Approximate times of physical changes after death.

Vehicle Searches

Like any other crime scene, a vehicle must be searched in a systematic manner. If a car is suspected to have been involved in a hit-and-run accident, the exterior and the undercarriage are of primary interest. The exterior is carefully searched one side at a time from front to rear and then back to the front again. If two officers are searching, they can switch sides and check each other's work to ensure completeness. The vehicle should be lifted on a hoist for the search of the undercarriage. The most thorough method is to segment the area and search segment by segment. Here the investigator is looking for traces that can connect the vehicle to the victim or to the accident scene. Such traces might include broken glass, soil, blood, hairs, fibers, and cloth weave impressions in the paint.

If the vehicle is being searched for hidden items such as weapons or drugs, the interior, trunk, and motor compartment are of primary interest, but the exterior and undercarriage should not be overlooked. Again, each area to be searched should be segmented into manageable units and each unit should be covered one at a time.

Clothing Searches

The search of clothing for minute items of trace evidence that might have been transferred between the victim and the suspect or between the suspect and items at the scene can best be conducted at the laboratory. This is equally true whether the clothing came from the suspect or from living or dead victims. Each item of clothing should be placed in a separate bag as it is removed in order to avoid cross contamination and in order to catch any bits of evidence that may be shaken off during transportation. The clothing is first searched carefully with a hand magnifying glass for visible evidence. Smaller bits of evidence down to microscopic size can be collected by pressing transparent adhesive tape against the clothing or by sweeping it with a vacuum sweeper equipped with a filter attachment (see Figure 5–2). The adhesive tape method has the advantage of showing specifically where on the clothing the evidence was found, but it has the disadvantage of being extremely painstaking and time-consuming.

If possible, it is best to avoid cutting clothing when removing it, but if the clothing cannot be removed any other way, care should be taken not to cut through any area where powder or shot patterns or evidential stains are likely to be present.

Crime Scene Photography

Crime scene photographs must be taken with a view to their admissibility in court. To be admissible, photographs must represent

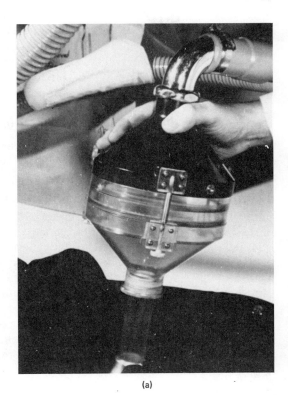

(a)

FIGURE 5–2 (a) Shows a vacuum sweeper with filter attachment being used to search a garment. (b) Shows trapped particles collected on the filter. The particles are separated and examined for evidential value under a stereoscopic microscope. (Courtesy of Wisconsin State Crime Laboratory)

(b)

the scene accurately. There must be no distortion and no trick photography. The presentation of a negative is considered sufficient proof that a photograph has not been altered. Photography should be straightforward, relevant to the investigation, and unsensational. If a court considers that a photograph will prejudice a jury by appealing unduly to its emotions, the photograph will not be admitted. For example, a color photograph of the bloody, mangled body of a child might be considered unacceptably prejudicial. If it were essential to the prosecution of the case, the same photograph might be acceptable in black and white because the visual impact of the blood and wounds is less startling.

For photographic purposes, the crime scene should be extended to include all possible approaches and the general surrounding area. External shots of a building in which a crime has occurred should be taken and if the case is important enough, it may be desirable to take aerial photographs.

The overall scene should be photographed in such a way that the positions and interrelationships of all objects present are clear. Nothing should be disturbed or removed and a detailed search should not begin until the scene has been photographed. Photography is also an integral part of the search and collection process. No item of evidence should be touched until it has been photographed. A first shot should be taken of the item in its undisturbed state followed by a second shot showing a ruler or other scale marker. This sequence is important because if the first shot is not taken, the defense can claim that the inclusion of a scale marker constitutes tampering with the scene.

Each photograph should be keyed to a crime scene sketch indicating the camera position and direction. The photographer should maintain a running log indicating the camera, lens, setting, direction, subject, and time of each shot. To avoid cluttering it is often advisable to make a photography sketch separate from the regular crime scene sketch or sketches. The photography sketch need show only the basic outlines of the room or scene and the focal point of the crime (i.e., a body or burglarized safe). The exact camera position can be shown in the sketch by indicating measured distances from the lens to immovable reference points such as corners, door jambs, trees, telephone poles, etc. The camera positions on the sketch should be numbered and the photographs should be keyed to those numbers.

Crime Scene Sketches

Although nothing can surpass photography for recording the details of a scene, photography has the disadvantage that it cannot accurately depict dimensions. Sketches compensate for this disadvantage by depicting overall views of the scene or parts of the scene and showing true distance relationships between objects. In sketches the investigator can portray the important elements of the scene and leave out the unessential details. If the scene is particularly complicated or confusing, the investigator may want to make several sketches depicting different aspects. Sketches should not be considered a substitute for photography. The two should complement each other to produce a clear picture of the scene.

Artistic ability is less important in a sketch than accuracy. Normally, the investigator draws a rough sketch at the scene without trying to maintain proportion. The correct placement of every object in the sketch is shown by indicating the measured distance from the object to immovable reference points in the scene. All pertinent dimensions of the scene itself, such as lengths of walls, distances from doors or windows to walls, and the sizes of objects, are also measured and indicated in the sketch. Later a finished drawing is made in which the proportions are corrected on the basis of the measured dimensions shown in the rough sketch. For this reason, all measurements must be carefully made with steel measuring tape and checked for accuracy.

In a rough sketch a dead body is depicted by a stick figure showing the approximate position. At least two measurements should be taken from the top of the head to fixed reference points; and the position of each foot should be similarly established by measurements shown in the sketch. These measurements should be taken before the body is removed, but if that is impossible, the outline of the body should be drawn with chalk or other marking material before removal and the measurements made from the outline.

The location of an evidence item should also be measured and included on the sketch before the item is collected. Evidence items need not be drawn in the sketch, but their locations should be indicated by letters or numbers which are keyed to the investigator's notes or to a legend at the bottom of the sketch. (see Figure 5-3).

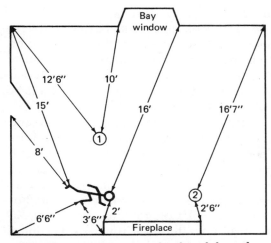

Case No. 78-1375
6/12/78
Stabbing Homicide
215 Rhodes Terrace Apt No. 5
Anytown, U.S.A.
Victim ID by neighbor
as tenant. John Doe.
Sketch by D/Sgt. Joe Zyx,
Anytown P.D.

N

① White handkerchief
with possible blood stains

② Kitchen knife, blade 7 3/4"
handle 5 1/4" with possible blood
on handle

FIGURE 5–3 Crime scene sketch with legend.

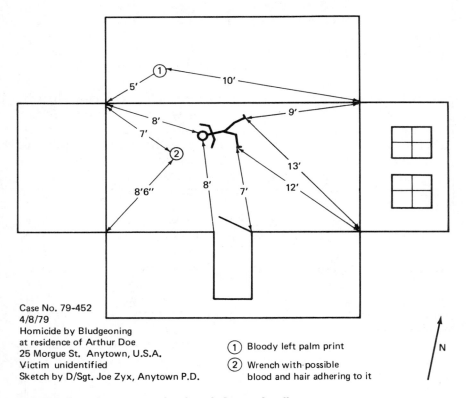

Case No. 79-452
4/8/79
Homicide by Bludgeoning
at residence of Arthur Doe   ① Bloody left palm print
25 Morgue St. Anytown, U.S.A.
Victim unidentified   ② Wrench with possible
Sketch by D/Sgt. Joe Zyx, Anytown P.D.   blood and hair adhering to it

N

FIGURE 5–4 Crime scene sketch with flattened walls.

Crime scene sketches are drawn as if they are being viewed from directly above so that a square room looks like a square in the sketch. If the walls do not figure evidentially into the scene, they need not be drawn. But if some evidence is found on a wall, for example a bullet hole, bloodstain, or other trace, the walls should be drawn as if flattened out and the measured dimensions from the evidence to the corners or other fixed points should be shown as in Figure 5–4.

Each sketch should be identified with the case number, date and time, a brief description of the crime, the address or location, and the name of the investigating officer. Compass north should be indicated off to one side. The legend or notebook reference, keyed by number or letter to each item of evidence, should fully identify the item by make, model, and serial number if appropriate or by a verbal description. For example, in the case of a firearm: 1. Pistol, Colt government model, .45 cal., ser. no. 234567; in the case of another item: 2. Crowbar, 18 in. long, probable dried bloodstain on hooked end with hairs adhering to stain.

Notes

The investigator's notes are used to relate chronologically the officer's actions at the scene, give a verbal description of the officer's observations and examinations of evidence, and identify the photographs and sketches. Notes serve as the starting point for the final written report, but the notes themselves are kept permanently on file, and the investigator uses them as a reference when it comes time to testify in court. Notes should always be clearly written, preferably in block letters. They should also be complete. No matter how good a memory an investigator may have, he or she should never rely on it. If there is any doubt whether or not an observation or event is pertinent, it is better to include it.

In addition to an overall description of the crime scene, the notes should identify any victims if possible and describe them in detail, including the type and location of wounds. Each item of evidence is described as it is discovered. The location is related to the sketch and all measurements are noted. Finally, the manner of collecting and packaging each item and any identification markings placed by the investigator on the item or on the package should be described briefly.

The notes for each case should be kept separate from those of all other cases. Each set should be identified by case number, the officer's name and rank, the date and time, the nature of the investigation, and the location. The names of all personnel aiding in the investigation should also be included. If one officer is appointed to collect all the evidence, he or she should be the one to maintain the notes.

Collection and Preservation of Evidence

The various types of evidence have their own peculiarities which must be taken into account during the collection process. Fingerprints, for example, are treated very differently from hairs and fibers. Specific collection and preservation methods for the individual items are treated separately in later chapters.

When investigators approach the scene of a crime, they must be prepared to handle any kind of evidence. They must have available an assortment of containers suitable for collecting the various items. These would include plastic and paper evidence bags of various sizes, boxes, plastic pill bottles, and envelopes. Glass jars that have tight rubber seals and clean metal paint cans can be used for liquid and volatile materials. The investigator should always be equipped with a magnifying glass, flashlight, tweezers or forceps (both plain and rubber tipped), a pocket knife, scissors, and a steel measuring tape. Pliers, wirecutters, and an assortment of standard household tools should be available when

71

needed. During the search and collection process it is advisable to wear rubber or cotton gloves in order to avoid contaminating evidence. For evidence like fingerprints, tire impressions, tool marks, and other impressions that cannot be removed from the scene, appropriate developing and casting materials must be available. A supply of the necessary basic materials may be kept in the investigator's cruiser or official vehicle; the investigator can call in to headquarters for specialized materials that are infrequently used. In larger jurisdictions that have high crime rates a special truck or van containing all necessary backup material for the investigator is usually available for dispatch to the scene.

Evidence Marking

When investigators testify in court, it is essential that they be able to state with certainty that a given courtroom exhibit is indeed the item of evidence that they collected at the crime scene in question. For that reason, investigators must mark or label the evidence when they collect it in a manner that they will be able to identify in court. If possible, a permanent identifying mark and the date of collection should be inscribed on the evidence itself. For metallic, plastic, or other hard objects, it is best to scratch the mark into the material with a hard-pointed stylus. Investigators can use their initials or badge numbers as a mark —never an "X." Plaster casts can be identified by indenting the mark in the plaster before it hardens. Fabrics can be identified with indelible ink. All marks should be made in an inconspicuous place where they do not interfere with other evidence that may be on the object. Items too small to be marked should be packaged in containers of appropriate size and sealed in evidence bags with special evidence tape, which shows any signs of tampering. The investigator can write his or her mark across the seals. In addition to the identifying mark, a label should be either tied onto the evidence itself or affixed to the package. The label should include the collecting officer's full name, rank, and badge number, the case number, the date and time of collection, and a description of the evidence.

The marking of objects for identification may sometimes conflict with the need to preserve fingerprints or other trace evidence on the object for laboratory identification. It is almost impossible to mark an object like a firearm, cartridge case, or tool without risking smudging fingerprints. If a fingerprint technician is available at the crime scene, the technician should check items for prints before they are handled by anyone else; then the item can be marked and packaged. If the evidence has to be sent to the laboratory for the fingerprint check, the evidence should not be marked. It should be packaged and sealed in an evidence container with as much care as possible to avoid destroying latent prints.

Preserving the Chain of Custody

An item of evidence must be accounted for from the moment it is collected until the time it appears in court; otherwise, the defense can claim it as inadmissible because it might have been tampered with.

Evidence should pass through as few hands as possible. The best practice is for the investigator to hand carry it to the evidence property room and personally pick it up from there when it is time to take it to court. Whenever an item passes from one person to another, the person giving it up should get a receipt for it, and a written entry should be made on the envelope stating who gave it to whom, the date and time, and the purpose of the exchange.

When evidence goes to the crime laboratory for examination, the laboratory scientist naturally has to open the package to gain access to the material. Since the field investigator's seal is evidence in itself, the laboratory examiner should avoid breaking it if possible. A paper envelope, for instance, can be slit open at the end opposite to the seal. If the only way a laboratory examiner can get access is by breaking the seal, it is a good idea to photograph the seal first for the record. Examiners must write on the package their name, the date and time they opened it, and the purpose of the examination. When they are finished with the package, they should reseal it, again indicating the date and time, and return it to the property room.

The property room is run by an evidence custodian who signs for every article received and must obtain a receipt for every article given out. The evidence custodian should also maintain a running property log indicating the date and time an object was received, the case number, from whom the object was received, and the storage location in the property room. When the evidence custodian releases the item, the log should reflect the date, time, and purpose of the transfer and the name of the officer receiving it.

Review Questions

1. The officer in charge of investigating a crime scene should
   a. Allow any police official who wants to to enter the crime scene as a matter of courtesy.

   b. Have any dead bodies removed before beginning the investigation
   c. Cordon the search area and post officers to keep out intruders
   d. Proceed to collect evidence even if the photographer has not arrived

2. Which of the following will *not* help in estimating the time of death?
   a. Rigor mortis
   b. Post-mortem lividity
   c. Body temperature
   d. Cadaveric spasm

3. The evacuation of the bowels and bladder upon death is caused by
   a. Rigor mortis
   b. Muscle relaxation
   c. Cadaveric spasm
   d. Chemical degeneration

4. (T, F) If a vehicle is found which is suspected to have been used in a hit-and-run accident, it should immediately be returned to the scene so that the accident can be reenacted.

5. When clothing is to be searched for evidence,
   a. It should be cut away in order to avoid unbuttoning buttons
   b. All items should be carefully folded and packed together in a large bag
   c. The search should be conducted at the crime scene if possible
   d. Each item should be packaged separately and removed to the laboratory

6. Crime scene photographs
   a. Should be prepared in conjunction with notes and sketches
   b. Should be as gory as possible in order to impress a jury
   c. Should be restricted to *corpus delicti* evidence
   d. Are generally not admissible in court

7. In making crime scene sketches
   a. Each item of evidence should be drawn in detail
   b. Distances between evidence items and fixed objects should be indicated
   c. Distances should be carefully paced off
   d. All the above

8. (T, F) Investigators may mark evidence with an "X" if they make an appropriate notation in their notebook.

9. Investigators put their mark on an item of evidence so that
   a. They can later claim it as a souvenir
   b. The evidence custodian will know who collected it
   c. They can later identify it in court
   d. Crime lab technicians will know whom to ask about it

CHAPTER SIX

—— PHOTOGRAPHY ——
FOR THE INVESTIGATOR

The collection of evidence from a crime scene is a highly skilled proceeding that entails close observation and painstaking attention to detail. But even the most skillful investigation is of little value if the details are not recorded in a way that can be presented in court. The principal recording methods are the investigator's notes, sketches, and photography. Each of these has advantages over the others, but there is probably no form of evidence record that can make as strong an impression on a jury as good photography.

The main advantages of photography are accuracy of detail, objectivity, and permanence. Although human vision may be more accurate at the moment of observation, human memory is faulty. It is often years after an investigation before a case comes to trial, and the investigating officer will have been involved in many other cases in the meanwhile. Nothing will refresh the investigator's memory of any given case better than the photographs that were taken at the time of the investigation.

Photography is appropriate to every kind of investigation from accidents, to crimes, to arson. Most police departments have officers who specialize in photography, and normally they will be the ones to provide the necessary photographic support to an investigation. Nevertheless, every investigator should understand the principles of photography and be able to photograph the scene of an investigation if necessary.

TYPES OF CAMERAS

There are many different types and makes of cameras available which the investigative photographer can use efficiently. Unfortunately, there is no single camera that can do everything, but high-quality cameras have interchangeable lenses and accessories that enable them to perform almost any job a photographer desires.

Press Cameras

Traditionally, police photographers have favored press-type cameras such as the Speed Graphic that has a large 4-inch by 5-inch format. *Format* refers to the negative size. The main advantage of a large format is that it enables the photographer to get more visual information into the picture without having to enlarge it. The more a print has to be enlarged, the more detail is lost. The large scale also makes the press camera excellent for 1:1 scale close-up shots of fingerprints and other small items of evidence when used with a special close-up attachment like the Faurot Foto Focuser. The standard press camera is designed to use cut film holders, which contain two sheets of film. But by changing the film holder the camera can be adapted to a film pack that holds from 12 to 16 pieces of film or to a roll film that takes more pictures but in a smaller format (2¼ inches by 2¾ inches) and in black and white only. It can also be adapted to a Polaroid Land holder, which will produce a finished 4-inch by 5-inch print in a few seconds.

35mm Cameras

A serious disadvantage of large format cameras is that they are big and heavy. There are times when investigative photographers have to move fast and take pictures from difficult angles and positions where a big camera would be too cumbersome. For this reason, smaller, lighter 35mm cameras are becoming increasingly popular. Although they have a smaller format (24mm X 36mm), excellent fine-grain films are available for them which permit enlargement without significant loss of detail. They are not well-suited to 1:1 scale photography of fingerprints because only one or two prints will appear on the negative, but smaller-scale photographs can easily be enlarged to life size. 35mm cameras take rolls of 20 or 36 exposures in both black and white and in color, which allows for more pictures without reloading than press cameras without any special attachments. The short focal length of the 35mm camera gives it greater depth of field than larger cameras, which means that a greater portion of the scene is in focus (focal length and depth of field are discussed later in the chapter). This is an important consideration in crime scene photography where it is often desirable to get a large portion of a room in focus. In addition to crime scene photography, 35mm cameras are especially well-suited to surveillance work because they are easy to carry around, are not very conspicuous, and are readily adaptable to changing conditions.

The 35mm camera is also commonly used for photomicrography (photography through a microscope). An adapter is used in place of a lens to mount the camera on the end of the microscope and the microscope itself becomes the lens. Photomicrography is an important function of the crime laboratory because a large percentage of the evidence used in criminalistics is examined through a microscope.

Many modern 35mm cameras have light meters built into them so that they read the light intensity through the lens. This feature is especially advantageous when filters are used because many filters reduce the light intensity and therefore necessitate a change in camera setting. If an external light meter is used, the change has to be calculated each time; if an internal meter is used, the change is made automatically.

Polaroid Land Cameras

The Polaroid Land camera has become increasingly popular in criminal investigation. Its greatest advantage is that it produces a finished print in seconds after the picture is taken. Formerly, its main disadvantage for investigative work was that there was no negative, but Polaroid now makes black-and-white positive/negative films which produce negatives in addition to the usual positive prints. The importance of the negative is that it can be held on file as a permanent record from which additional prints or enlargements can be made. The Polaroid Land camera enables the investigative photographer to know right away whether or not a photograph is successful. Some photographers take a preliminary picture with a Polaroid camera to test the lighting conditions and then take the record photograph with a press camera or a 35mm camera. The Land camera does not produce color negatives or color slides and cannot accommodate the wide range of film types and interchangeable lenses that can be used with other cameras.

Fingerprint Cameras

Another camera that must be included in a discussion of investigative and evidence photography is the fingerprint camera (see Figure 6–1). This camera has a fixed lens and a built-in flash designed for 1:1 scale photography of fingerprints or any small items. The photographer merely places the camera on top of the print and releases the shutter. The photographer never has to bother with focusing or lighting.

FIGURE 6–1 Fingerprint camera. (Courtesy of Sirchie Finger Print Laboratories)

PRINCIPLES OF PHOTOGRAPHY

Although many of the refinements of photography are technically very sophisticated, its basic principles are very simple. This section is designed to acquaint students with the fundamental chemical and optical principles so that they will understand what is happening when they take pictures.

Photographic Chemistry

Photography depends on the ability of light to bring about a visible chemical change on a film emulsion in which the degree of change is proportional to the intensity of the light. An emulsion is a thin layer of gelatin that holds light-sensitive chemicals in an even, solid suspension against a firm backing material. The principle is basically the same for both negative and positive materials. In negative materials, which are commonly referred to as *film,* the base is generally made of transparent cellulose acetate. Positive, or printing, materials have an opaque base, usually paper.

The light-sensitive chemicals used in black-and-white photography are various combinations of silver chloride (AgCl), silver bromide (AgBr), and silver iodide (AgI). Chlorine, bromine, and iodine are part of a group of elements known as *halogens.* Halogens readily combine with metallic elements to form crystalline salts known as *halides.* The silver salts of these elements, known as *silver halides,* are sensitive to light. When light strikes the silver halides held in suspension in a gelatin emulsion, the photons in the light sensitize the crystals by causing electron shifts to take place in their molecules. The degree of sensitization is proportional to the amount of light striking any given point so that the light reflected from the bright areas in the scene or object being photographed sensitizes more silver halide molecules than light reflected from the dark areas. Therefore, the light entering the camera when a picture is taken creates a pattern of sensitized silver halide crystals in the film emulsion corresponding to the varying intensities of the scene. This pattern is called a *latent image* because it is invisible to the naked eye. The word latent means hidden.

The latent image is made visible by the developing process. The developer is a chemical that causes silver halides to decompose into free silver and the elemental halogen (i.e., chlorine, bromine, or iodine). The decomposition takes place preferentially around the sensitized molecules that make up the latent image, thereby causing free silver to be deposited in the emulsion in a pattern corresponding to the latent image. Free elemental silver is black; therefore, the areas of heaviest deposits appear dark on the film, and lighter deposits appear in varying shades of gray. Since the heaviest silver deposits occur in the areas that were most intensely struck by light, the dark areas in the film correspond to the bright areas in the original scene and the bright areas in the film correspond to the dark areas in the scene. It is because of this reversal of light and dark areas that the developed film is called a *negative.*

When the development is complete, unused silver halides remain in the emulsion and will turn dark if exposed to light. These are removed by dissolving them in a solution of sodium thiosulphate, also known as *hyposulphite* or *hypo.* This process is known as *fixing.* The free silver is not soluble in hypo and therefore remains in place in the emulsion.

The printing of positives from negatives is based on the same principles as the production of negatives. The negative image is projected onto a light-sensitive silver halide emulsion, usually on white paper. Dark areas in the negative come through as light areas on the print, thereby producing a positive reproduction of the original scene.

The Camera

A camera is nothing more than a device to control the amount of light falling on a film. It is actually possible to take good pictures with a simple light-tight box that has a pinhole in the end opposite the film.

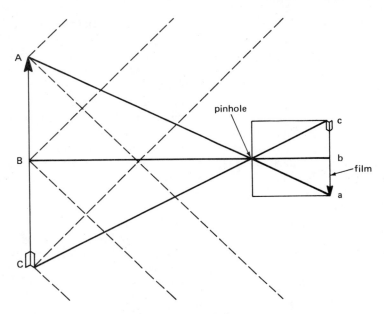

FIGURE 6–2 The principle of the pinhole camera.

To understand how this is possible, one must think of the object being photographed as being made up of innumerable tiny points each reflecting a wide beam of light. Figure 6–2 isolates three such points, *A*, *B*, and *C*. Because the pinhole is so small, it accepts only a very narrow portion of each beam, which sensitizes the silver halides on a single small spot on the film. If the pinhole were widened, a wider beam would strike the film from each point of light on the object. This would allow the beams to overlap each other on the film and put the picture out of focus.

The pinhole system is impractical in photography because it takes too long to expose each picture. The only way to speed up the process is to let in more light by widening the hole. This necessitates using a lens to focus the light rays.

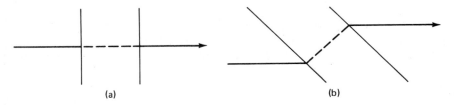

FIGURE 6–3 Illustration of refraction.

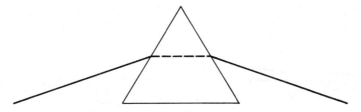

FIGURE 6–4   Light refracted by a prism.

Lenses

The purpose of a camera lens is to bend light rays back to a pinpoint focus at the point where they strike the film. Although most lenses are made of glass, some less expensive lenses are made of plastic; special-purpose lenses may be made of quartz or other materials. Because glass is denser than air, it refracts the light that passes through it. If the glass has parallel sides and the light strikes the glass at right angles, the glass slows down the speed of the light rays but it does not bend them [Figure 6–3(a)]. If the light strikes the same glass obliquely, that is, at an angle other than 90 degrees, the light is bent twice (once as it enters the glass and once as it exits) and it emerges into the air parallel to the original ray but displaced slightly to one side [Figure 6–3(b)].

If the sides of the glass are not parallel, as in a prism, the ray again is refracted twice but the entering and exiting rays are not parallel (see Figure 6–4). For the moment we will assume that no dispersion takes place but that a single ray of white light enters one side of the prism and exits the other. The degree to which the light is bent depends on

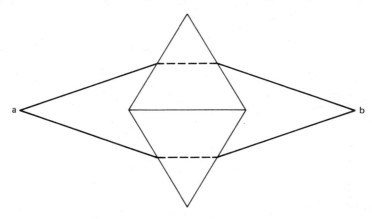

FIGURE 6–5   Light being focused by two prisms put together.

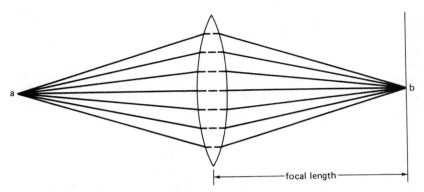

FIGURE 6–6 Light being focused by a convex lens.

the refractive index of the glass and the angle of the sides. If two prisms are put together as in Figure 6–5, we see that two light rays emanating from point A pass through and are focused at point B.

If the sides of this glass figure are ground into two smooth arcs, they form a lens, and the rays of light passing through at any point along its surface are focused at one point (See Figure 6–6). The distance between the optical center of the lens and the point where the light rays converge is the *focal length* of the lens. Figure 6–6 shows a ray coming from just one point, but a lens focuses the rays coming from all points on the object and pinpoints them in the same relative position on the film (see Figure 6–7).

If all light had the same wavelength, a single convex lens of the

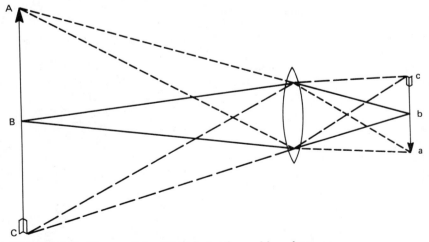

FIGURE 6–7 Three points of light being focused by a lens.

type shown in Figure 6–7 might be adequate for a camera. But as we saw earlier, a prism refracts light of different wavelengths at different angles. Therefore, if only one lens were used, the different colors would come into focus at different distances from the lens and the picture would be out of focus because of *chromatic aberration* [see Figure 3–5(b)]. Chromatic aberration can be corrected by using various combinations of lenses having different refractive indexes and degrees of curvature.

Another fault that may be present in lenses is *astigmatic aberration.* This is the inability of a lens to reproduce vertical and horizontal lines with the same degree of sharpness. One of the major criteria of quality and cost of a lens system is its ability to correct chromatic and astigmatic aberrations.

Focal Length

Earlier we defined the focal length of a lens as the distance between the optical center of the lens and the point where the light rays converge. In a camera this is the distance between the optical center of the lens and the film plane when the lens is focused on infinity. When identifying a lens the words *focal length* are generally not stated. So if one hears reference to a 50mm lens, this means that the lens has a focal length of 50mm.

The focal length of a camera lens bears an important relationship to the size of the negative. It is this relationship that determines the perspective distortion of a photograph. A lens that produces a photograph of approximately the same field of vision as the human eye with a minimum of distortion is called a *normal lens.* These are the all-purpose lenses that are usually sold with a camera. In general, the focal length of a normal lens is approximately the same as the diagonal of the negative. Thus the normal lens that goes with a 4-inch by 5-inch camera is approximately 6 inches, and the most common normal lens for a 35mm camera is 50mm.

Lenses having focal lengths significantly longer than normal are *telephoto lenses.* They have a narrower angle of vision and they have the property of enlarging the size of objects on the negative, thus making distant objects seem closer. Consequently, they are useful for surreptitious surveillance photography, which must often be conducted at a considerable distance from the subject.

Lenses having shorter than normal focal lengths are called *wide-angle lenses.* Because these lenses expand the angle of vision, they incorporate a wider view of a scene on the same negative and minimize the sizes of objects. Wide-angle lenses are very useful in indoor crime scene photography where space limitations prevent the photographer from backing away from the scene to include more of the scene in the picture. The disadvantage of wide-angle lenses is their tendency to grossly distort perspective, making objects in the foreground seem huge by comparison to more distant objects. The shorter the focal length, the greater the angle of vision (up to the 180-degree fish-eye) and the greater the tendency to distortion.

Depth of Field

In the discussion of lenses we saw that a lens bends the light rays so that they converge at a point. This is the point where the image is in exact focus. If a flat object like a document is being photographed, all parts of the object can be in perfect focus because all parts are the same distance from the lens. In most scenes to be photographed, however, there are objects at different distances from the lens that cannot all be in focus at the same time.

In Figure 6–8 we can see that at the distance where the light rays coming from point *A* are brought into focus by the lens, those from point *B* form a broad cone of light which would be out of focus, and the reverse is true at the point where *B* is in focus. These cones of light that appear on both sides of the focal point are called *circles of confusion*. It is the overlapping of these circles of confusion on a negative that causes a picture to appear out of focus. Since the human eye is not perfectly precise, it allows a certain amount of latitude on either side of the focal point in which an image will still appear to be in focus. In general, if the circle of confusion is no larger than 1/100 inch in diameter, the eye accepts it as being in focus. *Depth of field,* then, refers to the area in the scene being photographed in which objects at different distances from the lens are in acceptable focus. Thus, in Figure 6–8 if

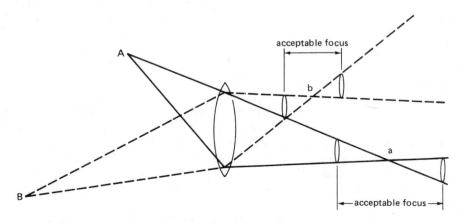

FIGURE 6–8   Circles of confusion and depth of field.

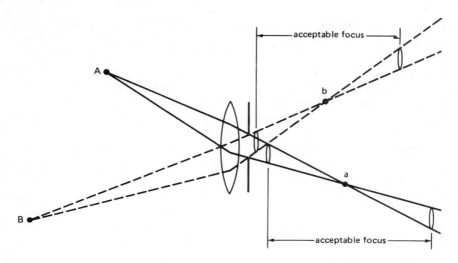

FIGURE 6–9 The smaller the aperture, the greater the depth of field.

the photographer were to focus on a point approximately halfway between *A* and *B*, neither *A* nor *B* would be in perfect focus but both would be in acceptable focus and both would be within the depth of field of the lens.

The possible depth of field varies with the focal length of the lens and the aperture setting. Lenses having short focal lengths have greater depths of field than do long lenses. Therefore, careful focusing is much more vital in telephoto photography than it is in normal or wide-angle photography. Also, the smaller the aperture (i.e., the larger the *f*/number), the greater the depth of field. Figure 6–9 illustrates the way a smaller aperture increases the depth of field of the situation shown in Figure 6–8 by flattening the cones of light.

A good rule of thumb in photographing scenes that contain objects at different distances from the lens is to set the lens at the smallest possible aperture and focus slightly in front of the halfway point between the nearest and most distant objects.

Exposure Controls

Exposure control means controlling the amount of light that reaches the film. This is done by means of the lens *diaphragm* and the *shutter speed*.

The Diaphragm

The diaphragm is a mechanism inside the lens which can be adjusted to control the size of the aperture through which the light passes into the camera. It corresponds to the iris in the human eye. The various diaphragm settings are given numerical values known as *f/numbers* (see Figure 6–10). The value of the f/number is determined by dividing the diameter of the diaphragm opening into the focal length of the lens. If the diaphragm of a 50mm lens is opened to 12.5mm, the f/number at that setting is 4 and is written $f/4$. The smaller the f/number, the larger the aperture. The largest aperture at which a lens can be set (i.e., the smallest number) is known as the *speed* of the lens, and the larger the maximum aperture, the faster the lens. Lens speed and focal length together are generally used to identify a lens. For example, a lens designated 2.8/50 has a lens speed of $f/2.8$ and a focal length of 50mm.

Most lenses are designed with a range of f/numbers indicating the diaphragm apertures at which they can be set. The f/numbers most commonly used are 1.4, 2, 2.8, 4, 5.6, 8, 11, 16, 22, 32, 45, and 64. The numbers in this series are known as *full stops*. They are so called because each higher number lets in just half as much light as the preceding number. Any number in between the full stops lets in proportionately less light than the preceding full stop and is known as an *intermediate stop*. While some lenses are designed to be faster than others, no lens combines the whole range of stops. A lens having a range of f/values from 2.8 to 16 is more than adequate for most forensic photography jobs. Since f/numbers are referred to as stops, it is common practice to speak of *stopping down* when reducing the size of the aperture.

Shutter Speed

The shutter controls the amount of time that light is allowed to pass into the camera. There are two basic types of shutter: the between-the-lens shutter and the focal plane shutter. The between-the-lens shutter is housed in the lens itself and works by means of a spring mechanism that opens a group of thin metal overlapping blades for a certain period of time and closes them automatically. The focal plane shutter is housed in the camera. It is a cloth or metal curtain that has an adjustable slit in it which shoots across the film plane under spring tension.

The amount of time the shutter stays open is known as the *shutter speed*. Different speeds are available on different make cameras. A typical range of speeds on a good 35mm camera that has a focal plane shutter is 1 second, 1/2 second, 1/4 second, 1/8 second, 1/15 second, 1/30 second, 1/60 second, 1/125 second, 1/250 second, 1/500 second, and 1/1,000 second. In this series each setting lets in one-half as much light as the next lower setting. Most cameras also have a B (bulb) setting in which the shutter stays open as long as the shutter release button is held down and closes when the button is let up. Many cameras also have

FIGURE 6–10   Top view of 35 mm camera shows shutter speed, f/number, and distance settings.

a T (time) setting in which the shutter opens when the release button is pushed the first time and closes when it is pushed a second time. The B and T settings are used when exposures longer than 1 second are needed.

Film Speed

Diaphragm settings and shutter speeds are used in combination with each other to bring about precise exposure control under varying conditions. When less light is available, either the diaphragm must be opened or the shutter speed must be slowed down, or both. The exact amount of light that is needed to photograph a given scene adequately depends on the speed of the film. Film speed is a measure of a film's sensitivity to light. Fast films are very sensitive and need relatively little light; slow films are less sensitive and need more light to photograph the same scene. For purposes of uniformity, all American film manufacturers recognize the *ASA* (American Standards Association) *exposure index system* for identifying film speed, and although different systems may be used in other countries, most foreign manufacturers also indicate the ASA number of their films. The *ASA number* is the basic reference point for the calibration of light meters and the calculation of exposure controls. The ASA number for every film is printed on the film package and on the data sheet that comes with every roll of film. The numbers may range from a very slow ASA 6 to an extremely fast ASA 1600 or higher.

Fast films, because they require little light, can be used in conjunction with fast shutter speeds to capture very rapid action scenes without blur, but they generally do this at the expense of fine detail. For the most part, the silver halide particles on fast film are relatively large. These large particles give rise to a "grainy" appearance on the finished photograph which is all the more pronounced if the print is enlarged.

Generally speaking, the slower the film, the finer the grain, and the finer the grain, the better the resolving power (i.e., the ability to capture fine detail). Because of their high resolving power, slow films are especially suitable for photographic enlargements. Except in surveillance cases, it is rare that the investigator needs to photograph moving objects. For the most part, all-purpose films having ASA ratings in the range of 50 to 125 used with artificial illumination for indoor work meet all the needs of crime scene photography. For surveillance photography, where the subjects may be in motion and available light must be used, films having speeds of ASA 400 or higher may be needed.

Light Meters

The best way to determine the appropriate f/stop and shutter speed for a given condition of light is to use a light meter. Most light meters operate on the basis of a photoelectric cell which sets up a small electrical current when light strikes it. The more intense the light, the stronger the current. The changes in light intensity are indicated by a needle moving across a calibrated dial. The meter is equipped with a conversion table that enables the user to calculate several combinations of f/numbers and shutter speeds from the light intensity reading. The conversion table must be calibrated on the basis of the ASA number of the film being used. Any of the f/number and shutter speed combinations shown on the meter for a given light intensity will transmit the right amount of light to the film. If there is motion in the scene, a combination with a fast shutter speed should be used Otherwise, it is generally best to use the smallest possible aperture since that will increase the depth of field.

When using a light meter one should bear in mind that most meters react to the average light intensity of a scene. Therefore, if a meter reading is taken of a scene containing mostly bright areas and a few dark areas, a photograph taken on the basis of that reading will tend to underexpose the dark areas. If the important part of the scene is in a dark area, the photographer must compensate by either opening the aperture or using a slower shutter speed. For example, in surveillance photography if the subject is standing in a dark doorway in an otherwise bright scene, it is important to adjust the camera settings on the basis of the amount of light in the doorway. The simplest method of ensuring correct camera settings is to walk up to the dark area and take a separate meter reading of it. This would obviously not be practical in a covert surveillance. In such a case the photographer should take several shots at successively wider openings. It is better to waste film than to lose the photograph.

Color Sensitivity of Film

While it is obvious that color film must have approximately the same sensitivity to color as the human eye if it is to reproduce a scene the way we see it, beginning photographers are generally not aware of the importance of color sensitivity in black-and-white films. Colors in black-and-white photography are reproduced as tones or shades of gray. A red blood spot comes out dark and a yellow shirt comes out light. In general-purpose photography it is important that the film have approximately the same sensitivity to the brightness of colors as the human eye. The silver halides in black-and-white emulsions are actually sensitive only to the blue, violet, and ultraviolet end of the light spectrum. This means that they do not record green, yellow, orange, and red wavelengths unless the film is chemically sensitized to them. Black-and-white films are classified into four groups based on their color sensitivity: monochromatic, orthochromatic, panchromatic, and infrared.

Monochromatic film is also called *color blind* because it is sensitive only to the blue, violet, and ultraviolet end of the spectrum. It is less expensive than films having greater sensitivity and can be used in applications such as photocopying in which tonal distinction is not necessary.

Orthochromatic film is sensitive to ultraviolet, violet, blue, green, and yellow-green but is blind to yellow, orange, and red. It is also used in copy work and can be used when some tonal distinction is desired.

Panchromatic film most closely resembles the sensitivity range of the human eye. It is not only sensitive to all the colors of the visible spectrum, but it also closely approaches the human eye in sensitivity to the intensity of the various colors. Panchromatic film is designed for all-purpose photography and comes in a wide range of speeds. It is subdivided into type B and type C emulsions, which are basically the same except that type C is more sensitive to the red end of the spectrum. Panchromatic type B film is suitable to almost all the needs of the investigative photographer.

Infrared film is special-purpose film that is sensitive to the deep red and invisible infrared portions of the spectrum. Like all silver halide emulsions, it is also sensitive to ultraviolet, violet, and blue.

Infrared and Ultraviolet Photography

Photography in the invisible regions of infrared and ultraviolet has many applications in investigative photography and criminalistics. By using infrared film and a source of infrared light it is possible to take surveillance photographs without the subject's being aware that his or her picture is being taken. Infrared camera traps can operate even in total darkness. The illumination is usually provided by a standard tungsten lamp, flashbulb, or electronic flash covered with a filter that allows only infrared rays to pass. If the surveillance subject happens to be looking directly at the light, he or she may notice a slight red glow. Otherwise, the infrared illumination is totally invisible.

Infrared photography may reveal items of evidence that are not visible to the naked eye. For example, powder patterns on dark-colored cloth show up dark in an infrared photograph, but the cloth comes out light (see Figure 15–8). Infrared is also useful in detecting alterations in documents. Although difrerent inks may look the same to the eye, they often reflect infrared rays in different amounts so that the original ink shows up differently from the ink used to make the alteration (see Figure 23–3). Similarly, infrared can be used to bring out the writing on charred documents.

Ultraviolet light can be used for many similar purposes to infrared. When ultraviolet light strikes certain substances, it chemically excites them in such a way that they luminesce (glow) with visible light. Many inks and pigments luminesce with different colors and intensities so that illumination of a document by ultraviolet light can often reveal forgeries and alterations. Luminescent fingerprint powders can be used to good advantage when it is otherwise difficult to differentiate a print from its background. In these processes, invisible ultraviolet light, sometimes called *black light,* is used to illuminate the subject, but a lens filter prevents the invisible ultraviolet light from entering the camera; only the visible luminescence is used to record the picture. This is known as *luminescence photography.* Pure ultraviolet photography, which does not depend on luminescence, can also be used since all black-and-white films are sensitive in the ultraviolet range. In these applications the subject is illuminated with ultraviolet light and a lens filter is used which allows only ultraviolet to enter the camera. The film records the varying amounts of ultraviolet reflected by the different substances being photographed.

Color Photography

Investigative agencies should not limit themselves to black-and-white photography because there are many subjects which can be adequately represented only in color. In arson photography, for example, flame color may be important evidence in itself. Color gives a more reliable portrayal of most crime scenes. Blood looks like blood instead of a dark spot. In cases in which the matching of paint chips or glass fragments is part of the evidence, a black-and-white photograph shows only the physical match of the contours whereas color photography also shows any color matches. Also, since black-and-white photography can only show tonal distinctions between colors of different intensities, two different colors of similar brightness come out the same shade of gray on a black-and-white print, but a color print reveals the difference.

Although color photography is usually more realistic than black-and-white, it does have some disadvantages. Color films have generally less resolving power than fine grained black-and-white films do and are therefore not as well-suited to enlargements. Color film is also less tolerant of exposure errors. Black-and-white film has considerable latitude in this respect and good prints can still be produced from negatives that are overexposed or underexposed, but a small amount of overexposure or underexposure ruins a color picture. This can be an important consideration in surveillances, where lighting conditions may change rapidly and the photographer has to make rapid estimates of exposure settings. When exposed and developed properly, color films have reasonably good color fidelity, but errors in either of these processes can result in color distortions that give inaccurate representations of the scenes.

It is good practice for an investigative photographer to have both a black-and-white and a color capability for every investigation in order to have the flexibility to take advantage of the assets of both.

Two types of color film are generally used in investigative photography: *color reversal film* and *color negative film*. Color reversal film is the type that is used in colored slides. It is called reversal film because in the developing process the negative is actually transformed into a positive transparency. The positive transparency can be projected directly onto a screen. Color negative film is used to make colored prints. The advantage of reversal film is that it is inexpensive since only one process is involved, but it has the disadvantage of requiring projection equipment to view it properly. This may become an advantage in a courtroom display where the projection enables the entire court to see the evidence at the same time. Color prints are more expensive than slides or black-and-white prints. For the sake of economy, black-and-white film should be used if there is no clear advantage in using color.

Artificial Illumination

Since most crime scenes are indoors, it is often necessary to use artificial illumination. The usual types are photo floodlamps, flashbulbs, or electronic flashes. When using artificial illumination, the photographer must calculate the appropriate f/number for any given distance on the basis of guide numbers. Guide numbers are provided in the data sheets that come with each type of film and in the instructional materials that come with the lighting equipment. The choice of shutter speed is important only for flash synchronization since the duration of the flash is shorter than all but the fastest shutter speeds. If the recommended shutter speed for the camera (usually 1/30 second or 1/60 second for a 35mm focal plane camera using an electronic flash) is used, the aperture must be opened wider for objects at greater distances from the lens because the amount of light provided by artificial lighting units diminishes rapidly with increased distance. To find the correct f/stop, one must divide the guide number by the distance in feet from the lens to the subject and set the camera on the f/number closest to the result of the division. For example, most electronic flash units are rated as to output in beam candlepower seconds (BCPS). For a film having a speed of ASA 125, the guide number for an electronic flash unit with 1,000 BCPS output is 80. If the subject is 10 feet away, the camera should be set at f/8 ($80 \div 10 = 8$).

If the scene to be photographed is a deep one that needs artificial illumination, the photographer can use several extension lamps to illuminate the whole scene. If the lamps are not available, the photographer can use a technique called *painting with light*. The camera is firmly mounted on a tripod and the shutter is held open in the time position. While an assistant holds something in front of the lens (being careful not to move the camera), the photographer takes the flash unit in front of the camera and makes a series of flashes in different parts of the scene. The assistant uncovers the lens when the photographer is ready to make a flash and then recovers it while the photographer takes a new position. Each flash must, of course, be made from the side so that the photographer's shadow does not appear in the picture.

Filters

The use of filters in photography can be rather complicated, and for most investigative purposes the beginning photographer can get adequate results without them. There are some situations, however, in which filters are indispensable. We have already seen how filters are used in the highly specialized areas of ultraviolet and infrared photography, and there are several other areas of criminalistics and crime scene photography where they can be useful. Most filters work by selectively absorbing certain wavelengths of light, thereby preventing them from entering the camera. In general-purpose photography four types of filters are commonly used:

Color correction filters
Color contrast filters
Neutral density filters
Polarizing filters

Color Correction Filters

Natural sunlight has more blue in it than artificial tungsten illumination (photo floodlamps), which has a higher concentration of the red end of the spectrum. Consequently, color films are manufactured with their color sensitivity balanced either for daylight or for tungsten. If daylight film is used in daylight, no filter is needed. Similarly, no filter is needed if tungsten film is used indoors with floodlamps. However, if daylight film is used with tungsten illumination or tungsten film in sunlight, a color correction filter is needed to compensate for the different balance of color sensitivity. Since blue flashbulbs and most electronic flash units are designed to reproduce daylight conditions rather than tungsten, daylight color film can be used in most situations without a filter.

Color Contrast Filters

Color contrast filters are used primarily in black-and-white photography. They are used to lighten or darken certain areas of a scene and to make the intensity of color brightness as recorded by film more like the brightness perceived by the human eye. The most commonly used contrast filters are red, green, yellow, and blue. Each filter allows wavelengths of its own color to pass into the camera and expose the film and absorbs (filters out) the wavelengths of its complementary colors. This means that in a photograph a filter causes its own color to appear lighter in the print and its complementary colors to appear darker. The

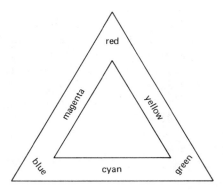

FIGURE 6–11 The triangle of primary and complementary colors. The complementary colors, on the sides of the triangle, are mixtures of the primaries on either side of them.

triangle in Figure 6–11 shows the primary colors at the corners and their complementary colors along the opposite sides.

Contrast filters are often used in crime scene photography to make the main subject of the photograph stand out against its background. For example, if bloodstains are found on a dark blue background, the eye can separate them because it distinguishes colors, but a black-and-white photograph, which renders different colors only as shades of gray, may see the dark red of the bloodstain as having the same brightness intensity as the dark blue background. If a blue filter is used, the blue portion of the scene is lightened in the photograph, thereby making the bloodstain stand out.

Neutral Density Filters

Neutral density filters partially absorb all wavelengths of light to the same degree. They are used to reduce the overall intensity of light in extremely bright scenes while maintaining normal color balance. Neutral density filters are often used in close-up flash photography. At the close distance, the flash puts out more light than necessary to illuminate the object. Since there is no convenient way to reduce the intensity of the flash, a neutral density filter can be used to prevent some of the light from entering the camera.

Polarizing Filters

Polarizing filters do not work by absorbing selective wavelengths of light. Instead, they allow only light waves vibrating in one plane to enter the camera. Their main use is in cutting out glare from nonmetallic surfaces. When ordinary light is reflected off a nonmetallic surface, such as water, glass, varnished wood, or glossy paint, it becomes polarized. That is, the reflected light vibrates only in the plane parallel to the surface. The polarizing filter can be turned at will so that its plane of polarization can be set at any angle to the vibratory plane of the polarized light. If the filter is set at right angles to the plane of the reflected light, the light in that plane does not enter the camera. Therefore, since the glare from shiny, nonmetallic surfaces is made up of polarized reflected light, it can be eliminated by using a polarizing filter. Because a polarizing filter eliminates a portion of the light entering the camera without changing the color balance, it can also double as a neutral density filter even when there is no problem with glare.

Filter Factors

All filters reduce to some extent the amount of light entering the camera. Therefore, when taking a picture with a filter, the photographer must make an exposure compensation either by opening the diaphragm aperture or by increasing the exposure time. The amount of compensation can be calculated by the *filter factor,* a number which is either engraved on the side of the filter or indicated in the instruction sheet that comes with the filter. The filter factor is multiplied times 1 to tell the additional amount of light needed. For example, if a filter has a factor of 2, twice as much light is needed to properly expose the negative as is needed to take the same picture without a filter. The adjustment can be made either by opening the aperture one full stop or by reducing the shutter speed by one-half. Some of the denser filters, such as the deep red 25A, have factors as high as 8. This means that eight times more light is needed with the filter than without it. This exposure increase can be achieved by opening the aperture three full stops or by multiplying the exposure time by eight or by some combination of the two. When one is using a filter one is not familiar with, it is a good practice to take three pictures of every subject: (1) one at the calculated exposure setting, (2) one at one full stop higher, and (3) one at one full stop lower than the calculated setting. This procedure is called *bracketing.*

CRIME SCENE PHOTOGRAPHY

Every crime scene has its own unique features. Therefore, the investigator must use common sense in deciding the photographic requirements of each case. There are, however, certain basic principles that are generally valid.

It is essential that the crime scene be photographed before any of the evidence is disturbed. Therefore, the scene should be protected from all intruders (including officials) until the photographs are taken. The only exception to this is the removal of living victims in order to save their lives. The first photographs taken should be of the undisturbed scene. That means that no rulers, tape measures, or other police equipment should appear in the picture. Courts have been known to refuse to accept such photographs on the grounds that even the presence of a ruler constitutes tampering with the scene. A second series of photographs should be taken to include scale indicators.

Photography must not be considered a substitute for the crime scene sketches. No matter how good the photographs are, they cannot accurately represent the relative dimensions and distances between objects. The sketches and the photographs should be done in conjunction with each other, and all camera positions should be indicated on a sketch.

Overall scenes should be photographed from normal eye level. Pictures should be taken from the point of view of an observer approaching the scene and also from the point of entry of the criminal if different from the normal entrance. In addition to the pictures of the scene, record shots should be taken of the exteriors of all premises where crimes have been committed.

Bodies should be photographed from at least two positions (preferably four if space permits) at 90 degrees to each other. A first series should be taken from eye level and a second series should be taken from above with the use of a step ladder. Then close-up shots should be taken of any wounds. After the corpse is removed, the spot where it lay should be photographed again to record any bloodstains or other evidence that may have been hidden by the body.

The photographer should make every effort to show perspective as close to natural as possible. This may be difficult when taking pictures in close quarters, especially when wide-angle lenses are used. The distortion of wide-angle lenses can often be corrected by enlarging the prints. This has the effect of bringing the viewer's eye closer to the scene, thus approximating the view that the camera sees through a lens that has a short focal length.

Every small item of evidence should be photographed close up: first as found in its undisturbed state and then with a ruler placed next to it for scale. Fingerprints should be photographed after development with powder or chemicals directly on the item of evidence on which they are found. If possible, the photograph should be used for identification purposes and the prints should be left on the item. If this is not possible and the prints must be lifted, they should be photographed after they are transferred to cards.

The photographer should keep a running log of every evidence picture he or she takes. Log references should include the case number, the date and time, the camera and lens used, the $f/$number and shutter speed, the type of film, and the position of the camera. For a photograph to be accepted in court, the photographer must be able to attest to its accuracy and to the circumstances in which it was taken.

Review Questions

1. The camera *format* refers to
   a. The size of the negative
   b. The design of the camera
   c. The distance between the lens and the object
   d. The focal length of the camera

2. (T, F) 35mm cameras are good for 1:1 scale close-up shots.

3. Which of the following are halogens?
   a. Silver, iodine, and sulfur
   b. Chlorine, mercury, and hypo
   c. Iodine, chlorine, and bromine
   d. Bromine, calcium, and silver iodide

4. (T, F) A latent image can be seen if the undeveloped film is held up to a light.

5. (T, F) A pinhole camera is useful as a backup camera in investigative photography.

6. A beam of light striking a pane of glass at a 33-degree angle is
   a. Diffused
   b. Refracted twice
   c. Refracted once
   d. Slowed down but not bent

7. The distance between the optical center of a lens and the point where the rays of light converge is
   a. The speed of the lens
   b. 35mm
   c. The refraction distance of the lens
   d. The focal length of the lens

8. (T, F) A high-quality lens is corrected for chromatic aberration and astigmatic aberration.

9. A telephoto lens
   a. Has greater depth of field than a normal lens does
   b. Increases the format of the negative
   c. Requires more careful focusing than a wide-angle lens does
   d. Is more subject to distortion than a wide angle lens

10. When one is photographing objects at different distances from the lens, it is best to focus

    a. On the nearest object
    b. Slightly in front of the halfway point between the nearest and most distant objects
    c. Slightly behind the halfway point between the nearest and most distant objects
    d. On the most distant object

11. (T, F) An aperture of $f/8$ lets in twice as much light as an aperture of $f/4$.

12. When fast film is being used,
    a. The negative is likely to be grainy
    b. A relatively large amount of light is needed
    c. It is possible to stop rapid action without a blur
    d. No light meter is necessary
    e. a and b
    f. a and c

13. Colorblind film is
    a. Panchromatic
    b. Used in general-purpose black-and-white photography
    c. Sensitive to ultraviolet and infrared light
    d. Monochromatic

14. Infrared photography can be used
    a. In total darkness
    b. In broad daylight
    c. To reveal powder patterns
    d. a and c
    e. a, b, and c

15. (T, F) Color slide film is also known as color reversal film.

16. If the guide number for a given combination of film and electronic flash is 160 and if the subject is 20 feet away from the lens, the $f/$number should be
    a. $f/2$
    b. $f/1.4$
    c. $f/16$
    d. $f/8$

17. When crime scenes are being photographed,
    a. The photographer's assistant should hold each evidence item up in front of the camera
    b. Bodies should be photographed from floor level
    c. Scale markers should not be used in order to avoid tampering with the scene
    d. Overall scenes should be photographed from normal eye level
    e. All the above

CHAPTER SEVEN

GLASS

Broken glass can be a major source of clues in many cases in which human testimony is either unavailable or unreliable. Burglars often have to break windows to reach their objectives, and car thieves sometimes get into automobiles by breaking in the side windows. Since there are usually no witnesses present to observe these crimes, investigators must derive most of their leads from the physical evidence.

Any time a person breaks a window, although it may appear that all the fragments fly in the direction of the blow, some tiny particles always fly backward. These particles can become embedded in the folds and fibers of the clothing of thieves without their being aware of them. If such particles are found on a suspect, they can be matched with the glass remaining at the crime scene. Similarly, particles embedded in the instrument used to break the glass may connect a criminal to a crime if the instrument is found in the criminal's possession.

Broken glass clues do not necessarily come from windows. Anytime there is violence, bottles, glasses, mirrors, eyeglasses, and other glass objects can be accidentally shattered, and fragments of these can also adhere to a criminal's clothing or the bottoms of the criminal's shoes. Whenever broken glass is present, even if it does not appear to have any connection with the crime, the investigator should bear in mind the possibility that the criminal walked through it and check the soles and heels of suspects' shoes.

In an automobile accident in which a driver flees without identifying himself or herself, broken glass left at the scene from headlights, taillights, and reflectors often plays an important role in identifying the vehicle. Although witnesses to hit-and-run crimes may often be present, it has been the experience of police that these witnesses' testimonies are extremely unreliable.

CHARACTERISTICS OF GLASS

Glass is a complex material that can vary greatly in its composition. It depends on the method of manufacture and the intended use. Ordinary glass was made by the ancient Egyptians many centuries before the Christian era. It is basically a mixture of the silicates of sodium and calcium (Na_2SiO_3 and $CaSiO_3$). The raw materials are sand (SiO_2), limestone ($CaCO_3$), and sodium carbonate (Na_2CO_3). If one wishes to produce glass of different properties, potassium may be substituted for sodium and the oxides of other metals may be added or substituted in various proportions for the calcium or silicon. The sand and other raw materials are melted together and cooled at a precise rate. The resulting glass is either a colloidal suspension or solid solution of the different compounds in each other. Unlike most other solid materials, glass does not crystallize when it hardens. It remains amorphous, that is, it retains the random distribution of molecules that is characteristic of liquids. In fact, glass can be described as a supercooled liquid, that is, a liquid that has been cooled below its freezing point without solidifying. Its apparent solidity is due to its extremely high viscosity (opposition to flow) and rigidity.

Strength

The tensile strength of glass is a function of the chemical bonding of the surface molecules. This is clearly demonstrated by the fact that it is possible to cut glass into any shape simply by scoring the surface with a glass cutter and breaking the glass under tension. Fiberglass owes its great strength to the large relative proportion of its surface area to its cross-sectional area. When the surface of glass is cracked or scratched, the glass becomes weak. Similarly, the effects of weather can weaken glass over a period of time by gradual erosion of the surface. For this reason, the older glass is, the weaker it is likely to be.

Physical Differences

There are great variations in the physical properties of glass that are due primarily to the different combinations of raw materials that go into its manufacture. Certain metals produce characteristic colors when added to the melt and other additives affect the strength and elasticity. Cobalt oxide (CoO), for example, produces a dark blue color popularly known as *cobalt blue;* and Pyrex, whose relatively low coefficient of expansion results in a high resistance to heat, is made by fusing borax ($Na_2B_4O_7$) and aluminum oxide (Al_2O_3) with sand.

Other variations in glass may be due to the presence of slight impurities or to differences in mechanical or heat treatments. Even a single type of glass is different from batch to batch because of the difficulty in reproducing the exact proportions. This is especially true of glasses that are made in small batches such as fine tableware and optical glass. Each individual batch is uniform and of very high quality but differs slightly in physical properties from other batches. Mass-produced glasses, like plate glass, window glass, and automobile glass, tend to have more uniformity of composition because of the continuous automatic feed of raw materials. Since the purity of the product is not so important as it is in the more expensive types of glass, incidental impurities from the raw materials are present and impart variations in physical properties that are sometimes observable even in different parts of the same glass product. Glass manufactured before mass production became commonplace (*ca.* 1940) shows even greater individual variation. By measuring these differences in physical properties crime laboratories can determine with a high degree of certainty whether or not different glass fragments have identical origins.

COLLECTION AND PRESERVATION

All broken glass at a crime scene should be photographed before it is handled by investigators. After the first photos are taken of the undisturbed evidence, the larger fragments should be numbered with a grease pencil on the side facing up and rephotographed or keyed to a sketch in order to facilitate a later reconstruction.

If a qualified fingerprint expert is present at the crime scene, the glass fragments should be checked for latent fingerprints before the fragments are collected and packed for transport to the laboratory. Otherwise, investigators should be careful to avoid destroying fingerprints when marking and handling the glass. Investigators should wear protective gloves to avoid leaving their own prints and they should pick up the fragments by the edges or with rubber-tipped tweezers.

All of the broken glass found at the scene of a crime or hit-and-run accident should be collected. The larger pieces should be carefully packaged in boxes with cotton or some other soft material between the pieces. Tiny particles from each individual area should be swept together and placed in pill bottles or other containers of suitable size. If possible, window frames containing the remaining jagged shards of a broken window should be brought to the laboratory intact. If the entire frame cannot be removed, the fragments should be numbered in place with a grease pencil and photographed and then carefully removed and packed in a separate box. All packages should be marked with the name or initials of the investigating officer, the date and time of collection, and the nature of the contents.

The clothing of victims and suspects should also be examined for glass particles. Cuffs and pockets should be turned out onto a sheet of clean white paper and the contents separately preserved in small vials or boxes. The clothing should then be vacuumed with a vacuum sweeper equipped with a filter attachment, and the filter should be forwarded to the laboratory. These containers should also be marked with appropriate identifying information.

INVESTIGATION OF GLASS

In one case of insurance fraud an individual attempted to simulate a robbery of some insured valuables by breaking a back window of his house and claiming that a burglar had broken in and stolen the articles. The owner had hidden the articles elsewhere. He thoughtlessly broke the window from the inside. He realized that he had made a mistake when he saw that the glass fragments had fallen outside. Therefore, he carefully picked up the pieces and deposited them under the broken window inside the house in order to make it appear that the window had been broken from the outside. In the course of the investigation a detective observed that, in spite of the apparent evidence of the fallen glass, the markings on the broken pieces remaining in the window frame indicated a blow from the inside. This inconsistency led the investigator to pursue his investigation until he found a pair of the homeowner's trousers in which there were tiny particles of glass stuck in the fold of a pocket. On examination in the laboratory these particles proved to have identical properties to the glass of the window. So it was clear that the man himself had broken the window and staged the crime.

Broken glass is frequently found as evidence in crimes. As the above case illustrates, the two areas in which it is particularly useful are in the ability to prove that bits of glass found in different places come from the same source and in determining from what direction a window is broken. Although some of the comparison work must be done in the laboratory, the investigating officer can derive much of the information right at the scene of the crime.

Field Investigation

When a pane of glass is broken by the force of a blow or a missile, the stresses involved cause cracks to develop which bear characteristic striations along their cross-sectional edges.

Radial Fractures

When an object strikes a flat piece of glass, the force causes the glass to bend outward in the direction it is pushed. Such a force stretches the surface molecules on the side away from the striking object; the surface molecules on the side of the blow are compressed. For simplicity, we will call the side opposite the impact the outer surface and the side of the impact the inner surface. Cracks begin to appear when the tension on the outer surface exceeds the elasticity of the surface molecules and the glass is actually pulled apart. These cracks first open on the outer surface and radiate outward like the spokes of a wheel in fairly straight lines from the point where the force was applied (see Figure 7-1). The progression of a radial fracture is faster on the outer surface than on the inner surface.

Concentric Fractures

As an object strikes a window, putting tension on the outer surface and compressing the inner surface at the point where it is struck, the outward bulging of the glass at the same time places tension on the

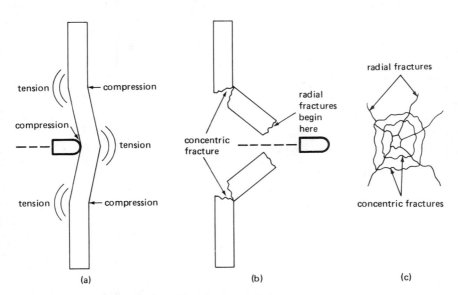

FIGURE 7-1 Formation of radial and concentric fractures.

inner surface of the glass in those areas surrounding the point of impact where the glass is forced to bend outward. This tension is often sufficient to cause cracks to appear in concentric rings around the point of impact. These cracks join the radial fractures and give rise to the formation of wedge-shaped fragments. When such fragments are found loose, it is helpful to remember that the point of the wedge always points toward the place where the glass was struck.

Rib Marks

As radial cracks progress outward from the point of impact, they make little pauses in their advance which cause conchoidal (shell-like) striations known as *rib marks* to be formed on the broken edge of the glass at each resting point (see Figure 7-2). The rib marks begin their formation perpendicular to the outer surface of the glass and arc backward toward the point of impact so that they touch the inner surface at a tangent. Thus, when examining radial fractures, one can easily determine the direction of the force causing the break by noting that the surface that the rib marks touch perpendicularly is the one opposite to the impact surface. Also, since the rib marks at the inner surface point back toward the place where the glass was struck, it is possible to determine the orientation of the glass fragments in relation to the point of impact.

Rib marks also appear in concentric fractures. Although they are similar in appearance to rib marks caused by radial fractures, they have the opposite orientation because the cracks first open on the inner surface. Therefore, the markings on the broken edge are perpendicular to the impact surface and are tangential to the outer surface (see Figure 7-3).

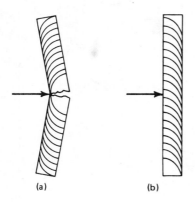

(a)   (b)

FIGURE 7–2 Formation of rib marks (a) in a radial fracture; (b) in a concentric fracture. Note opposite orientation of ribs.

FIGURE 7–3 Here two fragments of broken glass are being matched by comparing the orientation of their rib marks. (Courtesy of Wisconsin State Crime Laboratory)

Hackle Marks

In high-energy impacts, such as those caused by bullets, small, straight lines may appear perpendicular to the rib marks. These are termed *hackle marks* and are caused by the sudden strong shearing forces in the rupture (see Figure 7-4). Hackle marks are normally of less investigative significance than rib marks are, but since they sometimes appear when rib marks do not, they can be helpful in determining the impact surface.

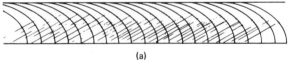

(a)

FIGURE 7–4 Drawing (a) shows the orientation of hackle marks to rib marks. As shown in photograph (b) hackle marks may be present when rib marks are absent. (Photograph courtesy of Wisconsin State Crime Laboratory)

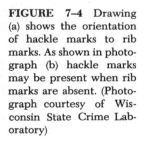

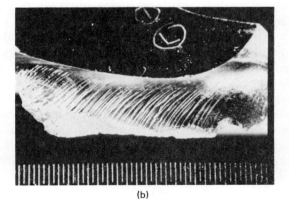

(b)

Safety Glass

There are two basic types of safety glass: *laminated* and *tempered.* Both are much stronger than ordinary glass and are commonly used in automobiles and construction.

Laminated glass consists of a piece of plastic sandwiched between two thin panes of glass. Laminated glass fractures in the same way that ordinary glass does, but the fragments stick to the plastic instead of shattering. Its construction makes it much more flexible than ordinary glass; therefore, it takes a more powerful blow to break it. Because of the greater tension produced on the inner surface, concentric fractures occur in safety glass more often than in ordinary glass. When cracks form in laminated safety glass, they often fail to go all the way through the glass. When this happens, the investigating officer can determine the direction of impact by running a fingernail or a sharp object across the cracks: if a radial crack can be felt on one side of the glass but not on the other, the side where the crack is felt is the one opposite to the blow. The reverse is true of concentric cracks: the side on which the crack can be felt is the impact side.

Tempered glass is manufactured in a single sheet, but it is made stronger than ordinary glass by a process of heating and sudden cooling. The fracture patterns described for other types of glass do not apply to tempered glass because it tends to break into little squares which do not have the dangerous sharp edges of other kinds of glass fragments.

Glass Hit by Missiles

If a small missile like a bullet or a stone strikes a pane of glass, small bits of glass are chipped off the exit side, leaving a cone-shaped crater of a larger diameter than the missile (see Figure 7-5). Even if the missile fails to penetrate the glass, its force may still cause such a crater to form on the opposite side, and it may also chip a hole smaller than its own diameter through the bottom of the crater.

If a bullet is fired at right angles to a pane of glass, the crater is roughly circular and the amount of glass chipped out is fairly even all around. If the bullet is fired at an angle, the crater is elongated in the direction of movement of the bullet. That is, if the bullet comes from the right (from the point of view of the shooter), it chips out more glass particles on the left-hand side of the crater than it does on the right. Conversely, if the bullet comes from the left, the crater is bigger on the right. By examining these effects an investigator can determine not only from which side of a window a shot was fired but also the approximate angle of fire.

If more than one bullet is fired through the same pane, regardless

106

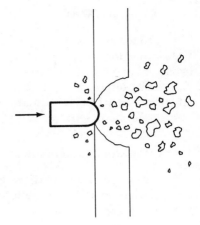

FIGURE 7-5 A missile striking a pane of glass forms a crater on the side opposite to the impact. Some glass chips also fly backward.

of direction, it is usually possible to tell which bullet strikes first. This might become an important consideration in a case in which a person claims self-defense in an exchange of gunfire through a window. The first bullet to penetrate causes the radial and possibly the concentric cracks described above. The second bullet also makes radial cracks, but their advance is stopped by any previously made cracks that lie in their path. Hence any fracture that is stopped by another fracture must have been made after the first fracture (see Figure 7-6).

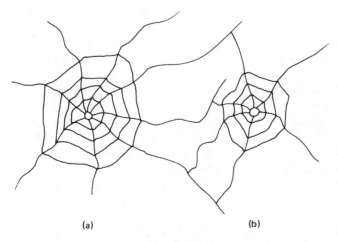

(a)   (b)

FIGURE 7-6 Penetration sequence. Bullet hole (b) was made after bullet hole (a).

Fractures Caused by Heat

Fractures that seem to occur spontaneously without the force of a blow may be caused by exposure to heat on one side of the glass. These fractures are easily recognizable because the cracks are random and wavy. The heat causes the molecules to stretch on one side and eventually break apart. When fragments fall out, they usually fall in the direction of the heat source.

Laboratory Examinations

Laboratory examinations are primarily concerned with determining whether or not fragments or small particles of glass came from a specific source.

Reconstructing Fragments

Although gross matches of large fragments by color or by shape can sometimes be readily made in the field by the crime scene investigator, the less obvious matches of small fragments are ordinarily done in the laboratory in connection with a detailed reconstruction of the glass object (see Figure 7-7). This work takes more patience than it does scientific expertise. The pieces are fitted together like a jigsaw puzzle according to size, shape, and pattern, if any. When a piece fits into its right place, the striations of its edges mesh snugly with those of the piece against which it is fitted. If it feels right, it almost certainly is right because the probability of two nonmatching pieces having exactly the same shape and pattern of striations along their edges is so slight as to approach impossibility.

A flat piece of glass is reconstructed on a portable flat surface, such as a wooden board or piece of cardboard, to which the fragments are glued or taped in place for use as a courtroom exhibit. If the frame of a broken window is available, it should be the starting point for the reconstruction.

The one glass object that requires reconstruction more than any other is the automobile headlight lens, which is, of course, curved. Reconstruction is greatly simplified if enough fragments are collected to identify the type of lens from the manufacturer's markings. In that case one can make a plaster cast of the inner surface of an unbroken lens of the same type and use it as a base on which to mount the fragments. If the type cannot be determined from the fragments, the curvature and circumference can be roughly approximated by using a Geneva gauge on the available fragments. Since headlight lenses have become

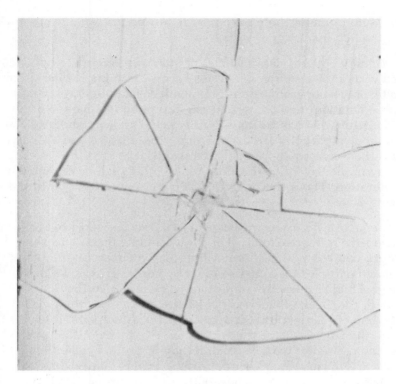

FIGURE 7–7   Reconstruction of a pane of glass jigsaw puzzle fashion. (Courtesy of Wisconsin State Crime Laboratory)

so standardized in recent years, a cast of almost any recent type can serve as a base until enough fragments are found to identify the model. The pieces are fitted together in the same manner as flat glass. Head-lights have an advantage over window panes in this regard because the prismatic patterns cast into the face of the lens help in the placement of the pieces.

Comparison of Physical Properties

Frequently the crime laboratory must deal with bits of glass that are too small to permit a gross physical match. This might occur in the comparison of tiny particles found on a burglary suspect's clothing with the glass of a broken window, the comparison of particles stuck to the soles of a suspect's shoes with broken glass found at the scene of a crime, or the comparison of window glass with particles found embedded in an object thought to have been used to break the window. The most efficient methods for these purposes are testing for *density* and testing for *refractive index.*

Density. When glass particles of unknown origin are being compared with known samples, it is not necessary to know their absolute density; only comparative density is needed. The simplest technique is the free flotation method, which was described in Chapter 2. After a liquid mixture that has the same density as the known standard is found, the unknown particles are dropped into the mixture and are allowed to find their own equilibrium. Those that float at the same level as the known sample have the same density. All others can be excluded from consideration. Those that match in density should then be tested for refractive index.

Refractive index. As with density, it is only necessary to test for the comparative refractive index. The most accurate technique is the temperature control method using a hot-stage microscope (see page 27) Unknown particles are immersed side by side with a known particle in a liquid of higher refractive index than the samples. As the temperature is raised, the Becke line behavior of the samples is observed. If the Becke line of the unknown disappears at the same point as that of the known, the particles have the same refractive index. Although it is not uncommon for glass particles of different origins to have either similar density or similar refractive index, it is extremely unusual for them to have both. Consequently, when both of these properties match, the probability of identical origin is very high.

Other tests. *Emission spectrography* is another technique that can be used effectively on glass. It destroys the sample, but only a small amount of sample is used. The spectrograph reveals all the metallic constituents present in glass, including minor trace elements and any contaminants that are present in different quantities and combinations in bits of glass from different sources. If the spectrograms of different samples show the same line spectra, the samples are of identical origin.

Fluorescence can also be a useful test, especially for exclusionary purposes. Almost all types of glass contain components that cause them to fluoresce when subjected to ultraviolet light. Since it is possible for pieces of glass from different origins to fluoresce with similar color and intensity, the test cannot be considered reliable for discriminating between samples. Fluorescence is a valuable preliminary test, however, because it is quick and easy. If two samples display visibly different fluorescent properties, they are clearly of different origin and no further tests need be made.

Review Questions

1. Glass fragments may be found in the suspect's
   a. Trousers
   b. Pockets
   c. Cuffs
   d. Shoes
   e. All the above

2. Glass is basically a mixture of
   a. Phosphates and carbonates
   b. Silicates and carbonates
   c. Oxides and metals
   d. None of the above

3. When glass hardens, it has the characteristics of
   a. A liquid
   b. Double refraction and birefringence
   c. A crystal
   d. A gas

4. When an object strikes a flat piece of glass and the glass remains whole, one can investigate the
   a. Conchoidal striations
   b. Radial fractures
   c. Concentric fractures
   d. a and c
   e. b and c

5. At the point where an object strikes a window, it puts
   a. Tension on the outer surface and compression on the inner surface
   b. Compression on the outer surface and tension on the inner surface
   c. Tension on both surfaces
   d. Compression on both surfaces

6. If a small missile strikes a pane of glass without penetrating, it leaves a cone-shaped crater
   a. Smaller than the diameter of the missile on the inner side of the glass
   b. Smaller than the diameter of the missile on the opposite side of the glass
   c. Larger than the diameter of the missile on the opposite side of the glass
   d. Larger than the diameter of the missile on the inner side of the glass

7. In a pane of glass in which there are two bullet holes when one radial fracture reaches another but does not pass through it, it was caused by
   a. Heat
   b. The first bullet
   c. The second bullet
   d. None of the above

8. If known and unknown pieces of glass are examined under a microscope and their Becke lines disappear at the same point, the refractive index of the unknown piece is
   a. Greater than the known
   b. Less than the known
   c. Equal to the known
   d. None of the above

CHAPTER EIGHT

—— SOIL AND —— BOTANICAL EVIDENCE

In general, soil and botanical substances can be useful as evidence in two ways. The first and by far the most important is their ability to connect a suspected individual, vehicle, or object with a specific crime scene. The second lies in their ability to place a person in a general area. The first is clearly within the province of the laboratory criminalist because it concerns the comparison of soil or vegetable materials found on a suspected person or object with like materials collected at a crime scene. The second would normally require the aid of a geologist or botanist. A geologist can tell in general terms what classes of soil and what mineralogical peculiarities can be expected in a given area. A botanist can provide the same expert knowledge about the varieties of plant life in an area. From this kind of information it is possible to tell whether or not soil or vegetable samples found on a suspect are consistent with those of an area where a crime has been committed, but it is not possible to place the suspect at the scene. If the samples are inconsistent with the area, then they may have exculpatory value.

SOIL EVIDENCE

In one case of sexual homicide a murderer assaulted and killed his victim in a secluded wooded area and then carried the body out into a field to bury it because he could not dig through the dense network

113

of tree roots in the woods. On later investigation dirt was found on the knees of the culprit's trousers which matched dirt collected from the place in the woods where investigators found signs of a struggle. Also, there was found in the trunk of the suspect's car a shovel caked with dirt which matched that of one portion of the grave site. The dirt on his trousers indicated that the suspect had at some time visited the scene of the crime and that he must have knelt on the ground, but it did not prove that he had committed the murder. However, that evidence combined with the dirt on the shovel not only placed him at the scene of the crime but had him digging at the grave site, an activity for which only the murderer had a plausible reason.

Because soil shows considerable variation in composition from one location to another (even between spots that are as little as a few feet or sometimes inches apart) the evidence it provides can be highly specific. In the case cited above, for example, the dirt on the man's trousers matched the dirt taken from the actual indentations in the ground which were indicative of a struggle. Samples collected for control purposes from other spots in the same vicinity all showed slightly different characteristics. Because a large number of constituents can go into the composition of soil and in infinitely variable percentages, the probability that soil samples from different locations would have precisely the same characteristics is extremely slight.

The same kind of evidence can sometimes be used to place vehicles at a certain place, although there are often difficulties in differentiating dirt suspected to have come from a crime scene from other road dirt. If a car never left well-traveled roads, it would be impossible to make a case from any dirt found on it. But if the car traveled through muddy terrain in connection with a crime, the mud flung up onto the body and undercarriage or stuck to the sides of the wheels would be susceptible to testing in the same way as mud found on a person's shoes or clothing.

Soil Composition

Soil is a complex mixture of organic and inorganic materials. The inorganic constituents are mineral particles that come from the decomposition of rocks. The disintegration of rock into ever smaller pieces is a continuous process of nature. Wind and weather steadily erode the rock, and changes in temperature crack and crumble the rock by continuously expanding and contracting the molecules. Tiny plants—some microscopic in size—help the process of decomposition by growing and decaying in the cracks and releasing acids which etch the rock. This and other decomposed vegetable matter, combined with decayed insect and animal wastes and various living microorganisms, comprise the organic part of soil, which is known as *humus.*

There is considerable variety in the kinds of rock that make up soil. Most rocks are mixtures of minerals ranging from quartz and feldspar to hornblende, mica, and calcite. Since some of these are more resistant to weathering than others and since they exist in different quantities in different areas, the production of soil is a very uneven process. When the chemical composition of the rocks in a given area is highly mixed, the resulting soil tends to be gravelly because of the uneven rate of decay. In areas where the composition is more uniform the more resistant rocks tend to produce a granular soil and the softer rocks tend to produce a silt-like soil.

The great variability of soil is due in large part to the wide diversity of available rocks and to the humus, which can vary greatly depending on the vegetation, insects, and other small animal life present in a given area. In addition, the components of soil can be moved great distances from their place of formation by the effects of wind and water and by the works of humans.

COLLECTING SOIL EVIDENCE

Because of the extreme diversity of soil the investigator must always collect enough samples from the area of the crime scene to be sure that the selection is representative. The samples need not be large (an amount equivalent to a heaping tablespoon is sufficient), but many samples should be taken. They should certainly be collected from all points with which the criminal or vehicle might have had direct contact. This would include foot and tire impressions, diggings, and any other places where there are signs of unusual human activity. In addition, samples should be taken from several other random points in the vicinity of the crime site for control purposes and to establish the degree of variability of the soil in the area. Soil samples must not be collected from footprints or tire impressions until all necessary photographs and casts have been made.

Samples should be placed in vials or pill bottles of appropriate size and labeled with the name or mark of the investigating officer, the date and time of acquisition, and the nature of the contents. Also, each sample should be keyed to a photograph or sketch of the crime scene showing the exact point from which the sample was collected (see Figure 8–1). In most cases samples should be taken from the surface because that is the soil with which the criminal would normally make

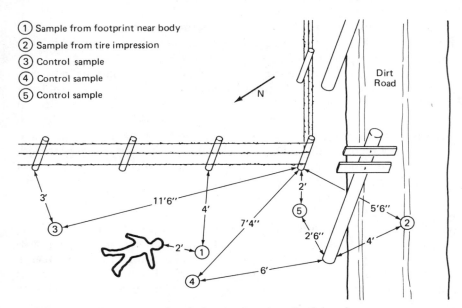

FIGURE 8–1 Crime scene sketch showing location of soil samples.

contact, but when digging is involved, as in the case study cited earlier, representative samples should be taken at different levels and from different parts of the dug area.

Soil found adhering to a suspect's shoes or clothing should be left intact if possible and the entire article should be carefully wrapped in paper and bagged for transmittal to the laboratory. If the suspect does not permit this, the investigator must carefully remove any clumps of dirt with a knife. The investigator must try not to crumble them. Samples from different parts of the clothing should be collected separately onto a piece of plain paper and funneled into vials. These again should have the appropriate identifying information including the part of the garment from which each sample was taken.

Similarly, representative dirt samples should be taken from the wheels, undercarriage, and body of suspect vehicles. Every effort should be made to keep clumps intact. Dirt deposits on the undercarriage are likely to be obscured by layers of innocent road dirt. However, when a vehicle is suspected to have been used in regular criminal activity over a long term, the layers themselves might be revealing.

LABORATORY EXAMINATION OF SOIL

The first step in comparing soil samples is a macroscopic examination for gross similarities in color and granularity. Since moisture can affect color, all samples should be thoroughly dried before examination. This simple preliminary step can often have exclusionary value. If the soil found on a suspect is visibly different from that found at the scene of the crime, it may remove the suspect from suspicion.

Soil Density

A useful but painstaking procedure for determining the identity of soil samples is Kirk's method of comparing density distributions.[1] After being dried, all samples to be compared should be sifted through a fine-meshed sieve to eliminate nonsoil particles and gravel. Density distribution is determined by the gradient tube method. The tubes are prepared by sealing 18-inch lengths of glass tubing at one end and filling them with liquids of increasingly lower densities. Each layer must be carefully floated onto the previous heavier layer by means of a pipette. The amounts of each layer must be the same in every tube. After the tubes have stood for 24 hours to allow the gradient liquids to reach equilibrium, equal amounts of each soil sample are added to the tops

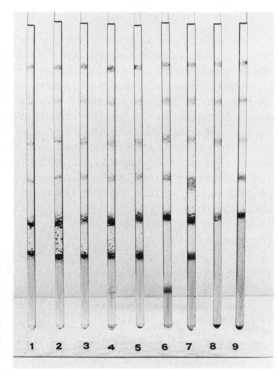

FIGURE 8–2 Comparison of soil samples by their distribution in gradient tubes. Sample 1 was found on a suspect's shoe; the other samples were collected from different parts of the crime scene. (Courtesy of Wisconsin State Crime Laboratory).

[1]Paul L. Kirk, *Crime Investigation,* 1st ed. (New York: Interscience Publishers, Inc., 1966), p. 681.

of the tubes. The soil particles sink and distribute themselves according to their densities: The lighter particles float higher than the heavier ones. If, after a few hours, two or more tubes show the same density distribution, the soil samples in them can be considered to be of identical origin. (See Figure 8–2.)

Spectrographic Analysis

In forensic applications, spectrography is especially useful for its ability to detect metallic trace elements in soil. The spectra of the common constituents are almost always present because of their general abundance. Therefore they can be ignored when making comparisons. It is in the elements that appear irregularly and in minute quantities that the differences can be seen. Since trace elements can be expected to occur in different combinations in soil from different locations, identical spectra for such elements would indicate identity of origin.

Enzyme Analysis

Although soil appears to be inert to the naked eye, it is in fact teeming with living microorganisms which manufacture great quantities of biochemical compounds. These include enzymes, which can be detected indirectly by adding chemical reagents that react specifically with the compounds produced by the catalytic activity of the enzymes.[2] The techniques for detecting enzymes are complicated and are rarely used in crime laboratories, but they can be useful if it is important to know the relative age of the soil samples. Enzyme activity changes over a period of time, but density and trace elements do not. Therefore, if two soil samples show identical enzyme levels, they must have the same origin and they must have been removed from their natural location at the same time.

BOTANICAL EVIDENCE

Botanical evidence includes any plant or plant product as well as plant residues like pollen, seeds, twigs, and fragments of bark and leaves. Plants of the same species are usually indistinguishable from each other regardless of their location. Thus the fact that some botanical material which is indigenous to the crime scene is found on a suspect's clothing does not prove that the suspect was there unless there is something

---

[2]J. I. Thornton and A. D. McLaren, "Enzymatic Characterization of Soil Evidence," *Journal of Forensic Sciences,* 20, no. 4 (1975), 674–92.

unique about the evidence. The rarer the material or combination of materials is the better the chances are of using it to connect a person to a place. But even when no unique set of circumstances exists to connect a suspect to a crime, botanical evidence can often lend weight to other evidence.

Wood

Wood occurs as evidence in criminal investigations more than any other plant product. It is especially significant because of the many wooden products that we encounter in daily life. If criminals jimmy open wooden doors or windows, bits of wood are likely to scatter and stick to their clothes. Also, bullets and other weapons can send chips flying, and burglars can easily pick up splinters while breaking and entering.

Examination of Wood

If the chips of wood brought into evidence are large enough, it may be possible to match them up physically with the object from which they were broken by fitting the broken edges together. In such a case a suspect may be linked directly to a crime. Irregular features in wood, such as knots, bruises, decay, cracks, and holes made by drills, nails, or screws, can be helpful in matching pieces together.

When a physical match is not possible, pieces of wood can be

FIGURE 8–3 The photograph shows the bases of two ornamental knobs used to decorate antique clocks. The one on the right was found on a stolen clock in the possession of a suspect; the one on the left remained in the clock maker's shop. The suspect claimed that the clock was not stolen but that he had bought it elsewhere. However, a comparison of the growth rings of the two knobs clearly shows that they were made from the same piece of wood. Therefore the clock can only have come from that particular shop. (Courtesy of Connecticut State Police Forensic Laboratory)

compared to see if they are of the same species. It is usually not necessary for forensic purposes to determine what the species is. If a piece of wood found on a suspect exhibits the same anatomical characteristics as a wooden object at the crime scene, the two pieces of wood are of the same species, even though they may not be of the same origin.

Growth rings can sometimes be used as a basis of comparison and identification if the wood is cut in cross section (see Figure 8–3). The rings reflect the availability of water throughout each year of a tree's growth. When water is plentiful, as in the spring, the wood cells grow rapidly and to a large size. When water is not so plentiful, as in the winter, the cells are smaller and more closely packed, thus causing a darkening of the wood. Pieces of wood can often be eliminated as possible evidence by a simple naked-eye comparison of the rings and of other gross characteristics such as color, grain, and texture [see Figure 8–4 (a) and (b)].

If the gross features are similar or when very minute pieces are involved, a microscopic examination is necessary [see Figure 8–4(c)].

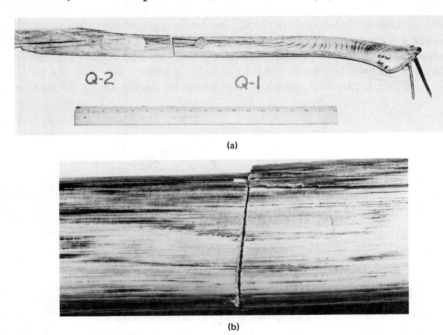

(a)

(b)

FIGURE 8–4 (a) Shows two parts of a sawed off ax handle. The right hand portion was used in an assault and left at the scene; the left hand portion was found at the suspect's home. A comparison of the grain (b) shows that the two pieces were from the same source. The match is confirmed by a cross sectional comparison of the pore structures (c). (Courtesy of Connecticut State Police Forensic Laboratory)

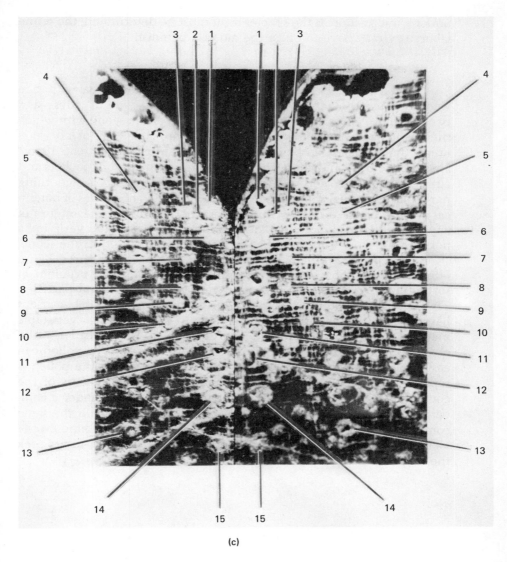

(c)

FIGURE 8–4 *continued*

Most wood cells grow longitudinally as the tree grows. This accounts for the grain of the wood. A small percentage of the wood cells grow radially, from the center of the tree outward, forming individual cellular patterns for each species. Also, hard woods have pores between the cells which are lacking in soft woods. These and other growth characteristics, which are distinctive for each species, can easily be compared under a microscope. If the species itself must be determined, the crime laboratory may have to enlist the aid of a botanist.

Plant Residues

Pollen and other plant residues are more difficult to deal with than wood because they are so widespread in nature—even in cities—and because there is usually no single object at the crime scene with which they can readily be compared. Thus they are generally of no value unless their species can be identified. Pollen, in particular, can almost always be found somewhere about a person—in the dust of pockets and cuffs, for example, and even in ear wax. Unless there is something particularly unusual about a species or combination of species of botanical residues found on a suspect or unless there is an unusual amount of any one kind, this kind of evidence is more often useful in verifying a person's usual environment than in tying the person to a crime scene.

Since pollen is usually found mixed in with pocket dirt or vacuum filter contents, the criminalist is usually faced with the problem of sorting and separating it from other microscopic dusts and particles. The most useful tool for this is the stereoscopic microscope because it has high enough magnification to be able to distinguish the vegetable material from the contaminants and low enough magnification to include a large number of particles in the field of view. The pollen can easily be sorted out with a needle-pointed probe. Once the pollen is separated out, it can be examined under the higher powers of the compound microscope or compared with other samples under a comparison microscope. The criminalist generally looks to see if the same combination of pollen types is found on a suspect as was found on the victim. If species identification is required, it may be necessary to seek the help of a botanist.

Review Questions

1. Soil and botanical evidence can be useful in
    a. Connecting a suspected object with a crime scene
    b. Determining the age of the crime scene
    c. Its ability to place a person in the general area
    d. a and c
    e. a, b, and c
2. If soil found on a suspect's clothing is consistent with the soil found at the crime scene, this would indicate

    a. That the suspect committed the crime
    b. That the suspect was in the area
    c. That the suspect was in the area at the time of the crime
    d. None of the above

3. Soil is
    a. A compound
    b. A solution
    c. A mixture
    d. An element

4. Soil is made by
    a. Disintegration of rock
    b. Erosion
    c. Weathering
    d. All the above

5. The organic part of soil is called
    a. Humus
    b. Feldspar
    c. Calcite
    d. Hornblende

6. At the crime scene soil samples should be taken from
    a. Any point with which the criminal might have come in direct contact
    b. Any point with which the criminal's vehicle might have come in direct contact
    c. Several random points around the crime scene
    d. a and b
    e. All the above

7. When comparing soil samples by macroscopic examination, one should
    a. Observe color
    b. Observe granularity
    c. Determine density
    d. Dry the samples
    e. a, b, and d

8. Which of the following techniques is used to compare trace elements found in soil?
    a. Spectrographic analysis
    b. Density
    c. Enzyme analysis
    d. Macroscopic examination

9. (T, F) Since soil from one place is much like soil from another place, soil has little value in connecting a suspect with a specific crime scene.

10. (T, F) The ability to physically match a chip of wood found on a suspect with the object from which it was broken is more useful as evidence than the ability to match the species.

11. (T, F) Criminalists are expected to be able to identify a species of plant from a microscopic examination of its pollen.

CHAPTER NINE

PAINT

The use of decorative and protective colorings is one of mankind's most ancient arts. Neolithic cave dwellers painted pictures of their prey in the dark recesses of their caves, and over a thousand years before Christ the Egyptians developed paints from natural oils and resins which were the direct precursors of modern oxidizing oil paints. Since paints have been such an integral part of human culture for so long, it is not surprising that they figure very prominently in crimes and, therefore, in the crime laboratory.

PAINT EVIDENCE

Because of the high incidence of crimes involving automobiles, especially hit-and-run accidents, chips and smears of paint from automobiles make up some of the most common forms of paint evidence. Chipping is usually the result of a sharp blow to the surface or a bending of the metal. Because of the hard and brittle nature of automobile paint it tends to break cleanly away from the metal surface in discrete segments which show all the layers. These chips can often be found on the ground at the site of an accident. They may also be found on a victim, in the folds or cuffs of the victim's clothing, or even in the victim's hair. When two vehicles are involved, chips from one vehicle may be found on the other vehicle.

Automobile paint can also be transferred to other objects and even to clothing in the form of smears, particularly when the collision is in the nature of a sideswipe or glancing blow. When one vehicle hits another or collides with another painted object, there is almost always some area of mutual paint transfer. Unlike chips, which can be brushed away, smears cling tenaciously to painted surfaces as well as to fabrics.

Paint evidence can also play an important role in other kinds of crimes. A burglar breaking into a house or other property almost inevitably comes into contact with painted surfaces. If the burglar has to jimmy open a window or a door, he or she is likely to chip off flakes of paint in the process, which may later be found in the cuffs or pockets of the burglar's clothing. Tools used to break into a premises or into painted safes or strongboxes often pick up paint smears by being forcefully pried against a painted surface.

If a criminal is unlucky enough to brush against wet paint, not only is the criminal's clothing smeared but the criminal also leaves fibers sticking to the paint. Although wet paint rarely occurs as evidence, it is useful when it does because it is difficult for the criminal to get rid of it and because it is usually transferred in larger quantities than dry smears are.

Because most house paints dry more slowly than automobile paints do and because they form a softer finish, they are less likely to chip, but they do flake and peel, especially when they are old or inexpertly applied. Some house paints that are designed to be self-cleaning by means of a continuous wearing away of the surface leave a chalky residue on anything that brushes against them. Similarly, paints designed for use on masonry and concrete surfaces, like whitewash, powder off when rubbed.

Because paint is used on so many items of everyday life, it very frequently occurs in conjunction with other forms of evidence. Window glass, for example, often has paint spatters on it where a frame was carelessly painted. Similarly, automobile headlights sometimes bear traces of sprayed paint. And, of course, wood almost always has some kind of protective coating.

Artists' colors may also constitute evidence in crimes like forgery and theft of valuable art works, but this is seldom a concern of the crime laboratory. The same examination techniques apply to artists' paints as apply to automotive and architectural paints, but spotting forgeries requires a highly specialized knowledge of the type and composition of the paints that individual artists actually used.

Paints, like synthetic textile fibers, are subject to ongoing research by manufacturers, who are continuously trying to improve their products and produce paints that have special characteristics. The introduction of new kinds of paint and the vast amount of old paint still in existence make it almost impossible for the forensic scientist to keep up with all developments. Nevertheless, the great variation that exists in paint composition improves the chances of being able to differentiate between random paint samples and it also increases the probability that samples having the same characteristics are of common origin.

In essence, paint consists of *pigments,* which give the paint color and opacity, and a *binder,* which hardens and holds the pigments in suspension while adhering to the paint surface. Other agents may be added in minor amounts to promote faster drying and special surface effects. Wet paint contains various thinners and solvents that evaporate in the drying process. Since a crime laboratory almost never receives wet paint as evidence, the components that the criminalist mainly has to deal with are pigments and binders.

Pigments

Paint pigments are insoluble particles held in suspension by the binder (see Figure 9–1). Approximately one-half of all the pigments available for use in automotive, architectural, and artistic applications are inorganic compounds. The rest are natural or synthetic organic compounds. Almost all white pigments in use today are inorganic, titanium dioxide (TiO_2) being by far the most common. In the colored pigments synthetic organic compounds are becoming increasingly important, and it is in this field that most new developments are taking place. In practical applications a good deal of mixing takes place to

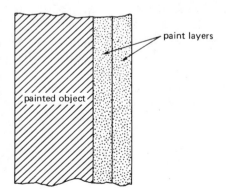

paint layers

painted object

FIGURE 9–1 Paint hardens on the surface of object holding the pigment granules in solid suspension.

produce different shades. Thus countless combinations of organic and inorganic pigments may exist in any given paint sample.

Pigments are differentiated from dyes in that dyes are soluble. Some dyes, however, have been used as pigments either by changing their composition to make them insoluble or by precipitating them onto existing pigments.

Binders

The binder, sometimes referred to as a *vehicle* because it carries the pigments, is the material that hardens into a thin film and holds the pigment particles in place across the painted surface. Binders are organic compounds and are classified into four overall groups according to whether they harden by *oxidation, polymerization, evaporation,* or *coagulation.* [1]

It should be noted that just as the different types of pigments can be mixed, there is a certain amount of overlap among the binders. For example, polymerization takes place as part of the hardening process of all modern paints even if that is not the primary drying method. In the chapter on fibers we saw that polymerization was the process by which many small molecules (monomers) of the same type join with each other to form long chain molecules with the same percentage composition of elements. In textiles the polymer chains are forced into parallel alignment in order to form fibers, but in paints the chains form in random directions and interweave with each other to create a hard surface. Under certain conditions polymer chains form chemical bonds, called *cross-linkages,* with adjacent chains. The more cross-linking that takes place between polymer chains, the tougher the paint finish is likely to be.

Oxidizing Binders

This category comprises *drying-oil* paints and enamels and *alkyd* paints and enamels. Enamels are distinguished from paints by their high resin content which imparts a harder, glossier surface.

The oldest known paints were of the drying-oil type. They consisted of natural oxidizing oils, such as linseed oil, mixed with natural pigments and resins. Modern drying-oil paints use both natural and synthetic unsaturated oils, which polymerize and harden on contact with the oxygen in the air. In the wet state these paints contain thinners, like turpentine, to facilitate application. These thinners evaporate in the drying process. Since the drying process of oil paints is normally

[1]David A. Crown *The Forensic Examination of Paints and Pigments* (Springfield, Ill.: Charles C Thomas), 1968.

slow, chemical driers are added to speed up the process. Drying-oil paints are most commonly used as house paints, especially on exteriors. Although they are also used on interiors, they have been largely superseded in this application by *latex* paints, which dry quickly and have little unpleasant odor.

Alkyds are highly cross-linked synthetic polyester chains. They are used on interior and exterior trim, metal finishes, and in automobile and aircraft applications. Alkyd enamels are used extensively on foreign import cars.

Polymerizing Binders

These are synthetic resin paints in which plasticizers are used for flexibility and toughness. Polymerizing binders are used in elastomers, or rubber paints, in some automobile finishes, and in silicone resins known for high heat resistance. The polymerization process may take place on contact with air or when the paint is heated.

Evaporating Solvent Binders

In these paints the binding material is dissolved in a solvent, such as acetone, which evaporates and leaves a hard, smooth, highly polymerized film. These paints include the various types of lacquers and cellulosic and acrylic paints and enamels. The lacquers and cellulose paints do not change their chemical composition when the solvent evaporates. Consequently, they can be easily redissolved on application of the appropriate solvent.

Nitrocellulose lacquers are used on automobile finishes, particularly on cars of non-U.S. manufacture. General Motors uses acrylic lacquers on their products. These automotive finishes are easily dissolved in acetone.

The other American automobile manufacturers, as well as some foreign producers, use acrylic enamels, which cannot be readily redissolved in their original solvents because when they are baked onto the car surfaces, the heat causes the polymer chains to develop extensive irreversible cross-linkages which make the surface coat extremely hard and chemically resistant.

Coagulating Binders

These are the water-based emulsion paints of which the latex types are most common. In these paints the pigments, monomeric resins, plasticizers, and oils are emulsified in water. That is, they are reduced to tiny droplets of colloidal dimensions and are dispersed in water where they are held in suspension. When the water evaporates, the droplets coagulate and the resins polymerize to form a painted surface. The resins most commonly used are the vinyl resins, such as polyvinyl acetate and polyvinyl chloride and the acrylic resins.

Emulsion paints are used primarily on architecture. Most of the interior paints sold today are of the latex variety, and since their weathering characteristics have become greatly improved in recent years, latex paints are being used more and more on exteriors.

Other water-based paints are those like whitewash, which are used on masonry and concrete, and distempers, which are mainly used in artistic applications. These paints are nonwashable, and the masonry paints have a powdery surface that rubs off on anything that comes into contact with it.

COLLECTION AND PRESERVATION OF PAINT

Most of the paint evidence with which the investigating officer has to deal is in the form of chips from automobile and architectural finishes. The investigator's first concern should be to keep the chips intact. Although it is rare that paint chips can be physically matched against the paint edge from which they were broken, when it can be done, it is the surest proof that the paint came from that particular place and therefore can be extremely valuable in connecting a vehicle to a hit-and-run accident or a criminal to a crime scene. Paint chips can be picked up intact with tweezers, with knife blade and forefinger, or by slipping a piece of paper under them. They should be packaged in such a way as to prevent further breakage. A box lined with cotton or other soft material is one suitable method. If there is more than one source of paint evidence at a crime scene, the collected samples should be packaged separately.

In collecting paint chips from clothing, the investigator should pick off large visible pieces with tweezers. The part of the clothing from which the paint chips came should be noted. If there are no visible chips but the possible presence of paint evidence is suspected, clothing can be swept with a vacuum sweeper equipped with a filter attachment. The filter with the contents still in it should be labeled and forwarded to the laboratory.

The investigator in the field should not attempt to remove chalked or smeared paint from clothing or portable objects such as tools or weapons. The entire object should be packaged and sent to the laboratory with the evidence undisturbed. If there is a paint smear on an automobile or other nonportable object, a sample of the smeared area should be removed along with an unsmeared sample from an adjacent area for control purposes. Paint samples taken from an automobile should be cut all the way down to the metal surface so that all layers are represented. Similarly, samples from other objects should be cut down to the original surface. The samples should be packaged in the same manner as paint chips and labeled to identify the exact location from which they were taken.

If a tool having paint smears on it is suspected to have been used in a break-in, not only should the tool be forwarded to the laboratory, but paint samples from surfaces where the tool might have been used should also be collected for comparison purposes.

LABORATORY EXAMINATION OF PAINT

With paint, as with most items of physical evidence, the criminalist's main concern is to compare samples of unknown origin with known standards for the purpose of connecting a suspect automobile to an accident or suspected persons or items to a crime. In the case of hit-and-run accidents, if no suspect vehicles are found through other investigative methods, the laboratory scientist may be called upon to identify the make, model, and year of a car from a paint chip. The accuracy of such identification depends on the scope of a laboratory's paint library. Automobile manufacturers make paint samples and information about the chemical composition of their paints available to crime laboratories, and the National Bureau of Standards Law Enforcement Standards Laboratory has made a collection of automobile paint colors which is also available to crime laboratories. If these libraries are kept up, it is possible to state the possible and probable makes, models, and years of cars to which a paint chip could belong. If a paint or combination of paints was used only once, it is possible to identify them precisely.

A large number of comparative and analytical techniques are possible in the examination of paint. The choice depends on the information required and the equipment available. Modern analytical instrumental techniques provide the most reliable results, but smaller laboratories that may not have the equipment can still get reasonably good results by less sophisticated methods, such as pigment distribution and density determinations. Wet chemical techniques can also be used, but they are laborious and time-consuming and the results generally do not justify the time spent on them.

Preliminary Examination

The purpose of the preliminary examination is to weed out any samples that can be seen by simple observation to be clearly different from the sample of known origin. Surface color and basic layer structure are compared macroscopically and under a stereoscopic binocular microscope with vertical illumination. In the future it may be possible to identify paint by an instrumental examination of the color alone, that is, by measuring the trichromatic coefficients of the surface. This would mean assigning a numerical value to the relative intensity of each of the three primary colors present in a sample. Today, however, the human eye is more sensitive than any instrument in distinguishing colors. But because human eye observations are highly subjective, they cannot be considered accurate enough for definitive identifications.

If both the color and the layer structure match, it is necessary to go on to other tests. If the layer structures do not match, it is still possible that the two samples come from the same source because the vehicle or object might have been partially repainted or retouched. For this reason, it is important to collect control samples as close to the area from which the paint was chipped as possible. If several control samples taken from an object agree with each other but differ from the unknown, then the unknown did not come from that object.

Matching Paint Chips

If large enough chips are available from the scene of a hit-and-run accident and a suspect vehicle is brought in, it is well worth the trouble to attempt to match the chips in jigsaw puzzle fashion against places on the car where paint has broken off (see Figure 9–2). Although it is seldom possible to make the pieces fit, when they do fit, the origin of the chip is proved and no further examination is required.

Layer Structure Examination

If the preliminary examination shows the possibility of identity and if several layers are present, the samples have to be mounted for a detailed examination of the edge. Soft chips can be mounted in a soft mounting medium like paraffin and sectioned with a microtome. Harder chips need a firmer mount such as Lucite, a clear plastic material that can be melted around the chip and then cut away to expose

FIGURE 9–2 Chips of paint found at a hit-and-run scene are matched jigsaw puzzle fashion on the hood of a suspect automobile. (Courtesy of Wisconsin State Crime Laboratory).

FIGURE 9–3 Microscopic examination of a paint chip in cross section. (Courtesy of Wisconsin State Crime Laboratory)

the edge. The surface of the paint edge must be polished in order to reveal the layers clearly (see Figure 9–3).

The prepared samples are viewed again in more detail under a comparison microscope at 30X to 50X magnification. The samples are compared layer by layer for correspondence of colors and layer thicknesses and the presence of debris between the layers. Although there is no accepted standard on how many matching layers must be present to prove identity, the greater the number, the greater the probability that the samples are identical.

Examination of Pigments

The preferred instrumental techniques for pigment analysis are *emission spectrography* and *X-ray diffraction.*

Emission spectrography is the most sensitive and rapid method of detecting metallic elements which is available in most crime laboratories. It is a destructive test, and even though it uses only small quantities of the sample material, it should not be performed until all desired nondestructive tests have been performed. If the spectra of the two samples being compared match, then it is proved that they contain the same metallic elements. Specific metals can be identified by comparing the spectrograms of the tested samples with known spectra for the different elements. Since some elements, like titanium, are fairly common in most paints, it is most fruitful to differentiate samples on the basis of minor metallic constituents. To obtain the most accurate results, it is best to separate the paint layers and test each layer individually against the corresponding layer of the second sample, but since the procedure of separating the layers is rather painstaking, criminalists must often content themselves with a spectrographic analysis of all the layers together. If a laser microprobe is available (see page 56), it is possible to analyze all the individual layers of paint spectrographically without physically separating them. The laser beam is simply focused on the edge of each layer. A disadvantage of emission spectrography is that if metallic contaminants are present, such as may be found in dirt, their line spectra appear in the spectrogram along with those of the metals in the paint.

X-ray diffraction is a good complementary technique to spectrography. It is nondestructive and instead of detecting metallic ions, it determines the crystalline structure of the chemical compounds. Since X-ray diffraction is not sensitive to minor components, contaminants present in small quantities do not interfere with it. It is especially useful in conjunction with emission spectrography because it differentiates compounds. Emission spectrography only detects elemental ions. Thus if a paint sample contained a mixture of barium chromate, titanium dioxide, lead chromate, and barium sulphate, X-ray diffraction would distinguish between all the compounds while spectrography would only reveal the presence of barium, chromium, titanium, and lead.

Neutron Activation Analysis

Neutron activation analysis (NAA) can also be used to detect metallic elements. Although neutron activation analysis is much more sensitive to metals present in trace quantities than is emission spectrography, it does not cover the range of all the metallic elements. Because of the expense and the need for access to a nuclear reactor it is impractical for routine criminalistics work.

Pigment Distribution

This is a technique of Kirk's[2] that can be used when analytical instruments are not available. The pigment particles are separated from the binder as much as possible by the use of solvents and grinding. Then the particles are viewed through a microscope that is equipped with a ruled ocular grid micrometer. All the particles of each color present are counted in a few random grids and the average percentages of each color are taken as the percentage composition of the pigment. The same procedure is carried out for each sample. Only one layer of paint is used at a time, and if the percentage composition corresponds through all the layers of two samples, they can be considered identical. Although there is a certain amount of subjectivity in this method, it provides a fairly accurate statistical range if enough different pigments are present.

[2]Paul L. Kirk, *Crime Investigation,* 1st ed. (New York: Interscience Publishers, Inc., 1966), p. 689.

Examination of Binders

The instrumental techniques most commonly used for identifying binders are *infrared spectrophotometry* and *pyrolysis-gas chromatography*.

Infrared spectrophotometry is a sensitive, rapid, and nondestructive method for analyzing the chemical structure of organic substances. The infrared spectra reflect the common groupings of atoms characteristic of organic compounds. Some inorganic compounds also absorb light in the infrared range; therefore when used on paint, the technique might include the identification of some pigments unless the binder is separated out by solution in an appropriate solvent. As long as all samples are tested in the same way, the pigment interference does not affect the results of a comparison.

Pyrolysis-gas chromatography, while destructive, can function with small quantities of a sample. In pyrolysis the organic compounds are vaporized or decomposed into simpler compounds under extreme heat in the absence of oxygen. The resulting volatile products are injected into a gas chromatograph, which analyzes them and records the results graphically on a chromatogram. Again, best results are obtained when the paint layers are separated and analyzed individually. Although pyrolysis-gas chromatography cannot identify constituents absolutely, it is excellent for comparisons because two identical samples analyzed by the same procedures result in identical chromatograms.

Solvent Tests

These are rather unsatisfactory tests that can be applied when instrumental equipment is not available. Every paint binder reacts in some way to some chemical reagent. The solvent tests are merely a matter of applying small amounts of a whole range of solvents, acids, and bases to the paint samples and observing all the reactions under a microscope. If two samples react in the same way to all the chemicals, the binders can at least be considered to belong to the same class. These tests are more suitable for their exclusionary value than for proving identity, for if the samples react differently to the solvents, they must be of different chemical composition.

Paint Density

Observation of the density distribution of paint is another somewhat unsatisfactory examination that can be used in the absence of more sophisticated instruments. Gradient tubes are prepared in the same manner as for soil. The paint chips are carefully separated by layers and each layer is ground as finely as possible. When the ground up paint particles are added to the gradients, the paint particles sink to the levels consistent with their specific gravity. Often one paint sample will distribute itself at several different gradient layers. A matter to bear in mind when using gradients is that some paint components react with the gradient liquids and change their behavior. Consequently, the same paint might give different readings if left immersed over a long period. This method is accurate only in a statistical sense, and even when two samples show similar density distribution, they cannot be considered with absolute certainty to be identical.

Review Questions

1. Paint evidence can play an important role in
   a. Hit-and-run accidents
   b. Automobile accidents
   c. Burglaries
   d. All the above

2. Paint evidence can be found
   a. In the cuffs of a suspect's clothing
   b. On tools
   c. On automobiles
   d. On all the above

3. Titanium dioxide is used in paint for
   a. Pigment
   b. Binder
   c. Dryer
   d. Solvent

4. Which of the following paints can be redissolved in their solvent after drying?
   a. Latex
   b. Lacquer
   c. Oil
   d. None of the above

5. In collecting paint chips from clothing, one may
   a. Wash the clothing to remove as much dirt as possible
   b. Use a vacuum sweeper equipped with a filter attachment
   c. Immerse the clothing in acetone to dissolve the paint chips
   d. None of the above

6. A nondestructive instrumental test to determine the crystalline structure of the chemical compounds in paint is called
   a. X-ray diffraction

    b. Emission spectrography

    c. Pyrolysis-gas chromatography

    d. Infrared spectrophotometry

7. (T, F) If an investigator finds paint chips at a crime scene, the investigator does not need to look for any other evidence.

8. (T, F) Wood and paint evidence are frequently found together.

9. (T, F) The two main components of paint that criminalists examine for comparison and identification are pigments and thinners.

10. (T, F) Since paint chips can seldom be physically matched with the area from which they were broken, it is not necessary to preserve them intact.

11. Latex paint

    a. Is relatively fast drying

    b. Is a colloidal suspension in water

    c. Hardens by coagulation

    d. All the above

    e. b and c

12. Drying oil paints

    a. Were used in ancient times

    b. Are soluble in acetone

    c. Harden by oxidation

    d. All the above

    e. a and c

CHAPTER TEN

— *HAIR* —

Throughout their daily lives people shed hair without being aware of it. They leave it on clothing, combs, chairs, floors, in cars—everywhere they go. Consequently, there is a good chance that even the most careful criminal will leave some hairs behind at the scene of a crime. The likelihood is greatly increased if there is violence associated with the crime. The victim's hair may be found adhering to the paint of a hit-and-run vehicle or to a murder weapon or to a murderer's clothing. A murderer's hair may be found in a victim's hand or under the victims's fingernails or elsewhere at the scene. In sex crimes an attacker will frequently leave pubic hairs behind or carry away some pubic hairs of the victim. The possibilities are almost unlimited, and an investigator who is not alert to them might easily overlook important hair evidence.

HAIR AS EVIDENCE

Hair is an especially important item of evidence because of the frequency with which it is found in connection with crimes. While all criminals know about fingerprints and are generally careful not to leave any behind, they seldom think about their hair. Its value is limited, however, because, in spite of its physiological origin, a hair sample usually cannot be absolutely identified as belonging to a given individual. Scalp hairs from the same person can vary considerably from one another depending on the part of the head they come from and their growth phase. Likewise, hairs from different people can show a great similarity, even under detailed laboratory examination. When a suspect's hair is compared with hair collected at the scene of a crime, laboratory tests can only indicate whether or not it is possible that they came from the same head. The probability of identity increases if a large population of evidence hairs can be compared to a similarly large population of hairs from suspects. Unfortunately, it is rare that a large number of evidence hairs are collected at a crime scene. If only two or three hairs are collected, as is often the case, the forensic scientist is not able to state with any confidence that they came from a certain individual, no matter how similar they may be to samples from that person's head, unless there is something unique about that individual's hair. If, however, the hairs are dissimilar enough, laboratory examinations may indicate that they are not from the same head. Therefore, the comparison of hair can either eliminate a suspect from suspicion or can lend weight to other evidence tying a suspect to the scene of a crime.

Hair has other evidentiary value aside from comparison tests. An experienced examiner can clearly tell whether a hair is of human or animal origin, whether it has been bleached or dyed, and whether it fell out naturally or was cut or pulled out. The examiner can identify foreign matter attached to it, such as blood, sweat, grease, or semen. And the examiner can sometimes make reasonable, though not conclusive, deductions as to the sex, race, and relative age of the person from whom it came. Also, since the hair of a large segment of the human population contains traces of the same ABO antigens found in blood, it is often possible to determine a person's blood group from his or her hair. (See Chapter 12 for a discussion of blood groups.)

The examination of hair can also be useful in reconstructing a crime. A blow from a blunt instrument tends to crush a hair shaft or split it lengthwise, whereas a sharp instrument cuts the end off squarely. In both cases the hair is likely to be matted with blood. The appearance of the root can be another indicator of violence. If the root is dry and shrunken, the hair probably fell out naturally, but if the root is fat and bulbous with bits of cell tissue adhering to it, this gives an indication that the hair was pulled out by force, thus suggesting some kind of struggle.

The human body tends to metabolize certain materials and excrete them as waste products in the hair. Perhaps the most notable of these in the field of criminal investigation is arsenic. Not only can it be detected in the hair in cases of arsenic poisoning but by relating its distribution in the hair to the average rate of hair growth, one can also determine the approximate dates the poison was administered. This technique was used in one case in which a woman was given small doses of arsenic by her husband over a long period of time. The women was eventually hospitalized for observation of an unknown ailment. Arsenic poisoning was not diagnosed at first. The woman's condition improved as long as her husband stayed away, but every time he visited her she had a relapse. After she died, an alert pathologist tested her hair for arsenic and found that the deposits of the poison roughly coincided with the dates of the husband's visits. Although this type of evidence is not conclusive in itself, it can point the way for further investigation and, when used as supporting evidence in court, can make a very strong impression on a jury.

CHARACTERISTICS OF HAIR

Hair has unique properties that make it readily distinguishable from all other materials. Hair is produced in the dermis, or underlayer of skin, by tiny organs called *follicles.* The follicles generate protein cells which harden and get pushed steadily outward by the continuing production of new cells. This hardened material, known as *keratin,* is the basic component of hair, fingernails and toenails, horn, and feathers. The newly formed living hair cells develop at the base of the follicles as long tight bundles of small filaments or fibrils until they become keratinized (hardened). The protoplasm of these cells is totally keratinized by the time hair emerges from the follicle, so that all of the hair shaft outside the follicle is made up of dead tissue.

Structure

All hair, whether animal or human, has the same basic structure. The proteinaceous material produced by the follicle develops into a rod-like shaft of elongated cells called the *cortex.* In the center of the cortex there is usually a hollow tube or core called the *medulla.* The exterior of the shaft is covered by flattened cells called *scales.* Collectively, the scales are referred to as the *cuticle.* Within this basic com-

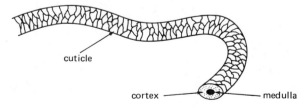

FIGURE 10–1 Illustration of a hair, showing the position of the cortex, medulla, and cuticle.

mon structure (see Figure 10-1), however, there are wide variations between individuals and between humans and animals.

The *cortex,* or main part of the shaft, is essentially a cylinder of long spindle-shaped cells that surrounds the medulla. In addition to keratin, the crystal-like protein of which its cells are primarily composed, cortical cells carry minor constituents such as uric acid, cholesterol, some vitamins, blood antigens, and trace elements as well as most of the pigmentary material which gives hair its color.

The *medulla* is essentially a tubular cavity in the middle of the cortex. In juvenile hair it forms a rod-like core of organic material, but as the hair matures the medullar cells disintegrate leaving a hollow tube, or *lumen.* Some patches of medullar cell detritus usually remain in the lumen which can appear black or brown under the microscope. The medulla is classified according to the microscopic appearance of the dark patches of medullar material along the hair as *continuous, intermittent,* or *fragmental* (see Figure 10-2). A continuous medulla shows an uninterrupted band of dark material throughout the length of the hair. In the intermittent medulla the medullar material is regularly interrupted by air spaces to form a symmetrical pattern along the core.

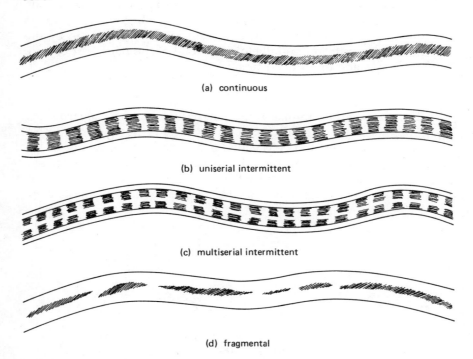

(a) continuous

(b) uniserial intermittent

(c) multiserial intermittent

(d) fragmental

FIGURE 10–2 Some typical medullas.

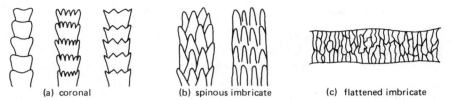

FIGURE 10–3 Some basic scale structures of hairs.

These patterns show great diversity and are of considerable value in species identification. The fragmental medulla displays non-uniform dashes of medullary material, which are irregularly interrupted by air spaces. In some hairs medullary material may be entirely absent.

The *cuticle* is made up of overlapping flattened scales on the exterior of the hair shaft. These scales are also made of keratin, but they have a higher sulfur content which makes them less chemically reactive and therefore tougher and more resistant to abrasion and dyeing. There is great variety in the scale patterns from person to person and from species to species, but they can be divided into two general classifications: *imbricate* (shingle-like) and *coronal* (crown-like) (see Figure 10-3). Imbricate scales, which most mammals possess, overlap each other in patterns similar to fish scales. In coronal patterns each scale forms a ring around the hair and overlaps the next distal ring. A hair having coronal scales is often compared to a stack of dixie cups. The individual patterns within these two overall classifications are similar for any given species, but sometimes the differences are so subtle that only an expert can recognize them. An adept examiner can often pick out patterns in the scales of human hair which are characteristic of individual people, but this examination is still not accurate enough to prove identity beyond doubt. With few exceptions, scale tips always point toward the tip of the hair.

Growth

Human scalp hair grows at an average rate of 2.33 millimeters a week. The end first emerges as a point and tapers to a diameter that is generally fairly uniform for the remainder of the length. Short hairs, like eyebrows and body hair, tend to taper continuously from tip to root. After a long period of steady growth (*anagen* phase), the hair ceases to get longer and stays in a short rest phase (*catagen* phase). Then the root begins to shrink and eventually the hair falls out naturally (*telogen* phase). The follicle then begins to produce a new hair. Since the cycle of each follicle is independent of all the others, a hair from any part of the head can be in any phase of growth.

Appearance

In cross section hair generally appears round, oval, triangular, or flat. Round and triangular hairs tend to be straight. Flat hairs are curly; the amount of curl is directly related to the flatness. A long, relatively straight hair of uniform diameter would probably be a head hair. Beard and moustache hair tends to be triangular in cross section and of greater average diameter than head hair. Pubic and armpit hairs are usually flat in cross section and kinky in appearance and can be variable in diameter. Other body hairs tend to be short and their diameters taper along the entire lengths. Curly hair is produced in the follicle by a rotating development of a flat side. As the hair emerges, this flat side describes a helix. The flat side is the result of the production of smaller cells that have a higher sulfur content.

Animal Hair

Most animals have a layer of fine, short *down* hair close to their skins for warmth and an outer layer of coarser *guard* hairs for protection against the elements and external hazards. Down hairs and guard hairs are different from each other and are different from eyelashes, whiskers, tails, and manes, but they exhibit common characteristics throughout the species. All animal hair can be readily differentiated from human hair. The diameter of a human head hair is generally uniform along the shaft. Most animal hairs widen to a certain point in their growth and then begin to narrow or show irregularities in diameter along the shaft. The measured diameter of animal hair can vary from less than one-half to more than double that of human hair. Also, the tip of the hair is pointed in animals, except in animals that are shorn, whereas human hair often exhibits a squared or blunt end from cutting. When uncut, human hair also has a pointed tip.

The medullas of animal hair are distinctive. When present, they often occupy more than one-half the diameter of the shaft (human medullas usually occupy no more than one-third the diameter of the shaft), and they often display symmetrical, sometimes ladder-like *intermittent* patterns that human hairs never have. Human hairs often have *fragmental* medullas; occasionally the medullation is entirely absent. Very rarely the medullation may be *continuous* (see Figure 10-4). In general, the pigment of animal hair tends to cluster around the medulla, but it can also be diffused throughout the cortex. Conversely, in human hair the pigment tends to distribute itself around the periphery of the cortex.

The cuticles of animal hair tend to be coarser and tend to protrude outward from the shaft more than those of human hair, which is rela-

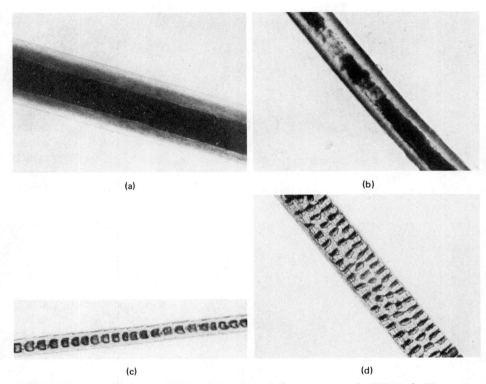

FIGURE 10–4 (a) Horsehair with continuous medulla (approximately 250 X); (b) Human hair with fragmental medulla (approximately 250 X); (c) Cat hair with intermittent (uniserial) medulla (approximately 250 X); (d) Pine mouse hair with intermittent (multiserial) medulla (approximately 250 X).

tively smooth. If known standards are available, the species of animal can be determined by comparing the cuticles (see Figure 10-5).

Although it is helpful to be familiar with the general characteristics of both human and animal hair, especially in deciding which hair types to select as samples, it must be stressed that these are only tendencies, and they can lead to confusion under cursory or inexpert examination. For example, Negroid scalp hairs may exhibit many of the same features as pubic hair, and sheep's wool is similar to human hair in many respects. It takes much experience to make accurate deductions.

COLLECTION AND PRESERVATION OF HAIR

An investigator should be careful not to disturb any hair evidence at the scene of a crime. Using a flashlight and tweezers, the investigator should

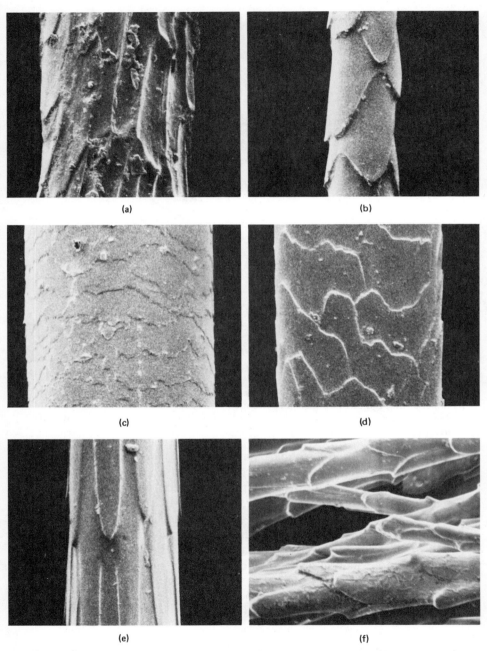

FIGURE 10–5   Scanning electron micrographs of some animal hairs (2200 X):(a) wolf, (b) leopard, (c) bobcat, (d) muskrat, (e) mink, (f) artic seal. (Courtesy of Leo Barish, FRL—An Albany International Co., Dedham, Mass.)

examine the floor, furniture, bedding, toilet facilities, and any other places where hair might be found. All collected hairs should be folded in clean sheets of paper and placed in envelopes. The investigator should state on each envelope *who* found the hair, *what* the evidence is, and *where* and *when* the evidence was found. The location should be marked on a sketch.

All hairs found at the crime scene should be collected and taken to the laboratory, but investigators should take care to avoid contaminating the evidence with their own hair. If the hairs have any foreign matter adhering to them, the matter should be left undisturbed for examination in the laboratory.

In homicides and sexual assaults the investigator should look for hair in the victim's hands and under the fingernails. Pubic hairs from the criminal may be found on the victim's clothing, on the floor or bed, or any place where the victim might have been lying. In rape cases such evidence should be collected from the victim's person by a doctor, nurse, or police woman.

When suspects are available, their clothing should be examined immediately. Even if the criminal makes no effort to brush the victim's hair from his or her clothing, much of the evidence can be lost just in casual wear. In rape or sexual murder cases the suspects should be examined by a doctor. The doctor should be alerted not to allow the suspect to interfere with the evidence.

When head hairs are taken from a murder victim for comparison purposes, they should be representative of all parts of the head. A vigorous, thorough combing is an efficient method for general collection, but hairs should also be clipped from the temples, neck, and crown, and some hairs should be pulled. At least 100 samples should be taken in all. These should be placed in separate envelopes or test tubes and labeled as to the places from which they were taken and whether they were cut, combed, or pulled. When the samples are forwarded to the laboratory, a brief description of the general condition of the victim's hair should be included (i.e., general hair color, baldness, visible signs of bleaching or dyeing, how firmly the hair is attached). The same hair samples should be taken from living victims and suspects if possible, but, especially in the case of women, the work should be done by a doctor or a nurse. When fatalities are involved, the investigating officer should make sure that hair samples are collected from the victim before burial even if hair evidence does not seem immediately pertinent to the case. It is much easier to have the samples on hand than to get an exhumation order later. In most cases the pathologist takes the samples during the autopsy.

Representative animal hairs can be easily collected by pulling at all parts of the coat with the fingers. Hair samples from animals should be packaged and labeled in the same manner as human hair.

LABORATORY EXAMINATION OF HAIR

The task that the laboratory examiner most commonly has to perform with regard to hair is to compare unknown hairs found at a crime scene with samples from suspects. When there are no suspects, the examiner may be called upon to provide leads by making deductions from unidentified hairs as to the age, sex, and race of the person who shed them. When animals are involved, the examiner may have to distinguish their hair from human hair. The great majority of this work is done by microscopic examination of the hair structure.

Preliminary Examination

A preliminary microscopic examination is made at low magnification to note the general condition of the hair: color, texture, curl, effects of bleach or dyes, condition of roots and tips, damage, and adhesion of other materials to be removed for separate testing.

Microscopic Comparison

Known sample hairs are compared with unknown hairs under a comparison microscope. Dry slide mounts are used for comparison of external features such as diameter, scale appearance, and the general conditions noted in the preliminary examination. At this point some suspect samples may be eliminated because of obvious gross differences from the unknown hairs. If the color, scale appearance, and other gross characteristics coincide, more detailed comparisons should be made.

Liquid slide mounting media, which render the hair translucent, are used to examine the interior structure under the microscope, particularly the pigment distribution, medullation, and air bubbles if they occur. Commercial mineral oil makes an excellent temporary mounting medium because it has a suitable refractive index for hair study. Diaphane or Permount may be used for permanent mounts. Although there are some differences, the patterns of the internal characteristics of hairs from the same source are generally similar over a wide enough range of samples. Therefore, it is important to collect as many hairs as possible. Unless a large number of evidence hairs are available, they should not be immersed in any mounting media or other fluids until it is determined that no tests other than microscopic are required. The

FIGURE 10–6 Scanning electron micrograph of human hair (2200 X). (Courtesy of Leo Barish, FRL—An Albany International Co., Dedham, Mass.)

liquids can remove surface materials or alter their chemical compositon.

In laboratories so equipped, detailed studies of the cuticle can best be made by using a scanning electron microscope (see Figures 10-5 and 10-6). Otherwise, *scale casts* can be used for the study of the exterior. Scale casts are most easily made by coating a microscope slide with Polaroid black-and-white print coater or clear fingernail polish and gently pressing the hair into it while it is still wet. When the fluid dries, the hair is removed intact, leaving an exact impression of the scale structure in the hardened material. In addition to comparing the overall appearance of the cuticles, scale counts may be taken and compared. This is done by using a microscope equipped with a calibrated ocular micrometer or by using a microprojector. The scales from a random segment of a hair are counted along a given portion of the micrometer and the count corrected for a standard length. The counts from the hairs of suspects are compared with those of the unknown hairs, and, again, if there are enough samples to work from, the mean count over the range will tend to indicate identity.

Other Microscopic Examinations

As we saw earlier, animal hairs can be distinguished with great certainty from human hairs when their separate characteristics are known. Animal hairs are examined in essentially the same manner as human hair: Dry mounts are used to study the color, diameter, and tips; liquid mounts are used for the medulla; and the scanning electron microscope or scale casts are used for the scales and other surface characteristics.

The determination of age, sex, and race is far from certain; it is more in the nature of educated guesswork. Below are some of the features an examiner can look for to aid in making deductions.

A white hair points to a person over middle age. A mixture of white and pigmented hairs may indicate a person whose hair is in the early stages of graying. When a person is turning bald, hairs taken from the edge of the bald area have different characteristics from other scalp hairs. The hair of a child before puberty is finer and not so fully developed as adult hair.

Even with today's freedom of hair styles, a very long hair is more likely to belong to a woman than to a man. Artificial waving (which twists the hair and produces an irregular diameter) and the use of dye or bleach also tend to indicate a woman, but men should not be excluded from consideration. These processes as well as continuous vigorous brushing tend to produce split ends. A man's hair more often shows squared ends from more frequent cutting.

Among the different races caucasoid hair shows the widest diversity. Straight, light-colored hair almost certainly belongs to a white person, but dark curly hair may belong to almost any race. Negroid hair tends to be flat, dark, and kinky and the medulla is often slightly off center. American Indians and Orientals generally have straight or wavy hair which is round or triangular in cross section. The medulla is centrally placed, and the dark pigment is seen in clumps around the periphery of the cortex.

Chemical Properties of Hair

Hair chemistry is at present of relatively little value in criminal investigations. Keratin, whose chemical composition is well known, is essentially the same in all hair and therefore worthless for identification purposes, and too little is known about pigment and medullation materials for them to be of much use. Also, when chemical tests are made, they generally destroy the sample. One chemical test that is sometimes used to determine the age of a hair source is to drop a hair into a concentrated solution of potassium hydroxide. If the root dissolves quickly, it is more likely from a young child because the roots of adult hair are more resistant.

Approximately 75 percent of the human race secrete blood antigens of the ABO groups into their hair, bones, and other body tissues. In these cases blood types can be determined from hair by absorption-elution techniques similar to those described in Chapter 12 for typing dried blood.

Arsenic and other poisons can be detected in the hair by chemical means if they are present in sufficient quantities, but for more accurate readings and detection of minute quantities, atomic absorption spectrophotometry is preferable.

Physical Properties of Hair

If enough hairs are available, the *density* of known samples can be compared to the density of unknown hair by the same gradient method used to examine soil. At least 50 representative segments approximately 1 millimeter long are placed in separate test tubes with uniform gradient solutions. Segments without medulla must be used because the presence of medullary material significantly alters the density. After equilibrium is reached (in about 24 hours) hairs from the same source will show the same mean and range density.

Similar comparisons can be made of *refractive indexes* of hair by using a liquid immersion method in conjunction with a microscope as described for glass examinations. The Becke line behavior of hair should be observed at a cut end so that the reading is from the cortex instead of the cuticle. Since it is not a pure compound, hair shows differences in refractive index from sample to sample. Although there are small random differences in hairs from the same source, the agreement is very close. This agreement, as well as that shown for density, is valid only in a statistical sense. It is only when the statistical probabilities become so overwhelming as to be beyond doubt (as with fingerprints) that these methods will be of truly positive value to the criminal laboratory scientist. So far, no such degree of probability has been reached in any study of hair.

Instrumental Analyses

Instrumental methods have generally not proved as useful in the analysis of hair as have microscopic examinations and comparisons of physical properties. Emission spectrography and neutron activation analysis can be used to determine the presence of metallic trace elements. And atomic absorption spectrophotometry can be used to trace the distribution of a single element along a hair by cutting the hair into small segments and testing each segment for the presence and concentration of the element.

Although these techniques can result in accurate measurements of the elements in the tested hairs, they cannot distinguish between metabolized trace elements and elements absorbed from the atmosphere, and they cannot take into account the effects of a change of diet or environment on a suspect's hair. Consequently, if a considerable amount of time has elapsed between the commission of the crime and the examination, the validity of any comparisons can be called into question. Also, since the tests are not reliable unless they are carried out on a large range of samples, the time-consuming and complicated nature of the instrumental processes reduces their practicality in busy crime laboratories.

The major problem in analyzing human hair is its great variability. All of the individual characteristics—diameter, color, scale frequency, size and nature of the medulla, pigment distribution, etc.—vary greatly in the population of hairs found on a single head or body. For head hair especially, it is important to realize that when only a single hair or a few hairs are available as evidence, they must be evaluated against the *population* of hair found on a head and cannot be compared directly to one or a few selected hairs from that head.

Review Questions

1. (T, F) Hair evidence is frequently found at crime scenes.
2. When hair collected at a crime scene is compared with hair from a suspect,
   a. It can prove that the suspect was at the crime scene
   b. It can indicate that the suspect might have been at the crime scene
   c. The probability of making a correct match increases with the number of evidence hairs available
   d. a, b, and c
   e. b and c
3. (T, F) An experienced examiner can always tell a person's race from a hair.
4. Hair is made up primarily of
   a. Follicles
   b. Dermis
   c. Keratin
   d. Arsenic
5. Hair scales are collectively known as
   a. Cuticle
   b. Follicle
   c. Cortex
   d. Medulla
6. Medullar material can be
   a. Continuous, intermittent, or coronal
   b. Imbricate, fragmental, or continuous
   c. Continuous, fragmental, or overlapping
   d. Continuous, intermittent, or fragmental
7. Animal hair
   a. Has a uniform diameter along its shaft
   b. Can seldom be reliably differentiated from human hair

   c. Rarely has a medulla

   d. Often has a medulla greater than one-half the diameter of the shaft

8. When collecting evidence hairs, an investigator

   a. Should enclose some of his or her own hair with the evidence as a reference

   b. Should indicate where each hair was found

   c. Can ignore any hair not found in the same room as the victim

   d. Should carefully wipe the dirt and contaminating material off hairs before packaging them

9. (T, F) An inexperienced examiner might mistake sheep's wool for human hair.

10. The best way to examine hair scales is with a

   a. Scanning electron microscope

   b. Infrared spectrophotometer

   c. Mineral oil mount

   d. Atomic absorpotion spectrophotometer

11. (T, F) By using both density and refractive index determinations it is possible to positively identify a hair as belonging to an individual.

CHAPTER ELEVEN

—————— *FIBERS* ——————

Fibers are the basic building materials of countless items of everyday life to which people never give a second thought. The plant world is essentially fibrous; consequently wood, paper, and much of the food we eat is made up of fiber. In connection with crime, fiber most often appears in the form of textiles—whether as clothing worn by the persons involved or bedding, drapery, rugs, and upholstery. Other fibrous items often found in evidence in criminal cases are ropes, strings, sacks, and wrapping materials that a criminal might have used to bind a victim or transport some equipment.

FIBER AS EVIDENCE

Fiber evidence is by no means limited to criminal cases. Fiber evidence is also used in other types of litigation such as actions brought against textile manufacturers over violations of health and flammability standards or civil suits against hit-and-run drivers. However, the situations in which the criminal investigator is most likely to encounter fiber evidence are those in which either some fabric has rubbed or caught against something else, leaving a bit of fabric behind, or some form of rope or cord was used in the commission of a crime.

In crimes involving breaking and entering burglars often have to perform some fairly acrobatic activity in order to gain entrance. In so doing, they may easily catch their clothing on a nail or a splinter and leave visible bits of fabric behind. They will certainly leave microscopic bits of fiber adhering to other objects with which their clothing comes into contact. Similarly, in the case of a car theft the thief will leave fibers from his or her apparel on the upholstery of the stolen car, and in a crime involving a struggle there will be a reciprocal transfer of fibers between the clothing of the assailant and that of the victim. Fiber transferences like these are usually invisible to the naked eye. Therefore, all clothing and cloth articles found in connection with crimes should be handled as if they carry fiber evidence.

Fiber evidence is almost always present at crime scenes and sometimes it is the only evidence available, but it has some serious limitations. Since so many textiles, ropes, and sacking materials are mass produced, the very commonness of such items reduces the evidential value of any fibers derived from them. Blue jeans are a good example. Even though different pairs may show microscopic variations in color, dye, and fading, a prosecutor would have to be able to match some very distinctive peculiarity between fibers found at the scene of a crime and blue jeans worn by a suspect before the prosecutor could use such evidence to connect that suspect with the crime. The comparison of fibers found at the scene of a crime with known samples taken from suspects can be of great value in eliminating innocent people from suspicion when the two samples are dissimilar. But when the known and unknown samples are similar, their value in placing an individual at the crime scene is directly proportional to their rarity.

Another limitation is the difficulty of identifying unknown fibers in the laboratory. In addition to the natural fibers, many of which have been used for thousands of years and are relatively easy to identify, there are large numbers of synthetic fibers on the market, and new ones are being created all the time. Since these synthetic fibers may vary greatly in their microscopic appearance and their chemical and physical properties, it is difficult even for experts to keep up with developments.

CHARACTERISTICS OF FIBERS

Chemically, fibers are made up of long, chain-like structures known as *polymers,* which result from the combination of two or more single molecules *(monomers)* of the same kind (see Figure 11-1). The long molecules of the polymers retain the same percentage composition of elements as the monomers.

To the criminal investigator the term fiber generally means any

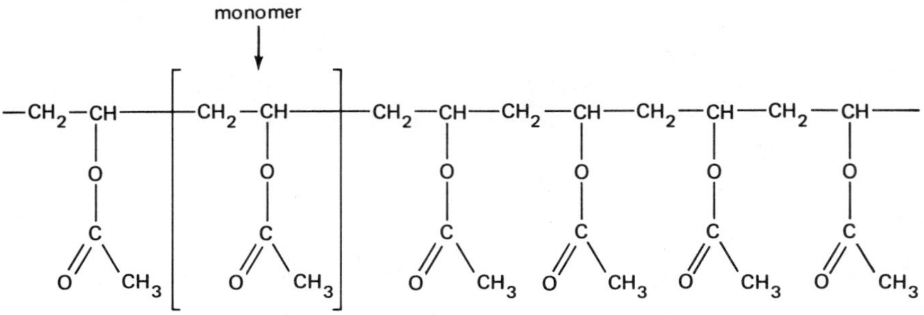

monomer

$$-CH_2-CH\left[\begin{matrix}-CH_2-CH-\\\ |\\\ O\\\ |\\\ C\\\ O^{/\!/}\ {}^{\backslash}CH_3\end{matrix}\right]-CH_2-CH-CH_2-CH-CH_2-CH-CH_2-CH-$$

FIGURE 11-1 Chemical structure of a polyvinylacetate polymer. The vinyl acetate monomer repeats itself thousands of times to form one long chain molecule.

tough, pliable, filament-like substance that can be spun or woven. To the textile manufacturer a fiber is the smallest visible unit from which a fabric is made. Fibers are spun into thread and yarn, which in turn are woven, knitted, or otherwise combined to produce a textile. Short fibers, which have to be spun to form yarn (⅜ inch to 2½ inches in the case of cotton), are known as *staple,* and fibers of extreme length, like silk from undamaged cocoons and some synthetics whose length is controlled by the manufacturing process, are called *filament.*

Fibers fall into two overall classifications: (1) those that occur in nature in the form in which they are used commercially (natural fibers) and (2) those that are artificially produced (man-made fibers).

Natural Fibers

Most natural fibers come from vegetable or animal sources. Only one mineral, asbestos, is found in nature in fibrous form. Asbestos is a hydrous silicate of magnesium or iron. The fibers are fine and are usually gray or greenish-white, but they can also be yellow, lavender, or blue in color.

Vegetable fibers are made up of polymers of cellulose and can come from the seed, stem, or leaves of plants. Cotton is the best known of the seed fibers. Cotton is the vegetable fiber most commonly found in criminal evidence because it is still used in so many types of clothing. Cotton is soft and short and under a microscope it looks like a flat band with a corkscrew twist (see Figure 11-2). Linen used to be the most important of the stem fibers (also known as *bast* and *soft* fibers). Linen comes from the flax plant and is the strongest of the vegetable fibers. Since it has been almost entirely replaced in clothing by man-made materials, linen seldom appears in evidence. Its main use today is in fine tablecloths, napkins, and handkerchiefs. Under the microscope linen shows distinctive cross bands that resemble bamboo nodes and its fibril-

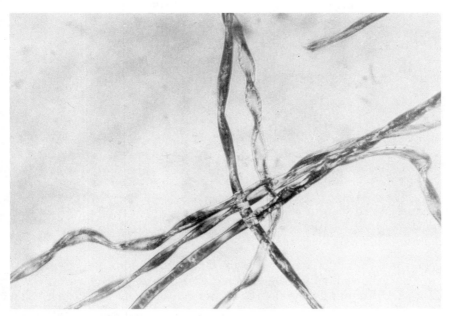

FIGURE 11–2 Cotton fibers (approximately 400 X).

lar structure is clearly visible. Some other stem fibers are jute and hemp. Jute is coarse and stiff and its colors range from yellow to brown. Jute is used in inexpensive woven mats, burlap, and some linoleums. Hemp, which is lighter than jute, is used in ropes, cord, sacks, and tarpaulins. Some examples of leaf (or *hard*) fibers are Manila hemp and sisal. Manila hemp, which is pale yellow to light brown in color, is used for twine and rope. Sisal, which is yellow-white and has a fine gloss, is used to make coarse mats as well as rope and string.

The natural animal fibers are all proteinaceous, and all except silk are the hair of animals. By far the most common is sheep's wool. Other less common varieties are fibers from Angora goats (mohair), cashmere goats, camels, alpacas, llamas, and vicunas. All of these, though varying greatly from each other, possess the characteristic cortex, medulla, pigment, and cuticle of hair (hair is described in greater detail in Chapter 10). In sheep's wool the medulla may be fragmental or absent (though in some breeds it is more evident and very broad) and the scales vary from indistinct in the coarser hairs to very pronounced in the finer hairs. (See Figure 11-3).

Silk is a long continuous fiber which the silkworm secretes as a viscous fluid to build its cocoon. Silk is made up of two filaments, each triangular in cross section, bound together by a gelatinous protein

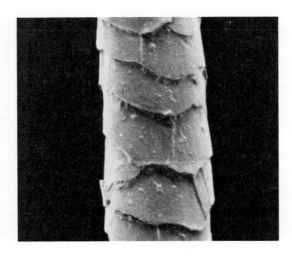

FIGURE 11-3 Scanning electron micrograph of wool (2200 X). (Courtesy of Leo Barish, FRL—An Albany International Co., Dedham, Mass.)

called *sericin,* which hardens in air. Under the microscope its surface structure shows highly irregular creases, folds, and lumps (see Figure 11-4), and frequently the double strand can be seen. Degummed silk, from which the sericin has been removed, is smooth and structureless, but because it is the lightest of textile fibers, it is usually commercially weighted with tin oxide, which can be identified chemically. To produce the silk yarns used in textiles from 3 to 24 filaments are combined into strands (strands of 12 filaments are the most common), and then from 3 to 8 of these combined strands are twisted into yarn.

Man-Made Fibers

Man-made fibers can be classified in various complicated ways according to their chemical, physical, microscopic, and biological properties. Nevertheless, they can be simply divided into two overall categories:

1. *Regenerated fibers* are made from natural polymers that have been broken down and restructured into usable fibers. Although structurally different, these fibers retain the same basic chemical composition as the original material.
2. *Synthetic fibers* are made from manufactured, originally nonfibrous substances that are artificially processed into fiber form.

Regenerated Fibers

The most common of the regenerated fibers is rayon, which is regenerated from cellulose by one of two processes known as *viscose* and *cuprammonium,* of which viscose is the most widely used. The

FIGURE 11-4 Silk (approximately 300 X).

cellulose may come from wood, cotton, or other plants. When cotton cellulose is used, both viscose and cuprammonium rayon have the same chemical composition as cotton fiber, but their microscopic structure and physical properties are very different. Cuprammonium rayon has an almost cylindrical and smooth surface, which is not found in any natural fiber; viscose rayon is very uneven with deep longitudinal striations that are more exaggerated than any irregularities found in natural plant fibers (see Figure 11-5).

Other regenerated fibers are those belonging to the *azlon* group. These fibers are regenerated from naturally occurring proteins such as casein from skim milk, zein from corn, and the proteins of peanuts, soya beans, and cotton seed. Casein fiber is white; zein fiber is yellow; soya bean fiber is white to tan; and peanut fiber is creamy white to light tan. All the azlons are wool-like in quality.

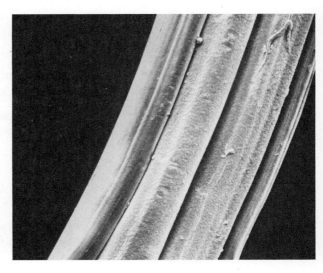

FIGURE 11-5 Scanning electron micrograph of viscose rayon (2200 X). (Courtesy of Leo Barish, FRL—An Albany International Co., Dedham, Mass.)

Synthetic Fibers

It is in this category that most of the complications arise for the laboratory scientist. Synthetic fibers fall into several different chemical categories, and new ones are being invented all the time. To make matters more complicated, different types of fibers may be spun together to produce yarns having certain desired characteristics, and each manufacturer may assign its own trade name to the same product. The following are some of the main categories of synthetic fibers.

Acetate. All types of acetate are made by acetylating cellulose, that is, by treating cellulose with acetic acid in the presence of sulfuric acid and acetic anhydride. The major source of cellulose is wood pulp. Because of the cellulose base there have been some objections to including acetates among the synthetics, but their chemical properties are more akin to those of synthetic fibers than to pure cellulose products. Acetate is mostly produced in filament form and, when undyed, is pure white.

Nylon. Nylon is one of the most common synthetic fibers. Nylon is tough, pliable, and lustrous. It is white in color, translucent, and primarily produced in filament form. In addition to its wide use in garments, nylon is often used in ropes and fishing line because of its great tensile strength.

Acrylics. Acrylics are known for their softness and are generally used in fabrics. Orlon is one of the best-known examples. Acrylics are produced in both staple and filament form. They are silky in filament form and wool-like when spun from staple. The undyed fibers are white.

Polyesters. Because of their high resistance to wrinkling, polyesters are largely used in wash-and-wear clothing. The fibers are white and opaque and are produced in staple and filament length.

Saran. This fiber is water repellent and spot resistant. It is used mainly in rugs, lawn furniture, and industrial fabrics.

Spandex. Spandex is light, soft, and elastic. It is used in stretch garments such as foundation garments and swimwear. The fiber is white and dull-lustered.

Vinyon. Vinyon fibers are strong and are easily heat-bonded to other fibers. This latter property makes it especially suitable for the manufacture of nonwoven fabrics. Vinyon is made only in staple form.

Olefins. Olefins are polypropylene and polyethylene polymers. They are the most common upholstery fiber in use today. They are also commonly used in nonwoven applications such as twine, cordage, and fish nets.

Rubber fibers. Rubber fibers can be made from natural or synthetic rubber and they are used in elastic applications. Usually, rubber fiber forms the core of the yarn and there is an outer covering of some other fiber.

Mineral fibers. Mineral fibers can be made from glass or metals coated with plastic or plastic coated with metal. The metal is usually aluminum foil. Glass fibers are used largely in drapery material. Metallic yarns, such as lamé, are used in combination with conventional fibers to create special effects in clothing.

FIBER PRODUCTS

Yarn

Since most fabrics are made from fibers in yarn form, knowledge of the construction of yarn is essential in scientific investigations, especially in comparison work. Yarns may be made by twisting a number of fibers together (spinning), by laying filaments together with or without twist, or they may be a single filament with or without twist. Single strands of yarn made directly from fibers are called *single-ply* or *one-ply* yarns. Yarns made from two or more one-ply yarns twisted together are called *multiple* or *ply* yarns, such as 2 ply, 3 ply, etc. Different types of fibers can be blended in various ways to create desired qualities in yarns and fabrics, such as softness and wrinkle resistance. The twisting process, which makes the yarn strong enough to use in fabrics, can be varied for different surface effects. Sewing thread, for example, is a type of ply yarn that has been twisted in such a way as to create a compact but flexible strand. A clockwise twist is known as an "S" twist; a counterclockwise twist is called a "Z" twist. Twist is measured in turns per inch. One of the most important developments in recent years is the so-called textured yarn in which the fibers are crimped by any of several processes in order to produce a more bulky yarn. Textured yarn is almost always used in polyester knit fabrics, carpets, and many other structures.

Other points of comparison in yarns are count systems borrowed from the textile industry, which express the linear density of the yarn. Yarns made from filament silk and most man-made fibers are measured in *deniers* (the number of grams per 9,000 meters of length). Yarns made from spun silk, glass, asbestos, and most natural fibers are measured in terms of the yardage necessary to make up one pound in weight.

Fabrics

Although some fabrics are made directly from fibers either by felting (physically matting the fibers together), by bonding (holding the fibers together by chemical cementing or fusing), or by needling (tangling fibers together by transverse punching with barbed needles), most fabrics are made from yarn. The most traditional of these are produced by weaving which, in simple terms, consists of laying out parallel strands of yarn (called the *warp*) on a loom and filling them in by interlacing other strands of yarn through them at right angles. These strands are called *filling strands* or (collectively) the *woof* or *weft*. In plain weaving the warp and the woof pass alternately over and under each other, but there can be variations for special effects. The count of a woven fabric is the number of warp and woof yarns per inch.

In recent years knitted fabrics have become as common as woven fabrics. This is because knitted fabrics can be made more rapidly and less expensively, because they provide more stretch and comfort, and because complicated fabric design patterns, such as double knits, are more easily made by knitting than by weaving. Knitting is a process of interlacing single yarns by means of various patterns of loops.

Other fabrics in which yarn is used but not woven or knitted are braids, nets, laces, and imitation furs.

Finishing

All commercial fabrics undergo some kind of finishing treatment to make them more useful or more attractive. Yarns and fibers can also be treated before anything is made of them. The treatments involve the application of heat, pressure, and a variety of chemicals, depending on the desired characteristics, and may include such processes as delustering, scouring, bleaching, stiffening, sizing and desizing, singeing, softening, and weighting. Other special processes are used to make fabrics mothproof and waterproof, flame resistant or flame retardant, antiseptic, and mildew resistant. Since all these processes produce characteristic changes in the fibers that can be detected in the laboratory, they can figure prominently in fiber identification.

Rope and Cordage

Rope is distinguished from cordage (cords, twine, string) by the manner of contruction. In rope construction the fibers are twisted into threads, which are in turn twisted into strands. The strands are then twisted or plaited into rope. The various forms of cord are made by simple spinning. Most ropes and cord were formerly made from natural vegetable fibers, and many still are, but man-made fibers (largely nylon,

160

polyester, and propylene) now dominate. Manila hemp and sisal are the natural fibers most commonly used in rope. Cord, twine, and some light ropes are commonly made from cotton, jute, and hemp. Ropes and cords made from man-made fibers utilize fibers designed for specific applications. Thus, polypropylene is commonly used for fish nets because it has a density of less than one and it floats. Nylon is used whenever great strength combined with light weight and some shock-absorbing elasticity are required, as in mountain climbing ropes, parachute cords, and towing hawsers. Polyester provides rope with high chemical resistance and maximum abrasion resistance.

The principal characteristics to be examined in the identification and comparison of rope are its diameter, direction of twist ("S" or "Z" as in yarns), the number of twists per unit length, construction material, the number of strands, the number of threads per strand, and the average number of fibers per thread.

Cords are of less evidential significance than rope because cords are so commonly found in everyday usage. They can be examined for diameter, direction of twist, twists per unit length, and construction material. They may be useful as evidence if they have some unusual feature or if they have picked up some debris that may be connected to the crime scene. Cords are more likely to be of value than rope in the latter respect because their relatively loose construction enables them to pick up and hold small particles.

COLLECTION AND PRESERVATION OF FIBERS

Fiber evidence can be found almost anywhere at the scene of a crime. Consequently, investigators must always be alert not just to finding it but to avoid contaminating it with fibers from their own clothing.

Pieces of fabric, rope, or cordage should be photographed where they are found before they are picked up. Then they should be placed in evidence bags or envelopes of appropriate size on which the investigator writes his or her name or identifying mark and states what the evidence is and where it was found. Each item should be placed in a separate container to avoid mutual contamination.

Fibers found in the hands or under the fingernails of victims of violent crimes should be carefully collected with tweezers and folded in pieces of plain paper, which are then placed in envelopes with the appropriate identifying notations mentioned above. Individual strands or fibers visible on the floor, on heavy furniture, or on other objects that cannot be brought to the laboratory should be treated in the same way. No attempt should be made to remove fibers from clothing or other transportable fabrics at the scene of the crime. The fiber-bearing article should be appropriately bagged and transported to the laboratory. When all visible fibers and bits of fabric have been collected and properly packaged, the whole crime scene should be vacuumed with a vacuum sweeper equipped with a filter and the filter contents taken to the lab for separation and examination.

Whenever possible, fibers should be removed from clothing and other fabrics under laboratory conditions because much of this evidence is microscopic. Also, it might be important to know on what part of the article the fiber was found. The most efficient method of removing loose fibers from other fabrics is to press the adhesive side of transparent tape against the article. The tape picks up an extremely large percent of the loose fibers and has the additional advantage of pinpointing the spot where a specific fiber was found. The disadvantages of this method are that a high adhesive tape picks up a large number of background fibers from the material itself and that very fine fibers may be difficult to remove from the adhesive surface. Other methods are shaking, vacuuming, and brushing, but none of these has either the collecting qualities or the specificity of tape. The tape process is also the best for collecting fibers from the clothing of suspects. It is very important to collect such samples as soon as possible after the crime since foreign fibers can be shed quickly just through normal wear.

LABORATORY EXAMINATION OF FIBERS

Because of the large array of existing fibers and the continuous development of new synthetics, fiber analysis is an extremely complex field requiring considerable expertise on the part of the laboratory scientist. Fiber examiners have a great number of laboratory techniques at their disposal, and their choice of technique is determined by the individual needs of the case and the amount of evidence available. When, as in most criminal cases, only a small amount of fiber evidence is found, the analyst is limited to tests that do not destroy the evidence. Very often a detailed microscopic examination is adequate for identification without any further testing. Other nondestructive techniques include the determination of density, refractive index, and birefringence. If further testing is called for and enough samples are available, the scientist has recourse to cross-section microscopic examination, chemical tests, determination of melting point, ash analysis, infrared spectrophotometry, and pyrolysis-gas chromatography.

Since most of the work of a fiber analyst in a crime laboratory consists of comparing sample fibers from suspects with fibers found at the scene of the crime, it is usually only necessary to determine whether or not the two samples match. It is not strictly necessary to identify the fiber. In these cases a microscopic examination and comparison of the longitudinal appearance of the fiber, including the presence of bleaches, dyes, and other finishing processes, are usually sufficient. When whole pieces of fabric are involved, as when a criminal leaves a bit of torn clothing at the crime scene, a gross examination by naked eye may be enough to establish a match because the tear pattern of the missing piece should match that of the place from which it was torn. The results of such macroscopic (naked eye) examinations can be confirmed by comparing the thread counts of the fabrics, the fiber composition of the yarn, the direction of twist of the threads, and the weaving and dying patterns and by matching broken yarn ends of the evidence sample to yarn ends from the garment. Since yarns break at different spots and protrude from the fabric at different lengths, a match of several yarn ends provides strong proof of identity.

The examiner's task can be much more complicated if he or she is required to identify a completely unknown fiber. Fiber properties fall into various groups which sometimes overlap. The examiner proceeds by eliminating those fibers that do not fit into the observed groups, thus narrowing down the range of possible alternatives. Textile manufacturers have published detailed descriptive materials against which the examiner can check the observations. Some of these publications are listed in the bibliography. Generally, a skilled fiber analyst can identify the generic type of textile fibers (polyester, acrylic, nylon, etc.) if given a sufficient sample. Identification of specific brand names (Orlon acrylic, Acrilon acrylic, etc.) is more difficult and sometimes impossible.

Heat and Flame Tests

Since these tests destroy the fibers, they are used only when a large number of samples are available, but when they can be used, they are very helpful because they may permit the rapid elimination of many classes of fibers even before the microscopic examination is begun. The tests consist of observing the behavior of a fiber as it approaches a flame, when it is in the flame, and after it is removed from the flame. Natural vegetable fibers, for example, do not fuse near the flame and they burn without melting. Synthetic fibers react differently according to their composition, but most synthetic fibers tend to fuse before reaching the flame and to melt while burning in the flame. The various types of fibers also leave characteristic ashes or other charred remains when removed from the flame, and some have characteristic odors when burned.

Microscopic Examination

Because there are rarely enough fibers for the heat and flame tests, the microscopic examination is usually the first step in identification. Fibers are first observed longitudinally in dry mount under low power

(50X to 60X). Fibers showing surface scales are natural animal fibers and can be identified by detailed microscopic comparison with animal hairs known to be used in textiles. Cross markings or nodes indicate vascular fibers such as flax or hemp; and the appearance of a twist along with an internal cellular structure indicates cotton. Asbestos and glass have very small diameters, and the latter is very uniform. Silk is slightly non-uniform; if it is not degummed, it exhibits fine striations. Some synthetics which are round in cross sections have a smooth, structureless appearance and relatively great width, but many man-made fibers, such as rayon, are striated.

Almost all natural fibers and many synthetics can be positively identified by detailed (250X to 500X) microscopic inspection of their longitudinal appearance. If sufficient samples are available, the identification can be further narrowed down by examining the cross-sectional appearance. For example, natural animal fibers (except silk) show the typical hair structure of medulla, cortex, and cuticle; silk is triangular and often the double strand can be seen; Orlon-21 is T-shaped; Lycra, Orlon, and Verel are dumbbell or dog-bone shaped; acetate generally has a rough cloverleaf shape; Qiana is trilobal; and polyesters can be round, trilobal or eight-lobed (see Figure 11–6). Many of the synthetics fall into the nondescript grouping of round or nearly round. When

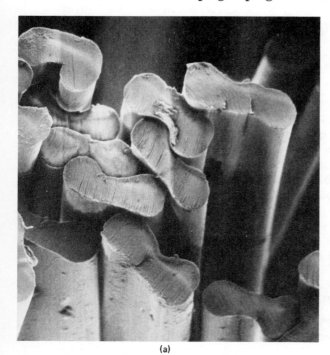

(a)

FIGURE 11–6 Scanning electron micrographs of textile fibers: (a) dumbell shaped Orlon Acrylic, (b) trilobal Quiana, (c) octalobal polyester (2200 X). (Courtesy of Leo Barish, FRL—An Albany International Co., Dedham, Mass.)

(b)

FIGURE 11–6 *continued*

(c)

there is more than one fiber in a given group, the fibers must be differentiated by other means.

Other Nondestructive Tests

Since almost all undyed fibers are transparent or translucent, they have the property of refracting light, and their refractive indexes can be determined by the use of a polarizing microscope and the Becke line test. Refractive index is useful only in comparisons made in the same laboratory because of the difficulty in reproducing exact conditions in different laboratories. A more accurate measurement, however, is that of birefringence (see page 40), which is the difference between the longitudinal and perpendicular refractive indexes of a fiber. Regardless of the different readings for refractive index that may be obtained under different laboratory conditions, the relationship between the longitudinal and the perpendicular readings is always the same. Therefore, the birefringence measurement is reproducible from laboratory to laboratory and can be stated as a constant property of a fiber. But this holds true only for synthetics that are manufactured under constant, controlled conditions. Birefringence cannot be determined for all synthetic fibers.

Density within a given range is another constant property of fibers, but the presence of finishing treatments or of medullary material in animal fibers may make density determination difficult. Density is most easily found by means of gradients (a graduated column of different liquids that have different, known specific gravities in which a bit of fiber floats at a level consistent with its own specific gravity). The density values are determined by means of calibration beads. Density ranges are available in the publications of the textile manufacturers listed in the bibliography.

Chemical Tests

Chemical tests are used primarily to confirm identifications made by microscopic examination or to differentiate fibers within a group having similar structural properties. The tests consist of solubility tests, which divide fibers into chemical groups according to their susceptibility to disintegrate in various chemical agents, and stain tests, in which some fibers exhibit characteristic color changes when treated with certain chemicals. The appropriate solvents and staining chemicals for given fibers are listed in textile publications. Stain tests are not applicable for dyed fibers. Stain tests on undyed fibers should be verified, if possible, by other tests. Stain test results may be variable because of prior chemical treatment during finishing.

Melting Point

Testing the melting point, especially of synthetic fibers, can help confirm identifications made by other means. However, since the determination of melting point can be a rather imprecise measurement for some fibers, with variations for a single fiber of as much as 5°C, it must generally be regarded only as an approximation. The advantage of melting point values is that they are generally unaffected by the presence of finishing materials.

Instrumental Tests

Infrared spectrophotometry and pyrolysis-gas chromatography can be valuable in providing accurate fiber identifications. Infrared spectrophotometry is used mainly in the comparison of synthetic fibers. The chemical compounds that make up the fiber polymers absorb infrared light in characteristic ways that can be recorded by the spectrophotometer. Although it is sometimes difficult to tell what a single fiber is from its spectrogram, it is relatively easy to compare two spectrograms. If they match, the fibers are identical. Pyrolysis-gas chromatography is especially useful in comparing fibers that are heavily pigmented with dyes or finishing materials. The pyrolysis (extreme heat in the absence of oxygen) breaks down all the organic compounds present, including the finishing materials; the resulting volatile compounds are analyzed by the gas chromatograph. Since all the fibers from the same garment have received the same finishing treatment, the presence of such materials does not invalidate a comparison.

No single one of these laboratory techniques is adequate to identify all fibers. When complications arise, various methods must be used in combination. Fiber analysis is a field that requires a great deal of experience in bringing together diverse testing procedures and making reasoned conclusions from their results. Even the most experienced examiners cannot always be absolutely certain of the accuracy of their conclusions.

Review Questions

1. Fiber can be found in
   a. Wood
   b. Rope

  c. Food
  d. All the above
  e. a and b

2. (T, F) A commonplace fiber is more valuable as evidence than a rare fiber is because the examiner is more likely to recognize it.

3. Short fibers that have to be spun into yarn are called
  a. Filament
  b. Staple
  c. Monomers
  d. Natural

4. Under a microscope cotton fiber is
  a. Trilobal
  b. Round and has deep longitudinal striations
  c. Flat with a corkscrew twist
  d. Indistinguishable from rayon

5. Which of the following is a regenerated fiber?
  a. Rayon
  b. Sericin
  c. Nylon
  d. Second-growth mink

6. Acetate is made from
  a. Polyvinyl
  b. Soya beans
  c. Wood pulp
  d. Polyethylene glycol

7. In cross section synthetic fibers can appear
  a. Round
  b. Dogbone-shaped
  c. Octalobal
  d. Trilobal
  e. All the above

8. Glass fibers are considered
  a. Regenerated
  b. Natural
  c. Elastic
  d. Mineral

9. Multiple ply yarns are made from
  a. Two or more one-ply yarns
  b. Two or more strands twisted together
  c. Two or more filaments
  d. Fibers with a "Z" twist

10. (T, F) A "Z" twist is counterclockwise.

11. The majority of fabrics are made from
  a. Felt

    b. Bonded fibers
    c. Yarn
    d. Needled fibers

12. All textile fabrics are
    a. Woven
    b. Synthetic
    c. Moth resistant
    d. Subjected to finishing treatment

13. Polypropylene is used in fish nets because
    a. It attracts fish
    b. It floats
    c. It is elastic
    d. It has a high density

14. Microscopic fibers are best collected from clothing by means of
    a. Transparent adhesive tape
    b. A thorough brushing
    c. Shaking the article into a bag
    d. Tweezers

15. Heat and flame tests can be used
    a. When few fiber samples are available
    b. To eliminate classes of fibers
    c. In place of microscopic examinations
    d. Only on synthetic fibers

16. The instrumental analyses most useful for identification of synthetic fibers are
    a. X-ray diffraction and gas chromatography
    b. Mass spectrometry and emission spectrography
    c. Pyrolysis and atomic absorption spectrophotometry
    d. Infrared spectrophotometry and pyrolysis-gas chromatography

CHAPTER TWELVE

———— *BLOOD* ————

When blood comes out of a wound, it is a dense, viscous, red fluid which begins to congeal immediately upon contact with the air. If whole blood is spun in a centrifuge, it separates into a pale straw-colored fluid called *plasma* and a reddish-brown sediment of solid materials called *formed elements.*

Blood plasma is mostly water in which small amounts of salts and approximately 9 percent by weight of various blood proteins are carried in solution. One of these proteins is *fibrinogen* which, when converted to *fibrin* at the site of a wound, causes the blood to clot.

The formed elements, which account for 45 percent of the volume of whole blood, consist mainly of red blood corpuscles *(erythrocytes),* white corpuscles *(leukocytes),* and platelets *(thrombocytes).* The red corpuscles (cells) which are almost a thousand times more numerous than the white cells, carry hemoglobin, a red-pigmented compound of iron and protein that picks up oxygen in the lungs and delivers it to the body tissues. The white cells are colorless and transparent and are larger than the erythrocytes. They have the capability of moving actively to an infected area where they gather in large numbers to fight the infection. The platelets are the smallest of the blood particles. They release a chemical at the site of a wound that causes the fibrinogen in the plasma to precipitate out in the form of fibrin. The fibrin precipitate is a sticky substance which binds the red blood cells together to form clots. The yellowish liquid that remains after the fibrin is removed from the plasma is known as *serum.*

BLOOD AS EVIDENCE

In one spectacular case patrolmen answered a possible homicide call and found five people murdered in a quiet suburban residence. The scene was one of frightening disorder, and there were clear signs of the victims' struggles to escape their attackers evident in the overwhelming amount of blood that was scattered around the house and grounds. There were several pools of still undried blood on the premises; there were bloody tracks in the house, which might have been made by the killers; and the walls and even the outside shrubbery were liberally spattered with blood. A mountain of potential evidence lay in all that blood and disarray. As it turned out, however, much of the evidence was obscured by the army of largely unnecessary police officials who tracked their own footprints through the blood in their curiosity to see what had happened. Although the killers were ultimately caught and convicted through betrayal by one of their confederates, proper use of the physical evidence, most of which concerned blood in some way, would have led to the same result much more quickly.

Blood Transfers

Transfers of wet blood can be very helpful forms of evidence. If a criminal gets wet blood on his or her person while commiting the crime and then touches something, he or she may leave bloody finger or hand prints, footprints, fabric weave patterns, or contact imprints of tools or weapons. Any of these might help connect a criminal with a crime.

Blood Distribution

A skillful investigator can learn much by observing the distribution of blood at the scene of a crime. A large pool of blood under a body indicates that the victim was not moved from the place where he or she was killed, whereas if only flakes of dried blood are found around the body, it probably means that the victim was killed elsewhere and moved to the place where the body was found. In such a case the blood would have had time to coagulate and the flakes would have been knocked free by the movement of the body.

After death blood pressure is reduced to zero and a body no longer bleeds. Instead it drains, and the drainage must follow the law of gravity. Hence, any signs of drainage from a wound which are contrary to gravity prove that the body was moved after the blood had congealed.

Inside the body the blood settles through the force of gravity into the lowest tissues, where it coagulates and creates a purple-red discoloration known as *post-mortem lividity.* This process begins between one-half hour and one hour after death and is completed by 12 hours. Since the blood cannot move once it has coagulated, if signs of post-mortem lividity are seen in any but the lowest parts of the body, the body has been moved.

The distribution of spattered blood can be highly significant. Blood spattering is generally caused by blows to a part of the body that is already bleeding. The first blow might open a wound. Subsequent blows strike the flowing blood with sufficient force to cause drops to break free and fly laterally out from the wound. The flying blood drops tend to strike the floor and walls at oblique angles, and when they hit a hard, flat surface, they leave characteristically elongated spots from which tiny droplets radiate outward in the direction of travel (See Figure 12–1). The direction can easily be determined by observing the shape of the spot and the radiation pattern of the droplets.

Another source of flying blood drops can be the murder weapon itself. In a bludgeoning or knifing murder if the assailant strikes repeated blows, the victim's blood adheres to the weapon, and as the murderer swings it back to strike again, drops fly off it under centrifugal force and form a pattern dictated by the arc of the swing and the last jerk before the weapon begins to come forward again.

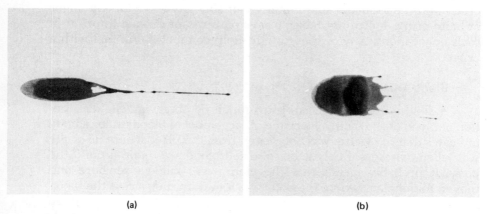

(a)   (b)

FIGURE 12–1   The direction of travel of both blood spots is from left to right; (a) struck the surface at a 30° angle, and (b) struck the surface at a 45° angle.

Blood splashing can also be caused by arterial bleeding. When an artery is severed, blood spurts out of it with each heartbeat. Arterial bleeding can often be recognized by the fact that the drops are larger than those propelled by the greater force of a blow and they tend to fall in an oval pattern.

Because the high viscosity of blood makes its molecules tend to cling together, it takes more force to produce small drops than to produce large ones. Consequently, the drops that fall freely from wounds or blood-covered objects are larger (⅝ inch to ¾ inch in diameter on hard, flat surfaces) than those propelled by force. Drops propelled at medium velocity, as by a hammer or axe blow, are ⅛ inch or less in diameter. Those propelled at high velocity, as from a gunshot, tend to form a mist-like spray pattern of droplets less than ⅛ inch in diameter mixed with tiny particles sometimes smaller than 1/1000 inch in diameter.

Free-falling blood drops also tend to form characteristic spots when they fall perpendicularly onto hard, flat surfaces. If they fall from a height of up to 20 inches, the spots are round and clearly defined. Above 8 inches the edges take on a scalloped effect which becomes more pronounced with greater distance. Between 20 inches and 54 inches the points splash out like sun rays, and tiny droplets, loosened by the force of the fall, radiate out in all directions from the spot. (See Figure 12–2.)

The investigator must be very careful about drawing any conclusions from a bloodstain about the distance the blood drop has fallen because the appearance of the drop is influenced much more by the texture of the surface on which it lands than by the distance. A drop that has fallen onto a hard, smooth, nonporous surface like glass or plastic shows little or no scalloping of the edges even from a great distance,

(a)   (b)   (c)

FIGURE 12–2 Blood drops that have fallen straight down onto a piece of paper (a) 6 inches, (b) 12 inches, (c) 36 inches.

whereas a drop that has fallen only a few inches onto a desk blotter shows considerable scalloping and radiation of droplets. The rougher the surface, the more it tends to break the viscosity of the blood. Long practice might enable an experienced crime scene investigator to form a reasonable hunch, but the only way to obtain accurate estimates is to make laboratory tests using surfaces of the same materials as those on which the stains under investigation are found.

In the majority of cases the blood found at the scene of a homicide is that of the victim or victims. Observation of its distribution can be very helpful in reconstructing the crime. The position and direction of movement of the spots may make it possible to determine where the assault occurred. An area free of blood spots might indicate the place where the murderer stood because the flying blood would have landed on the murderer rather than on the floor. The way the blood flowed out of the wound can help determine the position of the body at the time of the attack and whether the body was moved. Swipe marks left on surfaces by blood-soaked hair or cloth may also suggest the movement of the body or the direction of the victim's fall. It may also be possible to tell how many blows were struck and whether the victim put up a struggle.

Experienced investigators can sometimes get a general idea of how much time has passed since the commission of the crime from the condition of the blood. If the stain is still fresh and fluid, the elapsed time is probably less than an hour. When the stain begins to get jelly-like, showing that fibrin has formed, and when the stain begins to pucker and crack around the edges, it becomes more difficult to draw accurate conclusions because such factors as humidity, temperature, the color and intensity of the light, and the kind of material on which the stain appears can affect the speed of the chemical reactions that cause blood to alter its consistency. Nevertheless, through experience investigators can develop a sense for making rough estimates which, while having no official significance, may help them proceed with the investigation.

BLOOD TYPES

The effectiveness of blood evidence depends on its ability to connect a suspect with a crime. This is usually a matter of linking the blood of a victim to bloodstains on clothing or other possessions of the criminal. But in cases in which there might have been a struggle between victim and murderer or in which a burglar may have incurred an injury while breaking and entering, then the culprit's own blood may connect him or her to the crime. The blood of different people is differentiated by means of testing for blood *types* or blood *groups*. The terms are used interchangeably. There are over 100 known ways in which blood can be typed, at least 12 of which are based on the red cells, but the ones that are of current significance in criminal investigations are the ABO system, the MN system, and to a lesser extent, the Rh system (which derives its name from the fact that it was first discovered in the blood of the Rhesus monkey).

The ABO System

The ABO system divides the human race into four blood types: A, B, AB, and O. It is actually possible to arrive at further subdivisions within the ABO system because different types of blood have been discovered, which are referred to as A_1, A_2, and an extremely rare A_3. However, since all of these test out as group A and more refined procedures are required to differentiate among them, they receive little attention in crime laboratories. In the population of the United States 43 percent are type O, 40 percent are type A, 14 percent are type B, and 3 percent are type AB. If a criminal's blood found at the scene of a crime turns out to be type O or A, it is of relatively little value as evidence because there are so many other people who have the same type. But if the blood turns out to be type B or type AB, its value is proportionately greater because it greatly narrows down the range of possible suspects. If the blood of both perpetrator and victim is shed at the scene of a crime, the blood can, of course, be distinguished only if the perpetrator and the victim have different blood types.

The MN System

In the MN system there are three possible types: M, N, and MN. Their approximate distribution among the white population of the United States is: M, 30 percent; N, 27 percent; and MN, 43 percent. When the MN system is used, it is a valuable adjunct to the ABO system because it operates entirely independently of the ABO system. Therefore, any one of the four ABO groups can be further subdivided into the three MN groups, thus creating 12 possible subgroups.

The Rh System

The ABO and MN systems are especially useful in criminal investigations because they can both be applied to dried blood stains as well as to fresh blood. The Rh system is effective only with fresh blood or a relatively fresh stain. It is expressed simply in terms of Rh positive or Rh negative, depending on whether or not an Rh factor is present in the blood. Approximately 85 percent of the white population of the United States and almost 100 percent of some other races are Rh positive.

When all three systems of typing blood can be applied to an unidentified blood spot at the scene of a crime, the subgroup to which the owner must belong is narrowed down to 1 out of 24. Although this considerably reduces the population of suspects who could have shed the blood, it is not sufficient to pinpoint the individual. If a suspect is found whose blood matches all the types of the unidentified blood, it is only *possible* that the suspect is the criminal. If, however, the suspect's blood fails to match the type of the unidentified spot in any single respect, the suspect can be absolutely eliminated from suspicion.

Antigens, Antibodies, and Lectins

The ABO typing system is based on the presence in the blood of chemical substances called *antigens* and *antibodies*,[1] which combine with each other and cause agglutination (clumping) of the red cells when blood of two different groups is mixed together (See Figure 12–3). The antigens, which are attached to the surface of the red blood cells, determine the blood type. A person who has A antigens is type A; a person who has B antigens is type B; a person who has both A and B antigens is type AB; and a person who has neither is type O. The antibodies, which are designated anti-A and anti-B and are contained in the blood serum, react specifically against the antigens with which they are incompatible. A person with type A blood has naturally occurring anti-B antibodies in his or her serum; a person with type B blood has anti-A antibodies; a person with AB blood has neither antibody; and a person with type O blood has both. Thus if type B blood is mixed with type A blood, the anti-A antibodies in the type B blood agglutinate all the red corpuscles bearing A antigens, and the anti-B antibodies in the type A blood agglutinate the type B corpuscles. If type A blood is mixed with type AB blood, while the A factors are compatible with each other, the anti-B antibodies in the type A blood combine with the B factor of the type AB blood and cause the cells to clump. The converse is, of course, true if types B and AB blood are mixed. Similarly, if either type A, B, or AB blood is mixed with type O blood, since the serum of type O blood contains both anti-A and anti-B, the appropriate one agglutinates whichever antigens are introduced. In addition to the anti-A and

[1]Antigens are sometimes known as *agglutinogens,* and antibodies are sometimes called *agglutinins.* For the sake of simplicity, antigen and antibody are used throughout this text.

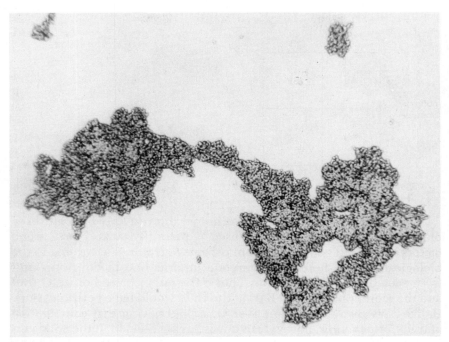

FIGURE 12–3 Agglutinated red blood cells (approximately 400 X). (Courtesy of Boston Police Technical Services Section)

anti-B antibodies, which occur naturally in the serum, an antibody known as anti-H has been derived from vegetable protein sources which specifically agglutinates type O cells. Such antibodies from vegetable sources are known as *lectins.* Consequently, typing whole blood is simply a matter of introducing anti-A and anti-B sera and anti-H lectin to the blood and watching the agglutination behavior. All three are available commercially.

As in the ABO system, M, N, and Rh antigens are attached to the red blood corpuscles. Their specific antibodies, however, do not occur naturally in the serum. Anti-M and N antibodies are obtained by using the serum of animals that have been immunized against M and N antigens. These as well as anti-M and anti-N lectins are available commercially for typing purposes. It is also possible to test for the various Rh antigens that may be present in the red cells by means of commercially produced antibodies, but since most blood found at crime scenes has had time to dry out before investigators arrive, Rh testing is of little practical significance in forensic work.

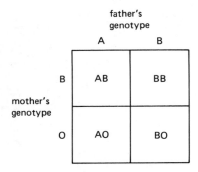

FIGURE 12–4

Heredity

An area of more legal than criminal interest in which all three blood grouping systems can be used is paternity suits. Blood group factors are passed genetically from parents to children according to the biological laws of heredity. Everyone inherits one blood group trait from each of his or her parents. Thus if the father passed on an O trait and the mother passed on a B trait, the child would have both, and since B, like A, is always dominant over O, a child having that combination of traits, or *genotype*, always tests out as having B blood. If the child gets an A trait from one parent and a B trait from the other, the child's genotype is AB and so is the child's tested blood group, or *phenotype*. Two A traits or an A and an O always produce an A phenotype, just as two B's or a B and an O produce a B. The only way to get type O blood is to receive an O trait from each parent. Parents can pass either of their genotype traits on to their children. Thus if an AB father and a BO mother have a child, that child has a 50 percent chance of having type B blood, a 25 percent chance of having type A blood, and a 25 percent chance of having type AB blood. These possibilities are illustrated in Figure 12–4.

It would be impossible for these two parents to have a type O child. Therefore, if the woman bore a type O baby, the AB man cannot have been the father. The application of these laws to paternity suits is obvious. By applying the MN and Rh systems, one can greatly narrow down the possibilities of who the father might be. Although it is never possible to tell specifically who the father was on the basis of blood types, it is possible to absolutely exclude some men from consideration.

FIELD INVESTIGATION

In the multiple murder case cited earlier in this chapter it is impossible to calculate the amount of evidence that was lost through the carelessness of the investigating officers. By a painstaking comparison of the shoes of everyone who had been present during the investigation against photographs of the multitude of footprints tracked through the house, it was finally possible to isolate a few tracks that might have been made by the murderers. Even then it was impossible to be sure since by the time the comparison was made, some of the officers could not remember what shoes they had been wearing on that day. Proper protection and collection of evidence may seem tedious, but if they are done in a professional manner, they can save much more tedious work later, and they may make the difference between having and not having a case that will stand up in court.

The blood evidence at the scene of a violent murder can be a terrible mess. The first thing an investigating officer must do is consider it dispassionately, trying to sort out the various blood distribution patterns and the probable sequence of events. This will help the investigator decide what photographic shots and angles will most clearly depict the scene. If a police photographer is called in, the investigating officer can instruct the photographer just how the scene is to be photographed. Pictures should include not only the victim but also the bloodstain patterns. After photographs have been taken of the undisturbed scene, the rest of the investigation can proceed.

In most cases all of the bloodstains are dry by the time the police arrive. Sometimes, however, large pools of blood may still be liquid. Samples of all liquid blood should be taken with a medicine dropper and placed into a test tube or appropriate glass container with an anticoagulant. Then it should either be refrigerated or taken without delay to the laboratory. Blood components continue to deteriorate as long as they are exposed to air, light, or high temperatures.

Dried bloodstains found on portable objects should be left intact and the entire object removed to the laboratory. Samples of dry stains on floors or immovable objects should be scraped into a vial or onto a clean piece of paper and folded into an envelope. All clothing or other fabrics on which the blood has dried should be packaged separately in plastic bags to avoid mutual contamination.

Bloodsoaked clothing that is still wet should be air-dried out of direct sunlight before packaging. If that is not possible, the articles should be packaged in well-ventilated bags or boxes. If they are packaged in airtight containers, the moisture in the warm, enclosed atmosphere will accelerate the decay process, and the laboratory personnel may be subjected to the stench of putrefaction when they open the packages.

Each article and sample collected should bear a label showing the investigator's mark, the date and time of collection, a description of the evidential material, and the exact location where it was found with reference to notes, sketches, or photographs. If some of the blood is later found to belong to a different group from that of the victim, it is essential to be able to pinpoint its exact location.

Whenever blood has been shed at the scene of a crime or when an investigating officer otherwise foresees that blood group determination may be an important factor, the officer should make arrangements to take samples from all victims as well as all suspects.

Blood samples from deceased persons are usually taken as part of the autopsy, and in some states that is the only time it can legally be done. It is the investigating officer's responsibility to make sure that it is done before the body is embalmed.

Blood samples from living persons should be taken only by medical personnel. If a suspect refuses to allow a sample to be taken or if there is some other reason why it cannot be done, hospital or military records can be checked for blood type. Otherwise, such records should not be relied on; military records in particular have proved to be notoriously inaccurate in regard to blood typing.

The presence of blood may not always be obvious, for example when a criminal has been able to clean up the area before the crime is discovered or has had a chance to wash his or her own clothing after leaving the scene. It is almost impossible to wash away all traces of blood, even from smooth, hard surfaces. Even though blood may not be visible, chemical presumptive tests are sensitive enough to detect its presence after numerous washings. Therefore, the clothing of suspects should be tested even if no blood is apparent. Similarly, if there is reason to believe that blood has been shed, hidden areas should be tested. These might include water in the traps of sinks and bathtubs where the criminal may have washed his or her hands and towels, rags, or even curtains on which the criminal may have wiped them.

FIELD TESTING OF BLOOD

Ideally, all testing of blood should be done in the laboratory by experienced chemists. But there are times, particularly when searching for hidden blood or examining stains on immovable objects, when tests must be performed at the scene. Even in the field the chemical tests for ascertaining the presence of blood should be carried out by trained laboratory technicians dispatched to the scene for that purpose. Investigating officers do not normally perform them unless they are specifically trained to do so.

Presumptive Tests for Blood

Benzidine[2]

The field test most commonly used is the benzidine test. It is called presumptive because, while highly sensitive to blood, it can react to a few other substances. Therefore, a positive reaction constitutes a strong presumption but not proof of the presence of blood. The benzidine test is based on the catalytic activity of peroxidase, one of the enzymes found in blood. When an oxidizing agent, such as hydrogen peroxide or sodium perborate, is mixed with benzidine, the oxidizer begins to react slowly with the benzidine. But when blood is added, the peroxidase enzyme acts as a catalyst to accelerate the reaction so that it takes place almost instantaneously. The reaction produces a characteristic bluish-green color, which is taken as a presumptive indication of the presence of blood.

Benzidine is extremely sensitive to minute quantities of blood and can detect traces on an item even after it has been washed. Because benzidine destroys blood, it should never be used directly on a questioned stain or item suspected of having blood on it. If a piece of filter paper, either dry or dampened with distilled water, is rubbed against the stain, the paper picks up enough blood so that the test can be carried out on the filter paper.

PROCEDURE FOR BENZIDINE TEST

A. Reagents
   1. Benzidine
      (a) 0.25 gram benzidine or tetramethylbenzidine
      (b) 175 milliliters glacial acetic acid
   2. 3 percent hydrogen peroxide: available in any drugstore.
B. Conducting the test
   1. Reagents 1 and 2 are kept in separate dropper bottles.
   2. A piece of filter paper is rubbed on the questioned stain or item.
   3. A few drops of benzidine reagent are placed onto the filter paper.
   4. A few drops of hydrogen peroxide are added to the benzidine on the filter paper.
   5. Observation: If blood is present, a bluish-green stain appears

---

[2]Benzidine has been found to cause cancer in rats and is no longer commercially available, though many police laboratories are still using their existing stocks. A noncarcinogenic reagent, 3,3' 5,5' tetramethylbenzidine has been synthesized which has approximately the same sensitivity as benzidine and is used in the same way.

almost instantaneously (yellow-green if tetramethylbenzidine is used).

C. An alternate method is to mix the oxidizing agent (hydrogen peroxide or sodium perborate) in with the benzidine just before using. Once the oxidizer is added, the reagent begins to deteriorate; therefore, it should be used immediately after mixing.

Luminol

The luminol test is a presumptive test that indicates the presence of blood by luminescence instead of by a color reaction. As with benzidine, the blood peroxidase catalyzes a reaction between the luminol reagent and an oxidizing agent. Luminol is more commonly used when a large area must be checked for the presence of hidden blood. Because it relies on luminescence, luminol can be used only in the dark. The reagent is sprayed onto the area to be tested, and any spots where blood is present glow in the dark. Like benzidine, luminol destroys blood for further testing; therefore, it should be used only after all possible blood evidence has been collected and removed from the scene.

PROCEDURE FOR LUMINOL TEST

A. Reagents
    1. 0.1 gram luminol (3-aminophthalhydrazide)
    2. 5.0 grams sodium carbonate
    3. 0.7 gram sodium perborate (oxidizing agent)
    4. 100 milliliters distilled water
B. Conducting the test
    1. Ingredients 1, 2, and 3 are carried in dry form and dissolved in the water immediately before use.
    2. After mixing, the reagent is sprayed onto the test area.
    3. The area is darkened and observed for spots of luminescence. If the area cannot be darkened, the test must be conducted at night.

Other Presumptive Tests

Other color tests that are sometimes used are the *leuko-malachite* and the *phenolphthalein* tests. Leuko-malachite turns green when blood is added and phenolphthalein turns pink in the presence of blood. Benzidine is used more often because it is easier to prepare and because most criminal lawyers have heard of it. Even though the other reagents are equally effective, a defense lawyer may attempt to discredit the testimony of an investigator or criminalist who fails to use benzidine.

None of the color or luminescence tests is specific for blood. All of the reagents react positively to some other substances. Benzidine, for example, can get false positive reactions from milk, certain fresh vegetable materials and animal tissues, and some microorganisms. A negative reaction almost certainly indicates the absence of blood, but there are a few substances which, when mixed with blood, will cause it to give a weak or negative reaction. Much experience is required to be able to accurately evaluate weak reactions.

LABORATORY EXAMINATION OF BLOOD

Crystal Tests

The presumptive tests for the presence of blood can be confirmed in the laboratory, usually by microcrystalline tests. The two most commonly used are the *Takayama* and *Teichmann* tests. When the reagent is added to blood on a slide, characteristic crystals form which can be viewed under a microscope. The Takayama test forms reddish feather-like crystals of pyridine hemochromogen (see Figure 12–5), and the Teichmann test forms yellow-brown rhomboid crystals of hemin. Only a very small amount of blood is needed for the tests, but if the blood is diluted, the concentration must generally be strong enough for the reddish blood color to be visible. The Teichmann test is sometimes not effective if the blood has been collected from wood or leather because these materials contain certain tannins that interfere with the reaction. The Takayama test is not affected by these tannins. The procedure for conducting the tests is the same for both reagents.

FIGURE 12–5 Pyridine hemochromogen (Takayama) crystals (approximately 500 X). (Courtesy of Boston Police Technical Services Section)

PROCEDURE FOR TAKAYAMA AND TEICHMANN TESTS

A. Reagents
   1. Takayama (shelf life approximately two weeks; keep in amber bottle)
      (a) 3 milliliters saturated solution of dextrose
      (b) 3 milliliters 10 percent solution of sodium hydroxide (10 grams NaOH dissolved in 100 milliliters distilled water)
      (c) 3 milliliters pyridine
      (d) 7 milliliters distilled water
   2. Teichmann
      (a) 0.1 gram potassium chloride
      (b) 0.1 gram potassium bromide
      (c) 0.1 gram potassium iodide
      (d) 100 milliliters glacial acetic acid
B. Conducting the test
   1. Cut out a small section of stained material or scrape off a small bit of crust and place onto a microscope slide.
   2. Add two or three drops of reagent and cover with a cover slide.
   3. Warm slide on a slide warmer or by passing through the flame of an alcohol burner.
   4. Allow to cool and observe formation of crystals under a microscope.

Microscopic Tests

The presence of blood can also be confirmed microscopically if it is fresh enough. Red corpuscles can easily be identified under a microscope if they are still intact, but they disintegrate rapidly with drying. They are also destroyed by water because the difference in tonicity (concentration of dissolved salts and proteins) between the water and the interior of the cell causes the cell wall to burst. Red cells can be preserved in a 0.9 percent saline solution.

Spectroscopic Tests

The absorption spectrum of hemoglobin or one of its derivatives can be identified if the blood is fairly fresh, but these are difficult to identify once the blood has begun to decompose because the decomposition products of hemoglobin have very different spectra.

Species Testing

Sometimes it is necessary to determine if blood samples are of human or animal origin. This may occur in connection with hunting violations or in cases in which a murder suspect claims that blood found on his or her clothing came from an animal. If the sample in question is animal blood, it may also be necessary to determine the species. The method normally used for these purposes is the *precipitin* test.

Every species of animal, including the human, has proteins in its blood that are unique to it. If the serum of one animal is injected into the body of an animal of another species, the blood of the recipient animal forms specific antibodies to immunize it from the invasion by the foreign protein. This process is similar to the body's natural defenses against disease. If human blood serum is injected into a test animal (usually a rabbit), the animal produces antihuman antibodies that can be recovered by drawing its blood and separating out the serum. A serum containing specific antibodies against human proteins is called *antihuman antiserum.* Antisera are available commercially for several species, including humans, dogs, cats, deer, cattle, and others.

There are several variations of precipitin test procedures. In each of them a layer of a saline solution of the sample bloodstain is floated onto a layer of antihuman (or other) antiserum. If the sample is human blood, the antiserum precipitates the human proteins in the form of a thin white cloud or ring at the point where the two liquids meet.[3] If a suspect claims that a stain on his or her clothing is animal blood, the stain should be tested for control purposes with the antiserum of that animal even if the stain has reacted positively as human blood. Also, a control test should be run on each bottle of antihuman antiserum with known human blood. Most antisera are obtained commercially and are very expensive. The following procedure for the precipitin test is recommended for teaching laboratories and crime laboratories whose budgets are limited because only a very small amount of antiserum is used in each test.

PROCEDURE FOR PRECIPITIN TEST

A. Prepare in advance
   1. A capillary (Pasteur) pipette
      (a) Seal the narrow end of the pipette by holding it briefly in the flame of a Bunsen burner.
      (b) Break the pipette approximately ½ inch above the point where it starts to taper by scoring it once with a triangular file and snapping it with the fingers [See Figure 12–6(a)].
   2. Physiological saline solution: Add 9 grams sodium chloride (NaCl)

---

[3]The blood protein composition of higher primates is similar to that of humans and can react to antihuman antiserum. Although the chances are remote, it is conceivable that this similarity could be a source of confusion.

to 1000 milliliters distilled water or purchase from a commercial hospital or chemical supplier.

3. Saline preparation of questioned bloodstain: Cut out a small sample of the stained material (approximately 5 millimeters square) or scrape off a small bit of crust and put it into a test tube. Add a few drps of physiological saline solution and briefly agitate.

4. Human (or other) antiserum: Purchase commercially.

B. Conducting the test

1. Using a capillary tube, take a drop of antiserum from its bottle and place it into the sealed narrow end of the prepared pipette. The liquid will be transferred from the tube to the pipette by capillary action.

2. Using an eyedropper, carefully place one drop of the saline blood sample inside the wide end of the pipette close to the antiserum so that it flows gently over the antiserum, forming a layer [See Figure 12–6(b)].

3. Keep the pipette upright by sticking it into a block of Styrofoam.

4. Observe under indirect lighting. If the bloodstain is human, a white precipitate will appear at the interface of the two liquids [see Figure 12–6(c)].

A newer procedure for the precipitin test, which is still less often used than the standard test-tube method in most crime laboratories, takes advantage of the fact that proteins have electric charges. This technique is called *electrophoresis.* The test sample and the antiserum are placed opposite each other on a plate that is coated with a gel medium and are forced to move toward each other through the application of an electric charge to the plate. If the antiserum is specific to the species of the sample, a visible line of precipitate forms where the two substances meet.

Typing of Dried Blood

As stated earlier, fresh blood is very easily typed by adding the anti-A, anti-B, and anti-H antisera to it and observing the agglutination reactions. The typing of dried blood is a somewhat more complicated process because the red corpuscles disintegrate in the drying process, and without them there is nothing in the stain to be agglutinated.

Various typing methods have been devised, some of which test for the presence of antigens and some for the presence of antibodies, but the standard technique used in most crime laboratories is the *absorption-elution* method (see Figure 12–7). Even though the red cells dete-

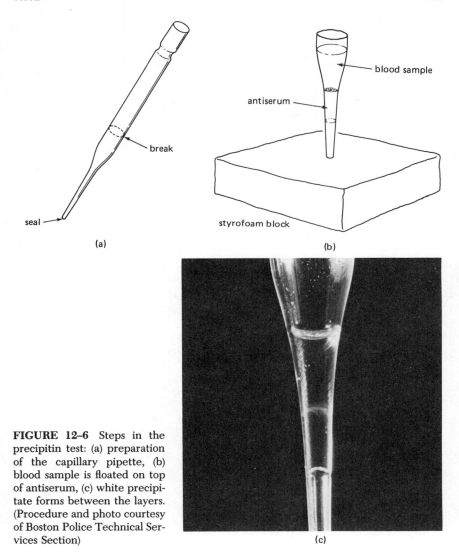

FIGURE 12–6 Steps in the precipitin test: (a) preparation of the capillary pipette, (b) blood sample is floated on top of antiserum, (c) white precipitate forms between the layers. (Procedure and photo courtesy of Boston Police Technical Services Section)

riorate rapidly when blood dries, the antigens that were attached to them remain intact for a long time. A and B antigens have been known to survive as long as 15 years in dried blood and MN antigens as long as 9 months. In the absorption-elution test anti-A, anti-B, and anti-H antisera are added to separate samples of the stain to be tested. The samples are incubated overnight at 4°C to allow the antibodies in the antisera to combine with their specific antigens. After incubation the samples are rinsed several times in cold saline solution in order to wash

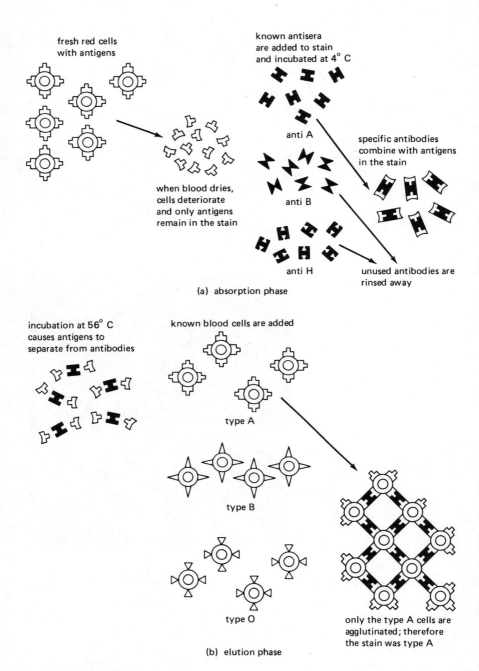

fresh red cells
with antigens

when blood dries,
cells deteriorate
and only antigens
remain in the stain

known antisera
are added to stain
and incubated at 4° C

anti A

anti B

anti H

specific antibodies
combine with antigens
in the stain

unused antibodies are
rinsed away

(a) absorption phase

incubation at 56° C
causes antigens to
separate from antibodies

known blood cells are added

type A

type B

type O

only the type A cells are
agglutinated; therefore
the stain was type A

(b) elution phase

FIGURE 12–7 Schematic representation of the absorption-elution test.

away excess antibodies. At this point the antigens in the stain are combined only with the antibodies of their corresponding type (i.e., A with anti-A, etc.) and all other antibodies have been removed. This is the absorption phase. The next step is the elution phase, which consists of adding a small amount of saline solution to the stain samples and incubating them for 20 minutes at 56°C. The heat forces the antibodies to break free from the antigens, thus producing an antiserum specific to the blood type of the stain. All that remains is to add known A, B, and O cells, which are available commercially, and observe which ones are agglutinated. If only A cells are agglutinated, the stain was type A; if only B cells are agglutinated, it was type B; and if only O cells are agglutinated, it was type O. If both A and B cells show clumping, the stain was AB.

Other Tests

Microscopic Test

It is sometimes possible to pinpoint by means of microscopic examination the specific part of the body from which blood has come if identifiable impurities are present. For example, blood from the nose may be identified by discovery of nasal secretions and hair in the sample, or menstrual blood may be identified by the presence of pubic hairs and epithelial cells from the vagina.

Electrophoresis

Electrophoresis is a relatively simple and not very time-consuming technique for identifying blood enzymes and proteins, known as genetic markers. Every blood protein has a characteristic electric charge that is not duplicated by any other. Consequently, when a protein solution such as blood serum is placed on a gel medium in an electric field, the electric potential causes the different proteins present to separate and move across the gel to places in the field that are compatible with their own charge. When the movement of the proteins is completed, the proteins can be stained for observation; their separation patterns provide a fingerprint of each individual protein. Hundreds of whole blood proteins have been identified in this manner, including serum proteins, red cell enzymes, and hemoglobin variants. Some genetic markers have been found that are able to survive in dried blood for significant periods of time. The four enzyme marker systems that are the most promising for forensic applications are adenylate kinase (AK) and phosphoglucomutase (PGM), which have been found under certain conditions to be identifiable after 26 weeks of aging, and erythrocyte acid phosphatase (EAP) and adenosine deaminase (ADA), which have been identified at up to 13 weeks of aging.[4]

Variants of hemoglobin are also likely to prove useful in forensic work in the future. Some are found exclusively in certain racial groups. For example, the sickle-cell variant, HbS, occurs only in the black population and to a slight extent in people of Mediterranean ancestry. Also, fetal blood can be distinguished by a hemoglobin variant, HbF, which the body ceases to manufacture after birth.

Since the various blood proteins and variants exist in different combinations in different people, it is very possible that once enough of them become reliably identifiable, blood typing will become as specific in identifying individuals as fingerprinting is today.

Review Questions

1. White blood cells are
   a. Erythrocytes
   b. Leukocytes
   c. Iron compounds
   d. Thrombocytes

2. When whole blood is spun in a centrifuge, it separates into formed elements and
   a. Serum
   b. Fibrin
   c. Corpuscles
   d. Plasma

3. If a body found lying on its back shows signs of post-mortem lividity on the front, it indicates that
   a. Death was instantaneous
   b. The body was moved
   c. There was little bleeding
   d. Death occurred less than an hour earlier

4. If spattered blood is mist-like, it indicates
   a. A gunshot wound
   b. A blow from a blunt object
   c. A knife wound
   d. Arterial bleeding

[4]G. C. Denault, H. H. Takimoto, Q. Y. Kwan, and A. Pallos, *Detectability of Selected Genetic Markers in Dried Blood Upon Aging* (Washington, D.C.: U.S. Government Printing Office, 1978).

5. (T, F)   The form of a blood drop is influenced more by the texture of the surface than the distance it fell.

6. (T, F)   A person who has type A blood has anti-O antibodies in his or her serum.

7. If type A blood and type B blood are mixed,
   a. The A antigens agglutinate the B antigens
   b. The anti-B antibodies in the type A blood agglutinate the B antigens
   c. The anti-A antibodies in the type B blood agglutinate the A antigens
   d. The A antibodies agglutinate the B antibodies
   e. a and d
   f. b and c

8. (T, F)   A person who has type AB blood has both anti-A and anti-B antibodies.

9. If a father's genotype is OO and a mother's genotype is BB, their children
   a. Have a 25 percent change of having type B blood
   b. Have a 50 percent chance of having type O blood
   c. Will all have type B blood
   d. Will all have type O blood

10. (T, F)   An anticoagulant prevents blood from deteriorating.

11. Which of the following is *not* a presumptive test for blood?
    a. Electrophoresis
    b. Benzidene
    c. Phenolphthalein
    d. Luminol

12. Teichmann crystals are inhibited by
    a. Sweat
    b. Tannins
    c. Glacial acetic acid
    d. Red paint

13. Dried blood stains are typed primarily by means of
    a. The precipitin test
    b. Adding anti-A and anti-B antisera to the stain
    c. Electrophoresis
    d. Absorption-elution

14. Electrophoresis can be used to identify which blood component?
    a. Takayama crystals
    b. Anti-H lectin
    c. Erythrocytes
    d. Enzymes

CHAPTER THIRTEEN

BODY FLUIDS OTHER THAN BLOOD

Although other body fluids and their stains do not occur as evidence in crimes as frequently as blood does, the investigator should nevertheless be alert to their possible presence. Because of the high incidence of sex-related crimes, semen is encountered more often than any physiological fluid except blood. However, urine, perspiration, saliva, and other body fluids may occasionally have evidential significance.

SECRETORS

In approximately 75 percent to 80 percent of the human population antigens of the ABO blood typing system are found in other cells of the body, including semen, saliva, perspiration, vaginal secretions, gastric juices, hair, and bone. People in whom this phenomenon occurs are known as *secretors,* and their blood type within the ABO system can be reliably determined from those body substances by means of absorption-elution techniques similar to those used in typing dried blood. All secretors display the presence of H antigens in their body fluids. In addition, people who have type A blood secrete A antigens; people who have B blood secrete B antigens; and those who have type AB blood secrete both. People who have type O blood secrete only the H antigen. If there is no positive reaction to anti-A, anti-B, and anti-H sera, the individual tested is not a secretor. People are secretors or nonsecretors from birth and never change from one status to the other.

SEMEN

When fresh, semen is a viscous, creamy fluid that has a tacky consistency. The average ejaculate of a human male contains approximately from 2.5 cubic centimeters to 5 cubic centimers of seminal fluid. In the normal man slightly under 10 percent of the volume of the fluid is made up of *spermatozoa* (or *sperm*), the male reproductive cells, which are generated in the testes. The rest is seminal plasma, a combination of chemical substances produced in the prostate gland and seminal vesicles, which bind and protect the sperm cells. Spermatozoa, if undamaged, can be easily recognized under a microscope by their characteristic tadpole shape (a broad, round head tapering into a long, thin tail) (see Figure 13–1). In fresh semen they are alive and motile (wiggling).

Attempts have been made to fix the time of intercourse by the death rate of the spermatozoa, but the length of time that a sperm cell can survive after ejaculation varies so greatly with differences in temperature, humidity, and environment that it is of little use as a means of estimation. Since vaginal secretions are hostile to sperm cells, a spermatozoon normally survives in the vagina of a living woman for only 30 minutes to 4 hours, but motility after several days is still possible.

Fresh semen is rarely available as evidence. Far more often it is found in the form of dry stains. Dried semen is gray-white in color and stiff on cloth; it has the sugary look of dried spittle. It becomes flaky if

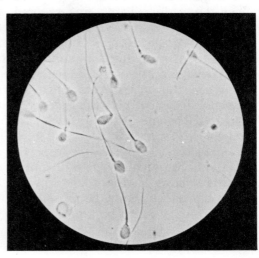

FIGURE 13–1 Human spermatozoa (500 X). (Courtesy of Dr. Michael J. Camp, Northeastern University)

rubbed and it may not be distinguishable to the naked eye if it is contaminated with blood or other substances. Although live spermatozoa are very hardy, they become very brittle when dry and can easily be broken up if material carrying semen stains is rubbed or folded.

Collection and Preservation

The investigator should look for semen evidence in any crime in which sexual activity has occurred or is suspected to have occurred. Stains may be found on the clothing and underclothing of both the victim and the criminal. Bedding, towels, handkerchiefs, and automobile upholstery may bear stains. In a fatality the area under the victim's body should be checked.

A simple and effective preliminary test for the presence of semen on articles that have not been laundered with detergents is examination under ultraviolet light. Semen stains fluoresce strongly with a bluish-white color. Ultraviolet light is useless on any materials that have been laundered because all modern detergents contain strongly fluorescent chemical brighteners. Since stains other than semen may fluoresce, fluorescence does not prove the presence of semen. No fluorescence, however, does prove the absence of semen. If semen is suspected to be present on laundered items, the items must be sent to the laboratory for microscopic and chemical testing. When ultraviolet light is ineffective or unavailable, the investigator most look for the characteristic crusty appearance and stiff feel of stained cloth.

Vaginal smears should always be taken in rape and assault cases. When the victim is living, smears should be taken only by a doctor. A pathologist takes smears from a dead victim during the autopsy. The pathologist should also check other areas of the victim's body for semen, such as the mouth, buttocks, anus, and thighs.

When submitting articles with semen evidence to the laboratory, the investigator must take care to avoid rubbing, folding, or wrinkling the stained area. Otherwise, the dry, brittle spermatozoa may break apart and become unrecognizable. Items should be packaged separately to avoid contamination, and if the entire article cannot be transported to the laboratory, the suspected stain should be cut out and forwarded. If suspects are found, samples of their spittle should be sent to the laboratory in order to determine whether or not they are secretors. If the semen shows the presence of any of the ABO antigens and a suspect turns out to be a nonsecretor, then the semen in the stain cannot be his. Investigators must be very careful not to contaminate samples with their own body fluids. If a semen stain is from a type A secretor and the investigator is a type B secretor, perspiration from the investigator's hands may cause the stain to test falsely as type AB.

Laboratory Examination

Microscopic Tests

The only really sure proof that a substance is semen is the presence of spermatozoa. One cubic centimer of semen from a normal man contains an average of 100 million sperm cells. Small numbers of spermatozoa may also be found in urine stains, but if there is any question, these can be eliminated by testing for urine. Spermatozoa can be seen under a microscope at approximately 400X magnification with or without staining. In the rare case in which the semen sample is fresh, a smear of it can be observed directly on a slide. When the stain is dry, as is usually the case, a bit of the crusted material is scraped onto a slide and dissolved in a few drops of dilute hydrochloric acid or in a drop of clear liquid detergent to which a few drops of distilled water are added after soaking for 15 minutes. The examiner should not conclude that the substance is semen unless a number of whole sperm cells are identified since other contaminating materials can give a false appearance of sperm heads or bits of the tail. If the sperm cells are all broken up from bacterial action, sunlight, or rough handling, one of the chemical tests should be used for confirmation.

Because the structure of the sperm cell varies from species to species, it is possible to differentiate the semen of different animals by microscopic examination. This may occasionally be necessary in rare cases of bestiality. Also, human spermatozoa may show abnormalities that can help identify individual men. These types of examination require a great deal of skill and expertise on the part of the laboratory scientist, both in the preparation of the slides and in the interpretation of the results.

Chemical Tests

Although the presence of a large number of spermatozoa is a sure indicator of semen, their absence does not necessarily mean that the stain is not semen. As was mentioned earlier, the sperm cells in an old, dry stain may be too badly damaged to be recognizable. Also, semen evidence may reflect a low sperm count *(oligospermia)* or be completely lacking in spermatozoa *(aspermia)* as a result of natural sterility or vasectomy. In these cases the laboratory scientist has to rely on chemical tests. None of the chemical tests can be considered positive proof of semen.

Acid Phosphatase Test

This is the most reliable of the chemical tests and is almost as conclusive in identifying semen as the presence of sperm. Acid phosphatase is an enzyme that occurs in several body fluids and in some plants, but in semen it exists in concentrations up to 400 times higher than in other materials. Since it is produced in the prostate gland, it is entirely independent of sperm production and is lacking only in the extremely unusual circumstances in which a criminal has had his prostate gland surgically removed. Although some other body fluids and some vegetable materials give positive reactions to the test, the reactions are not nearly as strong as the reaction produced by seminal acid phosphatase. The test relies on the ability of the acid phosphatase enzyme to catalyze a reaction between calcium alpha-naphthyl phosphate and a diazonium dye salt to produce a color reaction.

Procedure for Acid Phosphatase Test

A. Reagents
   1. Acetate buffer solution of pH 5.0: Dissolve 2 grams sodium acetate in 100 milliliters of 1 percent acetic acid (1 milliliter glacial acetic acid in 99 milliliters distilled water).
   2. Saturated solution of calcium alpha-naphthyl phosphate in buffer mixture 1: Keep adding reagent powder to the buffer until no more will go into solution; then filter.
   3. Saturated solution of anthraquinone-1-diazonium chloride: Prepare the same as for reagent 2.
B. Conducting the test
   1. Cut out three small pieces from questioned stained material and place them on separate pieces of filter paper.
   2. Add a few drops of reagent 2 to one piece of material.
   3. Add a few drops of reagent 3 to the second piece.
   4. Add a few drops of both reagents 2 and 3 to the third piece of material.
   5. If acid phosphatase is present, an orange-red stain appears in step 4 (the purpose of steps 2 and 3 is to eliminate the possibility of false positive reactions).
   6. For control purposes, add a few drops of reagents 2 and 3 to a bit of unstained material from the same garment and to a bit of material that has a known semen stain.

Several other diazonium dye salts may be used instead of anthraquinone-1-diazonium chloride. Among these are Fast Black Salt K and Fast Blue B. Either of these produces a purple or bluish-purple color reaction in step 4.

The acid phosphatase test is also useful in searching clothing or bedding for the presence of semen when no visible stain is present. This is done by rubbing a piece of filter paper dampened with distilled water over the article and testing it with reagents 2 and 3.

Vaginal smears, usually taken with cotton-tipped applicators and preserved in physiological saline solution in test tubes, can be tested by adding a drop each of reagents 2 and 3 to a drop of the specimen solution either in a test tube or on a piece of filter paper. Vaginal smears must be taken only by a physician. A strong reaction to a vaginal smear can be considered presumptive evidence of recent coitus, but since the vaginal secretions themselves contain low levels of acid phosphatase even when semen is not present, a weak reaction should be confirmed by other tests. A weak reaction does not necessarily rule out the possibility of the presence of semen. Acid phosphatase activity can be inhibited by menstruation, the use of douches or suppositories, or the presence of some urogenital pathologies. The acid phosphatase found in semen can be differentiated from that found in vaginal secretions and other materials by means of electrophoresis, but such refinements find little use as yet in most overworked crime laboratories.

Florence and Barbeiros Tests

These are microcrystalline tests which identify the substance *choline* by means of crystalline formations. Like acid phosphatase, choline exists in several biological fluids but in smaller concentrations than in semen. The Florence and Barbeiros tests are both conducted in the same way.

Procedure for Florence and Barbeiros Tests

A. Florence reagent
   1. 1.65 grams potassium iodide
   2. 2.54 grams iodine
   3. 30 milliliters distilled water
   4. Dissolve potassium iodide in water; then dissolve iodine in the potassium iodide solution.
B. Barbeiros reagent
   1. Saturated aqueous solution of picric acid (keep adding picric acid to water until no more will go into solution).
C. Conducting the test
   1. Cut out a small sample of the material with the questioned stain on it and place the sample on a microscope slide.

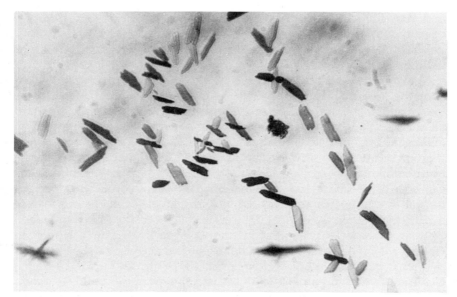

FIGURE 13–2 Florence Crystals (approximately 500 X). (Courtesy of Boston Police Technical Services Section)

2. Add a few drops of reagent and cover with a cover slide.
3. Observe crystal formation under microscope. The Florence test produces notched brown rhombic crystals (see Figure 13–2). The Barbeiros test forms yellow prisms.

Sometimes the tests may show negative results because of chemical interferences with the reaction. This problem can often be eliminated by covering a small sample of stained material with physiological saline solution in a test tube and incubating it overnight in a refrigerator. After incubation, a drop of the saline solution can be tested with a drop of reagent on a microscope slide.

None of the semen tests can tell the investigator when the stain was made or whether or not it bears any relation to the crime under investigation. Bedding or clothing may carry semen stains from earlier legitimate sexual activity and may give positive reactions even after washing.

Semen Typing

As stated before, the ABO antigens in the semen and other body fluids of secretors can be typed by absorption-elution methods in the same manner as dried bloodstains. Typing is a useful investigative tool, but it must be used with caution. False typing can easily occur if a stain is contaminated by the body fluids of other people. For example, if a semen stain from a nonsecretor is found on a garment in which a secretor has perspired, the semen may falsely appear to contain the antigens in the perspiration; or if a woman had had legitimate intercourse a few hours before being raped, the earlier semen deposit could contaminate that of the rapist; and also, since women as well as men can be secretors, antigens in a woman's own vaginal secretions can cause false readings on a vaginal smear. There are many combinations of possibilities. Investigating officers as well as laboratory serologists should be aware of them not only so that the investigating officers can avoid contaminating the samples by their own actions but also so that when they are investigating the crime scene, they can be alert to any indications of contamination and thereby facilitate the serologist's work.

URINE

Urine stains fluoresce a yellowish color under ultraviolet light, but this fact is of little value since such stains are most likely to appear on items that have been laundered. Although urine can be identified by chemical means through testing for sulphate and phosphate ions, the simplest and most practical test is to heat a bit of the stained material and note the characteristic urine odor. The urine of secretors cannot be reliably typed for blood group antigens.

PERSPIRATION

The perspiration of secretors contains ABO antigens that can be typed. The ability to determine blood type is probably the most important investigative use of perspiration. Although it is similar to urine in composition and fluorescent quality, perspiration can usually be differentiated visually by the position of the stains in places where people are likely to sweat. Urine is the only other body fluid with which perspiration is likely to be confused. Perspiration can be easily differentiated by heating a sample and testing for the characteristic odor, which is distinct and different from that of urine.

SALIVA

As with perspiration, the main significance of saliva in investigations is the ability to determine blood groups from it. Saliva fluoresces with a whitish color. It is usually identified by its location on objects that come in contact with a person's mouth, such as cigarette and cigar butts, toothpicks, bottles and glasses, handerchiefs, and pieces of cloth used as gags. The presence of large amounts of spittle around a crime scene may indicate that the criminal is a nervous spitter or a heavy smoker or that he or she has a cold. Blood groups can be determined from items with saliva on them even if they are contaminated with lipstick, tobacco juice, or other foreign materials.

OTHER BODY EXCRETIONS

Vomit and Feces

These seldom have great investigative significance. Stomach contents vomited at the scene of a crime can suggest areas for investigation if some distinctive kind of food is discovered. Vomit is highly acidic and contains numerous enzymes that can be chemically identified if necessary. Blood groups can also be determined from gastric juices. Feces may have more value as psychological clues than as direct evidence. Their presence at a crime scene may be a gesture of contempt on the part of the criminal or the result of nervous strain or superstition.

Serum and Pus

Serum exudes from a wound when the blood has clotted inside the body, as after internal hemorrhaging. It is yellow and viscous when wet and stiff when dry. Because hemogloblin is present, serum gives the same chemical reactions as blood. It can also be identified electrophoretically through the serum proteins. Pus is serum that contains high concentrations of white blood corpuscles and dead bacteria. These can be easily identified by staining and microscopic examination.

Vaginal Secretions

These may sometimes have to be identified in order to determine whether or not they have contaminated a semen sample for blood grouping. They can be identified under a microscope by a pathologist or experienced examiner from the presence of characteristic epithelial cells and other organisms normally found in the vagina.

Review Questions

1. People whose ABO antigens are found in their saliva are known as
   a. Salivators
   b. Secretors

    c. Nonsecretors

    d. Crossovers

2. Spermatazoa
    a. Are generated in the prostate gland
    b. Make up approximately 10 percent of the seminal fluid
    c. Often survive in the vagina of a living woman for weeks
    d. Are very hardy in dried stains
    e. All the above

3. (T, F) Semen stains on clothing should not be folded or rubbed.

4. If spermatazoa are not detectable in a suspected semen stain,
    a. It proves that the stain is not semen
    b. It means that they were destroyed by rough handling
    c. The stain should be tested for acid phosphatase
    d. The stain should be tested for ABO antibodies

5. Which of the following body fluids *cannot* be reliably typed for ABO antigens?
    a. Urine
    b. Perspiration
    c. Blood
    d. Saliva

CHAPTER FOURTEEN

—————— *METALS* ——————

In a suburb of a large American city a store owner was found bludgeoned to death in the office of his store. The office safe had been drilled open and metal shavings were scattered around it. Surprised in the act of robbing the safe, the thief overpowered and killed the owner and escaped with the cash from the safe. As far as the detectives investigating the scene could tell, the criminal had left no clues to his identity. As part of the routine crime scene search they collected the metal shavings around the safe and forwarded them to the crime laboratory with the idea that if some of the same type filings were found on a suspect's clothing, they would connect the suspect to the crime. At first the crime laboratory found no leads in any of the physical evidence collected at the crime scene. However, without really expecting to find anything useful, one of the laboratory criminalists decided to give the drill shavings from the safe a closer look, and among them he found two or three shavings that did not seem to fit in with the others. Spectrographic analysis indicated that the odd shavings were an alloy of aluminum containing approximately 5 percent copper, less than 1 percent each of magnesium and manganese, and some trace level metallic impurities. Since the safe was made of steel, the examiner speculated that the criminal himself had brought the aluminum shavings to the scene, probably on his clothes. By checking with metallurgical references, the examiner found that an aluminum alloy of approximately those proportions was used in making screws. There was only one screw factory in the vicinity, and the owner of the factory confirmed that his factory did use that particular alloy. By comparing the machining marks on the shavings found at the crime scene with those from each of the screw machines in the factory, the criminalist was able to identify the actual machine that had made them. This trail led to the eventual arrest and conviction of one of the men who regularly operated that machine.

Although criminalists are not expected to be experts in metallurgy, there are occasions when it is important for them to have a basic knowledge of the nature and properties of metals. Investigating officers must likewise be aware of the ways metals can be used as evidence. The case described above was a rather unusual combination of good laboratory work and good luck, but it was not luck that led the crime scene investigator to collect the shavings from the safe. Even though they were used in a way he had not foreseen, they provided the essential lead in the case.

METALS AS EVIDENCE

Metals appear as evidence most frequently in connection with the markings made by firearms and tools, which are covered separately in Chapters 15 and 17. In this chapter we are concerned with the metals themselves and the basic metallographic operations of interest to the criminalist. Perhaps the most important of these in crime investigation is the restoration of serial numbers. Almost all appliances, firearms, electronic equipment, and machinery have serial numbers stamped or engraved on some metal part. The serial numbers are recorded when the items are sold and they serve as a means of identifying the items and tracing their owners if they are stolen or used in the commission of a crime. In an attempt to make such objects untraceable criminals often file away or grind down the serial numbers until they are no longer distinguishable to the naked eye. In highly professional operations, like some car theft rings, the criminals repolish the metal after removing the serial numbers and stamp in new numbers. With patience and careful technique criminalists can often restore the obliterated serial numbers by polishing the metal and etching it with appropriate chemical reagents. The force used to stamp numbers into metal not only affects the surface of the metal but it also alters the underlying crystalline structure so that when the etching reagents are applied, they react either faster or slower on the altered portion than on the surrounding metal, thus bringing the numbers to light. Similar metallographic etching techniques can be used to compare the crystal structure of two or more pieces of metal to help determine if they are of identical origin.

Identifying bits of metal such as filings, drill shavings, and broken chips and fragments found at a crime scene and comparing them with similar bits found on suspects are important ways of using metal evidence that do not require an extensive knowledge of metallurgy. Such comparison work can include metallographic chemical tests, instrumental analyses like those used in the above case history, and the simple matching of broken fragments. Investigators should be alert for metal fragments that may have snapped off a tool or knife blade used in breaking and entering. If the corresponding pieces can be found in the possession of a suspect, they can constitute very important evidence. These physical matches are made in the same way that pieces of glass are matched. The broken edges are placed together to see if the granular surfaces mesh together snugly. When they do mesh and the pieces do not move from side to side, the evidence of common origin is conclusive and no further comparisons are needed.

An area which is usually the province of the metallurgist but which occasionally concerns the criminalist is that of metal fatigue and failure. When accidents caused by metal failure result in court action, they are usually matters of civil litigation, but when there is a possibility that an accident was rigged, it becomes a criminal matter and therefore of interest to the crime laboratory.

True metal fatigue is a gradual process that begins as *slippage* in the crystal structure, usually at some discontinuity in the surface of the metal such as a machined corner or a corrosion pit. Under repeated

FIGURE 14–1 Metal fatigue failure showing beach marks. (Courtesy of American Society for Metals)

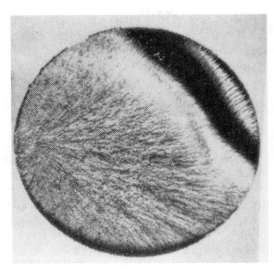

FIGURE 14–2 Fatigue fracture of brittle metal showing radial markings pointing back to the point of failure. (Courtesy of American Society for Metals)

stresses, which are small enough that any one application has no apparent effect, the point of slippage develops into a crack, which grows bigger and bigger until the remaining sound metal cannot withstand the stress any longer and snaps. The fracture surfaces of broken parts reveal the history of the events that led up to the failure. By examining them at low magnification or even with the naked eye, an analyst can usually determine the point at which the failure began. The area of slow crack growth is often revealed by curved, roughly parallel lines called *beach marks* (see Figure 14-1). Beach marks originate at the point where the failure began and reflect the progressive stopping points of the crack up to the point where the remaining sound metal snapped under the stress. When sound metal snaps, it has a rough granular appearance and may have radial markings that point back toward the locus of the failure (see Figure 14-2). Once the point of origin of the failure is located, it is easy to see whether it was caused by a design defect, faulty machining, corrosion, or sabotage. Instantaneous fractures, caused by the sudden application of a strong force on sound metal, show the granular appearance across the entire fracture area and are more likely to be the result of an accident than the cause of one.

This description, although generally accurate, is something of an oversimplification. There can actually be considerable variation in the appearance of fracture surfaces, depending on the hardness of the material, variations in heat treatment, and the type of stress causing the fracture (tensile, compressive, or torsional). For example, ductile (soft) metals, like copper and aluminum and their alloys, tend to become deformed more than the more brittle metals like cast iron and steel.

The ductile metals stretch when broken under tension. The more brittle a metal is, the cleaner it breaks off. Metal fracture analysis is a specialized area, and in most cases crime laboratory examiners would be wise to have their conclusions verified by a metallurgist trained in this field.

CHARACTERISTICS OF METALS

When in the liquid or molten state, metals, like other liquids, are characterized by a random distribution of atoms. These atoms are free to move in any direction. When they go from the liquid to the solid state, they crystallize. That is, their atoms line up in symmetrical, three-dimensional patterns that are repeated at regular intervals. These patterns are termed *space lattices* or *crystal lattices* because they are generally represented pictorially as having a latticework of lines connecting the atoms (see Figure 2–4).

Whether in the liquid or crystal state, metals are *monatomic;* that is, their structure consists of individual atoms, not molecules. As soon as a metal atom reacts chemically with other elements, it becomes a compound and can no longer be properly termed a metal. This is important in understanding the nature of alloys, which are the form in which metals are most commonly used. When alloying elements are mixed with metals in the liquid state, they dissolve in each other and harden to form solid solutions. When this occurs, the space lattice of the pure metal is altered, causing the alloy to have different properties from the metal. The solid solutions of alloys can be either *substitutional* or *interstitial.* Substitutional solid solutions occur when the atoms of the alloying elements are approximately the same size as those of the base metal and displace them in the lattice. In interstitial solutions the atoms of the alloying elements are small enough to slip in between the lattice of the base metal.

Although metals tend to crystallize in regular patterns, no single piece of metal is ever a perfect crystal. As the molten mass of metal begins to solidify, crystal formations begin simultaneously at many points throughout the melt and grow in *dendritic* (tree-like) fashion as more and more atoms align themselves. Within each dendritic crystal the space lattice is perfectly symmetrical, but since the crystals are growing in a three-dimensional system, one does not necessarily line up with the one next to it. The crystals formed in this manner are called the *grain* of a piece of metal and the points were they meet are called *grain boundaries* (see Figure 14-3). Most metal failure caused by corrosion originates at a grain boundary. The rough granular appearance of

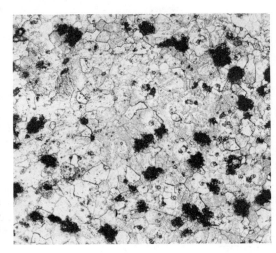

FIGURE 14–3 Malleable iron surface polished and etched to reveal grain boundaries (200 X). (Courtesy of Wai K. Chin)

metal that has snapped under force is caused by its separation along grain boundaries. However, the beach marks, which are characteristic of the progressive cracks of metal fatigue, occur as a result of slippage of two planes of the space lattice, and, consequently, they cut through the grains. The size of the grain can be controlled in modern metallurgical processes, usually by means of careful temperature control. The larger the grain of a metal, the more brittle it is.

COLLECTION AND PRESERVATION OF METAL EVIDENCE

Metal evidence is usually fairly obvious at a crime scene. When it is present, its position should be photographed before collection and indicated on a sketch. Metal filings, drill shavings, and small chips should be swept up and placed in suitable-sized plastic containers. Larger pieces of metal such as broken knife blades, tools, and weapons should be handled with gloves both to avoid leaving fingerprints and to avoid spoiling any that may be on them.

Articles of clothing containing particles of metallic evidence should be placed in bags and forwarded to the laboratory intact. If for some reason that is impossible, the larger particles should be removed with tweezers and their position on the article noted. Then the clothing should be swept with a vacuum sweeper with a filter attachment and the filter forwarded to the laboratory. All packages should be appropriately marked with the collecting officer's name, the date, time, and exact place of collection, and the contents.

Emission Spectrography

The forensic scientist's most valuable tool in the analysis and comparison of metals is the spectrograph. All metals, when excited, display line spectra of constant wavelengths. The metals present in an unknown alloy can be identified by comparing its spectrogram with the published spectra of the various metals (see Figure 4–9). A general, though not completely accurate, idea of the percentage composition of the component metals can be determined from the intensity of the lines. In most of the cases that arise in the crime laboratory, identifying the components of an unknown sample is not so important as comparing its composition to that of samples collected at the crime scene. The case study cited earlier in this chapter is unusual in that respect because the criminalist actually identified the components of the metal shavings and used that knowledge to advance the investigation. In comparison work it is only necessary to ensure that the samples are tested under the same conditions. If their spectra are the same, they can be considered to have a common source. The greatest value of the spectrograph lies in its ability to detect the minor alloying components and contaminating elements that are present only in trace quantities. Impurities are present in almost all commercial metals and alloys, but since these impurities do not impair their effectiveness in the vast majority of applications, it would be needlessly expensive to remove them. Consequently, different batches of the same type of alloy can be differentiated from each other spectrographically through their trace contaminants.

Neutron Activation Analysis

Aside from its expense and inconvenience, neutron activation analysis is not as useful for metal identification as spectrography is because it cannot detect the whole range of metals. It can, however, be especially useful in comparing bullets that are too badly damaged to compare by their markings. Since neutron activation analysis is completely insensitive to lead but very sensitive to many of the trace elements that may be present in bullets, it can discriminate among bullets on the basis of minor components alone.

X-Ray Diffraction

Since all metals are crystalline in structure, X-ray diffraction is an excellent nondestructive way to differentiate among them (see Figure 4–11). Scientists trained in metallurgy can deduce the basic shape and orientation of metallic crystals from the position of the beams in the diffraction pattern. Even without having an extensive knowledge of metallography the criminalist can use these patterns for comparing metal samples. Also by comparing the patterns made by unknown samples with published standard patterns for metals, the criminalist can identify the types of metal present.

Microchemical Investigations

Chemical etching techniques were developed by the metallurgical industry to investigate metal failure. The same techniques can be useful to the criminalist, who can use them to compare the behavior of different metal samples when treated with etching solutions. The samples to be examined must be encased in thermoplastic, which is then cut away down to the metal. The metal is ground and polished by successively finer abrasive materials until it is mirror smooth and no polish marks can be seen under a microscope. After the metal is polished, a suitable etching reagent is applied to the metal. This can be any of a number of acid and alkaline solutions, depending on the type of metal being tested. The etchant attacks the grain boundaries and highlights the dendritic crystal formations. It also reveals metal fatigue, which appears as pits and minute cracks filled with corrosion products. The mirror smooth polishing is essential because if even a microscopic scratch is present, the reagent tends to follow it instead of reacting along the grain boundaries. With experience an examiner can recognize the structural differences and similarities between different samples and come to reasonable conclusions about their origin.

RESTORATION OF SERIAL NUMBERS

As explained earlier in this chapter, the force required to stamp numbers or other identifying marks into metal alters the alignment of the crystal structure of the metal immediately beneath the numbers. This crystal alteration takes place for approximately one-half the depth of the original indentations. When criminals file or grind off serial numbers from stolen goods, they usually go just deep enough to remove the visible portion. By using techniques derived from metallographic investigations of metal fatigue, criminalists can "develop" the altered underlying crystal structure and restore the numbers. For the most part, only marks that have been stamped into the metal can be restored. Engraving normally does not cause sufficient crystal alteration to permit restoration.

Etching

Etching is the simplest and most reliable method crime laboratories use to restore numbers. As mentioned above, different reagents are suitable for the different metals; therefore, examiners must know what type of metal they are working with in order to select the right one. All etching solutions are caustic and should not come in contact with the skin.

Since most attempts at number obliteration are crudely done with a file, it is easy to find the location of the serial number by the file markings. More professional criminals, however, may take the trouble to smooth and polish the spot. In these cases it may be necessary to consult the manufacturers' manuals for the location of serial numbers. Sometimes criminals stamp a different number in the place where the old one was. In these cases the criminalist must not attempt to remove the new number but must try to develop and read the old number around it.

Etching Reagents

Different metals and alloys require different reagents for best results. Although many more possible etching solutions exist, the following are generally successful:

1. Iron and steel
   (a) 5 grams copper sulfate
      60 milliliters water
      30 milliliters concentrated ammonium hydroxide
      60 milliliters concentrated hydrochloric acid
      Dissolve the copper sulfate in the water; slowly add the ammonium hydroxide; then slowly add the hydrochloric acid. Because this solution creates caustic fumes, this and other etching reagents should be mixed in a ventilated hood.
   (b) 1 gram cupric ammonium chloride
      12 grams ferric chloride
      50 milliliters concentrated hydrochloric acid
      25 milliliters water
      Dissolve the cupric ammonium chloride and the ferric chloride separately in water; then combine and add the acid slowly to the solution.
2. Aluminum
   Dissolve 1 part nitric acid in 9 parts ethyl alcohol

3. Copper and its alloys
   Slowly add 25 parts nitric acid and 2 parts sulfuric acid to 73 parts water. Because of its extremely vigorous reaction, this solution should be watched closely and not continued beyond 20 minutes.
4. Gold and its alloys
   Slowly add 1 part nitric acid and 1 part hydrochloric acid to 2 parts water.

ETCHING PROCEDURE

1. Clean the area of restoration with an organic solvent such as acetone, alcohol, or benzene.
2. Photograph it.
3. Smooth the surface by carefully polishing with an electric polishing tool or by sanding with successively finer grades of emery cloth.
4. Clean again with organic solvent. Do not touch the area with bare fingers because fingerprints can interfere with the reaction.
5. Enclose the area of restoration with modeling clay or paraffin [see Figure 14-4 (b)].
6. Add the reagent with an eyedropper and renew every 10 or 15 minutes.
7. When the serial number appears, make a note of it immediately and then take several photographs of it with different angles of illumination [see Figure 14-4(c)].

Note: Depending on the nature of the alloy, it can take from a few minutes to over an hour for a number to appear. If one of the above reagents does not work within two or three hours, concentrated hydrochloric acid may be used to bring out the number. Since the reaction can be very rapid, it must be watched closely. Once the etchant eats below the point where the crystalline structure of the metal has been altered by the stamping process, the number is lost forever.

Other Methods

Electrolytic etching is a more sophisticated technique based on the principle that if two metals are immersed in an electrolyte bath and a direct current is passed through them, metal will be removed from the anode (positive pole) and deposited on the cathode (negative pole). The process is essentially the reverse of electroplating. The object being tested becomes the anode, and under controlled conditions the metal with the altered crystal structure where the serial number was is de-

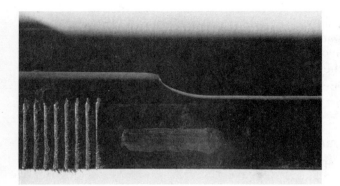

(a)

(b)

(c)

FIGURE 14–4 Restoration of a serial number on the slide of a Baretta semi-automatic pistol: (a) the ground down serial number before restoration, (b) dam of modeling clay to hold the etchant in place, (c) the restored serial number.

plated at a different rate than the surrounding metal. Because the procedure is more difficult than chemical etching and often not as effective, it is not often used in crime laboratories. Its main advantage is that it makes it unnecessary to select an appropriate etching solution for a given metal.

Magnetic particle methods have been used with some success in number restorations on ferromagnetic materials such as iron and steel. These methods were developed by the metallurgical industry as ways of detecting cracks in these metals. After the surface is polished, the piece is magnetized, covered with powder-fine magnetic particles, and vibrated. The particles adhere differentially to the surface discontinuities, including the altered crystal structure, and thereby reveal the number. Since this method can be used only on iron and steel, it is of limited value and is not generally used in crime laboratories. Its main advantage is that it is nondestructive.

Review Questions

1. Serial number restoration is possible because
   a. Criminals seldom grind away the entire serial number
   b. The grinding process impresses microscopic metal shavings into the metal which follow the outlines of the number
   c. The force used to stamp the number into the metal changes the underlying crystalline structure
   d. The metal underlying the serial number is amorphous

2. Which of the following may constitute metal evidence?
   a. Filings
   b. Drill shavings
   c. A broken knife blade
   d. All the above

3. Fractures caused by metal fatigue
   a. Begin as slippage in the crystal structure
   b. Happen instantaneously
   c. May display beach marks on the fracture surface
   d. Are the result of the application of a sudden strong force
   e. All the above
   f. a and c

4. (T, F) When a mass of molten metal solidifies, it forms one symmetrical crystal.

5. When ductile metals break under tension, they
   a. Tend to become stretched
   b. Display beach marks

   c. Break off cleanly

   d. Were probably sabotaged

6. Metals in the solid state are

   a. Amorphous

   b. Birefringent

   c. Monatomic

   d. Cool to the touch

7. The instrument that criminalists use most often in metal identification is

   a. The mass spectrometer

   b. The spectrograph

   c. Neutron activiation analysis

   d. The infrared spectrophotometer

8. When restoring a serial number, the criminalist

   a. Applies the etchant with a fingertip

   b. Lets the etchant sit on the metal overnight

   c. Uses the same reagent for iron, copper, and aluminum

   d. Records the number photographically

CHAPTER FIFTEEN

—— *FIREARMS* ——

Ever since the days of the first pioneers firearms have played an important role in American life. Even though they are no longer the absolute necessity for survival that they were to the early settlers, guns continue to enjoy great popularity among Americans, whether for sport, hunting, hobby, or home defense. In view of their abundance in the United States, it is not surprising that firearms appear as evidence in a great number of criminal investigations from robbery and assault to murder and suicide.

FIREARMS EVIDENCE

Firearms identification is an extremely broad field requiring much training and experience. Although investigating officers are not expected to be experts, they must be familiar with the weapons and ammunition they are most likely to encounter and the evidence they produce. The types of firearms most frequently used in crimes are pistols and revolvers, particularly in urban areas. Rifles and shotguns are used to a lesser extent but still appear in significant numbers of crimes. Their incidence is somewhat higher in rural areas than in towns and cities. However, sawed-off rifles and shotguns, often converted into pistols, are very popular with city gangs. Fully automatic weapons like machine pistols and submachine guns appear infrequently as evidence. Since they are much more strictly controlled by federal law than are rifles, shotguns, and handguns, there are fewer of them in general circulation. Other unusual firearms may be encountered on some occasions, such as antique weapons, converted tear gas pen guns, and weapons disguised as other objects.

The kinds of evidence that may appear in firearms investigations include the weapons themselves, bullets, cartridge cases (shells), powder residues, scorches, and shot patterns. Through these items of evidence it may be possible to determine whether bullets and cartridge cases found at the scene of a crime were fired by a certain gun, what type of weapon was used, approximately what distance from the victim a shot was fired, and whether a suspect has recently fired a gun.

Bullets and cartridge cases can be tied to the weapon that fired them by comparing them under a comparison microscope with standards fired under controlled conditions from the same weapon. Various mechanical parts of a firearm, especially the barrel, firing pin, breech block, extractor, and ejector, leave markings on the bullet and shells which are distinctive for each weapon. If a weapon used in a crime is recovered before corrosion or subsequent firings have had a chance to change the microscopic configuration of the mechanical surfaces and if the evidence bullets are not too badly damaged, the markings on the standards will be the same as those on the evidence. Under ideal conditions these comparisons can be as conclusive in identifying weapons as fingerprints are in identifying people. But, unfortunately, bullets fired in crimes are all too often disfigured by hitting bones or other hard objects to the point where they are not suitable for comparison. Cartridge cases are usually in better condition, but they are found less often because they are left at the scene only when auto-loading or military-type manual loading weapons are involved, and even then some criminals, knowing their value as evidence, pick up the ejected shells. When revolvers are used, as is the case in a large percentage of crimes, the used shells remain in the cylinder and are carried away with the gun.

CHARACTERISTICS OF FIREARMS AND AMMUNITION

Because of the tremendous number of different types of firearms, both domestic and foreign, that are in circulation in the United States, it would be futile to attempt anything like a complete description of them all. This section deals with the basic types of weapons that are most often encountered by investigators: pistols, revolvers, rifles, and shotguns.

Pistols

Pistols can be either single-shot or auto-loading repeating hand-guns (see Figure 15–1). In single-shot pistols the shooter generally has to open the action after each shot and manually eject the used shell and reload a new cartridge, but there are some single shots that automatically eject the used shell. Auto-loading pistols, sometimes called *semiautomatics* or (erroneously) *automatics,* make use of the recoil energy generated in the explosion to mechanically eject the used cartridge case and reload the next round. After each reloading operation the hammer is usually left in the cocked position, ready for firing. One round is fired every time the trigger is pulled. As each shot is fired, the cartridges are fed into the automatic reloading mechanism by a magazine, which usually fits into the grip of the weapon.

Revolvers

A revolver is a repeating handgun with a cylinder that holds several cartridges and mechanically rotates to place each successive bullet in firing position when the weapon is cocked (see Figure 15–2). Revolvers can be single-action or double-action. A single-action revolver has to be cocked for each shot by pulling the hammer back against spring

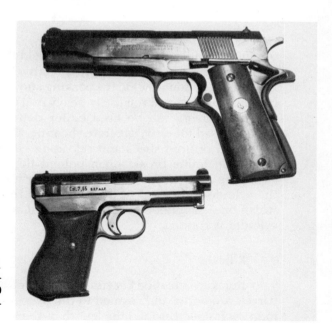

FIGURE 15–1 Top: 1911A1 Government Model .45 cal. automatic pistol. Bottom: 1910 Mauser 7.65 mm pocket automatic.

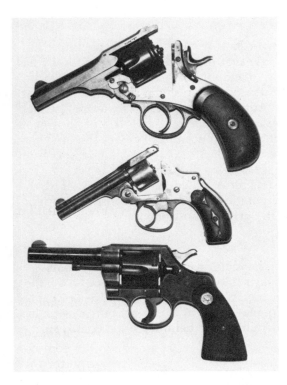

FIGURE 15–2 Top: Webley .455 cal. Mark V revolver, shown with frame broken open for reloading. Center: Smith and Wesson "New Departure" safety hammerless .32 S&W short revolver, shown with frame broken open. Bottom: Colt Official Police Service revolver, cal. .38 special.

tension until it clicks into place and is held there by the trigger mechanism. On firing, it is released by a relatively light pull on the trigger. In a double-action weapon the cocking and firing actions are performed by a single, long, and relatively heavy pull on the trigger. Most double-action revolvers can be fired either double or single action. Single action is used for slow, accurate shooting. Revolvers can be opened for extraction of fired shells and reloading either by a hinged action, in which the frame breaks open behind the cylinder and the cylinder swings up to expose the chambers, or by a swing-out action, in which the cylinder drops out to the side, or by the side ejection position, in which one chamber at a time is exposed at the side of the gun as the cylinder is rotated.

Rifles

Rifles are so called because their barrels are rifled. That is, after the barrels are bored and reamed to the proper diameter, *grooves* are cut in spiral fashion through the length of the bore, leaving corresponding raised spirals of uncut metal called *lands.* When a fired bullet is engaged in the lands, the lands impart a spin to the bullet which gives it stability in flight and thus improves accuracy. It was the invention of rifling that made possible the use of elongated and pointed projectiles. All modern rifles, as well as pistols and revolvers, have rifled barrels.

Like pistols, rifles can be single-shot or repeating. Repeating rifles use various methods for the successive ejection of fired shells and reloading of new rounds. The manual methods include lever, bolt, and pump actions; automatic and semiautomatic methods use recoil energy or gas pressure to perform the ejecting and reloading functions. Semiautomatic weapons fire one shot every time the trigger is pulled; fully automatic weapons continue firing at a very rapid rate as long as the trigger is pressed. Most fully automatic weapons were designed for military applications and are rarely encountered in criminal investigations.

Shotguns

Shotguns usually fire a load of round lead pellets called *shot* instead of single projectiles, and their barrels are not rifled. The most popular shotguns in current production are pump-type repeaters and semiautomatic, auto-loading shotguns. Formerly the most common shotguns were of the break frame type where the barrel breaks forward on a hinge to expose the breech, into which live cartridges are manually inserted and from which fired shells are extracted. These can be single-barreled or double-barreled. Shotgun barrels usually have a muzzle of slightly smaller diameter than the rest of the bore. This is called the *choke* and is designed to hold the shot pattern together over a long distance. Different barrels can have varying degrees of choke.

Bullets

Bullets are generally made of lead or lead alloyed with tin or antimony. The lead slugs are sometimes electroplated with a thin coating of copper or (rarely) cadmium. In high-powered rifles and in automatic and semiautomatic firearms of all kinds, commercial ammunition is made up of a hard metal jacket (usually a copper alloy) and a lead core. The hard jacket is needed to withstand the high velocities and the battering that a bullet receives in an automatic weapon when it is fed from the magazine into the breech. A variant designed for hunting is the jacketed bullet that has an exposed lead point which mushrooms on impact to provide greater shocking power.

Caliber

The primary identifying feature of rifle and handgun ammunition is the caliber of the bullet. Caliber can refer to both the weapon and the ammunition. In reference to weapons it means the diameter of the bore as measured between the lands; in reference to ammunition it means the diameter of the slug. In American ammunition caliber is normally stated in hundredths of an inch, for example, .22, .38, .45 but thousandths are also occasionally used, as in .357 magnum. British calibers are usually stated in thousandths of an inch; other European calibers are expressed in millimeters, for example, 7.62, 9 millimeter parabellum. Other numbers or word designations are often added to the caliber to identify individual bullet types. In .30–30 and .38–40 the second number designates the original load of black powder in grains; .30–06 indicates the year the bullet was adopted; .45 ACP (automatic Colt pistol) indicates the weapon for which the bullet was developed; .22 Nieder shows the name of the designer; such names as .44 Magnum and .500 Express indicate high power; and in 7.92 X 57 the first number is the caliber and the second is the case length in millimeters.

Calibers can sometimes be misleading since they do not necessarily reflect the true diameter either of the bore or of the bullet. For example, .22-caliber weapons may vary in actual diameter from .22 inch to .219 inch and the bullets may measure from .223 inch to .224 inch. A revolver firing a .38 Special cartridge may have a bore diameter of from .346 inch to .347 inch and the bullets may measure from .354 inch to .359 inch. When attempting to determine the caliber of a spent bullet found in evidence, an examiner should measure land and groove diameters by using a microscope equipped with an ocular micrometer. Mathews[1] gives comprehensive lists of bore and groove dimensions to which the examiner may refer.

Weight

The weight of the bullet, traditionally given in grains,[2] should also be considered in ammunition identification. This is particularly important when the bullet is too badly disfigured to determine the caliber. Even when the caliber can be measured, the weight is usually necessary to determine the type of ammunition. A firearms identification manual such as Mathews can be used to help to identify the bullet or narrow it down to a few choices if caliber and weight are known. The examiner

[1]J. Howard Mathews, *Firearms Identification* (Springfield, Ill.: Charles C Thomas, Publisher, 1973).
[2]One grain equals 64.8 milligrams.

must bear in mind, however, that a bullet may easily lose some pieces when it hits something and therefore lose weight.

Bullet Shape

The length of the bullet and the configuration of the point and the base may be helpful in identifying ammunition. The usual tips are rounded, sharp-pointed, or flat. Rounded points are the most common for general use, sharp points are used in most military ammunition, and flat points are used for police and some hunting ammunition for their increased stopping power. Hollow-points, or "dum-dums," are used in hunting because of their mushrooming effect, which causes larger wounds and severe shock. Wad-cutters, used in target shooting, have a flat face that cuts a clean hole in paper. The base of most bullets is flat, but some bases are made concave so that the pressure of the explosion forces them to expand against the grooves and prevent the escape of gas around the bullet. The base of a bullet may also have one or more grooves called *cannelures* around the outside circumference. Cannelures serve as a means to hold lubrication in lead bullets and as a crimping groove on some jacketed and lead bullets, into which the neck of the case is crimped to hold the bullet in place.

Shotgun Ammunition

The diameter of shotgun barrels and their corresponding ammunition is designated by *gauge,* a term left over from the days of smoothbore musketry. Gauge refers to the number of single round lead balls fitting in a firearm that it would take to make up a pound in weight. A 12-gauge gun fired a ball weighing 1/12 pound. Thus the larger the gauge of a gun, the smaller the diameter of the bore. An exception is the so-called .410-gauge shotgun; here the .410 refers to the diameter of the bore in thousandths of an inch. Although shotguns normally fire shot, single-ball cartridges are also manufactured for them. These cartridges have a diameter slightly smaller than that of the bore. Shot is made of lead, lead alloys, or steel and is sometimes copper coated. Shot ranges in size from 00, 0, 1, 2, etc., through number 12, which is the smallest of the numbered shot. The larger shot (i.e., the lower numbers) is often called buckshot and the smaller shot is called birdshot. Dust shot, which is smaller than number 12, is the smallest of all.

Cartridge Cases

Cartridge cases, or shells, are found at crime scenes when autoloading or manual repeating weapons are used or in the rare instance in which a criminal has to reload a revolver. Cartridge cases are identified in various ways. Almost all modern versions are made of brass, but some copper cases in .22, .25, and .41 calibers are still in circulation and some pistol cartridge cases are nickel-plated. Shotgun cartridges can be made of paper or plastic with a brass head or all plastic. Plastic shotgun cartridges are the most common today. Some .410 cartridges are all aluminum. All high-velocity cartridges and most other ammunition are *centerfire;* that is, the primer is located in the center of the head. Ordinary .22s and a few other small-caliber cartridges have the primer material embedded in the rim and are called *rimfire.*

In centerfire cartridges the caliber and a manufacturer's symbol are usually stamped on the head around the primer. Rimfire cartridges do not usually show the caliber, but they do have a manufacturer's symbol in the center of the head.

The base of a cartridge case can be either rimmed, semirimmed, or rimless. In a rimmed cartridge there is a projecting shoulder that

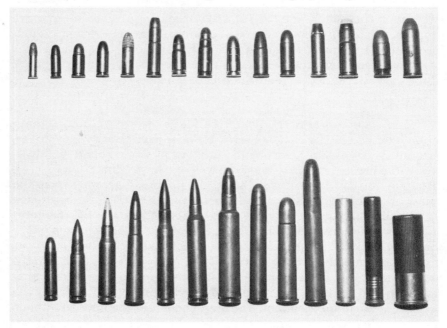

FIGURE 15–3 Top row, handgun cartridges, left to right: .22 long rifle (also used in rifles), .25 ACP (6.35mm), .32 S&W short, .32 ACP (7.65 mm), .32 long rimfire, .32/20 Winchester (also used in rifles), .30 Luger (7.65 mm), .30 Mauser (7.63 mm), 9 mm Luger, .380/200 (.38 S&W), .38 Super ACP, .38 special, .38/40 Winchester (also used in rifles), .45 ACP, .45 long Colt. Bottom row, rifle and shotgun cartriges, left to right: .30 Ml U.S. carbine, 7.62X39 Russian, 7.62X51 NATO (.308 Winchester), .303 British, .30–06 U.S., .300 Winchester magnum, .378 Wetherby magnum, .405 Winchester, .45/70, .450 nitro express, .410 3 inch aluminum shot shell, .410 3 inch paper shot shell, #12 gauge shot shell.

keeps the bullet from going too far into the chamber. The rimmed cartridge is currently considered unsuitable for military rifles and auto-loading weapons (although it has been used in them in the past) because the rim tends to get in the way when the bullets are fed from the magazine into the breech. A rimless cartridge was designed for these types of weapons; here the rim is flush with the body of the cartridge and an extractor groove is indented behind it around the circumference of the cartridge case. The semirimmed cartridge is a modification in which the rim extends only slightly beyond the body of the cartridge case.

In some cartridges a cannelure is crimped around the neck of the case to hold the bullet in place.

Reloads

Reloading ammunition is an increasingly popular money-saving practice among target shooters and sportsmen. Manufacturers sell bullets, cases, primers, shot cups, shot, and powder separately for home reloading purposes. Some reloaders cast their own lead and lead alloy bullets. Consequently, both the investigator and the laboratory examiner should be aware that because of the possibility of mixing parts, reusing old cartridge cases, and using nonstandard powder loads, there may be discrepancies from commercial ammunition.

EVIDENTIAL MARKINGS ON BULLETS AND CARTRIDGE CASES

As stated earlier, all modern firearms have spiral grooves called *rifling* cut into the bore of their barrels (see Figure 15–4). Various machining processes are used to produce rifling. Barrels must be reamed to the appropriate diameter before they can be rifled. One mass-production rifling technique passes a broach cutter through the barrel. This is a hard steel tool having a series of successively broader concentric rings that are shaped and aligned so as to cut the desired number of grooves. The cutter is turned during the operation in order to produce the spirals; one pass is sufficient to rifle a barrel. Other cutting systems, such as the older hook cutter, may require several passes to complete the job. In addition to the cutting systems, there are pressure methods for rifling. In one method an extremely hard tool, called a *button swage,* is forced through the reamed barrel at pressures high enough to displace the metal in the grooves. In another method, called *cold forming,* the barrel is formed by pounding it under pressure around a stationary mandrel. The mandrel is a negative image of the desired land and groove pattern which is impressed into the steel of the bore.

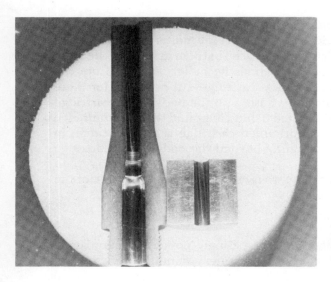

FIGURE 15–4 Sectioned rifle barrel showing the rifling. (Courtesy of Colt Firearms)

Bullets

Tool marks and imperfections in the rifling produce the striations on fired bullets which enable examiners to state whether a bullet was fired by a certain gun. Since bullets are of larger diameter than the groove-to-groove diameter of the weapons that fire them, the slug fills the grooves as it is forced through the barrel and picks up a reverse image of any tool marks or flaws in the metal of the bore. Although it might seem that two barrels rifled by the same tool would have the same tool marks and therefore produce identical striations, the fact is that there are always microscopic differences in the tool marks even in barrels rifled one after another by the same tool. The cutting tools change the character of their edge every time they are sharpened, and they also push minute metal shavings along as they cut, which in turn make tiny random cuts in the bore. Since the pressure methods of rifling displace the metal rather than cut it, it is much more difficult to find unique characteristics in those barrels when they are new. Nevertheless, with very careful examination it is sometimes possible to identify bullets fired from these barrels. After a weapon leaves the factory and goes into use, the treatment it receives adds markings to the barrel. Corrosion, shooting, and the use of cleaning tools gradually cause small changes in the bore which further individualize it. Because these markings constantly change under use, it is important that a firearm used in a crime be recovered fairly soon after the incident. As more time elapses, the chances become greater that a match cannot be made between a bullet and the gun that fired it.

Since there is no convenient way of comparing a bullet directly with a barrel, the simplest method is to fire several test bullets and compare them with the bullet in evidence. The preferred method is to fire the test bullets into a tank of water. Boxes filled with cotton waste or other soft materials are sometimes used, but it has been found that the cotton fibers impress their own markings into lead bullets and sometimes wipe off parts of the tool marks. Several test bullets of the same type ammunition as the evidence bullet should be fired. If the chamber is not perfectly lined up with the barrel, as is often the case in old, worn revolvers, the bullet may sometimes be forced more strongly against one side of the barrel than the other, thereby causing a slightly different pattern of striations. If several test shots are fired, there is a greater chance of getting one that corresponds to the evidence bullet. Different types of ammunition may have different muzzle velocities and internal pressures that could cause different striations to appear.

The evidence bullet is mounted at one side of a comparison microscope and a test bullet is mounted at the other side. They are mounted to face the same direction and aligned so that the front half of one lines up with the rear half of the other. One bullet remains stationary and the other bullet is turned until the striation patterns match up. Then both bullets are turned together to ensure that the match continues all the way around (see Figure 15–5). Since evidence bullets are often damaged from striking hard objects, it may not be possible to match the striations around the entire circumference. There is no rule stating the number of points of comparison necessary to prove a match. The examiner's experience plays a role here, but when there is a match, even when it can be seen only in a small area, it is usually obvious enough so that there is little question. Of course, if the evidence bullet is badly enough damaged, there may be no basis of comparison at all.

When no firearm is recovered after a shooting crime, the markings on the bullet may give some clues to the type and condition of the weapon involved. Sometimes the rifling marks are wider toward the front of the bullet than at the rear. This phenomenon, called *slippage,* occurs because the bullet starts off moving straight ahead without spin and it is well into the barrel before the rifling engages it and starts it spinning. This results in the widened pattern of markings at the front of the bullet. The effects of slippage tend to be more pronounced in revolvers than in auto-loading weapons because the bullet travels farther before becoming engaged in the rifling. It is also more pronounced in old weapons in which the bore is extremely worn. Consequently, unusually wide slippage marks may indicate a revolver or an old gun.

Manufacturers all have their own standards as to the number of lands and grooves and their pitch. *Pitch* is the degree of twist in the

(a)

(b)

FIGURE 15–5 Some examples of land and groove striations matched under the comparison microscope. Evidence bullet is on the left; test bullet on the right. (Courtesy of Connecticut State Police Forensic Laboratory)

spiral and is measured according to the distance a bullet must travel to complete one revolution. These elements are constant for each caliber of a given manufacturer. The width of the grooves and the direction of the twist are also different in different manufacturers. While most weapons have rifling that twists to the right, weapons made by Colt all twist to the left. Hence all Colt products can immediately be excluded if the bullet in evidence shows striations that twist to the right. The best aid a crime laboratory can have in identifying the makes and models of weapons from bullet markings is an extensive collection of bullet samples that show the characteristic marks made by various weapons. Although it is not always possible to pinpoint the exact make and model, it is possible to greatly narrow down the possibilities.

Cartridge Cases

Cartridge cases (shells) from all types of weapons are subject to the same type of comparison as bullets. The breech block is that part of a weapon that fits up against the head of a cartridge to prevent its backward movement. The breech block is a machined part that sometimes

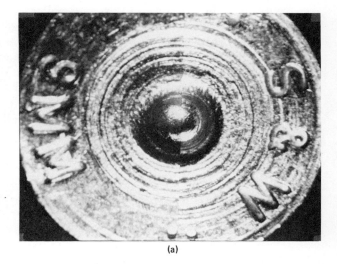

(a)

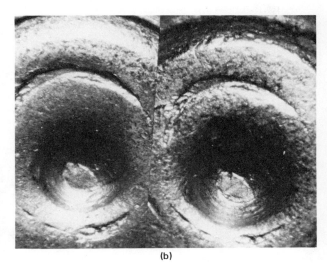

FIGURE 15–6 Some examples of breech block markings on cartridge heads matched under the comparison microscope. (Courtesy of Connecticut State Police Forensic Laboratory)

(b)

has a cast surface. Consequently, the breech block bears machining or casting marks on its face. When a bullet is fired, the shell is slammed back with great force against the breech block and since the shell is made of a softer metal, it picks up an impression of any marks made by machining or corrosion (see Figure 15–6). These marks are never identical on different guns.

A similar situation arises with markings made by the firing pin, extractor, ejector, and the magazine. Although firing pins are of various designs (some are part of the hammer and some are separate pieces pushed forward by the hammer), all firing pins have to strike the primer with considerable force to fire the bullet. In centerfire cartridges the primer is in the center of the shell head and in rimfire cartridges the primer is embedded all the way around the hollow rim. In either case, when the firing pin stikes, it makes an indentation in the metal of the primer which stamps an impression of any tool marks or other distinctive markings on the point of the firing pin into the primer metal.

The extractor is a hook-like part found in most rifles and autoloading pistols. The extractor draws the shell out of the breech after firing in order to make room for the next round. In most guns the extractor pulls the shell rapidly back against the ejector, a protruding part in the face of the breech block, which flips the empty shell case out of the gun. Often these actions are done with sufficient force to leave impressions of their tool marks on the shell. Extractor marks are made either on the rim or in the extractor groove behind the rim. Ejector marks are made on the shell head. During the loading process in automatic weapons, shells can pick up scratch marks as they are scraped against the lip of the magazine and the breech as well as from the loading ramp, which guides the bullet into the chamber. These scratches may also show sufficient uniformity of detail to permit comparisons (see Figure 15–7).

FIGURE 15–7   Striations scratched on the side of cartridge cases by an irregularity in the breech of the pistol that fired them matched under the comparison microscope. (Courtesy of Connecticut State Police Forensic Laboratory)

DISTANCE ESTIMATION

In addition to identifying weapons and ammunition, firearms examiners are often called upon to estimate the distance from a victim that a shot was fired. This can be very helpful in reconstructing the crime and it is especially important in making suicide determinations. Powder patterns and shot patterns are the main indicators of firing distance.

Powder Patterns

All modern firearms use smokeless powder, which is basically nitrocellulose with other minor additives to control the speed of the explosion. A slower burning rate is needed in rifle ammunition than in handguns because the pressure must be sustained over a longer period. Regardless of the weapon or powder type, the powder is never completely consumed in a gunshot. Tiny bits and pieces of unburned and partially burned powder are always propelled forward along with the bullet. Because of their light weight they do not travel very far, but for the short distance that they do travel they describe a roughly conical pattern out from the muzzle. These patterns can vary considerably from each other, depending on the type and amount of powder, the weight of the bullet, and the characteristics of the gun. Nevertheless, several shots of a single type of ammunition fired from the same gun produce patterns that are generally similar.

It is from these patterns made by bits of unburned powder around bullet entrance holes that examiners can estimate distances. If the weapon is recovered and if the type of ammunition is known, it is possible to make approximate determinations of distance. Several test firings are made at various distances with the same gun and ammunition type. Then the powder patterns made in the tests are compared with those found on the victim's clothing. Ideally, the tests should be carried out on the same type of material as the evidence, but a white cotton cloth gives reasonably good results.

Sometimes the powder patterns can be observed with the naked eye or with a low-power stereoscopic microscope. But when there is insufficient color contrast between the powder and the material or when the pattern is obscured by blood or dirt or when the visible flakes have been shaken off through careless handling of the garment, the powder pattern can often be highlighted by infrared photography or developed by chemical means.

Infrared Photography

When infrared photography is used to bring out powder patterns, the camera (loaded with infrared film) is positioned directly above the

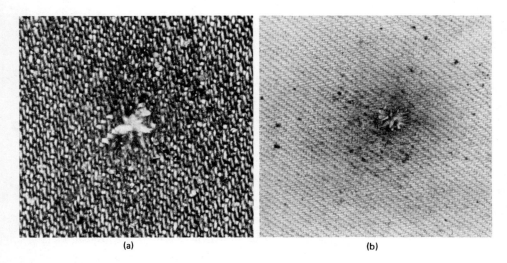

(a)   (b)

FIGURE 15–8   A powder pattern revealed by infrared photography: (a) shows a bullet hole in blue jeans photographed with black and white panchromatic film; (b) shows the same bullet hole photographed with infrared film and with a Kodak Wratten No. 87 filter held in front of the camera lens.

bullet entrance hole. The garment is illuminated by any source of white light, and an infrared filter (Kodak Wratten No. 87) is held in front of the camera lens so that only the infrared wavelengths are allowed to pass into the camera. It is usually a good idea to adjust the f/stop to the smallest possible aperture in order to ensure good focus, and since it is difficult to estimate the correct exposure for infrared, several shots should be made at different shutter speeds. (See Figure 15-8).

Chemical Development

Chemical procedures for developing powder patterns depend on a color reaction taking place between a reagent and a substance in the powder residue. Two methods are commonly used. One method uses a reagent that reacts specifically with *nitrites*. Nitrites (NO_2) are products of the incomplete combustion of nitrocellulose (gunpowder) or other compounds containing nitrates (NO_3). Since the pioneering work in the 1930s of Joseph T. Walker of the Massachusetts Department of Public Safety several reagents have been used. The one most commonly used today is the *Griess test* (see Figure 15–9). The other chemical method is the *Rhodizonate test,* which identifies lead and barium in the powder residue.

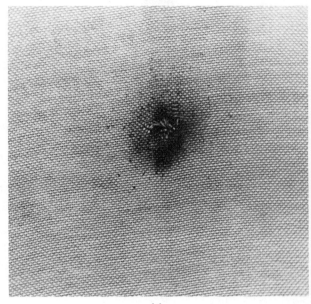

(a)

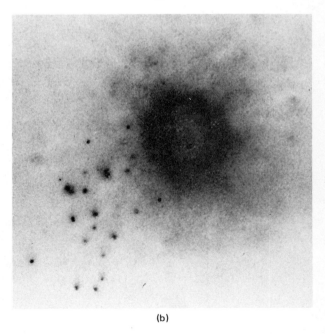

FIGURE 15–9   (a) Visible powder pattern of a gunshot fired at 6 inches from a .32 cal. semiautomatic pistol. (b) Same powder pattern developed by the Griess Test. (Courtesy of Boston Police Technical Services Section)

(b)

PROCEDURE FOR THE GRIESS TEST (PROTECTIVE GLOVES SHOULD BE WORN WHEN HANDLING REAGENTS)

A. Prepare in advance
   1. 0.5 percent solution of sulfanilic acid. Place 0.75 gram into a graduated cylinder and fill with distilled water to 150 milliliters.
   2. 0.5 percent solution of N-(1-naphthyl)-ethylene-diaminedihydro-chloride (Marshall's reagent). Place 0.75 gram into a graduated cylinder and fill with methyl alcohol (methanol) to 150 milliliters.
   3. Mix reagents 1 and 2 in a bottle and keep sealed.
   4. Fix photographic paper in hypo to remove all silver halides, wash thoroughly to remove hypo, and dry. This leaves a sheet of paper coated with a plain gelatin emulsion. Dip the paper in reagent mixture 3 so that those chemicals can soak into the emulsion. Dry the paper.
   5. 15 percent acetic acid solution. Combine 150 milliliters glacial acetic acid with 850 milliliters distilled water
   6. 5 percent hydrochloric acid solution. Slowly add 50 milliliters concentrated hydrochloric acid to 950 milliliters distilled water.

B. Conducting the test
   1. Place a sheet of treated photographic paper (emulsion side up) on the work area. Lay the garment on top of the paper with the bullet entrance hole against the paper.
   2. Place a piece of cheesecloth, which has been dipped in 15 percent acetic acid solution and wrung out, on top of the garment and press with a warm iron. Thicker garments require longer application of heat.
   3. The acetic acid reacts with the nitrites to form nitrous acid (HNO_2), which is transferred to the treated photographic paper. The nitrous acid reacts with the chemicals in the paper to produce orange-red spots. These spots correspond to the nitrite deposits in the garment. After the paper is dried, spray the paper with a 5 percent solution of hydrochloric acid. This solution causes the orange-red spots to turn to a permanent blue color.

PROCEDURE FOR THE RHODIZONATE TEST[3]

A. Prepare in advance
   1. 10 percent acetic acid solution. Combine 100 milliliters glacial acetic acid with 900 milliliters distilled water.
   2. Saturated sodium rhodizonate solution. Keep adding sodium

[3]R. D. Guy and B. D. Pate, "Studies of the Trace Element Content of Bullet Lead and Jacket Material." *Journal of Forensic Sciences,* 18, no. 2 (April 1973), 87–92.

rhodizonate to distilled water until no more will go into solution.

3. pH 2.8 tartaric acid buffer. 1.9 grams sodium bitartrate and 1.5 grams tartaric acid in 100 milliliters distilled water.

B. Conducting the test

1. Soak a large piece of filter paper in 10 percent acetic acid and blot to remove excess wetness.

2. Place the treated paper over the bullet entrance hole, cover it with several pieces of dry filter paper, and press it with a hot iron.

3. Air dry the garment and the filter paper.

4. Spray the filter paper with the sodium rhodizonate solution; then immediately spray with pH 2.8 tartaric acid buffer.

5. Observation: Lead becomes visible as a bright pink reaction and barium as an orange color. The tartaric acid buffer clears up the background and renders the expected reactions more visible.

After the tests have been conducted both on the evidence garment and on the fabrics prepared by firing at different known distances, the results are compared. The known distance pattern that is most like that of the evidence garment gives an approximate indication of the distance at which the weapon was fired in the crime.

If the weapon is not recovered, distance determinations are of necessity very rough and generally limited to a statement as to whether or not a shot *could* have been fired within a certain distance. Recognizable powder patterns are usually not found at distances greater than from 18 inches to 24 inches from the barrel, but powder tattooing on skin can be caused by certain types of smokeless powder as far as 36 inches. If the barrel is sawed off, the distance can be even greater. Powder charges are designed to burn in so many inches of barrel; therefore, the shorter the barrel, the more unburned powder there is. Old-fashioned black powder, which is seldom seen anymore in crimes, can deposit unburned powder as far as 6 feet from the muzzle.

If there is no weapon, the examiner must rely on experience. In addition to powder deposits, the examiner can use observations of tear patterns in clothing, scorching from muzzle flash, and smoke darkening to aid in making an estimate. At contact a gunshot often makes a star-shaped tear in clothing (see Figure 15–10) and leaves considerable scorching. Also at contact there may be little or no unburned powder deposits because the pressure drives the powder particles into the wound. Scorching seldom occurs at distances greater than 4 inches; and smoke darkening does not occur more than 12 inches to 18 inches from the muzzle.

FIGURE 15–10 Contact gunshot, showing scorching and star-shaped tear. (Courtesy of Boston Police Technical Services Section)

Shot Patterns

In cases of shotgun wounds distances can be roughly estimated by the degree of dispersion of the shot. As the shot comes out of the muzzle, it is packed into a tight group by the choke, but as soon as the shot leaves the barrel, it begins to disperse. As with powder patterns, accurate estimations can be made only by comparisons made with the same gun and ammunition type. Otherwise, the variables of the type of powder, type of load, length of barrel, and degree of choke are too great and only a very rough estimate can be made. Test patterns can be made by shooting shots at varying distances through white cloth or cardboard.

Shotgun cartridges used to be packed with a top wad to hold the shot in place. Many of these old-fashioned cartridges are still in existence. When the shotgun is fired, the top wad travels with the shot for a few feet before it is scattered and lost. If the top wad is found in the wound, it is an indication of a close shot. Most modern plastic cartridges hold the shot in place by crimping the top of the plastic case over the load; no top wad is needed. However, there is usually a light plastic shot cup in modern cartridges, which separates the shot from the powder. Some manufacturers cushion the shot pellets with a polyethylene filler material. If either the shot cup or any bits of filler material are found in the wound, they also indicate a very close shot.

POWDER RESIDUES ON THE SHOOTER'S GUN HAND

Although the only sure way to connect a suspect to a firearm used in a crime is by finding the suspect's fingerprints on it, it is nevertheless a very valuable investigative tool to be able to prove that an individual has recently fired a gun. Whenever a gun is fired, not only do particles of unburned powder fly forward out of the barrel, but small quantities also fly backward from the breech and become deposited on the shooter's gun hand.

For many years the standard method of detecting these residues was the *dermal nitrate* test, popularly known as the *paraffin* test. The dermal nitrate test is a chemical method of detecting nitrates present in unburned powder. The technique consists of pouring or brushing melted paraffin onto the suspect's hand, removing the paraffin after it has hardened, and testing it with a solution of diphenylamine in sulfuric acid and distilled water. Whenever nitrates are present, a vivid blue color appears on the paraffin.

Experience has proved that the results of the dermal nitrate test can be very dubious because people who are known to have recently fired a gun sometimes do not have any nitrates on their hands, and people who have not fired guns sometimes have nitrates on their hands from other sources such as tobacco, fertilizer, urine, some cosmetics, and some chemicals.

In recent years other tests have been devised which detect trace residues of barium, antimony, and sometimes copper and lead. All present-day centerfire cartridges and many .22 rimfire cartridges have primers that contain compounds of barium and antimony. These elements can almost always be found on a shooter's gun hand if the tests are conducted soon enough after the shooting. Studies have shown that residues of barium and antimony on the skin become reduced to insignificant levels after approximately 2 hours of normal activity. Any attempt to wash or wipe the residues off results in an immediate significant decrease in their levels.[4]

The most sensitive methods of detecting barium and antimony are neutron activation analysis (NAA) and flameless atomic absorption spectrophotometry (FAAS). As we have seen in other chapters, neutron activation analysis is costly, time-consuming, and not readily available to most laboratories. FAAS has approximately the same sensitivity and is within the cost range of most crime laboratories. Because the light source in FAAS must be of the same wavelength as the characteristic wavelength of the element being detected, the lamps have to be changed for every element and only one element can be detected at a time. Although this may be a drawback in the analysis of completely unknown materials, it makes FAAS eminently suitable for primer residue examinations in which the object is to test for the presence of a few specific elements.

[4] J. W. Kilty, "Activity after Shooting and Its Effect on the Retention of Primer Residue," *Journal of Forensic Sciences*, 20, no. 2 (1975), 219–30.

Several different techniques are available for collecting the residues from the suspect's hands. The paraffin method described above for use in the dermal nitrate test is also effective for FAAS, but it is too clumsy for investigating officers to use in the field. Some other techniques in wide use are wiping the hand with cotton balls or filter paper moistened with dilute nitric acid, having the suspect rinse his or her hands in a plastic bag full of dilute nitric acid, or using "film-lift," a film-forming polymer of cellulose acetate which hardens quickly on the hand and is then peeled off. According to studies made by the Bureau of Alcohol, Tobacco, and Firearms of the United States Treasury Department,[5] the simplest and most effective collection method is to press transparent adhesive tape several times against the web portion of the hand between the thumb and forefinger. The tape sample is easily taken in the field with a minimum of equipment. After the sample is collected, it is folded in half and placed in a plastic pill bottle, which is appropriately labeled and sent to the laboratory. The adhesive tape method has the additional advantage that it can be readily viewed under a microscope for signs of nitrate deposits. The adhesive tape used must be tested to make sure that its own possible levels of barium and antimony do not interfere with the test. Whenever powder residue samples are taken, a piece of plain tape should be sent along with samples to the laboratory for control purposes.

TRACE METAL DETECTION TECHNIQUE

Since the tests for powder residues on a suspect's hands cannot prove conclusively that he or she has fired a weapon, it is useful to perform another test to help confirm that the suspect has recently held a firearm. The Trace Metal Detection Technique (TMDT)[6] is a chemical method for determining whether one has recently held something metallic in one's hands. The reagent is a 0.1 percent to 0.2 percent solution of 8-hydroxyquinoline in isopropanol (200 milligrams of 8-hydroxyquinoline powder dissolved in 100 milliliters isopropanol). The reagent is sprayed onto the palms of the suspect's hands, and if the suspect has been holding a firearm or other metallic object, the reagent reacts with traces of the metallic oxide deposited on the hand. When the hand is then held under ultraviolet light, the area of metal deposit fluoresces

    [5]J. A. Goleb and C. R. Midkiff, "Firearms Discharge Residue Sample Collection Techniques," *Journal of Forensic Sciences,* 20, no. 4 (1975), 701–7.
    [6]"Trace Metal Detection Technique in Law Enforcement," Pamphlet No. 71–1, NILE & CJ, LEAA (Washington, D.C.: U.S. Government Printing Office, 1970).

with characteristic colors for different metals. Some of the observed fluorescences are:

Steel and iron: blackish-purple
Brass and copper: purple
Aluminum: mottled dull yellow
Lead: tannish flesh color

Although the reaction will occur if the subject has been holding any metal object, firearms tend to leave recognizable patterns because of their characteristic shapes and because one finger usually comes in contact with the trigger. By comparing the suspect pattern with known standards, it is sometimes possible to make a reasonable guess as to the make and model of firearm used. Similarly, when metallic objects other than firearms are used as weapons, their characteristic patterns may help identify them.

The main disadvantages of TMDT are the inconvenience of using untraviolet light to bring up the pattern and the difficulty of photographing with ultraviolet illumination. A newer trace metal detection test is available which identifies iron and steel deposits under visible light.[7] The reagent is a 0.1 percent solution of 3-(2-pyridyl)-5,6-diphenyl-1,2,4-triazine-p,p'-disulphonic acid, disodium salt trihydrate in methanol (100 milligrams of the powder dissoved in 100 milliliters of methanol). The reagent is commonly known as PDT, or Ferrozine, and like the TMDT reagent, it is sprayed onto the hands. If the suspect has held a ferrous metal (iron or steel), a magenta stain begins to appear within one minute and intensifies over a period of one to two hours or more rapidly if exposed to long wavelength ultraviolet light. Since the stain is visible in visible light, it can easily be photographed by using any common illumination source.

In both of these tests the strength of the reaction is dependent on the length of time the metallic object was held and the amount of perspiration on the hands. Perspiration increases the amount of oxidation of the metal and therefore the amount of oxide deposited on the hand. A weapon that has been freshly oiled may yield a weak reaction because the oil protects the metal from oxidation. The test should always be made on both hands in case the reaction might have come from some other source normal to the suspect's daily life. For control purposes, a test should be carried out on the hands of a person who is known not to have held a firearm within the past several days.

[7]B. S. Goldman and J. I. Thornton, "A New Trace Ferrous Metal Detection Reagent," *Journal of Forensic Sciences*, 21, no. 3 (1976), 625–28.

Firearms

Investigators must exercise extreme caution when handling firearms found at crime scenes. Because firearms are usually loaded, they should not be picked up so that they point at anyone.

Ideally, a fingerprint expert should be present at the crime scene search to examine the weapon for latent prints before it is unloaded or handled by anyone else. The fingerprint expert should then unload the weapon and test the remaining bullets and empty cartridge cases for prints. In most cases, however, a fingerprint expert is not at the crime scene and the weapon must be sent to the laboratory for fingerprint examination.

Although obtaining usable prints from a firearm is very difficult and rarely successful, any weapon found at a crime scene should be treated as if it carried prints. One of the major difficulties of the investigating officer is how to transmit the weapon to the laboratory since any time something rubs against the weapon, any prints may be smudged. The first rule is that no one should handle the weapon any more than is absolutely necessary for purposes of transmittal. The weapon should be transmitted loaded because it is almost impossible to unload a firearm without rubbing portions where prints may be present. The transmittal package should be clearly marked to indicate that it contains a loaded weapon, and laboratory personnel should be trained to expect loaded weapons. After checking the exterior of the weapon for prints, laboratory personnel should carefully unload the weapon and check the cartridges.

A handgun can be picked up by the checkered grips or the trigger guard because these areas do not normally hold fingerprints. A rifle or shotgun can be picked up by the sling (if there is one), by any checkered part, or by a firm grip with the fingers on the trigger guard. A weapon should never be lifted by sticking a pencil or other object into the barrel. This could disturb or destroy such evidence as blood or fibers that may be present in close-range shootings, dirt or rust particles that might indicate that the weapon had not been fired recently, and any deposits of powder, dirt, or rust that may affect the striation pattern of the bore.

The investigating officer should attach a tag to any recovered firearms, usually to the trigger guard, indicating the make, model, caliber, serial number, finish, date and time of recovery, and the investigating officer's name. When packaging a weapon for transmittal the main consideration is to avoid any rubbing. The weapon should never be wrapped in cloth. One method for a pistol or a revolver is to lay it carefully into a box and wedge it against the side of the box with a piece of wood. Many investigators package handguns in a plain brown paper bag. If that method is used, the weapon should not be dropped into the bag but carefully placed in the bottom. Whatever type of packaging is used, the package should be carried carefully to prevent the weapon from sliding around inside.

When a revolver is unloaded, whether in the laboratory or by the fingerprint technician in the field, the position of the chamber facing the barrel should be marked with a scratch and a diagram should be drawn that shows the chamber positions of each of the cartridges and empty shells removed from the weapon. This may be helpful later in reconstructing the sequence of events.

Cartridges

Bullets embedded in walls or other objects should be removed with care in order to avoid destroying any striations. The entire area around the bullet should be cut out and the bullet with its surrounding material sent to the laboratory for careful removal. Bullets in bodies are removed only by medical personnel, usually during the autopsy. The investigating officer's initials should be scratched in bullets and shell cases with an inscribing tool (see Figure 15–11). In the case of a bullet the initials should go either on the point or on the base (never on the side where they might interfere with striations). A cartridge case should be marked on the inside of the mouth if the caliber is large enough to permit it; otherwise, it should be marked on the outside body near the mouth. In the case of a shotgun shell the initials should be scratched or written with indelible ink on the side or scratched into the brass portion. No marks of any kind should be placed on the head.

When a shotgun has been used, the investigator should always look for the shot cup or the top wad. They can provide clues as to the type of ammunition used and, as mentioned earlier, if they are inside the wound they indicate a close-range shot.

All bullets and cartridge cases recovered at a crime scene should be individually wrapped in pieces of cloth and placed in a box so that they cannot jostle against each other. Bullets and shell cases from different guns should be placed in separate boxes and labeled accordingly. The boxes should also show the date, time, and place of collection and the investigator's initials.

Powder Residues

The clothing of a gunshot victim should always be presumed to carry gunpowder residues. The clothing should be folded and packaged

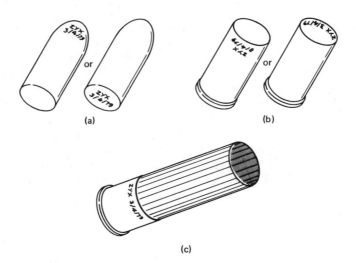

(a)   (b)

(c)

(d)

FIGURE 15–11 Identification markings (a) on bullets, (b) on pistol and rifle cartridges, (c) on shotgun shells, (d) a good example of how *not* to mark a bullet. (Photograph (d) courtesy of Connecticut State Police Forensic Laboratory)

carefully for transmittal to the laboratory so that the pattern is neither disturbed nor altered. If clothing has to be cut off a victim, the cut should not pass through the potential area of residue.

When a suspect's hands are to be tested for powder residues, the sample should be collected as soon as possible because of the great perishability of the evidence. As stated earlier, the adhesive tape method is the simplest and most effective for field use by investigators. Samples should always be taken from both of the suspect's hands to preclude the possibility that the suspect has acquired barium, antimony, or nitrate deposits from some source other than the gunshot. Whatever collection method is used, the investigator should submit unused samples of the collecting materials to the laboratory along with the evidence for control purposes.

Review Questions

1. The firearms most frequently used in crimes are
   a. Submachine guns
   b. Shotguns
   c. Handguns
   d. Rifles

2. Which of the following would *not* be considered a form of firearms evidence?
   a. Powder residues
   b. Matted hair stuck to a rifle butt
   c. Shot patterns
   d. Cartridge cases

3. A semiautomatic pistol
   a. Operates by recoil energy
   b. Keeps firing as long as the shooter holds the trigger down
   c. Is manual loading
   d. retains the fired cartridge cases in the cylinder

4. (T, F) Pistols and revolvers are rifled.

5. The choke of a shotgun barrel
   a. Is increased when it is sawed off
   b. Holds the shot pattern together
   c. Is due to the rifling
   d. Is the same on all shotguns of the same caliber

6. (T, F) Most American calibers are stated in hundredths of an inch.

7. In making bullet identifications the criminalist can consider
   a. Weight
   b. Shape
   c. Caliber
   d. Cannelures

e. All the above
f. a, b, and c

8. (T, F) Most cartridge cases are made of aluminum.

9. The striations the barrel makes on a fired bullet
   a. Cannot be individualized on new weapons
   b. Always remain the same throughout the life of the weapon
   c. Are affected by corrosion
   d. Are caused by the casting of the barrel

10. Bullet striations are most commonly examined with
    a. A comparison microscope
    b. A polarizing microscope
    c. Emission spectrography
    d. An X-ray diffraction camera

11. (T, F) Firearms made by Colt have rifling that twists to the left.

12. Evidential markings on a cartridge case can appear
    a. On the inner lip
    b. On the ejector
    c. On the head
    d. In the extractor groove
    e. a and b
    f. c and d

13. Powder patterns can be examined
    a. With the naked eye
    b. With a stereoscopic microscope
    c. By infrared photography
    d. By the Griess test
    e. All the above
    f. c and d

14. The paraffin test
    a. Proves that a person is guilty
    b. Is sensitive to barium and antimony
    c. Is sensitive to paraffin
    d. Is sensitive to nitrates

15. A handgun should be picked up
    a. By sticking a pencil into the barrel
    b. By wrapping it in a clean handkerchief
    c. By the checkered grips
    d. By the barrel

CHAPTER SIXTEEN

——— *TRACKS* ———
AND IMPRESSIONS

Most of the evidence we have studied up to now has concerned physical items that a criminal either leaves at the scene of a crime or inadvertently carries away from it. Very often, however, criminals leave discernible signs of their presence in the form of tracks and impressions, such as fingerprints, tool marks, shoe prints, tire tracks, and others, which can be equally effective means of connecting a suspect to a crime scene. The most significant of these are tool marks and fingerprints which, because of the unique complexities they present, are covered in more detail in separate chapters.

TRACKS AND IMPRESSIONS AS EVIDENCE

The tracks and impressions that an investigator is likely to find at a crime scene can be either in the form of indented impressions or residues. Indented impressions are those appearing in some yielding substance, such as mud, soft clay, wet sand, or snow, that record in relief the surface characteristics of the object making the print. Shoe prints and tire tracks at outdoor crime scenes and compression tool marks are perhaps the most common of these. Other examples are fingerprints pressed into some malleable material like soft candle wax, bite marks in flesh, and marks made in earth by an object being dragged. Residue prints are those recorded on a relatively hard surface by an object that has deposited some visible or detectable material onto it. Most finger-prints found in evidence are residue prints made by the deposit of oily secretions from the fingertips onto smooth surfaces. If a criminal steps in blood, wet paint, spilled cosmetic powder, or flour, there is a good chance that residue tracks of these substances will be deposited as the criminal continues walking.

These types of evidence are very often made on surfaces that cannot be transported to the laboratory because they are either built into the premises or are too massive to move or because moving them would result in destruction of the evidence. Although it is always pref-erable to take physical evidence to the laboratory intact if possible, in those cases in which tracks and impressions cannot be moved, they must be recorded at the scene by methods that will preserve them for laboratory investigation and future court testimony.

Apart from their value in connecting a criminal to a crime scene, tracks and impressions can sometimes be useful in reconstructing the crime and making deductions about the criminal. For example, the presence of different shoe prints may indicate that more than one criminal was involved. One track superimposed on another can help give an idea of the sequence of events. Running prints can often be differentiated from walking prints by the depth of the heel indenta-tions. Deductions about a person's height and weight can sometimes be made from the distance between the prints if enough prints are avail-able. A person of average weight normally walks in such a way that a straight line can be drawn through the person's heel marks. An over-weight person or someone carrying a heavy load tends to waddle some-what and place the feet farther apart from side to side so that the heel marks appear well to either side of a straight line drawn between them. The examiner must be careful not to place too much significance on conclusions drawn from this type of evidence because one observation may be susceptible to different interpretations.

RECORDING TRACKS AND IMPRESSIONS

Tracks and impressions can be recorded by means of photography, casting, or lifting. All imprints should be photographed before any other recording technique is used. Casting is used for indented impressions in order to capture the three-dimensional detail. Lifting techniques are used for residue-type prints.

Photography

Photographs should be taken both at a distance from the impression, to show the setting in which it occurs, and close up, to record the detail. Close-up pictures should be taken with the plane of the film parallel to the plane of the imprint in order to avoid angular distortion. Illumination should be oblique so that the details are highlighted by light and shadow. Several shots should be taken at different angles of illumination to ensure the best possible result. In the close-up shots a ruler should be laid next to the print to indicate proportions, and a piece of paper on which the date, time, and the investigator's initials are written should also be shown.

Casting

Although photographs are important records of the evidence and should always be taken in case the casts are unsuccessful or accidentally destroyed, good casts have an advantage for comparison purposes because they reproduce in three dimension the details of the object that made the impression. For example, the cast of a shoe print is in effect a positive replica of the shoe sole itself, and a direct, side-by-side comparison can be made when a suspect shoe is brought in. When dealing with tool impressions, casts are the only means of reproducing the microscopic details necessary for comparison and identification.

Gross Impressions

These are impressions like shoe prints and tire marks made in wet dirt, sand, or other soft materials that are incapable of capturing microscopic detail (see Figure 16–1). The best casting material for these prints is a fine-grade plaster of Paris, which is excellent for reproducing gross visible details and is relatively simple to use. Other materials are available for casts requiring microscopic precision.

Before a cast is made of the print, any foreign debris must be carefully picked out of the print with tweezers without disturbing the print itself. A hypodermic syringe can be used to draw out standing water. Since dirt or sand may tend to crumble easily, impressions are reinforced by a spray of a 50 percent solution of shellac dissolved in alcohol or by a commercial clear shellac spray. The spray is held a few feet above the print so that the shellac settles gently into it. If the spray is held too close, the air pressure may disturb the distinctive features of the impression. It is a good practice to make a test print in the same surface material in order to determine how many layers of shellac are

245

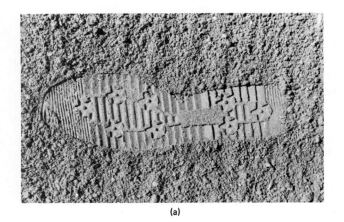

(a)

(b)

(c)

FIGURE 16–1 Plaster casting: (a) shoe print in dirt, (b) plaster hardening in a field expedient retaining frame made of strips of cardboard, (c) the finished cast compared side by side with the shoe that made the print.

needed to strengthen the print. When the shellac is dry, a thin coat of light oil is sprayed over it so that it does not adhere to the plaster. A frame to retain the wet plaster is built around the print before the plaster is poured. The frame can be made of wood, cardboard, mud, or any material that can form a retaining wall. The inner sides of this frame are sprayed with a light coat of oil to prevent the plaster from sticking to it.

The plaster is mixed according to the manufacturer's directions. The powder is stirred gradually into the water until the mixture reaches the correct consistency. Seven parts powder to four parts water is usually about right, but the person making the cast may want to vary this. A thick mixture hardens more quickly than a thin one, but a thin mixture gives better detail. One-half teaspoon of table salt can be added to the mixture for each pint of water to speed up the setting rate. If the officer needs more time to work on the cast, the setting time can be extended by adding a saturated solution of borax. It is best if the powder has been sifted; when it is not, the lumps must be removed or broken up by hand.

The plaster is never allowed to fall directly into the impression. Instead, the plaster is poured against some kind of baffle like a spoon or one's hand from which it can flow gently into the print. After a first layer of plaster has been poured to a thickness of from ½ inch to ¾ inch, a reinforcing material is added because hardened plaster is very brittle. Chicken wire is excellent for this purpose, but sticks, nails, or other odd pieces of wire can be used as field expedients. Then more plaster is poured on top of the reinforcements until the impression is completely filled. When the cast has thoroughly set, it must be carefully removed with due regard for its fragility. The film of shellac is peeled away and any bits of dirt clinging to the cast can be removed by rinsing it under a gentle stream of water or by brushing it with a soft brush.

When a plaster of Paris cast is to be made in snow, the procedure for reinforcing the print is slightly different. Since the hardening of plaster is an exothermic (heat producing) reaction, the heat melts the print if the print is not well protected. For purposes of insulation, a light layer of talcum powder is shaken into the print before the shellac is sprayed, and more talcum powder is spread between each layer of shellac. Because snow is such a delicate medium, test prints should definitely be made to see how many layers of shellac and powder are needed or whether another method might be more suitable. One other method is to dust a thin coat of plaster powder directly into the print, spray it with water, and as it begins to harden add the regular plaster mixture. Another is to pour molten sulfur directly into the print. The sulfur is melted in a pan and then allowed to begin cooling. As the first signs of crystallization begin to appear, but before it actually starts to harden, the sulphur is poured gently onto the print using a baffle as with plaster. It may seem surprising that this process does not melt the snow, but the crystallization of sulphur is in fact an endothermic (heat absorbing) reaction; therefore, the sulfur actually draws heat from the snow as it sets.

The officer who makes the cast should mark it with the date and time and his or her initials. This information should be scratched into the plaster before it has completely set. The position and orientation of the cast should be indicated on the crime scene sketch, and if more than one cast is made, each cast should be numbered and keyed to the sketch.

Shoe Prints

A three-dimensional cast of an indented impression is a replica of the object that made it. In the case of shoe prints the cast can be compared directly with suspect shoes. It is very common for the prints, and therefore the casts, to vary slightly in size from the shoes that made them. This difference may be due to the manner in which the impression was made. For example, prints made while running or struggling are likely to be enlarged. Or the difference may be due to the medium in which the print is found. Wet earth and clay contract when they dry. Prints in snow are inclined to enlarge because the edges melt slightly. If the size of the suspect shoe is significantly different from that of the cast, then, of course, that shoe cannot have made the print. Normally, old, worn shoes are more profitably compared with a cast than new shoes because it is the correspondence of unusual features that makes identification possible. These might include the wear pattern of the heel, holes in the sole, nicks, cuts, protruding nails, and manufacturer's symbols. If the shoes are too new to have any distinctive features, the best an examiner can do is state whether or not a certain shoe *could* have made a print. Also, the sooner a shoe is recovered after the crime, the greater the chances are of proving that it was that shoe that made a questioned mark, for much additional wear can obliterate the identifying features.

Tire Tracks

The examination of tire tracks entails similar considerations to shoe prints. A new tire is less likely to be identified than an old one, for road use not only wears a tread but adds distinctive nicks and cuts that serve to individualize a tire. Unlike shoes, a suspect tire should not be compared directly with a cast because a tire flattens considerably when it bears the weight of an automobile, thus making the track appear wider than the tire. Instead, test tracks should be made with the suspect vehicle and casts should be made of them. These casts can then be compared with the casts made of the evidence.

When casts of tire tracks are being made, a length showing the entire circumference of the tire should be cast if possible. The cast can be anywhere from 5 feet to 8 feet. If a single distinguishing mark appears in the impression, the point where this mark reappears indicates where the tire has completed a full turn. If this point cannot be seen, as much of the track as possible (up to 8 feet) should be cast. Since a single cast 8 feet in length would be clearly unmanageable, the casting must be done in sections. Each section must be labeled so that the sections can be layed out in correct order for examination or courtroom display.

Sometimes, when an automobile makes a turn, all four tires make marks that can be separately distinguished. If their tread patterns are different, it may be possible to identify the vehicle from the position of the tires even if the tracks show no unique signs of wear.

When no vehicle is recovered, it may be desirable to identify the make of a tire from its tracks. This can be done only if the laboratory maintains an up-to-date collection of tread samples for comparison purposes. Samples can be obtained from tire manufacturers or even from junkyards. Maintenance of such a collection entails some effort, but the rewards in the form of successful identifications make it worthwhile.

Other Tracks

Occasionally other tire treads, such as those made by bicycles, motorcycles, wagons, and other vehicles, must be investigated. These are handled in essentially the same way as automobile tire tracks.

Animal tracks are infrequent evidence in criminal investigations and they call for specialized knowledge. The more common animal tracks are those of cattle and horses which can be distinctive both in size and character. Cows have cloven hooves, larger than those of sheep, and horses' hooves are not only larger but usually solid and ordinarily shod. Hooves and horseshoes can show flaws and irregularities in the same way that shoes and tires do.

Microscopic Impressions

The reproduction of microscopic detail becomes necessary primarily in the examination of tool marks and hair scales. Since plaster of Paris cannot reproduce such fine detail, it is not suitable for these purposes.

Liquid silicone rubber is probably the most popular casting material today for use on tool marks. It is one of the easiest materials to use, and it faithfully reproduces the finest details. There are only two ingredients: a liquid rubber base and a catalyst that causes the base to harden by polymerization. The rubber base and the catalyst are mixed in proportions specified by the manufacturers. A first coat of the mixture is carefully brushed into the mark to make sure that no air bubbles are present, and more is poured in to fill the impression. The silicone rubber mixture begins to set in minutes at room temperature. The final casts are rubbery and very durable. Because no heat is involved, liquid silicone is also well suited for casting parts of the body. Silicone rubber is generally used to make negative casts, that is, reverse images of the object or impression, and normally negative casts are sufficient for tool mark comparison. If positive replicas are desired, positive moulage material or epoxy casting resin can be used with a silicone negative, or a silicone positive can be made from a moulage negative.

Moulage-agar compositions, originally developed for dental casting, were for a long time the traditional materials used for casting microscopic details in criminal work, but in modern practice they have been largely superseded by silicone because silicone is so much easier to use. Moulage can be used for the same purposes as silicone rubber, but since it is prepared by heating, it must be allowed to cool before casting body parts of living persons.

Moulage negative, which comes in powder or strips, is heated with water in the top of a double boiler. It can be made thinner by adding more water and thicker by adding more moulage material. The consistency of thick oatmeal is about right. Because moulage negative material begins to deteriorate soon after it sets, it can be used only as a mold from which casts of moulage positive can be made. If a permanent negative is desired, as often in the case of tool marks, positive moulage material can be used directly in an impression. Negative moulage is painted with a brush onto the impression to be cast and each successive layer is added before the previous one is dry. Careful brushing ensures that no air bubbles are trapped in it.

Moulage positive is a wax composition that can be melted in a pan directly over low heat. Because of the perishability of the negative material, the positive should be prepared immediately after the negative mold is completed. After the positive is melted, it is allowed to cool until it reaches a glue-like consistency and then it is poured into the negative mold. If it is poured too soon, its heat could melt the negative. If the replica is large, it should be reinforced with wire mesh. The completed positive cast can be readily tinted for photographic purposes to resemble the original object.

In the days before photography was as accessible as it is now moulage was used to make both life and death masks for identification purposes. Although this is seldom done today, moulage or silicone may still be used on body parts to record bite marks and other wounds and scars, the casts of which can then be compared with a set of teeth or a weapon. Casts of moulage and silicone can also be used in place of photography to record impressions that are difficult to reach with a camera. A serial number on an engine block is one example. When any of the liquid materials are used on corners or vertical surfaces, sheet metal molds can be used to hold the liquid in place while it sets. If these are not available, molds from pieces of cardboard can be fashioned by the investigator and held in place with an adhesive tape.

Thermoplastic materials such as Lucite can also be used to advantage in certain casting situations. These are clear plastic materials that melt and flow when heated. Their main advantage is that they are translucent and therefore can be used directly under a microscope with transmitted light. One such application is in the casting of hairs. A piece of thermoplastic the size of a microscope slide is placed on top of a hair or other small object to be cast and heated until it melts and flows around the object. Thermoplastic generally comes in thin strips and consequently is not very suitable for deep impressions. Silicone rubber or moulage materials are better adapted for these cases because, being liquid in their soft state, they fill an impression and provide a three-dimensional replica when they set.

Residue Prints

Residue tracks and prints are generally recorded by photography or a combination of photography and a lifting process. If the print shows sufficient color contrast with its background surface, as, for example, a bloody footprint on a light-colored floor, a photograph is the simplest and best means of reproduction. When a suspect shoe is recovered, a test print of it can be made for comparison purposes by rolling fingerprinting ink on its sole and heel and pressing it onto a sheet of plain white paper. The inked print can then be compared with a photograph of the evidence. Since the photograph would probably not be life-size, dimensions must be calculated on the basis of the ruler scale which should be included in all photographs. The examiner looks for the same kinds of flaws and irregularities that are used to identify impression prints.

Residue prints made with some loose substance like dust, talcum powder, or flour should be photographed where they are found if they are in good contrast to their backgrounds. Otherwise, they can be lifted by using sheets of commercial rubber lifter of the type used to lift latent fingerprints. The lifter is a sheet of black or white rubber that has one sticky side. The sticky side is carefully pressed onto the print and then

FIGURE 16–2 A residue footprint picked up with a transparent lifter. (Courtesy of Sirchie Finger Print Laboratories)

lifted. The material adhering to the rubber makes an excellent reproduction of the print. If the residue material is light colored, a black lifter should be used. If the residue material is dark colored, a white lifter should be used. Another method that can be used with a dark-colored residue is to pour a thin coat of liquid silicone rubber over it. After it has set, the silicone rubber is peeled up. The print comes up with it. The print should always be photographed before lifting in case the lift fails. A photograph in poor contrast is better than no evidence at all. After the print has been lifted, a permanent record of it can be made by photographing it on the lifter. (See Figure 16–2.)

Review Questions

1. Which of the following could not be considered a residue print?
   a. A bloody handprint
   b. Tracks made after walking through spilled flour
   c. Tire tracks made on pavement after driving through oil
   d. Tire tracks made in mud

2. A person carrying a heavy load
   a. Tends to walk in such a way that a straight line can be drawn between the person's heel marks without touching them
   b. Tends to walk in such a way that a straight line can be drawn through the person's heel marks
   c. Walks no differently from when the person is not carrying a heavy load
   d. Tends to walk in an "S" pattern

3. Photographs of tracks and impressions should be taken
   a. Before any other recording techniques are attempted
   b. With the film plane parallel to the print
   c. With a scale indicator
   d. All the above

4. (T, F) Molten sulfur cannot be used to make casts in snow because it melts the snow.

5. When a cast is being made with plaster of Paris,
   a. The plaster should be poured directly from the mixing bowl into the impression
   b. A thin mixture will record microscopic details
   c. The print should be reinforced by spraying shellac into it.
   d. Salt can be added to the mixture to retard the setting rate

6. A cast made of a shoe print in mud
   a. Is a positive replica of the impression
   b. Is a positive replica of the shoe
   c. Is exactly the same size as the shoe
   d. Can be compared directly with the impression

7. In the examination of tire tracks
   a. A single cast 8 feet long should be made of each track
   b. The cast should be compared directly with the suspect tire
   c. A cast of the evidence track should be compared with the cast of a track made by the suspect tire
   d. Nicks and irregularities caused by wear are used to identify the make and model of the tire

8. Microscopic details can be captured in casts made with
   a. Liquid silicone rubber
   b. High quality plaster
   c. Moulage
   d. Lucite
   e. a, c, and d
   f. a, b, and c

9. If a light-colored residue print is found against a light background, the print
   a. Should be lifted with a dark lifter
   b. Should be lifted with transparent adhesive tape
   c. Should be lifted with liquid silicone rubber
   d. Should not be lifted

CHAPTER SEVENTEEN

—— TOOL MARKS ——

The investigation of tool marks raises problems analagous to those encountered in firearms investigations. The characteristic markings that a gun leaves on bullets and cartridge cases are the result of a soft material being pressed or scraped forcefully against a harder material, thereby picking up an impression of its surface irregularities. The situation is the same in the case of tools; in fact, the marks left by firearms can be considered a specialized form of tool mark. However, the marks made by tools tend to be less consistent and therefore more difficult to identify than those made by firearms.

TOOL MARK EVIDENCE

Tool marks are often present in crimes involving breaking and entering. They may be found on the locks of doors or windows that a criminal has picked or jimmied in order to gain entrance, and they may be found on drawers, safes, strongboxes, and cash registers that have been pried open (see Figure 17–1).

Almost any kind of tool can play a role in crimes. Tools used for prying and leverage, such as knives, screwdrivers, chisels, crowbars, and tire irons, are probably the most common. Knives and screwdrivers are very often used because they are easy to conceal. Bolt cutters are

FIGURE 17-1 Scraping tool marks on a steel door that was pried open with a crowbar. (Courtesy of Connecticut State Police Forensic Laboratory)

often used to snap the hasps of padlocks, and hammers, saws, drill bits, augers, pliers, wrenches, and metal cutters have all been used at some time in connection with crimes.

The principal evidentiary value of tool marks lies in the possibility of matching them with the tool that made them. If a tool found in the possession of a suspect can be proved to have made the marks discovered at the scene of a crime, it becomes seriously incriminating evidence against that person. As in the case of firearms, tool marks are matched with the tools that made them by comparing the evidence marks found at the scene with test marks made under controlled laboratory conditions. In order to do this the tool must, of course, be recovered, and even then it is not always possible to prove a match. Marks made by saws and files, for example, are almost impossible to match up with the tools because tools like these are applied over and over again in the same spot so that each pass obscures the marks previously made. Sometimes the material in which the mark is made does not hold a clear impression. One is less likely to find identifiable tool marks on unpainted wood than on painted wood because the paint itself holds an impression while wood fibers tend to spring back slightly after an indentation is made in them.

Even when a perfect match cannot be proved or when the tool is not recovered, the marks can still constitute useful evidence. From the size and appearance of a mark the examiner may be able to state whether or not a certain tool *could* have made the mark, and the examiner may be able to exclude certain classes of tools from consideration. The examiner may also be able to deduce from the way the mark was made whether the criminal is right-handed or left-handed and whether or not the criminal is experienced in the use of the tool.

The probative value of a tool mark depends on the individual edge characteristics of the tool, for it is usually the working edge of the tool that makes the identifying marks. If a tool is old, the combination of corrosion and use will have given its edge a unique pattern, and the marks the tool makes will be quite distinctive. Tools that are machined or hand forged have unique characteristics even when they are new. The laboratory scientist must proceed with caution when examining new mass-produced tools. Some of them are so similar when they come from the factory that their edges are virtually indistinguishable from each other, and it is not until they receive some wear that they become individualized.

CHARACTERISTICS OF TOOL MARKS

Tool marks can be made by *compression, scraping,* and *shearing* or some combination of these. Compression marks are caused either by a sharp blow from an instrument, such as a hammer, or by pressing a tool forcibly into a softer material, as when the edge of a crowbar is gouged into paint or wood under leverage. Compression marks result in a negative image of the tool being impressed into the material (see Figure 17-2). Scraping marks are caused either by the lateral movement of a tool's edge across the surface of a softer material or by the shearing action of a cutting tool. These actions result in a series of parallel scratches that reflect the irregularities in the tool's edge.

Generally speaking, compression marks do not make as valuable evidence as scraping and shearing marks do. This is true partly because compression marks are most often found in wood, which tends not to hold a very faithful reproduction of the tool in its fine details, and partly because there is rarely a single clear-cut indentation. Most often there is a series of dents and gouges superimposed on each other that confuse the marks. If the face or edge of the tool has irregularities that are sufficiently pronounced and if the marks are not too badly obscured, in some cases it may be possible to identify the tool from the marks. Otherwise, the examiner may be limited to judging whether or not the tool could have made the mark.

Another compression mark is the type made by machinists' dies used to stamp serial numbers into metal. Some highly organized criminals, especially gangs specializing in car theft, grind down manufacturers' serial numbers and stamp new numbers in their places. When the dies used for these alterations are found on the premises of a suspect, they represent valuable evidence. Photographs and casts should be made of such marks before any attempt is made to restore the original serial numbers.

Scraping and shearing marks have proved more useful in criminal investigations because they can be more readily associated with the tool. When a tool is scraped laterally across a surface, it makes parallel scratches. These scratches are actually alternating ridges and valleys cut into the surface by minute irregularities in the metal, and they are

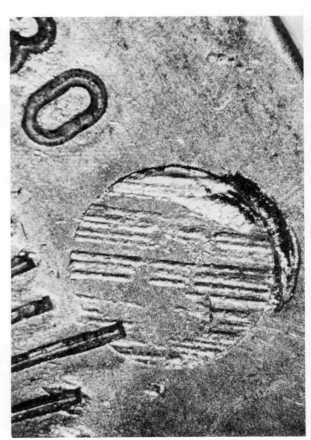

FIGURE 17-2 (a) Punch mark made on the dial of a burglarized safe; (b) test mark made in lead with a recovered suspect punch; (c) comparison of the striations of the evidence mark and the test mark. (Courtesy of Boston Police Technical Services Section)

(a)

(b)

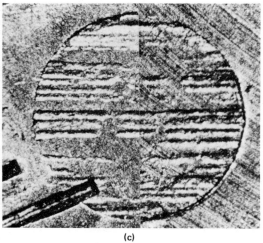

(c)

FIGURE 17–2 *continued*

duplicated every time the tool is used in the same manner until something happens to alter the tool's edge characteristics. These kinds of marks are found more often on painted surfaces and on metal, particularly door locks. Both of these surfaces clearly retain the microscopic details needed to prove that the scratches were made by a particular tool.

Shearing marks are made by cutting tools. Knives and other bladed tools may leave identifiable marks when they are used to cut with a sideways motion. If the motion is saw-like, the marks probably have no evidentiary value. The shearing marks that are probably found most frequently in criminal investigations are those made by the various forms of wire cutters. These range from pliers used to cut light-weight wires to bolt cutters used to cut heavy fence wire or padlock hasps. These tools, which actually pinch the metal in two, usually have irregular cutting edges that leave very distinct impressions.

Many tool marks are produced by a combination of compression and scraping. Hammer blows, for example, usually glance slightly to one side or the other when they strike. When a crowbar, screwdriver, or other tool is used to pry open a door or window, it makes scraping marks as it is forced into a suitable position for leverage. The gouge that the tool makes in the wood is basically a compression mark, but the tool also produces scraping marks along the side of the gouge as it digs in.

FIELD INVESTIGATION OF TOOL MARKS

Officers should be alert for tool marks whenever they are investigating crimes involving breaking and entering or the forcible opening of a container.

Any marks found at a scene should be photographed, first at a sufficient distance to show their general location and then in close-up to show the detail.

If possible, the object bearing the tool marks should be brought to the laboratory and the marks themselves protected from contact with anything that might alter them. If the object is part of the permanent installation of the premises or is otherwise too massive to transport, a laboratory technician or an investigating officer trained in casting techniques should make several casts of the marks out of some suitable material such as liquid silicone or dental moulage. Casting techniques are described in Chapter 16.

In compression marks investigators may be tempted to insert a tool recovered at the scene into the impression to see if it fits. This is a dangerous practice, for even a light touch of the tool could alter some of the microscopic features of the marks. No foreign object, including a suspect tool, must be allowed to touch tool marks until all photographs and casts have been made. If the marks are on a portable object, nothing should be allowed to touch the object before it reaches the laboratory.

LABORATORY INVESTIGATION

As with markings made by firearms, the laboratory examination of tool marks consists of comparing evidence marks with standard marks made with suspect tools in the laboratory. When the edge of a tool is damaged or grossly irregular from misuse, the marks it makes may sometimes reflect these irregularities so clearly that it is possible to make a direct visual comparison between the marks and the tool. In these circumstances the two can be photographed side by side to show the way the irregularities match. The more common procedure, however, is to duplicate the evidence marks as clearly as possible with the suspect tool and then compare the different sets of marks.

In the preliminary examination the criminalist checks the tool under low powers of a microscope for the presence of any trace evidence like paint smears or particles of metal or wood which might serve as clues. Then the criminalist makes overall visual comparisons to see if the tool is of the right general size and type to have made the mark in question.

If the criminalist decides that the suspect tool could have made the mark, the next step is to try to determine just how the mark was made. With experience and close observation it is often possible to tell what kind of motion was used in applying the tool. If it is a bladed tool like a knife or screwdriver, there is usually no way of telling which side of the blade was used. When the examiner has made as close a determination as possible about the nature of the mark, the examiner must make a series of marks with the suspect tool in different positions in the expectation that some of them will be similar enough to the evidence mark to allow a comparison. In the case of wire cutters or other cutting tools, sample cuts must be made all along the blade since any part of the blade could have been used on the evidence samples.

Whenever possible, the standard marks should be made in the same type of material as the evidence marks were made. If the evidence is a compression mark in wood, no other material can duplicate it in quite the same way, and even different kinds of wood give different results. If the evidence marks are in a soft metal, the same type of metal should be used for the standards, but if they are in steel or some other hard metal, the standards should be made in a soft metal like lead or aluminum, because it gives a similar photographic appearance but is not so likely to alter the edge of the tool.

Compression Marks

Compression marks are usually identified by comparing a photograph of the evidence with photographs taken of the standards. If the impression is especially deep, casts can be made of both the evidence and the standard marks and compared to each other, or a cast of the evidence impression can be compared directly with the tool itself. These procedures allow a comparison in three dimensions that can reveal irregularities in the overall shape of the tool as well as in its face. Each set of photographs must be taken under exactly the same conditions so that the relationships of the irregularities to each other can be measured and compared. In this regard it is sometimes useful to use photographic transparencies because they can be laid one over the other to see if the irregular features coincide.

Scraping and Shearing Marks

Scraping and shearing marks can best be identified under a comparison microscope in the same manner as bullet striations. If possible, the actual mark should be compared directly with the standard marks made in the laboratory. If the object bearing the marks cannot be brought to the laboratory or if it is too bulky to fit under the microscope, casts have to be used. Since the casts will be compared under a microscope, it is important to use casting materials that will produce the minutest details. Liquid silicone rubber is well adapted for making negative casts and is relatively easy to apply. Silicones have largely replaced dental moulage because the latter is more complicated, but moulage is excellent for reproducing fine details and may still be used when positive casts are desired.

Either positives or negatives can be used as long as both samples are the same in any given comparison. The evidence mark or its cast is placed on one stage of a comparison microscope and the standard is placed on the other. They must be placed at the same distance from the objective and arranged so that one-half the evidence mark and one-half the standard appear in the eyepiece. The illumination must be oblique and perpendicular to the direction of the lines so that the ridges and valleys appear as lines of light and shadow. The samples are adjusted so that the scratch lines are oriented in the same direction, and the standard is moved around until a significant number of the lines in the two halves of the picture seem to flow into each other. (See Figure 17-3.)

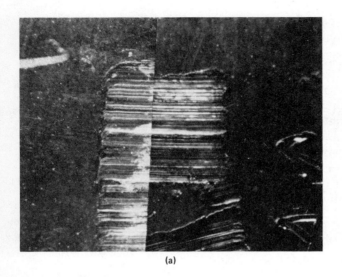

(a)

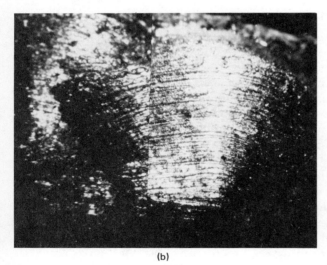

(b)

FIGURE 17-3 Some examples of scraping tool marks matched under the comparison microscope. Evidence marks are on the left, test marks on the right. Mark (a) was made with a screwdriver; mark (b) is a turning from milling machine. (Courtesy of Connecticut State Police Forensic Laboratory)

Because there are so many possible variations in the way a tool can make marks, it is rare that the lines of any two samples correspond across the entire mark. If one definite area of correspondence is found, it is accepted as virtual proof of identity, and usually if one such area is found, others can be found with further observation. There is no fixed rule as to how many lines must coincide to prove a match. When there is a match, it is usually clear enough to be beyond doubt. In questionable cases the examiner can have another examiner repeat the observation, but in the end it comes down to a matter of experience and judgment.

Review Questions

1. The principal evidential value of tool marks
   a. Lies in the possibility of matching the tool marks with the tool that made them
   b. Is to identify the type of tool that made the mark
   c. Is to connect a suspect with the scene of a crime
   d. a and c

2. Which of the following tools probably produce the least valuable evidence marks?
   a. Bolt cutters
   b. Crowbars
   c. Screwdrivers
   d. Files

3. Two newly mass-produced tools of the same type can best be distinguished from each other
   a. By their wear marks
   b. By their corrosion marks
   c. After they have received some wear
   d. By compression marks

4. (T, F) The examination of tool marks involves problems similar to those in the examination of striations found on fired bullets.

5. Tool marks can be made by
   a. Compression
   b. Scraping
   c. Shearing
   d. All the above

6. A clear tool mark can be found on which type of surface?
   a. Metal
   b. Wood
   c. Painted wood
   d. a and c
   e. a, b, and c

7. Which of the following should the criminalist *not* do to a tool mark?
   a. Take a photograph of the tool mark
   b. Make a cast of the tool mark
   c. Insert a tool to see if it fits the tool mark
   d. Transport the tool mark to the laboratory

8. In the preliminary examination the criminalist
   a. Checks the tool for trace evidence
   b. Sees whether or not the tool is the right general size and shape to have made the mark
   c. Tries to determine just how the mark was made
   d. All the above

9. If the tool mark was made in steel, the standard should be made in
   a. Steel
   b. Wood
   c. Lead
   d. Any of the above

10. (T, F) By examining a tool mark carefully, a criminalist can always tell whether it was made by a right-handed or left-handed person.

11. (T, F) A tool mark made on a portable object should be first photographed and then cast before it is transported to the laboratory.

12. (T, F) The scanning electron microscope is the best instrument for examining tool marks.

CHAPTER EIGHTEEN

—— FINGERPRINTS ——

Fingerprints, through the influence of movies, television, and detective fiction, are the form of physical evidence with which the public has become most familiar. This general familiarity with the subject tends to lend a greater importance to fingerprints in the mind of the public than they actually have in criminal investigation. Many people think they leave a fingerprint every time they touch something. This is far from true. The chances of leaving a readable print depend on the surface of the item that is touched, the condition of the fingers, and the way one handles the item. A great many of the materials with which a criminal may come into contact are unlikely to receive fingerprints of sufficient clarity to be useful as evidence. When fingerprints are found at a crime scene, the majority of the prints are unreadable smudges or fragmentary prints of dubious value. Moreover, since criminals are as aware as anybody else of the incriminating nature of fingerprints, if they are going to make any effort at all to avoid leaving clues, that is the one thing they will surely be careful about.

In spite of these limitations, it is fair to say that when clear fingerprints are found at a crime scene, they surpass all other physical evidence in their ability to identify the person who left them. Although other kinds of trace evidence, such as blood and hair, may be unique to each person, there is as yet no way of readily individualizing and classifying them, and they may undergo changes in the course of a person's life. Fingerprints, however, are completely individual characteristics. No two fingers have ever been found to have identical prints, and it is an overwhelming mathematical probability that no two ever will be found to match. Human fingerprints are formed in the human fetus before birth and remain the same throughout a person's life and after death until they are lost through decomposition. Moreover, fingerprints are made up of a number of easily recognizable features that permit them to be classified and filed for later reference. Thus it is possible, when the prints are on file, to identify not only criminals but also amnesia victims and unidentified corpses.

CHARACTERISTICS OF FINGERPRINTS

Fingerprints are impressions produced by the roughly parallel raised lines of skin which come together to form a pattern in the central portion of the end joints of the fingers. These raised lines, known as *friction ridges,* also exist on the palms of the hands and on the bottoms of the feet. Palm prints and bare footprints are also unique to each individual, and when such impressions found at a crime scene are compared with like prints taken from suspects, they are as conclusive as fingerprints in proving identity. Friction ridges are so called because they aid in grasping and holding in much the same way that an automobile tire tread grasps and holds. Along each of these ridges is a series of pores, which are connected by ducts to sweat glands in the dermis, or underlayer of the skin. These pores continuously exude small amounts of perspiration.

The patterns formed by the ridges never change throughout a person's life. Criminals have often tried to change or destroy their fingerprints, but without success. The fingerprints always grow back in exactly the same pattern, or if the damage is severe enough, they are replaced by patches of scar tissue, which themselves form identifiable patterns.

Fingerprints found at a crime scene appear in three different forms: *visible, plastic,* and *latent.* Visible fingerprints, sometimes also called *contaminated fingerprints,* are a form of residue print. They appear when the friction ridges deposit some visible material like ink, blood, grease, or dirt onto a surface, thereby reproducing their pattern. Plastic fingerprints are those made in some soft material like tacky paint, soft wax, putty, or partially congealed blood, which retains a negative impression of the ridge pattern. The word plastic in this sense refers to something that is capable of being molded. In this type of print the valleys in the impression correspond to the ridges of the finger. A related kind of print is that made in dust. The sweat-moistened friction ridges remove dust from a surface and leave lines of dust corresponding to the valleys between the ridges of the fingers. The fingerprints most commonly found in criminal investigations are the latent type. The word latent means hidden, and the prints are so called because they are invisible or not readily visible and must be developed either by the use of powders or by chemical means to make them useful as evidence. Latent prints are usually the result of perspiration, often combined with natural body oils, being deposited on a surface. Perspiration is approximately 98 percent water with small amounts of acids, urea, and mineral salts, including ordinary sodium chloride, in solution. The sweat glands of the hands and feet do not produce oils themselves, but oils are almost always present on the fingers from touching other parts of the body which do produce them.

In general, latent prints can be most easily developed when they occur on smooth, nonporous surfaces like metal, plastic, glass, and painted objects. Latents made on paper, bare wood, and occasionally even fabrics can also be valuable as evidence, but the tendency of these porous materials to absorb the oils and perspiration can result in a loss of line clarity.

CLASSIFICATION

The purpose of classifying fingerprints is so that they can be filed and retrieved when needed to make identifications. The various classifications systems used throughout the world are based on all ten fingers. Single-finger files are kept only on a limited number of known criminals. Consequently, for the most part, it is impossible to make an identification from fingerprint files on the basis of a single print found at the scene of a crime. The FBI system used in the United States is a modification of the Henry system, which was first devised in England at the beginning of this century. Fingerprint classification is a complicated procedure and entails a whole course of study in itself. Here we will confine ourselves to the fundamental principals.

The FBI and other classification systems are based on the patterns formed by the friction ridges in the center of the fingertips. These patterns fall into three general classes called *arches, loops,* and *whorls.*

Arches are the simplest patterns and also the rarest. There are two types: *plain arches* and *tented arches* (see Figure 18-1). In both types the ridge lines flow into the print from one side, rise in the middle of the pattern, and flow out the other side of the print. Plain arches show a gradual rise. Tented arches rise more sharply and form an angle of less than 90 degrees at the top. Tented arches sometimes have a single ridge

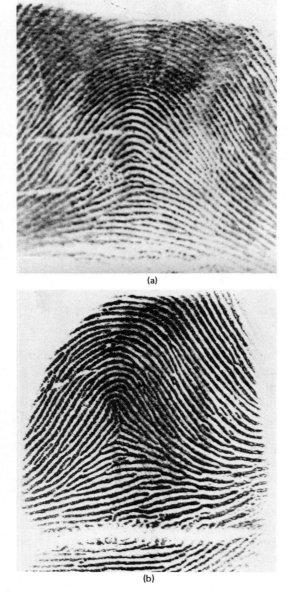

(a)

(b)

FIGURE 18–1 (a) Plain arch, (b) tented arch. (Courtesy of Boston Police Technical Services Section)

line rising up to the center of the arch which gives the appearance of a tent pole.

Loops are formed by ridge lines that flow in from one side of the print, sweep up in the center like a tented arch, and then curve back around and flow out or tend to flow out on the side where they entered

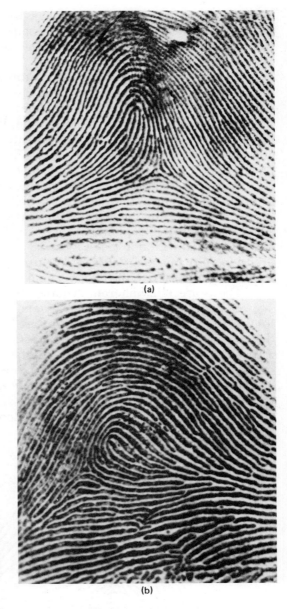

FIGURE 18–2 Two examples of loops (a) with ridge lines entering from the left; (b) with ridge lines entering from the right. (Courtesy of Boston Police Technical Services Section)

(see Figure 18-2). Loops are designated as being either *radial* or *ulnar*, depending on which side of the finger the lines enter. These terms refer to the two bones of the human forearm, the *radius* and the *ulna*. The radius is the bone that lies on the same side of the arm as the thumb; consequently, a radial loop is one in which the ridge lines enter and exit in the direction of the thumb. The ulna is the bone that lies on the same side of the arm as the little finger; consequently, the loops that enter from that direction are called ulnar. The loop is the most common of all the patterns.

Every fingerprint having a loop pattern also contains a *delta* and a *core*. Although the ridges that form the loop enter and exit on the same side of the print, other ridge lines which are not part of the pattern itself enter from the opposite side. Where these lines run into the recurving line of the loop, they spread apart like a fork in a river and tend to surround the pattern area. The point where they spread open is called the delta because of its somewhat triangular appearance (like the Greek letter Δ). The two innermost ridges which spread apart to begin surrounding the pattern are called *type lines.* The core is simply the approximate center of the pattern as defined either by the top of the innermost looping ridge or by single straight ridge lines called *rods* contained within it. (See Figure 18-3.) For a pattern to be considered a loop, an imaginary straight line drawn from the core to the delta must cross at least one of the recurving ridge lines.

There are four different whorl patterns: the *plain whorl,* the *central pocket loop,* the *double loop,* and the *accidental whorl* (see Figure 18-4). Their common features are that they have at least two deltas and one or more of the ridge lines curves around the core to form a circle or spiral or other rounded, constantly curving form.

In a plain whorl one or more ridges make a complete circle, and an imaginary line drawn between the two deltas must touch or pass through at least one of them.

The central pocket loop is like a plain loop except that one or more

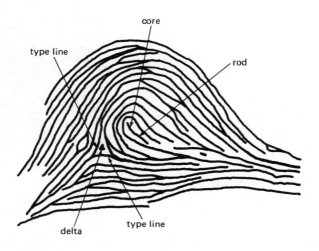

FIGURE 18–3

of the innermost lines curves around to enclose the core in a circle, or pocket. A line drawn between the deltas of a central pocket loop may not cross any of the lines forming the pocket.

The double loop is a pattern containing two distinct loops. In addition to the two deltas, this pattern has two separate cores, one in

(a)

FIGURE 18–4 (a) Plain whorl; (b) double loop; (c) central pocket loop; (d) accidental whorl. (Courtesy of Boston Police Technical Services Section)

(b)

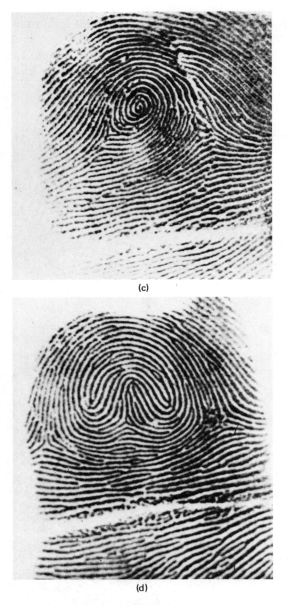

(c)

(d)   **FIGURE 18-4**   *continued*

each loop. The accidental whorl can be any pattern or combination of
patterns that does not fit into any of the above classifications.

The FBI ten-finger classification system is broken down into seven
possible subdivisions based on the way these patterns appear on the
different fingers. When an identification is made from fingerprint files,

each successive subdivision further narrows down the possibilities until the number of choices is small enough to permit the final identification to be made by a visual comparison of the prints. The FBI and the principal law enforcement agencies of other countries have converted or are in the process of converting to computerized filing systems that can read, classify, and retrieve prints automatically. Although the computer systems greatly speed up the identification process, they still do not eliminate the identification officer who must make the final determination by point-by-point comparison.

COMPARING FINGERPRINTS

A major task of a fingerprint identification officer is to compare the fingerprints found at a crime scene with those of known criminals and samples taken from suspects. Although the pattern classification described above quickly eliminates most nonmatching prints, many partial prints found in criminal investigations are so fragmental that the pattern areas do not show up at all. Identifications must be based on more detailed examination of the ridge characteristics, which are independent of the patterns (see Figure 18-5). Some of the features that the examiner looks for are ridge endings, bifurcations (forks), dots, enclosures, and others. If a sufficient number of these characteristics are found in the same relative position to each other on evidence prints and on prints taken from a suspect and if no differences are seen, the prints are considered to be from the same finger. There is no absolute established standard for the number of matching ridge characteristics, or *points,* that must be present to prove identity. Most authorities require at least 8 points and some require 12 or more points (see Figure 18-6). But a correspondence of fewer points might still constitute virtual proof, if not legal proof, and therefore be useful for investigative purposes. This is most likely to be true in the case of small partials in which there may simply not be many points available for reference.

Another possible means of identification lies in the position of the

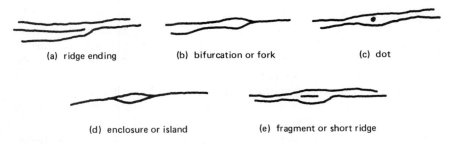

(a) ridge ending   (b) bifurcation or fork   (c) dot

(d) enclosure or island   (e) fragment or short ridge

FIGURE 18-5

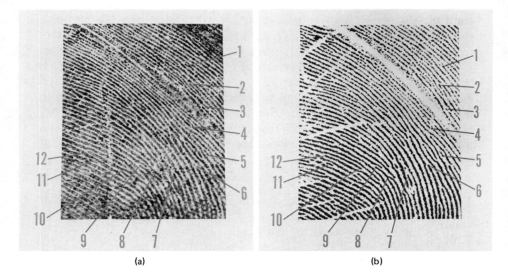

(a)   (b)

FIGURE 18–6   (a) A partial latent print recovered at a crime scene; (b) is the corresponding portion of a suspect's inked print. The 12 matching points with no other discrepancies constitute legal proof of identity. (Courtesy of Connecticut State Police Forensic Laboratory)

pores along the friction ridges. The pore patterns are completely individual and can be successfully used to make identifications from a small fragment of the print. The problem is that conventional developing and lifting methods are generally not sensitive enough to record the pore arrangements with sufficient fidelity to permit a comparison.

DEVELOPING LATENT PRINTS

The development, or *raising,* of fingerprints is a matter of providing color contrast between the print and its background so that it can be photographed or otherwise preserved for later comparison. Visible and plastic prints can generally be photographed as they are found and therefore do not need to be developed. Although a visible print may require some attention if the residue is the same color as the background, it is usually the latent print that needs to be developed. Latents are traditionally developed by powders or by chemical means, and the latest advance in the field involves the detection of prints by laser-induced luminescence. For the traditional methods, it is the nature of the surface on which the prints are found that dictates which method to use. In general, powders are used to develop prints on smooth, nonporous surfaces and chemicals are used to develop prints on absorbent materials like paper, wood, or cloth. The laser technique is effective on all surfaces and may work when other techniques fail.

Powders

A considerable variety of fingerprint powders is produced commercially in different colors, and there will normally be several different ones in an investigator's kit. The choice depends primarily on the background color of the surface. For the most part, black powders are used on light-colored surfaces (see Figure 18-7) and white or gray powders are used on dark backgrounds, but there may be situations in which a powder of a different color provides the best contrast. One problem that sometimes arises is in raising a print on a variegated background where none of the usual colored powders provides an adequate contrast. In such a case the print can be developed with a fluorescent powder which can be photographed using ultraviolet illumination.

All fingerprint powders work by adhering to the perspiration or oily residues deposited by the friction ridges. Normally, the powder is applied by means of a soft-bristled camel's hair brush. Magnetic brushes are also available. These are pencil-shaped devices with one magnetized end which picks up a loose clump of special magnetic powder. The clump of powder is applied to the print in the same manner as

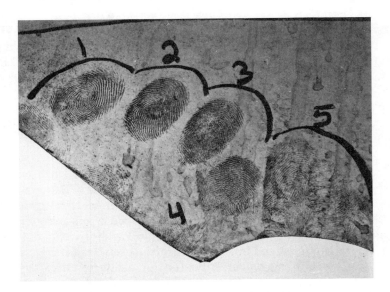

FIGURE 18–7 Fingerprints developed with black powder on a fragment of broken glass found at the scene of a breaking and entering. (Courtesy of Connecticut State Police Forensic Laboratory)

powder from a camel's hair brush. The magnetic brush can then be demagnetized to return unused powder to the bottle. Since the magnetic brush has no bristles, there is no possibility of spoiling the print by brushing too hard. However, the standard camel's hair brushes do an excellent job if used properly, and most investigators still use them. To dust a print with a brush, one pours a small amount of powder into a jar cap or other flat, shallow receptacle and the ends of the bristles are dipped lightly into it. Only a small amount of powder is needed. This is brushed lightly onto the print, following the ridge lines as much as possible. After the print is powdered, the remaining powder is knocked off the brush and the clean brush is used to remove excess powder from the print. Again, the brush motion follows the lines of the print pattern. Different colored powders should never be used on the same brush.

Chemical Methods

Although powders can sometimes be used successfully on paper if the prints are relatively fresh, chemical methods are more commonly used because they do not rely on moisture remaining in the print but rather on a chemical reaction taking place between the developer and organic or inorganic compounds in the deposit. Powders are not at all suitable for more absorbent and porous materials like cloth and wood.

The chemicals most commonly used for developing old prints and prints on porous materials are *ninhydrin* and *silver nitrate.* While these reagents can produce excellent results, prints developed by them often come out with a fragmentary, spotty look. This uneven effect is due to differences in the amount of reactive materials deposited in the print. The constituents of perspiration can vary considerably from person to person and from one time to another in the same person. Therefore, an examiner cannot always expect satisfactory results when chemical methods are used.

Ninhydrin

Ninhydrin is an all-purpose developer that reacts with amino acids deposited in the perspiration. It is an easy method to use and it is capable of raising prints that are many months old. A 0.3 percent to 0.6 percent solution of the reagent in acetone (300 milligrams to 600 milligrams ninhydrin dissolved in 100 milliliters acetone) is usually sprayed onto the print and the object is heated for a few minutes at 110°C (225°F). The prints appear as a light purple-red color. If the object cannot be conveniently heated, the print generally emerges at room temperature in an hour or two, but if the reaction is weak, it may not appear for over 24 hours. One disadvantage of the ninhydrin test is that when it is used to develop prints on documents, the acetone dissolves most inks and causes them to run.

Silver Nitrate

This is one of the older chemical procedures that is still in wide use for prints from several weeks to several years old. A 3 percent to 5 percent solution of silver nitrate ($AgNO_3$) in distilled water (3 grams to 5 grams $AgNO_3$ dissolved in 100 milliliters H_2O) is brushed lightly onto the print, or the print-bearing item can be dipped into the solution. The silver nitrate reacts with the common salt (NaCl) which is present to some degree in all perspiration, and insoluble silver chloride (AgCl) is precipitated along the ridge lines. The paper or object that bears the print is washed to remove the excess silver nitrate solution and then it is allowed to dry in darkness. Later, the print is exposed to light. The light causes the silver chloride to break down into chlorine gas and free silver, which outlines the pattern of ridges in black. When the print has reached its optimum darkness, it can be fixed with photographic hypo, which removes any remaining silver chloride that has not been broken down by the light. If it is not fixed, the print continues to grow blacker and blacker as long as it is exposed to light until the lines are no longer clear.

Ninhydrin and silver nitrate can both be used on the same print, but ninhydrin should always be used first because the silver nitrate solution removes the amino acids from the print but ninhydrin does not affect the sodium chloride.

Iodine Fuming

This is an old but still useful method of temporarily making a print visible. It is not strictly a chemical technique because a chemical reaction does not take place. Iodine vapor is readily absorbed by the oily residues deposited in fingerprints, and as long as the iodine is retained by the oils it outlines the ridge patterns in a brownish-yellow color. However, the iodine evaporates very quickly from the prints after they stop being fumed. If the investigator wants to use iodine as the only developer, he or she must be ready with a camera to photograph the prints before they fade. Fumed prints can be preserved by treating them with starch or sealing them off from the air, but since it is so much easier to make a lasting development with ninhydrin, the only practical use that iodine still retains is in testing surfaces for the presence of fingerprints. If the objects suspected to bear prints are small enough, they can be tested by being enclosed in a cabinet along with iodine crystals, which will give off vapors when slightly heated. Otherwise, a fuming gun can be used. A simple fuming gun can be made by packing

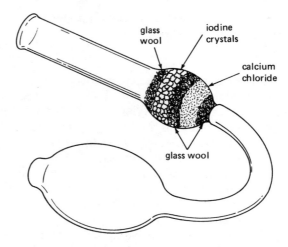

FIGURE 18–8   Iodine fuming gun.

iodine crystals between layers of glass wool in a plastic or glass drying tube and pumping air through it with a rubber bulb. Calcium chloride or some other drying agent should be packed between the iodine crystals and the air source in order to remove the moisture from the air (see Figure 18-8). By placing one's hand around the portion of the tube containing the iodine, the crystals become warm enough to cause them to emit vapors, which can be directed onto the area to be tested.

Laser Luminescence

This latest method, developed in Canada by the Ontario Provincial Police and the Xerox Research Center of Canada,[1] has been found to be effective on very old fingerprints and on prints appearing on surfaces that would normally not yield usable prints. The principle of the technique is based on the ability of highly energetic laser light to induce luminescence in latent prints. A continuous wave argon-ion laser, which produces a beam of light at a wavelength of 514.5 nanometers, is used. The beam is projected through a lens that disperses the beam to cover an area of approximately 65 cm²(10 in²). When excited by the laser light, materials in the fingerprint deposit luminesce in a range from yellow-green to orange. Fresh prints luminesce in the yellow-green range while older prints luminesce more in the orange range. The luminescence can be observed visually if the viewer wears safety goggles that are opaque to the laser wavelength. The lumines-

[1]B. E. Dalrymple, J. M. Duff, and E. R. Menzel, "Inherent Fingerprint Luminescence—Detection by Laser," *Journal of Forensic Sciences,* 22, no. 1 (1977) 106–15.

cent prints can also be recorded photographically. When prints illuminated by laser luminescence are to be photographed, a special filter must be used which absorbs light at 514.5 nanometers but allows light in the yellow-green to orange range to pass into the camera. The reason for this is that the laser light, being so much more intense than the luminescence, would obscure the luminescence if it were allowed to strike the film. The only time the laser luminescence technique is not effective is when the fingerprint appears on a surface that luminesces with the same color as the print. Of course, no technique can be effective if the print itself is unclear.

PRESERVING FINGERPRINT EVIDENCE

A good rule to follow in dealing with fingerprints is not to tamper with them any more than is absolutely necessary. Therefore, if prints appear with good contrast on a small, portable object, it is best to retain the object itself as evidence instead of trying to treat the prints separately. However, many fingerprints appear on fixed locations which make it necessary to preserve the print apart from the object on which it is found. The principal method of preservation is photography. Every fingerprint should be photographed both as it is found at the crime scene and after development. In most cases a light source almost parallel to the plane of the print gives the best results, but prints on clear glass can be illuminated by back lighting, and glass containers can be filled with dark- or light-colored liquids as needed for contrast. The simplest camera to use is the fingerprint camera which is specifically designed for this purpose and which produces a picture in the same scale as the print, but a 35mm or other camera that has a suitable close-up lens can be used with good results.

When prints are dusted with powder and the background does not provide good contrast for photography, lifters can be used to pick the print up off the object. Various kinds of opaque and transparent lifters are available. The most common opaque lifters are sheets of either black or white rubber that have one sticky side. The sticky side is protected with a clear plastic cover sheet. In lifting a print, a piece of the lifter is cut to the appropriate size for the print, the plastic cover is pulled back, and the lifter is pressed against the print. The powder adheres to the sticky rubber and the plastic strip is replaced to protect the impression. A white lifter is used on a print developed with a dark powder, and a black lifter is used for white or gray powder. Several lifts can usually be taken from the same print, and often the second and third lifts are clearer than the first lift because the powder is not too thick. Prints lifted with opaque lifters are mirror images of the prints found at the scene; therefore, they must be photographed and printed with the negative reversed so that they are oriented correctly for comparison. Also, it is customary to photographically reverse the colors of prints developed with white powder because examiners are accustomed to associating the dark lines with the friction ridges and the white lines with the spaces between them.

Transparent lifters come either in rolls of adhesive tape or in sheets which, like the opaque lifters, have one sticky side protected by a thin plastic strip. The sheets are used in the same manner as the opaque rubber sheets, the only difference being that the print can be examined through the lifter in its proper orientation. Transparent tape lifters must be unrolled smoothly because any hesitation causes a line to appear across the adhesive material. The tape must be pressed onto the print with a smooth motion to avoid trapping air bubbles under it. When the tape is lifted, the print comes up with it and can be preserved by pressing the tape onto a piece of clear glass or a smooth white plastic. Tape should never be used to lift prints from paper because the tape pulls up paper fibers along with the fingerprint.

Iodine-fumed prints can be lifted by pressing a piece of thin polished silver plate against the fumed print and then exposing the plate to sunlight or ultraviolet light. The iodine combines with the silver to form silver iodide, and the light converts this to iodine vapor and free metallic silver, which appears black against the polished silver plate. Although iodine-fumed prints are seldom lifted any more, this technique can still be useful for prints on greasy surfaces where powders cannot be used and there is insufficient color contrast for other chemical means which can be preserved only by photography.

SEARCHING THE CRIME SCENE

The investigator searching the crime scene for fingerprints should proceed systematically and should use common sense. It is usually good practice to start at the entrance and proceed clockwise around the area, gradually working toward the center. All objects and surfaces that the criminal is likely to have touched should be checked. This might include glasses, silverware, articles of furniture, walls, doors, and windows in a house and door handles and rearview mirrors in an automobile. Steering wheels and dashboards should also be checked, but they seldom yield good prints. A good strong flashlight is an invaluable aid because many latent prints show up when observed with an oblique light.

The investigator can often tell from impressions in a rug, uneven dust deposits, or scratches on a floor whether articles of furniture were moved, and the investigator should pay attention to possible fingerprints on the undersides of such articles.

The entire crime scene should be photographed before the search begins so that the exact unaltered location of any object bearing fingerprints can be seen. Prints should be photographed both before and after developing and their exact position should be recorded in the investigator's notes and indicated in a sketch of the scene.

Investigators should wear rubber gloves while processing the scene in order to avoid leaving their own prints.[2] They must also be sure to record the fingerprints of all persons having legitimate access to the scene so that these persons' prints can be eliminated from the investigation.

When fingerprint technicians are not available at the crime scene, portable objects bearing fingerprints should be sent to the laboratory for processing. When such objects are being prepared for transmittal, they should never be wrapped in cloth or paper because these materials are more likely to smear a print than protect it. It is best to try to wedge the object snugly in a strong box in such a way that the surface bearing the print is not touched by the packing materials. The box should be labeled with the usual information concerning the date, the time, and the place of recovery and the investigator's identifying mark. The label should also clearly indicate the nature of the evidence so that anyone opening the box will not destroy the prints.

Review Questions

1. (T, F) Most fingerprints found at crime scenes are of great evidential value.
2. A person's identity can be determined by
   a. Bare footprints
   b. Palm prints
   c. Fingerprints
   d. All the above
3. Fingerprints found at a crime scene can appear as
   a. Visible
   b. Plastic
   c. Latent.
   d. All the above

[2]Not all investigators agree with this. Some feel that if they accidentally leave a print, they at least know whose print it is, whereas if they wear gloves, the gloves can leave unidentifiable smudges that can confuse the evidence.

4. Latent prints are usually the result of perspiration, which is made up of
   a. Water
   b. Mineral salts
   c. Blood
   d. Urea
   e. a, b, and d

5. Latent prints can be most easily developed on
   a. Wood
   b. Fabrics
   c. Glass
   d. Paper

6. The patterns formed by the friction ridges in the center of the fingerprint are called
   a. Circles
   b. Arches
   c. Loops
   d. Whorls
   e. b, c, and d

7. (T, F) Investigative agencies can usually identify a person from fingerprint files on the basis of a single print.

8. When two ridge lines come together to form a triangular appearance, they are called
   a. Arches
   b. Loops
   c. Whorls
   d. Delta

9. Iodine fumes adhere to
   a. Oil
   b. Amino acids
   c. Sodium chloride
   d. Proteins

10. Which of the following may be used for developing old prints?
    a. Powder
    b. Silver nitrate
    c. Iodine fuming
    d. Ninhydrin
    e. b and d

11. Prints lifted with opaque lifters
    a. Do not need to be photographed
    b. Must be photographically reversed
    c. Are compared directly with standard prints taken from a suspect
    d. Should be removed from the lifter with transparent adhesive tape

CHAPTER NINETEEN

——— *VOICE PRINTS* ———

One of the never-ending requirements of forensic science is to find new ways to identify criminals and associate them with their crimes. Most methods deal with physical items or impressions, and, of course, fingerprints, when available, are the most reliable of these. But many crimes are committed in which fingerprints and other kinds of physical evidence are either inadequate or totally lacking, and with a rise in the incidence of terrorism, kidnapping, and extortion, an increasing number of crimes involve the use of the telephone. A favorite trick of extremist groups is to telephone false bomb threats to the police. In this case the telephone call itself is the crime and the voice of the caller is the only evidence. If the bomb threat is real and if the device goes off, the available physical evidence may be destroyed in the explosion. Ransom demands and blackmail threats are most commonly relayed by telephone, and the telephone message is frequently the only link to the culprit.

To combat these and other crimes in which the criminal's voice can be recorded, the *sound spectrograph,* or *voice print,* was devised in order to provide a system of visual voice individualization comparable to the fingerprint (see Figure 19-1). The first experiments in voice spectrograph were conducted by Bell Laboratories during World War II in response to a military requirement to track the movement of

FIGURE 19-1   Sound spectrograph. (Courtesy of Audio Intelligence Devices, Ft. Lauderdale, Fla.)

enemy units by identifying the voices of radio operators. Although these first attempts were too crude to be useful, one of the Bell scientists, L. G. Kersta, continued the research on his own and by the 1960s had developed a workable sound spectrograph system that was made available to law enforcement agencies.

PRINCIPLES OF THE SOUND SPECTROGRAPH

To understand how the sound spectrograph works we must first know something about the production of human vocal sounds. The body organs that combine to produce intelligible speech are the lungs and windpipe; the larynx, or voice box; the pharnyx, or upper throat; the mouth; and the nasal cavities.

The lungs and windpipe provide the steady stream of air which is the energy base of speech. While in normal breathing the time devoted to inhalation and exhalation are approximately equal, when a person is speaking he or she extends the exhalation rate up to six or seven times normal to adjust for the requirements of speech.

The larynx is a complex set of muscles, including the vocal chords, which controls the air flow from the lungs. When a person speaks, the muscles of the vocal chords close and the pressure of air from the lungs pushes through them causing them to flutter rapidly. This fluttering effect causes the basic, or *first-formant,* frequency of the voice, which can be anywhere from 60 cycles per second to 500 cycles per second but which averages out to between 100 cycles per second and 250 cycles per second. As this basic vocal tone progresses up into the throat, mouth, and nasal cavities, it is modulated by an extremely complex combination of muscular actions that produces the resonances, harmonic overtones, and stops and starts that characterize intelligible speech. The harmonic frequencies superimposed on the fundamental frequency can go up as high as 5,000 cycles per second.

Since it is highly improbable that any two people have the same configuration of vocal organs or use them in exactly the same way, every time a person utters a sound, the set of vocal patterns that is produced is unique to that person. Because of the extreme complexity of these patterns, it would be impractical to attempt to analyze them completely. The sound spectrograph is designed to analyze three separate components of human speech sounds: *frequency, duration,* and *amplitude.*

Starting with a standard magnetic tape recording of the voice to be analyzed, a small segment (approximately 2.4 seconds) is selected and rerecorded on a loop of magnetic tape in the sound spectrograph instrument. The loop of tape plays this short segment over and over again into the analyzing circuit of the spectrograph. Each time the segment is played, it is analyzed at a slightly higher frequency band. When the frequency of the voice in any part of the taped segment corresponds to a given frequency band, the fact is visually recorded by a stylus (pen), which inks a small line on electrically sensitive paper. This paper is mounted on a drum that rotates at the same rate as the loop of magnetic tape. As the successive frequency bands move higher and higher each time the segment is played, the stylus moves mechanically to a correspondingly higher position on the paper until the speech segment has been analyzed throughout the whole range of voice frequencies. On the finished chart the frequency values are shown by the vertical position of the lines. The closer they are to the top of the chart, the higher the frequency of the sound. The duration, or length of time a given frequency appears in the segment, is depicted from left to right across the chart. And the amplitude, or loudness, is roughly shown by the relative darkness of the line. The darker the line, the greater the amplitude (see Figure 19-2).

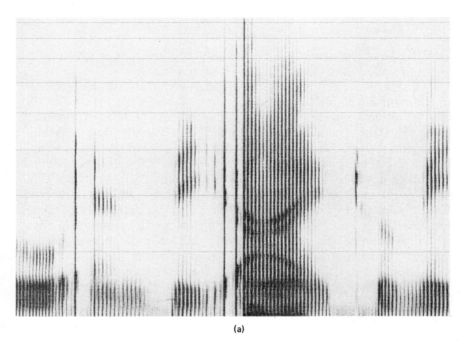

(a)

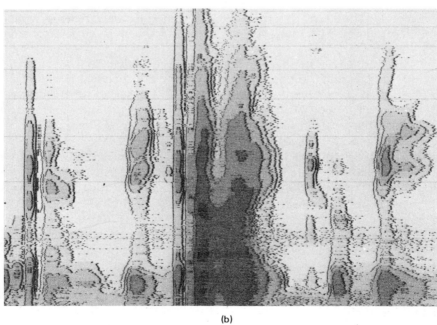

(b)

FIGURE 19–2 Sound spectrograph charts: (a) normal, (b) contour. (Courtesy of Audio Intelligence Devices, Ft. Lauderdale, Fla.)

286

Investigative Use of Voice Prints

The voice print identification system consists of visually comparing charts made by the procedure described above. A chart, or *sound spectrogram,* of an unknown criminal's voice, usually recorded over the telephone, is compared with the voice of a known suspect. If a suspect is willingly submitting to a voice print test, the suspect can be asked to record any sequence of words selected from the unknown recording. If the suspect is unaware that his or her voice is being taped for comparison purposes, the investigators must do their best to match words or word sequences from the unknown recording with the recording of the known suspect. Since people tend to have habitual speech patterns, it is often possible to get the same short sequence of words if the recorded conversations are long enough.

For the sound spectrograph to be effective in identifying people, each individual's vocal frequency pattern must not only be unique to that individual, but it must also be constant. That is, it must not change significantly over a period of time and under different circumstances. It is here that the weakness of voice prints lies. Although each person's voice pattern is indeed unique, it can be considerably affected by a number of factors. Unlike fingerprints, the configuration of the vocal organs can change to some extent as a person ages. Therefore, it would be impractical to keep voice prints permanently on file. Other factors that can alter the voice enough to make it difficult to match voice prints are emotional stress, colds and laryngitis, attempts to disguise the voice, and even a change in the amount of moisture lining the throat and vocal chords. Other difficulties not attributable to the voice are differences in quality of recording equipment, background noise, and poor telephone connections.

Any of these conditions may alter voice prints made by the same individual beyond recognition, and even when a match exists, an examiner may not see it. Because of these difficulties, voice prints have received only limited acceptance in courts. Nevertheless, even if they generally cannot be used directly as evidence, voice prints have proved to be of great value as an investigative aid to police in eliminating innocent suspects and focusing their other investigative resources on the correct suspect.

At the present state of sound spectrograph development the most important factor in voice print interpretation is how much training and experience the examiner has had. The more experience the examiner has, the more likely the examiner is to spot matching voice prints. An experienced examiner can often make successful matches even when criminals attempt to disguise their voices. Because of the differences that exist in the abilities of examiners, the interpretation of voice prints is more in the nature of an art than a science. Research is currently underway to refine and quantify sound spectrographs to the point where they can be analyzed by computer. Although it is doubtful that voice prints will ever enjoy the same degree of acceptance as fingerprints, if the computer analyses result in a high percentage of correct matches in spite of all the possibilities of confusion, voice prints will probably become more widely admitted in courts.

Review Questions

1. Voice prints are most likely to be used in connection with
   a. Hairs and fibers
   b. Line spectra
   c. Bomb threats
   d. Forgeries

2. Which of the following organs does *not* contribute to speech production?
   a. Lungs
   b. Heart
   c. Larynx
   d. Nose

3. The first-formant frequency of the voice can go as high as
   a. 50 cycles per second
   b. 500 cycles per second
   c. 5,000 cycles per second
   d. 50,000 cycles per second

4. (T, F) Voice prints are as effective as fingerprints in identifying an individual.

5. In a sound spectrogram the lower the line appears on the chart,
   a. The greater the amplitude
   b. The higher the frequency
   c. The shorter the duration
   d. The lower the frequency

6. (T, F) Little experience is needed to interpret voice prints.

7. Voice prints can be affected by
   a. Age
   b. Emotional stress
   c. The amount of moisture lining the throat
   d. Background noise
   e. All the above
   f. b and d

CHAPTER TWENTY

—— FIRE EVIDENCE ——

The primary responsibility of the fire investigator is to determine from an on-site inspection whether or not a crime has been committed. If the evidence at the scene points to arson, then all clues must be carefully exploited in order to identify the culprit. It is in the latter aspect of the investigation that the laboratory scientist can play a role by analyzing residues of flammable materials and performing the usual laboratory examinations of other trace evidence that the arsonist may have left behind. But it is the investigating officer in the field who plays the major role in tying the threads of evidence together into a coherent investigation. To be able to perform this job properly, the officer should be skilled not only in the investigation of fire itself but also in all-around crime scene search procedures. Knowledge of fire behavior may answer the first question of whether a fire was accidental or intentional, but the ability of the investigator to recognize other kinds of trace evidence and an awareness of the capabilities of the laboratory can be as valuable to the fire investigator as they are to the burglary investigator in associating a suspect with the scene.

Perhaps the most obvious difficulty that an arson investigator has to face is the fact that the crime tends to destroy its own evidence. Although this is a happy circumstance from the arsonist's point of view, it is nevertheless very rare for the destruction to be so complete as to wipe out all traces of the arsonist's actions, and the competent investigator is usually able to tell whether or not a fire was of accidental or incendiary origin. What can be even more frustrating to the investigator than the destruction of evidence by fire is the destruction of evidence by human beings after the fire. Ideally, the investigator should be present at the scene while the fire is still in progress in order to observe the fire's behavior and be ready to begin the investigation as soon as the fire has been put out. Unfortunately, it seldom works out that way in actual practice. It may be days or even weeks before a thorough investigation is conducted. In that time valuable evidence may have been cleared up along with the debris; traces of uncombusted accelerants may have evaporated; and the arsonist may even have taken measures to cover up the crime.

THE NATURE OF COMBUSTION

People usually think of fire as a primarily destructive phenomenon. Indeed, from a practical point of view, the burning of one's property is destruction. From a chemical point of view, however, matter is never destroyed; it is only transformed into other kinds of matter. The transformation that takes place in a fire consists of adding oxygen to a combustible compound. In the presence of heat that compound breaks down and recombines with the oxygen to form new compounds. This process, called *oxidation,* can be illustrated by showing what happens when methane (CH_4) is burned. Methane is the simplest of a group of organic compounds known as *hydrocarbons,* which are so called because they contain only atoms of hydrogen and carbon. Methane, with one carbon atom and four hydrogen atoms, can be depicted chemically as

$$
\begin{array}{c}
H \\
| \\
H - C - H \\
| \\
H
\end{array}
$$

Oxygen exists freely in air as a diatomic gas, O_2, that is, a gas made up of molecules formed by the combination of two atoms. It is depicted as

$$O = O$$

A single oxygen atom is too unstable to exist in uncombined form.

The same is true of hygrogen gas (H_2). So when something happens to break the bonds by which the atoms are attached to each other, the atoms immediately seek to recombine into more stable compounds. In fires this process of recombination is initiated when enough energy is added in the form of heat to overcome the internal energy that holds the original molecule together. Thus when methane is ignited with a match or other heat source, the following reaction occurs:

$$
\begin{array}{ccccccc}
\text{H} & & & & & & \text{H}-\text{O}-\text{H} \\
| & & \text{O}=\text{O} & & & & \\
\text{H}-\text{C}-\text{H} & + & & \rightarrow & \text{O}=\text{C}=\text{O} & + & \\
| & & \text{O}=\text{O} & & & & \text{H}-\text{O}-\text{H} \\
\text{H} & & & & & & \\
\text{methane} & + \text{ oxygen} & \text{yields} & & \text{carbon} & + & \text{water} \\
& & & & \text{dioxide} & & \text{vapor}
\end{array}
$$

Note that two oxygen molecules are needed for each methane molecule in order to make enough oxygen available to combine with the carbon atom and all four hydrogen atoms. The same formula can be written in simplified form as

$$CH_4 + 2\ O_2 \rightarrow CO_2 + 2\ H_2O$$

Methane, the principal component of natural gas, burns with a blue flame, which is indicative of complete combustion.

The new compounds that are formed, in this case carbon dioxide and water, are called *combustion products.* Because their molecules are more stable than those of the original compounds, they do not need as much internal energy to hold them together. The excess energy is released into the atmosphere as the heat and light which are always associated with fire. In the process of combustion some heat is absorbed to start the reaction and more heat is released as the reaction completes itself. Any chemical reaction that emits more heat than it absorbs is said to be *exothermic.* In fires the degree of heat needed to initiate the reaction is known as the *ignition temperature* or *ignition point* of the fuel and the heat given off is known as the *heat of combustion.* The heat of combustion, being higher in temperature than the heat required for ignition, breaks down more methane and oxygen molecules which in turn recombine into carbon dioxide and water, thereby producing more heat. The reaction continues to regenerate itself indefinitely in this manner as long as fuel and oxygen are available.

The same general principles hold true for any kind of fire, regardless of the fuel. For example, the hydrocarbon octane, which is one of

the main components of gasoline and has a molecular structure based
on a chain of eight carbon atoms

$$
\begin{array}{cccccccc}
H & H & H & H & H & H & H & H \\
| & | & | & | & | & | & | & | \\
H-C-C-C-C-C-C-C-C-H \\
| & | & | & | & | & | & | & | \\
H & H & H & H & H & H & H & H
\end{array}
$$

burns with the following reaction:

$$C_8H_{18} + 12.5\ O_2 \rightarrow 8\ CO_2 + 9\ H_2O$$

If we compare the reaction of octane with that of methane, we can
see that the longer the hydrocarbon molecule is, the greater the volume
of oxygen that is required to complete the combustion. While only 2
molecules of oxygen are needed to burn 1 molecule of methane, 12.5
molecules of oxygen are needed to burn 1 molecule of octane. Since
there is only a limited amount of free oxygen in a given volume of air
(approximately 20 percent), organic fuels that have a high carbon content generally cannot get enough oxygen to allow for complete oxidation of all the carbon and hydrogen atoms. The result is that
considerable quantities of carbon monoxide (CO) and uncombusted
carbon particles are produced along with the carbon dioxide and water.
The unoxidized carbon, or soot, is of significance to the investigator
because it is the source of flame and black smoke. The carbon particles,
made red-hot by the heat of combustion and driven upward by convection, make up the orange flame we see in fires, and as the carbon
particles continue to rise and cool off, they become black and form
smoke.

Heavy black smoke is characteristic of the burning of most liquid
hydrocarbons, such as gasoline, kerosene, and organic thinners and
solvents. These hydrocarbons are frequently used by arsonists to spread
and intensify a fire. When used in this manner, such combustible liquids
are known as *accelerants.* Thus when heavy black smoke is observed in
the early stages of a fire, it is a strong indication that accelerants have
been used and therefore that the fire is probably the result of arson.

Combustion Ingredients

From the above discussion we can see that three ingredients must
be present for a fire to take place: fuel, oxygen, and heat. These ingredients are often referred to as the fire triangle (see Figure 20–1). The fire

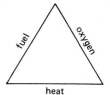

FIGURE 20-1 The fire triangle.

produces its own heat once it gets started; so if there is sufficient ventilation to continuously renew the oxygen supply and if there is no outside intervention, the fire burns until all the fuel is consumed. All fire fighting procedures are based on the principle of removing or reducing one or more of these ingredients. Water, the most common fire fighting tool, works by cooling the fuel below its ignition point; chemical foams smother the fire by denying the access of fresh oxygen; and fuel is often removed from forest fires by stripping or burning away areas of forest in the path of the flames.

Flammable Materials

Up to now we have been using the word combustion almost synonymously with fire. Combustion actually encompasses any exothermic oxidation reaction. Some combustion reactions, like the drying of oxidizing oil paints and the rusting of iron, are so slow that we are not aware of the heat they produce. Oxidizing oils can be a factor in spontaneous combustion, which will be discussed later, but for the most part such slow reactions are of no interest either to the fire fighter or the fire investigator. The kinds of combustion which we think of as fire are the extremely rapid reactions which can take the form of *flaming fires* or *glowing fires*.

Flammable materials, or fuels, exist in the form of gases, liquids, or solids, but only gases can burn with a flaming fire. Liquids and solids can oxidize slowly on the surface, and some solids like charcoal and coke can burn with a glowing fire, which is a rapid form of surface oxidation, but they both must be converted into gas form before they can burn with flames.

The flames produced by gas fires are a result of the speed and vigor of the reaction. This rapid reaction occurs because the gas molecules intermix thoroughly with molecules of air, thus presenting a tremendous surface area for reacting with the oxygen. The ratio of gas to air is important; if it is either too rich (too much gas) or too lean (too little gas), it will not burn.

The leanest mixture of a given gas with air that will still burn is known as the *lower flammable limit* of the gas. The richest mixture of

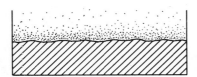

FIGURE 20–2 At constant temperature and pressure the vapor layer above a flammable liquid tends to maintain a uniform concentration. As molecules dissipate into the atmosphere, more molecules escape from the liquid to keep the vapor/air mixture constant.

the gas with air that will burn is the *upper flammable limit* of the gas. These limits are expressed in percentages by volume of the gas in air. For example, the lower flammable limit of methane in air is 5.3 percent and its upper limit is 13.9 percent. The span between these limits is known as the *flammable range.* Any ratio of methane to air that falls within the flammable range forms a *flammable mixture.*[1]

One of the common properties of combustible liquids is that their molecules continuously escape from the surface to form a vapor layer in the air above (see Figure 20–2). These vapors are gases and therefore burn like gases when they exist in a suitable ratio to air. The richness of the vapor/air mixture is related to the weight of the molecule and the temperature of the environment. The higher the temperature the more vapor is given off from the surface, and lighter molecules are given off faster than heavier molecules. For every flammable liquid there is a temperature below which too little vapor escapes into the air to form a flammable mixture. The lowest temperature at which the vapor/air mixture is rich enough to be ignited is known as the *flash point* of that liquid. For example, the flash point of gasoline is approximately –45°C. A gasoline motor that has been standing in an environment colder than –45°C will not run unless the fuel is warmed up because the gasoline will not ignite. Liquids of lighter molecular weight have lower flash points than heavier liquids. At temperatures below its flash point a liquid cannot be ignited without being warmed up. Once ignited, the heat of the reaction continues to raise the temperature of the liquid until the liquid reaches its boiling point, and it stays at that temperature until it is completely vaporized.

For solids to support flaming fires somewhat different conditions must be met. Although some metals can be made to burn if they are finely divided or if unusually high temperatures are reached, the fire investigator is normally concerned with organic solids such as wood, paper, rubber, linoleum, and fabric materials. Unlike liquids, solids do not give off vapor at normal temperatures. Consequently, in order to make them burn they must be heated to a point where the complex molecules at the surface of the solid material are forced to decompose

[1]The terms *explosive limit, explosive range,* and *explosive mixture* are often used instead of *flammable limit* etc. In this context the words *flammable* and *explosive* are interchangeable.

into simpler volatile molecules, or gases. This process is called *pyrolysis.* It is actually the gaseous products of pyrolysis and not the solid materials themselves that burn.

The solid that provides the most abundant source of fuel in most fires is wood. Wood is a complex combination of substances made up primarily of *cellulose,* which forms the fibrous material, *lignin,* which is a natural plastic that binds the fibers, and small amounts of mineral salts, sugar, fats, resins, and proteins. Wood burns with a predominantly orange flame and in the absence of hydrocarbons or other contaminants burns with a gray to white smoke. Because of its complex structure wood does not burn very efficiently. In addition to carbon dioxide and steam, wood fires give off significant quantities of carbon monoxide, sulfur dioxide (SO_2), nitrogen dioxide (NO_2), and hydrogen cyanide (HCN), all of which are either poisonous or irritating to human beings and therefore dangerous to fire fighters. After the easily pyrolyzed, volatile gases are burned off, a large amount of carbonaceous residue, or charcoal, remains. When the flames have died down, charcoal continues to burn with a glowing fire, producing a mixture of carbon monoxide and carbon dioxide. This type of combustion indicates that a fire is going through the last steps of the chemical process and is typical of the last stages of most fires.

An exception to this is the fire that glows from the start because there is not enough oxygen to support flames. Some examples of this slow combustion are smoldering fires in mattresses and hay in barns. These can continue to burn in this manner for a long time until they reach a place of adequate ventilation and burst into flame.

Heat Transmittal

If a fire is to continue to burn, there must be a transfer of heat to new fuel sources. Heat can be transmitted by *conduction, convection,* or *radiation,* or by combinations of the three.

Conduction

Conduction is the transfer of heat from one solid object to another or from one part of an object to another part by direct transmittal of heat energy from molecule to molecule (see Figure 20–3). We normally think of conduction as taking place in metals, where if one part is heated, other parts not exposed to the heat source also become hot. For conduction to take place between two objects, the objects must touch each other. If the temperature of a piece of metal rises above the ignition point of any combustible material touching it, that material will become ignited even if it is some distance from the original heat source.

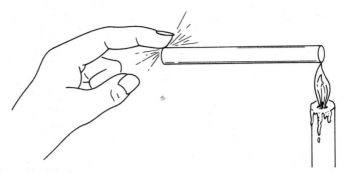

FIGURE 20–3 Conduction.

Perhaps the most common example of this phenomenon occurs in electrical short circuits in which the hot copper wire may set its insulation on fire at a considerable distance from the point of the short circuit. The ability of materials to conduct heat is known as *thermal conductivity.* In general, metals tend to be better conductors than nonmetals, and such common fuels as wood and paper are among the worst. That is why we can hold a lighted match until the flame reaches our fingers, but we cannot hold the end of a pin very long if the other end of the pin is held in a flame.

Convection

Convection is the physical movement of heated molecules from one place to another, and it can occur only in liquids and gases (see Figure 20–4). Everyone is familiar with the sight of flames rising up a chimney. Flames rise because the gases produced in the reaction expand and become lighter when they are heated. As they rise, they tend to create a vacuum at their base, which cooler air rushes in to fill, bringing with it a fresh supply of oxygen. The same thing happens with liquids. Even though water is a poor conductor, a pot of water held over a flame heats evenly throughout because the molecules rise as they are heated and displace cooler molecules at the top, which are forced downward to be heated in turn. This tendency of heated molecules to rise and be replaced by cooler molecules results in currents known as *convection currents.*

Convection currents are extremely important in understanding the behavior of fire. A fire always tends to burn straight upward unless it is prevented by an obstacle in its path or lateral air currents are introduced. Therefore, a fire started in an enclosed room tends to burn relatively slowly. If a window and door are opened, a lateral wind current may be introduced which can speed the progress of the fire into

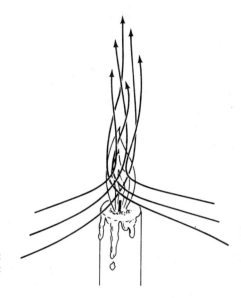

FIGURE 20-4 Convection. As the hot air rises, cooler air rushes in to replace it thereby creating convection currents.

the interior of the structure. And if the fire reaches a natural chimney, like a stairwell or elevator shaft, the fire burns with great violence and sets up strong convection currents.

Most of the heat of fires is transmitted by a combination of convection and conduction. The convection currents carry hot gas molecules and hot airborne particles to new sources of fuel, which they ignite through direct transmittal of their heat by conduction.

Radiation

Radiation is the transmittal of heat energy in the form of infrared rays (see Figure 20-5). Infrared radiation is the portion of the electromagnetic spectrum below visible light, and like all other electromagnetic emissions, infrared radiation travels at the speed of light. Heat transferral in this fashion is not dependent upon direct contact between objects or movement of molecules. The heat we receive from the sun is radiant heat, and everything on Earth is continuously radiating and absorbing heat. If we absorb more heat than we radiate, we feel warm; if we radiate more heat than we absorb, we feel cold.

Large amounts of heat radiation are associated with all fires, and the bigger the fire, the more radiation it produces. In large structural fires it is not uncommon for neighboring buildings to burst apparently spontaneously into flames. In these cases the burning building produces enough radiant heat to pyrolyze the surface of the nearby structure. The gases thus produced may be ignited by the radiation, if it raises

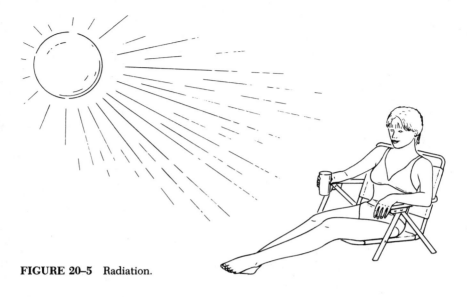

FIGURE 20–5   Radiation.

them to their ignition temperature, or the gases may waft over to the fire and be ignited directly by the flames, or they may be ignited by a hot particle carried by air currents from the fire.

The same thing can happen in an enclosed area. If a fire is burning on one side of a closed room, radiant heat from the fire can pyrolyze the opposite walls. If the resulting gases become sufficiently diffused in the atmosphere of the room, they can actually cause an explosion when they ignite. This situation can be extremely dangerous for fire fighters who may be in the room, and it can prove confusing to the fire investigator since the means by which the fire migrated from one area to another may not be immediately clear.

FIRE INVESTIGATION

As stated earlier, the fire investigator's first interest is to determine whether or not a crime has been committed. As in any criminal investigation, it is important to begin the investigation as soon as possible in order to preclude the possible destruction of evidence. Ideally, the investigation should begin while the fire is still burning so that its progress can be observed. If that is impossible, the investigator should arrive at the scene as soon as possible after the fire is out.

The first step in determining whether a fire was accidental or intentional is to locate the point where the fire started. As we noted earlier, convection tends to make a fire burn upward. Therefore, in structural fires, which are the ones most commonly of interest to investigators, the lowest area where there are signs of burning is likely to be the starting point. Although this is a good rule of thumb, it is sometimes an oversimplification. Accelerants may obscure the true origin by dripping through cracks and carrying the fire to lower levels or by spreading the fire simultaneously to multiple fuel sources. The flames can also be carried to lower levels by the natural actions of the fire, as, for example, when a falling timber crashes through a floor.

Under ordinary circumstances, a fire burns upward and outward from its point of origin to form a triangular or cone-shaped burn pattern. If there is lateral ventilation, the fire is forced in the direction of the air current. If the investigator can find the point of the cone pattern, that is likely to be the starting point.

After locating the origin, the investigator looks for evidence as to the cause of the fire. The cause of an accidental fire always has some kind of logic to it because there must be both a means of ignition and an adequate source of fuel which are natural to the setting. For example, a wastepaper basket fire started by a lighted match or cigarette in the middle of a room is unlikely to spread into a general blaze because there is no fuel above it, but the same wastepaper basket fire under a curtain and next to a wood-paneled wall can spread very easily. In such a situation the investigator would probably find that the charring of the wall began at a point above the rim of the wastepaper basket and spread upward and outward from there. Such a triangular char pattern rising from the point of origin is typical of accidental fires and is an indication that no liquid accelerant was used.

Intentionally set fires have a different kind of logic. Since the intention of most arsonists is to cause as much destruction as possible, they usually take measures to ensure that result. The most common of these is the use of accelerants to intensify and spread the fire. Also, especially in large structures, arsonists often arrange several starting points, which they may ignite separately on the way out or which they may connect by means of *trailers,* usually of flammable liquids (see Figure 20–6). The liquids most commonly used for these purposes are gasoline and kerosene because they are easy to acquire in large quantities without arousing suspicion.

The presence of accelerants can usually be deduced from char patterns (see Figure 20–6). Since accelerants are liquids, they spread out and soak into porous surfaces like wood, and they seep into cracks along walls. Consequently, when the accelerants are ignited, they burn along a broad expanse of floor and tend to char walls uniformly from the floor up without leaving a triangular pattern (see Figure 20-7). Moreover, although accelerants produce a hot flame, the surfaces on which they

FIGURE 20–6 The discoloration of the floorboards leading from one room to another indicates the use of a trailer to connect the two fuel sources.

burn do not get any hotter than the boiling point of the liquid and are not subject to charring until the liquid has completely boiled off. Similarly, porous materials like rags that have been doused with a hydrocarbon often act as wicks for the liquid but do not themselves burn. Consequently, the presence of walls charred evenly all the way down to the floor, floors showing clearly defined patches of discoloration and minor charring, and unconsumed bits of cloth or rags are good visual evidence of the use of accelerants.

Because hydrocarbons have a tendency to soak into porous materials, they are seldom completely consumed in a fire. Therefore, if investigating officers begin the investigation immediately, before the accelerant residues can evaporate, they can usually discover the presence of the residues by using a commercial hydrocarbon detector, or "sniffer." Sometimes a good sense of smell may be all that an investigator needs.

Whenever the use of accelerants is suspected, investigators must collect samples of any materials that might have soaked up some of the liquid. Because of the volatility of these liquids, they must be packaged in airtight containers. Wide-mouthed canning jars are good for this purpose. Some investigators use new metal paint cans. Any airtight container will do.

Because of the many different circumstances that can lead to arson there is considerable variation in the way fires are set. Most arsons are either rather hastily planned or carried out on a sudden impulse. Fires set under such conditions usually reflect the arsonist's haste. Accelerants are often scattered around carelessly or if no accelerant is used,

FIGURE 20–7 Deep, even charring along the wall starting at floor level indicates the use of an accelerant.

some other hasty kindling arrangement may be made, such as distributing piles of crumpled paper around the premises and lighting them or piling some flammable materials against the side of a building and lighting them. More often than not a match or lighter is used to start the blaze, and the culprit does not have a chance to get very far away before the fire is reported. Fire arrangements made without accelerants are often ineffective, and the fires either go out by themselves or are extinguished before significant damage is done. Occasionally, the match used to light the fire is found and if it has unusual characteristics or if it can be matched with a book of matches found on the suspect, it can provide valuable evidence.

Another fairly common method of ignition is the Molotov cocktail. This is usually a glass bottle filled with an accelerant. A rag soaked in the accelerant is wrapped around the bottle and lit. When the bottle is thrown against a hard surface, the bottle shatters and flaming accelerant is spread in all directions. The evidence of the use of Molotov cocktails is usually clear. The shattered glass generally remains intact throughout the fire, and the rag itself may also remain unconsumed if it serves as a wick for the hydrocarbon.

When more careful planning has gone into a fire, it is probable that the arsonist took steps to make sure that the destruction would be thorough and that he or she would not be in the area when the fire started. To ensure destruction, the arsonist almost always uses accelerants, often in several different places, and sets the fire in a low part of the building. Fires that start in the upper floors of buildings are likely to be either the result of an accident or the result of ignorance or haste on the part of the arsonist since the lower stories will usually escape any severe damage. Experienced arsonists may also try to conceal their crime by spreading the accelerant near an appliance like an electric heater or stove, which might, without thorough investigation, be considered responsible for the fire. In such cases the investigator must remember that the accelerant will still spread out across the floor and cause uniform charring on walls from the floor level up.

The careful arsonist is also likely to use some kind of timing device to ignite the fire after a safe period of time has elapsed. Such devices may be rather crude as, for example, a lighted cigarette stuck between layers of paper matches, or they may be more complicated mechanisms incorporating clocks or wristwatches for timers and batteries and blasting caps to ignite a flammable or explosive substance. Chemical fuses may also be used. In one of these, sulfuric acid eats through a barrier which separates the acid from another chemical with which it will react violently. (See Figure 21–2.) The officer investigating the scene should be especially alert for any signs of an ignition device. These might include stray bits of wire, clock mechanisms, batteries, or any stray materials which do not seem to fit naturally into the setting where the fire originated. If such evidence is found, it is clear proof of arson. Moreover, the use of such devices narrows down the range of possible suspects since only a limited number of people may have the requisite knowledge or access to the parts.

Spontaneous Combustion

Sometimes an arsonist tries to claim that a fire was started by spontaneous combustion. Although spontaneous combustion does sometimes occur, it is very rare. The investigator should question a person who makes such a claim very carefully about the circumstances under which the fire supposedly began. Most of us have heard at one time or another that we should avoid leaving oily rags lying around in poorly ventilated places. What is not generally known is that this precaution applies to a limited number of substances such as linseed oil and turpentine that are subject to oxidation at room temperature. The oxidation of these materials is an exothermic reaction, and if there is insufficient ventilation, the small amount of heat given off does not dissipate and causes the oxidation to take place more rapidly. This generates more heat, which in turn speeds up the reaction even more. If this cycle continues, the heat emitted may reach the ignition point of the oil and start a fire. The reason that it is more likely to happen in rags is that the fibers provide a large surface area for the reaction. Spontaneous combustion does not occur with petroleum based oils or highly saturated household oils; so if the suspect says that the rags were soaked in motor oil, the suspect is a very good candidate for further investigation.

Another form of spontaneous combustion can occur in damp, closely packed hay. In this case the activity of living microorganisms generates the initial heat which starts oxidation reactions in the hay itself. These reactions build up over a period of time in the same manner as in oily rags and they initiate a smoldering fire in the interior of the hay pack. When the smoldering fire works its way to a point where it receives adequate ventilation, it can burst suddenly into a violent blaze. Spontaneous combustion in hay is very rare because farmers are generally careful not to pack wet hay in a barn.

Motives for Arson

Once investigators have determined that a fire is the result of arson, they must consider who benefits from the act. Probably the most common benefit derived from arson is financial gain, usually in the form of insurance fraud, but sometimes arson is used to eliminate business competition. A person may burn a building simply because it is too old to renovate or sell at a profit. In this case there is a good chance the owner has recently raised the insurance on the building to an amount in excess of its true value. Insurance companies are often lax about verifying the value of a property when insurance is taken out on it. Another type of insurance fraud involves putting in a false claim for goods that were allegedly destroyed in a fire. Since fires are seldom totally destructive, there should be some remaining signs of such goods in the rubble. If the investigator can find none, the claim is probably fraudulent and a strong case for arson exists.

The benefit from a fire is not always financial. Fires have been known to be set for reasons of hatred and revenge, and if no other motive is apparent, the investigator should inquire into the victim's personal relationships. The revenge motive might not necessarily be against an individual but may be directed against an organization or "the establishment." In the latter case the arsonist may take public credit for the fire in the name of some extremist group.

On occasion the act of arson is secondary to another crime. For example, if a person has committed murder, the person may try to conceal that crime by setting fire to the building in the hope that the flames will destroy or conceal the evidence of murder. For this reason, dead bodies found in burned buildings should be examined for causes of death other than burning or asphyxiation. Most victims of fires die of asphyxiation or poisoning by toxic gases before the flames reach them, and their blood should show high levels of carbon monoxide and their lungs should be lined with soot. If these indicators are not found in the autopsy, the victim must have died before the fire started. This part of the investigation is carried out by the medical examiner.

Sometimes there is no rational motive. The *pyromaniac,* or "fire-bug," is a psychotic personality who derives great pleasure, often with sexual overtones, from simply watching the flames and destruction. Such cases are difficult to prove because there is no prior connection between the arsonist and the building. However, these people are always in the crowd watching the fire. Therefore, if investigators arrive on the scene while the fire is still in progress, they should take some photographs of the crowd. If the same face appears at several different fires, that person is a likely suspect.

Investigating the Scene

As with other types of criminal investigation, photography is of paramount importance. It is the only way to preserve the appearance of the scene as it was before clean-up operations began. Photography, especially in color, of the fire in progress can be valuable in depicting the nature of the flames and the smoke and in tracing the progress of the fire. After the fire is out, a preliminary photograph should be taken of the overall scene. When the point or points of origin are located, they should be photographed from different angles. Any evidentiary materials should be photographed exactly as they are found. Also, the position of all evidence should be indicated on a sketch for orientation purposes.

As indicated earlier, the investigator should check the area for accelerants, preferably with a hydrocarbon detector, and any materials suspected of containing accelerants should packaged in airtight containers and forwarded to the laboratory. Also, any cans or bottles that might have been used to transport accelerants should be preserved for laboratory examination. If possible, they should be sealed in order to retain any possible vapors or unused liquids.

In addition to having knowledge of the kinds of evidence that are directly associated with fires and arson, fire investigators should have a good knowledge of all-around criminal investigation. Unless a fire is set by the owner of an establishment or with the owner's connivance, the arsonist usually has to break into the premises, and in so doing is likely to produce the same kinds of evidence as ordinary burglars. All items of physical evidence should be handled with due regard for the preservation of fingerprints. It is wrong to assume that fingerprints are automatically destroyed by the fire. Also, broken glass, tool marks, footprints, and other clues should be collected and preserved just as rigorously as they would be in any other investigation.

The prompt interrogation of witnesses can be very valuable in arson investigations. Since it is unlikely that the investigator will have observed the early stages of the fire, witnesses may be able to provide information on the color of the first smoke and flames that were seen, what part of the building they came from, or whether they came from several parts of the building at the same time. Witnesses may also be able to tell whether anyone suspicious was seen entering or leaving the premises.

The investigator should make a careful check for valuables and other items that might become the basis for insurance claims. Safes and strongboxes should be checked for smaller valuables and documents that might throw light on the victim's affairs. If badly charred documents are found, they should be carefully packaged in a box large enough to eliminate the danger of pressure, and if the documents are very fragile, a layer of thin lacquer can be gently sprayed on them with an atomizer in order to strengthen the pieces and permit handling.

LABORATORY EXAMINATION

The work of the crime laboratory in supporting arson investigations can encompass almost the entire range of criminalistic examinations. The extent of the criminalist's role depends on the activities of the arsonist and the kinds of evidence the arsonist leaves behind, the amount of evidence that survives the fire, and the investigator's skill in recognizing and collecting the evidence. Those aspects of the criminalist's job that are directly connected with fire investigation generally include the examination of ignition devices and the identification of accelerants.

The most commonly used ignition device is the match. Although they are usually consumed in the fire, matches occasionally do survive to be recovered by investigators. If the match has been torn out of a book of matches and the unused remainder of the book is found in the possession of a suspect, it is sometimes possible to match the torn end of the match with the corresponding part of the matchbook. This would entail a simple visual examination made under the low powers of a microscope. Wooden matches can be distinctive because of the different manufacturers and because of the different species of wood used in various parts of the country. If the match used to start a fire was not indigenous to the area, it could indicate that the arsonist was from another part of the country. These kinds of determinations would probably necessitate consultations with match manufacturers.

The remains of other ignition devices must be carefully examined for any clues that might point to the arsonist. If a Molotov cocktail were used, the rag used as a wick might bear identifying information, for example an old laundry mark. When more sophisticated devices of unusual nature are used, a careful examination of the recovered parts may lead to individual suppliers who could give the names of people who had recently purchased such parts.

The task that the criminalist is most often called upon to perform in arson investigations is to determine whether or not accelerants were used and to identify the accelerants as closely as possible. The great majority of accelerants used by arsonists are hydrocarbons, with gasoline and kerosene predominating. Gas chromatography is the most commonly used method for analyzing hydrocarbons. It is available in most crime laboratories; it is easy to use; and it is sensitive to very small amounts of hydrocarbons both in liquid and vapor form.

Normally, the laboratory receives the evidence in the form of debris from a fire packaged in an airtight container. If the container has a metal lid, a small hole can be punched in it and a gas syringe inserted to draw off the vapors that have accumulated in the head space above the evidence material. The material can also be transferred to a container sealed with a *septum* (i.e., a piece of rubber in the lid which reseals itself after the passage of a syringe) and the vapors drawn off through it. These vapors are injected directly into the injection port of the gas chromatograph. On rare occasions a liquid sample may be brought into the laboratory for analysis. Liquid hydrocarbons can also be injected directly into the chromatograph since the temperature of the injection port is high enough to vaporize the sample instantly. When performing analyses of head space vapors, the laboratory examiner may have to warm up the evidence container to cause the vaporization of some of the heavier hydrocarbons. All commercial hydrocarbons are actually made up of a mixture of many different hydrocarbons, all having different boiling points and rates of vaporization related to their molecular weights. The gas chromatograph separates the molecules of a hydrocarbon mixture according to their molecular weights. Each peak on the chromatogram represents an individual compound (see Figure 20–8).

Because of their extreme volatility, many of the lighter components dissipate into the air before the evidence can be collected. Consequently, no hydrocarbon evidence ever has exactly the same composition that the original material had when the arsonist used it. For this reason it is almost impossible to compare an evidence sample with samples found in the possession of a suspect in the hope of finding an exact match. The gas chromatograph is able to distinguish between gasoline and kerosene and other commercial hydrocarbons because the components of each tend to have molecular weights within a certain

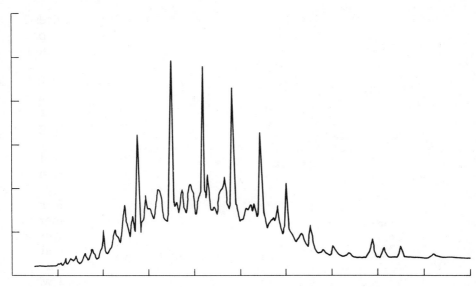

FIGURE 20–8   Gas chromatogram of kerosene. Compare Figure 4–2.

range, which are reflected in the peak retention times of the chromatogram. However, because of the uneven rates of volatilization and also because of the practice of blending and mixing that goes on among distributors, it is generally impossible to identify a hydrocarbon by brand. The dyes that the different companies use can sometimes be helpful in this regard, but when a gasoline has soaked into dirt or rags or wood, those dyes are often leached out by the filtering action of the materials. For the most part, the best a criminalist can do with these types of evidence is to state that the chromatogram of a given sample is consistent with that shown by gasoline or some other hydrocarbon.

Review Questions

1. It is the responsibility of a fire investigator to determine whether or not a crime has been committed
   a. From an on-site inspection
   b. From the fire department reports
   c. From the police department reports
   d. From newspaper reports

2. The person in the field who plays the major role in bringing the evidence together is the
   a. Fire fighter
   b. Building owner
   c. Criminalist
   d. Investigating officer

3. The most frustrating thing to an investigator is
   a. Weather
   b. Total destruction of the evidence in the fire
   c. Destruction of the evidence by the fire department
   d. Evaporation of uncombustible accelerants

4. The simplest hydrocarbon is
   a. Gasoline
   b. Methane
   c. Octane
   d. Benzene

5. The degree of heat needed to start a material on fire is its
   a. Ignition temperature
   b. Flash point
   c. Heat of combustion
   d. Fire point

6. Flammable materials can burn only in the
   a. Solid state
   b. Liquid state
   c. Gas state
   d. All the above

7. The lowest temperature at which a liquid produces enough vapors to form a combustible mixture is called the
   a. Flash point
   b. Ignition temperature
   c. Fire point
   d. Heat of combustion

8. A glowing fire indicates
   a. The last stages of the fire
   b. Insufficient oxygen
   c. Slow combustion
   d. All the above

9. Heat can be transmitted by
   a. Conduction
   b. Convection
   c. Radiation
   d. All the above

10. An accidental fire usually burns in what kind of pattern?
    a. Square
    b. Triangular

    c. Rectangular

    d. Circular

11. When gasoline is ignited on a wooden floor, the temperature of the floor underneath the gasoline is

    a. The same as the flame

    b. Hotter than the boiling point of gasoline

    c. No hotter than the boiling point of gasoline

    d. None of the above

12. Evidence suspected of containing accelerants should be packaged in

    a. A paper bag

    b. A plastic bag

    c. A glass jar

    d. Any of the above

13. Which of the following liquids would be most likely to start a fire by spontaneous combustion?

    a. Linseed oil

    b. Gasoline

    c. Kerosene

    d. Carbon tetrachloride

14. Arson fires are set

    a. For financial gain

    b. To eliminate business competition

    c. For hatred and revenge

    d. a and b

    e. All the above

15. Which of the following instruments is most commonly used to analyze hydrocarbons?

    a. Breathalyzer

    b. Spectrophotometer

    c. pH meter

    d. Gas chromatograph

CHAPTER TWENTY-ONE

—— *EXPLOSIVES* ——

Explosives have been an important tool to humans for several hundred years. Their tremendous energy has been applied to large-scale engineering tasks like drilling through mountains and clearing away obstacles, and their destructive potential has formed the basis of the most important advances in modern warfare. A conventional artillery shell, to give only one example, is propelled by one kind of explosive and does its damage by the detonation of another kind of explosive; still other explosives are needed to ignite the propellant and to detonate the main bursting charge when the shell lands.

In peacetime, for the most part, explosives have posed a threat only to people who work around them: manufacturers, users, and transporters. But when explosives are used in connection with arson or for purposes of political terrorism, they become a random hazard to anyone who happens to be in the vicinity. Since the incidence of this kind of political violence has risen considerably in recent years, the investigation of explosions has become a matter of increasing concern to police departments, especially in urban areas where these kinds of crimes are more likely to occur.

It is not uncommon for explosions to occur in connection with fires. Explosions can be the means of igniting a fire or they can be set off by a fire in progress. Consequently, scenes of explosions are often very much like fire scenes in many ways, but there are also important differences. With proper training, investigating officers at the scene can differentiate between different types of explosions, and they can generally determine whether the explosions were accidental or deliberate. The crime laboratory can help confirm the investigator's findings and identify the type of explosive used by examining explosive residues.

TYPES OF EXPLOSIONS AND EXPLOSIVE MATERIALS

To a casual observer all explosions may seem much alike. They make a lot of noise; they emit heat, light, and rapidly expanding gases; and they cause varying degrees of damage. Explosive reactions happen so fast that human senses cannot discriminate among them. Their effects, however, can be very different, depending on whether they are caused by the reaction of diffuse gases or dusts with oxygen in the air or whether they are caused by thermal decomposition of concentrated chemical explosives.

Gaseous or Diffuse Explosions

In Chapter 20 on fire investigation we noted that if pyrolyzed gases become sufficiently dispersed throughout the air of a room, they can explode when they are ignited. The same is true of all flammable gases as well as other combustible materials that are capable of being so finely divided and diffused in the air that they act like gases. A good example of the latter situation is the explosion of coal dust that sometimes takes place in mines. In gaseous explosions the chemical reactions are exactly the same as those that take place in fires, but while fires are continuous and self-sustaining after ignition, explosions are so rapid that they seem instantaneous. The difference lies in the degree of diffusion of the fuel in the air. When gas molecules are released into the air, they tend to intermix thoroughly with molecules of air. When the ratio of gas to air is within the explosive limits of the given gas, the gas can be ignited. If the gas is fed to the fire from a controlled source like a Bunsen burner or a gas stove, the gas combusts at a sustained rate, which we think of as burning. But if the gas is allowed to disperse throughout a room until it reaches its explosive limit and then lit, the entire volume of gas throughout the room ignites almost instantaneously to cause an explosion.

We saw in Chapter 20 that combustible liquids do not burn directly but that their vapors burn. Likewise they do not explode unless their vapors become widely diffused throughout an enclosed area. As long as adequate ventilation is available to prevent the vapors from reaching explosive concentrations, explosions cannot occur. Gasoline in a tank is a good example. Gasoline itself does not explode but the fumes that collect in the top of the tank above the liquid can explode if subjected to a spark or a flame. Often the fumes are too rich and there is not enough oxygen mixed in with the fumes to support an explosion, but when such explosions do occur, they can blow the tank apart and spread flaming gasoline in all directions. It also sometimes happens that the force of the explosion is just sufficient to blow oxygen away from the opening, thereby extinguishing itself and preventing any further fires.

We also saw that coal burns only with a flameless, glowing fire because coal presents a relatively small surface area to the oxygen in the air. But when coal becomes so finely divided that it can be diffused through the air in the form of dust, if offers a tremendous surface area for the oxygen to react with and consequently is capable of exploding like a gas. The same principle is true of other solids that burn poorly or do not burn at all in bulk. The dusts of aluminum, magnesium, grain, flour, and other solids can explode violently when diffused in the air in the right ratio and ignited.

Gaseous explosions are almost always accidental and they are generally easy to identify. They are often due to negligence and can occur as a result of leaky gas fixtures, gasoline containers left standing open in poorly ventilated spaces, unsafe levels of dust being allowed to build up in factories and mines, and many other situations which are easily prevented by observance of basic safety standards. Such accidental explosions can be ignited by a variety of means, some of the most common of which are careless use of matches, sparks from machinery, and electrical arcs. By recognizing the conditions of negligence the investigator can often pinpoint the cause of the explosion.

Investigators can recognize gaseous explosions from their effects. When gaseous explosions occur in a room, they tend to blow the walls outward, thereby causing the roof to cave in (see Figure 21–1). They do not leave craters. Objects inside a room may sustain little or no damage because the explosive forces exist equally on all sides. If, however, the gas and air mixture is richer in some parts of the room than in others, the explosive forces are unequal and will cause apparently random destruction within the room. Gases that are lighter than air, like methane, tend to rise and form richer mixtures near the ceiling. Heavier gases, like gasoline vapors, tend to sink to the floor and into low places. Consequently, if the walls are blown out at the top, the chances are that the explosion was caused by natural gas; if they are blown out at the bottom or if the explosion has occurred in low-lying drains, the fuel must have been a heavier than air vapor.

Gaseous explosions produce the same combustion products that the same fuel would have produced in a fire. For example, hydrocarbon

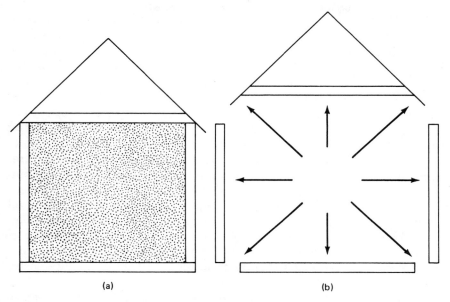

(a)   (b)

FIGURE 21-1 If an explosive mixture of flammable vapors or dust diffuses evenly throughout an enclosed space (a) and is ignited, the forces of the expanding gases act equally in all directions (b). If some parts of the structure are relatively weak, such as windows, they will be blown outward and dissipate the force of the explosion.

vapors produce carbon monoxide, carbon dioxide, and water; coal dust produces carbon monoxide and carbon dioxide; and the dusts of metals that would not normally burn in their solid state produce the oxides of the metals. During an explosion these combustion products expand rapidly outward, tending to create a vacuum, which fresh air then rushes in to fill. If there are any hot, uncombusted gases remaining after the explosion, as might be the case if the mixture was rich, the fresh incoming oxygen may react with them, creating a strong whooshing sound and a violent rolling fire.

Concentrated Explosions

Although various gases and dusts can give rise to explosions when ignited under the right circumstances, the fuels themselves are not generally thought of as explosives. True explosives are materials which explode in concentrated form entirely as a result of internal molecular decomposition and need no contact with the oxygen in the air. The oxygen necessary for the explosive reaction is contained within the compound or mixture itself. Explosive materials can be organic, inorganic, or a mixture of both. They are all highly unstable. When subjected to varying degrees of heat or shock, they decompose instantaneously with a tremendous release of heat, light, and rapidly expanding gases. Because the heat is so intense, these gases expand to much greater volumes and at a much faster rate than those of gaseous explosions.

The sudden localized increase in atmospheric pressure caused by the expanding gases produces the effect known as *blast*. Most of the damage and injuries from explosions are caused by blast and associated flying debris. Another important property of extremely rapidly detonating concentrated explosives is the shattering effect of shock and noise called *brisance*. It is the high brisance of the plastic explosives and nitroglycerin that make them attractive to the safecracker because a small amount of the explosive has a strong potential for shattering metal without causing blast damage to other objects or people in the room.

The great instability of explosives is caused by the presence of certain functional groups of atoms called *explosophores*,[1] which, when excited by heat or shock, instantly decompose and attack any fuel material with which they come in contact, causing them to break their molecular bonds and rearrange themselves in simpler, more stable forms. When nitroglycerin explodes, for example, it produces carbon dioxide, steam, nitrogen, and oxygen:

$$
\begin{array}{c}
\text{H} \\
| \\
\text{H} - \text{C} - \text{ONO}_2 \\
| \\
4\ \text{H} - \text{C} - \text{ONO}_2 \quad \rightarrow \quad 12\ \text{CO}_2\ +\ 10\ \text{H}_2\text{O}\ +\ 6\ \text{N}_2\ +\ \text{O}_2 \\
| \qquad\qquad\qquad\qquad\ \text{carbon}\qquad\ \text{water}\qquad\ \text{nitrogen}\quad\ \text{oxygen} \\
\text{H} - \text{C} - \text{ONO}_2 \qquad\ \text{dioxide}\qquad\qquad\qquad\quad\ \text{gas}\qquad\quad \text{gas} \\
| \\
\text{H}
\end{array}
$$

nitroglycerin

In this case the nitrate ion (ONO_2, also written NO_3) is the explosophore. It and the nitrite ion, or nitro group (NO_2), are by far the most common. One or the other is present in dynamite, TNT, black powder, nitrocellulose, cyclonite, tetryl, PETN, and others. These groups furnish the explosive instability, which is inherent in many nitrogen compounds, and they also provide the internal oxygen supply. Some other

[1]T. Urbanski, *Chemistry and Technology of Explosives Volume I* (New York: Pergamon Press, 1964).

common explosophores are azides (N_3), fulminates (CNO), chlorates ($OClO_2$), perchlorates ($OClO_3$) and peroxides (—O—O—).

Types of Explosives

Explosives are generally classified as *high* or *low,* depending on their rate of thermal decomposition. High explosives can detonate as fast as 8 kilometers per second whereas the detonation rate of low explosives can be slower than the speed of sound (331 meters per second).

Low Explosives

Black powder, smokeless powder (nitrocellulose), and mixtures of potassium chlorate with sugar or some other fuel material are some of the low explosives most commonly found in criminal investigations. Low explosives are frequently used in homemade bombs because the constituents are easy to obtain. Any child who has a chemistry set can make black powder, which is a mixture of 1 part sulfur (S), 1.5 parts charcoal (C), and 7.5 parts potassium nitrate (KNO_3). When the mixture explodes, it produces a variety of gaseous decomposition products:

$$6\ KNO_3 \quad + \quad 5\ C \quad + \quad 4\ S \quad \rightarrow$$

potassium nitrate   charcoal   sulfur   yields

$$2\ K_2CO_3 \quad + \quad 3\ SO_2 \quad + \quad K_2S \quad + \quad 3\ CO_2 \quad + \quad 3\ N_2$$

potassium carbonate   sulfur dioxide   potassium sulfide   carbon dioxide   nitrogen

Note that in this reaction, as well as in the reaction of nitroglycerin which we saw earlier, the nitrogen always ends up as a free diatomic gas (N_2). This gas, which makes up approximately four-fifths of the volume of air, is extremely stable. It is because of the strong preference of nitrogen for this stable state that many compounds of nitrogen are explosively unstable.

Nitrocellulose and to a lesser extent black powder are used commercially as propellants for fireworks and ammunition. Because they burn at a relatively slow rate, they give a constant steady push to a projectile as it leaves the barrel. The burning rate of nitrocellulose can be varied for different types of ammunition by mixing it with nitroglycerin.

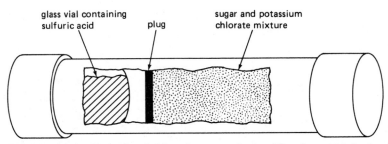

FIGURE 21-2 One type of delayed ignition device. The glass vial is broken by rapping the pipe against something hard. The acid eats through the plug and reacts explosively with the potassium chlorate/sugar mixture.

A mixture of potassium chlorate and sugar is often used as a delayed ignition device. A typical device uses a tube which is divided into two sections by a metal plug. The potassium chlorate and sugar mixture is enclosed in one section and a glass vial of sulfuric acid is enclosed in the other section. The device is activated by breaking the glass vial, which allows the sulfuric acid to come in contact with the metal divider. The delay mechanism is the time that it takes the acid to eat through the divider. When the acid reaches the mixture, it reacts with the sugar, creating enough heat to initiate the thermal decomposition of the potassium chlorate. From that point on the mixture combusts explosively with the sugar providing the fuel. (See Figure 21-2.)

The fact that these are low explosives does not mean that they cannot do a great deal of damage, but in order to attain their full destructive potential, they must be closely confined as, for example, in a length of metal pipe. The confinement forces the expanding gases to build up a tremendous amount of energy in order to burst the walls of the container. This built-up energy can often equal or surpass that of high explosives. If low explosives are ignited without being confined, they simply burn.

High Explosives

High explosives are divided into two categories: *primary* explosives, also known as *initiating* explosives, and *secondary* explosives. Primary explosives are extremely sensitive to heat and shock. They are regularly used to detonate other less sensitive explosives. They make good ammunition primers because the blow from a firing pin is sufficient to detonate them, and they in turn ignite the propellant charge. They are also used in percussion caps and artillery impact detonators. Some of the most common primary explosives are mercury fulminate, $Hg(CNO)_2$, and lead azide, $Pb(N_3)_2$. These materials will explode in large or small quantities whether they are confined or not.

Secondary explosives do not have to be confined to explode, but confinement increases their destructive capacity. Most of them have to be detonated by a primary explosive; they merely burn if they are spread out and lit with a match. The major exception is nitroglycerin, which is almost as sensitive to heat and shock as primary explosives are. Nitroglycerin is one of the principal constituents of most dynamites. In 1867 Alfred Nobel, a Swedish engineer and the founder of the Nobel prizes, discovered that when nitroglycerin was absorbed into some porous filling material, it became stable enough to handle safely without losing its explosive power. This is the basis of dynamite. Nobel used a siliceous earth as a filler, but modern fillers generally consist of combustible organic waste materials like wood pulp and sawdust.

Dynamite is found in connection with criminal investigations more than any other high explosive. In spite of the controls placed on its sale and use, dynamite is still the most easily accessible high explosive. Commercial dynamites are modified by the addition of various materials, usually oxidizing agents. *Straight* dynamite, which is the most brisant, has sodium nitrate as an additive for oxygen balance. *Ammonia* dynamite has ammonium nitrate, and *gelatin* dynamite is mixed with gelatinized nitrocellulose. Gelatin dynamite is water resistant and is therefore commonly used in underwater applications. Ethylene glycol dinitrate (EGDN) is added to most dynamites in order to lower their freezing points.

Several other high explosives occasionally appear as evidence in crimes, but much less often than dynamite because of the relative difficulty in obtaining them. TNT (trinitrotoluene) is used both commercially in mining work and as a military explosive. RDX (cyclotrimethylenetrinitrate) is primarily a military explosive having high brisance. RDX is used in demolitions and is the main component of plastic explosives. Its military designation is Composition C-4. Tetryl (2, 4, 6 trinitrophenylmethylnitramine) is a military explosive used in artillery shells. PETN (pentaerythritoltetranitrate) is used mainly in primacord, a detonating fuse which explodes so rapidly that it can detonate widely separated explosive charges almost simultaneously.

INVESTIGATING EXPLOSIONS

Since gaseous explosions are generally accidental, they are usually of less concern to an investigating officer than explosions caused by concentrated explosives. High and low explosives are almost always detonated intentionally for the purpose of producing destruction. The only times their explosions are likely to be accidental are when they occur during transport or as the result of a fire in an industry that deals with explosive materials. One example is ammonium nitrate fertilizer. Although ammonium nitrate is relatively stable, it explodes violently when it is heated to its ignition point. Thermal decomposition explosions can always be recognized and differentiated from gaseous explosions. Whereas the explosive fuels in gaseous explosions are spread thinly throughout an enclosed area, those of thermal decomposition explosives are concentrated in compact form. When they detonate, concentrated explosives emit energy and gases with equal force in all directions, including downward. Consequently, in addition to the damage they do laterally, they also generally leave craters. Gaseous explosions are not sufficiently concentrated in one spot to make craters.

For the most part, the blast effects of concentrated explosives show a pattern of destruction that radiates outward from the central point where the explosive was planted, and most of the breakage and flying debris is away from that point. This pattern can be disturbed, however, by a suction effect sometimes found in very rapidly detonating high explosives. This suction effect is caused by the sudden decrease in atmospheric pressure after the passage of the blast wave. This and the deflection of smaller objects off larger ones can cause debris to land in ways that are apparently inconsistent with the main direction of force of the explosion. Usually, the point of origin of the explosion is clear from the position of the crater and the predominating signs of blast damage. Investigators must be careful not to let these apparent inconsistencies confuse their conclusions.

As with fire scenes, it is essential that the scene of a bombing be thoroughly photographed. The overall area should be photographed from various angles, and each individual discovery of evidence should be photographed before it is touched. Photographs of the scene before the explosion should be obtained if they exist because they can be helpful in gauging the extent and nature of the damage.

Recovery of Evidence

Similar rules hold true for the collection of evidence from bomb scenes as for fire scenes. The investigator must not only be alert to evidence directly connected with the bomb itself but also to any possible evidence of forced entry and other personal trace evidence that the bomber may have left behind.

As far as evidence from the bomb itself is concerned, the investigator should concentrate on finding unexploded residues of the explosive itself and any bits and pieces of fuses, detonators, and timing devices.

The first and most obvious place to look for these items is in and around the crater. Even if no clues are visible to the naked eye, soil and debris samples from the crater area should be packaged in plastic bags or containers that can be closed off tightly and sent to the laboratory for close examination. Unexploded residues are often embedded in soil, wood, and other soft objects, but they can also adhere to metals and nonporous items.

Searching for parts of timing devices, fuses, and bomb casings can be a long, laborious job, but it is essential that it be done thoroughly. The best method is to sift the soil, ash, and debris through a wire mesh screen. Since an explosion can hurl this type of evidence considerable distances, the debris from the entire scene should be sifted systematically area by area. Although this is a tedious process, it is well worth the effort because the evidence recovered often provides the most important leads to the culprits. The clues to look for are odd bits of wire, clock parts, fragments of metal that do not seem to belong to the scene, bits of paper that may have been used for wrapping, and glass fragments that might have been part of a bottle containing nitroglycerin or a hydrocarbon.

LABORATORY EXAMINATION

The purpose of laboratory examinations of evidence from bomb scenes is to verify the investigating officer's assessment that an explosive was used and to identify the explosive.

The first step is to find unexploded residues of the explosive material. This is best done by examining the soil and debris under a low-power stereomicroscope. When residue particles are found, they are carefully separated (with a fine-pointed probe or tweezers) from the material in which they are embedded. Explosive residues are not always visible even under the microscope. In those cases they can be extracted by soaking some debris samples in acetone, which dissolves most explosive materials. The acetone is then filtered and allowed to air dry on a glass plate, leaving a small residue of the desired explosive sample. Heat should not be used to speed the drying process because heat can cause some explosives to decompose.

A wide variety of chemical and instrumental techniques is available to the criminalist for identifying explosive residues. The simplest and most satisfactory method is a two-step procedure in which the first step is a general screening by chemical spot tests that narrow down the possibilities by eliminating certain classes of explosives. The second step is to identify the evidence sample by comparing it with known samples of those explosives that have not been eliminated by the spot tests.

TABLE 21–1. Spot Test Reagents

Substance tested	Reagent				
	Aniline sulfate	*Barium chloride*	*Brucine*	*Cupric tetrapyridine*	*Diphenylamine*
Bromide	yellow to yellow-orange	NR	yellow to orange	NR	yellow[a] NR[b]
Carbonate	NCD	white precipitate	NCD	NCD	NCD
Chlorate	yellow to orange	NR	orange to red	NR	blue to blue-black
Chloride	NCD	NR	NR	NR	NR
Iodide	brown to purple to black	NR	brown to purple to black	brown precipitate	purple
Nitrate	light yellow to yellow	NR	orange to yellow	NR	blue to blue-black
Nitrite	NR[a] yellow[b]	NR	orange to red	green	blue-black
Nitrocellulose	NR	NR	orange to red	NR	blue-black
Nitroglycerin	NR	NR	orange to red	NR	blue to blue-black
Nitrostarch	NR	NR	orange to red	NR	blue-black
Perchlorate	NR	NR	NR	purple crystalline precipitate	NR
PETN	NR	NR	orange to red	NR	blue
RDX	NR	NR	orange to red	NR	NR
Sulfate	NR	white precipitate	NR	NR	NR
Tetryl	NR	NR	orange-red	NR	blue
TNT; 2,4-DNT; 2,6-DNT;	NR	NR	NR	NR	NR

NR = no reaction
NCD = no color development
[a] Solid.
[b] Aqueous.

			Reagent			
Griess	J-acid	Nessler	Nitron	Methylene blue	Silver nitrate	Sulfuric acid
NR	dirty orange[a] NRb	NCD	NR	light purple[a] NR[b]	creamy white precipitate	yellow to yellow-orange
NCD	NCD	NCD	NR	NCD	creamy white precipitate	NCD
NCD	orange-brown	NR	dirty white precipitate	NR	NR	yellow
NR	NCD	NR	NR	NR	white precipitate	NCD
NR	brown to purple	NR	dirty white precipitate	purple	yellow precipitate	brown to purple to black
pink to red	orange-brown	NR	white precipitate	NR	NR	NR
red to yellow	NR[a] brown-orange[b]	NR	dirty white precipitate	NR	white precipitate	NR
pink	orange-brown	NR	NR	NR	NR	NR
pink to red	orange-brown	NR	light, dirty white precipitate	NR	NR	NR
pink	orange-brown	NR	NR	NR	NR	NR
NR	NR	NR	white precipitate turns gray-white	purple to purple precipitate	NR	NR
pink to red	orange-brown to red	NR	NR	NR	NR	NR
pink to red	orange-brown	NR	NR	NR	NR	NR
NR	NR	NR	NR	NR	NR	NR
pink to red	yellow to orange-brown	NR	NR	orange to red	NR	NR
NR	NR	NR	NR	NR	NR	NR

R. G. Parker, M. O. Stephenson, J. M. McOwen, and J. A. Cherolis, "Analysis of Explosives and Explosive Residues. Part 1: Chemical Tests." Reprinted, with permission, from the *Journal of Forensic Sciences*, Jan. 1975. Copyright American Society for Testing and Materials, 1916 Race Street, Philadelphia, PA 19103.

Color Spot Tests

To perform the spot tests the samples are first dissolved in acetone. Drops of the acetone solution are placed on a spot plate and air dried. One spot plate is prepared for each test. A drop of each test reagent is added to the residue spot and any color reaction is noted. Table 21–1 gives a comprehensive list of reagents that can be used and the color reactions to be expected from different explosives. Since it would be impractical to apply all the reagents for each test, the two reagents that have proved the most useful are the Griess reagent[2] and diphenylamine.[3] In addition, TNT shows a red reaction to a reagent of alcoholic potassium hydroxide (10 grams of KOH dissolved in 100 milliliters of absolute alcohol).

Identification

Once the field of choices is narrowed by means of the spot tests, the samples can be compared in various ways with samples of explosives. The most satisfactory method is by thin-layer chromatography (TLC). A drop of concentrated acetone solution of the evidence sample is spotted onto a TLC plate (i.e., a glass plate coated with a thin layer of silica gel) along with a drop of a known standard, which is also in acetone solution. The samples can then be migrated with chloroform and the Rf values compared to those of the known standards.

Confirmation can be made by infrared spectrophotometry for organic materials and inorganic nitrates, chlorates, and perchlorates. The identification of crystalline materials can be confirmed by X-ray diffraction. Normally, the criminalist's job is limited to identifying the type of explosive (e.g., dynamite, TNT, PETN, etc.), but in the extremely unusual circumstance in which explosives are found in the subject's possession, the criminalist may have to give an opinion as to whether or not those explosives and the residues found at the scene of a bombing have a common origin. Since most explosives have some metallic compounds in them, either in the form of manufacturer's additives or trace impurities, such comparisons can best be made by emission spectroscopy or neutron activation analysis.

[2]Griess reagent: Step 1: Dissolve 1 gram sulfanilic acid in 100 milliliters 30 percent acetic acid. Step 2: Dissolve 1 gram alphanaphthylamine in 230 milliliters boiling distilled water. Let cool and decant supernatant liquid, which is mixed with 100 milliliters glacial acetic acid. Add both solutions along with a few milligrams of zinc to sample.

[3]Diphenylamine reagent: Dissolve 1 gram diphenylamine in 100 milliliters concentrated sulfuric acid.

Review Questions

1. When an explosive explodes, it produces
   a. Noise
   b. Heat
   c. Light
   d. Expanding gases
   e. a, b, and d
   f. All the above

2. Which of the following materials can produce explosive mixtures with air?
   a. Coal dust
   b. Aluminum dust
   c. Methane
   d. All the above

3. Which of the following is *not* an explosophore?
   a. Nitrate
   b. Chloride
   c. Azide
   d. Fulminate

4. (T, F) Explosions of nitrate compounds always result in the production of nitrogen gas.

5. Black powder consists of
   a. Potassium nitrate, sulfur, and charcoal
   b. Potassium chlorate, sulfur, and charcoal
   c. Potassium chlorate and sugar
   d. Nitrocellulose

6. Investigations of explosions have become more frequent in recent years because of
   a. Inadequate transportation facilities for explosives
   b. Increased availability of explosives
   c. Terrorism
   d. Military experiments

7. When coal dust becomes diffused throughout the air, it has the explosive properties of
   a. Dynamite
   b. Nitric acid
   c. C4
   d. A gas

8. In the potassium chlorate delayed ignition device the fuel material is
   a. Sugar
   b. Potassium

   c. Chlorine
   d. Sulfuric acid

9. The presence of a crater indicates
   a. A gaseous explosion
   b. A thermal decomposition explosion
   c. An accidental explosion
   d. An explosion in low-lying drains

10. (T, F) Explosive residues can be identified by a combination of spot tests and thin-layer chromatography.

————— *DRUGS* —————
AND POISONS

The cells of the human body teem with billions of chemical reactions which are closely interrelated to strike the delicate balance needed to maintain normal life. Drugs and poisons produce their effects by interfering in some way with these reactions, thereby throwing the body chemistry out of balance. The distinction between drugs and poisons is not always a clear one. Although some drugs, like heroin and hashish, have no current medical uses in the United States, many drugs have important therapeutic value. If they are taken under controlled medical conditions, they can help to restore and maintain normal body functions when the normal chemical balances have somehow been lost. But when taken in sufficient overdoses to cause injury or death, the same drugs in effect become poisons.

Most of the poisons used in suicide and murder cases have legitimate uses either as prescription drugs or in agriculture and industry or, like carbon monoxide, they are products of everyday life. Since the more exotic poisons are simply not available to the average person, they very seldom appear in criminal cases.

Investigative agencies are interested only in the criminal aspects of drugs and poisons. Police investigators are in the forefront of the battle to control the illegal distribution and use of drugs, and they have the responsibility to solve cases of suicide or murder by poisoning. Their main concern is with the evidentiary value of substances collected in the course of their investigations. Since a drug is useless as evidence unless it is properly identified, the investigative officer must work in close cooperation with the forensic chemist, whose job is to analyze substances brought into the laboratory. In the case of drug overdoses or deaths by poisoning the identification becomes the province of the toxicologist, who must extract and identify substances from the blood and urine of living victims and from various organs and body fluids of dead ones.

Since police and investigating officers are usually the first on the scene of a drug or poisoning case, they should be sufficiently familiar with the nature of the substances most commonly encountered in such cases to be able to recognize their effects on people and take the necessary steps to save lives and preserve evidence.

DRUGS

Although much is known about the physical and social effects of drug abuse, the reasons for addiction are still poorly understood. The main difficulty lies in understanding the nature of the psychological dependence that drugs induce. Taking drugs can produce strong feelings of pleasure and satisfaction, and some people can develop a powerful psychological drive to preserve and renew these sensations. This pursuit of pleasure tends to lead people to take larger than therapeutic doses. With many drugs this results in a physical dependence characterized by extreme physical discomfort when the drug is withdrawn. The physical dependence can be cured in all cases in a matter of a few days or a few weeks, but even after the physical cure is complete, the psychological need almost always remains strong. There are many drugs, particularly of the stimulant type, which do not produce physical dependence, but the psychological drive to use and abuse them can be just as compelling as it is when a physical dependence is present. All different kinds of people can become addicted to drugs. It is not clear to what extent psychological dependence is caused by the drug itself or by the individual's own susceptibility. There is no way of predicting whether any given person will become addicted.

A characteristic of some drugs, which is often related to physical dependence, is a tendency to induce tolerance. Tolerance is a state of physical adaptation to a drug, which requires that increasingly larger doses be taken in order to achieve the same level of pleasure. If it were not for the phenomenon of tolerance, many drugs could be taken indefinitely in small doses without doing any appreciable harm. But the fact that developing addicts need ever-increasing doses just to maintain their habits makes these kinds of drugs particularly dangerous to society. When addicts run out of money to buy the drug, they resort to crime, and the more drug they need, the more crimes they must commit.

The various classes of drugs have different characteristics with regard to physical and psychological dependence and also with regard to tolerance.

Narcotics

The word *narcotics* is often misused to mean drugs in general. It actually refers to any substance that induces stupor, and in current usage it refers to opium and its derivatives. Narcotics are important therapeutically because they have powerful analgesic (pain-killing) properties without causing loss of motor coordination or slurred speech as is the case with central nervous system depressants. The reason for the pain-killing effects of narcotics is not completely understood.

The drugs in this class include natural, semisynthetic, and synthetic substances. Natural narcotics are alkaloids which are used in the same chemical form in which they occur in nature. For the most part, they come from the opium poppy plant, *Papaver somniferum.* Among the most important narcotics are opium itself, morphine, and codeine. Opium finds little use in its raw form in the United States. It is primarily used as a raw material from which other natural and semisynthetic drugs are made.

The semisynthetics are derived from opium but there are certain chemical changes. The most commonly abused semisynthetic is heroin. Heroin is an especially chancy drug for the addict because it has no medicinal use today in this country and all the heroin available to users has been made in clandestine laboratories in which there is no control over the quality of the product. In addition, heroin is generally cut to anywhere from 1 percent to 10 percent of its strength before it reaches the street. It is usually diluted with lactose (milk sugar), sugar, starch, or powdered milk.

The synthetic narcotics, although chemically related to the opium derivatives, are produced entirely in the laboratory. The most common ones are meperidine and methadone, both of which are analgesics. Methadone has been widely used in programs to detoxify heroin addicts because although its addictive effects are similar to those of heroin, the feeling of well-being that it induces is more stable. Therefore, the user can take one daily oral dose and function normally in the world instead of having to shoot up four times a day.

Most of the narcotics produce strong physical as well as psychological dependence, and they also induce tolerance. It may be difficult to spot an individual who is under the influence of a narcotic because a maintenance dose does not give rise to any abnormal behavior. The user may experience reduced vision due to pinpoint pupils caused by the drug. Long-time users can often be identified by needle marks in various parts of their bodies but most commonly on their arms. They may also suffer from malnutrition, infections, and general personal neglect. There is a particular danger of contracting hepatitis from the communal use of unsterilized needles. If a user has hepatitis, he or she may have a yellowish cast to the skin color and to the whites of the eyes.

If a user takes more than the amount needed just to maintain a high, the user may seem drowsy and apathetic. A mild overdose can produce a stupor or deep sleep, and a large overdose can result in coma, in slow, shallow breathing, and in cold, clammy skin. If the overdose is large enough, it can cause convulsions and death from respiratory failure. But it is not always a matter of the size of the dose. Sometimes a group of heroin addicts get together and shoot up the same dose but only one addict suffers respiratory collapse. These cases seem to be the result of a reaction between the heroin and alcohol or barbiturates already in the addict's system instead of an overdose of heroin.

Narcotics can be administered by eating, sniffing, smoking, and injecting. The user who reaches the point of injecting a drug usually starts by injecting small amounts just under the skin ("skin popping"). The user then progresses to intramuscular and finally intravenous injections ("mainlining").

If the narcotic abruptly ceases to be administered, the addict experiences a broad range of withdrawal symptoms, including anxiety, restlessness, yawning, perspiration, watery eyes, running nose, loss of appetite, nausea, goose flesh, insomnia, stomach cramps and other body aches, elevated heart beat and blood pressure, diarrhea, and muscle spasms. The symptoms last from 7 to 10 days if the withdrawal of the drug is sudden and complete ("cold turkey"). The worst of the symptoms can be avoided if the drug dosages are reduced gradually over a period of 2 or 3 weeks. The psychological dependence, however, may remain for an indefinite period.

Depressants

The class of drugs known as depressants operates by inhibiting the transmission of neurological signals within the central nervous system (CNS). Housed in the brain and spinal cord, the central nervous system controls and coordinates all of the voluntary and involuntary bodily functions. Consequently, depressant drugs can affect perception, motor coordination, and the functioning of internal organs.

Taken in prescribed doses, depressants are useful in the treatment of anxiety, insomnia, and tension. The effects vary in their intensity in different people, but large doses can lead to sedation, stupor, coma, and death.

Barbiturates

These drugs, which are derived from barbituric acid, make up the group of CNS depressants most widely used in medicine and, except for alcohol, they are also the most commonly abused of the depressants. The barbiturates include such brand names as Amytal, Nembutal, Luminal, and Seconal. They are generally taken orally in tablet form, but they are also sometimes injected by thrill seekers.

When barbiturates are taken on a continuous basis in greater than therapeutic doses, they induce strong dependence, both physical and psychological. One of the dangers of barbiturates is that tolerance can develop quickly at relatively low doses so that people who use them continuously even for legitimate purposes like combating insomnia may find that they need stronger and stronger doses to get the desired effect.

The use of barbiturates produces effects that differ from person to person and even within the same person, depending on the person's emotional state and the social setting in which the barbiturates are taken. At one time the drug may induce a mild euphoria (feeling of well-being); at another time the drug may induce hostility and aggression. Moderate doses result in slurred speech, slow reaction times, and impaired memory. Barbiturates may also cause a distorted perception of time which can lead users to take an accidental overdose because they forgot when they took the last dose.

Withdrawal symptoms from barbiturate addiction are extremely severe and they can be fatal if the withdrawal is not carried out gradually. The "cold turkey" approach should never be used with barbiturate users. Withdrawal symptoms include anxiety, muscle tremors and twitching, dizziness, visual distortion, nausea, insomnia, rapid weight loss, convulsions similar to epilepsy, and psychotic delirium with paranoia, hallucinations, and panic.

Nonbarbiturate Depressants

Although chemically different from the barbiturates, the other depressants have similar effects on the central nervous system, and in varying degrees of severity they are also similar with respect to dependence, tolerance, and withdrawal symptoms.

The oldest of the depressants is chloral hydrate, which has become famous in detective fiction as knockout drops or as a "Mickey Finn."

Some brand names include Noctec and Somnos. It induces moderate dependence and is not widely used as a street drug.

Glutethimide (brand name Doriden) and methaqualone (Optimil, Quaalude, Sopor, and others) are sedatives with strong potential for physical and psychological dependence and tolerance.

The tranquilizers, including Librium, Miltown, Serax, Tranxene, and Valium, are primarily anti-anxiety drugs with only moderate potential for dependence. They all produce some tolerance.

Alcohol

Consumed in the form of wine, liquor, and beer, grain alcohol (ethyl alcohol or ethanol) is not generally thought of as a drug, but it is in fact a central nervous system depressant that has properties remarkably similar to barbiturates. Alcohol is the single most abused drug of any class or type.

Because alcohol is readily available and socially acceptable, it is not easy to tell where social drinking ends and dependence begins. Although most people agree that drinking a few glasses of wine with a meal does not constitute alcohol abuse, if a person comes to miss those few glasses when they are not available, that person is already beginning to experience a mild form of psychological dependence. Psychological dependence can exist in varying degrees and may only become evident when people stand out by drinking significantly more than is acceptable in their cultural setting. Dependence begins with the feeling that one needs a drink for some reason, whether to stimulate the appetite, have the courage to face social situations, relieve anxiety, alleviate boredom, or other reasons.

The symptoms of alcohol intoxication are similar to those of barbiturates: loss of motor coordination, slurred speech, impaired mental performance. Like barbiturates, alcohol can induce happy or hostile feelings, depending on the individual's personality, emotional state, and setting. Although physical dependence on alcohol does not develop as readily as with barbiturates, it definitely exists when alcohol is consumed regularly in large quantities. Alcohol users can also develop a certain amount of tolerance, which is largely manifested in the ability of the alcoholic to appear to be less drunk than the nondrinker who has the same blood alcohol content.

When a high degree of physical dependence has developed, the withdrawal syndrome can be very severe. At its worst it is characterized by tremors, sweating, nausea, thready elevated heart rate and low blood pressure, convulsions, and delirium with delusions and hallucinations. These symptoms are similar to those of barbiturate withdrawal and to some extent the ingestion of barbiturates can reduce the severity of alcohol withdrawal symptoms. Similarly, the consumption of alcohol can help ease barbiturate withdrawal symptoms.

The use of alcohol together with barbiturates or other drugs poses a serious threat to the user because of the problem of *potentiation.* This refers to the tendency of one drug to intensify the effects of another drug when the two drugs are taken together. Because of the potentiating property of alcohol, the dose of barbiturate that a person could normally tolerate could become a lethal overdose if taken after drinking alcohol.

Stimulants

As the name suggests, this class of drugs has its effect by stimulating the neurological activity of the central nervous system. The most commonly abused stimulants are cocaine and amphetamine (Benzedrine, Dexedrine, Biphetamine, and others). Cocaine is a natural alkaloid extracted from the leaves of the coca plant *(Erythroxylon coca)* which grows in the high Andes in South America. Cocaine was formerly used widely as a local anesthetic, but it has very little medical use today. As a street drug cocaine generally comes in the form of a white powder which, like heroin, is likely to be of uncertain purity.

Amphetamine and other closely related drugs, popularly known as "speed," were originally developed to combat narcolepsy, a disease characterized by an overpowering desire for sleep. It was later discovered that amphetamine is useful in weight control because it diminishes the appetite and, surprisingly, that it has a tendency to calm down hyperactive children. This calming effect, which is the reverse of what one might expect, was discovered by accident and the reasons for it are not fully understood. Amphetamine is still prescribed for those purposes, but most states strictly control the amounts. Recent experience indicates that the dangers of amphetamine far outweigh any value it may have in diet control.

Stimulants can be taken orally, sniffed, or diluted and injected. The strongest sensations come from intravenous injection, which brings about a sudden ecstatic flash when the drug hits the brain.

People under the influence of stimulants are abnormally energetic, wakeful, and hyperactive. Continuous large doses can lead to obsessive behavior, paranoia, and hallucinations. Overdoses can lead to dizziness, tremors, agitation, hostility, panic, headache, flushed skin, chest pains, palpitations, vomiting and cramps, convulsions, and finally death due to cardiovascular collapse.

Although the psychological dependence on stimulants is strong, there appears to be no physical dependence and no development of tolerance. However, withdrawal of the drug does result in apathy and depression that can last for several days. As stimulants are metabolized quickly, the episodes do not last very long, and frequent readministration of the drug may be necessary to maintain the desired sensations. To avoid the depressive effects when the drug finally wears off, users may sedate themselves with a narcotic or depressant and they often alternate between them. Users may also inject a mixture of cocaine and heroin, known as a "speedball," to get the simultaneous antagonistic effects of the two drugs.

Hallucinogens

Hallucinogens, which can be of either natural or synthetic origin, have the effect on the user of distorting perception and creating sensory illusions, which may include both auditory and visual hallucinations. The effects of hallucinogens are unpredictable. On one occasion they may produce a pleasantly altered state of consciousness and on another a severe psychotic episode that can last or recur even after the drug has worn off. There can be considerable variations in mood from euphoria to depressive anxiety during a single drug-taking experience. Heavy overdoses can be fatal. At present there are no medical uses for hallucinogens.

The major natural hallucinogens are peyote, mescaline, psilocybin, and psilocyn. Peyote and mescaline come from the peyote cactus, which grows in northern Mexico and the southwestern United States. The button of the cactus can be chewed or ground into powder and eaten. Mescaline is the same as peyote, but it is refined and concentrated into stronger doses. Psilocybin and psilocyn are derived from mushrooms that also grow in Mexico. Psilocybin and psilocyn as well as peyote have been used in Indian religious ceremonies for centuries.

Perhaps the most popular of all hallucinogens is LSD (lysergic acid diethylamide), a semisynthetic substance synthesized from ergot, a fungus of rye. Some other synthetic hallucinogens are DOM (5-dimethyloxyamphetamine) which combines its hallucinogenic effect with the stimulant effect of amphetamine, DMT (dimethyltryptamine), DET (diethyltryptamine), and PCP (phencyclidine). PCP ("angel dust") currently rivals LSD in popularity among young users. It is produced legally in limited quantities as a veterinary anesthetic, but because it is relatively easy to make, many clandestine laboratories are producing it illicitly in large quantities. The clandestine product is often highly contaminated. PCP usage can induce various perceptual distortions, including hallucinations and a feeling of being outside one's own body. Reactions can range from apathy to homicidal violence.

None of the hallucinogens has been found to induce physical dependence. Consequently, there are no withdrawal symptoms. LSD and psilocybin produce a high degree of tolerance if they are taken continuously, but the tolerance disappears rapidly after the drugs are stopped.

Cannabis

Cannabis sativa is the hemp plant. It is cultivated for its stem fibers, which are used primarily in making rope. Cannabis grows like a weed in tropical and warm temperate climates. When smoked or eaten it produces relaxation and a carefree attitude that is sometimes combined with perceptual distortions which users describe as mind expanding. The use of cannabis makes the senses seem more acute in that tasting, seeing, and hearing produce vivid sensations. It also lowers the blood sugar content, which results in a craving for food, especially sweets.

Cannabis is used in three forms, marihuana, hashish, and hashish oil, each of which is of successively greater strength. The psychoactive ingredient is THC (delta-9-tetrahydrocannabinol). Marihuana is the dried leaves and flowering tops of the cannabis plant. Seeds and bits of stem are also sometimes mixed in, but they have little hallucinogenic effect. Marihuana contains between 0.2 percent and 2.0 percent THC. Hashish is a dried resin secreted from cannabis flowers. It contains from 5 percent to 12 percent THC. Hashish oil is a thick, dark liquid made by repeated extraction and concentration of hashish. It may contain between 20 percent and 60 percent THC.

There is some controversy over whether or not cannabis produces physical dependence. There is a set of withdrawal symptoms after prolonged heavy use; these symptoms are characterized by insomnia, irritability, hyperactivity, decreased appetite and weight loss, sweating, and increased salivation. Although there is a moderate psychological dependence, the principal danger of cannabis seems to be that it introduces neophyte users to the illicit drug environment, which may lead them to try more addictive drugs.

POISONS

The majority of poisonings that criminal investigators encounter today involve overdoses of the drugs mentioned in the previous section, but suicides and homicides still do occur in which other types of poisons are used. One reason for the comparatively limited number of poisonings is the general unfamiliarity of suitable poisons. There are many highly toxic materials readily at hand in everyday life, but for the most part they are either naturally repugnant or such large doses are needed to cause death that they are not suitable for murder and they would require an extraordinary amount of determination to be used in a suicide.

Inorganic Poisons

Heavy Elements

Although some heavy metallic elements are essential constituents of the human diet in trace quantities, many metallic compounds are extremely toxic in amounts which are greater than trace levels but still very small.

Perhaps the most famous of all the metallic poisons is arsenic trioxide (As_2O_3), which has historically been a popular murder weapon. Today arsenic compounds are widely used as agricultural pesticides, rodenticides, and herbicides. If arsenic is found to be the cause of death in a homicide, one important line of investigation would be to trace people who had access to such materials. These compounds of arsenic having industrial and agricultural applications can also be the cause of accidental poisonings. Some symptoms of arsenic poisoning are nausea and violent vomiting, stomach pains, thirst, an odor of garlic on the breath, inability to urinate, cold clammy skin, and eventual death.

Lead poisoning, although rarely encountered in murders and suicides, is responsible for a large number of accidental poisonings, especially among children, because of the presence of lead and its compounds in old paint, water pipes, and gasoline. Tetraethyl lead, the gasoline antiknock additive, is readily absorbed through the skin. It is highly toxic and cumulative and can cause serious illness and death if leaded gasoline is used frequently as a hand-washing solvent.

Some other toxic metals that may occasionally be encountered because of their use in industry are mercury, thallium, beryllium, antimony, and their compounds. The heavy metallic poisons generally operate by attacking the sulfur in certain enzymes and proteins in the body, thereby altering their structure and destroying their ability to function properly.

Cyanide

The cyanide compounds have long been well known for their highly toxic properties. They have a wide range of commercial uses from rodenticides to metallurgy. Hydrogen cyanide (HCN) is an extremely toxic gas which can pose a serious hazard to fire fighters and workers in chemical or metal plants. When it enters the bloodstream, it attacks certain enzymes necessary for the transfer of oxygen to the cells, thereby causing the body tissues to be destroyed by oxygen starvation. The cyanide compounds most commonly used in intentional poisonings are sodium cyanide (NaCN) and potassium cyanide (KCN), which can be obtained in solid pellet form. When either sodium cyanide or potassium cyanide is ingested, it reacts with hydrochloric acid in the stomach to produce hydrogen cyanide (NaCN + HCl → NaCl + HCN), which is quickly absorbed into the bloodstream with the deadly results noted above. Cyanide poisoning is very rapid and death can occur in a few minutes after ingestion.

Symptoms of cyanide poisoning are rapid, labored breathing, heart palpitations, tightness in the chest, and bluish tinge to the skin from the lack of oxygenation. The odor of oil of bitter almonds on the breath is another symptom that has been popularized in detective fiction. It is not especially helpful because the odor is not always easy to detect and most people have never smelled oil of bitter almonds.

Organic Poisons

Organic poisons include all the drugs described in the drug section of this chapter. In addition to ethyl alcohol, which was mentioned earlier as a central nervous system depressant, other alcohols and organic solvents are highly toxic. If they are ingested, they cause severe gastrointestinal corrosion and pain. They are seldom found in intentional poisonings. Severe alcoholics sometimes drink wood alcohol or rubbing alcohol when they are desperate for a drink. Methanol causes blindness but otherwise it is no more toxic than ethanol. The heavier alcohols (propanol, isopropanol, butanol, isobutanol, etc.), however, can cause serious illness and death. The lethal dose of isopropanol (rubbing alcohol) is approximately 240 milliliters.

Aside from the natural drugs, there are other plant poisons that may come to the attention of the toxicologist. Strychnine is an alkaloid extracted from the *Strychnos nux-vomica,* a nut that grows in Indonesia and Malaysia. It has been used medicinally in small doses as a stimulant. Doses of over 20 milligrams can cause symptoms of stiffness, twitching, violent convulsions, and finally death due to spasms of the respiratory system and exhaustion. Nicotine, which acts as a mild stimulant when inhaled with tobacco smoke, is highly toxic in high concentration (from 40 milligrams to 60 milligrams can be fatal). Digitalis is a mixture of sugar-derivative substances called glycosides extracted from the dried leaf of the purple foxglove *(Digitalis purpurea),* a plant that grows in temperate climates. Digitalis in therapeutic doses is commonly used as a heart stimulant. In larger doses it can cause death by cardiac arrest.

Carbon Monoxide

Although many gases, such as hydrogen cyanide, hydrogen sulfide, sulfur dioxide, and others, can be highly toxic when inhaled, they are more likely to be associated with industrial accidents and fires than criminal cases. The one gas that is of major importance in criminal investigations is carbon monoxide because of the frequency of its occurrence in suicides, accidental deaths, and occasionally homicides. Carbon monoxide is produced as the result of the incomplete combustion of carbon. Whenever there is a fire, carbon monoxide is produced, and in urban areas large amounts are generated by motor vehicles. Suicides by carbon monoxide poisoning are most commonly carried out by sitting in a closed garage with a car motor running or by extending a hose from the exhaust pipe of a car to the interior and sitting inside the car with the windows closed and the motor running. Accidental carbon monoxide poisoning can occur any time there is a fire in a poorly ventilated area.

Carbon monoxide works as a poison by interfering with the delivery of oxygen to the body tissues. The body's mechanism for transporting oxygen is hemoglobin, a complex component of the red blood cells, which picks up oxygen molecules from the air drawn into the lungs and transports them through the blood stream to all the cells of the body. When oxygen is bound molecularly to hemoglobin, the compound formed thereby is called *oxyhemoglobin*. When the hemoglobin delivers the oxygen to the cells, its oxygen-carrying sites become free to pick up carbon dioxide, which the cells return as a waste product. The blood carries the carbon dioxide back to the lungs where it is expelled into the air. When quantities of carbon monoxide are present in the air, its molecules occupy the sites on the hemoglobin that are normally taken by oxygen. The compound that results from the combination of carbon monoxide and hemoglobin is *carboxyhemoglobin*. The high toxicity of carbon monoxide is due to the fact that carboxyhemoglobin is a much more stable compound than oxyhemoglobin, and hemoglobin has a more than 200 times greater preference for carbon monoxide than it does for oxygen. The degree of danger of carbon monoxide depends on its concentration in the air. A concentration of 100 ppm (parts per million) or 0.01 percent causes no ill effects, but 1,000 ppm, or 0.1 percent, can cause headaches in a short time and can be fatal over a period of hours. A concentration of over 2,000 ppm is extremely hazardous and can cause death in less than an hour.

The human body can tolerate a 10 percent carboxyhemoglobin saturation in the blood without ill effects. Heavy smokers may have concentrations between 5 percent and 10 percent. Between 10 percent and 40 percent blood saturation can cause throbbing headaches, dizziness, vomiting, and collapse. Concentrations from 40 percent to 60 percent can intensify the above symptoms and bring about convulsions. Above 50 percent they can cause coma and rapid death. These figures are generalizations. The toxicity of carbon monoxide can vary considerably from person to person, depending on the individual's metabolism and state of health. Also, the consumption of alcohol has a potentiating effect on carbon monoxide poisoning.

It is the hemoglobin that imparts the red color to the blood, and carboxyhemoglobin is a deeper red than oxyhemoglobin. Therefore, people who have been exposed to dangerous concentrations of carbon monoxide often have a ruddy skin color that gives the appearance of good health. A person who has collapsed from carbon monoxide poisoning rapidly returns to normal when brought into fresh air. However, if the exposure is long enough, there may be permanent damage to the brain and respiratory and nervous systems.

INVESTIGATION OF POISONINGS AND OVERDOSES

In the case of a fatal poisoning or drug overdose it is the job of the toxicologist to determine the exact cause of death by analysis of the post-mortem remains. This can be like searching for a needle in a haystack if the toxicologist has no clue to what the poison might be. The investigating officer can often make such analyses incomparably easier by thoroughly observing the scene and carefully collecting evidence.

If the poison or drug was self-administered, there is almost always some trace remaining in the vicinity of the victim. It may be in the form of empty medicine bottles, a hypodermic syringe and associated paraphernalia, an envelope that has traces of powder adhering to it, a glass in which there are liquid remains, or some other container that may not fit into the scene. If the poison container or the means of administering the poison are not clearly evident, it is advisable to collect all the medicine containers and pill bottles found on the premises in order to provide the toxicologist with some basis for beginning the analysis without having to screen for every type of drug. It may happen that a person poisons himself or herself, either intentionally or accidentally, in one place and then goes to another location before the poison takes effect. The investigator may be able to learn the probable nature of the poison by questioning relatives and friends, who may be able to provide information about drugs the victim might have had legally through a doctor's prescription or about poisons to which the victim may have had access through a job.

If remaining traces of the substance are found on the scene, they should be collected with care to preserve them. Liquids should be collected in airtight containers such as Mason jars or perhaps in their original containers. Tablets and powders should be packaged in plastic pill bottles or other containers of suitable size to prevent the loss of any of the evidence. Again, it may be possible to use the original drugstore container. Blood samples should be kept in airtight bottles with an anticoagulant and a preservative and should be refrigerated as soon as possible.

If no signs of the poison are on the premises, the substance is likely to have been administered by someone other than the victim. Again, questioning of friends, relatives, and neighbors may reveal who among the victim's acquaintances had access to drugs or poisons, perhaps through their work. Investigators should also search the immediate neighborhood of the poisoning in case the murderer threw away incriminating materials while leaving the scene.

All evidence collected should be properly labeled with the name of the investigating officer, the date, time and place of discovery, and the nature of the evidence.

LABORATORY IDENTIFICATION OF DRUGS AND POISONS

A number of techniques are available to the crime laboratory for identifying drugs and poisons. The main difficulties lie in pinpointing the specific toxic substances from the large array of possibilities and in isolating them from contaminating materials. In general, the drug chemist has an easier task than the toxicologist does. The job of the drug chemist is to analyze suspected drugs which are recovered as evidence in the course of drug-related investigations. For the most part, the drug chemist will have relatively large amounts of the evidence to work with. The toxicologist, on the other hand, must often deal with minute amounts of a drug or poison extracted in trace quantities from the organs or body fluids of the victim. The difficulties of the toxicologist are intensified by the fact that drug abusers often seek new thrills by mixing their drugs so there is often more than one drug to be identified. Another problem is that the metabolic processes of the human body change the chemical nature of many drugs. Heroin, for example, is quickly metabolized into morphine once it gets into the bloodstream. Other drugs may be metabolized into four or five substances with which the toxicologist must be familiar in order to identify the original drug.

Drug Extractions

The ability to identify a drug correctly is to a large extent dependent on the drug's extraction from contaminating materials. This is especially true for toxicologists because of the minute amounts of toxic materials with which they must work. For the drug chemist, who normally receives the unknown drug in the form of a brown or white powder, the extraction process is made relatively simple by the fact that most drugs are soluble in organic solvents like methanol, ethanol, chloroform, and ether. Sugar, starch, and lactose, which are the diluents most commonly used to cut street drugs, are not soluble in organic solvents. Consequently, if the unknown powder is mixed with a solvent, the insoluble powders sink to the bottom and the drug in fairly pure form remains in solution. After separation from the insoluble portion, the solution can be evaporated to recover the drug.

The situation becomes more complicated if more than one drug is present, as is often the case with street drugs. To isolate the drugs from the diluents and from each other, the chemist takes advantage of the fact that the different drugs are of varying degrees of acidity and basicity. As we saw in Chapter 2 (page 20) an acid is a substance that increases the concentration of positive hydrogen ions (H^+) in a solution and a base is a substance that increases the concentration of negative hydroxide ions (OH^-).

Drugs can be acidic, neutral, basic, or amphoteric (i.e., able to act either as an acid or a base). To separate acidic drugs from basic drugs, the chemist first dissolves the unknown powder in an aqueous (water) solution. Water, being neutral, has a pH of 7. To extract the acidic drugs, the chemist adds an acid (usually hydrochloric or acetic) to the water solution. This has the effect of increasing the concentration of H^+ ions in the solution, thereby making it more difficult for the acidic drugs to give off their own H^+ ions. When forced to retain their H^+ ions, the molecules of the drug become depolarized, i.e., lacking any electrical charge. Nonpolar molecules have a much greater solubility in organic solvents than they do in water. Therefore, if some chloroform or ether is added to the solution and the whole mixture shaken up, the acidic drugs migrate to the organic solvent while the polarized basic drugs remain behind in the water solution. Since chloroform is heavier than water and ether is lighter, they separate into layers and the organic layer is easily separated from the aqueous layer. Methanol and ethanol cannot be used for extractions from aqueous solutions because they are soluble in water and consequently do not form layers.

When a basic drug is being extracted, a strong base like ammonium hydroxide or sodium hydroxide is added to the aqueous solution, thereby furnishing an excess of OH^- ions. This has the effect of depolarizing the basic drugs just as the excess of H^+ ions depolarizes the acid drugs. Once again chloroform or ether is added; this time the basic drugs migrate to the organic layer.

The extraction of acid and basic drugs from body organs works on essentially the same principle as extraction from an aqueous solution, but the procedure is made much more difficult by the fact that the drugs are bound up in the cellular tissue of the organs. If the drugs are to be released, the tissues have to be macerated, chemically digested, and filtered several times in order to obtain a very small amount of drug in an aqueous solution. Once the aqueous solution is separated from the tissues, acid and basic drugs can be extracted according to the principles described above. Volatile drugs and poisons, such as alcohols, alde-

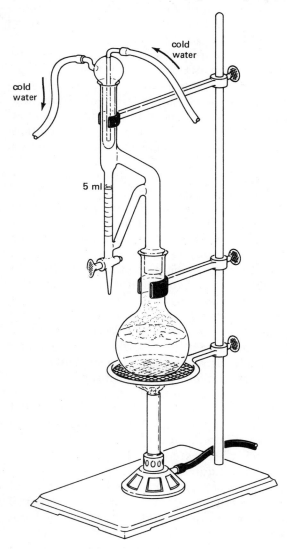

FIGURE 22–1 Steam distillation apparatus.

hydes, phenols, cyanides, amphetamine, and hydrocarbons, can be separated by steam distillation. The tissue is macerated, mixed with water, and steam distilled (see Figure 22-1). As with other extraction processes, the slurry (tissue mixture) can be made acid or basic prior to distillation in order to selectively distill acid and basic volatile poisons.

The great majority of abused drugs are basic. Barbiturates, aspirin, and lysergic acid are a few of the acid ones, and most of the rest are basic. Consequently, when drugs are mixed, more than one drug is likely to be extracted in the basic fraction. This is not a drawback since the main purpose of extraction is not identification but a preliminary isolation of drugs from contaminants. The separation into acidic and basic fractions is a first step toward identification. Once extracted, the drugs can be identified by the methods described below.

Identification Methods

Microscopic Examinations

To a limited extent microscopic examinations can be used to separate poisons from contaminating materials. This is only true when visually detectable amounts of a poison are found in the undigested stomach contents of a victim. Once a substance has entered the bloodstream, microscopic detection is no longer possible.

Most drugs in their solid state are crystalline in nature and can be at least tentatively identified by microcrystalline tests, that is, by observing the drug's manner of crystal formation under a microscope and comparing the crystal behavior of the unknown with that of known drugs. Microcrystalline tests are laborious and time-consuming, but they can be useful in small laboratories that do not have advanced instrumentation.

For some plant materials a microscopic examination is sufficient for a positive identification. Fragments of marihuana leaf (see Figure 22-2) can be identified by the presence of tiny thorn-shaped protrusions of calcium carbonate called *cystolithic hairs* on their surface. Although other plants have similar leaf hairs, an experienced examiner can usually tell the difference, and the other plants are not likely to be found in connection with drug investigations. If there is any doubt, the identification of marihuana can be confirmed by other tests.

Chemical Tests

Chemical tests are carried out by treating the unknown drug with a variety of reagents that will bring about known color reactions when they come into contact with certain drugs. For the most part chemical

FIGURE 22-2 Scanning electron micrograph of a marihuana leaf showing cystolithic hairs (approximately 200 X). (Courtesy of Dr. Michael J. Camp, Northeastern University)

tests are used as screening methods or field tests to arrive at possible and probable identifications.

The field of chemical spot tests is too vast to be within the scope of this chapter, but some of the more commonly used reagents are as follows:

Marquis reagent (10 milliliters of 40 percent formaldehyde added to 100 milliliters of concentrated sulfuric acid). Produces different color reactions for a variety of drugs, including most of the narcotics, amphetamines, barbiturates, and hallucinogens.

Cobalt thiocyanate (2.0 grams dissolved in 100 milliliters of distilled water). Produces various color reactions for some amphetamines, cocaine, some depressants, and some narcotics.

Dille–Koppanyi reagent (Solution 1: 0.1 milliliter cobalt acetate dihydrate dissolved in 100 milliliters methanol plus 0.2 milliliter glacial acetic acid. Solution 2: 5 milliliters isopropylamine added to 95 milliliters methanol). Produces purple reaction to pentobarbital, phenobarbital, and secobarbital.

Duquenois–Levine reagent (Solution 1: 2.5 milliliters acetaldehyde and 2.0 grams vanillin added to 100 milliliters 95 percent ethanol. Solution 2: concentrated hydrochloric acid. Solution 3: chloroform). Produces purple-violet color for marihuana and hashish.

Mandelin reagent (1.0 gram of ammonium vanadate dissolved in 100 milliliters concentrated sulfuric acid). Produces different color reactions for some amphetamines, narcotics, and hallucinogens.

Nitric acid. Produces different color reactions for most narcotics, hallucinogens, and some other drugs.

Many other reagents are available. Although the chemical spot tests are good indicators for presumptive identification of the various drugs, they cannot be considered positive for any specific drug. Some of the reagents are good only for narrowing down the choices to certain classes of drugs. Others give the same or similar color reactions with different drugs. In addition, since color perception is highly subjective and some of the color reactions vary only slightly from each other, one observer's opinion of a result may be different from that of another observer.

Thin-Layer Chromatography

TLC is an excellent screening method which can eliminate the need for chemical spot tests. Because of its sensitivity TLC is especially useful for extractions from body organs, in which the amount of drug present tends to be very minute. In a general screening for an unknown drug the organic extract is spotted onto a TLC plate, allowed to migrate, and developed by spraying. The color reactions to the developing sprays and the Rf values are compared with known values for drugs

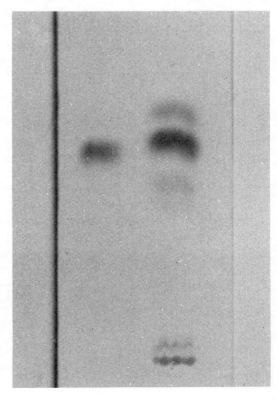

FIGURE 22–3 A presumptive identification of marihuana by thin layer chromatography. The spot on the left is a known standard of tetrahydrocannabinol (THC); the spots on the right, from a suspected marihuana sample, indicate the presence of THC and some contaminants. (Courtesy of Dr. Michael J. Camp, Northeastern University)

(comprehensive lists of known values are given by Clarke[1]) and the substance is tentatively identified or narrowed down to a range of possibilities. If more than one drug is present in the extract, the drugs separate on the TLC plate unless they have very close Rf values. Once the possible choices are reduced to manageable numbers, the unknown can be compared directly on a TLC plate with samples of known standards and a presumptive identification can be obtained (see Figure 22-3). If the same drug is tested with different solvent systems and sprayed with different reagents, the cumulative observations can result in positive identifications.

Confirmatory Tests

After the probable identification is arrived at through spot tests or TLC, the results can be confirmed by instrumental methods, including gas chromatography, mass spectrometry, and ultraviolet and infrared spectrophotometry (see Figure 4-6). In each case the unknown must be compared with known samples under identical conditions. Because infrared spectrophotometry is especially sensitive to contamination, it is useful only if the extracted drug is close to 100 percent pure. A suitable state of purity can be attained by scraping an unsprayed spot of the substance off a TLC plate and dissolving it in chloroform. The insoluble silica gel sinks to the bottom of the solution and the chloroform can be poured off and evaporated to yield the pure drug.

Heavy Elements

On the rare occasions when one of the heavy metallic poisons is the cause of death, the poison can be identified without elaborate extraction procedures. If a heavy element is suspected, the stomach contents and body tissues can be screened for the presence of most metallic poisons by means of the *Reinsch* test. Dilute hydrochloric acid is added to the macerated organs or stomach contents and the mixture is boiled with a thin strip of clean copper foil or copper wire in it. If arsenic, mercury, bismuth, antimony, or others is present, a dark-colored deposit forms on the copper. This metallic deposit can be tested for the nature of the poison by subjecting it to emission spectrography, atomic absorption spectrophotometry, or neutron activation analysis.

Blood Alcohol Analysis

For most of the drugs and poisons extracted by the forensic toxicologist, there is no convenient way to determine the dosage from the amount of material extracted from the organs, and for the most part

[1]E. G. C. Clarke, *Isolation and Identification of Drugs in Pharmaceuticals, Body Fluids, and Post-Mortem Material* (London: The Pharmaceutical Press, 1974).

such quantitative estimations are not necessary. But, because of the large role that alcohol-related crimes play in law enforcement, especially drunken driving, it has become necessary to arrive at some kind of quantitative standard for determining the degree of intoxication. The most commonly used standard is the measurement of ethanol concentration in the blood, which is calculated in terms of the percent of ethanol measured in grams per 100 milliliters of blood. In most of the United States the maximum allowable blood alcohol concentration for driving a motor vehicle is 0.10 percent, or 0.10 gram of alcohol per 100 milliliters of blood. In some states the legal limit is 0.08 percent.

Aside from direct analysis of the blood itself, blood alcohol concentration can be calculated from the amount of alcohol found in the breath, saliva, urine, and organs. Most states rely on breath or blood analysis or both. Although direct analysis of the blood is more accurate, it has the disadvantage of requiring a doctor or nurse to draw the blood and a trained toxicologist to perform the analysis. The moment alcohol enters the bloodstream, the body begins oxidizing it to acetaldehyde, acetic acid, carbon dioxide, and water. This is the body's main method of getting rid of the alcohol, although a small percentage is expelled in the breath and the urine. The blood alcohol concentration increases faster than it can be oxidized as long as alcohol is being absorbed from the stomach and small intestine. As soon as the alcohol is completely absorbed, the level steadily decreases until all the alcohol has been oxidized. If blood analysis is used to determine the blood alcohol concentration, a long delay between the arrest and the time a qualified person can be found to draw the blood will result in an inaccurate reading. The approximate concentration for the time of arrest can be calculated on the basis of an average oxidation rate, but since different people metabolize alcohol at different rates, such a calculation could be challenged in court. Breath analysis methods do not require the presence of medical personnel, and they can be used by the police officer right at the time of the arrest.

Breath Alcohol Analysis

There are several breath analysis instruments in use today, most of which measure the amount of alcohol vapor in a known volume of breath and convert that to a blood alcohol concentration. The conversion is based on the fact that 2,100 milliliters of air from the deep lungs contain the same amount of alcohol as 1 milliliter of blood.

The most widely used device for measuring the breath alcohol content is the Breathalyzer® (see Figures 22-4 and 22-5). The device is set on "take" and the subject expels a deep breath through a tube into a cylinder that holds a measured volume of air. The air that enters the cylinder pushes up a piston; when the piston reaches the top of the

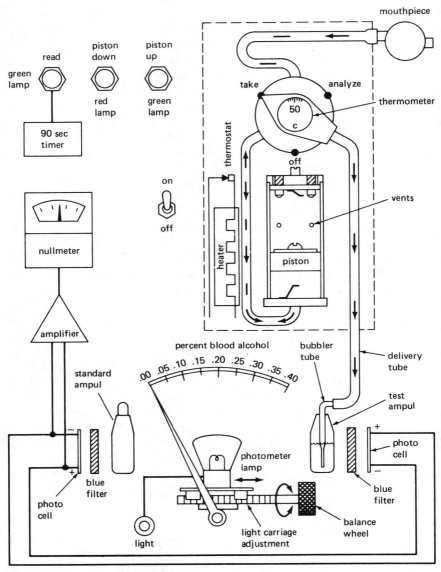

FIGURE 22–4 Schematic diagram of the Breathalyzer®.

cylinder, it exposes two vent holes which release the first part of the breath content into the outside air, thereby ensuring that the air remaining in the cylinder is from the deep lungs. The device is then set on "analyze" and the air collected in the cylinder is bubbled over a period of 90 seconds through a glass ampul containing 0.25 percent potassium dichromate ($K_2Cr_2O_7$) and 0.25 percent silver nitrate

(AgNO$_3$) in a 50 percent solution of sulfuric acid (H$_2$SO$_4$) at a temperature of 50°C. During this process the potassium dichromate oxidizes the alcohol and converts it to acetic acid (CH$_3$COOH). At the same time the potassium dichromate and sulfuric acid are chemically converted to chromium sulfate [Cr$_2$(SO$_4$)$_3$] and potassium sulfate (K$_2$SO$_4$) and water. The silver nitrate acts as a catalyst and undergoes no change. The entire reaction is as follows:

$$3\ CH_3CH_2OH\ +\ 2\ K_2Cr_2O_7\ +\ 8\ H_2SO_4\ \rightarrow$$

ethanol   potassium   sulfuric   yields
                  dichromate   acid

$$3\ CH_3COOH\ +\ 2\ Cr_2(SO_4)_3\ +\ 2\ K_2SO_4\ +\ 11\ H_2O$$

acetic   chromium   potassium   water
acid   sulfate   sulfate

As the chemical reaction takes place, the potassium dichromate solution undergoes a color change from yellow to colorless. The extent

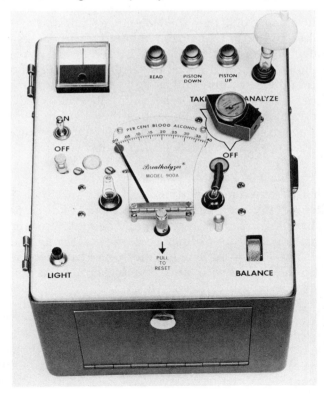

FIGURE 22–5
Breathalyzer®.

of the color change is directly proportional to the amount of potassium dichromate used to oxidize the alcohol. The reaction continues until all the alcohol is oxidized. Consequently, the amount of alcohol in the air sample is calculated indirectly by measuring the extent of color change.

The color change is measured by a spectrophotometric method. Inside the instrument, in addition to the test ampul through which the air is bubbled, there is another sealed ampul containing the same combination of chemicals as the test ampul. Whereas the test ampul is changed every time an analysis is made, the sealed ampul remains as a reference standard. Between the two ampuls is a light source, which at the beginning of the examination is centered between the test ampul and the reference ampul. A beam of white light shines through each of the ampuls and through a blue filter behind each ampul and strikes a photocell behind each filter. The light striking the photocells sets up an electric current that is measured by a galvanometer. At the beginning of the test the electric currents from the photocells behind each ampul are equal and balance each other so that the galvanometer registers zero. Since yellow and blue are complementary to each other, the yellow potassium dichromate solution absorbs light in the blue range. As the yellow color of the test ampul begins to turn colorless, an increasing amount of light in the blue range is allowed to pass through the blue filter and hit the photocell behind it. This causes an imbalance in the electrical current, which is registered by the galvanometer. The galvanometer is brought back to zero by physically moving the light away from the test ampul and closer to the standard ampul. The mechanism that moves the light is mechanically connected to a pointer, which moves along a scale calibrated directly in terms of percent blood alcohol concentration. The farther the light must be moved, the higher the reading is on the blood alcohol scale.

Although breath analysis methods are very accurate for measuring breath alcohol content, the accuracy of that relationship to blood alcohol is sometimes questionable. Small variations in body and breath temperature can cause a certain amount of discrepancy, and there is no absolute guarantee of getting the deepest lung air. In addition, breath analysis does not distinguish between ethanol and other alcohols and volatile liquids. Although it rarely happens, people do occasionally poison themselves with other liquids that react in the same way that alcohol does in a breath analysis.

Blood Alcohol Analysis

Blood alcohol concentrations can be determined either instrumentally, by using the gas chromatograph, or chemically. The gas chromatographic technique is highly accurate and relatively simple. It involves comparing a given quantity of unknown blood with the same quantity of prepared standards containing known quantities of ethanol. If the legal limit is 0.10 percent (0.10 gram per 100 milliliters), standards are prepared with 0.05 percent, 0.10 percent, 0.15 percent, and 0.20 percent. A fixed amount of propanol is added to each of the standards as well as to the unknown sample. The propanol concentration must be the same for all the samples. All of the samples are sealed in glass vials (the vials must have rubber septums) of the same size. The samples are incubated at 37°C (body temperature) for approximately 20 minutes. Then an equal amount of vapor is drawn out of the headspace (i.e., the air space above the liquid in the vial) of each sample with a gas syringe and injected into the gas chromatograph. The chromatograph separates the propanol from the ethanol; the propanol and the ethanol appear as two separate peaks on the chart. Since the propanol concentration is constant for each sample, including the unknown, it serves as a reference. The ratio of the peak heights of ethanol to propanol for each sample is plotted on a graph. The point where the unknown fits into the graph indicates its percent concentration of ethanol. Apart from its ease and accuracy, another advantage of the gas chromatograph method is that if other alcohols or volatile poisons are present, they are shown as separate peaks on the chart.

To perform the analysis by traditional chemical methods, the chemist must distill the sample in order to extract the ethanol from the water and protein material. The distillate is tested by adding a measured quantity of potassium dichromate solution in sulfuric acid to the sample. The solution is added drop by drop (a process known as *titration*) until a color indicator shows that all the ethanol has been oxidized to acetic acid. By comparing the amount of potassium dichromate solution used to oxidize the unknown sample with amounts used to oxidize standards of known ethanol concentration the ethanol level of the unknown can be determined.

It is important for the investigator and the toxicologist to be aware that significant ethanol losses can occur if the blood sample is not stored properly. Since the analysis does not usually take place immediately after the blood is drawn, sodium fluoride preservative should always be added to the sample to prevent loss of alcohol due to microorganismic activity. The temperature factor is also important because ethanol steadily oxidizes to acetaldehyde at room temperature. It is not enough to seal the sample in an airtight container because the ethanol can be oxidized by the oxygen present in the oxyhemoglobin. To ensure the preservation of the blood alcohol, the sample must be kept under refrigeration.

Review Questions

1. (T, F) Drugs and poisons work by interfering with the body's normal chemistry.
2. The most perplexing aspect of drug addiction is understanding the nature of
   a. Physical dependence
   b. Psychological dependence
   c. Tolerance
   d. Potentiation
3. An analgesic is
   a. A narcotic
   b. A depressant
   c. A stimulant
   d. A pain killer
4. (T, F) Because heroin is in such common use it is a relatively safe drug to take.
5. Alcohol belongs to the class of drugs known as
   a. Alkaloids
   b. Narcotics
   c. Depressants
   d. Stimulants
6. (T, F) A person who is dependent on barbiturates should be locked up until the withdrawal symptoms pass.
7. One of the most serious problems connected with alcohol is
   a. Blood sugar
   b. Dizziness
   c. Slurred speech
   d. Potentiation
8. Which of the following is *not* a stimulant?
   a. PCP
   b. Dexedrine
   c. Cocaine
   d. Amphetamine
9. The effects of hallucinogens are
   a. Stimulating
   b. Unpredictable
   c. Unpleasant
   d. Violent
10. Hashish is made from
    a. Castor oil
    b. LSD
    c. Peyote
    d. Hemp
11. An odor of garlic on the breath of a poison victim indicates
    a. Tetraethyl lead

   b. Rubbing alcohol

   c. Mercury

   d. Arsenic

12. Strychnine is
   a. Organic
   b. Inorganic
   c. Unsafe in any amount
   d. A depressant

13. Carboxyhemoglobin is a compound of hemoglobin and
   a. Carbon dioxide
   b. Oxygen
   c. Carbon monoxide
   d. Nitrogen

14. When investigating suspected poisonings, investigators should be alert for
   a. Hypodermic syringes
   b. Pill bottles
   c. Liquids remaining in glasses
   d. All the above

15. Which of the following can be used to extract acid drugs from an aqueous solution?
   a. Methanol and hydrochloric acid
   b. Chloroform and acetic acid
   c. Chloroform and ammonium hydroxide
   d. Ethanol and sodium hydroxide

16. Before drugs can be extracted from body organs the organs have to be
   a. Washed and dried
   b. Steam distilled
   c. Macerated and chemically digested
   d. Immersed in dilute nitric acid

17. Cystolythic hairs are associated with
   a. Marihuana
   b. Peyote
   c. Purple foxglove
   d. Poppies

18. (T,F) The Breathalyzer® is a form of spectrophotometer.

19. The most accurate blood alcohol analysis is done by
   a. Titration
   b. Infrared spectrophotometry
   c. Breathalyzer
   d. Gas chromatography

CHAPTER TWENTY-THREE

— DOCUMENT — EXAMINATIONS

Documents make up a broad class of physical evidence that can come to the attention of investigative agencies in a variety of forms. Checks, wills, passports, automobile registrations, driver's licenses, identity documents, letters, deeds, military records, and many others may at some time become suspect and have to be examined by the crime laboratory. The most common document-related crimes involve some kind of falsification, either by forgery or by alteration of legitimate documents. Ordinarily, documents are falsified for fraudulent monetary gain, as in the case of a forged check or will, but there are other motives. A suicide note may be forged to cover up a murder. Driver's licenses, birth certificates, passports, and other identity documents may be falsified in order to conceal a person's true identity. Documents may be mutilated or destroyed to prevent true facts from coming to light. For example, if a true inventory of goods is destroyed in a fire, a building owner may try to claim the loss of items that never existed. Other documents that may appear as evidence include anonymous, threatening, and obscene letters, anonymous confessions, and occasionally even notes left by criminals at the scene of a crime.

The document examiner uses documents in much the same way that criminalists use other forms of evidence. By comparing features of questioned documents such as handwriting, typescripts, paper, and inks, against standards found in the possession of suspects, the examiner may be able to connect an individual to a crime. And by carefully observing internal clues in documents, the examiner may be able to develop leads to a criminal's identity or to the solution of a crime.

HANDWRITING

Like other kinds of evidence, handwriting exhibits both class characteristics and individual characteristics. The class characteristics come about as a result of the handwriting system that a person learned in school. Most Americans living today learned some version of what are known as modern business hands, the most prominent of which is the Palmer system. Schoolchildren first learn handwriting by copying, and the writing of different children tends to be rather similar throughout elementary school because the children are primarily under the influence of the learned system. But as they grow older, people tend to develop individual handwriting characteristics. The ways in which these characteristics develop are very much a function of each individual's nervous system, motor coordination, and personality. By the time a person reaches adulthood he or she will have developed a style of handwriting that is unique in small details but similar to other people's generally.

Expert document examiners must be familiar with the systems taught both in their own country and in other countries. This is especially true in the United States, which attracts such a mixture of nationalities. In addition, examiners must be trained to observe the individual characteristics. For the most part, people are entirely unconscious of the individual stylistic features of their own or other people's handwriting. A person's familiarity with a certain handwriting is usually based on gross external characteristics, and if the person is confronted with similar styles he or she might find it difficult to tell the difference. Even bank tellers, who are supposed to be able to verify the identity of their clients on the basis of their handwriting, usually judge a signature by its overall appearance.

Handwriting Variations and Disguise

Not only is it possible for different people to have very similar handwriting in outward appearances, but it is also possible for the same person to show so much variation in his or her own handwriting under different circumstances that a casual observer may think that the specimens were written by different people. The cases of most concern to the document examiner are intentional attempts to disguise one's handwriting, but other factors can cause people inadvertently to change the outward appearance of their handwriting. Some of these factors may be hand injuries or other physical discomforts, awkward writing positions, illness, old age, bad lighting, and the different gliding characteristics of different writing implements.

It is easy to disguise one's handwriting so that it has a different appearance from one's normal handwriting. The most common method is to change the slant. A person who normally writes with a forward slant may affect an upright or a backward slant and vice versa. Other disguising features may include adopting a childish or awkward handwriting, block printing, changing one's normal pattern of connecting letters, particularly capitals, changing the r's and the e's, changing size and angularity, and changing the nature of initial and terminal strokes. The main difficulty for people attempting to disguise their writing is that the individual features of their normal handwriting are so deeply ingrained into their nervous system that it is almost impossible to sustain any but the most obvious features of the disguise over a period of time.

Handwriting Identification

Even experts cannot identify a handwriting sample on the basis of a cursory glance. Comparing an unknown specimen with a sample from a suspect requires painstaking work. The examiner's principal aids are magnifying glasses, a stereoscopic microscope, and a variety of grids, templates, and measuring devices. Although the field of handwriting identification is far too broad to be treated in depth here, the student should be aware of some of the characteristics that an examiner looks for.

Although the slant and angularity of the writing are fairly easy to disguise, it is very difficult to control relative letter size and spacing. Anyone can write larger or smaller letters at will and the size of the writing is often relative to the available space, but when one changes the size, the ratio of tall letters to short letters tends to remain the same. Also, the proximity of letters to letters and words to words tends to be a constant factor in a person's handwriting. The presence or absence of initial and terminal strokes and their length and angles in relation to the letter are characteristics that people usually neglect to disguise. The same is true of connecting strokes between letters. Other characteristics that tend to be very personal and unconscious are penlifts and gaps between letters in certain combinations, relative alignment of letters and of entire lines, use and position of punctuation, and the dotting of i's and crossing of t's. These are just a few of the individual handwriting characteristics that are not easily disguised.

Although it is dangerous to try to draw any firm conclusions about an unknown person from his or her handwriting, some tentative indications can sometimes be derived. A foreign primary education can often be reliably recognized if characteristics of a foreign system are present. The sex of a writer is far more difficult to tell because some men have very "feminine" handwriting and some women have "masculine" handwriting. Still, it is sometimes possible to make a guess, as long as it is recognized as a guess, on the basis of style and point of view. If, for example, a sexually explicit obscene letter were written from a man's point of view, it is a safe guess that the writer was a man. Old age or disease may be indicated by a quavering script. And the educational level may be deduced from the level of word usage, spelling, and punctuation. Although well educated people can to some extent disguise their education by intentionally using ungrammatical constructions and misspellings, they are sometimes inconsistent, and small signs of their school training tend to slip through.

Handwriting Exemplars

When attempting to associate a suspect with an evidence document, the document examiner should collect exemplars, or specimens, of the suspect's handwriting (see Figure 23–1). The best way to obtain exemplars is to have the suspect write out a dictated passage that has been prepared in advance. The passage should not have the same wording as the evidence specimen, but it should contain the same letter combinations in different words. The suspect should be given a writing implement as similar as possible to the one used in the evidence document. The suspect should be made to write and sign the dictation several times. Each time the suspect writes an exemplar the previous exemplar should be removed from sight so that the suspect cannot see how he or she wrote something the last time. The dictation should be given at a rapid pace to make it difficult for the suspect to concentrate on disguising the writing. Under these circumstances, it is almost impossible for people to avoid letting features of their true handwriting slip into the sample. Even bearing in mind the possibilities of variation in a person's normal handwriting, the expert examiner can always tell when disguise is being attempted. Since people trying to disguise their writing have to concentrate closely on what they are doing, disguised writing tends to have a labored appearance which is seen under a microscope as a loss of fluency and smooth line quality.

If handwriting exemplars cannot be taken directly from a suspect, investigators may have to find specimens without the suspect's knowledge or cooperation. Some possible sources of handwriting specimens are bank records, letters, applications, military records, school papers, deeds, and contracts.

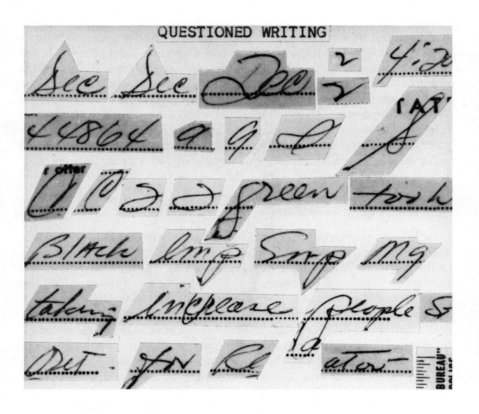

(a)

FIGURE 23–1 Writing samples taken from a questioned document (a) are compared with corresponding samples of known writing (b) from an exemplar which was written on request. Some variation is normal and is to be expected in the known writing, but the *D* in the first *Dec* and the closed *4s* are some of the attempts at deception in the exemplar. (Courtesy of Connecticut State Police Forensic Laboratory)

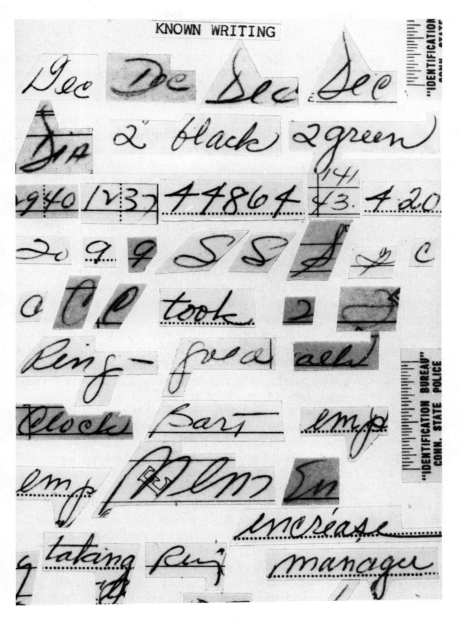

(b)

TYPEWRITING

As with handwriting, the expert examination of typewriting requires a great deal of training and experience. The document examiner is generally called upon to solve three kinds of problems concerning typescript: (1) In the absence of any suspect typewriters, the examiner may have to identify the make, model, and the approximate year of the machine that typed a certain evidence document; (2) the examiner may have to determine whether two separate documents were typed on the same typewriter; and (3) if suspect machines are available, the examiner may be asked to determine if the evidence document was typed on any one of them.

In order to be able to state the make, model, and date of a machine from its type characteristics, a crime laboratory must maintain an extensive reference collection of typeface samples produced by different manufacturers. As with other reference standards, the typeface collection must be continuously maintained and updated since manufacturers change their designs from time to time. It is because of these design changes that examiners are able to estimate approximate years of manufacture. Fortunately, most American typewriter manufacturers design their own typefaces. Therefore, except for some rebuilt typewriters, a given type design can generally be expected to be consistent within a certain make and model. This is not necessarily true of European machines since the keys are often made by separate firms and several manufacturers may purchase the same design.

Document examiners can identify typefaces through a wide variety of small design differences. The first criterion is the amount of space the characters occupy, which can vary from 6 characters to 16 characters to the inch. In the United States the most popular type size is the *pica,* which is 10 characters to the inch, and the next most popular size is the *elite,* which is 12 characters to the inch. In addition, the expert examines the differences in the height and width of each character, the relative sizes of capitals and small letters, the degrees of internal curvatures, slopes, and angles of the various letters and numbers, and many other features which constitute the class characteristics of the typeface. Although the examiner can never state with absolute certainty that a certain make and model machine typed a document in evidence, if an adequate reference collection is available, the examiner will be right a large percentage of the time and will at least be able to narrow down the possibilities.

The problem of ascertaining whether an evidence document was written on a specific machine or whether two different documents were

written on the same machine is one of identifying the individual characteristics of the typeface. The relative ease or difficulty of this task usually
depends on the amount of wear a typewriter has had. A typewriter
consists of thousands of interconnected parts all of which come from the
factory in perfect alignment. As the machine gets used, the positions of
the keys gradually slip in relation to each other, and they begin to
produce a slightly uneven type pattern. Some letters may fall higher or
lower than the normal alignment, and some letters may begin crowding
other letters to one side or the other. The keys may become twisted so
that a letter is turned slightly on the page or prints darker on one side
than on the other. In addition, some of the typefaces may develop small
nicks and irregularities as a result of the keys striking against each other.
This kind of damage is more likely to occur in typewriters used by
inexpert typists.

Every machine develops a pattern of irregularities that is unique
to that machine. If it is a matter of matching a document with a machine, the examiner or investigator types exemplars on all the suspect
machines, trying as much as possible to duplicate the conditions of the
evidence document. For example, if the evidence document was typed
with a worn ribbon, the exemplar should also be typed with a worn
ribbon; or if the evidence document is a carbon copy, the exemplar
should also be a carbon copy.

For control purposes a second exemplar should be typed using a
plain piece of carbon paper against a sheet of typing paper with the
ribbon set on the stencil setting. This will give the characters their
clearest definition. The text of the exemplar should be the same as
that of the evidence document so that the letter combinations will be
the same. When determining whether two evidence documents
were typed on the same machine, the examiner checks them both
to see whether the same individual irregularities occur in both documents.

Examiners can run into difficulties in determining the identity of
typewriters and documents if the typewriter used was too new to have
developed observable characteristics. Even when such characteristics
exist, they may be difficult or impossible to spot if a new ribbon is used
because the thick ink may obscure irregularities in the typeface. Another case in which it is usually impossible to find individual identifying
characteristics is when an IBM Selectric or other typewriter having a
rotating steel ball instead of keys is used. Because the characters on a
steel ball are spun into place electrically there are no mechanical parts
to wear and get out of alignment, and since there are no keys to strike
nicks into each other, the only way individual irregularities would be

likely to develop would be if the typist removed the ball and dropped it.

Document specialists conduct most of their examinations under a magnifying glass or a stereoscopic microscope. They may also use a comparison microscope under low magnification for matching individual characters. Higher powers of magnification are rarely used because it is usually necessary to have an entire character and its surroundings in view. Examiners are normally equipped with clear plastic sheets that have lined grids laid out on them for pica, elite, and other type sizes. They may also use a reticle, a special eyepiece with engraved lines, for making close measurements.

Forgery

The great majority of forgery problems that a document examiner has to deal with concern forged signatures. Forged signatures fall for the most part into the following categories:

1. Forgeries in which no attempt is made to imitate the genuine signature
2. Attempts to duplicate a genuine signature by tracing
3. Attempts to copy a genuine signature by freehand writing

The first of these categories is the most common and also the easiest to solve. Typically, a forger obtains a person's checkbook and writes checks to himself or herself or to an accomplice in that person's name. Because forgers do not usually have access to a sample of the checkowner's signature, they usually sign the name in a disguised handwriting. Sometimes forgers do not even bother to disguise their own handwriting in the signature. If the culprit is caught, the forgery can usually be tied to him or her by means of handwriting comparison techniques.

Traced signatures are usually done in one of two ways. The forger rigs a makeshift light table and places the document to be forged over a genuine signature and traces the forgery directly on to the document. Or the forger traces the genuine signature through a piece of carbon paper on to the spurious document. The latter method is crude and rarely meets with much success.

Although the first tracing method can make a good reproduction, a document examiner can usually tell that it was traced. Genuine signatures are written with a speed and fluency that produce a certain line quality. Viewed under the stereoscopic microscope, tracings almost always show a wavering, unsteady line. Microscopic observations also reveal slight overlaps and build-ups of ink which indicate the points where the pen stopped or changed direction. The pen lifts and changes in direction in the forged signature will not be in the same places as in the genuine signature. If a tracing is made with a ball point pen and if the genuine signature from which it was made can be found, further evidence of the tracing may be present in the form of indentations along the lines of the genuine signature in the paper on which the genuine signature occurs.

The most expert forgeries are normally done freehand. Nevertheless, even the best freehand forgeries rarely duplicate the line quality of a genuine signature. The pen lifts and changes of direction are different, and the forgers have a difficult time keeping out subtle characteristics of their own handwriting. Freehand forgers often practice a signature several times on a separate sheet of paper before attempting the actual forgery. If investigators should find a sheet with practice signatures on it, they should be alert to the possibility of forgery. If the practice signatures are written on a pad, even if the original practice sheet has been destroyed, a backup sheet may still be found that bears indented fascimiles of the signature.

INDENTED WRITING

When a message is written on a pad of paper with a pencil or a ball point pen, the message is often reproduced in indented impressions in the next few sheets lying under the sheet on which the message was written. Similarly, typewritten messages can come through on backup sheets. When they are available, samples of indented writing can be valuable forms of evidence either to prove that a certain message was written in a certain place or to reveal information that criminals hoped to keep concealed. During their crime scene search investigators should routinely check any pads or stray pieces of paper for indented writing. It can usually be easily discovered by holding the paper up to a light so that the light grazes the paper almost parallel to the surface. Both sides of the sheet should be checked.

Although it is usually fairly easy to ascertain the presence of indented writing, indented writing is not always easy to read. The sheet can be observed more closely in the laboratory. The illumination should be from the side and almost parallel to the paper. The illumination should be shined onto the sample from different directions until the best results are obtained (see Figure 23–2). Indented writing can sometimes be brought out by fuming the paper with iodine vapors. The same type of fuming gun that is used in fingerprint searches can be used to bring out indented writing (see Figure 18–7). The disturbed paper fibers in the indented areas often absorb iodine vapor at a different rate from the normal fibers, thereby revealing the lines of the message. If the iodine fuming is successful, the examiner must be ready with a camera to photograph the revealed writing before the vapors dissipate. Often indented writing can also be read by means of closeup photography in which a polarizing lens filter is used with grazing illumination. Such photography can often reveal the writing more clearly than the naked eye can because the polarizing filter reduces glare, which can interfere with the eye's perception.

ALTERATIONS

Document examiners are frequently confronted with alterations of genuine documents. The alterations normally take the form of *additions, erasures,* and *obliterations.*

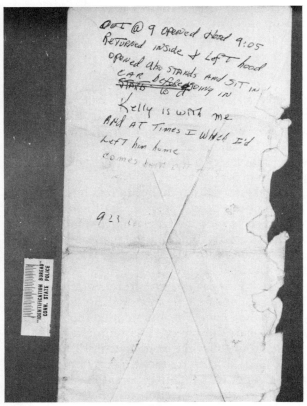

(a)

FIGURE 23–2 Indented writing revealed by side lighting: (a) shows the document illuminated from above; (b) shows the document illuminated with grazing light from the side. (Courtesy of Connecticut State Police Forensic Laboratory)

FIGURE 23–2 *continued*   (b)

Additions

Perhaps the most common of all document falsifications is the "raised" check. This is usually a petty crime in which the culprit increases the amount of a check by adding a zero to the numeral and a "ty" to a six, seven, or nine or a "y" to eight. Fraudulent additions can profitably be made to wills, receipts, contracts, and other documents.

In a case in which an amount is raised by adding onto existing words, the additions can usually be spotted under microscopic examination. Unless the same pen is used, there are likely to be slight differences in the color and line appearance of the ink. Also, when the added part must be joined to an existing word, for example, a "ty" to a seven, there is likely to be a small ink buildup at the join that can be seen under magnification. If different inks are used, even if they appear the same to the naked eye, they often have different fluorescence characteristics that show up under ultraviolet light. In addition, different inks tend to absorb and reflect infrared radiation to differing degrees. These differences can be revealed by infrared photography (see Figures 23–3 and 23–4).

When it is suspected that additions have been made to a docu-

(a)

(b)

FIGURE 23–3 A document alteration revealed by reflected infrared photography. In (a) a check was photographed using normal black and white film, white light, and no filter; in (b) white light was also used but the camera was loaded with infrared sensitive film and a filter was held in front of the lens which allows only infrared light to enter the camera. The original ink reflects infrared light and shows up strongly in the photograph; the ink used to make the alteration reflects infrared only slightly and can barely be seen in the photograph. (Courtesy of Connecticut State Police Forensic Laboratory)

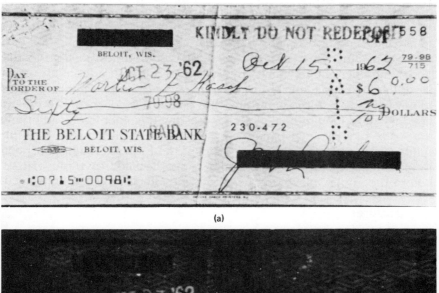

(a)

(b)

FIGURE 23–4 A document alteration revealed by infrared luminescence photography. Some inks emit luminescence in the infrared range when excited by high-energy ultraviolet light. In (a) a check was photographed as it would appear to the naked eye. In (b) the same check was illuminated with ultraviolet light, but the camera was loaded with infrared film, and a filter that transmits only infrared light was held in front of the lens. In this case the ink used to make the alteration luminesced in the infrared range when excited by ultraviolet light, and the original did not. Therefore, only the alteration shows up in the photograph. (Courtesy of Wisconsin State Crime Laboratory)

ment, it may be necessary to determine the relative age of the different parts of the text or the order in which the parts were written. It is not usually possible to assess the relative ages of two writing specimens unless the difference is very great. Most inks either fade or change color over long periods of time, but these aging characteristics are very much influenced by temperature, humidity, and the degree to which the document has been exposed to air. If an addition were made many years after the original document was written, it might be possible to determine that one ink had aged more than another.

When lines of writing intersect, it is sometimes possible to tell under the microscope which line was written first. If a fountain pen is used, the ink from a newer line crossing an older line sometimes tends to flow slightly into the older line. If a pencil is used, the more recent line may show longitudinal scratches crossing the older line. If additions are made to a piece of paper that has been folded, fountain pen ink tends to flow into the disturbed fibers of the fold, and ball point pens tend to deposit a small lump of ink against the fold. Anything written before the paper was folded would not be affected by the folds.

Erasures

Erasures can be made by abrasion of the paper surface or by chemical means. In the case of pencil marks, abrasive erasures rub away the deposit of "lead." The so-called lead of pencils is a mixture of graphite and clay. Soft pencils have a relatively high graphite content, and hard pencils have a relatively greater clay content. Since pencil writing is deposited predominantly on the surface of the paper fibers, it can be erased with relatively non-abrasive materials. Inks on the other hand sink into fibers so that a more highly abrasive erasure is needed to rub away the fibers themselves. Abrasive erasures of inks and typescript can often be detected simply by holding a paper up to a light to look for thin spots. However, sometimes it is possible to resize these spots by carefully applying starch.

Chemical erasures are almost always made by applying oxidizing agents that bleach the dyes. Chemical erasures and erasures that have been resized with starch can almost always be detected by examining them under ultraviolet light because the spread of the chemicals or starch into the paper changes its fluorescence characteristics. Iodine fuming is another method of detecting chemical erasures.

Erased pencil writing can sometimes be deciphered if erasure was incomplete by observing the area under the stereoscopic microscope. Pencil erasures may also be deciphered by infrared photography. Some erased inks, especially if the inks contain iron compounds, can also be deciphered by infrared photography.

Obliterations

Sometimes bits of writing that might be important evidence are intentionally or inadvertently obliterated by inkblots or by being crossed out or written over. If the desired writing is to be deciphered, it must be discriminated from the unwanted markings that obscure it. The major discriminating methods are ultraviolet, fluorescence, and infrared photography and photography using contrasting lens filters.

Direct ultraviolet photography discriminates the different inks by their differential reflection of ultraviolet light. The sample is illuminated with ultraviolet light and a lens filter is used which allows only ultraviolet to enter the camera. If the hidden ink reflects ultraviolet more strongly than the obscuring ink, the message is recorded on film.

Fluorescence photography takes advantage of the fact that some inks fluoresce in the visible range when they are illuminated with ultraviolet light. The sample is illuminated with ultraviolet but a filter is used which allows only visible light to enter the camera. If the hidden ink emits visible fluorescence and the obscuring ink does not, the film picks up the hidden words.

Infrared film will likewise record the different abilities of inks to reflect infrared light. The samples can be illuminated with white light since most white light contains some infrared, and a lens filter (Wratten number 87) is used which allows only infrared light to enter the camera.

If the hidden ink is obscured by inks of different colors, color contrast filters can be used to suppress the unwanted background. For example, if the hidden writing is in red and the obscuring marks are in blue, a blue lens filter can be used which allows the wavelengths of the blue ink and white paper to enter the camera but blocks the red. The blue and white expose the film and come out light in the print; the hidden red writing, which did not expose the negative, stands out in a dark shade in the print.

Sometimes inks that appear to the eye to be the same color are actually made up of different mixtures of wavelengths that can be reinforced or suppressed by filters. There is no way of knowing which of these techniques will be the most suitable for a given document problem. The examiner must experiment until the one that works best is found.

CHARRED DOCUMENTS

Examiners sometimes face a special obliteration problem with charred documents. If the paper is only partially charred, the writing may still be visible and can be photographed with ordinary reflected light. If a paper has charred entirely to ash and has curled without crumbling, the first task is to deal with the fragility of the ash. The ash can be collected by carefully slipping a piece of paper under it. It can then be packaged in a box which will not subject it to pressure and carefully transported to the laboratory. The ash can be strengthened by a very careful appli-

(a)

(b)

FIGURE 23–5 Charred documents. In (a) the writing can be seen under ordinary visible light. In (b) no writing can be seen under visible light, but the writing is revealed in (c) when reflected infrared photography is used. [(a) Courtesy of Connecticut State Police Forensic Laboratory; (b) and (c) Courtesy of Wisconsin State Crime Laboratory]

FIGURE 23–5   *continued*   (c)

cation of polyvinyl acetate in acetone solution. When the acetone evaporates, the polyvinyl acetate plasticizes and gives the ash enough stability so that it can be flattened. Despite the burning, ink residues may remain in place and can often be read by reflected light. If the writing cannot be read by visible light, infrared and ultraviolet photographic techniques should be used (see Figure 23–5).

INK IDENTIFICATION

In addition to comparing documents on the basis of handwriting, typewriting, and other observable characteristics, it is sometimes necessary to compare inks by their chemical composition. Most fountain pen inks are solutions or suspensions of metallic pigments and synthetic organic dyes in water. The water evaporates and the colored materials are left behind. Ball point inks are mostly made up of synthetic organic dyes dissolved or suspended in a binder that polymerizes on contact with the air and adheres to the paper along with the colored constituents. Another important category of inks are carbon inks like India ink which are suspensions of finely divided carbon in a binder. Carbon inks, which are generally used by artists and draftsmen, are rarely encountered in the crime laboratory.

Because of the great prevalence of ball point pens since World War II, these are the inks which laboratory examiners most frequently have to compare or identify. The most suitable method in use today for identifying ball point inks is thin-layer chromagraphy (see Figure 23–6).

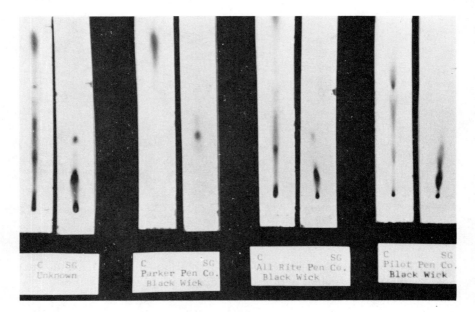

FIGURE 23–6 Thin layer chromatography of inks. An unknown ink (left) is compared with several known standards. (Courtesy of Wisconsin State Crime Laboratory)

The ink can be conveniently removed without causing significant damage to the document by punching out a small dot from the center of an inked line. This can be done by filing the point of a pin flat and pressing it into the inked line against a thick rubber backing. The ink can then be dissolved and spotted onto a TLC plate. Identifications are made by comparing the ink with standard chromatograms prepared under identical conditions. If the laboratory maintains an ink reference library, the unknown can be identified by make and model of pen, and since ball point pen manufacturers frequently change composition of their inks, the identification can often serve to date the sample.

Review Questions

1. Documents can be altered
   a. To conceal identity
   b. For monetary gain

   c. To cover up a murder
   d. To exclude a rival from a will
   e. All the above

2. Individual handwriting characteristics result from
   a. One's nervous system
   b. One's personality
   c. Attempts at disguise
   d. All the above
   e. a and b

3. (T, F)　Most bank tellers are expert handwriting analysts.

4. (T, F)　The sex of a writer can be determined by the masculine or feminine characteristics of the handwriting.

5. When a suspect writes out a dictated passage, he or she should
   a. Be given plenty of time
   b. Be encouraged to ask questions about it
   c. Not be allowed to see previous exemplars
   d. Always use a pencil

6. The class characteristics of a typescript can identify
   a. A specific typewriter
   b. The make and model of a typewriter
   c. The typist
   d. A specific document

7. Pica type is
   a. Twelve characters to the inch
   b. Rarely encountered in the United States
   c. The same height as elite
   d. None of the above

8. (T, F)　IBM Selectric typewriters are easily identified by irregularities in their typeface.

9. The most expert forgeries are done
   a. By tracing
   b. Freehand
   c. With a light table
   d. With carbon paper

10. Indented writing may be deciphered by
   a. Ultraviolet photography
   b. Iodine fuming
   c. Photography under grazing illumination with a polarizing filter
   d. Thin-layer chromatography
   e. a, b, and c
   f. b and c

11. Document alterations can often be deciphered by
   a. Infrared photography

   b. Luminescence photography
   c. Photography using contrasting filters
   d. All the above

12. Charred documents can be strengthened with
   a. Polyvinyl acetate in acetone solution
   b. Concentrated sulfuric acid
   c. Isopropanol
   d. Scotch tape

13. Ball point ink can best be identified by
   a. Atomic absorption spectrophotometry
   b. Thin-layer chromatography
   c. Pyrolysis-gas chromatography
   d. Microscopic examination

CHAPTER TWENTY FOUR

—— LIE DETECTION: ——
THE POLYGRAPH AND
THE PSYCHOLOGICAL
STRESS EVALUATOR

Throughout history people have looked for ways to determine if suspects are lying or telling the truth. According to legends dating back before 1000 BC the ancient Chinese recognized that fear or anxiety caused the human body to stop producing saliva. Consequently, the Chinese made suspects chew dried rice powder and then spit it out. If the powder was still dry, the individual was considered guilty. Other ancient civilizations reportedly took the more drastic step of touching the suspect's tongue with a hot sword. If the sword sizzled from the presence of saliva, the person was thought to be telling the truth. If the sword burned the tongue, the person was thought to be lying. Although based on a physiological phenomenon this latter method probably had a strong enough psychological effect to make most guilty persons confess before the blade was put to their tongues.

These ancient methods, although crude and of doubtful reliability, were based on the correct observation that the human body undergoes certain involuntary reactions in the face of fear, guilt, anxiety, or other forms of stress. Modern lie detection methods rely on the same principle, and to understand how they work, we must know something about the human nervous system.

The human nervous system is a complex combination of separate systems that controls the many functions and activities of the body and responds to external stimuli. The *central nervous system* (CNS), which is housed in the brain and spinal cord, integrates and coordinates the other systems so that they work in harmony with each other. The *peripheral nervous system* is made up of *motor nerves, sensory nerves,* and the *autonomic nervous system.* The sensory nerves transmit the external stimuli of the senses (sight, smell, hearing, touch, and taste) to the central nervous system. The central nervous system in turn sends messages to the muscles by way of the motor nerves. The sensory and motor nerves work in combination with each other and actually follow the same pathways within the body. In coordination with the central nervous system the sensory and motor nerves control our voluntary actions such as walking, talking, picking things up, and all forms of muscular activity that emanate from decisions made in the brain.

The autonomic nervous system is made up of the *sympathetic* and *parasympathetic* nerves, which follow separate pathways to the central nervous system. Working in conjunction with the central nervous system, they control our involuntary actions such as heartbeat, involuntary breathing, digestion, and the function of the liver, kidneys, and other internal organs. When a person is not being subjected to stress, the sympathetic and parasympathetic nerves balance each other and maintain the body functions at their normal, stable level, called *homeostasis.* But when a person is confronted with a threatening situation, the sympathetic nerves stimulate the body organs to react in ways designed to meet the threat. This is commonly known as the "fight or flight" reaction. The adrenal glands secrete adrenalin into the bloodstream and the liver secretes sugar. The heartbeat becomes faster and stronger in order to deliver more oxygen to the muscles. The rate of breathing increases so that the blood can pick up the increased amount of oxygen. Various changes occur at the surface of the skin, most notably an increase in perspiration. The digestive system stops working so that all the blood can be made available to the muscles that need it. This is what causes the saliva to stop flowing. These reactions and many others occur in response to stimuli from the autonomic nervous system and are completely involuntary. When the threatening situation passes, the parasympathetic nerves take over and send messages to the organs to stop their emergency output. The body then returns to homeostasis.

THE POLYGRAPH

The polygraph is an instrument designed to detect and measure some of the above responses. Although some variations of the polygraph are used for medical and research purposes, the instrument used by investigative agencies for the detection of deception uses three separate mea-

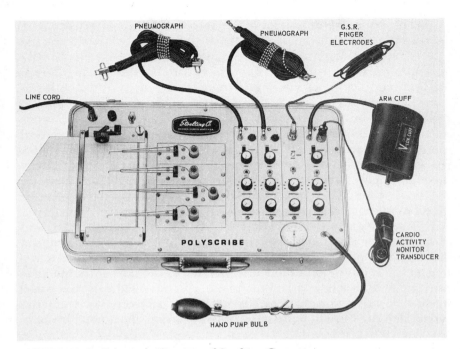

FIGURE 24–1   Polygraph (Courtesy of Stoelting Company)

suring units: the *cardiosphygmograph,* the *pneumograph,* and the *galvanograph* (see Figure 24–1).

The cardiosphygmograph records any changes in the blood volume and in the strength and rate of the pulse. A pressure cuff similar to the type used to take blood pressure readings is wrapped around the upper arm and inflated by means of a bulb pump to a point where it begins to constrict the blood flow without cutting it off. A wrist cuff is also available for people who find the arm cuff too uncomfortable. The pressure cuff is connected by means of an airtight rubber tube to a bellows unit in the polygraph instrument. As the blood volume increases, the brachial (arm) artery swells, thereby slightly increasing the air pressure in the cuff. The increased pressure is transmitted by a column of compressed air in the rubber tube to the bellows and causes the bellows to expand. The bellows movement is transmitted mechanically to a stylus, or pen, which records the movement on a moving chart. The pulse recording works in the same manner. The artery expands and contracts rapidly with each heartbeat and has the same effect on the recording unit as the more gradual changes in blood volume. The strength of the pulse is measured by the amplitude, or height, of each pulse stroke as recorded on the chart.

The pneumograph records the rate and depth of breathing. It works on a principle similar to that of the cardiosphygmograph. An accordion-like airtight rubber tube is fastened around the chest with a chain. As the chest expands and contracts with breathing, the tube also expands and contracts, causing changes in the air pressure inside it. These changes are transmitted through a length of rubber tubing to a bellows unit in the instrument, and the movement of the bellows is recorded by another stylus on the chart. If only one chest attachment is used, it is placed around either the upper or lower chest, depending on which part shows the greater expansion. The newer polygraph instruments have two attachments, one for the upper chest and one for the lower chest. There are separate styluses to record the movement of each on the chart (see Figure 24–2).

The galvanograph is the only unit that is run electronically rather than mechanically. Electrodes are attached to two fingers, usually the index finger and ring finger. A direct current too weak for the subject to feel is passed through the electrodes across the skin of the subject's hand. The skin acts as a resistor to the current flow. The amount of resistance in the skin decreases when the subject is under emotional stress, thereby causing more current to flow. This change in skin resistance is known as the *galvanic skin response* (GSR). The cause of the galvanic skin response is not entirely clear. It is partially the result of an increase in perspiration level, but it is also thought that the skin itself undergoes a slight physiological change which results in a change in resistance. The GSR current passes through a Wheatstone bridge, which is an electrical circuit designed to measure resistance. The slight fluctuations in current caused by the changes in skin resistance are amplified and transmitted to a galvanometer recorder. A galvanometer is a device that visually displays a change in electrical current. In the polygraph it is electronically connected to a stylus, which records the changes on the moving chart paper.

The Polygraph Examination

Polygraph examinations may be given for a variety of reasons. The most common is the pre-employment test generally used by businesses to screen prospective employees for false statements on their employment applications. They are also used by private companies to determine the guilt or innocence of employees in internal matters like cash thefts or destruction of machinery. The polygraph is also widely used by law enforcement agencies as an investigative aid. Although the testing procedures are basically the same regardless of the reason for the

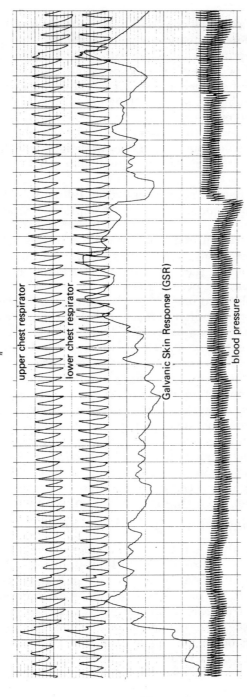

FIGURE 24-2 Sample polygraph chart. Top line: upper chest respirator; second line: lower chest respirator; third line: galvanic skin response (GSR); bottom line: blood pressure. (Courtesy of Stoelting Company)

examination, there are some considerations that pertain particularly to examinations made in connection with criminal investigations.

For the examination to be effective, the act of lying must cause the subject to feel guilt or anxiety or some psychological stress. There are some criminals who have become so hardened that they feel no guilt either for their criminal acts or for their lies. There are also cases of pathological liars and mental defectives who have no sense of wrongdoing when they lie. Since these people experience no psychological stress, the autonomic nervous system does not trigger the fight or flight reaction in them, and they give no indication of deception on polygraph examinations.

The amount of stress people feel when telling a lie is related to their fear of the consequences of their deception. People who have spent a long time in jail may become indifferent to consequences because they realize that nothing much worse can happen to them. Also people who have been polygraphed many times tend to show weaker and weaker reactions as they become unconsciously aware that the instrument itself does not pose a threat.

The individuals mentioned above make poor polygraph subjects because they underreact or fail to react at all, but there are also people who test poorly because they overreact. There are a few rare individuals who seem to have guilt complexes about any subject and give strong reactions regardless of the questions asked or the truth or falsity of their answers. In most cases the examiner finds that these people are actually reacting to guilty recollections not at all related to the case being investigated. If, however, a person persists in showing guilty reactions to questions about crimes that he or she could not possibly have committed, the examiner knows that the person has a severe psychological problem and is probably not a suitable candidate for a polygraph examination. Many people are simply very nervous and show a heightened level of stress throughout. A competent examiner can usually calm such people down enough to be able to conduct an examination on them.

The Pre-Test Interview

Almost everybody is nervous to some degree when about to take a polygraph examination. Consequently, it is essential for the examiner to conduct a pre-test interview with the subject before beginning the actual examination. In the pre-test interview the examiner explains the workings of the instrument, soothes any fears the subject may have about it, and discusses the case under investigation. The pre-test interview not only calms down the subject, but it also helps the examiner formulate questions. Each individual is different, and the examiner must determine what kinds of questions will best elicit clear responses.

After deciding what questions to ask, the examiner goes over them with the subject to make sure that the subject understands the questions. This reassures the subject that there will be no surprise questions and lets guilty subjects know when the incriminating questions will come up so that they can start worrying about them. After the pre-test interview is completed, the units of the instrument are attached to the subject and the questioning begins.

Questioning Techniques

The actual questioning part of the examination takes only a few minutes even though several charts may be run on a subject. If the questioning goes on too long, the pressure cuff can become unbearably uncomfortable and the subject will start becoming less reactive. Usually no more than ten questions are asked per chart. All questions must be answerable by yes or no, and the types of questions asked may include irrelevant and relevant questions, control questions, and peak of tension (POT) questions.

Irrelevant questions have nothing to do with the matter under investigation and should have no other possible guilty associations for the subject. For example: "Is today Friday?" or "Is your name John?" These questions are designed to establish a base line of the subject's normal, guilt-free reaction patterns.

Relevant questions have a direct bearing on the case and are designed to draw out a stressed response from a guilty subject. Relevant questions may be worded directly: "Did you kill *(the victim)?*" or obliquely: "Do you know who killed *(the victim)?*"

Control questions, or *probable lie* questions, are interspersed among the relevant and irrelevant questions. Control questions are designed to evoke a deceptive response to a question not directly related to the case under investigation. One of the purposes of the pre-test interview is to enable the examiner to learn enough about the subject to determine appropriate control questions. Although the control questions should not be directly related to the crime being investigated, they may concern a similar situation. For example, in a rape murder case it might be appropriate to ask a suspect: "Since you were 18 years old have you ever seriously hurt anybody?" Or if it is a burglary: "Have you ever stolen anything of value?" Although this is something of an oversimplification, subjects are generally considered to be truthful if they react more strongly to the control questions than to the relevant questions.

Peak of tension questions may be part of a regular test or they may form the basis of a separate test. There are two types of peak of tension test. Type A is the known solution test, which may be used in criminal cases in which certain information relevant to the crime and known to the police has been held back from the public. Since the culprit would know the information, he or she can be expected to react when questions are asked about it. The examiner tries to build up the suspect's tension by asking a series of questions that come successively closer to the bit of guilty knowledge. The questions are meaningless to the innocent subject and do not generate any tension. The type B test is a searching POT test in which the criminal has guilty knowledge which the examiner does not know. For example, in a case in which a person is suspected of having killed someone and hidden the body, the examiner might mark a map of the area off in grids and question the suspect about each grid. If guilty the suspect usually begins to give stressful reactions as the examiner comes closer to the section in which the body is hidden.

After each test the examiner loosens the attachments and reviews the chart with the subject. It is especially important to clarify any signs of deception since an innocent subject might not have been reacting to the question itself but to some guilty association which the question triggered. Once the subject has given a satisfactory explanation for the reactions, the examiner runs another test in which the questions are reworded to account for the explanation. It is not unusual to run three or more charts on a subject during a single examination session.

THE PSYCHOLOGICAL STRESS EVALUATOR

The Psychological Stress Evaluator (PSE), formerly known as the Voice Stress Analyzer, is the most recent development in the field of lie detection (see Figure 24–3). Like the polygraph the PSE detects involuntary physiological changes that occur in reaction to the stress of fear, guilt, anger, or other emotions. However, the PSE has no physical attachments to the subject's body; it operates on changes in the voice alone.

To understand how the PSE works, we must return to the human nervous system. As we saw earlier, the muscles in the human body which react to our conscious desires are controlled from the central nervous system through the motor nerves. All of these muscles, even when relaxed, are in a constant state of tension which is necessary to keep them in readiness for instantaneous responses to signals from the brain. Whenever a voluntary muscle is used, its contraction is accompanied by a slight physiological tremor known as a *micro-tremor*. The physiological purpose of the micro-tremor is not completely understood, but it is thought to be the mechanism that maintains the appropriate amount of tension on a muscle in order to keep the muscle in a state of readiness. Although the tremor belongs to the complex of sys-

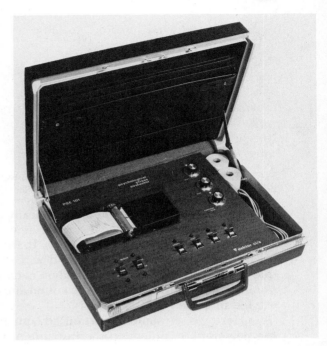

FIGURE 24–3 PSE-101.
(Courtesy of Dektor Counterintelligence and Security, Springfield, Virginia)

tems that control the voluntary muscles, the tremor itself is completely involuntary.

The muscles of the human throat and larynx, which are responsible for the formation of voice sounds, are subject to the micro-tremor as are any other voluntary muscles, and although the tremor cannot be heard in a person's speech, it can be detected electronically as an FM (frequency modulated) component of from 8 cycles per second to 12 cycles per second superimposed on the fundamental AM (amplitude modulated) voice frequency of from 100 cycles per second to 250 cycles per second.

The micro-tremor is always present in the normal, unstressed voice. But when a person is subjected to emotional stress, the sympathetic portion of the autonomic nervous system takes over and suppresses the tremor or even eliminates it completely. The degree of suppression is proportional to the amount of stress.

Operation of the PSE

The PSE is designed to selectively analyze those frequency components of the human voice that reveal the presence, suppression, or absence of the micro-tremor and to display them graphically on a moving chart similar to that of the polygraph (see Figure 24–4).

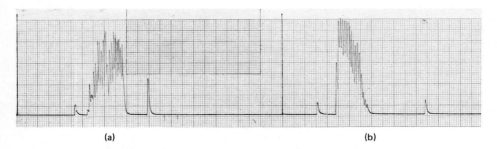

(a)   (b)

FIGURE 24–4 Sample PSE chart shows yes/no answers. Answer (a) is truthful; (b) is a lie. (Courtesy of Dektor Counterintelligence and Security, Springfield, Virginia)

The examination is conducted basically in the same manner as the polygraph examination (pre-test interview, examination proper, and review of each chart with the subject). In the examination phase, however, instead of attaching tubes and wires to the subject's body, the questions and answers are recorded on magnetic tape. When the questioning is completed, the tape is rewound and only the subject's answers are fed into the PSE for analysis.

Here we see some important advantages over the polygraph. In the polygraph examination the instrument itself and its necessary attachments are a source of stress which can invalidate the examination of some subjects. Also, some subjects, particularly obese ones, find the attachments extremely uncomfortable. The PSE examination can be conducted in a more relaxed atmosphere without any stress or discomfort being caused by the machine. Also while the polygraph is limited to yes or no answers, the PSE can analyze narrative answers, thereby making it more flexible.

The PSE can analyze the answers in several different modes. The questions and answers are recorded at a tape speed of 7½ inches per second. In Mode I the answers are fed into the PSE at the same speed. This does not give a detailed frequency pattern but visually records the amplitude, or loudness, of the voice. Using Mode I, the examiner can make a rapid check for certain gross indicators of deception that are often found in amplitude patterns.

In Mode II the answers are fed into the instrument at one-half the recording speed (3¾ inches per second) and the effects of the microtremor can be seen on the chart. At this speed the examiner can monitor the input because the voice, although distorted, remains intelligible.

Mode III is the most sensitive. The answers can be analyzed at one-quarter or one-eighth the recording speed (1⅞ inches per second or 15/16 inches per second), thus providing a clear display of the frequency patterns. It is often desirable to run female voices at 15/16 inches per second because of the higher fundamental frequency. At these speeds the voice is too distorted to be intelligible. So Mode III has the disadvantage that it requires the examiner to stop and start the tape at different speeds to make sure that the right portion is fed into the PSE.

Mode IV has the same function as Mode III except that the amplitude of the signal is dampened. This helps keep the pen centered on the chart and it is especially useful when dealing with subjects who exhibit a high level of stress throughout the examination.

While the different modes in the PSE permit the examiner to analyze doubtful answers in several different ways, they have the disadvantage of being time consuming. With the polygraph the entire readout is available immediately as the subject gives the answers, but the PSE examiner cannot get the results until the taped answers have been fed back into the instrument. Some investigators prefer the polygraph for this reason; other investigators feel that this disadvantage is offset by the other advantages of the PSE. In addition to the convenience of not having any physical attachments, the PSE makes a permanent record of the examination which can be checked and double checked as many times as necessary. If an examiner wants to get an independent opinion of the results of any given examination, the tape can be given to another examiner, or the taped interview can be transmitted over the telephone.

THE LIE DETECTOR

Knowing the way the polygraph and the Psychological Stress Evaluator work, we can see that it is incorrect to refer to either of them as "lie detectors." These instruments do not detect lies; they detect physiological changes in the human body. These changes can be caused by different kinds of stress. If there is a lie detector, it is the examiner. Examiners must determine through their manner of questioning and interpretation of the charts whether the stress is due to deception or something else. Unfortunately, this leaves considerable room for abuse if examiners do not have sufficient training and experience or if they are dishonest. Unscrupulous examiners can make anybody seem to be lying. No one can be compelled to take either a polygraph or a PSE examination; nevertheless, there is often an element of coercion in that a refusal tends to arouse an assumption of guilt. Competent examiners always keep the rights and interests of the subject in mind and go out of their way to be fair.

Review Questions

1. The peripheral nervous system
   a. Is housed in the spinal cord
   b. Follows the same pathways as the autonomic nervous system
   c. Contains motor nerves and sensory nerves
   d. Controls liver function

2. When faced with a threat, the body is stimulated into the fight or flight reaction by
   a. The sympathetic nerves
   b. The parasympathetic nerves
   c. The motor nerves
   d. Homeostasis

3. The cardiosphygmograph transmits blood volume information
   a. Electronically
   b. Dynamically
   c. Hydraulically
   d. Mechanically

4. The galvanic skin response is
   a. Goose flesh
   b. Caused by high voltage
   c. A change in the electrical resistance of the skin
   d. Transmitted mechanically

5. Polygraph examinations are not effective when
   a. The subject is nervous
   b. Lying causes no stress in the subject
   c. The subject is telling the truth
   d. b and c

6. (T, F) A subject is generally considered to be truthful if he or she reacts more strongly to the control questions than to the relevant questions.

7. In a searching peak of tension test
   a. The examiner knows that the culprit has guilty knowledge which the general public does not know
   b. The examiner knows that the subject is guilty
   c. The examiner and the culprit both share knowledge about the crime which the general public does not know
   d. None of the above

8. When a person is subjected to stress, the micro-tremor in the voice muscles
   a. Is suppressed by the parasympathetic nerves
   b. Becomes more intense
   c. Is suppressed by the sympathetic nerves
   d. Changes from FM to AM

9. The PSE-101 is most sensitive when it is operated in
   a. Mode IV
   b. Mode III
   c. Mode II
   d. Mode I

10. An advantage that the Psychological Stress Evaluator has over the polygraph is that
    a. The PSE can distinguish between stress caused by deception and stress caused by something else
    b. The PSE is portable
    c. There are no physical attachments to the subject
    d. The PSE can analyze a narrative response
    e. All the above
    f. c and d

CHAPTER TWENTY-FIVE

—— *DEVELOPMENTS* ——
IN CRIMINALISTICS

The central foundation of criminalistics is the premise that nature never exactly repeats itself. This premise, which has its basis in probability and is so far corroborated by empirical observation, postulates that every person, animal, and thing is in some way different from every other of its kind. Every development and every innovation in the field of criminalistics have been directed at finding ways to isolate and classify the unique features of objects and organisms so that they can be reliably identified.

PIONEERING WORK IN CRIMINALISTICS

In the late 1800s Alphonse Bertillon, a clerk in the identification division of the Paris police whose father was a noted anthropologist, used his familiarity with anthropology to devise the first orderly system of personal identification. The system, based on the observations of anthropologists that each human body is different from all others, was called *anthropometry* and used a series of bodily measurements to individualize and identify criminals who came to the attention of the police.

In the early 1900s Bertillon's system was superseded by fingerprinting, whose basic principle of biological uniqueness is exactly the same as principles underlying anthropometrics. A British anthropologist, Sir Francis Galton, was actually doing research on fingerprints during the same period that Bertillon was developing anthropometry, but it was not until Juan Vucetich of the Argentinian police and Sir Edward Henry developed workable filing and retrieval systems in the early twentieth century that fingerprints came into their own.

Another contribution of Bertillon, which is still used in some forms today, was the *portrait parlé*. A natural extension of anthropometry, the *portrait parlé* was a systematic method of classifying the features of the human face so that a verbal description of a criminal could be filed and later retrieved for comparison. The modern descendant of the *portrait parlé* is the *identikit*, a system of transparent plastic cards each with a single facial feature drawn on it. All different kinds of features are represented so that by superimposing the cards one on top of another a composite portrait of a criminal can be compiled on the basis of eyewitness descriptions.

The principle of the nonrepetitiveness of nature applies to inanimate items of evidence as well as to anthropological observations. In the early 1900s Edmond Locard, a French doctor working with the police department of Lyons, France, did pioneering work in the analysis of physical evidence and is especially famous for his discovery that the microscopic evidence transferred between the criminal and the victim or crime scene was uniquely identifiable.

The first major contribution of the United States to the field of criminalistics was the work of Charles Waite and Colonel Calvin Goddard in the 1920s to prove that a firearm could be positively identified by the unique marks it made on the bullets and cartridge cases that it fired. It was their work that gave rise directly to the development of the comparison microscope.

Through the middle years of this century and up to the present advances have continued to be made in scientific methods of individualizing and identifying evidence. Perhaps the most significant general trend of these years has been the gradual shift from primary reliance on the analytical techniques of "wet" chemistry to instrumental methods of analysis. The result of this shift has been a realization of more rapid and more accurate analyses of evidence materials. And despite the ever-increasing costs of technological advances, it is expected that even greater reliance will be placed on instrumentation in the future.

RESEARCH AND TECHNOLOGY

Since criminalistics is not a pure science but a field that borrows what it needs from the various sciences, there tends to be relatively little original research done in criminalistics, and much of the research that is done is spent in finding ways to apply existing technology to the problems of criminal investigation. Consequently, technical advances in criminalistics tend to lag behind other scientific fields. Spectrography, spectrophotometry, electrophoresis, chromatography, mass spectrometry, and other instrumental methods were all in use in other fields before it was realized that they could be profitably applied in the crime laboratory. Because of this lag we can look at some of the scientific advances and trends that are currently taking place in other fields and make fairly reasonable predictions of the future directions in criminalistics.

In the fields of medical and biological research science has come a long way since the turn of the century when Landsteiner discovered the ABO system of blood grouping. Hundreds of proteins and enzymes have already been identified in whole blood and other biological materials which prove that each person's blood and cellular tissue composition is unique. As this research in the field of dried blood proceeds and as rapid, accurate methods are devised for characterizing the samples, dried bloodstains will be able to be used with increasing precision to identify individuals.

Lasers

New research techniques are finding increasingly sensitive methods of dealing with the nature of matter at molecular and atomic levels. One such area lies in the field of laser technology. Laser systems have been developed that can pulsate at the unbelievably rapid rates at which chemical reactions occur. This development will soon permit scientists to observe chemical reactions as they take place and to learn precisely what individual molecules look like. When this kind of technology is applied to biological research, it seems entirely within the realm of probability that sometime in the future people will be able to be identified by their unique internal cellular structure and that criminals will be identified by name from any physiological material they happen to leave at the crime scene.

Space Exploration

Another field of applied research that will undoubtedly contribute its technology to advances in criminalistics is that of space exploration. The Viking spaceship that landed on Mars was equipped with an automated shovel which scooped up a soil sample from the surface of the planet and dumped it into a miniaturized instrument which thoroughly analyzed its constituents, tested it for signs of living organisms, and electronically communicated the results back to earth. This instrument, the result of a tremendous amount of research, incorporates the work of several instruments currently used in crime laboratories. Criminalists would have to run a soil sample through a number of different tests to get the same results. Now that the technology is available, it seems but a matter of time until a similar one-step instrument, one which will analyze the soil and give the result in a computer printout, is used in crime laboratories. It is not unthinkable that such an instrument could be modified to analyze glass, paint, hairs, fibers, metals, and combustion residues.

Computers

It can already be seen from current technology that the key to the advances of the future will be the computer. Spectrographs, spectrophotometers, chromatographs, and other instruments are already being equipped with computer attachments, and some instruments, like the chromatograph/mass spectrometer combination, provide so much information in such a short time that they cannot be effectively used without a computer. The computer attachments to these instruments give simplified digital readouts which eliminate the need for the sometimes difficult interpretation of spectra. In addition, they provide a means for automated storage and retrieval.

A major problem facing crime laboratories is the difficulty of maintaining reference collections. If a laboratory either maintains or has access to up-to-date libraries of reference standards, criminalists can identify the make, model, and year of many products with a reasonable degree of accuracy. Automobiles can be identified from paint chips, typewriters from typing samples, ball point pens from ink analyses, tires from tread patterns, bullets from their weight and dimensions, and so on. It is an extremely difficult task for each individual laboratory to maintain such collections; yet they have to if they want to make speedy identifications. In the future all such reference materials will be maintained and continuously updated in a central computer to which all individual crime laboratories will have access through remote terminals. As an example, the local laboratory will conduct a layer by layer laser microprobe analysis of an automobile paint chip; the spectrographic result, which will come out in digital form, can be fed directly into the computer; and the computer will return a printout listing all the makes, models, and years of cars that used that kind of paint. Eventually the same kind of identifications will be made of people on the basis of stored information on their cellular structure.

Computers are already being used to store fingerprint files of ten-finger print cards. In the future computers will be able to store and retrieve single-finger files to which local laboratories will have access through their terminals.

The central computer that will maintain reference standards, fingerprints, and other law enforcement records will also be able to conduct random samplings of the evidentiary information fed into it from all over the world. This will enable criminalists to make accurate calculations of the probability of occurrence of any type of evidence or evidence-related event.

The Future

At the same time that we let our imaginations play freely with the possibilities for a superefficient criminal justice system of the future, we must also bear in mind some of the following cold facts:

1. All scientific advances in the field of law enforcement have had to overcome considerable resistance from skeptical jurists and advocates of traditional investigative methods. Although a certain amount of skepticism is healthy because it forces innovations to prove their worth, there is also a kind of automatic antagonism to scientific investigation which is rooted partly in jealousy and partly in a reluctance to do things differently.
2. American citizens, mindful of their traditional rights of privacy, will undoubtedly oppose any attempts at universal computerization of fingerprints, cell structure patterns, and other personal information. There will probably have to be some trade-off between individual privacy and improved law enforcement, but it is difficult to predict how much the public will tolerate.
3. Scientific advances in criminalistics are already to some extent getting ahead of the ability of many crime laboratories to use them to full advantage. This situation can be improved by better education of both investigators and crime laboratory personnel, but at a time when the costs of technology are soaring and the disposable funds available to communities are shrinking, it is unlikely that funding will be readily forthcoming for advanced instrumentation that may be perceived as law enforcement frills. The eventual outcome will probably depend on the extent to which the federal government becomes involved in the development of local crime laboratories.

For the immediate future it would seem that the most useful technological advances will be the development of relatively inexpensive instruments that are accurate, easy to use, and applicable to a broad range of scientific examinations. Also, it seems likely that more ways will be developed to examine evidence at the scene of the crime. There are already in existence easy-to-use test kits for the presumptive identification of drugs at the crime scene. These tests will continue to improve, and the concept will probably extend to other areas.

Perhaps the most important developments of all for the future lie in the field of education, for no technological advances will be of any use if there is no one trained to take advantage of them. It is not only important that the technical personnel be well trained in all phases of criminalistics, but it is also essential that investigators and criminalists both receive enough education in each others' fields so that they will understand each others' capabilities and limitations and be able to work together in a spirit of cooperation.

GLOSSARY

ABO system	a blood typing system.
absorptiometry	a measurement of the ability of substances to absorb light.
absorption-elution test	a method of typing dried blood.
accelerant	a combustible liquid used to spread and intensify a fire.
acceptance angle	the angle at which light rays are received into the eye or into a lens.
acid	a compound that increases the concentration of positive hydrogen ions (H^+) in a solution.
acid phosphatase test	a presumptive test for semen.
adsorption	the adherence of one material to another through molecular surface attraction.
agglutination	the clumping of red blood corpuscles.
agglutinin	same as antibody.
agglutinogen	same as antigen.
alcohol	any of a group of organic compounds the simplest of which are straight chain hydrocarbons in which an OH group has replaced a hydrogen atom, as methanol, ethanol, propanol. In common use it refers to ethanol.
alkali	same as base.
amorphous	shapeless; said of substances like liquids whose atoms are randomly distributed rather than occurring in regular geometric configurations.
amphetamine	a stimulant drug.
amphoteric	able to act either as an acid or a base.
anagen phase	the growth period of hair.

393

anthropometrics a series of bodily measurements formerly used to individualize and identify criminals.

antibody a substance in the blood serum that reacts specifically with antigens of their own type to cause agglutination.

antigen a blood protein attached to the red blood corpuscles that determines blood type by specific reactions with antibodies.

arch a class of fingerprints characterized by friction ridges that enter the print from one side, rise in the middle of the pattern, and flow out the other side.

arsenic a metallic element found in many poisonous compounds.

ASA the exposure index that indentifies the speed of a film; it is used to calibrate light meters.

aspermia total lack of sperm; sterility in males.

astigmatic aberration the inability of a lens to resolve vertical and horizontal lines with the same degree of sharpness.

atom the smallest unit of matter that retains a unique and constant chemical identity.

atomic absorption spectrophotometer an instrument used to identify the metallic elements present in a substance through their absorption of characteristic wavelengths of light (see Chapter 4).

atomic number the number of protons contained in the nucleus of an atom.

auto-loading weapon a firearm that uses recoil pressure or gas pressure to automatically eject spent cartridge cases and reload new cartridges into the breech.

automatic weapon an auto-loading weapon that fires continuously as long as the trigger is pulled and until the ammunition runs out, as a machine gun.

autonomic nervous system the nerves that control the involuntary activities of the body, such as heartbeat, breathing, and organ function.

Barbeiros test a presumptive microcrystalline test for semen.

barbiturate any of several depressant drugs derived from barbituric acid.

base a compound that increases the concentration of negative hydroxide ions (OH^-) in a solution.

bast fiber a natural fiber from the stem of a plant.

beach marks curved, roughly parallel lines on the surface of a metal fracture indicative of fatigue failure.

Becke line the light halo seen around the edge of a translucent microscopic specimen when the refractive index of the specimen is different from that of the mounting medium.

benzidine a color reagent used as a presumptive test for the presence of blood.

binder a liquid that hardens into a thin film on contact with air and holds the pigmentary materials of paints and certain inks in suspension.

birefringence the difference between the highest and lowest refractive indexes of optically active crystals (compare double refraction).

blast a sudden localized wave of increased atmospheric pressure that radiates outward from an explosion causing destruction as it moves.

blood group same as blood type.

blood type any of several categories into which the blood of individuals may be divided according to specific agglutination reactions between antigens and antibodies.

bore   the interior of a firearm barrel.

Breathalyzer®   an instrument for measuring breath alcohol concentration.

breech   the rear part of a firearm barrel where the cartridge enters.

breech block   the part of a firearm that fits up against the head of a cartridge to prevent the cartridge from moving backward when fired.

brisance   a shattering shock effect of very rapidly detonating thermal decomposition explosions.

buffer   a solution that has been adjusted to a certain pH.

cadaveric spasm   a localized stiffening of a part of the body caused by a strong muscle tension at the moment of death.

caliber   the diameter of a bullet at its base or of a firearm barrel measured between the lands.

cannabis   a group of drugs extracted from the leaves and flowers of the hemp plant, *Cannabis sativa,* including marihuana, hashish, and hashish oil.

cannelure   grooves around the circumference of a bullet or around the neck of a cartridge case used to hold lubrication or to crimp the bullet into place.

carbon monoxide (CO)   a toxic gas.

carboxyhemoglobin   the compound formed by the chemical combination of carbon monoxide and hemoglobin.

cardiosphygmograph   the part of the polygraph that measures changes in heartbeat and blood pressure.

cartridge   a complete round of firearm ammunition, including bullet (or shot), cartridge case, powder, and primer.

catagen phase   the rest phase of hair after growth is completed.

Celsius   another name for centigrade; thermometer on whose scale the boiling point of water is 100° and the freezing point of water is 0°.

centerfire ammunition   ammunition that has the primer in the center of the head.

central nervous system   the main set of nerves housed in the brain and spinal cord that integrates and coordinates all the nervous responses of the body.

chemical properties   the characteristic ways in which a substance combines chemically with other substances.

chloral hydrate   a central nervous system depressant; knockout drops.

chromatic aberration   the tendency of a lens to focus light of different wavelengths at different distances from the lens.

chromatography   any of several analytical techniques whereby organic mixtures are separated into their component compounds by the differential attraction of their molecules to a stationary phase while being propelled by a mobile phase (see Chapter 4).

circles of confusion   the cones of light formed on both sides of the focal point of a lens that determine the area of acceptable focus.

class characteristics   characteristics of an item of evidence that serve to identify the general category to which the item of evidence belongs without identifying the specific item (compare individual characteristics).

coagulation   the change from a liquid state to a gel-like or solid state through chemical reaction; congealing.

cocaine   a natural alkaloid stimulant drug.

colloid	a particle larger than a molecule but small enough to remain in suspension without settling.
color contrast filter	a filter used to make its own color appear brighter and its complementary color appear darker in black-and-white photography.
color correction filter	a filter used to correct the color balance of daylight or tungsten color films.
compound	a substance resulting from the chemical combination of two or more elements.
compressive stress	a stress caused by pushing or squeezing forces.
concentrated explosion	an explosion produced by a thermal decomposition explosive.
concentric fracture	a crack in a pane of glass that forms a rough circle around the point where the glass was struck.
condenser	lens system under the microscope stage that focuses light through the slide onto the specimen.
conduction	the transmittal of heat by direct transfer of heat energy from molecule to molecule.
contaminated fingerprint	same as visible fingerprint.
convection	the transmittal of heat by the physical movement of heated molecules from one place to another.
convection currents	air currents caused by the tendency of heated molecules to rise and be replaced from below by cooler molecules.
core	in fingerprints, the center of a loop or whorl pattern.
coronal	crown-like, said of hair scales.
corpuscle	blood cell.
corpus delicti	the body, or essential elements, of a crime.
***corpus delicti* evidence**	evidence proving that a crime has occurred.
cortex	in hair, the main body of the hair shaft.
covalent bonding	the combination of atoms to form molecules by means of sharing electrons.
criminalistics	the use of scientific methods of observation and analysis to detect and interpret physical evidence.
crystal	a substance whose atoms or molecules are lined up in regular repeating geometrical configurations; most solids are crystalline.
crystal lattice	the geometrical configuration of atoms and molecules in crystalline solids.
cuticle	in hair, the collective term for the scales covering the exterior of animal hairs.
cyanide	any of a group of toxic compounds containing the CN^- ion, which work by inhibiting the transfer of oxygen from the blood to the body cells.
cystolythic hair	a thorn-shaped protrusion of calcium carbonate on marihuana leaves.
delta	in fingerprints, a roughly triangular pattern of ridge lines found in all loops and whorls.
dendritic	tree-like; used to describe the growth of crystals in metals.
denier	the number of grams of yarn per 9,000 meters of length; a measure of the fineness of the yarn.
density	the ratio of the mass of a substance to a unit of its volume.
depressant	a class of drugs that inhibits the activity of the central nervous system.

depth of field	the area in a scene being photographed in which objects at different distances from the lens are all in acceptable focus.
depth of focus	in microscopy, the thickness of a specimen that is in focus at a given magnification.
dermal nitrate test	test for determining the presence of nitrates on the hands of a person who has recently fired a handgun.
DET	a hallucinogen.
diaphragm	in photography, the adjustable aperture that controls the amount of light received into a camera.
diatomic molecule	a molecule formed by the combination of two atoms of the same kind.
digitalis	a powerful stimulant that causes death when taken in large doses.
diphenylamine reagent	a spot test reagent used to identify explosive residues.
dispersion	the separation of white light into its component wavelengths by a prism or diffraction grating.
DMT	a hallucinogen.
DOM	a hallucinogen.
double refraction	the optically active property exhibited by most crystals of having different refractive indexes when viewed at different axes under polarized light.
down hair	the fine short hairs of animals that grow close to the skin and provide body warmth.
ductile	soft, capable of being stretched, said of metals.
ejector	a spring-loaded part of a firearm that flips the spent cartridge case away from the firearm's loading mechanism after it is extracted from the breech.
electromagnetic spectrum	the entire range of radiant energy from the most energetic cosmic rays to the least energetic radio waves.
electron	a subatomic particle of almost negligible mass that flies around the nucleus of an atom and bears a negative electrical charge.
electrophoresis	a method of identifying proteins and enzymes by subjecting them to an electrical potential on a plate covered with a gel medium and observing the distance they migrate.
element	a substance made up entirely of atoms that have the same atomic number.
emission spectrography	an instrumental analytical method for identifying metallic elements by the characteristic wavelengths of light they emit when their atoms return from an excited state to their ground state (see Chapter 4).
emulsion	in photography, the thin layer of gelatin which holds light sensitive silver salts in place on film and photographic papers.
endothermic	characterized by the absorption of energy, usually in the form of heat.
erythrocyte	red blood corpuscle.
ethanol	a simple alcohol, C_2H_5OH; a central nervous system depressant; ethyl alcohol, grain alcohol; the spirituous ingredient of beers, wines, and liquors.
exemplar	a sample or specimen used for comparison, as a handwriting exemplar.

exothermic	characterized by the emission of energy, usually in the form of heat.
explosive mixture	same as flammable mixture.
explosive range	same as flammable range.
explosophore	any of a number of functional groups of atoms commonly occurring in explosives that decompose readily when subjected to heat or shock.
extractor	a hook-like part of a firearm that draws the cartridge case out of the breech.
eyepiece	same as ocular.
fibrin	a sticky precipitate that binds the red blood cells together to form clots.
fibrinogen	a blood protein that is converted to fibrin at the site of a wound.
filament fiber	a long textile fiber.
filter factor	a number indicating the additional amount of light needed to properly expose film when a given filter is used.
firebug	same as pyromaniac.
fire triangle	schematic representation of the three ingredients (fuel, oxygen, and heat) necessary for a fire to take place.
first-formant frequency	the fundamental frequency of human voice sounds as produced by vibration of the vocal cords.
fixer	sodium thiosulfate solution used to remove unused silver halides from photographic film and paper.
flaming fire	the rapid combustion of volatile materials with sufficient ventilation to produce flames.
flammable mixture	any concentration of a gas or vapor in air that is within the flammable range.
flammable range	the entire range of possible concentrations of a gas or vapor in air that is capable of burning. The span between the upper and lower flammable limits.
flash point	the minimum temperature at which a liquid gives off sufficient vapor to form an ignitable mixture with the air near the surface of the liquid.
Florence test	a presumptive microcrystalline test for semen.
fluorescence	the property of a substance of emitting one form of radiation while being excited by another form of radiation, as when a substance radiates visible light when bathed in ultraviolet light.
***f*/number**	the numerical value of a camera's diaphragm setting determined by dividing the focal length of the lens by the diameter of the aperture.
focal length	the distance between the optical center of a lens and the focal point of the light focused by it.
forensic science	the entire range of scientific methods of investigation, including criminalistics, forensic medicine, and forensic odontology.
format	in photography, the size of the negative.
frequency	the number of complete alternations of the waves of electromagnetic radiations occurring in a given space of time, usually 1 second.
friction ridges	raised lines of skin that form patterns on the tips of the fingers, the palms of the hands, and the bottoms of the feet.
***f*/stop**	same as *f*/number.

galvanograph   the part of the polygraph that measures changes in electrical skin resistance.

gas chromatography   a chromatographic system in which the mobile phase is a pressurized inert gas and the stationary phase is a long coiled metal column packed with a viscous liquid (compare chromatography).

gaseous explosion   an explosion in which fuel materials, such as gases or finely divided dust particles that have become thoroughly intermixed with air, are ignited and combine instantaneously with the oxygen in the air.

gauge   a measurement of the bore of shotguns; originally referring to the number of single round lead balls fitting the bore of a firearm that would make up 1 pound in weight.

genotype   the total genetic traits that an individual inherits from his or her parents (compare phenotype).

glowing fire   the slow surface combustion of a solid resulting from the lack of volatile components or insufficient ventilation.

gradient   a glass tube filled from bottom to top with liquids of successively lighter densities used to determine the density distribution of materials such as soil or paint.

grain   in photography, the size of the silver halide crystals. In metallurgy, metallic crystals.

grain alcohol   same as ethanol.

grain boundary   in metallurgy, the points where the crystals of a metal meet.

Griess reagent   a spot test reagent used to identify explosive residues.

Griess test   a chemical method for developing powder patterns, especially on clothing.

grooves   in firearms, the cut or low-lying portions of a rifled barrel (compare lands).

guard hair   the coarse outer hair of animals that protects against the elements and external hazards.

hackle marks   small straight striations that appear perpendicular to rib marks on the edge of broken glass.

halides   salts formed from the halogens.

hallucinogen   a class of drugs, either natural or synthetic in origin, having the effect on the user of distorting perception and creating sensory illusions.

halogens   the chemical elements fluorine, chlorine, bromine, and iodine.

hard fiber   a natural fiber from the leaf of a plant.

hashish   see cannabis.

head   the back or base of a cartridge.

heat of combustion   the degree of heat given off by a fire.

hemoglobin   a blood protein attached to the red blood cells that delivers oxygen from the lungs to the body cells and returns carbon dioxide as a waste material from the cells to the lungs.

high explosive   in general, an explosive whose detonation rate is faster than the speed of sound.

homeostasis   the normal, stable, unstimulated state of the body functions.

humus   the organic portion of soil.

hydrocarbon   a compound containing only hydrogen and carbon atoms.

hypo   same as fixer.

identikit a system of transparent plastic cards with facial features drawn on them that can be used to construct a composite picture of a criminal on the basis of eyewitness reports.

ignition temperature the minimum temperature required to initiate or cause self-sustained combustion without any further external application of heat.

imbricate shingle-like, said of hair scales.

individual characteristics characteristics which because of their unique features serve to identify a specific item of evidence (compare class characteristics).

infrared invisible long wavelengths of light below red in the visible spectrum.

initiating explosive same as primary explosive.

inorganic chemistry the chemistry of minerals, metals, and noncarbonaceous substances.

interstitial solution in metallurgy, an alloy in which the atoms of the alloying element are small enough to slip into the crystal lattice of the base metal without displacing its molecules.

iodine fuming a technique for temporarily visualizing latent fingerprints by subjecting them to iodine vapor.

ion an atom or group of atoms that has become either positively charged through losing an electron or negatively charged through gaining an electron.

ionic bonding the combination of atoms to form molecules by means of a transfer of electrons from one atom to another thereby causing an electrostatic attraction between them.

keratin the hard proteinaceous dead tissue of which hair, fingernails, horn, and feathers are primarily composed.

lands the raised portion that remains in a rifled gun barrel after the grooves have been cut out or formed.

larynx the voice box, including the vocal cords.

laser microprobe a spectrographic analytical technique that uses a laser beam to isolate a very small amount of a sample.

latent fingerprint a fingerprint made by the deposit of oils and perspiration by the friction ridges; usually invisible to the naked eye.

latent image the invisible pattern of sensitized silver halide crystals that occurs on photographic films or papers when light strikes them.

lectin antibody from a vegetable protein source.

lens speed the largest diaphragm setting of a lens.

leuco-malachite a color reagent used as a presumptive test for blood.

leukocyte white blood corpuscle.

lifter a black or white rubber sheet with one sticky side used to pick up and preserve dusted fingerprints and other residue prints.

line spectrum (pl.: spectra) the characteristic pattern of lines produced by a spectrograph by which metallic elements can be identified.

liquid silicone rubber a casting material used on tool marks and other impressions to capture fine detail.

livor mortis same as post-mortem lividity.

loops a class of fingerprints characterized by ridge lines that enter from one side of the pattern, rise in the center, and curve around to flow out the same side. Radial loops enter and exit on the side of the print facing the thumb. Ulnar loops enter and exit on the side facing the little finger.

lower explosive limit same as lower flammable limit.

lower flammable limit the smallest percentage by volume of a gas or vapor mixed with air that is capable of burning.

low explosive in general, an explosive whose detonation rate is slower than the speed of sound.

LSD a hallucinogen.

Lucite a type of thermoplastic.

lumen a hollow cavity in the center of all animal hairs.

luminol a reagent used as a presumptive test for blood.

macroscopic examined with the naked eye.

marihuana see cannabis.

mass spectrometry an instrumental analytical method of identifying organic compounds by breaking up their molecules into ionized fragments and measuring the mass to charge ratio of the fragments (see Chapter 4).

matter anything that has mass and occupies space.

medulla organic material that is sometimes present in the hollow cavity in the center of animal hairs.

mescaline a hallucinogen.

methanol a toxic simple alcohol CH_3OH; methyl alcohol, wood alcohol.

micro-tremor a physiological tremor that accompanies the contraction of any voluntary muscle; in the muscles of the larynx the micro-tremor disappears or diminishes under stress and can therefore give an indication of deception.

MN system a blood typing system (see Chapter 12).

Molotov cocktail usually a glass bottle full of gasoline around which a gasoline soaked rag is tied and ignited. When the bottle is thrown against a hard surface, it breaks and spreads flaming gasoline.

monatomic characterizing a structure, such as a metal, having one atom per molecule.

monochromatic characterizing light of a single wavelength.

monochromator a device for isolating individual wavelengths of light.

monomer one of the small molecules forming a polymer by combining with identical or similar molecules.

motor nerves nerves that transmit action messages from the central nervous system to the muscles.

moulage dental casting material; sometimes used to make casts of tool marks or other impressions to record fine detail.

multiple yarn yarn made from twisting two or more single-ply yarns together.

narcotic a drug that induces stupor, specifically opium and its derivatives.

neutral density filter a filter that reduces the amount of light entering a camera without changing the color balance.

neutron a subatomic particle in the nucleus of an atom that has the same mass as a proton but no charge.

neutron activation analysis an analytical technique for identifying metallic elements by measuring the characteristic gamma radiation of an element that has been made radioactive by neutron bombardment.

ninhydrin   a chemical reagent used to develop latent fingerprints by reacting with amino acids in the perspiration.

numerical aperture   a measure of the resolving power of a microscope objective.

objective   the lower lens of a microscope that is positioned directly over the specimen and performs the primary magnification.

ocular   the lens of a microscope into which the viewer looks; it provides secondary magnification of the image projected by the objective.

oligospermia   low sperm count.

organic chemistry   the chemistry of plant and animal compounds such as petroleum products, coal, wood, and animal matter.

oxidation   the chemical combination of oxygen with another element or compound.

oxyhemoglobin   the compound formed by the chemical combination of oxygen and hemoglobin.

panchromatic   characterizing black-and-white films that approximate the human eye in sensitivity to color brightness.

paraffin test   same as dermal nitrate test.

parasympathetic nerves   a set of nerves belonging to the autonomic nervous system that causes the stimulated body organs to return to homeostasis after a threat has passed (compare sympathetic nerves).

parcentered   characteristic of the ability of microscopes equipped with multiple objectives to keep the specimen in the center of the field of view when a different objective is rotated into position.

parfocal   characteristic of the ability of microscopes equipped with multiple objectives to keep the specimen approximately in focus when a different objective is rotated into position.

PCP   a hallucinogen.

peripheral nervous systems   the motor nerves, the sensory nerves, and the autonomic nervous system.

peyote   a hallucinogen.

pH   a scale of values expressing relative acidity or basicity. Substances having a pH of less than 7 are acidic; substances having a pH of greater than 7 are basic; and a pH of 7 is neutral.

pharynx   the upper part of the throat, which is important in forming voice sounds.

phenolphthalein   a color reagent used as a presumptive test for blood.

phenotype   the genetic traits actually displayed by an individual (compare genotype).

photomicrography   photography through a microscope.

photon   in quantum theory, a particle of light energy.

physical evidence   any object, substance, trace, or impression that helps to trace or identify a criminal or to prove that a crime has occurred.

physical properties   any identifying characteristics of a substance that do not involve a change in the substance's chemical structure (e.g., melting point, boiling point, color, texture, refractive index, density).

physiological saline solution   a 0.9 percent salt solution buffered to the body pH of 7.2.

pigment   organic or inorganic particles that impart color or opacity to otherwise colorless materials; pigments occur naturally in hair and skin and are used in paints and inks.

plasma	the liquid portion of blood that remains after the solids are spun off in a centrifuge.
plastic fingerprints	fingerprints impressed in a soft material such as wax.
platelets	transparent, disc-like blood solids, smaller than red or white corpuscles, which induce the coagulation of blood at the site of a wound by causing the precipitation of fibrin.
pneumograph	the part of the polygraph that measures changes in breathing rate.
points	fingerprint identification characteristics including ridge endings, bifurcations, dots, and enclosures.
polarization	the filtration of light to permit the passage of light waves vibrating in only one plane.
polarizing filter	a filter that allows only light vibrating in one plane to enter a camera; primarily used to reduce glare in a picture.
polygraph	an instrument that detects stress by measuring changes in heartbeat, blood pressure, breathing, and galvanic skin resistance.
polymer	a long chain-like molecule made up of a number of smaller molecules of the same kind. A polymer has the same percentage composition of elements as each of the smaller molecules (compare monomer).
portrait parlé	a composite sketch made of a criminal on the basis of eye-witness reports.
post-mortem lividity	a purplish discoloration in a dead body caused by gravitational draining and subsequent coagulation of blood in lower-lying tissues.
potentiation	the tendency of one drug to intensify the effects of another when both drugs are taken together.
precipitin test	a test for blood species (see Chapter 12).
primary explosive	a high explosive that is easily detonated by heat or shock.
propanol	a toxic simple alcohol C_3H_7OH; propyl alcohol.
proton	a subatomic particle existing in the nucleus of an atom bearing a positive electrical charge.
psilocybin	a hallucinogen.
psilocyn	a hallucinogen.
Psychological Stress Evaluator	an instrument that detects stress by measuring changes in the voice.
pyrolysis	the decomposition of solid materials usually under high heat into simpler volatile components.
pyromaniac	a psychotic personality who derives great pleasure from starting and watching fires.
quantum theory	a theory that holds that light is made up of measurable particles of energy called photons.
radial fracture	a crack in glass that extends outward like the spoke of a wheel from the point where the glass was struck.
radiation	a transmittal of energy in the form of electromagnetic rays.
reagent	a substance which, because of its characteristic chemical reactions, can be used to examine or identify other substances.
reflected illumination	in microscopy, illumination of a specimen from above, generally used for opaque specimens.
refraction	the bending of light rays as they pass from one medium to a medium of different density at an oblique angle.

refractive index   the ratio of the speed of light in a vacuum to the speed of light in a medium.

regenerated fibers   natural fibers that have been chemically restructured to possess the properties of synthetic fibers.

Reinsch test   a procedure for determining the presence of metallic poisons.

resolving power   the ability of a lens to distinguish small details.

reticle   a microscope eyepiece with fine lines engraved in it; used to make close measurements.

revolver   a handgun with a revolving cylinder that holds cartridges in chambers and successively rotates them into firing position.

rhodizonate test   a chemical method for developing powder patterns, especially on clothing.

Rh system   a blood typing system (see Chapter 12).

rib marks   conchoidal striations on the edge of broken glass that are perpendicular to the surface opposite the impact and tangential to the impact surface.

rifling   the spiral grooves cut or formed in the bore of a firearm barrel to impart spin to the bullet when it is fired.

rigor mortis   a general stiffening of the muscles of a dead body due to degenerative chemical activity in the cells. It begins between 3 hours and 6 hours after death and lasts approximately 12 hours.

rimfire ammunition   ammunition in which the primer material is in the rim of the head.

rod   in fingerprints, a straight ridge line in the center of the pattern.

scales   flattened overlapping cells covering the exterior of animal hairs, collectively known as the cuticle.

secondary explosive   a high explosive that generally has to be detonated by a primary explosive.

secretor   a person in whom ABO antigens occur in body fluids and tissues other than blood.

semiautomatic weapon   an auto-loading weapon that fires one round each time the trigger is pulled.

sensory nerves   nerves that transmit the external stimuli of the senses to the central nervous system.

septum   a rubber seal that permits the passage of a hypodermic syringe and then reseals itself when the syringe is removed.

sericin   the natural proteinaceous material that binds raw silk filaments together.

serology   the branch of science dealing with blood and body fluids.

serum   the fluid portion of blood after the blood solids and fibrin have been removed.

slippage   a widening of the rifling marks toward the nose end of a bullet due to the straight forward motion of the bullet before the rifling engages it and starts it spinning.

silicone rubber   see liquid silicone rubber.

silver nitrate   a chemical reagent used to develop latent fingerprints by its reaction with salt in the perspiration.

single-ply yarn   a strand of yarn made directly from fibers.

soft fiber   same as bast fiber.

solute   a substance dissolved in another substance.

solution	a mixture in which the molecules of one substance become thoroughly dispersed in another substance without combining chemically.
solvent	a substance in which other substances are dissolved.
sound spectrograph	a pictorial representation of the frequency, duration, and amplitude of human voice sounds.
space lattice	same as crystal lattice.
spectrograph	an analytical instrument that identifies metallic elements by their characteristic line spectra (compare emission spectrography).
spectrophotometry	an instrumental analytical method for identifying organic compounds by their selective absorption of different wavelengths of light (see Chapter 4).
spermatozoon (pl.: spermatozoa)	a male reproductive cell.
spherical aberration	the tendency of a lens to focus light passing through its center at a different distance from the lens than light passing through its edges.
spontaneous combustion	self-ignition of a substance through chemical or microorganismic action, as in the oxidation of oily rags.
spot test	a method of identifying substances by observing characteristic color reactions when various reagents are applied to them.
staple fibers	short fibers that have to be spun to form yarn.
steam distillation	a procedure for extracting the volatile components of a mixture.
stimulant	a class of drugs that work by stimulating the activity of the central nervous system.
strychnine	a natural toxic alkaloid that causes death by convulsions.
"S" twist	a clockwise twist in yarns, ropes, and cords.
substitutional solution	in metallurgy, an alloy made up of metals whose atoms are approximately the same size thereby causing the atoms of the alloying metal to displace those of the base metal in their crystal lattice.
suspension	a mixture in which particles larger than molecules become dispersed in another substance without reacting chemically with it.
sympathetic nerves	a set of nerves belonging to the autonomic nervous system that stimulates the body organs in specific ways to meet a threat (compare parasympathetic nerves).
synthetic fibers	fibers artificially created from originally nonfibrous materials.
Takayama test	a microcrystalline test for the presence of blood.
Teichmann test	a microcrystalline test for the presence of blood.
telephoto lens	a camera lens that has a long focal length in order to magnify distant objects.
telogen phase	the last period in the life of a hair in which it falls out naturally.
tensile stress	stress caused by pulling or stretching forces.
testimonial evidence	verbal evidence from witnesses.
THC	the psychoactive ingredient of cannabis.
thermal conductivity	the ability of materials to conduct heat.
thermal decomposition explosives	explosive materials that furnish both fuel and oxygen in their internal molecular composition and do not require contact with oxygen in the air to explode.

thermoplastic a plastic material that melts and flows when heated.

thin-layer chromatography a chromatographic system in which the stationary phase is a granular material coated onto a glass plate and the mobile phase is a solvent that migrates along the granular surface by capillary action (compare chromatography).

thrombocyte platelet.

titration a method for determining the concentration of a substance in a solution by adding the least amount of a reagent necessary to cause a visible chemical change.

torsional stress stress by twisting forces.

toxicology the branch of science dealing with poisons.

trailer combustible material used to spread a set fire to different parts of a structure.

transmitted illumination in microscopy, light that passes up from the condenser through the specimen into the objective; generally used with translucent and transparent specimens.

ultraviolet invisible short wavelengths of light beyond violet in the visible spectrum.

upper explosive limit same as upper flammable limit.

upper flammable limit the highest percentage by volume of a gas or vapor mixed with air that is capable of burning.

vehicle same as binder.

virtual image the enlarged apparent image that the eye seems to see at a distance of approximately 25 centimeters when an object is enlarged by a microscope.

visible fingerprint a fingerprint made when the friction ridges of a finger deposit a visible material onto a surface.

voice print same as sound spectrograph.

volatile easily vaporized.

warp in weaving, strands of yarn laid parallel lengthwise on a loom.

wavelength the distance from crest to crest of the waves of electromagnetic radiations.

wave theory a theory that describes light as a continuous wave of energy.

weft same as woof.

wet chemistry analytical techniques based on the application of chemical reagents, as opposed to instrumental analyses.

whorl a classification of fingerprints having circular or generally rounded patterns and two deltas; it includes the plain whorl, the central pocket loop, the double loop, and the accidental whorl.

wide-angle lens a camera lens with a short focal length which expands the angle of view to include more information on a negative than a normal lens would.

wood alcohol same as methanol.

woof the filling strands of yarn that are woven at right angles to the warp.

X-ray diffraction an instrumental analytical technique for identifying crystalline materials.

"Z" twist a counterclockwise twist in yarns, ropes, and cords.

——— BIBLIOGRAPHY ———

ABRAMS, STANLEY, "Polygraph Validity and Reliability: A Review," *Journal of Forensic Sciences,* 18, no. 2 (1973), 324.

"A Joint Study of Crime Laboratories for the Commonwealth of Massachusetts." Midwest Research Institute, 425 Volker Boulevard, Kansas City, Mo. 64110, 1971.

ALFORD, E. F., Jr., "Disguised Handwriting," *Journal of Forensic Sciences,* 15, no. 4 (October 1970), 476–488.

BAREFOOT, J. KIRK, ed., "The Polygraph Story." Publication of the American Polygraph Association, 1974.

BARNES, F. C., and R. A. HELSON, "An Empirical Study of Gunshot Residue Patterns," *Journal of Forensic Sciences,* 19, no. 3 (1974), 448–462.

BATTLE, BRENDAN P., and PAUL B. WESTON, *Arson, A Handbook of Detection and Investigation.* New York: Arco Publishing Co., Inc., 1975.

BLOCK, EUGENE, *Voice Printing.* New York: David McKay Co., Inc., 1975.

BORTNIAK, J. P., and E. H. SILD, "Differentiation of Microgram Quantities of Acrylic and Modacrylic Fibers Using Pyrolysis Gas-Liquid Chromatography," *Journal of Forensic Sciences,* 16, no. 2 (1971), 380.

BRADFORD, LOWEL L. W., and ARYEH H. SAMUEL, "Research and Development Needs in Criminalistics," published in *Law Enforcement Science and Technology III,* S. I. Cohn and W. B. McMahon, ed. Proceedings of the Third National Symposium on Law Enforcement Science and Technology. Sponsored by the National Institute of Law Enforcement and Criminal Justice/LEAA. Port City Press, Inc. (1970), 465–476.

BRODIE, THOMAS G., *Bombs and Bombing: A Handbook to Detection, Disposal, and Investigation for Police and Fire Departments.* Springfield, Ill.: Charles C Thomas, 1972.

BROWN, G. A., D. NEYLAN, W. J. REYNOLDS, and K. W. SMALLDON, "The Stability of Ethanol in Stored Blood," *Analytica Chimica Acta,* 66, no. 2 (1973), Part I: 271–283, Part II: 285–290.

BROWN, THEODORE L., and H. EUGENE LEMAY, Jr., *Chemistry, The Central Science.* Englewood Cliffs, N.J.: Prentice-Hall, Inc., 1977.

BRUNELLE, RICHARD L., and A. A. CANTU, "Ink Analysis—A Weapon Against Crime by Detection of Fraud," in *Forensic Science,* ed. Geoffrey Davis. Washington, D.C.: American Chemical Society, 1975.

CHOWDHRY, R., S. K. GUPTA, and H. L. BAMI, "Ink Differentiation and Infrared Techniques," *Journal of Forensic Sciences,* 18, no. 4 (October 1973), 418.

CLARKE, E. G. C., *Isolation and Identification of Drugs in Pharmaceuticals, Body Fluids, and Post-Mortem Material.* London: The Pharmaceutical Press, 1974.

"CNS Depressants," National Institute of Drug Abuse, U.S. Department of Health, Education and Welfare Publication No. (ADM) 75–149.

Criminal Investigation, Vol. I, *Basic Procedures,* and Vol. II, *Specific Offenses.* Gaithersburg, Md.: International Association of Chiefs of Police, 1975.

CROWN, DAVID A., *The Forensic Examination of Paints and Pigments.* Springfield, Ill.: Charles C Thomas, 1968.

CULLIFORD, BRYAN J., *The Examination and Typing of Bloodstains in the Crime Laboratory.* Washington, D.C.: U.S. Government Printing Office, 1971.

CURRY, A. S., *Poison Detection in Human Organs,* 3rd ed. Springfield, Ill.: Charles C Thomas, 1976.

DALRYMPLE, B. E., J. M. DUFF, and E. R. MENZEL, "Inherent Fingerprint Luminescence —Detection by Laser," *Journal of Forensic Sciences,* 22, no. 1 (1977), 106–115

DAVIS, J., *Toolmarks, Firearms, and the Striagraph.* Springfield, Ill.: Charles C Thomas, 1958.

DENAULT, G. C., H. H. TAKIMOTO, Q. Y. KWAN, and A. PALLOS, *Detectability of Selected Genetic Markers in Dried Blood upon Aging.* Washington, D.C.: U.S. Government Printing Office, 1978.

"Drugs of Abuse," U.S. Department of Justice, Drug Enforcement Administration Publication, undated.

EDDY, NATHAN B., H. HALBACH, HARRIS ISBELL, and MAURICE H. SEEVERS, "Drug Dependence: Its Significance and Characteristics," *Bulletin of the World Health Organization,* 32, no. 5 (1965), 721–733.

EDSON, ROBERT K., "The Dektor Psychological Stress Evaluator" (unpublished Master's thesis, Human Service College of the National Graduate University, April 1976). (Available from Dektor CI/S, Inc., 5508 Port Royal Road, Springfield, Va. 22151.)

FOX, RICHARD H., "Absorption-Elution Testing for ABO Group Factors: Preliminary Collaborative Study," *Journal of the Association of Official Analytical Chemists,* 57, no. 3 (1974), 666.

Fox, Richard H., and Carl L. Cunningham, *Crime Scene Search and Physical Evidence Handbook.* Washington, D.C.: U.S. Government Printing Office, 1973.

Gardner, D. D., K. M. Cano, R. S. Peimer, and T. E. Yeshion, "An Evaluation of Tetramethylbenzidine as a Presumptive Test for Blood," *Journal of Forensic Sciences,* 21, no. 4 (October 1976), 816–821.

Given, B. W., "Latent Fingerprints on Cartridges and Expended Cartridge Casings," *Journal of Forensic Sciences,* 21, no. 3 (1976), 587–594.

Goldman, B. S., and J. I. Thornton, "A New Trace Ferrous Metal Detection Reagent," *Journal of Forensic Sciences,* 21, no. 3 (July 1976), 625–628.

Goleb, J. A., and C. R. Midkiff, Jr., "Firearms Discharge Residue Sample Collection Techniques," *Journal of Forensic Sciences,* 20, no. 4 (1975), 701–707.

Goodwin, Gary L., "PSE: New Security Tool," *Burroughs Clearing House,* 59, no. 8 (May 1975), 29–30.

Green, Gion B., "Truth Verification," *Security World,* 10; no. 9 (October 1973), 38.

Grunbaum, B. W., "Some New Approaches to the Individualization of Fresh and Dried Bloodstains," *Journal of Forensic Sciences,* 21, no. 3 (July 1976), 488–497.

Gurgin, V. A., B. Parker and S. J. Betsch, "Criminalistics: Today and Tomorrow," *Journal of Forensic Sciences,* 19, no. 3 (1974), 518.

Guy, R. D., and B. D. Pate, "Studies of the Trace Element Content of Bullet Lead and Jacket Material," *Journal of Forensic Sciences,* 18, no. 2 (April 1973), 87–92.

Haas, M. A., M. J. Camp, and R. F. Dragen, "A Comparative Study of the Applicability of the Scanning Electron Microscope in the Examination of Vehicle Light Filaments," *Journal of Forensic Sciences,* 20, no. 1 (January 1975), 91.

Hackett, L. P., L. J. Dusci, and I. A. McDonald, "Extraction Procedures for Some Common Drugs in Clinical and Forensic Toxicology," *Journal of Forensic Sciences,* 21, no. 2 (1976), 263–274.

Hallcock, R. P., "Spermine and Choline Identification by Thin-Layer Chromatography," *Journal of Forensic Sciences,* 19, no. 1 (January 1974), 172–174.

Harrison, Wilson R., *Suspect Documents.* New York: Praeger Publishers, Inc., 1958.

Heisse, J. D., Jr., "Does Audio Stress Analysis Work?" *Security World,* 13, no. 5 (May 1976), 24.

Hilton, Ordway, *Scientific Examination of Questioned Documents.* Chicago: Callaghan and Co., 1956.

"Identification of Fibers in Textiles," Method D 276–72. American Society for Testing and Materials, 1916 Race St., Philadelphia, Pa. 19103, 1972.

Inbau, Fred E., *Scientific Police Investigation.* Radnor, Pa.: Chilton Book Company, 1972.

Kahn, Herbert L., "Principles and Practice of Atomic Absorption," *Advances in Chemistry Series,* no. 73, "Trace Inorganics in Water" (1968), 183–229.

Kaistha, K. K., and Jerome Jaffee, "TLC Techniques for Identification of Narcotics, Barbiturates, and CNS Stimulants in a Drug Abuse Screening Program," *Journal of Pharmaceutical Sciences,* 61, no. 5 (1972), 679–688.

Kersta, L. G., "Voiceprint Identification," *Nature,* 196, no. 4861 (1962), 1253–1257.

Kilty, J. W., "Activity After Shooting and Its Effect on the Retention of Primer Residue," *Journal of Forensic Sciences,* 20, no. 2 (1975), 219–230.

KIND, S. S., "The Acid Phosphatase Test," in *Methods of Forensic Science,* Vol. 3, ed. A. S. Curry. New York: Wiley-Interscience, 1964.

KIRK, PAUL L., *Crime Investigation,* lst ed. New York: Interscience Publishers, Inc., 1966.

——, *Crime Investigation,* 2nd ed. New York: John Wiley & Sons, Inc., 1974.

——, *Fire Investigation.* New York: John Wiley & Sons, Inc., 1969.

KIRK, PAUL L., and LOWELL W. BRADFORD, *The Crime Laboratory, Organization and Operation.* Springfield, Ill.: Charles C Thomas, 1965.

Kodak Data Book P-2. "Photography Through the Microscope," 1974.

Kodak Publication M-2, "Using Photography to Preserve Evidence," 1976.

Kodak Publication M-8, "Photographic Surveillance Techniques for Law Enforcement Agencies," 1973.

Kodak Publication M-67, "Fire and Arson Photography," 1977.

KRADZ, MICHAEL P., "The Psychological Stress Evaluator—A Study" (unpublished). (Available from Dektor CI/S, Inc., 5508 Port Royal Road, Springfield, Va. 22151.)

KRISHNAN, S. S., "Detection of Gunshot Residues on the Hands by Trace Element Analysis," *Journal of Forensic Sciences,* 22, no. 2 (1977), 304–323.

MACDONELL, HERBERT L., *Flight Characteristics and Stain Patterns of Human Blood.* Washington, D.C.: U.S. Government Printing Office, 1971.

MAES, D., and B. D. PATE, "The Spatial Distribution of Copper in Individual Human Hairs," *Journal of Forensic Sciences,* 21, no. 1 (January 1976), 127–149.

MANURA, JOHN L., and RICHARD SAFERSTEIN, "Examination of Automobile Paints by Laser Beam Emission Spectroscopy," *Journal of the Association of Official Analytical Chemists,* 56, no. 5 (1973), 1227–1233.

MASON, M. F., and K. M. DUBOWSKI, "Breath-Alcohol Analysis: Uses, Methods, and Some Forensic Problems—Review and Opinion," *Journal of Forensic Sciences,* 21, no. 1 (1976), 9–41.

MATHEWS, J. HOWARD, *Firearms Identification* (3 volumes). Springfield, Ill.: Charles C Thomas, 1973.

MAY, R. W., and J. PORTER, "An Evaluation of Common Methods of Paint Analysis," *Journal of the Forensic Science Society,* 15, no. 2 (1975), 137–146.

McCLOSKEY, K. L., G. C. MUSCILLO, and B. NOORDWIER, "Prostatic Acid Phosphatase Activity in the Postcoital Vagina," *Journal of Forensic Sciences,* 20, no. 4 (October 1975), 630–636.

McCRONE, W. C., "Characterization of Human Hair by Light Microscopy," *Microscope,* 25, no. 1 (1977), 15–30.

——, "Microscopical Characteristics of Glass Fragments, *Journal of the Association of Official Analytical Chemists,* 55, no. 4 (1972), 834–839.

——, "Collaborative Study of the Microscopical Characterization of Glass Fragments," *Journal of the Association of Official Analytical Chemists,* 56, no. 5 (1973), 1223–1226.

——, "Microscopical Characterization of Glass Fragments," *Journal of the Association of Official Analytical Chemists,* 57, no. 3 (1974), 668–670.

McCRONE, WALTER C., and JOHN G. DELLY, *The Particle Atlas,* 2nd ed. Ann Arbor, Mich.: Ann Arbor Science Publishers, Inc., 1973.

McJunkins, Steven P., and John I. Thornton, "Glass Fracture Analysis—a Review," *Forensic Science,* 2, no. 1 (1973), 1–27.

Meyer, Eugene, *Chemistry of Hazardous Materials.* Englewood Cliffs, N.J.: Prentice-Hall, Inc., 1977.

Midkiff, Charles R., and Willard D. Washington, "Gas Chromatographic Determination of Traces of Accelerants in Physical Evidence," *Journal of the Association of Official Analytical Chemists,* 55, no. 4 (1972), 840–845.

————, "Systematic Approach to the Detection of Explosive Residues, III. Commercial Dynamite," *Journal of the Association of Official Analytical Chemists,* 57, no. 5 (1974), 1092.

Moenssens, Andre A., *Fingerprints and the Law.* Radnor, Pa.: Chilton Book Company, 1969.

Montagna, William, and Richard A. Ellis, *The Biology of Hair Growth.* New York: Academic Press, Inc., 1958.

Murray, Raymond C., and John C. F. Tedrow, *Forensic Geology, Earth Sciences and Criminal Investigation.* New Brunswick, N.J.: Rutgers University Press, 1975.

Nash, Ernest W., "Voice Identification with the Aid of Spectrographic Analysis," *Journal of the Association of Official Analytical Chemists,* 56, no. 4 (1974), 944.

Nutt, Merle C., *Principles of Modern Metallurgy.* Columbus, Ohio: Charles E. Merrill Publishing Company, 1968.

O'Brien, Kevin P., and Robert C. Sullivan, *Criminalistics, Theory and Practice,* 2nd ed. Boston: Holbrook Press, Inc., 1976.

O'Hara, Charles E., and James W. Osterburg, *An Introduction to Criminalistics.* Bloomington: Indiana University Press, 1972.

Owen, G. W., and K. W. Smalldon, "Blood and Semen Stains on Outer Clothing and Shoes Not Related to Crime: Report of Survey Using Presumptive Tests," *Journal of Forensic Sciences,* 20, no. 2 (April 1975), 391–403.

Parker, R. G., "Analysis of Explosives and Explosive Residues. Part 3: Monomethylamine Nitrate," *Journal of Forensic Sciences,* 20, no. 2 (April 1975), 257.

Parker, R. G., J. M. McOwen, and J. A. Cherolis, "Analysis of Explosives and Explosive Residues. Part 2: Thin-Layer Chromatography," *Journal of Forensic Sciences,* 20, no. 2 (April 1975), 254.

Parker, R. G., M. O. Stephenson, J. M. McOwen, and J. A. Cherolis, "Analysis of Explosives and Explosive Residues. Part I: Chemical Tests," *Journal of Forensic Sciences,* 20, no. 1 (January 1975), 133.

Peterson, Jack E., *Industrial Health.* Englewood Cliffs, N.J.: Prentice-Hall, Inc., 1977.

Pollack, Herman, W., *Materials Science and Metallurgy,* 2nd ed. Reston, Va.: Reston Publishing Company, 1977.

Pounds, C. A., "The Recovery of Fibres from the Surface of Clothing for Forensic Examination," *Journal of the Forensic Science Society,* 15, no. 2 (1975), 127–132.

Pounds, C. A., and K. W. Smalldon, "The Transfer of Fibres Between Clothing and Materials During Simulated Contacts and Their Persistence During Wear. Part I—Fibre Transference. Part II—Fibre Persistence," *Journal of the Forensic Science Society,* 15, no. 1 (1975), 17–38.

"Quantitative Analysis of Textiles," Method D 629–72. American Society for Testing and Materials, 1916 Race Street, Philadelphia, Pa. 19103, 1972.

RASKIN, DAVID C., GORDON H. BARLAND, and JOHN A. PODLESNY, *Validity and Reliability of Detection and Deception.* Washington, D.C.: U.S. Government Printing Office, 1978.

REID, J. E., and F. E. INBAU, *Truth and Deception.* Baltimore: The Williams & Wilkins Company, 1966.

RHODES, E. F., and J. I. THORNTON, "The Interpretation of Impact Fractures in Glassy Polymers," *Journal of Forensic Sciences,* 20, no. 2 (1975), 274–282.

ROUEN, R. A., and V. C. REEVE, "A Comparison and Evaluation of Techniques for Identification of Synthetic Fibers," *Journal of Forensic Sciences,* 15, no. 3 (1970), 410–432.

RUDZITIS, E., and M. WAHLGREN, "Firearm Residue Detection by Instrumental Neutron Activation Analysis," *Journal of Forensic Sciences,* 20, no. 1 (1975), 119–124.

SAFERSTEIN, RICHARD, *Criminalistics: An Introduction to Forensic Science.* Englewood Cliffs, N.J.: Prentice-Hall, Inc., 1977.

SAHYUN, M. R. V., "Mechanisms in Photographic Chemistry," *Journal of Chemical Education,* 51, no. 2 (February 1974), 72–77.

SANSONE, SAM J., *Modern Photography for Police and Firemen.* Cincinnati: W. H. Anderson Company, 1971.

————, *Police Photography.* Cincinnati: Anderson Publishing Company, 1977.

SCHENK, GUSTAV, *The Book of Poisons.* London: Schenval Press, 1956.

Science of Fingerprints—Classification and Uses. Washington, D.C.: U.S. Government Printing Office, 1977.

SCHULTZ, DONALD O., *Crime Scene Investigation.* Englewood Cliffs, N.J.: Prentice-Hall, Inc., 1977.

SIEK, T. J., "Identification of Drugs and Other Toxic Compounds from Their Ultraviolet Spectra. Part I," *Journal of Forensic Sciences,* 19, no. 2 (1974), 193–214.

SIEK, T. J., and R. J. OSIEWICZ, "Identification of Drugs and Other Toxic Compounds from Their Ultraviolet Spectra. Part II," *Journal of Forensic Sciences,* 20, no. 1 (1975), 18–37.

SIEK, T. J., R. J. OSIEWICZ, and R. J. BATH, "Identification of Drugs and Other Toxic Compounds from Their Ultraviolet Spectra. Part III," *Journal of Forensic Sciences,* 21, no. 3 (1976), 525–551.

SILJANDER, RAYMOND P., *Applied Police and Fire Photography.* Springfield, Ill.: Charles C Thomas, 1976.

SIVARAM, S., "A Modified Azo-Dye Method for Identification of Seminal Stains," *Journal of Forensic Sciences,* 15, no. 1 (January 1970), 120–123.

SMITH, BURKE M., "The Polygraph," *Scientific American,* 216, no. 1 (January 1967), 25–31.

SMRKOVSKI, LONNIE L., "Collaborative Study of Speaker Identification by the Voiceprint Method," *Journal of the Association of Official Analytical Chemists,* 58, no. 3 (1975), 453.

STAHL, EGON, *Drug Analysis by Chromatography and Microscopy.* Ann Arbor, Mich.: Ann Arbor Science Publishers, 1973.

STEWART, W. D., "Pyrolysis-Gas Chromatographic Analysis of Automobile Paints," *Journal of Forensic Sciences,* 19, no. 1 (1974), 121–129.

Technical Manual of the American Association of Textile Chemists and Colorists, Vol. 50. American Association of Textile Chemists and Colorists, P.O. Box 12215, Research Triangle Park, N.C. 27709, 1974.

THORNTON, J. I., and A. D. MCLAREN, "Enzymatic Characterization of Soil Evidence," *Journal of Forensic Sciences,* 20, no. 4 (October 1975), 674–692.

TOSI, O., H. OYER, W. LASHBROOK, C. PEDREY, J. NICOL, and E. NASH, "Experiment in Voice Identification," *Journal of the Acoustical Society of America,* 51. no. 6 (part 2) (1972), 2030–2043.

"Trace Metal Detection Techniques in Law Enforcement," Pamphlet No. 71–1. National Institute of Law Enforcement and Criminal Justice, LEAA. Washington, D.C.: U.S. Government Printing Office, 1970.

TREPTOW, RICHARD S., "Determination of Alcohol in Breath for Law Enforcement," *Journal of Chemical Education,* 51, no. 10 (1974), 651.

———, *Handbook of Methods for the Restoration of Obliterated Serial Numbers,* National Aeronautics and Space Administration Contractor Report CR-135322. Washington, D.C.: NASA, 1978.

TURNER, W. W., consulting ed., *Criminalistics.* San Francisco: Aqueduct Books, 1965.

URBANSKI, TADEUSZ, *Chemistry and Technology of Explosives.* New York: Pergamon Press, Vol. 1, 1964; Vol. 2, 1965; Vol. 3, 1967.

U.S. Department of Justice, National Institute of Law Enforcement and Criminal Justice, *Speaker Identification Through Voice Prints: A Brief Review.* Washington, D.C.: U.S. Government Printing Office, 1973.

VAN NAME, F. W., JR., and DAVID FLORY, *Elementary Physics,* 2nd ed. Englewood Cliffs, N.J.: Prentice-Hall, Inc., 1974.

VASAN, VEL S., WILLIAM D. STEWART, JR., and J. BRUCE WAGNER, JR., "X-Ray Analysis of Forensic Samples Using a Scanning Electron Microscope," *Journal of the Association of Official Analytical Chemists,* 56, no. 5 (1973), 1206–1222.

VON BERGEN, WERNER, and WALTER KRAUSS, *Textile Fiber Atlas.* New York: Textile Book Publishers, 1949.

WALLS, H. J., *Forensic Science,* 2nd ed. New York: Praeger Publishers, Inc., 1974.

WASHINGTON, W. D., and C. R. MIDKIFF, "Systematic Approach to the Detection of Explosive Residues, I. Basic Techniques," *Journal of the Association of Official Analytical Chemists,* 55, no. 4 (1972), 811.

———, "Systematic Approach to the Detection of Explosive Residues, II. Trace Vapor Analysis," *Journal of the Association of Official Analytical Chemists,* 56, no. 5 (1973), 1239.

WESTON, PAUL B., and KENNETH M. WELLS, *Criminal Investigation, Basic Perspectives,* 2nd ed. Englewood Cliffs, N.J.: Prentice-Hall, Inc., 1974.

WHITE, HARVEY E., *Modern College Physics,* 6th ed. New York: Van Nostrand Reinhold Company, 1972.

WILLARD, HOBART H., LYNNE L. MERRITT, and JOHN A. DEAN, *Instrumental Methods of Analysis,* 5th ed. New York: Van Nostrand Reinhold Company, 1974.

WILLIAMS, RAY L., "Forensic Science—The Present," *Analytical Chemistry,* 45, no. 13 (1973), 1076–1089.

INDEX

Men and Women of Parapsychology

Men and Women
of Parapsychology:
Personal Reflections

Edited by
Rosemarie Pilkington
FOREWORD BY STANLEY KRIPPNER

McFarland & Company, Inc., Publishers
Jefferson, North Carolina, and London

Library of Congress Cataloguing-in-Publication Data

Men and women of parapsychology.

Bibliography: p. 161.
Includes index.
Contents: My life with the paranormal / Jule
Eisenbud—The world of psychic phenomena as I came
to know it / Montague Ullman—An autobiographic
fragment / Jan Ehrenwald—[etc.]
  1. Psychical research. I. Pilkington, Rosemarie.
BF1031.M537   1987   133.8   87-42517

ISBN 0-89950-260-1 (acid-free natural paper)

Printed in the United States of America.

McFarland   Box 611   Jefferson NC 28640

Contents

Preface

This book provides a personal look at some of the men and women who have devoted a large part of their lives to the investigation of psychic phenomena. It illustrates why and how these investigators have persisted in their attempts to understand these unusual yet universal occurrences, despite criticism — and at times slighting or censure — from adherents of the more traditional, materialistic paradigms of other scientific disciplines.

The idea for this anthology came to me during the 1983 Parapsychological Association (PA) Convention. That year we were mourning the loss of some of the pioneers and major contributors to the field, such as Laura Dale, Arthur Koestler, Gaither Pratt, and Louisa Rhine (whose husband, J.B. Rhine, had died three years before). Of this group I was personally acquainted only with Laura Dale and regretted never having met the others.

It has been my great pleasure and privilege to know many of the researchers and philosophers involved in psychical research. I have had the fortune of basking in their warmth and humor and have gained immeasurable insights from our informal social meetings and conversations. I felt it would be a pity if the younger generations missed out on what I had benefited by — knowing these fascinating people, sharing their personal experiences and witty anecdotes, and gaining new insights into their work, their thinking, and their fascination with the mind and its phenomena.

It occurred to me that a book such as this one, of personal reflections by the "elder statespersons" of the field, might be a means of sharing at least a little of their wisdom with those not fortunate enough to know them.

Ford Madox Ford said that the sole reason for writing one's memoirs was to paint a picture of one's time. I hoped that these essays would do that as well; to create a setting within which the drama, mystery, comedy, and intrigues of these researchers' stories would help us to understand their dedication to and fascination with parapsychology against the backdrop of the *Zeitgeist* of the last century.

I invited to participate only those researchers who had passed the age of 65 and who had devoted most of their careers to psychical research. Unfortunately not all those asked could spare the time from their busy schedules to contribute. I regret their omission.

I asked each contributor to address five topics:

(1) How they became intrigued with and involved in investigating the so-called paranormal.

(2) What they felt their most important contributions to the field have been.

(3) What they might have done differently, or what beliefs they had when they entered the field that were changed through their experiences.

(4) What unusual experiences they have had that exceeded even their "boggle threshold."

(5) What advice they would give to young people entering the field as to what areas are of utmost importance and as to pitfalls of which they should be aware.

As you will see they covered my questions, and more, with their usual four "E"'s: enthusiasm, eloquence, erudition, and esprit.

                                                                    R.P.

Foreword

by Stanley Krippner

Parapsychology is the scientific study of psi phenomena, those apparent anomalies of behavior and experience that exist apart from currently known explanatory mechanisms which account for organism-environment and organism-organism information and influence flow. When an event is classified as a psi phenomenon, it is claimed that all known channels for the apparent interaction have been eliminated. Therefore, it is clear that labeling an event as a psi phenomenon does not constitute an explanation of that event; it only indicates an event for which a scientific explanation needs to be sought. Phenomena occurring under these conditions are said to have taken place under "psi-task conditions."

Labels such as "extra-sensory perception" (ESP) and "psychokinesis" (PK) refer to the apparent direction of information or influence. The first, ESP, refers to situations in which, under psi-task conditions, an organism behaves as if it has information about the physical environment (as in "clairvoyance"), another organism's mental processes (as in "telepathy"), or a future event (as in "precognition"), while PK refers to situations in which, under psi-task conditions, an organism's physical environment changes in a way that appears to be related to the organism's mental or physiological processes.

A commitment to the study of psi phenomena does not require assuming the reality of "nonordinary" factors or processes. Many parapsychologists, myself included, dislike such terms as "ESP" because they do not constitute an explanation and carry implicit theoretical loadings which may not be justified. Regardless of what form the final explanations may take, however, the study of these phenomena is likely to expand scientific understanding of the processes often referred to as "consciousness" and "mind" as well as the nature of disciplined inquiry itself (Parapsychological Association, 1985).

It was this search for understanding, coupled with a commitment to rigorous standards of investigation, that resulted in the founding of the

1

Society for Psychical Research (in England, 1882), the American Society for Psychical Research (in 1885), and a number of similar organizations throughout the world. In 1957 the Parapsychological Association was founded, and became an affiliate member of the American Association for the Advancement of Science in 1969. By 1986 it consisted of approximately 300 members in some 30 different countries. The Parapsychological Association is a professional organization that has developed high membership standards, an ethics committee, and an information officer. Several affiliated, but independent, refereed journals serve as an outlet for some of the research articles of its members.

Critics of parapsychology often take the position that extrachance scores obtained by parapsychologists may be attributed to flawed experimental procedures or to the failure to report negative or nonsignificant findings. However, in 1975 the Parapsychological Association instituted a policy against the selected publication of only positive experiments. Defects in experimental procedures have been observed by parapsychologists themselves (e.g., Akers, 1984; Stanford & Palmer, 1972), and members of the association are devoted to improving the quality of their research. At the same time, Parapsychological Association members have often been in the forefront of exposing fraudulent practitioners who use the title "parapsychologist" without the knowledge of, or the commitment to, rigorous scientific standards.

Parapsychological Association conventions at Cambridge, England (in 1982), and Boston (in 1985) celebrated the centennials of the societies of psychical research that provided the original impetus to the study of psi phenomena. This splendid volume of personal essays, assiduously collected and skillfully edited by Rosemarie Pilkington, also provides a historical perspective.

Because parapsychology is a small field of endeavor, and because the parapsychological community is minuscule in comparison with other groups of scientists, each of the authors in this collection is known to me personally. Many of them have been close friends of mine for many years. Even so, I found myself making observations from their essays that I had not made over the decades I had known them. Indeed, there appeared to be a pattern to their entry into parapsychology, a field not exactly conducive to professional advancement, financial reward, or societal prestige. In the case of virtually every parapsychologist, there were factors that predisposed them to take an interest in the field, precipitating factors that led to a conscious decision to become deeply involved in psi research, and maintaining factors that provided the motivation and opportunity for them to continue this involvement. Without the presence of all three of these conditions, it is unlikely that these men and women would be represented in Pilkington's book. As Eileen Coly observes in her interview, parapsychology is the kind of subject in which people typically "would drop in and drop out."

Coly offers a splendid example of my proposed three factors. Her interest was predisposed because her mother was the celebrated medium Eileen Garrett; when the Parapsychology Foundation was founded, Coly was not directly involved but recalls following everything that took place. The patronizing attitude of some of her mother's admirers may have stifled any psychic gift Coly might have possessed, but it did not extinguish her interest in the topic, especially her admiration for parapsychological research.

The death of Garrett provided the precipitating factor for Coly's entry into the field. Even though Coly had not always been intimately associated with the Parapsychology Foundation, she knew the prominent people in the field and was determined to encourage the foundation's support of research. Her continued enthusiasm for the field serves as the maintaining factor; she sees the work as worthwhile and, in her interview, takes pride in the foundation's accomplishments during her years as president.

Sometimes the predisposing factors included environmental factors such as the country stories heard by Renée Haynes during her childhood and the folktales cited by Karlis Osis (even though his parents discounted them). Predisposing factors also included personality traits, e.g., the contrariness mentioned by Haynes, the curiosity cited by Joseph Rush, the fear and anxiety reported by George Zorab.

Precipitating factors were typically personal experiences, sometimes psi-related in nature. Zorab was terrified of death and even associated sleep with dying until, at the age of 12, he took part (despite parental protest) in a seance at which several deceased family members purportedly "announced themselves." Hans Bender, as a young man of 17, participated in a Ouija board session and was impressed by the messages although he doubted their "spirit" origin.

Jule Eisenbud was favorably disposed toward psi phenomena as a result of reading Freud's papers on the topic; his personal experiences as a psychoanalyst activated this interest. Jan Ehrenwald's observations during his apprenticeship years as a psychoanalyst propelled him into the field. Montague Ullman's remarkable group sessions with a purported entity took place when he was in college. Bernard Grad's reported early psi experiences date back to his childhood. Haynes recalled early psi experiences as well, including a "haunting" that she now suspects could have been more parsimoniously explained by the presence of underground water.

Karlis Osis reports a series of events that initiated him into the world of psi phenomena. One, during his adolescence, was an unusual experience with "living light" that corresponded with the death of his aunt. Another was a presumptively precognitive dream. Osis was also impressed with an early book by J. B. Rhine and had a blueprint company construct a deck of ESP cards for him; the significant results obtained by his fellow students "clinched" his interest.

The reading of psi-related material also appeared to serve as precipitating factors for Joseph Rush, Emilio Servadio, and Gertrude Schmeidler, the latter being intrigued by one of Rhine's books. Like the personal experiences noted, the reading of these books was accompanied by intense emotionality. It is quite likely that the strength of these inner feelings served to initiate behavior that eventually led the individual into the field.

Osis recalls designing an experiment with chickens, sending the results to Rhine, and being invited to Duke University to engage in a project involving animal psi. This could be seen as the final in a series of precipitating factors that led to what Osis considered the "Mecca" of parapsychology and, for him, what proved to be a long and productive career.

Employment opportunities certainly serve as maintaining factors. A number of individuals are predisposed toward psi research, have been moved by precipitating factors to enter the field, but have found no job openings. For Osis, groups such as the American Society for Psychical Research and individuals such as Chester F. Carlson provided the wherewithal for him to continue his research projects. Zorab was offered a series of organizational positions by Eileen Garrett while Bender and Schmeidler successfully introduced parapsychology into various academic settings.

For such psychoanalysts as Ehrenwald, Eisenbud, Servadio, and Ullman, parapsychological interest and identity were maintained by their psychotherapeutic practice. They felt that they observed psi at work both in their patients' lives and in their own interactions with their patients, as when a dream about the therapist's personal life would emerge during a psychoanalytic session. In the case of Eisenbud, there were "resistances" to "work through" before the commitment was made. In the case of Ullman, an opportunity to organize a sleep laboratory provided the chance to make an intensive study of anomalous dreams.

The success of their research projects served to maintain the interest of Grad and Schmeidler, among others. Rush's interest in the field was maintained not only by the "piling up of evidence" favorable to the psi hypothesis but by the congenial personal relationships he formed with fellow parapsychologists. Psi researchers have the opportunity to meet yearly at the annual conventions. In addition, each of the psychical research societies around the world holds regular meetings. The Parapsychology Foundation's annual conferences provide another opportunity for the sharing of data, experiences, and theoretical speculation.

It is likely that collegial reinforcement is a major factor in maintaining a parapsychologist's commitment to the field. Institutional attitudes have been hostile; Ehrenwald and Grad are two of many researchers who have faced extremely negative reactions from those around them. Many scientists (e.g., Radner & Radner, 1982) dismiss parapsychology as a pseudo-science while others (e.g., Zusne, 1985) suggest that its adherents often suffer from "irrationalism" and "magical thinking."

The readers of this book have the unique opportunity to make these judgments themselves. The essays and interviews are unusually candid, frank, and self-disclosing. My summary of predisposing, precipitating, and maintaining factors has only presented a few of the specific experiences, beliefs, and events that have led the men and women in this volume to participate in a scientific endeavor that would be of little interest to most of their colleagues. Only time will tell whether these parapsychologists and their colleagues are eccentric cranks who have misused and distorted their gifts of intelligence and creativity, or pioneers who have provided an opening of what Osis calls the "window to something more."

Jule Eisenbud

Jule Eisenbud was born in New York City, where he received his B.A. from Columbia College and his M.D. from the Columbia College of Physicians and Surgeons. He also earned the doctor of medical science degree from Columbia University. In 1938 he began private practice in psychiatry and psychoanalysis in New York and became an associate in psychiatry at the Columbia College of Physicians and Surgeons.

In New York Dr. Eisenbud joined with Jan Ehrenwald, Montague Ullman, and other physicians in forming the Medical Section of the American Society for Psychical Research.

In 1950 he moved his family to Denver, Colorado, where he continued his private practice and became associate clinical professor of psychiatry at the University of Colorado Health Sciences Center in Denver.

Dr. Eisenbud has written many fascinating and profound papers in psychiatry, psychoanalysis, anthropology, and parapsychology. He is respected and admired for his genius and keen wit and loved for his genuineness and warmth.

Dr. Eisenbud is a fellow of the American Psychiatric Association and a member of the American Psychoanalytic Association and the Parapsychological Association.

Jule Eisenbud

My Life with the Paranormal

I was early exposed to what would probably at the period have been
called mind-reading, except that in our household it was not called
anything. Following the mid-day meal on Sundays, my father would often
sit back and ask my mother, "What am I thinking?" The answers were usually, "You would like your slippers," or, "You're ready for your nap," or
something of the sort, and were invariably greeted with mock astonishment, as if the riddle of the Sphinx or something equally as recondite had
just been solved before our eyes. It seemed to me, however, that there were
times when my mother's answers were unexpectedly subtle and precisely
on the mark of some stray thought my father had just had, and at such times
my father's amazement knew no bounds.

Somehow I always took it for granted that wives and mothers did things
like this, and I was not overly surprised that my own wife, soon after our
marriage almost fifty years ago, began to do things like this regularly and
without my asking. I have long come to take it for granted, at any rate, that
my wife is a telepathist of no mean ability, since I early on gave up on the
the usual normal possibilities that could conceivably account for her now
routine feats in this area.

My first actual encounter with something that struck me as possibly
more than just home style mind-reading was at the age of 17. During an
overnight train ride from Cleveland, where I had been visiting relatives, I
dreamed that a younger cousin who had been ill for many months with
leukemia, had died. Upon my return (to New York), I was told that the child
had indeed died during the night. Whatever thoughts I might have had
about the strangeness of this coincidence were lost in the sadness of the
event; but it certainly didn't seem to presage for me what was later to
become a consuming interest.

The reason I say that this was my first *actual* encounter with the
possibly paranormal is because of a distinct memory of an earlier encounter
with at least the vague *idea* of something beyond the ordinary in the
psychic sphere. The memory, which seems always to have been with me
since the encounter in question, has certain of the characteristics of a

8

screen (at least partially false) memory in that it doesn't square with certain other facts of my life and in the fact that, despite its persistence, I have always been diffident about sharing it with anyone.

I recall, as if it were yesterday (one of the characteristics of a screen memory), standing on the sidewalk of my home in the Flatbush section of Brooklyn and engaging in conversation a somewhat older girl, who lived a block or two away, who had just come along on the way to her home. Aware that she had just begun college, I asked her what she had taken up. My memory goes that she said "psychic research," and that even though I didn't have the faintest idea what this was, a wild excitement passed through me. I have the impression that I have always had this perfectly clear memory— of the tall, lovely looking blond girl stopping to talk with me and telling me this—although I am fairly certain that I didn't know what psychic research was for many years, and never, at any rate, connected it with the dream of my young cousin's death.

About forty years afterward, however, I did connect it with a precognitive dream of one of my patients in which the name Phyllis—the name of the girl in my memory—figured crucially. I have reported this dream (in two stages,* as it were) along with material that figured significantly in its elucidation, without reference to its possible connection with my curiously persistent memory. Subsequently I have had a nagging sense of guilt about having omitted this detail, as if it might have contributed a significant dimension to the analysis of the dream (as well it might have). But such is the way of resistance (and of screen memories).

I don't recall having thought either of my excitement at my pretty neighbor's having mentioned the magical words "psychic research" or my subsequent dream about my young cousin's death at the time of my first official encounter with the subject of the paranormal in the literature. This was about 1935, during my medical internship, when I first came across Sigmund Freud's *New Introductory Lectures on Psycho-Analysis* (1933). This included a chapter on "Dreams and Occultism" in which the possibility of telepathy and its implications were treated quite favorably. I recall being singularly unimpressed with this chapter, although the rest of the volume fired my already considerable interest in the exciting domain of the unconscious. It was not until years later—not until, in fact, I had painfully worked through some of my resistances to the presumptively telepathic material I began to run up against in my own practice of psychoanalysis— that I was able to appreciate the penetrating insights into telepathy that Freud presented in his *New Introductory Lectures.*

My first glimpse of the dynamic side of psi came during my psychiatric residency in a dream I had of Freud's death. My grief was immense, but

*In Psi and Psychoanalysis (1970), and in Paranormal Foreknowledge (1983).

when I awoke I sensed that my grief was really for my father, who had died five years before, since the two had always been completely identified in my mind. That day I saw a newspaper announcement of the death of Alfred Adler, one of the chief thorns in Freud's side. I knew immediately what my ostensibly precognitive dream was all about. The dream came to be, I felt, because the prior knowledge of Adler's death, which I must have paranormally acquired, permitted me to experience tremendous relief at finding that it wasn't Freud after all who had died but one of his enemies, who had undoubtedly harbored death wishes against him. Through its latent equation of Freud and my father, moreover, the dream also provided a magical undoing of the latter's death, and its switch "fulfillment," thus, a denial of my own death wishes.

Whether or not anything like this was actually the case, nothing since has ever left me with a firmer sense of conviction as to the essential dynamics underlying psi-conditioned dreamwork.

My strong resistances against the paranormal were yet far from resolved, however. Not long afterward I encountered my first instance of an ostensibly precognitive dream in which the possibility of self-fulfillment seemed inescapable. The dream—my own—occurred just before Christmas of 1937, shortly after the birth of our first child. In the dream (which seems now perfectly transparent) some fluid was spilled and something was said about not crying over spilled milk. The following day, during a visit to my newly delivered wife and daughter in the hospital, I accidentally knocked over an open bottle of ink on the narrow table across my wife's bed. This was greeted by her saying, "Let's not cry over spilled ink" (a remark entirely typical of her elisions and her matter-of-fact attitude toward trivial disasters).

Since I was undergoing my personal analysis at the time (second hitch, after funds ran out on my first go-around several years earlier), this episode came up in my analytic hour but was passed over in stony silence by my analyst who, in strict conformity to the convention of the period, was not given to loquacity about anything. For some reason, nevertheless, I was gripped by the firm conviction that there must have been something "psychic" about the correspondence involved, despite its nonveridical aspect. At the same time, however, an indication of my still strong resistance against the paranormal could be seen in the fact that despite my revealing insight of some months earlier in connection with the Freud-Adler dream, I didn't myself subject this dream to the analytic process any more than did my uncomprehending analyst. I was not yet ready to confront my ambivalence to my chief rival now, my newborn daughter.

About eighteen months later came a real mind-blower. I dreamed of inspecting a sailboat and being told that there was a Packard engine in it. The following day, having bicycled some miles (with my infant daughter on board) and stopped for a rest at a boat dock, I saw a sleek sailboat tied up at a slip with someone working on it. Without any recollection of my dream whatsoever, I engaged the skipper in casual conversation and was told that the boat had a Packard engine in it. At the time I knew little about boats but had never heard of this particular tie-up (nor have I since).

On this occasion too I let the episode get away from me, as if it were something wholly apart from the real me, something I had just stumbled upon, like a particular view when coming out of the woods on a hike.

I must have mentioned this some days later at the luncheon table of the New York Psychiatric Institute, where I was then a resident, because it was there that a fellow resident told me about J. W. Dunne's *An Experiment with Time* (1927/1958) which I soon got hold of and read. I was impressed with Dunne's case material, but his theory was above my head (and still is).

It was shortly thereafter that I began my private practice of psychiatry and psychoanalysis where, almost from the beginning, my patients began to provide striking examples of dreams and associations to which the telepathy hypothesis was reasonably applicable. But it was at least a year before I finally overcame my resistance to doing anything but gawk at the strange occurrences. I had to almost literally take myself by the scruff of the neck and force myself to annotate what I was observing.

It was in this process, however, once I got going, that I began to glimpse the further correspondences that turned up in the latent content of dreams that appeared telepathic, and to discern myself as a shadowy figure behind what was going on. My excitement at the infinite subtlety of the unconscious processes involved—it was as if psychoanalysis, exciting and demanding enough as it was, had suddenly become multidimensional—opened up a vast subterranean landscape that I had never dreamed existed. Writing furiously every night till three or four a.m., following the associative threads that the burgeoning correspondences provided, I began to compile a growing corpus of case material that kept me—and, I must confess, my still far from wholly resolved resistances—constantly preoccupied.

At the beginning of 1942 I joined the Saturday afternoon sessions Gardner Murphy held for a few disciples—Laura Dale, Joseph Woodruff, Ernest Taves (who later left the fold) and Montague Ullman—and began to outline my observations on the psychodynamics behind telepathic experiences. I was delighted to discover that others—Hollós in Hungary, Servadio in Italy, Fodor in America—had made essentially similar observations, especially on the key role of the analyst and the transference situation in what was going on. Hollós, who reported that the frequency of telepathic episodes in his practice diminished considerably with his advancing years (an observation I can only confirm with my own advancing years), had unfortunately dropped out of sight by the time I caught up with his seminal 1933 paper. (I later heard that he was last reported seen standing naked on the bank of a river into which a multitude of Hungarians was being herded literally for liquidation by the Third Reich.) But I began corresponding with Servadio and meeting with Fodor, both of whom were happy to have confirmation of their independently arrived at discoveries.

Soon Jan Ehrenwald, Joost Meerloo, Bob Laidlaw and others joined our group, out of which the Medical Section of the American Society for Psychical Research was formed. Our monthly meetings provided a welcome forum in which we could present our case material and exchange views. It soon became apparent that these meetings somehow provided a catalyst for the occurrence of the very case material we were meeting to present. Something was in the air, all right, but the high point of these meetings was when Monte Ullman brought several friends of his adolescent years, now perfectly straight professionals and businessmen, to recount what went on during rainy days when they got tired of playing cards and had nothing else to do. They got into seances in which all sorts of marvelous paranormal occurrences took place, such as psychic photographs, and a card table rising almost up to the ceiling with several of them hanging on for dear life; but I will leave the rest for Monte to tell about.

Around this time I had my own first encounter with homegrown psychokinesis. A friend of mine, a young British composer, and I managed to get invited to a weekly table-turning session held by three elderly dowagers. In the substreet dining level of an East Side brownstone we all sat around a heavy card table which within minutes took on a personality of its own and soon began wild gyrations and movements back and forth across the length and width of the room, often backing one or another of us into a corner before dashing off to harass someone else. There was no doubt in my mind that the good dowagers started things off with almost deliberate muscular movements on their own part but, as far as I could see, once the table got fired up and began madly careening about, sometimes in response to a request for it to answer a question with some specified movement, there was no possibility at all that muscular aid on the part of any of the participants, who were doing their best just to hold a finger or two lightly on the table as it skidded across the bare floor, and scrambling furiously to keep up with it, could have been responsible for what took place.

The weekly meetings ended for the season after one session at the close of which the table, seemingly possessed by a stamping, whirling, rushing will of its own, led us out the door and up the steps and into the street and the startled gaze of a couple of dumbly uncomprehending passersby. I recall that we all, seemingly with one mind, abandoned the table frenziedly at this point and rushed back into the house and hopeful anonymity. I don't recall whether the now completely inert table was later retrieved or not, but I presume that it was. Curiously, my composer friend, his girl friend, and I were able to get very much the same results in later sessions held in the large living room of my own apartment, with my wife simply looking on but, for some reason, taking no part. We discontinued these sessions after only two or three go-arounds because it was always pretty much the same thing. (How blasé can one get?)

Meanwhile I got my first taste of what I was to encounter throughout my association with "the occult," as my psychoanalytic colleagues (following Freud at least this far) were wont to call psychic research. (The term "parapsychology" had not yet caught on as a widely used designation.) Most of the friends and colleagues to whom I let my growing interest be known managed somehow to separate their positive personal feelings about me from their negative feelings about the weird field I was getting into. But they preferred not to discuss the issues involved and would simply divert the conversation to other matters if I ever brought the subject up. It was not difficult for me to understand their attitude when I recalled that only a few years back I was as ignorant as they about parapsychology—and almost as resistant to it.

It was when I made so bold as to go public with my interest, however, that peer resistance became more manifest. In November, 1945, I presented my maiden paper in the field, "Telepathy and Problems of Psychoanalysis," to a meeting of the New York Psychoanalytic Society. (This was published a few months later in *The Psychoanalytic Quarterly* [1946].) Immediately a movement started to oust me from the Society. This, happily, was voted down but at the same time I was informed that I would not be allowed to become a training analyst, the goal to which every career-oriented psychoanalyst aspired. This I could completely sympathize with since if I were one of my colleagues I certainly wouldn't have wanted my sister or my child corrupted by the regressive magical thinking someone such as I was manifesting.

At this time, however, I felt that my colleagues would surely come closer to my point of view as they themselves began having experiences with patients similar to those I was having. I now believe differently. I have come to realize that few psychiatrists or analysts possess what I prefer to call (for lack of better words) psychically sensitive dispositions and do not, consequently, create—and thus have the occasion to observe—psi-conditioned experiences in their interactions with patients.

The most difficult situation to deal with was not, in any case, the outright snubbings that inevitably ensued—there were few of these—or the handful of cases that were steered away from my couch, but my virtually total inability to engage colleagues in discussion of the scientific problems that seemed to me very much at issue. My colleagues on the whole remained friendly but most made it plain that they had no interest in extrasensory perception (a term the entire subject soon came to be tagged with) or in discussing it. And while some bent over backwards in their show of open-mindedness (in 1948 William Menninger, then president of the American Psychoanalytic Association, appointed me chairman of the important Committee on the Evaluation of Psychoanalytic Results, a job I carried out until my move to Denver a couple of years later), most exhibited a somewhat awkward indifference to my peculiar aberration, much as they might have if I had developed epilepsy and was given to occasional seizures in public.

The general attitude could just about be summed up in the remark made to me by a friendly colleague when dismissing the subject of telepathy I had tried to bring into our conversation: "Look, you're a nice guy but you're crazy." I found this somewhat maddening, but at the same time not entirely unwelcome, as it forced me more and more into a position of semi-isolation which I knew would be necessary in order to pursue my investigation of the thoroughly frustrating but challenging field that had increasingly come to dominate my thinking.

In Denver, to which I moved my family in 1950, the same situation came to prevail. Not a soul showed the slightest interest in my work in parapsychology, despite another couple of papers on telepathy that had appeared, as well as a vigorous interchange in *The Psychiatric Quarterly* (1947), in which I was joined by Nandor Fodor and Geraldine Pederson-Krag, with the highly critical psychologist Albert Ellis, who had not yet become the sex guru of the soon to burst upon the world hippie generation.

Nobody snubbed me, however, in Denver and I was able to write my own ticket at the medical school, whose faculty I was invited to join on my own terms. (For several years I conducted a well-attended weekly case seminar at the school.) But there was a sort of unspoken gentleman's agreement that I was not to mention parapsychology. When I tried to make the most of a lengthy ride with a colleague on a ski lift to break the embargo, my captive audience of one just emphatically refused to discuss the subject, period, after which he retreated into an uncomfortable silence until we parted at the top. It was probably only coincidental but all the same noteworthy to me that soon afterward a reigning faculty member in the department of psychiatry, who had always been most cordial to me in social situations, nevertheless walked right by me and the empty seat beside me on a plane filling up for the trip from New York to Denver with a cool nod and an embarrassed look. Under no circumstances was he going to let himself be greybearded by some glittering-eyed ancient mariner from whom no escape would be possible. On the whole, however, cordial relations continued at the medical school; but it was 33 years before I was formally invited to talk there on my researches in parapsychology, and even this invitation, which was never followed by another, came about through a pure fluke.

The research that more than any other has affected my views about just about everything under the sun was my work with Ted Serios. This began in April, 1964, and has been dealt with in my book *The World of Ted Serios* (1967) and in a series of papers and chapters in books afterward. When I wrote on the opening page of the book that I little suspected "that I was slated to spend the next couple of years — and perhaps the rest of my life — trying to make sense" of the data provided by the unpredictable psychic genius who had come my way, this was little more than a figure of speech, a fancy. I really didn't imagine that I actually would be actively involved with Ted and his marvelous thoughtographs (I still don't have a better term for his psychic pictures) for the rest of my life. I now know differently. There is no escape for me either from the data and their far reaching implications or from the furor these have evoked on all sides.

My efforts currently are bent toward keeping Ted, who no longer is capable of producing thoughtographs, out of reach of those whose last resort would be to frame him in some compromising situation, as if this would have the slightest significance in regard to what he was able to accomplish at his peak. What he did, which has been well attested and documented, has never been duplicated by normal means. No one, in fact, has even tried to do so under careful observation (to say nothing of distance controls and target shots), even though the ante for a successful replication, as judged by an independent and even skeptical jury drawn from university faculties in the "hard" sciences, has been upped to $10,000.

At the same time, my continuing investigation of Ted's thoughtographs (I am still discovering facets in them that escaped me initially) has made it difficult for me to sustain a high degree of interest in other investigative work in the field, much of which I find trivial (in comparison, say, with the work of some of the great mediums) and misguided (in its efforts to win scientific approval, for example) and all of which I find subject to the inescapable ambiguity of the experimenter effect.

My work with thoughtography, about whose more than hundred year history and variegated data I have learned much more than I knew at the time *The World of Ted Serios* was written, has also brought to me more clearly the depth and tenacity of the resistance against psi on the part of science and scientists. It is more than ever clear to me that while scientific method may continue to be of use to parapsychology, science as a body of implicit and explicit assumptions about the nature of man and his world will most definitely not.

Real progress in parapsychology will be made, I feel, only when its practitioners untether themselves completely from science and scientific institutions in order to work their own garden in their own way. Instead of wasting their time trying to woo scientists, parapsychologists should beat the bushes for the assuredly numerous genuine psychics, both physical and cognitive, who tend to keep to themselves and go their own way not only because they have long been insulted and humiliated by scientifically indoctrinated psychic investigators, but because they seem to sense better than their investigators the inherent antagonism and irreconcilability of science and the psychic side of man.

It would, of course, be highly desirable to find a middle road which could provide the best of each, or to develop a brand of investigator who could lash himself to the mast of the really psychic while listening to the siren song of science; but this, I fear, is a pipe dream, not in the nature of things. The Gresham's law of parapsychology seems to be that bad psychic research will drive out good psychic research (under the pretense of being good science).

I do not, finally, regard parapsychology as the answer to the manifold problems that afflict our planet at this time. Were it to happen that a dozen superstars of the stature of D. D. Home or Mirabelli could today, through the use of the most up-to-date electronic and photographic technology, reach all the scientists in the world and compel their assent to the existence of the paranormal, there would be little difference in the extent of man's irrationality and his destructiveness. No moral revolution would ensue, simply a race (as can already be glimpsed) to use a new tool for getting rich, or new weaponry for the same age-old purposes.

I have attempted to outline some of the problems involved in this seemingly insoluble Catch-22 situation in my *Paranormal Foreknowledge* (1982) but I doubt that either knowledge or foreknowledge singularly will release us from the mark of Cain so patently on our brows and in our hearts. Perhaps something in nature itself may save us (or some of us) when all else fails, but this something may remain eternally inscrutable.

Bibliography for Jule Eisenbud

(1946). Telepathy and problems of psychoanalysis. *Psychoanalytic Quarterly*, **15**, 32–87. Reprinted in G. Devereux (ed.), *Psychoanalysis and the Occult* (New York: International Universities Press, 1953).

(1947). A telepathic *rêve à deux*. *Psychoanalytic Quarterly*, **16**, 1, 39–60.

(1947). A reply to Ellis. *Psychiatric Quarterly*, **21**, 26–40. Reprinted as The Eisenbud findings, in G. Devereux (ed.), *Psychoanalysis and the Occult* (New York: International Universities Press, 1953).

(1948). The analysis of a presumptively telepathic dream. *Psychiatric Quarterly*, **22**, 1, 103–135.

(1963). Psi and the nature of things. *International Journal of Parapsychology*, **5**, 245–248.*

(1963). Two approaches to spontaneous case material. *Journal of the American Society for Psychical Research*, **57**, 3, 118–135.

(1965). A test to determine the relationship of subliminal visual stimuli and ESP in a laboratory setting. *International Journal of Parapsychology*, **7**, 2, 161–181.

(1966). The problem of resistance to psi. *Proceedings of the Parapsychological Association*, **3**, 63–79.*

(1966–1967). Why psi? *Psychoanalytic Review*, **53**, 4, 647–653.*

(1967). *The World of Ted Serios*. New York: William Morrow.

(1967). The cruel, cruel world of Ted Serios. *Popular Photography*, **61**, 5, 31–32, 134.

(1969). Chronologically extraordinary psi correspondences in the psychoanalytic setting. *Psychoanalytic Review*, **56**, 1, 9–27.

(1970). *Psi and Psychoanalysis*. New York: Grune & Stratton.

(1972). Some notes on the psychology of the paranormal. *Journal of the American Society for Psychical Research*, **66**, 1, 27–41.*

(1972). The dilemma of the survival data. Comments on Professor Flew's "Is there a case for disembodied survival." *Journal of the American Society for Psychical Research*, **66**, 2, 145–153.

(1973). A transatlantic experiment in precognition with Gerard Croiset. *Journal of the American Society for Psychical Research*, **67**, 1, 1–25.

(1974). Psychic photography and thoughtography. In E. Mitchell & J. White (eds.), *Psychic Exploration: A Challenge for Science* (New York: Putnam).*

(1975). Correspondence [Psi and the test-tube production of amino acids]. *Psychoenergetic Systems*, **1**, 98.

(1975). The mind-matter interface. *Journal of the American Society for Psychical Research*, **69**, 2, 115–126.

(1975). Research in precognition. Presented at Symposium on Parapsychology, American Psychiatric Association meeting, Dallas, May 2, 1972. In S. Dean (ed.), *Psychiatry and Mysticism* (Chicago: Nelson-Hall).

(1976). Evolution and psi. *Journal of the American Society for Psychical Research*, **70**, 1, 35–53.

(1977). Paranormal photography. In B. Wolman (ed.), *Handbook of Parapsychology* (New York: Van Nostrand Reinhold).

(1979). How to make things null and void: An essay-review of Brian Inglis' *Natural and Supernatural*. *Journal of Parapsychology*, **43**, 2, 140–152.

(1980). Synchronicity, psychodynamics and psi. In W. G. Roll (ed.), *Research in Parapsychology 1979* (Metuchen, N.J.: Scarecrow Press).

(1982). The flight that failed. *Christian Parapsychologist*, **4**, 7, 211–217.

(1982). *Paranormal Foreknowledge: Problems and Perplexities.* New York: Human Sciences Press.

(1982). Some investigations of claims of PK effects on metal and film by Masuaki Kiyota: The Denver experiments. *Journal of the American Society for Psychical Research,* **76**, 3, 218–233.

(1982). Different adaptive roles of psi in primitive and nonprimitive societies. *Psychoanalytic Review,* **69**, 3, 367–377.*

(1982). Thoughtography. In I. Grattan-Guinness (ed.), *Psychical Research: A Guide to Its History, Principles and Practices; In Celebration of 100 Years of the Society for Psychical Research* (Wellingborough, Northamptonshire: Aquarian Press).

(1983). *Parapsychology and the Unconscious.* Berkeley, Calif.: North Atlantic Books.

(1984). Paranormal film forms and paleolithic rock engravings. *Archaeus,* **2**, Fall, 9–18.

(1985). Visions old and new: An addendum to "Paranormal film forms and rock engravings." *Archaeus,* **3**, Summer, 9–14.

(1967). With associates. Some unusual data from a session with Ted Serios. *Journal of the American Society for Psychical Research,* **61**, 3, 241–253.

(1968). With Merrill, F. B., Eller, J. J., & Liddon, S. C. Two experiments with Ted Serios. *Journal of the American Society for Psychical Research,* **62**, 3, 309–320.

(1981). With Pratt, J. G., & Stevenson, I. Distortions in the photographs of Ted Serios. *Journal of the American Society for Psychical Research,* **75**, 2, 143–153.

*Reprinted in Parapsychology and the Unconscious (*Berkeley, Calif.: North Atlantic Books, 1983).

Montague Ullman

Montague Ullman, M.D., noted psychiatrist, psychoanalyst, researcher, educator, and author, has been involved in psychic investigation for most of his life. He founded the Dream Laboratory at the Maimonides Medical Center in Brooklyn, New York, and has been devoted since then to dream research and the development of group approaches to dream work here and abroad. At present he is clinical professor of psychiatry, Albert Einstein College of Medicine.

Dr. Ullman is a past president of the Parapsychological Association and of the American Society for Psychical Research. He is a life fellow of the American Psychiatric Association and a charter fellow of the American Academy of Psychoanalysis.

Montague Ullman

The World of Psychic Phenomena
As I Came to Know It

People come to a deeply felt conviction of the importance of psychical research from very different starting points. It can be, as in the case of Gardner Murphy, that during the formative years one encounters inspiring figures who have had the courage to acknowledge publicly the reality of these phenomena. In Murphy's day it was William James and Walter Franklin Prince. His reading of Myers and others further fired his imagination and led him to his lifelong devotion to the subject.

I came to it through a different route, namely, by a direct encounter with almost all the classical phenomena of the seance as described in the literature of the late 19th and early 20th century. It came about in this way:

Sometime in the fall of 1932 a college friend, Leonard Lauer, told me of a series of strange events that had happened to a friend of his named Gilbert Roller. Leonard and I were about 16 at the time and just beginning our sophomore year. We were both taking pre-med courses and considered ourselves budding scientists. What Leonard confided to me that day was the beginning of my involvement with psychical research.

He told me that Gilbert at about the age of 11 or 12 was the focus around which poltergeist phenomena occurred. Small objects were thrown about the room, watch crystals were broken, writing done with a lipstick appeared on mirrors, etc. Leonard learned of these events several months prior to his talk with me. It led him to look up the literature on psychical research and then, along with Gilbert and two others, to an attempt to replicate some of the phenomena he was reading about. They met weekly and had a series of seances in which they sat around a table in the dark. According to Leonard there was a response in the form of tilting and some movement of the table. Leonard told me about this in the hope of starting the sittings again. I was interested and agreed to join in what turned out to be a regular Saturday night commitment to psychic phenomena. Leonard suggested some books on the subject to which I promptly reacted. My readings included Hudson's *The Law of Psychic Phenomena*, Myers, Lodge,

20

Lombroso, and Schrenck-Notzing. I must have been a "sheep" from the beginning because the reading enthralled me, particularly since the more I read the more impressed I was with how many great figures of the last century had ventured into the field.

So much for my beginning exposure to the literature. More exciting was what happened over almost a two-year period (1932–1933) as a consequence of a dedicated devotion to Saturday night seances. From time to time the circle increased as we drew friends into it. There were six "regulars."

On several occasions I have tried to write an account of what happened. I never succeeded to my complete satisfaction. To understand its meaning and impact one must take into account the unique circumstances under which it evolved. A group of teenagers, some in college, some not, began to meet regularly every Saturday night. They persisted at sitting, not for a month or two but for nearly two years with very few missed sessions. We stayed with it despite an unpredictable mix of successes and failures, spurred on by the slow evolution of ever more startling and exciting manifestations. Starting with uncertain knocks and tilting of a small end table around which we sat in the dark holding hands, we ended up after several months with a bridge table levitating and dancing around the room. The next step was the identification of the force involved as intelligent through coded rappings on the table. Spurred on by our continued reading we went on to produce photographs on unexposed plates which, in turn, led to successful experiments in thought photography.

By this time we were informed that we had made contact with a doctor named Bindelof, who had died in 1919 but who was still interested in healing people. We arranged a very striking communication system with him. We would sit around the end table, clasping each other's hands at the edge of the table, while a pencil and paper rested on a lower shelf of the table. Soon after the lights were out we would hear the pencil writing very fast for a few seconds and then it would be put down with a loud noise. This was a signal for us to turn on the lights and read the message. The messages were answers to our many naive questions about the nature of the phenomena, about life after death, and what we had to do to facilitate the force involved. Stopping at nothing we went on to try for materialization. The nearest we got was when all of us were touched consecutively and then at the same time by what felt like human fingers. Our efforts at healing through Dr. Bindelof's ministrations were not remarkable except for a few strange and noteworthy effects, as when a very nearsighted person felt that fingers were manipulating his eyeballs from within the orbit.

The question then as now is how genuine were all these effects. Those of us who formed the core group were deeply convinced that the effects were genuine although the interpretation of the effects differed (basically, whether or not we were into the issue of survival). We could point to certain objective evidence for the reality of the phenomena we witnessed, aside from the trust we had in each other and the powerful subjective impact of the experience. Despite our youth and inexperience we did take reasonable precautions at each phase of the process and were quite careful in our handling of the photographic plates. Because of certain effects that were generated at the last minute prior to getting an image on an unexposed plate I was certain that the plate could not have been doctored beforehand. During Dr. Bindelof's helping phase we would put questions to him and get the answers back as written messages. Since we were at an age where many vexing problems beset us we asked for and received permission to *think* rather than ask questions out loud. I can testify in my own case to the specificity and relevance of the answer.

In a cursory way this touches on the highlights of the experience. Thirty-three years after the experience I managed to bring the core group together to spend an entire day reminiscing about the experience, our varying interpretations of it and the impact it had had on our lives. That is a story in inself. In my case it resulted in a lifelong fascination with psychic phenomena and a deep conviction about their significance. None of us were tricksters or magicians and I doubt whether any of us were clever enough to have carried off a hoax over nearly a two-year period, displaying such a remarkable variety of phenomena, without evoking suspicion.

As adults we were divided into two camps: those who took the phenomena at face value, who believed that Dr. Bindelof was who he professed to be, a dead physician still interested in helping humanity, and who believed explicitly in the account he gave of life after death; and those who held to a minority view, offered by Leonard and myself, a view that looked upon the phenomena as paranormal but shaped by the unique circle we formed and its endurance in so dedicated a way over so long a time. We felt that the emotional turmoil each of us was in during this time of adolescence had played a significant role. More specifically, growing out of unmet needs in our homes was our individual and collective need for a benevolent, all-powerful father figure. Dr. Bindelof was seen as our creation, someone responsive to our needs, helping us when we were in trouble and bringing us to incredible levels of excitement through the enormous power at his disposal.

In our opinion (Leonard's and mine) there was no objective evidence that we were dealing with a real person who had died. Nevertheless, like the others, we were and remain convinced that the psychic phenomena that did occur, including the mysterious writings, were genuine. The core group continued to hold reunions yearly for four years, checking and cross-checking our memories, evaluating the residually available data, and writing up our individual accounts.

Having a career both in parapsychology and in psychiatry, I know how easy it is to be fooled, how easily subjective factors and belief systems can influence perception, but my conviction about the reality of the experience is unshaken. It rests on what happened as a group experience at that time, what happened to me personally, the artifacts that have endured, and my now fifty-year knowledge of the key participants. Over the years I have witnessed (or learned about) on a smaller scale many effects that, in some measure, were congruent with what we produced in the early thirties, e.g., the thought photography reported by Eisenbud, the table-moving experiments of Batcheldor, and the manifold effects of Kulagina, which included psychokinesis as well as effects on photographic plates and organ systems.

In the years that followed the Bindelof experience I made two abortive attempts to reproduce the kinds of physical effects I had known earlier. The first was in 1944 at which time I was stationed in an army hospital outside of Paris. I managed to impress three of my fellow medical officers with the story of my earlier experiences. On three or four occasions we spent the evening intermittently sitting around a table in the dark with hand contact. Nothing happened.

In 1945, while on terminal leave from the army, one of the first things I did on getting back to New York was to visit the American Society for Psychical Research (A.S.P.R.) which, at that time, was located on 34th Street. It was there that I first met Gardner Murphy. Within ten minutes of our meeting, responding to his openness and interest, the whole story of the Bindelof experience came pouring out. A year later I located two of the main participants, Gilbert and Leonard. This led to a series of evening sittings with Gardner which took place at my office. Again nothing happened.

Whatever happened in the thirties happened in relation to a powerfully charged emotional atmosphere. We were inspired, almost messianic in our zeal, to bring Dr. Bindelof's message to the world. Different as we were from each other we were all going through inner turmoil of the quality and intensity that only adolescents know. We were not the most stable group of adolescents, if that term has any meaning for that age group.

The distillate of that experience has stayed with me throughout the years. It biased me toward a concern with the emotional field involved in the pursuit of psi, to the importance of an open attitude, to the responsiveness of psi effects, to the existence of genuine human needs and, finally, to the importance of dedicating oneself to the pursuit of the phenomenon over time. Gross psi effects require a long incubation period. This developmental aspect is difficult to bring into the laboratory. An optimal emotional environment is also difficult to bring into the laboratory. I would characterize that environment as one of need, tension, heightened interest, belief, expectation, and commonality of goal.

The closest I have come to replicating this kind of atmosphere with some measure of success was in the recent studies in dream sharing conducted at the A.S.P.R. from 1978 to 1984. Here, again, a developmental effect was observed but in no way comparable to the Bindelof effects. Limited as it was to the realm of effects noted in dreams it was nevertheless clearly apparent and convincing to those of us who participated.

In some ways my own parapsychological journey paralleled the domiciliary moves of the A.S.P.R. At the time of the Bindelof experience Leonard and I visited its headquarters at the old Hyslop house on 23rd Street. There we sought to bring our "discoveries" to a broader scientific public. We unburdened ourselves to Frederick Bligh Bond, then the secretary of the Society. He listened politely but didn't seem interested or encouraging.

My next encounter with the A.S.P.R. was in 1946 when the Society was located on East 34th Street. Here I was introduced to Gardner Murphy, Laura Dale, George Hyslop, Lydia Allison and the other dedicated souls who were working against great odds to keep up scientific interest in psychical phenomena.

The Society then moved to Fifth Avenue and 69th Street. Psychical research became parapsychological research. Under Gardner's direction Laura and others were busy following through on some of the lines of research being opened up under J. B. Rhine's direction at Duke University. This didn't displace an open interest in the way the laity experienced the paranormal and attention was paid to collecting spontaneous case material. During this time Gardner and I, along with students he brought from city college, met weekly at my office for experiments using hypnosis for the ESP transfer of free drawings.

It was also at this time that Laura and I initiated our pilot exploration of dream telepathy. This took place before our knowledge of the REM state and its relationship to dreaming. Using a machine called the dormiphone we could be awakened at any preset time during the night to try to capture a dream. Laura and I alternated as subject and agent. We met every Friday to compare our dreams and diary report. The results were encouraging and led ultimately to the experimental investigation of dream telepathy at Maimonides Hospital. This coincided with the move of the A.S.P.R. to its current location. Earlier, Karlis Osis and Douglas Dean had joined with me and, through the good graces of Eileen Garrett and the Parapsychology Foundation, we carried out very promising pilot studies. When Stan Krippner joined the laboratory at Maimonides we were able finally to transform these initial efforts into a series of systematic and carefully designed experiments.

Sometime in 1948 Gardner and I discussed the creation of a Medical Section of the A.S.P.R. This was at a time when there was a spirit of interest among psychoanalysts and psychiatrists in the clinical significance of the telepathic dream: Jan Ehrenwald (1948) had published his first book on the subject, Jule Eisenbud had published an article in the *Psychoanalytic Quarterly* (1946), and Bob Laidlaw had been working with Eileen Garrett. For my part, though I had not published anything on the subject, I had been meeting with Gardner for weekly lunches and shared my excitement at being at the receiving end of telepathic dreams from patients.

The Medical Section meetings which took place about once a month beginning in March of 1948 and extending over the next five years were a memorable experience in many ways. Aside from consolidating lasting friendships (we were few against the many) sharing clinical psi experiences resulted in much cross fertilization of ideas and, I believe, acted as a kind of intangible influence that stimulated the rate of occurrence of psi effects between our patients and ourselves.

There is a special excitement generated when psi effects crop up in an analytic session. There is a heightened intensity of interest, a sense of discovery, an awareness of moving into uncharted areas. At the same time there is that strange feeling of someone able to see through you, seeing all the things you so carefully contrive to hide from view.

At our meetings we were mutually supportive rather than critical. There was a common base of acceptance based on commonly agreed upon objective criteria and the deeply felt uncanny quality of the experience. Ehrenwald had an unending series of striking examples. Eisenbud was bold enough and skillful enough to introduce the psi hypothesis to the patient in working through the dynamics of the experience. I was even brash enough to come out of the psychic closet and share my earlier college experience with the group. One of the unforeseen and far-flung consequences of that sharing was Eisenbud's ready response to the thought photography of Ted Serios.

Teaching and working with dreams for over four decades I have been impressed with how much more we don't know than how much we do. Despite all the doors that have been opened since the resurgence of interest in dreams in the fifties, that interest has been pursued in a narrow way. We know more about the neurophysiology of sleep and dreams, more about some of the psychological features of the REM state, and have a new perspective on the phylogenesis of dreaming (Ullman, 1950–1980). But two significant areas remain largely unexplored: the psi dimension and the sociological dimension. It would not surprise me if we were some day to note a relationship between these two that may have a bearing on their relative neglect. As an example, consider this: The most striking psychological product of the industrial revolution is the view of the individual as an historic discrete entity, an atomic structure bouncing off other atomic structures. This is far from the optimal arrangement for the emergence of the human potential for moral, emotional, and creative fulfill-ment. The price we pay for this is a gradual increase in social entropy in parallel with the possibility of nuclear annihilation.

There are sufficient clues about the way psi operates to speculate about the relationship of this state of affairs to psi. In the therapeutic rela-tionship we witness one form of psi, its availability as an emergency measure in the interest of holding on to some vital form of contact. At the other extreme, laboratory studies have showed the healthier personality structure as more apt to come up with psi effects. Isolated reports on primitive tribes go further and suggest the appearance of psi abilities as a more or less natural communicative medium. For the most part these are also forms of social organization where there is much more social cohesiveness than the kind of individualism and discreteness that characterizes modern society. Psi then seems to be an emergency mechanism for the individual adrift in a technological society and an available and useful form of adaptation in societies that have escaped that evolutionary route. Perhaps psi in its full and palpable form will never appear in industrialized societies as they are now organized except in tiny quantitative doses, sporadic anecdotal accounts, and occasional freakish outbursts.

The future of psychic research is an intriguing question. In the wake of two recent centennial celebrations (the S.P.R. and the A.S.P.R.), this question looms larger than ever. We seem to have moved through two rather distinct epochs. The earlier one was characterized by direct observation of gross effect, best exemplified in the pursuit of the great mediums, and the more recent one where, with the benefit of advanced scientific techniques, paranormal effects could be teased out on a quantitative basis.

Each approach was a product of its age. Each reflected certain pre-vailing trends, the reaction to a materialist view of man in the case of the first and the belief in the power of the scientific approach as it has been derived from the biological and physical sciences.

I think the time is approaching when we will have to reorient ourselves to a third phase. Without a broader conceptual frame of reference I don't think that staying with approaches developed in the second phase will significantly alter the picture. Progress may continue in the same desultory way but I don't think the field will emerge successfully from its closeted existence into full public and scientific view as a central issue for our time.

I can offer only a rather speculative vision of what that third phase might look like.

Just as the first phase was shaped as a reaction to a particular view of man so, too, was the second phase. This time, however, the situation was a bit more complex, and contradictory trends emerged that have persisted throughout the second phase. The same antimaterialist and ill-concealed dualistic bias shaped the founding of the new science of parapsychology. There was, however, the realization that in order for further progress to be made there had to be interest and acceptance by orthodox science. The scientific method had to be applied with a rigor and fastidiousness that surpassed ordinary standards. A measure of repeatability did result—by no means a minor accomplishment. At the same time progress was frustratingly slow and in in no way brought us any closer to understanding the essential nature of the phenomena under investigation.

If the third phase is to introduce a fundamental difference it would seem to me that the central issue would revolve about a question that exists independent of psi, namely, the adequacy of the scientific method as it has evolved, to address issues that have the kind of complex interactive and social components that characterize human affairs. In these matters we have to note the extent to which our scientific pursuit of psi has followed rather than challenged the Leitmotif of individualism that colors both art and science in the twentieth century. This individualistic orientation in its culmination in a present epoch characterized by fragmentation of the human species in every way has brought us to the point of facing an uncertain survival for the entire species.

David Bohm, a distinguished theoretical physicist, taking note of this state of affairs, feels that even our approach to physical phenomena is basically wrong and should be reversed. Instead of emphasis on the discreteness of manifest entities in the physical world the emphasis should be placed on the interconnectedness of all matter and its rootedness in a common ground of being, which he refers to as the implicate order.

In retrospect the second phase, despite its many constructive features, had a kind of will-o'-the-wisp quality to it. It was like chasing a phantom with a slide rule. Sometimes we got close enough to take a few measurements but never did we get near enough to penetrate to the heart of the mystery.

My projection for the third phase would be to start with the most pressing need facing humanity today. How do we close ranks and re-experience ourselves as members of a single species? How do we overcome the fragmentation and begin to foster compassion and communion, neither of which can flourish in the pursuit of a specious individualism?

What has all this got to do with psi? Psi effects seem to occur (as I interpret my own experience) either when external factors impede significant contact or when internal factors result in the impedance. I believe this to be the essential nature of the psi capacity despite the fact that at times trivial items may be the ones being picked up.

What are the systems in which psi emerges as an integral part, and can they lend themselves to careful study? There have been three basic approaches to psi and I think all of them suggest a systemic effect: the laboratory approach, the clinical approach, and the anecdotal approach.

In the case of the laboratory approach we decide on the limits of the system we wish to study only to find ourselves enmeshed in a supraordinate system which, by adding its own influence, contaminates the original system. The experimenter effect would be an example. In the case of the clinical approach all that has been written about it points to an interactive effect whereby psi capacities are mobilized as a kind of covert contact between two or more individuals. In the case of the anecdotal material it is as if, under the pressure of the emotional stress of a given situation, the covert contact becomes overt regardless of whether it is accepted as such or not.

If reports of psi communication among aborigines are correct it might prove a fertile natural system to explore. My own experience, notably that of my youth and, more recently, in group dream work, has convinced me that psi can evolve in natural systems when there is an interest in psi and a persistence in its pursuit. Essential to such an endeavor would be the humility and sensitivity to follow where psi effects lead us instead of what I sometimes think is a certain degree of scientific arrogance in thinking we can trap psi by one of our ingenious experimental designs.

My work with dream telepathy is a good example. The most exciting and stimulating time was during the free-wheeling pilot phase. As we then shifted to designs to prove rather than to investigate dream telepathy the results, while they came through statistically, were divorced from an understanding of the human context from which they arose. Finally, when the big experimental push was made to prove dream telepathy under the impetus of a National Institute of Mental Health grant the result was a dismal failure. All this cannot be accounted for by the looseness of the controls initially and the subsequent tightening of them per se, but rather that as the goal became proof rather than understanding something was lost that otherwise would have given personal meaning to each discrete psi event that cropped up.

When it comes to human affairs the search for knowledge must include an aesthetic component, i.e., it has to be concerned with questions of fit, order, and the role of intuition. It no longer is possible to package truth in the form of cold impersonal facts. In the way people deal with each other truth registers as a felt response aside from the question of whether it is attended to or not, admitted, or denied. In gathering facts about the physical world this aspect of the truth is often set aside as irrelevant. In the truly innovative scientific projections, however, they often start with an intuitive flash that is aesthetically illuminating. In my opinion the third phase will be more productive if it can find a way to align itself with this aesthetic component without sacrificing the vigor of scientific exploration.

What are some of the implications of this point of view for the third phase?

1. We have to define any experiment in psi as embedded in a series of systems—ordinate and supraordinate system relationships. This means attending to the question of which system is implicated in the psi event, the system we are attempting to manipulate or the larger supraordinate system of which the system is a part.

2. If the supraordinate system is implicated, the effect has to be seen as a system effect rather than, as heretofore considered, the "experimenter effect." This is so because the experimenter is part of the system supraordinate to the designated experimental system one where his motivation, needs, and ways of interacting with others are all brought into play.

3. The recent theoretical contributions of David Bohm have highlighted these system relations which arise from and lead to the emphasis on the interconnectedness of all things.

The importance of Bohm's thinking lies in the radical shift in emphasis from our way of taking for granted the discreteness of things to realigning our sights so that more attention is paid to field phenomena that betray this essential interconnectedness. Certainly in the pursuit of psi effects much is lost if field effects aren't taken into account and it may even be that we have made a difficult situation even more difficult by this neglect. Gardner Murphy touched on this in his approach to the survival problem as did William Roll in his analysis of poltergeist phenomena.

Since most experimental efforts involve interacting human beings and each carries along its own supraordinate system the field approach can become quite complicated and removed from the ideal goal of controlling definable variables. As I have suggested, one way of approaching this problem is to devote some effort to cultivating psi in as naturalistic a setting as possible and, if successful, then to begin to explore and identify the field effects at the various levels of organization at which they occur: physical, biological, psychological, small group, large group, and so on. To add to the power of the endeavor we would include a temporal field by planning studies that develop over time. The complexity of the field may very well require an interdisciplinary approach. Such an approach has been conspicuously lacking in parapsychological research. Whatever other disciplines have been involved have either made contributions shaped by their own field of interest or have simply caried over and applied techniques originating in parapsychological laboratories to their own specialty.

Drawing on my own experience I feel there is much to be gained from a slow, free-wheeling developmental approach over an extended period of time. Two experiences almost forty years apart have convinced me of this. The first goes back to 1948 when, under Gardner Murphy's guidance I started, at first quite informally, a series of meetings with Lois Murphy in which she was the percipient and I the agent, using free drawings. We met weekly at my office for over a year before it was terminated by the Murphys' move to Topeka. During this time I had the feeling that I was working with someone who was slowly beginning to get in touch with her psi capacity and learning how to move into that state of mind that led to some degree of conviction around the target. She would let herself go into what she described as a free-wheeling stage which, in effect, was letting her thoughts and feelings go off in any direction at all. This was then followed by what she referred to as being "in gear," during which a number of images would come to mind that, varied as they might be, left her feeling that they were clustering around the target. There were many failures but some of the successes were spectacular.

The second example occurred more recently. In the course of several years of dream sharing in a small group that met weekly, one of the participants, Barbara Shelp, did develop psi ability in a rather striking way. This happened to someone who had no prior firsthand experience with psi. These effects appeared in her dreams and were manifested in distinctly different ways; in relation to other members of the group this reflected something of the specifics of her differing relationship with each. She also began to be aware of the increasing role that psi was playing in her personal life outside the group. While each of us experienced something from time to time that we would informally accept as psi it became obvious that something rather special was happening with Barbara. There was something analogous in what we were doing with dreams to what the Toronto group did in conjuring up Philip and to Batcheldor's approach to table movement. It provided the combination of spontaneity, informality, deep interest, a cohesive focus, and a temporal dimension. All of this would make for useful ingredients in the approach to the third phase. In a sense the third phase would be a replay of the first phase but at a higher level utilizing more sophisticated psychological, group, and technological techniques.

In sum I have had four close encounters with psi: first at a personal level in the early Bindelof experiences, and occasionally thereafter (a few sporadic dreams that struck me as either telepathic or precognitive); secondly, in the course of my psychoanalytic practice; thirdly, in the course of the experimental work at Maimonides; and, most recently, in the informal dream-sharing sessions conducted over the past several years at the A.S.P.R. The earliest were by far the most powerful and most lasting. They remain deeply embedded in my psyche, a continuing source of wonderment and mystery and unanswered questions pertaining not to their actuality as paranormal experiences but to their nature. I remain, a half century later, just as unresolved as I was then as to any particular explanatory point of view.

The psychoanalytic experiences reawakened that sense of excitement and challenge. They convinced me that we do possess an ability, perhaps developed unevenly in the population, of tapping into our psi abilities in the interest of working our interpersonal tensions.

My feelings are mixed about the outcome of the experimental dream studies. On the one hand I think we were able to induce telepathic and precognitive dreaming under well-controlled laboratory conditions. On the other hand the price we paid for orienting our work toward quantitative results led away from rather than toward any deeper understanding of the phenomena we were dealing with. The free-wheeling pilot studies carried out in the fifties under the auspices of the Parapsychological Foundation were truly exciting, raising as they did the possibility of an experimental approach. Being an active participant, inspired enough to stay up all night to monitor the dreams of the sleeping subject and witnessing the dramatic correspondences between the drawings and pictures we used as targets and the subject's dreams, generated a sense of involvement, immediacy, and spontaneity that was impossible to replicate when following a preordered experimental protocol. The results far exceeded my expectations. They certainly influenced my decision to give up practice and move into a situation where further research would be possible.

Once we began to formalize the approach, and introduced all the constraints necessary for a tight methodology, we did succeed in getting statistically significant results but, to put it simply, the fun was gone. It became another well-controlled parapsychological experiment designed to add further laboratory proof of the reality of psi. I was involved in proving rather than investigating the paranormal dream. The responsibility for running a department of psychiatry and a developing community mental health center diverted my energies and distanced me from the actual experimental work. Interested as I was, I no longer felt as personally involved as I had been during the pilot phase of the work.

My most recent pursuit of the paranormal dream began in the late seventies and came about in conjunction with my growing interest in group dream work. I again went back to an informal exploratory approach using a small group process in which dream sharing and experiential dream work took place. This opened up the possibility of seeking out psi correspondences through the sharing of both daytime and nocturnal experiences. Based on the encouraging results we obtained I feel that studies such as this pursued over a period of time can add a significant longitudinal developmental dimension as well as adding to our awareness of some of the psychological factors involved. It represents an attempt at cultivating psi in a natural and evolving interpersonal field.

On rereading what I have written I realize how one-sided this account has been. Biased by my own experiences I became an explorer, from within outward. Since I started with a deep conviction and an intuitive sense of the circumstances I consider favorable toward psi, I gravitated toward what might be more or less congruent with that approach, bypassing on the way other experimental approaches and theoretical possibilities. These I have left for others.

Bibliography for Montague Ullman

(1949). On the nature of psi processes. *Journal of Parapsychology*, **13**, 1.

(1950). On the occurrence of telepathic dreams. *Journal of the American Society for Psychical Research*, **53**, 2.

(1955). The dream, schizophrenia and psi phenomena. *Proceedings of the First International Conference of Parapsychological Studies, Utrecht, the Netherlands, July–August, 1953*. Massachusetts: Colonial Press.

(1966). An experimental study of the telepathic dream. *Corrective Psychiatry and Journal of Social Therapy*, **12**, 2.

(1966). An experimental approach to dreams and telepathy: Methodology and preliminary findings. *Archives of General Psychiatry*, **12**, June.

(1966). A nocturnal approach to psi. In W. Roll (ed.), *Proceedings of the Parapsychological Association*, **3** (Durham, N.C.: Parapsychological Association).

(1967). Rapid eye movement monitoring techniques in current research. *Transactions of the New York Academy of Sciences*, **30**, 2, 265–270.

(1970). Telepathy and dreams: A controlled experiment with electroencephalogram-oculogram monitoring. *Journal of Nervous and Mental Disease*, **151**, 6.

(1971). Fragments of a parapsychological journey. *Newsletter of the Academy of Psychoanalysis*, **15**, 3.

(1973). A theory of vigilance and dreaming. In V. Zigmund (ed.), *The Oculomotor System and Brain Functions* (London: Butterworth's).

(1980). Psi communication through dream sharing. In B. Shapin & L. Coly (eds.), *Communication and Parapsychology* (New York: Parapsychological Foundation).

(1966). With Krippner, S., & Feldstein, S. Experimentally induced telepathic dreams: Two studies using EEG–REM monitoring techniques. *International Journal of Parapsychology*, **8**, 4.

(1968). With Cavanna, R. Dreams and psi: The experimental decision. In *Proceedings of an International Conference on Hypnosis, Drugs, Dreams, and Psi, June, 1967* (New York: Garrett Press).

(1970). With Krippner, S. E.S.P. in the night. *Psychology Today*, **4**, 1, 46.

(1970). With Krippner, S. *Dream Studies and Telepathy* (New York: Parapsychology Foundation).

(1971). With Krippner, S., & Honorton, C. Electrophysiological studies of ESP in dreams. An investigation into the nature of psi-processing in dreams. In W. G. Roll, R. L. Morris & J. D. Morris (eds.), *Proceedings of the Parapsychological Association, 6,* 1969 (Durham, N.C.: The Association).

(1973). With Krippner, S., & Vaughan, A. *Dream Telepathy.* New York: Macmillan.

(1977). With Wolman, B. (ed.), Dale, L., & Schmeidler, G. (assoc. eds.). *Handbook of Parapsychology.* New York: Van Nostrand Reinhold.

(1979). With Tolaas, J. Extrasensory communication and dreams. In B. Wolman (ed.), *Handbook of Dreams* (New York: Van Nostrand Reinhold).

(1985). With Zimmerman, N. *Working with Dreams.* Los Angeles: J. P. Tarcher (orig. pub., 1979).

(1986). With Wolman, B. (ed.). *State of Consciousness.* New York: Van Nostrand Reinhold.

Jan Ehrenwald

Jan Ehrenwald, M.D., psychiatrist, philosopher, theorist, playwright, poet, and lecturer, has published nine books and hundreds of articles in journals, handbooks, and anthologies. He is currently (as of mid-1987) at work on a new book tentatively entitled *Three Models of Minds, Neuroscience, Psychoanalysis, and Psychical Research: A Quest for Integration.*

Dr. Ehrenwald, who was born on March 13, 1900, earned his M.D. at the University of Prague and received his neuropsychiatric and psychoanalytic training at the universities of Prague and Vienna. After emigrating to England he settled in New York where he maintained a private practice and served as a consulting psychiatrist at Roosevelt Hospital until his retirement. Dr. Ehrenwald is a diplomate of the American Board of Psychiatry and Neurology, life fellow of the American Association of Social Psychiatry, fellow of the New York Academy of Medicine, past president of the Schilder Society of Psychotherapy and Psychopathology, and former trustee of the American Society for Psychical Research.

His theories and insights into mental processes, especially as regards psychic functioning, are highly respected by parapsychologists and his playful puns and ready wit are a constant source of delight to his audiences. Among Dr. Ehrenwald's contributions to the field are his theories regarding "doctrinal compliance" and what he has labeled "need-determined" and "flaw-determined" psychic manifestations. More recently he has been concerned with the distinctions between right- and left-hemisphere processes and their relationship to psi.

Though "retired" he is presently lecturing at the Institute of New Dimensions in Lake Worth, Florida, during the winter and at the Westchester Institute for Training in Psychotherapy in Mt. Kisco, New York, during the summer and fall.

His contribution here includes letters written to him by G. B. Shaw and Alfred Einstein which, Dr. Ehrenwald remarks, serve as "raisins in the cake."

35

Jan Ehrenwald

An Autobiographic Fragment

How and when and why did I first get interested in psychical research? Maybe I am merely covering up a hidden mystical bent when I say that my curiosity was first aroused in the late 1920s during my apprenticeship in neuropsychiatry at the University Hospital in Vienna. It was a curiosity which, on the face of it, was worlds apart from the lure of the occult.

At that time, I was engaged in the study of such diverse neurological disturbances as aphasia, alexia, and acalculia, that is, impairment of language, reading, and the ability to calculate, when I came across the case of Ilga K., a nine-year-old mentally defective girl, published by Ferdinand von Neureiter, a professor of forensic medicine. Ilga was unable to read more than a few disjointed letters: She was a case of alexia or dyslexia in the clinical sense. But when her mother, separated from her in another room, was reading a given text "under her breath," the child would chime in and vocalize the passage read by her mother in a flat tone of voice and in a totally uncomprehending manner.

Although critical objections were raised to a telepathic interpretation of her performance, it suggested to me that Ilga's mother, a tense and emotional woman, had tried to compensate for her offspring's inability in precisely that area of functioning in which her debility happened to be the most glaring: Mrs. K. tried to function vicariously on her daughter's behalf, to make up for her "minus function" by mobilizing a substitute "plus function" in the child's mental organization. I hinted that even if she was doing so by means of involuntary subliminal whispering, this merely illustrated the intensity of her motivations. It may have weakened the case for the telepathy hypothesis, but it offered a clue for a testable hypothesis of its mode of operation.

The fact is that I soon turned my attention to my psychiatric patients in search of further clues in the same direction. Paranoid schizophrenics were known to be shut-in, withdrawn types of personality trying to insulate and numb themselves against hurts, real or imaginary, emanating from their friends and relations. At the same time they are vulnerable and indeed hypersensitive to the slightest cue of hostility in their social

36

environment. In short, I asked myself whether their delusions of persecution did not contain a grain of truth after all. Were they in effect "reading" (or misreading) the thoughts of their purported detractors and persecutors?

My emigration to England in 1939 put a temporary halt to this exploration, but on my arrival in London I hastened to put my half-baked new theory of the part played by telepathy in schizophrenia into a paper and dispatched the manuscript to Professor Freud who had already established residence in England. To my dismay, the manuscript was soon returned to me with the sad news of Freud's death. My secret hopes for a nod of approval or even a word of encouragement from a fellow exile and the highest authority in the field of psychiatry, who also had a tangential interest in the occult, were dashed.

It was in the midst of this personal predicament and of the ominous developments in the war effort and of the London Blitz to which my family and I were exposed, that I obtained employment as assistant medical officer in a mental hospital in London. Apparently I had taken some of my turmoil and anxieties along on my first round in the hospital. As it happened, adding insult to injury, a disturbed woman patient in a back ward greeted me with a hefty slap in the face! Had she become aware of my insecurity and vulnerability in a telepathic way?

The fact is that it was in the early months at Springfield Mental Hospital that I made my first observation of apparent telepathy in schizophrenic patients, suggesting once more a pattern of minus function and its pathological compensation.*

Another incident occurred during one of the dark days when the tide of war seemed to have turned against the allies, when the London Blitz had become a daily or nightly routine, when my own state of health was going through a crisis, and when despite a show of a stiff upper lip, suicide had been on my mind. That morning, as I passed one of my disturbed schizophrenics, a woman in her late forties, on my round, she seemed to be coming out of her shell. She looked straight at me and said in a flat, affectless tone of voice, "Don't do it, sir, . . . don't commit suicide." Both of us, the patient and myself, received a puzzled look from the hospital attendant who accompanied me. We proceeded in silence to the next patient. For obvious reasons I did not make a note of the incident in the hospital chart and I did not make a point of asking the attendant for its

---

These observations are recorded in my book Telepathy and Medical Psychology *(1948), and later revised and elaborated on in my article "The Telepathy Hypothesis and Schizophrenia" (1966). Both publications featured my own feelings of guilt, anxiety, and related preoccupations, which were apparently picked up and expressed by my hospital patients.*

confirmation. But it was the macabre response of a disturbed schizophrenic which served as one of the most persuasive observations upon which my subsequent work on the telepathic aspects of schizophrenia and other publications were based.

When I sought to obtain the official permission needed for publishing my material I met a stone wall. Touching upon such an unorthodox topic as telepathy and related phenomena in a British hospital was strictly *verboten*. I refused to budge and had to resign as a result of my refusal.

It was also about that time that I decided to seek succor from another outside authority: I sent the introductory chapter of my book, *Telepathy and Medical Psychology* (1948), to George Bernard Shaw with a request for advice, particularly about publication of the manuscript.

A week or so later, the following letter, apparently typed by G. B. S. himself, was delivered to my house:

24th October, 1941

Dear Dr. Ehrenwald,

I know of no way in which I can be of any service to you in the matter of your book. I am not a publisher; and it is waste of time to send MSS to anyone but a publisher. When publishers come to me they come for my own books, and to get nothing from me but a recommendation of someone else's books would infuriate them.

I have read the chapter you sent me. Nothing would induce me to read the rest because, being a very old man, and a contemporary of Fraser, I am completely tired of travellers' tales which are heaped up with the entirely unscientific object of smashing the Bible and getting rid of Jehovah. For me that sort of thing is out of date and unreadable. Your object is to establish a science of telepathy; but you have tried to do so by the Fraserian method, which has really nothing to do with it. The day before yesterday I suddenly asked my secretary, *a propos des bottes*, what had become of Maurice Baring and whether he was alive or dead. Nothing had occurred to remind me of him for years. Yesterday I received a letter from him. Apparently he, by writing a letter to me, reminded me of him before the letter arrived. This occurs so often that it may be worth enquiring whether there is not more in it than coincidence, though the number of coincidences must be enormous and the cases few.

Another experience of mine is more interesting. I spoke at a meeting in King's College in London. I was in perfect health and at the top of my form. I sat down amid hearty applause, very well satisfied with myself. Presently the meeting ended and I rose to go. To my amazement and consternation I found that something had happened to my spine — something blasting and blighting. I managed to conceal my condition and get home, but with great difficulty; and I remained in this state for a month, at the end of which, at the same hour, the blight ceased as suddenly as it had begun and left me again in perfect health.

There was only one way of accounting for this. I learnt that a lady who very strongly disapproved of me and who was intensely angered by certain

personal references in my speech, had been sitting behind me on the platform. My spine was within point blank range of her face, which expressed
concentrated hatred. Her curse damaged me as the curse of the Bishop of
Rheims damaged the jackdaw who stole his ring. And possibly my recovery
may have been due to the prayers of some of my friends. Anyhow it was a
clear case of a telepathic curse.

I tell you all this because for me such cases are alive and interesting; but
attempts to correlate them with Fraserian legends are intolerable. I can read
Malinowski because he describes contemporary facts which sometimes suggest that Polynesians have more *savoir faire* than we have, and never bores
me by hanging his facts on to worn-out fables.

That is why, I repeat, nothing can induce me to read any more of your
book. And it does not matter a scrap, as my reading would not get you a step
farther. I can only advise you to forget Fraser and write the book over again
in the form of clinical lectures.

Faithfully
(signed: G. Bernard Shaw)

I have not been able to find a copy of my answer to Shaw's letter and
I know of no reason to bemoan its loss. Yet there is one passage which
deserves being brought back from oblivion because it had in turn elicited
a reply from G. B. S. My letter acknowledged with due respect his advice
and concluded with what I thought to be a perfectly legitimate inquiry a
to whether or not there had been a *draft* in the lecture hall at Kings College
where Shaw had suddenly been stricken with an attack of lumbago. A draft,
I ventured to say, may have been a more plausible explanation of his affliction than black magic wrought by the lady with the evil eye. By return mail
the postman brought a postcard containing the following blast of four irate
Shavian monosyllables:

There was no draft.

Another attempt at obtaining the nod from a higher authority resulted
in a brief correspondence with Albert Einstein that remained unpublished
until 1978, when it was discovered among Einstein's letters by his executors.
This is the text in my own translation:

EINSTEIN LETTER, MAY 1946

Sehr geehrter Dr. Ehrenwald:

. . . A few years ago I read the book by Dr. Rhine. I could find no explanation whatsoever to account for the data reported by him. But what alienated
[befremdet] me is that in statistical experiments the subject's spatial distance
proved wholly irrelevant to the success of the procedure. This strongly indicates to me that a hitherto undetected systematic source of error may have
been at play.

I wrote the introductory notes for Upton Sinclair's book owing to [our]
personal friendship in such a way that it did not express my lack of conviction
without compelling me to sacrifice my honesty in doing so. I must openly
confess to you my skepticism due not so much to a closer acquaintance with

the relevant empirical observations and experiences but to my lifelong activity in the field of physics. I must also confess that I have not had any experiences in my own life that would point to interpersonal relationships that were not occasioned by sensory cues [durch die Sinne veranlasst]. When I add that the public tends to attribute more weight to my utterances than would be justified in view of my ignorance in so many things, I feel all the more dutybound to exercise utmost caution and reserve in these areas. . . .

Mit ausgezeichneter Hochachtung
Albert Einstein

A second Einstein letter reached me some two months later:

EINSTEIN LETTER OF JULY 1946

Sehr geehrter Herr Ehrenwald:

I read your book [*Telepathy and Medical Psychology*] with great interest. It is certainly a good presentation of the problem, and I do not doubt that it will find a broad circle of readers. I can judge as a layman only, and cannot state that I arrived at an affirmative or negative conclusion. In any case, it appears to me that from the physicist's point of view, we have no right to rule out a priori the possibility of telepathy. For that the foundations of our science are too uncertain and incomplete.

My impressions regarding the card experiments which are amenable to numerical treatment is as follows: On the one hand I have no objection to the reliability of the method. Yet I find suspicious that "clairvoyance" [tests] yield the same probabilities as "telepathy," and that the subject's distance from the target cards, i.e., from the agent, should have no influence upon results. This is improbable to the highest degree and consequently the result is suspicious.

Yet very interesting, and actually of greater significance to me, are the tests with the nine-year-old girl, Ilga K. . . . Also the experiments with drawings [Upton Sinclair, 1930/1962] seem to me to be of greater weight than the large-scale statistical experiments in which the discovery of a minute systematic error may upset everything.

Your finding that the productions of patients in the psychoanalytic situation are dependent on the respective analyst's "school" [of thought] appears to be important to me. This part of your book alone is deserving of special attention. I cannot leave unmentioned that in some of the experiences mentioned by you a strong suspicion may be raised by the reader that unconscious sensory influences instead of telepathy may have been involved.

In any case, your book was very stimulating to me and has somewhat "softened up" my attitude which from the onset was distinctly negative towards the whole problem. One should not go through this world with blinders. . . .

You may show this letter "privatim" to other people. . . .

Mit vorzüglicher Hochachtung
Albert Einstein

I did not, in Einstein's lifetime, have the courage to engage in a debate with one of the greatest minds of our age. However, some 32 years later I felt ready to do so, addressing my letter to "The Late Professor Albert Einstein, Elysian Fields, please forward."

In my letter, published in the May 1978 issue of the *Journal of Parapsychology*, I sought to salvage the credibility of psi phenomena by reference to cases of well-established spontaneous evidence versus the erratic, unpredictable experimental evidence of the card-calling or dice-throwing type, with its precarious similarity to random, essentially meaningless quantum mechanical events. I respectfully hinted that it was this frustrating characteristic of the Duke type of incidents which was responsible for their blanket rejection by Professor Einstein.

At the same time, I suggested that the very affinity of psi and quantum physical events was an argument for the reality of psi phenomena. My argument culminated in proposing a basic principle of *indeterminacy in the behavioral sciences*, e.g., in terms of what I called doctrinal compliance by the subject with the observer's (or therapist's) pet scientific doctrines or emotionally charged expectations. I closed my letter by paraphrasing a statement by Sir Arthur Eddington: "Before you can accept parapsychological observations, they have to be confirmed by theory."

In my books and in numerous journal articles I tried to spell out these ideas in what I now perceive to be an uphill track towards growing insight. But let me state once more that all these faltering attempts at coming to grips with psi had been predicated on my earlier neuropsychiatric and psychoanalytic training that had brought my interest in the *modus operandi* of the right hemisphere into sharper focus in the first place. As early as the 1920s I published several cases of left-sided hemiplegia who showed a peculiar reaction to their affliction: They were wholly unaware of the defect, even denied its existence. At the same time, the affected left side had become ego-alien, strange, and repulsive to them. Significantly this is a response totally absent in right-sided stroke victims.

Today most neuroscientists concur that the brain's hemispheres allow an individual to operate in two different cognitive styles. The left is more active during the use of propositional language and analytic reasoning and when the individual focuses on factual detail; the right is more active in many types of music processing and during mental activity that is holistic, intuitive, creative, largely preverbal, given to metaphorical thinking, to poetic diction, and to flights of fancy. I described their respective psychological corollaries in terms of a dominant left hemispheric *Ego One*, versus a nondominant, vastly underrated right hemispheric *Ego Two*, with the left hemisphere (Ego One) responsible for "repressing" the supposedly intellectually inferior productions of the right brain—including psi.

The fact is that—my present focus on psychical research notwithstanding—I never considered myself a dyed-in-the-wool parapsychologist.

My interest in psi phenomena has formed only one of several strands which went into the making of my personal equation. Indeed, on looking back from a vantage point close to the end of the century at whose beginning I was born, I am intrigued by the crazy quilt of influences and ideas that were crowding in on me. There was, first, the earliest strand of a humanistic Hungarian upbringing in my native Pozsony, Pressburg, or Bratislava as it was later known. There was the Viennese strand from my mother's side. There was an intellectual father, turned businessman and Hungarian patriot of "German tongue" as he put it. There was the venerable tradition of the German University of Prague where I studied art history and philosophy under Christian von Ehrenfels before going into medicine. There were my postgraduate years in Vienna where I followed my teacher, Otto Poetzl, on his appointment as chairman to the University Clinic for Psychiatry and Neurology. It was this intellectual climate in which I had my training in Freudian analysis, Adlerian Individual psychology, and in Paul Schilder's existentially tinged neuropsychiatry.

Thus psychical research was just one of the strands that went into the making of the finished (or unfinished?) product. Maybe it was the very multiplicity of cultural influences, cognitive styles, "languages of discourse," frames of reference (Euclidian and non-Euclidian, Newtonian and Einsteinian), together with the freedom to effect what I described as "freewheeling existential shifts" from one frame of reference, or hemisphere, to another, that had helped me to absorb psychoanalysis, neuroscience, a bit of physics, and psychical research into one multifarious mix and to try to bring them together in an integrated whole.

It would be presumptuous to think of psychical research as the capstone in such an overarching scheme. But leaving psi altogether out of the equation would be wholly indefensible. Filling in all the remaining gaps and arriving at a unified theory of human behavior are still a distant goal. Nevertheless, I feel that my groping attempts in that direction—the journey, even short of the arrival—have been highly rewarding. It is even possible that the wholly unplanned and unintended liberation of my right hemispheric potential (or creativity?) from the rigorous demands of the left hemisphere has been one of the unexpected spin-offs of these labors. This "liberation" may have been further aided by my semiretirement from private practice in 1979, which seems to have gone hand in hand with a resurgence of right-hemispheric creativity, documented by a number of journal articles, lectures, and symposia since that time.

My book *The ESP Experience* (1978) goes back to the preretirement period. It was followed by *Anatomy of Genius: Split Brains and Global Minds* in 1984. At the same time, I tried my hand at the libretto of a comic opera, *The Secret Life of Pablo Picasso;* a play entitled *The Loves and Letters of Dr. Freudjung;* another play entitled *Honeymoon in Meyerling;* and a morality play entitled *Mengele and the Trial of God*, all as yet unpublished and unperformed.

This belated, essentially right-hemispheric output may well have been facilitated by my relative good health, financial security, and, last but not least, the singular good fortune of having shared more than fifty years of my life with a congenial mate. Of course, I cannot tell whether and how far such a consummation can be credited to the cultivation of both my right- and left-hemispheric potentials over the years. Still, my advice, if such is asked for, to a new generation of parapsychologists would be to do the same: to live up to the demands of their left cerebral hemisphere but also to preserve the spontaneity and integrity of their innate right-hemispheric endowments. This may conceivably diminish their chances of having their findings published in a refereed scientific periodical, but it is likely to increase the probability of encountering genuine psi phenomena on their way. It goes without saying, however, that such a prescription is by no means linked with a guarantee of a prolonged life expectancy—nor with my wife, Anny's, making herself available as an extramarital fountain of youth.

Bibliography for Jan Ehrenwald

(1948). *Telepathy and Medical Psychology*. New York: W. W. Norton.

(1950). Presumptively telepathic incidents during analysis. *Psychiatric Quarterly*, **24**, 726–743.

(1954). *New Dimensions of Deep Analysis*. New York: Grune and Stratton. (2nd ed., New York: Arno Press, 1975.)

(1954). Telepathy and the child-parent relationship. *Journal of the American Society for Psychical Research*, **48**, 2.

(1960). Schizophrenia, neurotic compliance, and the psi hypothesis. *Psychoanalytic Review*, **47**, 43–54.

(1963). *Neurosis in the Family: A Study of Psychiatric Epidemiology*. New York: Harper and Row.

(1966). *Psychotherapy: Myth and Method, an Integrative Approach*. New York: Grune and Stratton.

(1966). The telepathy hypothesis and schizophrenia. *Journal of the American Academy of Psychoanalysis*, **2**, 159–169.

(1967). Precognition, prophecy, and self-fulfillment in Greco-Roman, Hebrew and Aztec antiquity. *International Journal of Parapsychology*, **9**.

(1968). Human personality and the nature of psi phenomena. *Journal of the American Society for Psychical Research*, **62**, 4.

(1971). Mother-child symbiosis: Cradle of ESP. *Psychoanalytic Review*, **58**, 3.

(1971). Psi phenomena and the existential shift. *Journal of the American Society for Psychical Research, 65*, 2.

(1978). *The ESP Experience: A Psychiatric Validation.* New York: Basic Books.

(1978). Einstein skeptical of ESP? Postscript to a correspondence. *Journal of Parapsychology, 2*, 137–142.

(1984). *Anatomy of Genius: Split Brains and Global Minds.* New York: Human Sciences Press.

(1984). Right- versus left-hemispheric approach to psychical research. *Journal of the American Society for Psychical Research, 78*, 1.

Eileen Coly

Eileen Coly was born April 3, 1916, in London, England. She was educated in British boarding schools and at the end of her formal schooling traveled extensively with her mother, Eileen J. Garrett, the world-famous psychic and founder of the Parapsychology Foundation, Inc. The younger Eileen, known as Babs to her close friends, spent the war years in England experiencing the bombing of London and meeting and marrying her husband of 45 years, a French fighter pilot, Robert Coly.

After the war she settled in the United States and worked in Creative Age Press and on *Tomorrow* magazine, also founded by Eileen J. Garrett. She joined the Parapsychology Foundation and worked as Mrs. Garrett's assistant for several years before her mother's death in 1970, when she was elected to become the second president of the Foundation.

The field of parapsychology is indebted to Babs Coly and the Foundation for their support and encouragement of meaningful research and for providing a forum for interdisciplinary dialogue essential for understanding.

This interview took place at the Parapsychology Foundation's lovely Manhattan town house office, 228 East 71st Street, which houses the Eileen J. Garrett library, one of the most complete parapsychological libraries in the United States, a great boon to psychical researchers for which we are also most grateful.

Eileen Coly

Interview, January 20, 1986

Rosemarie Pilkington: What attitudes or beliefs did you have when you began work in this field that were changed through your experience?

Eileen Coly: I haven't really changed my attitude very much since I was a kid trailing around with the very much sought after Eileen Garrett and being subjected to dear old ducks asking, "Do you have your mother's gifts, dear?" I had my own way of dealing with that and my own thoughts, if I bothered to think about the subject, and I find that they're pretty much the same today. You see, Spiritualism was firmly established in England in the 1920s, and still is for that matter, so the mention of psychic gifts suggests communication with the dead. I was interested because I felt very sorry for the people who were in a state of grief and sadness, but even at that early age I felt, well, that's fine if you could tell yourself that you could meet again your loved one in a few weeks or a few years or something—it's a wonderful state. Then you can put away all that total grief. I felt that even as a kid.

I was interested, however, in other things: not the future, not the fortune-telling side of it even, but the telepathy angle, knowing what someone in another country, perhaps, is doing. Somebody's son who was climbing a mountain for instance. Garrett could tell his mother, "Oh, that's all right. He slipped and fell but he's OK now." That type of thing interested me to the point where if I asked a question, it would possibly be, "What about that kind of sixth sense?" But otherwise I set aside the survival question as another religious belief.

Garrett's personality was such that she never tried to impose any point of view on anyone close to her and in bringing up her own offspring, she would say, go ahead, if you want to smoke, if you want to drink, or do this or that—just be aware that this could possibly happen that might not turn out so well. But if you want to do it, it's your life, you do it. So I was not pushed into any particular point of view. But being of a very practical nature—you know you have to prove it to me first—I never got carried away with emotional issues so it was rather automatic that the down-to-earth individuals and the research angles would appeal to me in the early

46

days of Garrett's experiments in psychical research before this organization was founded more than 35 years ago.

R.P.: How did the PF come into being?

E.C.: Garrett, even in those very early days in England where she started to look for reasons for the strange visions and experiences that had recurred from early childhood, wanted answers to this whole psychic puzzle. Her whole life she vacillated. One day she would say "I don't believe a word of it. No, there is no continuation, there is no survival after death." Then she would give a person some incredible information that was deemed impossible for anybody living on this earth to know and she would say, "Well, maybe there's something in it after all." But she wouldn't accept it completely. She wanted to know the why and wherefore; why should it happen, and if it did, let's control it—which she learned to do in the case of trance mediumship—let's examine it, let's investigate it, let's run research on it.

That is why the Foundation came to be established in 1951, to encourage and support impartial scientific inquiry into the psychical aspects of human behavior. I stress the word *impartial* as the Foundation has no official "belief" when it comes to the paranormal. We are not trying to prove the existence of psi or its nonexistence; rather we are merely trying to find explanations, no matter what they may be and where they may lead, to the many diverse and as yet unanswerable questions presented to us in psychical research as to what and how psi works, if it works at all.

R.P.: I'm interested in your attitude toward your mother, in your relationship with her. Would you like to say anything about that?

E.C.: We had an easy-going relationship. Garrett treated her work much as an office job: You go to work at nine in the morning and you leave at five. You leave the job on the desk, you go out, have a drink, and go to the theater. It's discipline. She didn't take this psychic interest with her. In fact, people who met her socially were absolutely amazed to learn about all this psychic activity. It was the other side of the coin.

R.P.: So she made that dichotomy.

E.C.: Yes, very much so. Then too, Garrett didn't tiptoe around saying, "Oh, it's a gift," and "Oh, this is so wonderful," and "I am so blessed." On the contrary, she just said, "Well, I don't know. Make what you like of it." Because of her irreverent attitude people were suspicious of her. In addition she was very flamboyant, so that people wouldn't associate anything as serious or profound as this research with her because she was colorful in her dress, she was up to date on all the latest literature, she was a first-nighter at the theater—she was just "with it." Way before women's lib, too (see Garrett, 1968).

R.P.: As a child were you aware of her psychic studies?

E.C.: Yes, but it didn't occur to me that there was anything very unusual about such an occupation. I met all types of people, and attended some of the physiological tests carried out with her to determine what difference, if any, existed between Garrett in her normal waking state, and in trance with the control Uvani, an Arab who apparently only manifested through Garrett's trance state, and referred to himself as "the Gatekeeper," and Abdul Latif, a Persian physician who appeared during trance sessions with other mediums. Hereward Carrington (1957) and Nandor Fodor (1938) conducted quite a lot of tests with Garrett during the 1930s and this interested me because they maintained a scientific attitude. I didn't want to deal with those who were emotionally involved because of a need they had for alleged contact with the dead.

Eileen Garrett started the Foundation because she was interested in testing her own abilities as well as other psychic subjects. She was involved in other research programs as well. She went down to Duke University to work with J. B. Rhine in the 1930s. She was always offering herself as a guinea pig because she realized that there must be other people in the world who had this — really somewhat unwanted — gift, if you will, and wanted to know just what it was, how to handle it, and how to get rid of it if it was no good to anybody, or how to develop it if it had any useful aspects.

But don't forget that at that time it was a subject that was very much under wraps; you didn't talk about psychic things. People had images of these sittings or seances in the dark, with trumpet voices whispering and specters flying around in sheets. It was certainly an interesting way of meeting people — in the dark! There was a lot of activity. The procedure in those days, in the twenties, was to invite perhaps eight or ten people to attend a seance. The medium would be tied down in a chair in a curtained "cabinet" and the sitters would form a circle holding hands so that contact would be maintained between all "sitters." But what can be achieved in the dark is really rather remarkable. You could back out and join the hands of the people on either side of you and you were free to move around, as I did!

R.P.: What did you do at these seances? Did you run around?

E.C.: It was quite possible to crawl around. I suppose I shouldn't make such a statement but my personal feeling is that all that trumpet business was rather entertaining. The trumpet would be supposedly flying around the room independently, but there was generally a hand or something substantial attached to that trumpet. Sometimes if you tried to pull it you got a resistance, and maybe you could snatch it and take it to the other side of the room. And of course the "spirit voice" would kind of disappear or drift away. It was very funny. However, this type of activity, which lends itself so easily to fraud, is not included in any of the Foundation research programs!

Eileen Garrett's attitude about her own work was similar to her raising of children who were anxious to try their wings. She'd point out that if you do such and such, this, that, or the other could happen, so think about it. Therefore, when people would come to her and she'd go into trance and bring them all this solace she would simply say, "Look, it's up to you to believe it or not. I make no guarantee of where it comes from or if it's even so. It's up to you." She would warn people to be practical, too. Especially in developing one's psychic gifts. She would say, "Now don't play with Ouija boards; don't open doors that you're not prepared to walk through." That's darned good advice—in any line of endeavor.

R.P.: And, of course, part of that integrity was forming the organization to study psi scientifically.

E.C.: Right. To take this whole thing out of those awful seance rooms, in the dark or semidark, all that nonsense that went on. She wanted an explanation, one way or the other.

As I started to say, in those days one didn't talk about psychic things so if there were one or two investigators, well known in their various disciplines, who wanted to investigate psychic phenomena, they couldn't even come out and tell the world—not even their own academic world—that they were interested enough to pursue a research program in order to try to find out what this psychic business was all about. Even in the world of publishing there were relatively few opportunities for publication of texts on the subject of psychic phenomena. It wasn't respectable.

Garrett published *Tomorrow* magazine in the fifties to offer a forum for such works. She was also a partner in Garrett Publications which during its lifetime in the fifties and sixties published approximately twenty titles dealing with psychic topics at a time when the psychic world was relatively unknown in publishing circles and certainly not commercially successful. I might add that at my mother's death until the dissolution of Garrett Publications I also had that part of my mother's legacy passed on to me in addition to my work at the Foundation.

So Garrett's ambition became to find the people who were willing to do the experiments and the research, to find the money, and to create a respectable organization that would sponsor such work. Many, many years before she had met Frances P. Bolton, who was tremendously wealthy. She was really a rather great woman. She had done an awful lot of good for many causes, financially and otherwise, and particularly for the world of nursing during peace time and war time. She had her own private interest in psychic phenomena, but not the emotional interest in contacting loved ones who had died. She, too, wanted to know what this was all about, to

try to put psychical research on a decent footing, to have it become respectable, to give people a chance to do research; because she was a very rich
lady, she was able to provide financial help to launch a research organization. So between them, Garrett and Bolton set up the Parapsychology
Foundation.

Of course, Garrett had enough to live on but nothing comparable to
the fortune of Bolton, who could put so much money into it, which was
necessary, because the money had to come from somewhere. Although the
original idea was to set it up in such a way as to have a lot of donors, there
just didn't happen to be a lot of donors and the organization became pretty
much reliant on Mrs. Bolton. And, God bless her, she was very generous
and wonderful. She looked forward to the same goal of bringing psychical
research out of the seance rooms, out of all this mushy, rather murky
atmosphere, and putting it into a respectable, clean, research laboratory
atmosphere. That's how this place was born. And that's how it has continued.

R.P.: When your mother passed on in 1970 you took over. Was it your
desire to do so and continue what she had started?

E.C.: Yes. Actually, I hadn't been actively connected with the place
from its inception, but I'd followed everything that was going on. I think I
knew most of the people—I'd attended many of the meetings and conferences—so I was pretty conversant with it and having been, if you will,
born into this psychic subject it didn't shock me to become closely identified with it, and the nice, clean research attitude pleased me immensely.
I was glad to take it over and continue that way because a lot of time and
effort, not to mention money, had been put into setting this up, largely
due to Garrett's efforts because Bolton was too busy as a representative
of Ohio in the United States Congress, to spend a lot of time on the
mechanics of it. But Garrett, with that wild personality, could attract people from the darnedest walks of life. She'd walk down the street and just
happen to smile sympathetically at someone, for no apparent reason and
people would respond to her. I used to call her "The Presence." She had an
insatiable curiosity about people, not gossip about who they slept with or
why—she didn't care if they slept with a totem pole—but what made them
tick.

R.P.: That was probably the impetus of her psychic behavior. It's a
common denominator of good psychics; they really want to know about
people.

E.C.: Exactly. So people were drawn to her even without knowing that
there was anything psychic there, just on pure personality as you see it when
it walks into a room. She really did like children, but then she liked
everybody, of all ages. She was amazing with kids and animals. There was
something about her; that she was no threat to them and she could have

the most intelligent philosophical conversations with five-year-olds. She never talked down to them, or to anyone. She talked on a level that they both understood and apparently enjoyed. And with adults, I guess she did the same thing that she did with a five-year-old. And she just had this sixth sense about people who had a genuine interest and who could really contribute some original thoughts and possibly research, so that practically everyone in the field today came in contact with her and she encouraged them to go their own way.

R.P.: When you took over the Foundation what changes did you make? How have you done things differently or kept them the same?

E.C.: I wanted to continue in the same spirit, but not having Garrett's remarkable gifts—and Lord knows she had a whole bag full of gifts of one kind or another—and being of a very practical turn of mind anyway—my main problem was that I had always been in her shadow: "Oh, this is my daughter, Babs." I had been used to this instant dismissal all my life. In the thirties Garrett went down to Durham to see the Rhines and I accompanied her as usual. The last time I saw J.B. Rhine, not too long before he died, he still remembered that he met us at the train and he said, "I remember little Babs looking so shy." I was a youngster a little out of water; strange country, strange habits, strange people, certainly strange trains because you could step off a high train right in the middle of town, not as in Europe where you always went into a station!

Now little Babs had to come back, behind the desk, and start showing that little Babs had a mind of her own, so for two or three years I travelled around meeting people in the field and renewing acquaintances. I suppose little by little it became apparent that if I do dig my heels in they stay dug.

But mostly I hope I've achieved a fair attitude. The research must go on and anyone who has anything important to offer and will do their very best should receive as much attention, and support, as possible. If they have a worthwhile program to present that's for the cause, as it were, not just to advance Dr. Joe Doakes, but as a contribution and, where possible, original—the more original the better—we will try to fund them. We can't stop because we haven't solved the mystery of psychic phenomena yet. It's got to be out there somewhere—but little by little the information is still being sifted and brought in.

So, as soon as I was elected to the job I decided that the Foundation was going to go on. I think what I did was to firm things up a bit because Garrett was a little loose. She was extremely generous, and she could be very touched by the overwhelming need that most researchers had anyway. Instead of thinking financially, that at the end of the year you had better still have something left in the kitty, she was rather apt to say, "Oh, my dear, whatever you need. . . ." Let us say she was a "good touch."

R.P.: You had to develop executive abilities in order to manage what became, then, a much larger more complex organization.

E.C.: Yes. Our main problem, of course, has been the fact that when Garrett was alive there was always Mrs. Bolton there. So when something came up particularly worthy of support that the general coffers couldn't handle, if Bolton really felt that it was worthwhile she would chip in a bit more to sweeten the pot. Well, that was wonderful. It gave Garrett a lot of leeway that we do not have. We have to live on a smaller income and make every dollar count. There is just no way we can take a high flier on anything. Which is just as well because Garrett would have, I think, gone "down the drain" because of her generosity and her enthusiasm. Well, I'm not impulsive, not particularly generous, and my enthusiasm is carefully scaled down!

R.P.: I think you're being too hard on yourself especially as regards enthusiasm because, certainly, you would not have maintained the organization as you have if you did not still have that enthusiasm toward the field.

E.C.: That I do. I do think the field, the work, is worthwhile, having seen so many odd facets of it all my life. The emotional side, the rather strange happenings, especially PK, and all that kind of thing. Oh yes, I am enthusiastic, I'm interested. I'd like to see more applications of it but we don't have a solid enough explanation of it yet. Another thing: the healing aspects of it. I would be very much in favor of that except that somehow I can't quite see it as being psychic. I think it is very much psychological, so that I can't accept healing as a part of the psychic manifestation.

R.P.: You mentioned "odd facets" and "strange happenings" a while ago. What were you referring to?

E.C.: Poltergeists, the "noisy ghosts," hauntings, apparitions and such. I went along on one of the most dramatic poltergeist manifestations, known as the Ghost of Ash Manor (Garrett, 1952). Nandor Fodor, then research officer of the International Institute for Psychical Research in London, had received an appeal for help from the owner of a lovely old house in the south of England who was troubled by sounds of footsteps, moaning noises, and even the apparition of a man in his bedroom on a couple of occasions. Fodor arranged for a meeting at Ash Manor with the owners and invited Garrett, E. Lindsay, an independent researcher, and myself as note taker, to participate in the inquiry into the nature of the disturbance.

Garrett had taken part in many poltergeist investigations and the procedure generally took much the same course. Garrett was given no information about the disturbing events and was simply instructed to give any impressions she might have of unusual events connected with the house and grounds, and then go into trance in an effort to gain information as to former occupants who might be said to haunt the scene of past unhappiness or tragedy. So, at Ash Manor in the master bedroom where most of the disturbances seemed to have occurred, Garrett went into trance. The control, Uvani, explained that indeed there was the personality of a man, that we should address this entity and offer him comfort, endeavor to explain that he is free of the bonds of imprisonment and pain and should go in peace.

The personality of this haunting entity took over and the most startling change came over the medium. Sinking to her knees, she was holding her throat and choking in an effort to speak. There was nothing of Garrett in this being who seemed to have taken over her body. In halting terms in the English language of several centuries back, the drama unfolded and our ghost identified himself as Lord Henley, mentioning family names, places; his suffering through the confiscation of all his possessions, the death of wife and son, and the pain of being tortured and left to die in agony. When the trance was finished we all felt that we had brought peace to this disturbed entity and there would be no more trouble. But no! The next day, Lindsay was having a sitting with another medium in London when Lord Henley appeared and accused Lindsay of breaking his promise to come back to the house and talk to him again.

That evening, the apparition appeared to the master of Ash Manor and another appointment was quickly made for all of us to return to the house. In the meantime, Fodor organized a research team to check on the information Lord Henley had given us during the Garrett trance. It appeared that a great deal of Lord Henley's story was confirmed by the historical records. Lord Henley did not trouble anyone again. The ghost left, and the highly emotional occupants of the house — man, wife, and 16-year-old daughter — who were in constant conflict and vying with one another for attention, possibly decided not to dabble any more with forces that seemed to get out of control, and the house became peaceful again.

That was a very interesting case because it was so dramatic, and I think that if you have a lot of drama connected with something it makes a tremendous impression on you. And whether you want to believe it or however you want to handle it, it stays there because of the dramatics of it. But here again, this leaves me wondering, "Well, what was that all about anyway?" Garrett also wondered about it: "This is probably something in my unconscious. Maybe with this psychic gift I picked up some traces of the tragedy of this man who was chained and left to die."

According to the records, Lord Henley was connected to the reigning house of England and at that time there were many intrigues and plots against the throne. Garrett felt that this psychic gift of hers allowed her to pick up impressions, that these "imprints" are left on the atmosphere and you can pick them up and weave the whole story of it out of them. I can accept that.

R.P.: Did she have any explanation for the apparition itself? That this might have been a thought form produced by someone in the house, the 16-year-old perhaps, who might also have picked up the vibrations unconsciously?

E.C.: There is an energy that is drawn upon by some individuals.

R.P.: In other words a super-psi explanation.

E.C.: Yes. But she was ambivalent, as we are here today as well. That's very much how this subject stands, and that was Garrett's idea: This is what we know, these are the possibilities, make what you like of it, and do your own thing.

R.P.: I would say she was being totally honest with herself and with others. She must have been a person with a great deal of integrity. And that holds true with you, Babs.

E.C.: Well, thank you, but I think it shows concern, otherwise you kind of set yourself up as a little god.

R.P.: You made a comment before on the many people who ask you if you have not inherited your mother's gift. Do you think you have repressed whatever psychic ability you might have?

E.C.: That has become my opinion, that I did, that I did negate it completely. Even my daughter, Lisette, who is now the vice president of the Parapsychology Foundation, was a little hounded when people at school found out she had this psychic grandmother. You can imagine how I reacted in the twenties.

R.P.: It must have been a burden for you to bear.

E.C.: In a way, yes. I didn't like being looked up and down by these old dowagers and sort of dismissed. It was still the tail end of the children-should-be-seen-and-not-heard era. You had to be about eighteen before you could dare come right out and spontaneously express your opinion. It was not done! So I didn't care for that whole attitude and I think unconsciously negated the whole thing to such a point that for years and years I would say, "No, no, no, no, I have no psychic gift, and I wouldn't want it anyway." And I was so successful that I just cut it right out. I'm sure that it was the reaction to those early days.

R.P.: There had to be some negative reaction on your part. But luckily for the field you didn't turn away from it. You took the obligation that was given to you, and with enthusiasm I think.

E.C.: Well don't forget that I was travelling around with Garrett for many, many years, about ten I think. I was doing her secretarial work, her appointments, throughout the late twenties and thirties, so that I was exposed to all these things. Whenever anything that looked like research came along, such as the Duke University work with J.B. Rhine (1934), Hereward Carrington (1957), Nandor Fodor (1938), etc. I thoroughly approved of that and felt that was the right direction so that the other spiritual element really didn't bother me because obviously I had learned to set that aside.

My interest developed and grew in the research area. So it was no effort whatsoever to drop into this presidency because in the last three years before Garrett died I was active here. Her secretary left and she tried several who didn't work out, so I pitched in and spent more and more time until it became full time. Actually she had wanted me here before that, but I was raising my family. By the time the children, Lisette and Robert, were in their teens we had a housekeeper who was a part of the family so it was no problem to just take off and spend the days with Garrett and then be home in the evening. The children were perfectly safe and happy.

R.P.: Would you like to say something about what the organization is doing at present?

E.C.: Well, the general tightening up can be observed in our conferences now. Garrett had the right idea, to get people from other disciplines together to exchange ideas and viewpoints. That was pretty well unique at the time. I saw the necessity to carry that on. To this day a lot of the researchers will tell us that it is useful to do it quietly in the format we do — and I think we are the only ones that achieve that.

R.P.: Yes, members of the Parapschological Association have expressed that opinion very strongly, that we need the exchange of ideas and the input from scientists from other disciplines.

E.C.: Yes, very much. For several years we have rather dwelt in one discipline at a time, trying to extract the maximum psychical content. We concentrated on parapsychology's role in the scientific disciplines and the discussions arising from these meetings contributed considerably to demonstrating parapsychology's place in the hard sciences. Quantum Physics and Parapsychology in 1974 was one of the early conferences to examine the relationship between these two disciplines (Oteri, 1975). Every year the PF sponsors a conference devoted to a specific theme and this is recorded and the proceedings published in book form by the Foundation. Some of the individual papers are published as well in the bi-monthly *Parapsychology Review*, also published by the PF, which contains articles, book reviews, and news notes on events in parapsychology around the world. But now we will turn once again to the interdisciplinary approach in the themes of coming conferences rather than concentrating on one particular aspect. We have to try to look farther out there and see what new contacts, new insights and widening viewpoints we can gather in.

We are trying to pay more attention to the students now. For a long time parapsychology was the kind of subject in which people would drop in and drop out, so we hesitated to fund students because one didn't know what the payoff would be, whether their interest was serious and they would stay in the field or not. But now we have initiated the Eileen J. Garrett scholarship program to encourage students to take up studies in parapsychology. The Parapsychology Foundation for many years has funded educational programs at various universities in an effort to promote parapsychological studies, but unfortunately when we withdraw support the institutions often drop the courses.

Some are maintained, however, and continue to broaden the scope of their studies, as in the case of John F. Kennedy University, Orinda, California, where a parapsychology program in the School of Consciousness Studies, originally introduced by John Palmer as the Eileen J. Garrett Professor of Parapsychology, has not only survived but has gone on to offer a master's degree in parapsychology. They have also organized some brilliant PK research there, with a fine research team, again partly aided by the PF. Another successful education project among many funded by the Foundation was the program devised and administered by Robert Morris at the University of California, Santa Barbara. Unfortunately, the University discontinued the parapsychology program after the PF ceased to support it. Then we also helped establish the Psi Communications Laboratory in the Syracuse University School of Computer and Information Sciences. Dr. Morris joined the laboratory and introduced some original courses and projects in psi communication. He has since been elected to the Koestler Chair of Parapsychology at Edinburgh, Scotland.

R.P.: Is that where you feel the future of your organization is going?

E.C.: The interdisciplinary exchange and the support to education in parapsychology are absolutely essential. We've got to spur the interest and add to the working knowledge of the youngsters because otherwise who's going to carry the banner? Many of our fine, reputable people are getting to an age where they're going to be dropping out and not actively working in the field, and suddenly we will be bereft of perhaps 60 percent of our established members, scholars, and leaders.

It was difficult to take over the Foundation when I did because at that time there were many loose ends. That was also the time of the occult explosion, the boom of interest in altered states of consciousness that carried over from the drug generation. And, then too, nobody could succeed a personality like Garrett's. She was magnetic. She was self-reliant. She was ahead of her time and saw nothing unusual in a woman's being a top executive. She was very earthy and had a wonderful sense of humor, but she could also be the *grande dame*. If you overstepped your bounds that British hauteur would emerge. Men were very attracted to her and there was always a great deal of excitement around her, here in the Foundation as well. It was very hard to keep things in order with that whirlwind going. I had to come along and tidy up. The trouble is that now nobody stirs up so much. It's a little too sterile. Perhaps Lisette will stir it up. She has served her apprenticeship in much the same way I did, and although it was not designed to be a family affair, it seems to have evolved that way.

R.P.: You really have made quite a contribution then in keeping this organization from going under, keeping it going, and keeping the funding flowing out.

E.C.: It is something of a clearinghouse for information in the field. You would be surprised at how many people stop by here. People call if they're passing through New York. We get, at the very least, a phone call.

R.P.: What advice would you give to young people entering the field today?

E.C.: Just warn them not to become emotionally involved and to try and stand back and keep an objective attitude. Even if an exciting piece of research presents itself, don't get so absolutely tied up with blinkers on so that you can't see where you're going. Keep your feet on the ground. Take a lot of time to observe. Don't just rush in and start mixing it up. Stand back; look at the whole situation and give it some mature thought.

Careers in parapsychology have to be worked out by the individuals since one cannot just choose a university and proceed to work toward a major in parapsychology. Only in the last few years have courses been developed dealing exclusively with parapsychology, and even today the choice is limited. Therefore my advice to the young student is still to select the main area of study required for a future career and design his or her own study pattern by introducing parapsychological elements into the chosen courses, keeping in mind that there are only a handful of full-time parapsychologists around the world, and those who are the respected leaders in the field generally have a full-time salaried job, and research and experiments in parapsychology are generally part-time, spare-time, non-paying activities that may well involve a certain outlay of the individual's own funds rather than any remuneration. However, many have successfully integrated parapsychological interests with their careers and life styles. Because, after all, there are so many facets that it is a fascinating subject to study.

The work of the Foundation will keep moving along. We will continue to encourage and support where possible the search for solutions through modern scientific techniques and interdisciplinary studies and research in all aspects of human experience—and through acceptance of psychic manifestations as part of "normal" existence rather than "abnormal." Educational programs to promote understanding and communication between disciplines and many other areas of psychic studies should be explored and examined to give us answers on how to deal with psychic phenomena and also put it to good use for the benefit of all.

Publications by the
Parapsychology Foundation
Under the Presidency of Eileen Coly

Proceedings of International Conferences of the
Parapsychology Foundation (in chronological order):

Angoff, A., & Shapin, B. (eds.). (1973). *Parapsychology Today: A Geographic View.*
Angoff, A., & Shapin B. (eds.). (1974). *Parapsychology and the Sciences.*
Angoff, A., & Barth, D. (eds.). (1974). *Parapsychology and Anthropology.*
Oteri, L. (ed.). (1975). *Quantum Physics and Parapsychology.*
Shapin, B., & Coly, L. (eds.). (1976). *Education in Parapsychology.*
Shapin, B., & Coly, L. (eds.). (1977). *The Philosophy of Parapsychology.*
Shapin, B., & Coly, L. (eds.). (1978). *Psi and States of Awareness.*
Shapin, B., & Coly, L. (eds.). (1979). *Brain/Mind and Parapsychology.*
Shapin, B., & Coly, L. (eds.). (1980). *Communication and Parapsychology.*
Shapin, B., & Coly, L. (eds.). (1981). *Concepts and Theories of Parapsychology.*
Shapin, B., & Coly, L. (eds.). (1982). *Parapsychology and the Experimental Method.*
Shapin, B., & Coly, L. (eds.). (1983). *Parapsychology's Second Century.*
Shapin, B., & Coly, L. (eds.). (1985). *The Repeatability Problem in Parapsychology.*
Shapin, B., & Coly, L. (eds.). (1986). *Current Trends in Psi Research.*

Parapsychological Monographs

Ullman, M., & Krippner, S. (1970). *Dream Studies and Telepathy.*
Sailaja, P., & Rao, K. R. (1973). *Experimental Studies of the Differential Effect in Life Setting.*
Rogo, D. S. (1973). *Methods and Models for Education in Parapsychology.*
Tart, C. (1975). *The Application of Learning Theory to ESP Performance.*
Duplessis, Y. (1975). *The Paranormal Perception of Color.*
Sargent, C. L. (1980). *Exploring Psi in the Ganzfeld.*
Kelly, E. F., & Locke, R. G. (1981). *Altered States of Consciousness and Psi: An Historical Survey and Research Prospectus.*

Joseph H. Rush

Joseph H. Rush is a physicist and science writer who long has been intrigued by the radical questions posed by parapsychological research. His professional career has involved him in the wartime atomic bomb project and in the scientists' political movement afterward. He has taught at Texas Tech University, Denison University, and the University of Colorado, where he also participated in the "Condon Committee" investigation of UFOs. His principal work has been with the National Center for Atmospheric Research, where he was active in solar research and optical instrumentation. He is author of *The Dawn of Life* and many popular articles on scientific topics.

During these activities, Dr. Rush has maintained a steadfast interest in psychic phenomena. This preoccupation has led to several published papers and book chapters, some experiments, and—as his chapter here indicates—much wondering.

Joseph H. Rush

Parapsychology:
Some Personal Observations

Many parapsychologists trace their involvement to personal psychic experiences. I came in by the intellectual back door while sitting out the 1930s depression as a radio operator in the Dallas Police Department. Night shifts in a secluded cubbyhole in the city hall attic allowed a lot of time for reading, and the library was across the street. In the process of bookworming my way through it, more or less, about 1936 I blundered into the shelf on psychical research.

That discovery changed my world view. I found Gurney, Myers and Podmore's *Phantasms of the Living*, Richet's *Twenty Years*, Myers' *Human Personality and Its Survival of Bodily Death*, J.B. Rhine's *Extra-sensory Perception*, and a miscellany of other books. Of course I had heard tales of ghosts and poltergeists, fortune telling and mind reading, but in my childhood context such topics had been considered beneath serious discussion. Now, for the first time, I became aware that scientists and scholars of distinction in other fields had been taking these disreputable claims seriously.

A few months later I met Chester Howard, a geologist who by a recent spontaneous experience — an apparition of his dead father — had been converted from scoffing skeptic to sky's-the-limit believer. He invited me to attend the amateur psychic circle over which he presided. Our experimental sessions yielded some intriguing effects, but little that impressed me as evidential. However, they made me acquainted with Ann Jensen, whose casually conversational "readings" astonished me then and still do.

There I also met James Crumbaugh, who was developing a master's thesis around card-guessing ESP tests. Through him I learned much about J.B. Rhine's controversial work and the statistical approach to psi experimentation.

This brief summary indicates how I became seriously involved in parapsychology, but not why. Other interests have come and gone, but this preoccupation with psi phenomena and their implications has persisted

60

undiminished. The key lies, I believe, in those implications. My interest in science is essentially philosophical. I love a mystery; and what mystery can compare with the layered enigma that is our universe? (One of my professors, the late Gregory Wannier, once helped clarify my self-image by remarking, "Rush is interested in things that don't work!")

The psi phenomena "don't work," and their implications run deep. When intractable data will not go away, they imply a flaw in the theoretical structure. They suggest that the world is not made quite the way we think it is. More pointedly, psi offers the prospect of fresh insight into the ancient mind-body problem, the role of mind and consciousness in the cosmos.

During nearly fifty years of reading, observing, experiencing and experimenting, questioning, analyzing, and endlessly wondering, I have found no reason to abandon my conviction of the reality and the fundamental importance of psi phenomena. Yet there is a curious other-worldly feeling about the field. I have been involved primarily with other matters, and weeks or sometimes months may pass without my giving serious attention to parapsychology. When I think of it at all, it has an air of unreality, like the memories of a hurried foreign trip. I feel as if I am living in two worlds that are hardly on speaking terms.

At such times I may find myself wondering—for the thousandth time—whether I have overlooked some fatal flaw in the evidence or have yielded to wishful thinking. Then I become involved in an experiment or a meeting of parapsychologists, or experience another odd happening that should not have happened, or have to reexamine my position as I am doing now, and I am overwhelmed anew by discordant feelings of reality and strangeness. Nevertheless, despite the will-o'-the-wisp capriciousness of the manifestations, the sometimes cogent criticisms of parapsychologists' reports, and even the few disheartening instances of fraud by respected experimenters, my basic conviction holds. Again, why?

From an objective standpoint, obviously the most impressive evidence for psi is in the professional parapsychological literature. Here I want to mention several experimental reports that particularly impress me. I make no attempt to select the "best experiments" or to rank those I mention, but only indicate the kind of evidence that I think is collectively compelling.

A psychologist, John E. Coover (1917/1975) at Stanford University, carried out a long series of card-guessing "telepathy" tests, and in his elaborate report he interpreted the results as nonsignificant. However, apparently dismissing the possibility of clairvoyance, he had compared his telepathy scores with "control" scores from trials that were open to clairvoyance! Actually, his combined scores exceeded theoretical chance expectation significantly. Thus he unwittingly confirmed the effect he apparently had hoped not to find.

Another psychologist, George H. Estabrooks (1927/1961), while a graduate student at Harvard obtained highly significant scores by student subjects who guessed colors and suits of playing cards. But he also noted the tendency of the success rates to decline, and he commented on the positive influence of a casual, friendly atmosphere. He found that indifferent subjects did better than those who were enthusiastic or otherwise involved. ("The very worst type . . . is the instructor in psychology.")

Of the many ESP tests reported by Duke University Parapsychology Laboratory, the Pearce-Pratt series (Palmer, 1978; Rhine & Pratt, 1954) is especially impressive. Very high scores were obtained in card-guessing trials with subject and experimenter in separate campus buildings. Criticisms of this experiment (e.g., Hansel, 1961) appear to have been effectively rebutted (Rhine & Pratt, 1961), and the high scoring rate accords with that in other tests with Pearce.

Gertrude Schmeidler's "sheep vs. goat" experiments demonstrated positive correlations between ESP scores and subjects' belief or nonbelief in the possibility of ESP in the experiment (Palmer, 1978; Schmeidler & McConnell, 1958/1973). Attempts to replicate these results have been unusually successful.

Turning to PK experiments, I like the elegance of A. M. Mitchell and G. W. Fisk's (1953) successful dice-throwing experiment in which the best subject was 170 miles from Fisk, who alone knew the trial targets.

The decline effect in PK dice tests, first reported from the Duke laboratory, seems to me strongly evidential (Rhine & Humphrey, 1944a, 1944b; Rhine, Humphrey, & Pratt, 1945). It was unanticipated; it appeared with high consistency in data from diverse experimenters; and in most series it could not be accounted for by biased dice or recording errors. Here I think also of R.A. McConnell's machine-thrown dice series that showed strong decline effects despite nonsignificant overall scores (McConnell, Snowdon, & Powell, 1955).

Bernard Grad (1965), a biologist at McGill University, developed some remarkably well-controlled laboratory tests of the powers of a reputed healer. In a series of multiple-blind experiments on barley seedlings, the healer did not handle the seedlings. He "treated" (by holding in his hands) only sealed bottles of saline solution that would be used to water the barley seeds. Germination and growth were significantly greater in the seedlings so treated than in controls watered with untreated saline.

Of the many excellent experiments in both ESP and PK modes using electronic random-event generators (REGs), Helmut Schmidt's (1969, 1973, 1976) are sufficiently representative. Besides demonstrating highly significant scores, his tests compared simple vs. complex REG machines, different rates of presenting target events, and on-line vs. prerecorded target series. Successful experiments with REGs are particularly impressive, because in competent hands these versatile machines practically eliminate artifacts caused by sensory cues, recording errors, or nonrandom target sequences.

It is clear from these examples that I attach more significance to evidence of meaningful relationships or contexts than to extrachance scores alone. Coover got significant scores despite his negative approach. Estabrooks, Schmeidler, the Duke decline studies, McConnell, Grad, and many REG experimenters found correlations between scoring rates and experimental variables. The Pearce-Pratt and Mitchell-Fisk experiments succeeded over unusually great distances.

These incidental relationships are important. Highly significant scores frequently are attained by low extrachance scoring rates sustained through thousands of trials. In such a procedure, it is very difficult to exclude the possibility of some slight, undetected systematic bias that can produce any desired level of statistical significance simply by piling up trials. Further, the *interpretation* of a probability value—the concept of statistical significance itself—is inescapably subjective. An experimental score yielding a probability of .01 means that, on average, the observed deviation (or greater) from chance expectation will occur purely by chance once in a hundred such experiments. But the probability value does not tell whether *that* particular score occurred by chance. The judgment of what level of probability is "statistically significant" is therefore a subjective appraisal deriving from both theory and common experience. Coover demanded a probability of 2×10^{-5} or less for significance. In the heyday of J.B. Rhine's investigations it was taken to be about .01. Today a probability of .05 is sometimes cited as signifying an extrachance effect.

For these and other reasons, scoring rates that decline systematically or vary with subjects' attitudes or other factors impress me more than highly significant scores that are derived from marginal scoring rates.

Having gotten into parapsychology by the intellectual back door, I necessarily rely primarily upon the experimental literature for scientific evidence in the field. Personal conviction in any matter, however, involves more than objective, scientifically definable evidence. My conviction of the reality of psi phenomena is strongly reinforced by personal observations and experiences. Among other effects, these have influenced my evaluation of the evidence from reports of spontaneous psi episodes. Though the findings in several major case studies are remarkably consistent (Schouten, 1979, 1981, 1982), such reports are of less evidential value than the experimental results, for well known reasons. However, I believe that such evidence has been too much depreciated.

I want to mention several incidents here, simply to indicate the kinds of experiences that have impressed me. About June, 1938, the *Doctor IQ* quiz program opened at the Palace Theater in Dallas with a format that included twelve true-or-false statements that anyone in the audience could try, for cash prizes. Under strong motivation to find the means to go back to college, I attended every week; but always there were several statements that I could only guess blindly. Then about the end of July came a night when something was different. On each statement that I did not know I felt a definite mental prompting of either "true" or "false." I wrote and never looked back. I won; and a month later, after more sessions of blind guessing, I repeated the experience for another prize. What impresses me is not merely that I won something—a sufficient anomaly in itself!—but that I knew on each occasion that I was functioning differently from my usual guessing.

Ann Jensen, whom I mentioned earlier, has given many "readings," often including specific predictions. She is not infallible, but her batting average seems to me to challenge severely the chance hypothesis. One example will suffice:

Early in 1941, at the University of Texas in Austin, I mentioned in a letter to Ann that I would be doing my thesis research on the wavelengths of starlight from some telescopic photographs supplied by McDonald Observatory. I did not elaborate, knowing her aversion to the disciplined tedium of the scientific enterprise ("What use does a humming bird have for crutches?"). Somewhere in the middle of her next letter she remarked:

> One of the plates furnished you by the McDonald Observatory has an error. I am at a loss to explain because I know absolutely nothing of the starlight (except how kind it can be) or astronomy but there is something wrong there.

Weeks later, during the laborious process of measuring the spectral lines, I discovered that one of the eight plates had somehow shifted during the long exposure in the telescope, so that it was double-exposed and useless. A lucky shot? Maybe. But time on a big telescope is precious, and great care is taken to avoid such accidents. In any case, the error should have been detected before the spectrograms were sent to me. The odds for a lucky guess had not been good.

Meanwhile, I had become intrigued by Mary Sinclair's account of the subjective technique she had developed for her "telepathic" drawings experiments (Sinclair, 1930/1962). Having a similar propensity for trying things for myself, I proposed to Ann Jensen, 200 miles (320 kilometers) distant, that we run a series of drawing tests in which we would take turns "sending" and "receiving" (Rush & Jensen, 1949). She was quite successful, which was not surprising; and I also achieved a respectable degree of success, which did surprise me. Independent statistical evaluation yielded a probability of .002 for the series; but that result, though satisfying, gives no intimation of the *subjective* experience of relaxing, blanking the mental field, and trying not to interfere with the dim shapes that evolve on the visual screen. Again, it is the correlation of process with result, not merely the resemblances between drawings, that impresses me.

Anyone must note incidents—the letters that cross in the mail, the phone that is answered before it rings—that leave one wondering at the workings of chance. Over the years, however, I have accumulated a few unlikely experiences that, taken in context, suggest that something other than chance is involved. One fine day I was at my desk at home, deeply absorbed in some task, while my six-year-old daughter was in the yard tossing a toy glider. I had no view of the yard. Presently in she came: "Daddy, come help me find my airplane."

"Okay." I got up and walked out with her in a trancelike state, my mind still back at the desk. I did not question her, but walked straight to one of several flower beds, parted the tall plants, and picked up the glider.

Once I was afflicted with a throat infection that affected me mentally, making me feel dull and "flighty," unable to concentrate. I called the medical clinic and was given an appointment with a Dr. Marbry. I didn't know him, and as I approached the receptionist I realized that I had forgotten his name. Marquand . . . Marquard? Too sick to worry about it, I asked for Dr. Marquard. The receptionist, puzzled, suggested Marbry. "Oh, yes, of course." While I sat in the waiting room dully thumbing a magazine, a man stepped up to the desk when the receptionist asked his name. He spoke in a clear, incisive voice: "Marquard!"

Chance coincidence? Maybe. But the name is not common, and patients in a doctor's office do not usually speak out clearly. I am inclined to believe that, in mentally reaching for my doctor's name in my flighty, disoriented state, I overshot and picked up the similar name that I would hear with sharp clarity a bit later. Each of these two incidents occurred while I was in an altered state of consciousness, a detachment comparable to that which I had deliberately induced for the drawings tests.

The experiences that have most impressed me, sometimes to the point of shocked disbelief, are a series of apparently paranormal dreams. One of the first parapsychological books I had read was J. W. Dunne's (1927/1958) *An Experiment with Time.* Over the years I had looked for the sort of precognitive correspondences that he had described, but none had appeared. Then in 1956 something I read, suggesting that precognitive dreams usually are "future memories" of the dreamer's later experiences, fired me with the idea of trying to induce such dreams by autosuggestion at the edge of sleep. Apparently this technique worked. During the next 15 years I recorded about a dozen dreams that seem to me to fit the prescribed pattern. Two will serve to illustrate their characteristics.

One morning, in a brief flash somewhere between sleeping and waking—probably more hypnopompic imagery than dream—I saw a cage or wall of horizontal and vertical slats. A pathetic-looking little brown bear had its head and one foreleg through a break in the slats, trying to get out.

While perusing that day's *Denver Post* (February 28, 1960) I was shocked to see on the cover of *This Week* magazine the picture of my vision. It was a crossword puzzle grid, illustrating an article about people who devise crossword puzzles. The center of the grid was burst open, and the brown animal (a bearlike potto, beloved of puzzle makers) was coming out, head and one foreleg visible just as I had seen it.

On the 6th of January, 1957, I finished a book I had been working on intensively for several months. I felt very tired, blank, "washed out," and slept poorly that night. While dozing early the next morning I had a dream, brief but clear and in color, suggesting to me that it might be precognitive. I am with some other people—vague, unidentified—at a country house on a knoll overlooking a flat grassy meadow. We watch apprehensively as an "airplane" approaches, trying to land. I see only a straight wing with rounded, *turned-up* tips; but, in the manner of dreams, I know it is an airplane and feel that one of my sons is the pilot. He overshoots the meadow and circles for another approach. Now I see the pilot, standing on a trapeze-like bar underneath the wing with his arms extended, holding onto the wing or trapeze supports. He overshoots the meadow again and crashes in rough, brushy ground beyond, disappearing in the foliage under a cloud of white dust. I feel sudden relief; he is hurt, but not dangerously.

About ten days earlier I had watched from our house, situated on a slope, as my 12-year-old younger son had tried to fly his new control-line model airplane in a meadow below. He overcontrolled; the plane zoomed and dived erratically through two or three circles, then crashed. I felt keenly his frustration and disappointment.

Twelve days after the dream the same boy tried skiing for the first time. I watched from the lodge as he and other beginners practiced in a shallow bowl below. He soon got the feel of it and made several good passes. Then someone crossed in front of him, and he tangled his skis and broke a leg.

This dream, situated roughly midway in time between two incidents having several elements of similarity, to me suggests that the dream process—whatever the underlying motivation—drew its material impartially from symmetrical past and future events. The physical settings were similar. In each situation the same boy was attempting a skill involving swift, soaring motion; and each ended in disaster. In the dream, the "airplane" resembled a composite of two skis, and the pilot hung beneath it in a stance suggestive of a skier. Though he crashed in green foliage, a cloud of white dust (snow?) rose. In each case my emotions were deeply involved.

Besides the correspondences between this series of dreams and their apparent real-life counterparts, the dreams themselves are marked by certain common characteristics. I rarely dream in color; but all of these paranormal dreams were in color except one that I related to a black-and-white picture. In ordinary dreams the dreamer usually is the central figure, an active protagonist; but in most of these, though not all, I was a passive spectator.

I emphasize again that these personal incidents are not offered as proof of anything, but as illustrations of certain types of experiences that, taken in their full contexts, strongly reinforce my conviction of the reality of psi phenomena. I have tried to imagine what my attitude would be if I had had no relevant personal observations or experiences. Certainly I would be more skeptical, though I do not believe I could explain away the experimental literature. Such considerations have made me more tolerant of the honest critics. The skeptic is entitled to suspect that I cheated in my drawings experiments or made up my dream anecdotes. I have the advantage of knowing that I did not. Such assurance greatly reduces the inevitable burden of doubt in a controversial field. Unfortunately, it is not transferable.

Against that personal background, how does parapsychology appear to me today?

The evolution of any science is a complex interplay of observation and insight, of opportunism and challenge. Some problems are solvable but trivial. Others of profound significance may be methodologically inaccessible. Between these extremes, scientists concentrate upon problems that appear most accessible and rewarding to experimental or theoretical elucidation.

The result, described clearly by T. S. Kuhn (1962/1970), is modification of the subject matter of a field as some problems are put aside and new ones are discovered or defined. Electromagnetic science began with investigations of the peculiar phenomena of lodestone and rubbed amber; but the research soon shifted into voltaic electricity, electrostatic generators, and electromagnetic effects. The phenomena of lodestone and amber were clarified only much later with the advent of solid-state physics. In their continual quest for exploitable clues, scientists remind us of the proverbial naif who loses something indoors but looks for it outside because the light is better there.

Parapsychology emerged a century ago out of preoccupation with the question of survival of death. The early research was intermingled with and influenced by spiritistic concepts and practices, and it relied heavily upon the "natural history" type of investigation. Now survival appears to be impossible in principle to establish rigorously. Spiritism has all but vanished from professional psi investigations, lingering in some aspects of poltergeists and in a few mediumistic studies. The experimental approach has largely replaced the investigation of spontaneous or mediumistic phenomena. Adopted first to establish convincing evidence for psi, it now is directed primarily to elucidating it by exploring its variations and relations to psychological and other variables.

In effect, the field of parapsychology has been defining itself by the selection process mentioned above, by which investigators pursue those problems and questions that promise significant answers and abandon those (e.g., survival) that do not. This evolution of concepts and goals has amounted literally to inventing a field of inquiry. From an investigation of survival through spontaneous and mediumistic experiences, parapsychology has become an esoteric field devoted to investigating problems most of which could not have occurred to the early psychical researchers. Thus modern parapsychology is not a more advanced phase of the investigations begun by the Society for Psychical Research in 1882, but is literally a new field that has evolved from those investigations into greatly altered methods, directions, and concepts.

A science that pursues fundamental questions becomes esoteric because it must follow its clues, and they lead necessarily from the commonplace to the bizarre, the ineffable, delineated only in the enigmatic traces of mathematical equations. Physics began with familiar intuitive notions of matter and space, force, motion, and time. Yet from these innocent concepts it has evolved the outlandish worlds of relativity and quantum mechanics.

Parapsychology began with simplistic notions of survival of death and of transmission of information from mind to mind. It cut its teeth on ghosts and poltergeists, psychic rods and ectoplasm, mental radio, spirit messages and cryptesthesia. Out of this wilderness experimental research evolved an orderly set of discrete concepts arranged by analogy with familiar sensorimotor functions: ESP and PK—telepathy and clairvoyance in contemporaneous or precognitive modes, and the undifferentiated concept of psychokinesis. ESP has been imagined to serve as psychic "eyes" to guide the PK force, again analogous to a sensorimotor servo loop. Experiments were conceived, again by analogy, in terms of detached experimenter and compliant subject. Psi effects, as Jule Eisenbud (1963) pungently noted, were assumed to conform obediently to the experimental design.

Meanwhile, disquieting evidence accumulated. The experimenter, it appeared, could be an active and even dominant participant in the psi manifestations. Psi appeared to be indifferent to complexity of the experimental task, as if oblivious of the steps that logically intervened between intention and goal. Conceptual ambiguities developed, as between PK and precognitive clairvoyance; telepathy became operationally undefinable. These developments have led to the emergence of holistic concepts in which psi is seen as a pervasive, impersonal, goal-serving tendency that involves mutual interactions among experimenter, subject, and sometimes others. Current experiments routinely test concepts that would not have been intelligible to the pioneers of psychical research. We are reminded again of J.B.S. Haldane's remark that nature is not only queerer than anyone has imagined — it is queerer than anyone *can* imagine.

Despite these conceptual advances, parapsychology still is not converging so rapidly as a new scientific field usually does. Two factors are recognized as the principal handicaps: the exasperating inconsistencies in experimental results, and the lack of a theoretical model that could relate psi phenomena to established science. The former difficulty is at least partly responsible for the latter, since it is difficult to formulate and test theories without consistent data. Nevertheless, findings have been sufficiently repeatable to sustain serious interest in the field for more than a century and to instigate the evolution of concepts outlined earlier. A principle generally overlooked by critics is that inconsistent results from well conducted experiments do not cancel each other. Rather, they suggest the influence of unrecognized variables. Null results do not invalidate positive results obtained in similar experiments under clean conditions; they pose questions for further investigation. Such inconsistencies, however, hinder the convergence toward consensus that is essential to the development of a science.

I suspect that repeatability in psi experiments may be intimately dependent upon the level of performance, or scoring rate. If the psi component in an experiment is very weak, it may be obstructed or otherwise perturbed by weak, unrecognized influences in the experimental situation, whereas a strong psi component will be less affected by such perturbations.

For that and other reasons, I believe that the most rewarding advance in the field would be the enhancement of experimental psi scoring rates or other manifestations — an idea that obviously is not original! Of several possible approaches, three seem to me to be particularly promising. The first is wider and more varied work with teams of subjects, to make use of some of the principles advanced by Batcheldor (1984) and possibly other advantages. A lone subject is "on the spot," particularly in the stereotyped experimenter-subject relation.

For openers, has anyone ever tried having two subjects use a Ouija board to call card symbols or other targets? This simple, easily tested idea could be adapted to more than two subjects and to more sophisticated apparatus. The help-or-hinder PK experiments are equivalent in principle. An interesting variation would be to have two or more subjects simultaneously throw dice for the same (unspecified) face, or do something equivalent with other apparatus. Such a task would remove the dichotomy of experimenter challenging subject, replacing it with a premium on cooperation between equals.

The second approach is to introduce more effective motivations. In the famed Brugmans-Heymans experiment (Schouten & Kelly, 1978) the subject tried to point to the target square on a board, while the experimenter watched from another room. The subject had complete motor freedom but no relevant sensory input, while the experimenter had ample sensory input but no effective motor freedom. It occurred to me that this interrupted servo loop might have evoked a strong, primitive motivation for psi to close the gap. I devised an ESP test apparatus (named "Rushian roulette" by a student!) that was equivalent to the Brugmans-Heymans arrangement and obtained some good results with it (Rush, 1979). However, the motivational hypothesis has not been tested explicitly.

This motivational situation relates to a more general hypothesis of "lead-in and frustration" that I had proposed earlier (Rush, 1964): namely that, if a motivated sensory or motor effort is frustrated short of its goal, psi intervention will be facilitated. While any psi test necessarily involves such frustration to some degree, I believe that results might be improved by creating test situations (such as those mentioned above) in which the motivation and frustration are more specific. Stanford devised such a situation to test his similar PMIR principle — i.e., unconscious, goal-oriented psi intervention (Stanford, Zenhausern, Taylor, & Dwyer, 1975).

My third suggestion is to devise methods for subjective development and awareness of psi functioning. My belief that this can be done, at least with adaptable subjects, derives from personal observations and experience, as well as from some of the literature (e.g., Sinclair, 1930/1962; Warcollier, 1938/1975). I have mentioned earlier my success in applying Mary Sinclair's concentration technique for ESP drawings tests. Another ESP technique is precisely that which everyone uses for recalling a name that is "blocked": you wait until your attention has turned to other matters. Then the name comes through spontaneously or when you revert to it. I have used this trick with some success in calling cards. It is tedious and difficult to continue for many trials, but the subjective difference between these distinct promptings and mere guesses is striking.

The "Rushian roulette" apparatus mentioned earlier provided for the subject to turn a knob so as to set a remote pointer, at the experimenter's station, to a randomly determined target location. Again and again I watched, exasperated, as a subject would rotate the pointer past the target, stop, hesitate, cross back over the target — and then spin the pointer rapidly away from that vicinity as if in relief! The implication of response to the target at some mental level was inescapable. I suspect that, by suitable coaching on such an apparatus, some subjects might learn to identify these subtle intimations. In broader terms, it might be profitable to give more attention to devising other experimental situations that would permit continuous monitoring of the development of a subject's response. Such techniques are slow, but they facilitate qualitative insights that might lead to enhanced performance.

Parapsychology is past the time when piling up more statistical evidence of the occurrence of psi phenomena could be of much use. Those who are unconvinced will not be convinced by more of such evidence. The best evidence lies in the development of consistent relationships between the phenomena and psychological and other variables. I believe that further advance requires an investment of faith as in any exploratory enterprise, a moderation of the preoccupation with proof that has dominated the field until recently, a pragmatic try-it-and-see approach. In that light, current attempts at sophisticated practical applications of psi take on particular interest. If they succeed, it will not be the first time that pragmatic utilization of a technique or phenomenon has preceded fundamental insight.

When as a brash young physicist I first became aware of parapsychology, I was quite excited by the possibilities for research. What was needed, I thought, was to get some first-rate scientists interested, develop some definitive experiments, and—*Voila!*—a new science would emerge as did electromagnetism or quantum mechanics. Everything I have learned since then has pushed me steadily further from that naive view. The central impression that emerges from all the psi research is that these elusive phenomena are inextricably involved with mind. Attempts to demonstrate dependences upon distance or other physical variables have come to nothing. Such dependences as have been tentatively shown are all psychological, relating psi performance to motivation, state of consciousness, personality factors, and the like.

That observation does not imply that psi is "nonphysical." To me, it suggests rather that physics still has room to grow. The interaction between observer and observed is crucial in quantum theory. It has led to endless speculation and controversy and is still being explored. Several theorists have been trying to interpret psi in terms of quantum concepts (Rush, 1986).

If psi phenomena eventually are explained through extensions of physical theory, that accommodation probably will imply that psi phenomena should not be limited to living organisms. It will rather suggest a principle or agency that must influence inanimate situations as well. This possibility has been suggested by several parapsychologists, but the difficulty of demonstrating it is obvious: how can the experimenter keep out of the experiment?

This concept of psi as a universal principle does not necessarily contradict the evidence of its association exclusively with humans and possibly other organisms. Other principles have been recognized first in living systems: e.g., Galvani's experiments with frog legs revealed the first clues to electrochemical activity. Bats and whales developed sonar distance ranging long before humans invented it. The accumulation of information, or order, is far more prominent in living organisms than in inanimate nature.

I am inclined to believe that the known psi phenomena are but the tip of a very large iceberg. Anomalous phenomena that "make no sense" are intimations of something far stranger and more fundamental than the immediate manifestations suggest. They make sense only when the principles to which they are but obscure clues are traced out and their implications understood. Further, the significance of a well verified anomaly tends to be proportional to its obscurity. An effect that is easily rationalized necessarily does not extend knowledge very much, but one that stubbornly resists explanation usually is an outcrop of a deep lode indeed. It resists explanation because it testifies to the existence of something too strange for present conception.

I believe that psi, if indeed it ever is elucidated, will prove to be strange beyond anything anyone has imagined. Everything we learn about it leads further from the familiar, even from the relatively familiar spontaneous psi phenomena themselves. Sometimes I feel that the key lies right before our eyes, that we are stumbling over it, but are too much bound by our cultural prejudices to see it. Yet I suspect that understanding will come, not through our direct pursuit of the phenomena, but through a convergence of developments in many fields that eventually will so alter the prevailing concept of the world that psi will become implicit. And people will read of our gropings with impatience: "But of course—why couldn't they see it?"

But there is a sense in which psi may be more common, if not more familiar, than we realize. If it is the manifestation of a pervasive natural principle, we must expect that its involvement in human and possibly other activities goes far beyond the sporadic manifestations that we presently recognize. It may seem illogical to suggest that so strange an agency as psi is actually pervasive and universal. But a fish might think water strange if he saw it in a test tube.

Bibliography for Joseph H. Rush

(1943). Some considerations as to a physical basis of ESP. *Journal of Parapsychology, 7*, 44–49.

(1960). The rediscovery of mind. *The Humanist*, May–June, 143–153.

(1964). *New Directions in Parapsychological Research.* (Parapsychological Monographs No. 4.) New York: Parapsychology Foundation.

(1973). Parapsychology's century of progress. In A. Angoff & B. Shapin (eds.), *Parapsychology Today: A Geographic View* (New York: Parapsychology Foundation).

(1976). Physical aspects of psi phenomena. In G. R. Schmeidler (ed.), *Parapsychology: Its Relation to Physics, Biology, Psychology, and Psychiatry* (Metuchen, N.J.: Scarecrow Press).

(1977). Problems and methods in psychokinesis research. In S. Krippner (ed.), *Advances in Parapsychological Research*, vol. 1 (New York: Plenum Press).

(1979). A non-verbal GESP study with continuous recording. In W. G. Roll (ed.), *Research in Parapsychology 1978* (Metuchen, N.J.: Scarecrow Press).

(1982). Problems and methods in psychokinesis research. In S. Krippner (ed.), *Advances in Parapsychological Research*, vol. 3 (New York: Plenum Press).

(1949). With Jensen, A. A reciprocal distance GESP test with drawings. *Journal of Parapsychology*, 13, 122–134.

(1986). With Edge, H. L., Morris, J., & Palmer, J. Physical and quasi-physical theories of psi. *Foundations of Parapsychology: Exploring the Boundaries of Human Capability*. London: Routledge & Kegan Paul.

Nonparapsychological Publications

(1951). Science and a free society. *Tomorrow*, May, 5–9.

(1952). Tree rings and sunspots. *Scientific American*, January, 54–58.

(1952). Yardsticks of the skies. *Colorado Quarterly*, Autumn, 177–178.

(1955). The speed of light. *Scientific American*, August, 62–67.

(1958). The next 10,000 years. *Saturday Review*, January 25, 11–13, 36.

(1960). Prometheus in Tennessee. *Saturday Review*, July 2, 10–11, 50.

(1962). *The Dawn of Life*. New York: New American Library (orig. pub. 1958).

Gertrude R. Schmeidler

Gertrude Raffel Schmeidler is an experimental psychologist who received her B.A. from Smith College in 1932, her M.A. a year later from Clark University, and her Ph.D. from Harvard in 1935. For most of her professional life she taught in the Department of Psychology of the City College of the City University of New York. She became professor emeritus after mandatory retirement in 1982 but continued to teach the graduate course in experimental psychology thereafter.

In 1942 while she was working at Harvard with Gordon W. Allport on civilian morale, Gardner Murphy aroused her interest in parapsychology. Since then she has done extensive research in parapsychology, especially in clairvoyance, telepathy, and the personality characteristics of the psychically gifted.

Dr. Schmeidler has long been admired by her colleagues for her inexhaustible store of creative ideas. She originated the now classic terms "sheep" and "goats" to describe those who accepted or rejected the possibility of paranormal phenomena, and initiated studies showing that these beliefs affect performance on ESP tests.

She illustrates how an academic who has had no personal psychic experiences can become involved in the field and remain interested and dedicated throughout her long and fruitful career. She was president of the Parapsychological Association in 1958 and again in 1971, and president of the American Society for Psychical Research from 1981 to 1985.

Dr. Schmeidler is currently working on her fourth book.

Gertrude R. Schmeidler

Questions and Attempts at Answers

Your editor asked me for answers to five questions and I rashly agreed to supply them — but as you'll see if you read on, one of her questions was too hard for me. I gave up on it and substituted three easier ones. Here come her five questions (and mine) and my best try at coping with them.

#1. How I "became intrigued with and involved in investigating the so-called paranormal?"

The story of how my interest first developed could also be called: "Why I didn't become involved in parapsychology." It began in the Reading Room of the Department of Psychology at Harvard, during the winter of 1934–1935. There was a rack of new books in the center of the front table of that Reading Room, and the new books always tempted us graduate students to dip into them instead of buckling down to work. A new book that year was J. B. Rhine's *Extra-Sensory Perception.* I yielded to temptation and read it.

The book was startling: a set of ideas that on the one hand were so wild that they couldn't really be taken seriously but that on the other hand seemed to deserve acceptance because they were based on careful work and had such impressive data to support them. Like most of the rest of us who read it, I decided to wait and see if someone else could find major flaws in it, and to suspend judgment meanwhile.

The notion of ESP was so stimulating that partly seriously, partly as a joke, I thought about its implications. One that came to mind was that the history of the Salem witchcraft trials might have to be rewritten. If what the book said was true, some of those accused witches might actually have afflicted their neighbors with strange sensations or made them jump and twitch. Maybe some of the witches *were* guilty!

Nothing came of this for a while because I was busy finishing a couple of experiments in perception and memory, my own areas of interest. But in 1935, with a new Ph.D. and a job at a junior college that had no psychology laboratory, I saw that the idea about the Salem witches could be tested even without apparatus. It needed only two subjects, and they were at hand. Two of the other instructors were close friends, were casually friendly with me, and agreed to give me some of their time.

76

We began by my watching one of them, Harriet, while she was reading. I recorded any incidental movements she made, like crossing her legs or twiddling her hair, then counted them up to find the five movements that were most frequent, and wrote each on a slip of paper.

Now we were ready to go. The other friend, Evelyn, sat upstairs. Her instructions were to select one of those slips (all face down, so she wouldn't know which was which) and to concentrate for five minutes on having Harriet make that movement. As soon as the five minutes were up, Evelyn was to choose another slip at random and concentrate on that movement, and so on. I sat downstairs with Harriet, who was reading as before, and recorded all her movements, marking them off into five-minute periods.

After a few sessions it was clear that Evelyn's messages corresponded almost perfectly with Harriet's most frequent movements. Taken at face value, it looked as if Evelyn was making Harriet move. But then I had a horrible thought. Might the two friends have cooked up a practical joke? Could they have agreed beforehand what the order of messages was to be?

This wasn't the sort of question I could ask them, and they weren't interested in having more sessions with a changed procedure. I let the whole thing drop until there was a chance to ask someone knowledgeable about whether it was worth pursuing.

That chance came a couple of years later. I'd stopped teaching when my husband and I were married, because the college was too far from where he worked. It was still the depth of the Depression; I couldn't find a job; and Professor Woodworth at the Columbia Department of Psychology graciously invited me to use that laboratory for another memory experiment and to attend the Department's Colloquia. One of the faculty members at the Colloquium was Gardner Murphy, who was known to be interested in parapsychology. He was, typically, kind enough to give me a few minutes of his time.

I described the procedure to him and my doubts about the results, to see if he'd encourage me to go on with it. His response was chilling. He was polite, but so noncommittal that the message that came through to me was, "Forget it!" And that's why I didn't become involved in parapsychology.

Then how did I become involved in it? Accidentally, and only because of World War II.

Less than a month after the attack on Pearl Harbor my husband was shipped overseas. I stayed at the air base where he'd been stationed, taking care of our three children. All of them were less than two years old, and my evenings were so empty that to fill them I needed something impersonal to think about. This made me write up to Harvard asking if they had a part-time job for me, one that would pay enough to hire part-time household help. The answer came quickly, inviting me to work with Gordon Allport in his project on civilian morale and the war effort.

Once the children and I were settled in Cambridge, it turned out that the job (and the schedule of the part-time nurse, a lovely, grandmotherly woman with whom the children were happy) left me with a couple of extra daytime hours. This was in the early summer of 1942 and two alluring ways of using those hours presented themselves. Lashley, a distinguished neuropsychologist whose work I'd admired for years, was offering a summer seminar; and Gardner Murphy was also up for the summer, offering a seminar on psychical research since William James.

Which should I audit? There wasn't time for both. I decided to sit in on Murphy's first lecture, because one session should be enough to convince me that the whole topic was nonsense. Then the way would be free to audit Lashley's seminar and have no regrets about missing the other one.

But it didn't work out that way. One session with Murphy convinced me that he was so well informed and sophisticated and critical that it would be well worth while to sit in on a second session. The second session left me with the same appraisal, and so did the next and the next. My empty evenings began to be filled with reading in Myers and the Sidgwicks and the other works that Murphy recommended. By the end of the seminar I was in a sadly ambivalent state. The findings from psychical research sounded as if they were too solid to ignore, but the conclusions those findings demanded were too implausible to accept. Was something wrong with the findings? I didn't know. When Dr. Murphy offered me some research funds to do an ESP experiment it was obviously an opportunity to see if ESP would show up under conditions that I knew at first-hand were well controlled. I accepted.

Pilot work began soon, in the hours left over from the morale project; and the sheep-goat hypothesis emerged from the pilot work. The hypothesis was that sheep, subjects who thought ESP *might* occur under the conditions of the experiment (even if they thought it very unlikely or were sure that they themselves couldn't show it) would have higher ESP scores than goats, subjects who were certain that under these conditions ESP was utterly impossible. I ran a series to test it (with a good part of the Harvard Psychology Department looking over my shoulder). Results came out as the hypothesis had predicted. I ran another series, and then another. By the time the third had also significantly supported the hypothesis, the data had dragged me, reluctant and resistant, to accepting the existence of ESP.

Does this answer Dr. Pilkington's question? Not quite; we have to start further back. From early in the 1930s I'd wanted to do research in experimental psychology. Why psychology? Because people interested me. Why experimental? Because the experimental method seemed to me (and still seems) the best way of finding the answers to interesting questions. What kind of research? The kind that studied the most fundamental, important, and mysterious problems about how we function. Memory and perception were good candidates for this, but parapsychology topped them on all counts. It was even more fundamental because it demanded revising the conventional materialistic views of the universe. It was more important because of its extraordinarily broad implications. It was even more mysterious, perhaps because it had been least explored. Once the affirmative ESP results had come in, the die was cast. Parapsychology seemed to me the most challenging area within psychology. I became involved with it, and have been involved ever since.

#2. What do I feel was my "most important contribution to the field?"

This one needs a crystal ball! I don't know that any of my work will be important in the long run. Let me pretend instead that there were three different questions along these lines and then speak to those three.

2a. What's been my most quoted work? No problem here; it's those sheep-goat studies, along with their continuation over the next several years.

2b. What do I think deserves to be remembered as an important contribution? This is easy too; it's the one where I've worked the hardest: a mix of theory and supporting data to show that—to put it simply—psi functions as our other abilities do.

But that's too simple to be accurate. It needs some phrase like *mutatis mutandis* added to it. Each ability has its own framework and limitations, and it's only within these specifics that any general rules apply. Even if fatigue or fever or encouragement or stress have comparable effects on solving mathematical problems or writing poetry or estimating time intervals or psi scoring, each ability will respond somewhat differently from the others. What is important, I think, is both the invitation to study motivations, moods, body states, etc., as determinants or modulators of how psi functions, and evidence that this is an invitation worth accepting—and such evidence comes from my own many affirmative findings in research projects that deal with variations on the theme.

Most of my projects studied fairly large groups of subjects and found that individual differences in achievement needs, mood, impulsiveness, or some other such variable related to ESP success or failure. But the invitation holds for special, gifted subjects too. Let me give you an example from a professional psychic, Mrs. Caroline Chapman, to show how it might be done.

Mrs. Chapman agreed to do "proxy sittings." In this double-blind method, she was asked for messages about one or another "absent sitter." The note-takers who asked her, the "proxy sitters," did not know the absent sitters. Messages were coded, then all were sent to each of the absent sitters. The absent sitters did not know which messages were intended for them, but scored every item to show whether it was true or false for themselves. Statistical analysis then showed if they had scored more items true in the messages intended for them than in the messages intended for others. Mrs. Chapman also took a Rorschach test.

The messages she gave were long and varied. They mixed general comments about personality with specifics, sometimes numerous and detailed specifics, about objects or events or other people associated with the absent sitter.

And how did her Rorschach come out? It also was long and varied. Sometimes her responses to the inkblots were uninteresting: vague or banal interpretations of the whole blot or of common details. Some of her responses were brilliantly original, with good form level, and these latter were typically based on a small, unusual detail that had captured Mrs. Chapman's attention.

What was especially interesting was that the ESP scores paralleled the Rorschach scores. General comments about the sitter's personality were negligibly interesting, but the detailed, well-elaborated descriptions, e.g., of a piece of furniture associated with the absent sitter, were often brilliantly successful; and when evaluated separately these latter were statistically significant.

Throwing everything into the same hopper obscured Mrs. Chapman's psi ability. If I had done originally what in fact I did only post hoc, and scored only the specific messages which corresponded to the times that her normal cognitive processes were best, it would have been a more appropriate way of handling the research.

The invitation to parapsychologists, then, is to begin research with a sympathetic study of a psychic — or a nonpsychic, for that matter — in order to find when the person functions most effectively in nonpsychic activities. The next step is to predict good psi scores only when the psi test is run under those conditions. We'd find, for example, that some people need long warm-ups and others need to give quick, spontaneous responses; some feel happier if they cooperate in planning the research and others if an authoritative experimenter tells them what to do; some benefit from hypnosis and others resist it; some prefer simple repetitive tasks and others prefer tasks that are varied and complex. I think we'd find that predictions were supported, and learn that no single procedure is likely to be appropriate for everyone.

Anyone who accepts this invitation can hope to find that when there are exceptions to a general rule, the exceptions are lawful too. Take the sheep-goat generalization. A shy, self-conscious sheep is likely to score low, as is a sheep who dislikes the experimenter or resents the particular method, or one with a bad headache; but on the other hand a goat who enjoys outlandish challenges might be expected to score high. The invitation is to recognize the complexity of all of us, to plan research accordingly, and thus to learn more about how psi functions.

2c. Which of the things I've done might turn out later to be important?

This is the question that's fun to answer, because it's such a free guess. It could be anything from the work that led to a peculiar theory of telepathy to a plan for research on the survival of personality after death. Here are five that may or may not eventually be considered important.

(i) Telepathy. My peculiar theory is that telepathy functions in two quite different ways. One is obvious: the transfer of specific bits of information. The other way is a telepathically induced profound change in how a person functions. You don't need examples of the first type, but I'll give you some for the second.

First, a formal experiment. There were fifty pairs of agents and percipients, each pair tested in widely separated rooms with closed doors. The percipient was to guess at four sets of colored ESP cards and expected the agent to send messages about each of the cards. In fact, though, the agent sent those messages for only two sets. On one set the agent hoped *without seeing the cards* that the percipient would get them right; and on one set the agent hoped *without seeing the cards* that the percipient would get them all wrong.

If telepathy were only transfer of bits of information, scores on the two runs where the agent did not see the cards should have been about the same, but they weren't. When the agent sent the message, "Get them wrong!" the ESP scores significantly reversed. Percipients who had scored high when the agent saw and tried to send the cards now scored worse than chance expectation; and percipients who had scored low when the agent tried to send, now scored high. The data seem to force us to conclude that a person's ordinary way of functioning can be changed to its opposite by telepathy.

The conclusion ties in with a good many other things that have been reported. One example is that for even the greatest psychics, like Mrs. Leonard, some sitters repeatedly found weak or no results while with other sitters the results were repeatedly strong. Perhaps the difference came only because some sitters were more pleasant socially, though this did not seem to be true. I suggest instead that some sitters produced a psychic helping and others a psychic hindering that directly affected performance. (Doesn't this have big implications for the effect of a friendly or a hostile social atmosphere? Or for psychic healing and hurting? Or for the experimenter effect?)

(ii) Theory of psychic space. On the troublesome question of how psi can be effective at a distance, I have been speculating that perhaps there is a psychic space that is different from physical space, and that psi works by changing relationships within psychic space so as to bring the target close. It would be as if psi produced a temporary warp in psychic space, a "rubber-sheet" effect. I speculated further along these lines: If there is such a warp, might it act as a bridge on which others can cross if they are in the same psychic space? It may be an absurd line of overambitious speculation, but at least it's a testable one. Unfortunately I've done only one small experiment to test it.

Any test of this theory requires, I think, two conditions. One is a cooperative psychic. The second is others who are so congenial with the psychic that he or she is willing to admit them to share his or her psychic space. Jane Goldberg helped me run the single test that was done (Schmeidler & Goldberg, 1974). Alan Vaughan was the psychic; he brought a group of friends to be the others. All tried at the same time (but in separate rooms) to respond to the same set of psychometric objects. Alan scored significantly well; his friends did not. On the items on which he succeeded, however, his friends had more success than on the items on which he failed. The results surely do not prove the theory but at least they are consistent with it, as far as they go. I've longed to repeat the research, but it hasn't been easy to find a psychic and a circle of associates who are all cooperative rather than competitive and who are willing to work under these conditions.

(iii) Precognition. Here, I think (though it sounds horribly conceited to say so) my data have clarified the problem enough to show that some popular theories are on the wrong track. These theories describe precognition as dependent on observation or feedback. Put briefly, they argue that the causal chain works backward. It starts with the person observing the event. Then that observation, as it were, travels backward in time so that the person learns about it before it happens. But my experiment (Schmeidler, 1964) found evidence for precognition when neither the subject nor anyone else ever observed what the event was.

It was an experiment where subjects made ESP calls. Weeks or months later, the calls were fed into a computer. The computer had made a random selection of targets. It then scored the calls against the targets, and for this key series it printed the total correct but never printed what the target was. No one ever knew the targets. The feedback or observational theories just don't mesh with the finding that precognition occurs under this condition. Instead we need a theory of psi and time which includes mental access to at least some future events which will never be observed, by anyone.

(iv) How PK functions. Some day—who knows?—a byproduct of the PK experiment that Ingo Swann did with me (Schmeidler, 1973) may be considered important for understanding PK. The experiment was designed to see if Ingo could make a distant object change its temperature. His target was a thermistor attached to a polygraph (a recording instrument). Ingo tried to make his target hotter or colder according to what I told him. The records showed that even when the thermistor was shielded, he succeeded.

Because the polygraph could record temperature change in four channels at once I had three other thermistors, nontargets, scattered around the room. Some were arranged so that they were near enough to the target for Ingo to associate them with the target, and they changed temperature as the target did. But the others were more interesting. When they were psychologically separated from the target (even if they were physically close) they showed temperature changes *opposite* to the target's. If the target became hotter, they became colder, and vice versa.

This implies that when Ingo made the target hotter, he was not somehow sending heat into the room, nor was he somehow pulling in heat when he made it colder. Rather he had been changing the balance among the random heat differences that were already present. He was acting like Maxwell's imaginary demon, who opened a trap door to admit the right kind of particle when it came along. It suggests that psi, like life itself, might be a reversal of entropy, an increase in the meaningfulness of the world.

(v) Survival of personality after death. The evidence for survival seems strong to some and weak to others. Surely one of the reasons for its seeming weak is that it is retrospective: The strongest cases are the ones that happen after a person dies, and can therefore be investigated only in retrospect. Another reason may be that when there is systematic research, the same expectations are made for everyone but evidence comes in for only a few. Critics then claim that the negative cases outweigh the positive ones.

The method that I proposed (Schmeidler, 1977) to cope with these two problems makes predictions, and the predictions are different for different people. It would be expensive to do and I've not been able to get it funded; but if some day someone uses it and it gives clear results, it may be considered an important contribution.

It involves having volunteers give a great deal of information about themselves to sympathetic and well-trained interviewers. We then predict, on the basis of this information, who (if there is survival after death) will give one type of message, who will give different types, who will give none at all. After the volunteers die, proxy sitters who know nothing about them or about the predictions will ask mediums for messages. Blind coders will sort the messages into the predictive categories. Simple statistics will show which predictions, if any, were accurate.

The pretty part of this is that almost any outcome could be meaningful. If all predictions fail or if all succeed, we know where we are. But if certain ones repeatedly succeed while others repeatedly fail, it could suggest what happens at and after death. Perhaps the personality traits on which successful predicitons are based represent an integral, stable part of ourselves, just as a small child's level of activity or of social responsiveness is likely to be rather stable over the years. But now consider the predictions that repeatedly fail. Perhaps the traits on which the failing predictions are based are so tied to everyday life or to one's body that they are altered at death, just as a toddler's lisp or way of walking will alter as the child grows older. Of course if no one ever picks up the idea and uses the method, it will not have been a contribution.

#3. What would I "have done differently" or "what beliefs . . . were changed?"

The beliefs part of this double question is easy. Before I worked in parapsychology I was a naive materialist; by now I'm not. (What am I now? Well, you might call me a tentative interactionist. Certainly the interactionist vocabulary is the most convenient one, but there's a hope that it can be translated into simpler, unitary terms after someone produces a grand, unified theory which embraces physics and psi, and of course brings in physiology and psychology too.)

What should I have done differently? I could have prevented one frustration, something that's annoyed me over the years and that I now see is my own fault. People sometimes cite my research, and that's fine; but hardly anyone ever pays attention to my theories. Probably that's because the theories are usually tucked into the Discussion section of research reports. What I should have done was to write more theoretical articles.

To make them effective, I now see, they should have been long-winded, polysyllabic, assertive, and immodest. They should have labeled any idea as a part of a Theory-with-a-capital-T. They should have pulled in lots of prior findings to show that the idea — oops, the Theory — is broadly explanatory. They should have mentioned others' theories only to show how inadequate the others were, but not mentioned this Theory's gaps. And each should be followed by another long, pompous article continuing the line of thought. (Maybe the book I'm working on now will help? Probably not; it's hard to change my style.)

#4. "What unusual experiences . . . exceeded even [my] 'boggle threshold?'"

The biggest boggles came for me when the data, no matter how I sliced them, shaped up to show that yes, there was ESP, or yes, there was precognition, or yes, there was PK; in other words, when other people's or my experiments forced me to recognize that my biases were wrong.

But this may not be what the question means. Maybe it really asks about personal events that I boggled at interpreting as psi. There were a few of these; here are four of the strongest.

When World War II ended, the army sent my husband and me for a few days of "R & R" in Atlantic City. One morning when I was up before my husband, we agreed to meet on the boardwalk opposite our hotel. After quite a while of gazing at the ocean I turned around, and that first time I turned was just when my husband was coming out of the hotel. The good timing couldn't have been knowledge of how long he'd nap and how long he'd take to dress. It might have been ESP, of course, but I boggle at thinking it was. It might have been just coincidence.

Years later, on a visit to Charles Honorton's laboratory, it turned out to my dismay that I was expected to play a psi game on one of Honorton's fancy computers. My score was significantly high—but after all, that's to be expected for about one person in twenty, just by chance.

One evening Dr. Irvin Child was kind enough to bring Bill Delmore and a group of Bill's friends to our home. Among other things he did, Bill took a deck of our cards and riffled through them so that one fell, face down, on the floor. He asked me what it was; I named a card; he flipped it over, and it was the one I had named. Here the odds against chance success are one in fifty-two and, especially in the context of the many remarkable things Bill did that evening, I wonder a little if it was only chance that I was right at such long odds.

But I can't help boggling also at the feeling I had at the time. The feeling was that Bill's rhythm had caught me up in his own way of responding, and that what I said wasn't so much my own impression as a response to Bill, or from Bill, or with Bill—that Bill was making something psychic happen through me. I shouldn't really boggle at this feeling though; it's consistent with my speculation that a psychic bridge can be created when a psychic makes a warp in psychic space.

The last and wildest experience I owe to Dr. Michael Grosso, who occasionally visited our parapsychology seminar at City College. One day he brought with him a piece of a helicopter which had killed the pilot when it crashed in South America. The helicopter was taken to New Jersey for examination and there had been various ghostly experiences while it was in the hangar there.

Mike passed the piece among us and asked for impressions. Many of our impressions were right. (The only one I remember is my own: a picture of high snowy fields in the Andes. I thought it couldn't be right because the air up there was too thin for a helicopter to fly, but when I asked Mike he said that yes, the crash was in the Andes, in the snow.) While we were still excited at the whole tale and at how correct our varied impressions had been, the bell in the building began jangling. This was the wrong time for it to ring: neither the beginning nor the end of a class period, nor a fire alarm, nor a fire drill (all of which anyhow would have been regular sounds, not these irregular ones). None of us could remember ever hearing it ring that way, although all of us except Dr. Grosso had worked in the building for years; nor have I heard it ring that way since. But I boggle at the thought of this being a psychic manifestation instead of a one-time electrical malfunction.

#5. "What advice [would I give] to young people entering the field as to what areas . . . are of utmost importance and as to what pitfalls to be aware of?"

Lots of advice. The most important is: Have a second string to your bow. Prepare to earn your living in some other line of work. Don't expect parapsychology to pay in money for the time you spend on it. It may repay you in intellectual excitement and emotional satisfaction and the feeling that you are advancing knowledge or helping others; but two things that it's not likely to give you are a decent income, and all the answers to all your questions.

If you can find a way to combine parapsychology with your paid work, you're fortunate (as I have been). If not, think of it as a demanding hobby, a hobby where the standards are so rigorous that unless you're very good, you're not good enough.

What area should you choose within parapsychology? Whichever you find most exciting, as long as it is practical in terms of the limitations of your own set-up.

How should you go about it? First plan out in detail what you want to do. But before you start, write to a parapsychologist or two. Describe the goal of the work, the planned method—in detail!—and ask for advice or comments. Then don't feel distressed if there's no answer; sometimes people are sick, or off on a trip. Instead send the same letter to another parapsychologist or two. Also, don't be distressed if a response suggests lots of changes in your plan. This is a field in which it's easy to make mistakes, and my guess is that every seasoned parapsychologist has learned the hard way some mistakes that you don't know of, yet.

One last kind of advice is for when you talk about parapsychology. Of course you must speak the truth as you see it, but this doesn't mean that you need to keep on talking until you've emphasized every part of the truth, to everyone. It's wise, I think, to adjust what you say (within the limits of honesty) according to your listener. For instance, if a skeptic becomes fiercely emotional, it's a good idea to stop the conversation (or to make some joke and shift to another topic as fast as you can) because factual or logical answers are a waste of words when emotions are strong. If the person you're talking with is an ardent, misty-eyed believer, you could be encouraging paranoia if you emphasize the statistical significance of psi's affirmative findings. You are more likely to be wise and helpful if instead you emphasize our ignorance about whether any single ESP guess will be a success or a failure.

I'll end with the advice that's hardest for me to follow. Even though you and I agree that parapsychology is the most interesting of all possible topics, don't let it monopolize a conversation. Stop talking about it as soon as someone else introduces another subject; concede that the other topic might be of some interest too.

Bibliography for Gertrude R. Schmeidler

(1943). Predicting good and bad scores in a clairvoyance experiment: A preliminary report. *Journal of the American Society for Psychical Research,* **17,** 103–110.

(1952). Rorschachs and ESP scores of patients suffering from cerebral concussion. *Journal of Parapsychology,* **16,** 80–89.

(1958). Analysis and evaluation of proxy sessions with Mrs. Caroline Chapman. *Journal of Parapsychology,* **22,** 137–155.

(1959). Exploring the parameters of research variables. *Journal of Parapsychology,* **23,** 238–250.

(1960). ESP in relation to Rorschach test evaluation. (Parapsychological Monographs, No. 2.) New York: Parapsychology Foundation.

(1961). Evidence for two kinds of telepathy. *International Journal of Parapsychology,* **3,** 5–48.

(1961). Are there two kinds of telepathy? *Journal of the American Society for Psychical Research,* **55,** 87–97.

(1962). ESP and tests of perception. *Journal of the American Society for Psychical Research,* **56,** 48–51.

(1964). An experiment in precognitive clairvoyance. Parts I-V. *Journal of Parapsychology,* **28,** 1–27; 93–125.

(1964). Scores related to feelings of success. Part V, Precognition. *Journal of Parapsychology,* **28,** 109–125.

(1966). Quantitative investigation of a "haunted house." *Journal of the American Society for Psychical Research,* **60,** 137–149.

(1967). ESP breakthroughs: Paranormal effects in real life. *Journal of the American Society for Psychical Research,* **61,** 306–325.

(1970). High ESP scores after a swami's brief instruction in meditation and breathing. *Journal of the American Society for Psychical Research,* **64,** 100–103.

(1971). Mood and attitude on a pretest as predictors of ESP retest performance. *Journal of the American Society for Psychical Research,* **65,** 324–335.

(1971). Respice, adspice, prospice. *Proceedings of the Parapsychological Association,* **8,** 117–145.

(1971). Parapsychologists' opinions about parapsychology, 1971. *Journal of Parapsychology,* **35,** 208–218.

(1973). PK effects upon continuously recorded temperature. *Journal of the American Society for Psychical Research,* **67,** 325–340.

(1977). Looking ahead: A method for research on survival. *Theta,* **5,** 2–6.

(1977). Methods for controlled research in ESP and PK. In B. Wolman (ed.), *Handbook of Parapsychology* (New York: Van Nostrand Reinhold), 131–159.

(1982). Individual subjects, differing groups, but general conclusions. *Parapsychology Review, 13*, 7–11.

(1982). A possible commonality among gifted psychics. *Journal of the American Society for Psychical Research, 76*, 53–58.

(1982). Psi and states of consciousness. *Theta, 10*, 6–9.

(1983). Psi scores and personality: Basic questions and a theory to encompass the answers. *Parapsychology Review, 14*, 1–3.

(1985). Field and stream: Background stimuli and the flow of ESP responses. *Journal of the American Society for Psychical Research, 79*, 13–26.

(1987). Psychokinesis: Recent studies and a possible paradigm shift. In S. Krippner (ed.), *Advances in Parapsychological Research, 5* (Jefferson, N.C.: McFarland).

(1958). With McConnell, R. A. *ESP and Personality Patterns*. New Haven: Yale University Press.

(1969). With Lewis, L. A search for feedback in ESP. Part III: The preferential effect and the impatience effect. *Journal of the American Society for Psychical Research, 63*, 60–68.

(1970). With LeShan, L. An aspect of body image related to ESP scores. *Journal of the American Society for Psychical Research, 64*, 211–218.

(1971). With Lewis L. Alpha relations with nonintentional and purposeful ESP after feedback. *Journal of the American Society for Psychical Research, 65*, 455–467.

(1974). With Goldberg, J. Evidence for selective telepathy in group psychometry. In W. G. Roll, R. L. Morris, & J. D. Morris (eds.), *Research in Parapsychology 1973* (Metuchen, N.J.: Scarecrow Press), 103–106.

(1975). With Brier, B., & Savits, B. Three experiments in clairvoyant diagnosis with Silva Mind Control graduates. *Journal of the American Society for Psychical Research, 69*, 263–272.

(1975). With Maher, M. Quantitative investigation of a recurrent apparition. *Journal of the American Society for Psychical Research, 69*, 341–352.

(1977). With Jackson, M., & Franzoi, S. Effects of feedback on ESP: A curious partial replication. *Journal of the American Society for Psychical Research, 71*, 147–155.

(1981). With Maher, M. Judges' responses to the nonverbal behavior of psi-conducive and psi-inhibitory experimenters. *Journal of the American Society for Psychical Research, 75*, 241–258.

Emilio Servadio

Emilio Servadio was born in Genoa in 1904. He received his doctoral degree in 1926 with a thesis on hypnosis in legal medicine. He was a pioneer of psychoanalysis in Italy and became a member of the International Psychoanalytic Association in 1935, an honorary professor of psychology in 1938, and from 1964 to 1969 was president of the Psychoanalytic Society of Italy, which he helped found in 1932. In 1962 he founded and served as president of the Psychoanalytic Center of Rome and became honorary president of the Società Psicoanalitica Italiana in 1982.

In 1937 he cofounded the Italian Society of Parapsychology from which he resigned in 1981 and became president of the Parapsychological Association of Italy the following year. He is also a member of the Parapsychological Association and European correspondent and advisor to the Parapsychology Foundation.

In addition, Professore Dottore Servadio is an honorary member of the American Academy of Psychoanalysis and an associate member of the (British) Royal Society of Medicine.

Professor Servadio has made an enormous contribution to the field. He, along with Jan Ehrenwald, Jule Eisenbud, and Montague Ullman, was a pioneer in the area of telepathy in the psychoanalytic setting. He is largely responsible for the organization of serious parapsychological research in Italy.

He speaks several languages fluently, including impeccable English, in which he has proved to be a witty and charming raconteur. He has a wide knowledge and deep affection for music and poetry, is a connoisseur of fine food, of wine, and of life.

It was my great pleasure to see Emilio again in August 1985 at the Parapsychology Foundation's conference in Rome. We sat in a rather noisy, bustling corner of the elegant Hilton and recorded the interview that follows.

Emilio Servadio

Interview, Rome, August 24, 1985

Rosemarie Pilkington: How did you first get interested in parapsychology?

Emilio Servadio: Well, first of all, as a young boy I attended some hypnotic performances on stage. I was fascinated by them. When these demonstrations were prohibited in Italy I started reading books on hypnosis and about the prehistory of hypnosis, which is the whole era of so-called Mesmerism, or animal magnetism. And then, lo and behold, I could see in the books that several *magnétiseurs* of the beginning of the eighteenth century and up to the nineteenth century had strange experiences during their magnetic endeavors: Some of their patients were telling them things that they couldn't possibly know otherwise. So that was called *lecture de pensée* or reading thoughts, but also clairvoyance or *lucidité*. But, I said, this is a fascinating realm also. It's not only hypnosis — there is something else. Of course it was psychical research, or *métapsychique* as it was called by the French since 1905. The book I came across immediately was the treatise by Richet, *Traité de Métapsychique*, which came out in 1922. I also started reading the *Revue Métapsychique* as well as some other publications.

But at the same time I was puzzled. I asked myself, "How can these things be approached?" because there was scant knowledge of psychology in Italian universities at that time and the books that I'd read in psychology taught me nothing about paranormal phenomena. Then I discovered a second book that had a great influence on me, the *New Introductory Lectures on Psycho-analysis* by Freud (1933). And then I said, "But this is real psychology; this is what I was thinking of." I then started to see if it was possible to use the psychoanalytic instrument as a tool to make a further approach to parapsychological phenomena. My first essay along these lines was published in the review *Imago*, which was edited by Freud, in 1935. It was a paper I had been bold enough to present to an International Congress of Psychoanalysis, in German. The title was *Psychoanalyse und Telepathie* (1935/1953). But I had published many articles before: My first article, on posthypnotic suggestion, was published when I was 17. These

90

were my "beginnings" to a subject that I have written and lectured on many other times.

R.P.: And so that's how you got to get into the field.

E.S.: Yes; then from those years onward I was always more or less informed about parapsychological endeavors and I've attended many parapsychological conferences; I've made innumerable speeches in several places in this world. I have had a great many publications in both fields, psychoanalysis and parapsychology. In fact, my next two books will comprise my scientific essays: one book, essays in psychoanalysis and the second on parapsychology.

R.P.: Did you have other personal experiences that intrigued you?

E.S.: Yes, of course, personal psi experiences, such as dreams and so on, but mainly the experiences that I could explore, which gave me plenty of food for thought, were those of my patients. Several of them produced telepathic phenomena in the psychoanalytic setting and I reported on some of these episodes in my papers.

R.P.: I was referring to your very early years, before you became an analyst.

E.S.: When I was 13 a wonderful book came under my eyes. That was *The Great Initiates* by Edouard Schure, a famous French essayist. This book deals with the major esoteric figures such as Hermes, Krishna, Jesus Christ, and so on, and I was extremely taken with it. But for a time I left this line aside because I wanted to be scientific. My thesis for my doctoral degree was on hypnosis, the medical-legal viewpoint. But then later, this interest in esoteric practices, theories, and conceptions, was revived and for many years I have been deep in reading Indo-traditional books and essays as well as books and papers belonging to other traditions.

I spent seven years in India; from 1938 to 1945. I had already read a great deal about Indian metaphysics and Indian tradition. But, of course, the Indian issue became extremely lively and, in the end, I continued after I came back to Italy in 1946, and I joined a group of very serious people who were rather busy in searching and practicing Yoga and other techniques, meditation, etc. This was and is still a very important realm for me.

R.P.: There was an allusion today to the LSD experiments you were involved in.

E.S.: Yes, I was one of the first to get interested in so-called psychedelic experiments. I took LSD three times. The first time I took it in the presence of Eileen Garrett at the Piol in France, which was then the seat of the Parapsychology Foundation. Then I took it twice more. I took also, five times, psilocybin which is a synthesis of the active chemical in the Mexican psychedelic mushrooms. So I did experiments on myself and then several people took LSD or psilocybin under my supervision. Then, due to the generosity of the Parapsychology Foundation, we conducted a series of experiments trying to see if these substances could promote or encourage extrasensory perception. This was a very difficult and long project. The results were published in book form by the Parapsychology Foundation in 1964.

R.P.: What do you feel was the most important thing that came out of that experimentation?

E.S.: Not much, to be quite frank. One particular subject gave some evidence of ESP but I still wonder if it was because of the drug we had given him or if he was just one of those subjects who can have ESP experiences with or without drugs. Certainly we did not all reach the point where we could state conclusively that LSD and/or psilocybin really have effects on extrasensory perception. This is absolutely in the negative. So these experiences have hardly been repeated. There were some other experiments in Holland and in Denmark but the results were not encouraging so they've stopped.

R.P.: You told me some time ago that you had taken LSD together with Eileen Garrett.

E.S.: Yes, I took LSD once and another time took psilocybin with Eileen Garrett. It was a remarkable experience because with Eileen I was so much attuned that this attunement became something almost extrasensory during our experiences. A glance or a smile could be sufficient to convey to the other person something one felt or thought. It was a most extraordinary experience.

R.P.: You mean you had complete communication between you?

E.S.: Yes, but this didn't happen the first time because that time Eileen didn't take LSD, only I took it—a rather high dose for me. I went through some nasty moments and some very beautiful ones. That was one of the only two peak experiences that I had in my life because at a certain point I was absolutely ecstatic under LSD and the medical man who attended this experiment asked, "What are you feeling?" and I said, "For the first time in my life I know what Love with a capital L is." The second time was in India while I was taking a walk in a field. It was approaching sunset. I was not thinking of anything in particular, just enjoying the afternoon, when suddenly, like a thunderbolt came this incredible experience—a cosmic experience which could not be expressed in words. It lasted only a couple of minutes but it is unforgettable. So I had these experiences twice; once under LSD and the other without any preparation of any kind.

R.P.: In your experience with Eileen Garrett: How did she react to the drugs?

E.S.: She liked LSD but she didn't like psilocybin very much. Eileen said that LSD made her fly and psilocybin was a bit reductive, or having to do with emotions, things like that. For me it was almost the contrary. For me LSD was ego-disruptive and psilocybin was affect-provoking. Under psilocybin everybody was so very kind and loveable and I was thinking that at some international conference, if psilocybin could be given the delegates they would immediately come to an agreement!

R.P.: It doesn't make you nauseated?

E.S.: No. It depends on the dosage. I like it. I took it once alone — all by myself, and I liked it. It's more difficult to obtain than LSD. If you know someone you can get some LSD ampules but not psilocybin.

R.P.: What ideas did you have as a young person when you came into the field that were later changed by your experience?

E.S.: It was a continuous process. I know, feel, and appreciate much more nowadays than I did, say, ten or twenty years ago. I think I have expressed this in my papers. Those who have read my recent papers have seen my progress. My recent work is much more valuable than my early writings. After all I have published more than 200 papers, eight or nine books, and innumerable popular articles for newspapers, magazines, etc.

R.P.: If I were a young person who hadn't read your works and wanted to know what the most important thing was, in your opinion, that you have contributed to this field, what would you tell me?

E.S.: From a scientific viewpoint, certainly it is the series of papers I've written about the psychoanalytic, psychodynamic approach to parapsychological problems. This is, I think, my major contribution in the field and has been widely recognized. You will find references to my works in any books by Ehrenwald or Eisenbud.

R.P.: Yes, in his chapter in this book Jule Eisenbud mentions you and how glad he was when he found that you, a kindred spirit, existed here in Italy.

E.S.: Oh yes, Jule and I are like brothers. I first met him in 1953 in Utrecht, at the big International Conference of the Parapsychology Foundation. We had already been corresponding. Jule and Jan Ehrenwald were there. It was an historic occasion.

R.P.: It must have been very exciting for all of you to meet each other. The three of you and Joost Meerloo.

E.S.: The encounter. Yes, very exciting. I remember that Jule quoted me in one of his addresses, and you know how eloquent he is. Mrs. Frances Bolton, who was one of the richest women in the United States and who gave great financial support to the Parapsychology Foundation was alive then as was Mrs. Garrett. It was a very grand occasion.

R.P.: One of the questions I have asked the other contributors to this book is if they have had any experiences that exceeded even their "boggle threshold," as Renée Haynes would say. Have you had any you'd like to share?

E.S.: Well, on more than one occasion I could see that a paranormal phenomenon produced either in or outside of the analytic setting was not interesting from a parapsychological viewpoint but it made sense in the context of the psychoanalytic situation because it was not just like a bolt from the blue; it was determined by an interpersonal moment, a moment in the interpersonal relationship. For instance, during a conference of the Parapsychology Foundation, I was able to report on a now famous case of a telepathic dream had by a young girl about a ring that her fiancé bought, not for her, but for his mother.

R.P.: Ah, yes, the "Guido and Luisa" case.

E.S.: Yes, it has been quoted many times. That was striking. I remember that Martin Ebon, who was then the secretary of the Parapsychology Foundation, was so enthusiastic about it that he sent a telegram to Mrs. Garrett saying that I had been the highlight of the conference with my report on the convergence of parapsychology and psychodynamics.

I have had deep-seated personal experiences of several kinds which cannot be made public because when I say that I had peak experiences that's all I can say; they cannot be expressed in words. I've had other experiences of many kinds, particularly in love relationships. But I still am persuaded that what I felt under LSD, Love with a capital L—dynamics, color, energy—was extraordinary.

R.P.: People seem to use LSD for different purposes.

E.S.: I know. But I always say to people who want to have an experience with LSD under my supervision, "You must have a purpose, an aim, not just want to see what happens." No, no, no, no.

Federico Fellini, who was very much involved in table tilting and mediumistic seances, wanted to make things a little clearer. So he took LSD under my supervision. And that was the beginning of his liquidation of spiritism and when he made the famous movie *Giulietta of the Spirits*.

R.P.: I don't understand what you mean by his "liquidation" of spiritism.

E.S.: He was a spiritist. He was convinced that those entities that came out during the sessions were real entities you see, but then after having realized, in the LSD experience, during which he was talking with those entities, and afterwards when we discussed the whole situation, that these entities were just projections of his own images, he stopped having spiritistic seances and he made the movie. In the movie the seances become ridiculous. The curious thing was this, that when the movie was shown in the cinema, several people asked me if Fellini had done something with LSD because the colors were so psychedelic.

R.P.: Fellini had been in analysis with you hadn't he?

E.S.: For a few months. Then he went to Dr. Bernhardt who was a Jungian because Fellini cannot do away with his fantastic world and Freudian analysis was too severe for him so he went into Jungian analysis instead.

R.P.: But the LSD experience he had with you must have opened his eyes quite a bit to a different world and must have been a valuable experience for him.

E.S.: Absolutely.

R.P.: Weren't you friends for a long time?

E.S.: We are still very close. A new book has been prepared about him now because he will receive the Golden Lion Award in Venice. I was asked to write my impressions of Fellini for it. I wrote one page and sent a copy to Federico. He wrote back to say that I had said the most acute things about him that had ever been said. He was absolutely taken with it.

R.P.: What advice would you give to young people who are coming into the field as to what you feel is important, what they should pursue, etc.?

E.S.: They should have a good scientific basis whatever they do because it is useless to try to make a difficult climb up a mountain without being sure of one's own muscles, heart, training, etc. So one cannot go into parapsychological realms without a good basic scientific preparation. The scientific method is only one approach. After one has really grasped, has digested the scientific method one can think that perhaps the scientific approach is not the only one possible to face certain phenomena. But this must come afterwards. Not immediately. Because otherwise you fall into amateur and irresponsible approaches like the great majority of people who say they are "interested" in parapsychology. They don't know one thing about science. On the other hand, there are scientists who have tunnel vision. They are positivistic, materialistic, mechanistic, etc. Still, one must have more than anything else a good philosophical base. It is not necessary that they be physicists, or mathematicians, but they should have a good grasp of the scientific method. Otherwise, it would be like doing something about one's own organism and then trying to make artistic gymnastics — one must start from the beginning.

R.P.: What area of parapsychology do you feel is the most important, that needs the most concentration?

E.S.: Well of course I was always interested in the psychodynamics of paranormal phenomena, and the psychoanalytical and psychodynamic study of them. This, to me, has been by far the most important line. I must confess I know very little about statistics. I respect the statistical approach but I don't feel that is my cup of tea at all. Much more, philosophical considerations and qualitative phenomena are of great interest to me — so-called spontaneous phenomena, which in my considered opinion are not spontaneous at all. They don't come like bolts from the blue; they have a certain conditioning of some kind.

These are my own interests. I don't say everybody should follow in my path. If a mathematician wants to experiment using the methods of J. B. Rhine, that's fine. But, nevertheless, for many years I've been convinced that so-called paranormal phenomena are just arrows pointing in the direction — not proving it — but indicating the direction of a Reality, with a big capital R. A reality that exists beyond our empirical reality of everyday life. In Eastern thought they say that this is a world of duality; that beyond this world of appearance is a world of the only unitarian reality. I think that paranormal phenomena give us some hints, as for thousands of years some of the great sages of the East have indicated, that this is a world of Maya, of appearance. And I repeat, I believe paranormal phenomena are indicative arrows that point to this assertion.

Bibliography for Emilio Servadio

(1937). Processes of identification and conversion phenomena in a mediumistic clairvoyant. *International Journal of Psychoanalysis,* 18, 89–90.

(1953). Psychoanalysis and telepathy. In G. Devereux (ed.), *Psychoanalysis and the Occult* (New York: International Universities Press; orig. pub. 1935).

(1955). A presumptively telepathic-precognitive dream during analysis. *International Journal of Psychoanalysis,* 36, 27–30.

(1956). Telepathy: a psychoanalytic view. *Tomorrow,* IV.

(1956). Transference and thought-transference. *International Journal of Psychoanalysis,* 27, 1–3.

(1958). Telepathy and psychoanalysis. *Journal of the American Society for Psychical Research,* 52, 127–133.

(1962). The normal and the paranormal dream. *International Journal of Parapsychology,* 4, 4, 5–23.

(1965). *Psychology Today.* New York: Garrett Publications (translation of Italian edition orig. pub. Milan: Longanesi, 1961).

(1966). The dynamics of so-called paranormal dreams. In G. E. von Grunebaum, & R. Caillois (eds.), *The Dream and Human Society* (Berkeley: University of California Press).

(1969). Preconscious process, ESP, and creativity. In A. Angoff & B. Shapin (eds.), *Proceedings of an International Conference on Psi Factors in Creativity* (New York: Parapsychology Foundation).

(1976). On the psychology of mediumistic states. *Parapsychology Review,* 7, 1, 26–28.

(1977). *Passi sulla via iniziatica* (Steps on the Way of Initiation). Rome: Edizioni Mediterranee.

(1978). Psiche e psicoanalisi. *Rivista di Psicoanalisi,* **24**, 327–335.

(1964). With Cavanna, R. *ESP Experiments with LSD 25 and Psilocybin: A Methodological Approach* (Parapsychological Monograph No. 5). New York: Parapsychology Foundation.

Zorab, G. (1974). A tribute to Emilio Servadio on his seventieth birthday. *Parapsychology Review,* **5**, 4, 7–11.

Renée Haynes

Renée Haynes, who was born on July 23, 1906, is "the eldest child of Edmund Sidney Pollock Haynes, lawyer, author, and defender of individual liberty, and Oriana Huxley Haynes (née Waller)," granddaughter of T. H. Huxley. She was educated in various day schools including an open air Theosophist establishment and the French *Lycée* in London. She read law and history at St. Hugh's College, Oxford, where she achieved bachelor's and master's degrees.

After graduation she wrote a novel, and worked as a magazine writer and publisher's assistant before her marriage, in 1929, to Jarrard Tickell, the journalist, novelist, and biographer. She continued writing novels and articles until joining a branch of the British Council during World War II.

Mrs. Tickell writes that during this time she hitchhiked the 12 miles to and from work initiating "a ghost story about a luminous redhead seen signalling on dark winter evenings beside a main road." It was she in "a red glove making hitchhiker's signs illuminated by a pocket torch."

She stayed on with the British Council after the war becoming founder and director of its Book Review Department, sending new books to foreign critics for review in their own countries' media. This was one of the ways through which she got in touch with overseas parapsychologists such as Emilio Servadio in Rome.

After her retirement in 1966 (the year her husband died) she became editor of the *Journal* and *Proceedings* of the Society for Psychical Research, which she had joined in the late 1940s. She is an elected member of its council and has written numerous articles about psychical research and related subjects.

Renée Haynes relates that when she married, Alec Waugh advised her to continue writing under her maiden name so as not to have her work confused with her husband's. She took his advice.

Mrs. Haynes' writing, like her conversation, is interesting, informative, and delightful, full of her charm and wit. She says she enjoys conversation, "high brow and otherwise, seeing new places, meeting people, cooking, eating, and family life."

Renée Haynes has authored numerous books and has contributed to many others as well as to symposia and various periodicals in Britain, Europe, and the United States. She has been heard on radio in Britain and has appeared on television there and in France.

Renée Haynes

Aspects of Psychical Research

My original interest in the paranormal may well have sprung from what British nannies used to call con-*trary*-ness, opposition to something generally accepted; in this case a family atmosphere of rationalism, implicit and explicit. It seemed to be taken for granted that the universe and all its manifestations would ultimately be explained in terms of scientific materialism, and that it was in general morally wrong to yield faith to any belief that could not be tested by scientific methods or justified by scientific standards. This dogma was most clearly set out for me by a much loved grandmother (daughter of T. H. Huxley, who had had to struggle for his own opinions and conclusions against such "religious" ideas as that the world had been created in 4004 B.C.). She talked to me about such matters of this sort quite early in my life.

My parents would, I think, have assented to her assumptions in general, but with many reservations. They did not usually discuss ideas and theories with me, and I was a teenager before I discovered that my father had had some vivid extrasensory experiences, one of a personal "haunting" (which did not deter him from writing a book on the whole critical of *The Belief in Personal Immortality* [1913/1925]), one of "voices" apparently talking Norman French in a very old house, and one of a crowd scene in a road, where the figures were all in early Victorian dress. These last two seem to have been of what may be called the "videotape recording" kind.

It was also in adolescence that I found out my mother had a marked capacity for psi. It is perhaps interesting that she had sporadic attacks of migraine which would keep her faint, sick and in pain for days at a time. Incidentally, her psi sensitivity did not necessarily coincide with her actual attacks of migraine. Later, after getting to know various other sufferers, I began to wonder whether this illness could be correlated with some talent for ESP. I do not know of any organized medical study of the possibility and have so far failed to stimulate any competent person or group to set one going.

Henri Bergson (1914), no less, first suggested that the separate senses had very probably been evolved to filter incoming impressions of all kinds, so that the perceiver should not be totally bewildered by an overwhelming

101

influx of undifferentiated "news." Since then Joel Elkes (1967) has written of the limbic system in the brain consisting of "remarkable cell groups able" in waking life "to choose and label what is useful" in incoming surges of information, "and to ignore what is irrelevant" (p. S7). Does migraine, I wonder, break down this ability to ignore, to reject, or at any rate to withhold attention from what is not immediately relevant, thus making it easier for paranormal data to rise into consciousness and heightening what has been called the Boggle Threshold?

Migraine is moreover believed to "run in families." Tradition has it, and observation seems to confirm tradition, that extrasensory capacities do so too. It would be most interesting to know whether any direct connection exists. I have tried to work out—but only on the most general and anecdotal basis—a pedigree recording the incidence both of extrasensory perception and of migraine in several generations of a family I know; but I do not have their entire medical history. Any general study would of course have to take into account the possibility that this talent is more easily recognized and accepted in such families, as musical talents were, say, among the Bachs, and that its incidence might not even be noticed in others, which could also repress any tendency of the kind, reprove it as "telling stories" or, more tolerantly, label it "fantasy" to be forgotten.

Where children in general are concerned Berthold Schwarz's (1971) systematic daily record of his own and his wife's experiences of telepathy with their offspring, from birth to adolescence, is an extraordinarily valuable source of information, in length, in careful detail, and in being the work of an eminent psychiatrist. Ernesto Spinelli's (1977) more formal experimental studies with small children have suggested, interestingly, that the psi factor seems to emerge in them before they learn to read, and comes to fade thereafter. (Here, of course, the reader must become aware of the importance of the "experimenter effect," a theory that includes the notion that certain types of warm, relaxed, open personalities obtain more significant results than other, more impersonal investigators.) One returns again to the supreme usefulness of what could be called Ecological Observation, records of how spontaneous extrasensory perception crops up, so to speak, in the context of daily living. I believe that—reasonably detached—mothers at home with their children could play a most valuable part in noting psi phenomena in their growing families, the background in which they appear, and the differences in age, temperament, and order (eldest, second, third . . .) in the young creatures involved. Celia Green (1960) discussed this last problem in a small-scale analysis of reported cases but more would be interesting.

Mothers of course tend to be overworked and exhausted by the vagaries of their young, especially temperamental toddlers, and may not have time or inclination to do this; but oddly enough, it can have a calming effect. I did it a little with my own children, and wish it had been possible to do more. It was fascinating to find that when one of them began to talk about "Uncle Bun," a rather erratic friend who only occasionally looked in, that "Uncle Bun" was liable to turn up within the next day or two—and equally so when another little boy, asked out to lunch by a small school friend, insisted that he *must* take a bunch of flowers for his hostess, got his way, and on return said he was quite right; he'd had no idea, but it had turned out to be her birthday.

I was also fascinated when one of my sisters told me that, counting (in one room with a door open to the landing) the family handkerchiefs to go to the laundry she had heard her three-year-old daughter next door—who could not have seen what was going on either directly or in a mirror—chanting the color of each as it was dropped on the pile, as it were "white, blue, white, green, yellow. . . ."

I am pretty sure that no one ever recorded instances of ESP during our childhood; but it is possible that what I now recognize in myself as small and rather trivial incidents of this sort may also have served to develop an interest in the paranormal. That they *are* trivial, and have no apparent usefulness (unlike Rosalind Heywood's [1964] impressions which could tell her, for instance, what time to meet an unexpectedly early war-time train) is in itself interesting because it suggests that psi experience is not always or necessarily dramatic or intensely meaningful, but is interwoven with the general nature of things.

Psi can flash with varied degrees of clarity into the minds of grown up human beings, especially those who have not been conditioned to use the "tunnel vision" narrowing of attention in which many academics are trained. It can crop up sporadically in children; and it seems to affect the behavior of animals, tame and wild. Witness the dog heard to howl at the time of his master's death far away; the cat left behind with neighbors when its owners move house, that treks directly across country to rejoin the family at the new house to which they have moved a long distance by road; the young stork of one species hatched from an egg placed by Dutch ornithologists in the nest of another and brought up with its foster brothers and sisters which when migration time came round left them—and their elders—to follow the different route of its ancestors. Note that however much birds may find their way by awareness of variations in the earth's magnetic field, some unexplained form of cognition must surely be involved if an individual joins the route at the point where these variations *begin* to operate.* This sort of behavior chimes well with the arguments of the late Sir Alister Hardy, F.R.S. (1966/1967), zoologist and parapsychologist, that different

---

*My late husband, Jerrard Tickell, heard about this episode when in Holland on business. I wrote it down at once but forgot to ask its source.—R.H.

species develop "group minds" to which those of individual members are telepathically linked and may contribute their own experience.

I began to notice my own odd little perceptions when, as an undergraduate I found that I was still aware—though 60 miles away—of my mother's sporadic and irregular attacks of migraine, during which I had helped to look after her when I was at home. I checked my impressions by letter.

I did not begin to write down any of my dreams until I came across J. W. Dunne's *Experiment with Time* (1927/1958) in the early 1930s. I have done so on and off ever since then, particularly if they were very vivid. Some remained completely without explanation. Others seemed partially to fit in with later events, like pieces from an incomplete mosaic. A few looked as if they were fulfilled in detail. Unfortunately some of the earlier records have vanished after several house moves, but here are three. On June 29, 1963, I dreamed of seeing from an upstairs window apes going by in a topless double decker bus. The dream seemed grotesque and pointless but I wrote it down. On July 16 one of my sons sat for an examination about which he was very anxious all the morning. In the afternoon, to cheer him up I took him to the zoo where we saw a collection of apes (who had taken part in an exhibition "tea party") being wheeled away in a tall-sided barrow. I immediately recognized those packed furry simian heads as part of my dream.

On October 20, 1979, I dreamed of a grassy green slope, at the top of which stood a beautiful Greek temple. A friend and I climbed up to it in bright sunshine and found young black and white bull calves playing around it. We played with them as if they had been kittens. On the 26th I went to stay with one of my sisters, then helping to run a large farming estate in the Cotswolds. She told me it had been decided that that year's Friesian bull calves should have the names of Greek gods beginning with P. She already had Pluto and Poseidon, what could I suggest: I put forward Priapus—very suitable for stud purposes—and Phoebus Apollo. Perhaps it should be noted that Friesian cattle are black and white.

These two were piecemeal dreams. The fulfillment of the third was witnessed and noted by another son at the time when it happened. I had gone to stay with him at a house he had been lent in Switzerland. The night I got there I dreamed we drove off to an open air swimming pool, and that just after our arrival, a party of mentally handicapped boys with satchels on their backs came shambling down to bathe, giving a rather gruesome impression. Next morning, when my grandsons clamored over breakfast to go swimming, their father picked out on a map—he did not know the district—what looked like a suitable place, and drove us all there. Before we set off I told him of the dream. As we approached the landscape became familiar; and just as we got there that orderly, sinister procession of mentally handicapped boys came shambling down with their satchels. It was all grotesquely uncanny.

My small capacity to receive psi impressions was once tested experimentally by the late Penelope Balagh, who successfully made me "hear" someone (herself) calling my name from 70 miles away (to my great anxiety, as I was alone in a house with a helpless invalid).

A few frightening episodes of apparent "haunting" in strange places made me anxious to find out and explain more about the paranormal. One of these, at some lodgings in Oxford, not far from the river Cherwell, where I repeatedly "heard footsteps" running along the passage outside my room and skipping outside the door, may, I now think, be an example of the "underground water" phenomenon noted by Guy Lambert (1955).

All this deals with two of the questions raised by Dr. Pilkington as to how the writers of these essays became intrigued with and involved in investigating this field, and what beliefs have been changed through their experiences. I ought perhaps to add that as I grew up I heard various country stories about such things: the noisy ghost once known at the manor of Compton Casey (again very likely explicable in Guy Lambert's terms), the odd things said to happen at Burford Priory, and the disturbances at the Old Rectory nearby (said to have been the background of a very ugly murder) which apparently went on into the years of World War II alarming the evacuee mothers and children sheltered there.

I do not think I was much influenced by the fact that Miss Jourdain, principal of my college, had written with her colleague, Miss Moberly, the famous *An Adventure* (1911/1932), an account of that postcognitive experiences of Versailles at the time of Marie Antoinette. The book's first impact was spent (though it has been revived and reinforced in recent years by able French investigators). Miss Jourdain died before I went up, and the only relevant thing I ever heard in this connection came from one or two older undergraduates who said her psychic talents had sometimes served to discover offenses against the then rather strict chaperonage rules.

Another matter for discussion was what I feel have been my chief contributions to psychical research. The first is in emphasizing how many disciplines are involved in it (listed in alphabetical order): aesthetics, anthropology, biology, ecology, electromagnetism, folklore, history, philosophy, physics, physiology, psychiatry, sociology, theology, zoology, and most significant of all in those concerned with humans, the two-way interaction between psyche and body.

From this multiplicity of approaches springs the need to discuss the subject in a language understood by experts in all the disciplines involved; a language comprehensible to all educated people, avoiding the allusive — and elusive — jargon, the technical "shorthand" vocabulary of any one specialty. Such shorthand may well be indispensable for fast communication between specialists researching in the same field, but it is no good for general use. Some of those unaccustomed to the idiom may misinterpret it if they comprehend it at all. Others may assume that it is very clever precisely because they do not understand it and accept without criticism arguments based on its findings. Most insidiously dangerous of all possibilities is that this jargon may be accepted and used as a status symbol, evidence that the user is one of an important elite. (Anyone who has ever used a "secret language"—like Ug-Ug or Pig Latin—at school will appreciate the situation, though of course researchers will not *originate* their language for the same motives.)

For all these reasons I have tried, wherever possible, to avoid and to oppose the use of jargon, which tends to spread like the creeper known in England as Old Man's Beard over the idioms of every activity from income taxation to insurance, from law to local government as well as parapsychology. If highly technical terms have to be used in print a clear glossary should appear at the end of every paper or book containing them. I would urge moreover where the concepts of mathematics and physics are involved, as is increasingly the case with psychical research, some attempt should be made to indicate their basic meaning which is often far from clear to those educated in the humanities. What used to be called the "Two Cultures"* do *not* coincide with the activities of the intuitive and the reasoning areas of the brain, as is sometimes taken for granted. They form a contrast between the results of experience — sensory, extrasensory, factual and emotional — and complex webs of abstract mathematical formulae, carefully constructed and tested in theory and in practice.

Reason and intuition occur in both cultures. Perhaps there may one day be a College of Translators from one mode of thought to the other. It should be dedicated to the demolition of ivory towers of Babel, and should bear in mind the old story of the two computers. One, used to translate English into Russian, had to deal with the sentence "The spirit is willing but the flesh is weak." The other, used to translate Russian into English, was given the result to translate back again. It reappeared as "The whisky is good but the meat is poor."

I hope to have illustrated the possibility of interaction between the two cultures in a biography of the eighteenth century Prospero Lambertini, later Pope Benedict XIV (Haynes, 1970), renowned for his learning, wisdom, open mindedness and honesty by contemporaries all over Europe, including Montesquieu and Voltaire. Born in Bologna, whose ancient and up to date university was vividly aware of the scientific and medical

---

One, that of the humanities—history, art, law, literature—and the other, that born of Descartes and Newton in which technology and statistical science are paramount.

developments of the time, Lambertini took a deep and informed interest in such subjects. (His own microscope is still to be seen in London at the Wellcome Institute for the History of Medicine.) Trained in law and history, he worked for many years as devil's advocate in canonization proceedings, pointing out why this or that candidate should not be recognized as a saint.

As Cardinal Archbishop of Bologna, Lambertini compiled and wrote with scholarly integrity a long treatise (1734, 1738) on the subject of psychical phenomena, some of whose findings are still in use. He wrote in Latin, the international language of learning at the time, used by scholars of most nations (who often published their work in their own languages as well). It was the general use of Latin that enabled him to read so widely. He distinguished very clearly between occurrences that could—or might later—be explained by science, occurrences due to paranormal causes, and occurrences that could be ascribed to the direct action of God in response to the prayers of people very close to Him, a response which would show that they should be recognized as saints, honored and imitated.

Paranormal activity—which he called "natural prophecy" and sometimes "the preternatural"—occurred in animals as well as in humans. Among the latter it was the illiterate, or the barely educated, who were likely to have "preternatural" experiences; it was rare among academics. In general a certain sort of temperament seemed to be involved. Where healing was concerned he considered very carefully the part played by suggestion, whether conveyed by medical placebos or by complete trust in the healer, and the influence of the mind—especially the imagination—on the body. There, as everywhere, he laid down detailed criteria to test and evaluate what were put forward as miracles, resulting from the direct action of God. He stressed the need to examine evidence, and those who gave it, with the strictest exactitude.

In general, though he distinguished very clearly between the preternatural and the miraculous, Lambertini did not consider paranormal abilities either essential to or incompatible with holiness. Thus, though at first he boggled at reports of the curious levitations of Joseph of Cupertino, he was finally convinced that they had indeed taken place by the evidence of a number of reliable and independent witnesses and canonized him, *not*, he said, on account of these peculiar flights, which were irrelevant, but because of his sanctity, his humility, and his love of God. Miracles acceptable in accordance with Lambertini's criteria had occurred to confirm this after his death.

Lambertini also discussed among many other themes telepathy, precognition, out-of-body experiences, phantasms of the living, and "ecstasy." This term included trances, voluntary and involuntary, hibernation (whose results are now known to resemble closely those of "transcendental medita-tion," lowering blood pressure, body temperature, and the rate of breathing) and the dissociated states of people concentrating on intellectual work, which, as the author points out, can have odd side effects, from dyspepsia, if the work is undertaken too soon after meals, to social solecisms and danger in time of war.

But I must not go on too much about Lambertini, whom I love for his scholarly integrity, his intellectual curiosity, his kindness, his wit, and the sense of justice rather than of feminism which made him nominate the brilliant young scientist Laura Bassi as a foundation member of a learned body, the Academia Benedettini, and persuaded the Senate of Bologna University to offer to the philosopher, linguist, and mathematician Maria Gaetani Agnesi the chair of mathematics.

It is startling to realize the extraordinary breadth and depth of his own knowledge, ranging from Greek thinkers to Aquinas to Descartes to Newton, from the nature of "strange occurrences in the sky" such as comets, to earthquakes. Citing astronomers such as Galileo and Tycho Brahe, he insisted that none of these phenomena is to be thought miraculous (though "a natural occurrence *may* be used as a supernatural sign"—an early hint, perhaps, at the idea of synchronicity). In medicine he cites most of the authorities of his day including Sydenham on gout, Harvey on the circulation of the blood, and Robert Boyle on his experimental work on respiration, and his curious definition, significant of that time and times to come, of the human body as "an hydraulico-mechanicall engine."

Lambertini had, of course, three points of reference in his study of psi phenomena: the natural, the paranormal, and the divine. This last could operate either directly or through one of the others. In our own times it is often assumed that only two such points remain. Each is in danger of transformation, by ardent excavators, into a pitfall.

One is the assumption that only experimental work, preferably carried out in laboratory conditions, and always examined by statistical methods is important, first to reiterate *ad infinitum* that psi really occurs, and then to test the climatic, physiological, psychological, and sociological conditions in which it emerges most clearly and massively.

The other is—taking the existence of psi for granted, which I should myself think justified by the results of over a century of careful research of every kind—to assume that whatever psi conveys would be accepted without question as good and valuable, and that sensitivity to it should be stimulated, increased, and trained as far as possible. This second pitfall has been dug, perhaps, by the growing reaction against purely mechanistic explanations of the universe "and all that therein is." Psychical research has after all done much to show that human beings are more than automated machines, producing consciousness as an odd and painful byproduct, machines whose workings can be understood, and whose reactions can all be predicted, after all the relevant data are assembled.

The first assumption ignores such facts as that persons differ from one another (as their fingerprints show very clearly), that paranormal capacities are at least as unpredictable as, say, talents for painting, and that to envisage individuals as no more than statistics fodder is to destroy valuable opportunities for investigation (as a builder could destroy the potentially important living plants of a field by concreting them over as the floor of a botanical research department).

This approach to parapsychology — and other disciplines — has brought about undue reverence for that sacred object the computer, undue faith that it is Always Right:

O who shall dispute a
Fallacious computer?
That harsh operator
Who queries its data.

Those data are exact and quantitative. They cannot include the temperament, or the inherited genes, or the intellectual background of any individual, label or measure the extent to which his family history and his personal life have influenced the emergence or nonemergence of paranormal faculties in him. They can blithely ignore historical circumstance, as when a learned attempt was made some years ago to assess whether some letters being attributed to Saint Paul had really originated with him. A computer was used to work out how often certain words occurred in them, and to see how the result compared with their frequency in letters known to be genuine. No one noted the fact that he often dictated his correspondence to secretaries: Witness his remark on one occasion, "You see how long a letter I have written to you *with my own hand*" (my italics). Nobody realized the other face, known to anyone who has ever dictated material to secretaries, that they sometimes take down, or read out a hastily scribbled script, the *sense* of what has been said rather than its exact wording (so that "beef" might replace "steak").

The second assumption, that all manifestations of psi should be given implicit faith and trust, is in its own way just as one-sided as the first. It excludes not only mathematical evidence but the use of ordinary observation, reason, and choice: reason, the power to appraise all suggestions, normal or paranormal, that may well up through the unconscious mind; and choice, the use of the will to ignore or to reject what may be said, from a longing to commit suicide to a compulsion to defraud.

Auntie Unconscious does *not* always know best. Impulses transmitted from extrasensory sources may, like any other impulses, be good, bad, or indifferent and need to be examined before they are carried out. We all know the results of Hitler's passionate plea for "thinking with the blood" nearly fifty years ago. Equally unfortunate may be a British para-psychologist's recent recommendation that all who seek paranormal heal-ing should adopt an uncritical attitude of relaxed "atavistic regression," uncritical faith in psi.

What has become of Lambertini's third point of reference, the direct action of God? It seems to have been covered up with rubble from the two pitfalls. From the mechanistic point of view, which ignores the problem of consciousness, it has become totally irrelevant. One remembers the story of what happened when a naked girl opened the front door of an advanced and trendy school, and the startled visitor said "Good God!" "There *is* no God," she replied, and shut the door.

From the other approach springs the idea that all that's numinous is in itself divine.

Each pitfall exhales its own smell, its own phosphorescence. The wind blows them all together to form the cloudy idea that all faiths are founded on the same basis: a basis despised as superstition on the one hand and reverenced as inspiration on the other.

The relationship of extrasensory experience to religion is an urgent question for psychical research. One aspect of this is what psychiatrists call "projection," the fact that where some people dream—as the chemist Kekule did—of the inspirations that may come to them, others *perceive* in waking life, as it were outside themselves, the images of this thought. Visualizers may "see," audiles may "hear" them.

Something very like this, but unrelated to anything objective, can occur when the chemistry of the brain goes wrong (as is thought may happen in schizophrenia). The mechanomorphics instantly assume that all the phenomena of "projection" can be ascribed to insanity.

Anatole France was perhaps the most distinguished of the turn-of-the-century "rationalists" to explain in this way the "voices" heard by Joan of Arc. It was left to Andrew Lang (1908), anthropologist, scholarly folklorist, and president of the Society for Psychical Research in 1911, to point out, after close study of the records of her trial, that there was no evidence of any other kind that could indicate mental illness. The point has been made that with all sensory hallucinations the need is to discover whether they are veridical, that is, correspond with any exterior reality.

Perfectly sane people have had veridical hallucinations. The archives of psychical research are full of well-authenticated cases in which indi-viduals had become aware by means of psi of matters going on far away of which they would otherwise have had no knowledge at the time. It is in-teresting that Joan's persecutors, like the pitfall diggers of our own time, had only two points of reference. Today, as happened with Anatole France, the possibility of direct divine action is omitted. In their era the neutral quality of paranormal phenomena—as in Lambertini's "natural prophecy"—was ignored. The alternative accusation brought against Joan was that if she was not insane, then she was a witch, and had learned, as shamans do, the techniques of developing and using psi as a source of power, techniques then believed to be essentially evil.

There is no need to accept either the paranoid fears of medieval lawyers or Margaret Murray's (1921) elaborate theories about widespread and highly organized witch cults, to regard with some unease the contention that all paranormally, or subconsciously, transmitted ideas and impulses should be accepted and carried out with simple faith in their goodness. It is over a hundred years since Charcot, at the Salpêtrière hospital in France, succeeded in inducing telepathy under hypnosis. Vasiliev (1963) and others in the U.S.S.R. have more recently demonstrated the same ability. Is there not some danger that urging obedience to apparently spontaneous ideas and impulses may, if it succeeds, eat away the ability to use judgment and common sense? And does it not follow that "psychic sensitivity" should *not* always be encouraged and trained to the greatest possible extent, unless this process is accompanied by some form of education in ethics, discrimination, and reasoning? This sort of education might also contribute to individual — and communal — stability, and to resistance to political and commercial propaganda (especially in the form of subliminal advertising).

I believe that parapsychological awareness, a faculty that like all other faculties can be used in conscious life for good, bad, or neutral purposes, is present in all sentient creatures, and may have played a part, as Rupert Sheldrake (1981) has argued, in developing their chemical and physical habitat. It is certainly present, as Alister Hardy (1966, 1967) has shown, in every living species including our own, in which it can appear as instinct, as flashes of precise knowledge, or as a means to the contemplation and service of God.

I am afraid I have ranged in this piece over many subjects in which I am not an expert, but perhaps it may be useful, if one cannot be a polymath, to function as an intellectual rag bag, some of whose contents may be pieced together to form a pattern.

Bibliography for Renée Haynes

(1967). *Telepathy and Allied Phenomena*, rev. ed. London: Society for Psychical Research.

(1970). *Philosopher King: The Humanist Pope Benedict XIV.* London: Weidenfeld & Nicolson.

(1970). Review of periodical literature, 1969. I. American. *Journal of the Society for Psychical Research,* **45**, 354–357.

(1972). *The Hidden Springs: An Enquiry into Extra-Sensory Perception*, rev. ed. Boston: Little, Brown (orig. pub. 1961, London: Hollis & Carter).

(1972). Postscript to Koestler, A. *The Roots of Coincidence* (New York: Random House).

(1976). *The Seeing Eye, the Seeing I: Perception, Sensory and Extra-Sensory.* New York: St. Martin's Press.

(1977). Philosophy and the unpredictable: A retrospect. In B. Shapin & L. Coly (eds.), *The Philosophy of Parapsychology: Proceedings of an International Conference Held in Copenhagen, Denmark, August 25–27, 1976* (New York: Parapsychology Foundation).

(1980). The trees and the wood: The importance of historical and legal evidence in psychical research. *Parapsychology Review,* **11**, 3, 17–21.

(1982). Either/or ... both/and ... plus. *Parapsychology Review,* **13**, 4, 9–12.

(1982). *The Society for Psychical Research 1882–1982: A History.* London: Macdonald.

(1983). Changing fashions in psychical research. *Parapsychology Review,* **14**, 4, 1–4.

(1984). Levitation. *Parapsychology Review,* **15**, 4, 13–15.

Hans Bender

Hans Bender was born in Freiburg in Breisgau, Germany, on February 5, 1907. Professor Bender, who holds doctoral degrees both in psychology and medicine, has been a professor of psychology, a prolific author, and a distinguished parapsychologist. His writings include works on many areas of psychical research such as ESP, mediumship, spiritual healing, and—what he is perhaps most noted for—psychokinesis, including metal bending and spontaneous phenomena (RSPK) or "poltergeists."

Dr. Bender was instrumental in integrating the study of parapsychology into the curriculum of the University of Freiburg and still heads the Institut für Grenzgebiete der Psychologie und Psychohygiene, (Institute for Border Areas of Psychology and Mental Hygiene), which he founded in the 1950s. Since that time, too, he has edited the *Zeitschrift für Parapsychologie und Grenzgebiete der Psychologie*. He was president of the Parapsychological Association in 1969, is an honorary member of the Società Italiana di Parapsicologia, and a corresponding member of the Society for Psychical Research.

Hans Bender

A Positive Critic of Superstition

I became involved in investigating the so-called paranormal by my "spiritual" constitution. Anyone who is interested in astrology may detect this in my chart. In the middle of my natal sky (*medium coeli*) is the planet Neptune, which in classical as well as modern astrology is significant for transcending the realm of the already known and accepted.

The trigger for this spiritual constitution was an experience I had in London when I was 17 years old. I was invited by a family who used to practice the Ouija board and who believed firmly in a contact with the beyond. I was impressed by the obvious "intelligent" production of messages but skeptical in regard to their alleged origin, namely "discarnate" entities. This primary experience influenced my life.

I followed the unforgettable courses of Pierre Janet in the College of France in Paris when I was studying there. Janet's classical work, *L' Automatisme Psychologique* (1930), provided me with the scientific framework for my observations. At the same time I was also impressed by the literary movement called Surrealism of Andre Breton, Nadja, and others, which claimed that unconscious productions have specific literary value. I soon found out that such productions were not produced by the unconscious but were artificial.

In the meantime I was engaged in experiments with automatic writing, automatic spelling, and so on. In the Psychological Institute at Bonn University I noticed that the unconscious "messages" I got by such techniques were different from the literary productions of the group of Surrealists.

In these experiments with automatisms I was confronted with the problem of extrasensory perception. Some of the automatic productions included traces of information which their producers could not have obtained through the normal senses. This preliminary research led to my Ph.D. thesis, which linked subconscious productions to extrasensory perception. It was the first thesis in the German academic world which approached the problem of paranormal information and yielded positive results. I am deeply grateful to the former director of the Psychological

Institue of Bonn University, Professor Erich Rothacker, who generously accepted this unorthodox work despite harsh criticisms by his colleagues.

It may be through synchronicity that the famous publication by J. B. Rhine, *Extra-sensory Perception* (1934), appeared at the same time. The Ph.D., on the basis of my work on *Psychische Automatismen*, was awarded me on February 12, 1936. This early involvement in parapsychological research determined my lifelong project: to integrate psychical research into the academic framework. In order to be as well equipped as possible to realize such a project I studied medicine in addition to my studies of psychology and philosophy.

I was especially motivated by my wish to introduce parapsychology into the university of my native town, Freiburg im Breisgau. The first step in this direction was to give an air of legitimacy to parapsychology, which at that time was far from being accepted by the scientific establishment. The representative frame had to be found — a difficult task considering my limited resources. I decided to become a businessman for four years to obtain enough funds to build an impressive institute, which was in a very generous way supported by the city of Freiburg.

The institute building on a hill over Freiburg was inaugurated in June, 1950, and was named the Institute für Grenzgebiete der Psychologie und Psychohygiene (Institute for Border areas of Psychology and Mental Hygiene). This dual focus stemmed from my understanding that dealing with the occult involved not only the problem of establishing psi as a reality through scientific methods but also the problem of changing the attitude of the general public towards the phenomena. This attitude seemed to be composed of different trends; negativism and skepticism on one side and irrational beliefs bordering on superstition on the other. I tried to cope with these different attitudes by promoting a slogan: "*Positive Kritik des Aberglaubens*" (positive criticism of superstition).

After the WWII, I returned to my native town and was nominated guest professor at Freiburg University. I began by teaching normal psychology and psychopathology. I slowly introduced the topic of parapsychology in my courses and lectures. The reactions of the students were very positive and the university authorities were tolerant and positive and finally decided to promote the establishment of a chair of psychology and border areas of psychology. This chair was transferred to me in 1953 and was transformed into a full professorship in 1967. Thus for the first time in German academic history parapsychology was fully integrated into the psychological curriculum.

When I retired in 1975 the chair was given to my successor, Professor Johannes Mischo, who had been my assistant at my Institute. At present there exist two institutions in Freiburg, the department of psychology and border areas of psychology at the University of Freiburg, and the independent institute which I founded myself and of which I am still the director.

I feel that my most important contribution to the field has been primarily the already mentioned integration of parapsychology into the university curriculum. In regard to research work I feel that I have realized a pluralistic approach: laboratory work on one side and — more important for me — field work on the other. I realized very early on that paranormal events are likely to occur in an emotional field and that pure laboratory work is difficult and does not succeed in creating such a field unless one is using strategies such as a situation of competition betwen subjects or providing a trusting, effective relationship between experimenter and subjects. If these factors were lacking, we soon realized, positive results were very rare and not at all outstanding.

Other highlights of my research work were: investigations regarding frequency and contents of paranormal experiences in the general population, empirical studies on psychic healing, investigations of astrology as a scientifically established diagnostic method, precognition in dreams, research in qualitative psychokinesis (PK), for example metal bending, and from the beginning of my work in the Freiburg Institute, research in so-called poltergeist phenomena.

In the last decades I was especially intrigued by problems of the documentation of such elusive phenomena; their reality, social context ("group mind"), the psychological constitution of the focus persons, the frequency of the phenomena, and the conditions which further their production.

Another major aspect of my work dealt with mediums. There are the famous "chair experiments" with the Dutch sensitive, Gerard Croiset (see Tenhaeff, 1960; Roy, 1982) who claimed, sometimes with success, to predict who at a future time would be sitting on a specific chair.

Closely connected with the scientific proof of the existence of psi phenomena is the problem of practical application. Numerous experiences with many mediums showed that no medium had a criterion by which to judge if her impressions were pure fantasy, contained some "psi flashes," or were a mixture of both. I feel it is of utmost importance that a medium be able to distinguish psi impressions from other intruding images and thoughts.

At the risk of seeming arrogant I must confess that I don't feel that I have made essential mistakes. Neither do I feel that beliefs that I had when I entered the field have been fundamentally changed because of my experiences. From the very beginning I expected that nearly all is possible in the "magic reality."

Some unusual experiences that exceeded even my "boggle threshold" occurred very recently. During the most unusual poltergeist case with which I was confronted, I heard a direct voice that I could register on tape. I now have reason to believe that the persons involved had, for weeks or even months, "conversations" with what they regarded as a "direct voice." I confess that I had some difficulty in realizing that the phenomenon of direct voice is not stranger than the "penetration of stones" into a closed room (an almost classical feature of poltergeist phenomena and a phenomenon which has very often been related to me).

I don't think that I can give general advice to young people who wish to enter the field, but I think that it is most important that young people should realize the illusions and challenges of psychical research and adopt a flexible attitude oscillating between emotional engagement on one side and cool distance on the other. This oscillation should accompany all research work in this most difficult field.

Bibliography for Hans Bender

(1936). *Psychische Automatismen. Zur Experimentalpsychologie des Unterbewusten und der ausersinnlichen Wahrnehmung.* Leipzig: Barth.

(1936). *Zum Problem der ausersinnlichen Wahrnehmung. Ein Beitrag zur Untersuchung des "räumlichen Hellsehens" mit Laboratoriumsmethoden.* Leipzig: Barth.

(1938). The case of Ilga K.: Report on a phenomenon of unusual perception. *Journal of Parapsychology, 2,* 5–22.

(1957). Praekognition im qualitativen Experiment. Zur Methodik der "Platzexperiments" mit dem Sensitiven Gerard Croiset. *Zeitschrift für Parapsychologie und Grenzbegiete der Psychologie, 1,* 5–36.

(1966). The Gotenhafen case of correspondence between dreams and future events: A study of motivation. *International Journal of Neuropsychiatry, 2,* 398–407.

(1970). Differential scoring of an outstanding subject on GESP and clairvoyance. *Journal of Parapsychology, 34,* 272–273.

(1971). An investigation of "poltergeist" occurrences. In W. G. Roll, R. L. Morris, & J. D. Morris (eds.), *Proceedings of the Parapsychological Association, 5, 1968,* 31–33.

(1971). New developments in poltergeist research. In W. G. Roll, R. L. Morris, & J. D. Morris (eds.), *Proceedings of the Parapsychological Association, 6, 1969,* 81–102.

(1972). The phenomena of Friedrich Jurgenson. *Journal of Paraphysics, 6,* 65–75.

(1973). Parapsychology in Germany. In A. Angoff & B. Shapin (eds.), *Parapsychology Today: A Geographic View* (New York: Parapsychology Foundation).

(1973). The gap between belief and proof. In W. G. Roll, R. L. Morris, & J. D. Morris (eds.). *Research in Parapsychology, 1972* (Metuchen, N.J.: Scarecrow Press).

(1974). Modern poltergeist research: A plea for an unprejudiced approach. In J. Beloff (ed.), *New Directions in Parapsychology* (London: Elek Science).

(1977). Meaningful coincidences in the light of Jung-Pauli's theory of synchronicity. In B. Shapin & L. Coly (eds.), *The Philosophy of Parapsychology* (New York: Parapsychology Foundation).

(1977). Further investigations of spontaneous and experimental PK by the Freiburg Institute. In J. D. Morris, W. G. Roll, & R. L. Morris (eds.), *Research in Parapsychology, 1976* (Metuchen, N.J.: Scarecrow Press).

(1980). Transcultural uniformity of poltergeist patterns as suggestive of an "archetypal" arrangement. In W. G. Roll (ed.), *Research in Parapsychology, 1979* (Metuchen, N.J.: Scarecrow Press).

(1982). Poltergeists. In I. Grattan-Guinness (ed.), *Psychical Research: A Guide to Its History, Principles and Practices* (Wellingborough, Northamptonshire: Aquarian Press).

(1983). Meaningful clairvoyant mistakes. In W. G. Roll, J. Beloff, & R. A. White (eds.), *Research in Parapsychology, 1982* (Metuchen, N.J.: Scarecrow Press).

(1976). With R. Vandrey & S. Wendlandt. The "Geller effect" in Western Germany and Switzerland: A preliminary report on a social and experimental study. In J. D. Morris, W. G. Roll, & W. L. Morris (eds.), *Research in Parapsychology, 1975* (Metuchen, N.J.: Scarecrow Press).

Secondary Bibliography

Adams, D. (1937). Bender on extra-sensory and sensory form perception. *Journal of Parapsychology*, 1, 52–62.

Gerster, G. (1956). Positive Kritik des Aberglaubens. In G. Gerster (ed.), *Eine Stunde mit Prof. Dr. Hans Bender* (Frankfurt am Main: Ullstein).

An interview with Professor Hans Bender. *ASPR Newsletter (1969)* No. 4, Autumn, 1–2.

Bauer, E. (ed.). (1974). *Psi und Psyche: Festschrift für Hans Bender.* Stuttgart: Deutsche Verlagsanstalt.

Bauer, E., & Lucadou, W. von (eds.). (1983). *Spektrum der Parapsychologie: Festschrift für Hans Bender zum 75 Geburtstag.* Freiburg im Breisgau: Aurum. (Contains complete bibliography up to 1982.)

Karlis Osis

Karlis Osis was born in Riga, Latvia, in 1917. He received his Ph.D. from the University of Munich in 1950, and was one of the first psychologists to have obtained a Ph.D. with a thesis dealing with extrasensory perception.

From 1951 to 1957 Dr. Osis was a research associate of J. B. Rhine's at the Parapsychology Laboratory at Duke University. There he performed some of the first ESP experiments with animals and studied, with human subjects, the strength of ESP over time and distance.

From 1957 to 1962, as director of research at the Parapsychology Foundation, Osis widened the scope of his activities, conducting experiments with mediums, exploring cases of apparitions and poltergeists, and compiling a survey of deathbed observations by physicians and nurses.

In 1962 he became director of research at the American Society for Psychical Research and, in 1976, their Chester F. Carlson Research Fellow (presently emeritus) until his retirement in 1983. During these years at the A.S.P.R. Osis conducted more pioneering studies, including his second survey on deathbed observations, interviews with creative artists to determine whether or not altered states of consciousness were related to psi-conducive states, a four-year project on meditation, and extensive laboratory experiments on out-of-body experiences.

With Erlendur Haraldsson he conducted a large-scale survey of the experiences of dying patients in India and the United States and psychic phenomena in selected yogis, particularly Sri Sathya Sai Baba, in southern India.

Dr. Osis is a past president of the Parapsychological Association, a member of the American Psychological Association, the Eastern Psychological Association, and the American Association for the Advancement of Science, and a fellow of the Society for the Scientific Study of Religion.

Karlis Osis

The Paranormal:
My Window to Something More

Psychic experiences and parapsychology, the science that concerns itself with such phenomena, are approached in surprisingly different ways by different people. For some, psi is just a curio to display at Friday night parties. For others it is as fearsome as anything which suddenly gushes up from the neglected, disorderly unconscious and is the stuff from which devils are made. For yet others, such experiences and knowledge about them can be very meaningful. The founding fathers of modern parapsychology, J. B. Rhine and Gardner Murphy, were foresighted enough to perceive the paranormal as an opening through which we could obtain new and important insights about who we really are and in what kind of universe we live—a needed correction for the crippling, one-sidedness of the so-called "modern" scientific world view. How we construe the paranormal depends on who we are, our roots, and our being. So I am telling my story in the hope that it might help some to see a little more clearly, more deeply, more personally, that side of the paranormal which enriches our humanity and expands our horizons. This is what heppened to me. We cannot *give* meaning of this kind to anybody; we just become aware of it in our own unique and very personal growth process.

I grew up in rural Latvia, one of the little Baltic countries south of Finland and north of Poland, now under Soviet rule. The devastations of World War I were still around me: bombed and burned structures, trenches with barbed wire hidden in long grass, and busy, busy adults rebuilding the scorched farmland. There was no time for idle speculation. Psychic experiences enmeshed in folk tales and superstition were summarily dismissed in my home. At that time in Latvia, no parapsychologists were around to disentangle the real from the unreal. We had not even heard of parapsychology.

Naturally, in such a milieu, I did not choose to study parapsychology—it was sprung on me as a total surprise. Just before I entered high school, I had tuberculosis. In those times (before antibiotics), one had a 50:50 chance of survival, if one was patient enough to lie in bed and rest. It was dusk in my room when it happened: All of a sudden a tremendous wave of joy, of such an unusual quality, came over me. I had not heard of anything like it before. The room seemed to fill with light; not something by which one can read, but "light" is the closest word I can find to describe it — living light — not only in the room but also in me, filling me up to my fingertips. Then the door opened and a relative announced, "Auntie just died." My experience and her death were surely simultaneous.

My aunt had been paralyzed by a stroke a few years before and my father had taken her in to care for her. She could not speak, which is why I was not particularly close to her; I just felt sorry for her and tried to help before I had become ill myself. A second stroke came and the doctor said that she would die within two weeks, the actual day or hour was not predictable. So while I knew that my aunt's death was imminent, I could not have guessed its exact moment.

I found similar experiential qualities described in the famous classic of comparative religion, Rudolph Otto's *Das Heilige* (The Idea of the Holy, 1958). Teenagers are said to experience "the call of the wild." For me, that was not the only call. The experience at the time of my aunt's death felt to me like a call of the mysteriously sublime. It happened to turn me onto the road of research. Belief was not enough; I had to *know*. My search turned out to be a trail full of hard work, and a thin pocketbook, but also one of deep fulfillment.

Straight ESP, without a spiritual component, is different. That too, popped up in my childhood. I still remember it was early on a Friday morning when I answered the phone: My grandfather was perplexed by a very unusual dream in which he had put on the boots of our president. That puzzled the old, white-bearded farmer. He had not met with the man for decades. My family made a joke about it: "Puss in President's Boots." But it was not just a dream. On Sunday, two days later, the president took a ride in the country, recognized my grandfather at the roadside, and got out of the car. A third of a century earlier, as a young agricultural expert, our president had taught local farmers new farming methods. Now he was pleased to see how well the farmers had used the new methods to achieve prosperity. Nostalgia, or something else, moved him. He returned on Monday bringing half the cabinet and the press with him. That made the front page, and so did my grandfather. I still have a photo of the event, which I recently took out and examined. The president wore no boots, just casual shoes. That is, the dream was entirely symbolic. Coincidence between the dream and the extremely unusual events that followed convinced me then, as it still does, that here was a case of real ESP.

This and many other ESP experiences are impressive but devoid of spiritual aspects. If I did not have my first experience at the time of my aunt's death I, too, might have been blind to this deeper side of parapsychology.

The core of the paranormal can be life-transforming in various ways, like gifts catered to our individuality. The greatest discoveries are always surprises, while the well-planned, controlled experiment comes like a second thought. Starting with "second thought" type of research often, but not always, ends up in trivialities. We become more perceptive, more open and creative through the immediacy of experiences, either our own or those of people who are close to us whom we love and trust deeply. Experience and knowledge are both essential for successful research, like the two wings of a bird. With just one wing, the bird can only tumble, it cannot fly. Neither experience nor book knowledge alone seems to be enough to give us a conviction of the reality of psi—at least, not for me.

When I was a student at the University of Munich, Rhine's *The Reach of the Mind* (1947) and other materials came into my hands. These works impressed me, but did not sway me. The cards, dice, statistics, and the dash of sales pitch felt a bit strange and lacked something. However, I had my own decks of Rhine's cards manufactured for me by a blueprint company. I was then able to experiment with my fellow students and the significant results that came under *my* nose clinched it.

The personal and the cognitive are intricately interwoven. Scientists are not completely objective, at least not insofar as their encounters with the paranormal are concerned.

The Mecca of Parapsychology

The road from engaging experiences to laboratory work is not short. First, I wrote my doctoral dissertation in psychology, at the University of Munich, on interpretations of ESP. A doctoral thesis about ESP was very risky in 1950, but mine was one of the few in the world which was accepted. I then immigrated to the United States under the displaced persons program. I had a shiny, brand new degree, poor English, and nothing else when I arrived in Tacoma, Washington, for assigned manual work. And then, out of the blue, the parapsychology laboratory at Duke University, which was then the Mecca for aspirants from all over the world, opened its doors to me.

This was a strange and unexpected coincidence, like the experience at the death of my aunt that captivated my interest years before in Latvia. At the time, struggling with my pitiful English, I had neither access to subjects for experiments, nor the necessary equipment. But there were a couple of miniature hens which I took care of. I thought, "How about using them as subjects instead of the humans who all seemed to be barricaded behind their smooth and easy English?" I designed a little experiment. At one end of a long table, I put two equal heaps of grain. I then released a hen at the middle position of the other end of the table. I wished the hens to go either to the right or to the left heap of grain. I chose the right side if a black playing card came up in a well-shuffled deck, and the left side if it was a red card. (I was thus using the color scheme of European parliaments where the "reds" sit on the left and the aristocratic "blacks" occupy the right side of the aisle.) The hen's choices, and their compliance or disregard of my guidance, were recorded. I statistically analyzed the results and, to my amazement, discovered that those charming little subjects had given me moderately significant scores.

Of course the experiment was very crude but I posted the results to Rhine anyway. At the time I had not the slightest notion that Rhine had quietly embarked on a large-scale program involving psi in animals, or "anpsi." Most of his staff combed the zoological and ornithological literature for possible clues on animal ESP. He and Gaither Pratt visited leading researchers in the United States and Europe, including the celebrated Conrad Lorenz and K. Von Frisch, the discoverer of the "language" of bees. Apparently my ESP experiment with the hens filled his bill and suddenly I was invited to come to Duke to work on animal ESP.

We investigated dogs and cats as potential subjects and settled for the charming felines. The experiment succeeded, was published (Osis, 1952; Osis & Foster, 1953), and later captured popular interest, earning even a picture in *Life* magazine. The same arrangement that worked for the hens was refined here. A cat had to go through runways and approach two cups, each containing a morsel of cat delicacies. My assistant or I wished the cat to go first either to the right or to the left cup according to prescribed random order. The possibility that the cat's sharp eyes could observe some unintentional cues from us was safely excluded by appropriate screening.

Only after the completion of this research did I find records of previous experiments with animals — all of which yielded no trace of ESP. Rhine had wisely withheld that information from me, which at the time offended me. Only later did I realize that knowledge of those dismal failures would have discouraged me to such an extent that nothing positive would have come out of my own work. Rhine knew that the experimenter's own ESP cannot be locked out of the experiment. Only years later did the celebrated Harvard psychologist Robert Rosenthal (1966) find slighter but somewhat similar "experimenter effects" in psychological experiments. Later still, the British sociologist Collins (1985) observed that skeptics rarely get positive results when they repeat an experiment about which they are skeptical. The moral is very simple: If deep down you quarrel with the phenomena you want to work with, don't set your foot on the path to Mecca; nothing will come of it except one more disappointed and grouchy scientist.

The Reach of Mind Over Great Distances

When I was preparing my thesis in the late 1940s Rhine's (1947) presentation of evidence for the far reaches of the mind greatly impressed me. His conception of a noble aspect of the human personality capable of transcending the physical dimensions of space and time appeared well supported by scientific research data. With World War II the roof fell in on Europe, exposing the brutal, cruel side of human nature in all its ugliness. The spiritual conceptions of man were challenged sharply as our sugar-coated culture was confronted by naked facts about man's capacity for ruthless destruction and oppression. I, like millions of others, felt the need for hard proof of a wiser, kinder, more humane side of our being. Rhine's (1947) empirically derived conceptions seemed to hand us just what we needed.

A young statistician, Malcolm Turner, had recalculated Rhine's distance data and found just the opposite of what we had expected: ESP significantly declined, became weaker and weaker, the further it had to reach. That ruffled me, and Turner and I argued fiercely. Another staff member and psychologist, Esther Foster, surveyed additional data and found the same trend: ESP scores went down with greater distances. Rhine argued that not all the data had been surveyed. He pointed out that such a drastic decline, if a true characteristic of ESP, would preclude good ESP results over very long distances, as he had found in his recently completed experiments with Marchesi between North Carolina and Yugoslavia. Subjects might have felt more at ease with cards sent from nearer locations, and that psychological effect alone might have caused the decline without distance having anything to do with the results. This indeed was a *possibility* but my belief in Rhine's *proof* of independence of ESP from space and time was shaken.

Clearly, to reach certainty we needed better designed experiments. I thought of a large-scale experiment in which subjects would not know (would be "blind" to) how far the ESP targets were from them, and the relevant factors, such as motivation, attitudes, emotional and attention states, etc., were measured and their influence statistically removed, leaving distance as the only independent variable. I realized that Rhine was, thus far, right; any lawful relationship (or lack thereof) with distance would enlighten us about the very essence of psi, that mysterious X factor which connects the knower (the subject) with the object known (for example Rhine's ESP cards). I called it "the ESP channel." It could be an energy not yet put on the map of science, a psychic energy that is akin to those conceptualized by Freud and Jung.

If we could describe the ESP channel qualitatively, and also mathematically with formulae, we might be able to understand it and use it more reliably. Electricity was also observable, as in lightning, but not usable until we learned such pertinent formulae as Ohm's law. Such possibilities fired me up to search out the ways and means for a new, high-quality project. Pilot experiments with persons in Finland, Germany, and even South Africa were performed. Distance seemed to decrease, but not mute, the little voice of ESP (Osis, 1956; Osis & Fahler, 1965). In a more formal experiment I learned that the "seven league boots" of ESP ran fast crossing the Atlantic to Rhodesia, Africa (7,500 miles) in no more than 10 seconds, probably less (Osis & Pienaar, 1956). My ally was that brilliant statistician Malcolm Turner. When I surveyed all the experiments published in English (Osis, 1965), Turner found that the decline was there but much slighter than the inverse square law of known energies would suggest. It looked more like the inverse of the square root of distance (Osis, 1965). We seemed to have something hot in our hands.

The inventor of Xerox, Chester F. Carlson, recognized the merits of such work and gave me a hand. We brainstormed at his home to sharpen our concepts, define our goals, and outline the ways to reach them. He sponsored a long-range project, which I directed at the American Society for Psychical Research. Four experiments were conducted over a several-year period. In three of them, a person travelled around the world exposing nature postcards at predetermined places and times in a clairvoyant situation. Subjects were kept ignorant regarding the locations of the targets. We took care of (controlled) 32 factors which could influence ESP. In a very sophisticated statistical assessment (stepwise multiple regression and canonical correlation analyses), we carefully separated distance effects from the effects on the date of various psychological variables such as personality, attitudes, motivation, attention, and others. It was the most elaborate research performed to determine the role of distance in ESP.

The technicalities were such a heavy burden to our subjects that they somewhat diminished ESP efficiency, but decline over distance was even found in several replications (Osis & Turner, 1968; Osis, Turner, & Carlson, 1971). The results were clearly against the expectations of established belief that ESP is independent of space and time. Without the influence of Murphy and Carlson these experiments would not have continued. Some of my interpretations and results were difficult to publish and appeared outside the regular parapsychological channels, for example, at a convention of the American Association for the Advancement of Science (Osis, 1970), in the proceedings of a conferencee on international computer communications (Osis, 1976), and also as a chapter in a book in German (Osis, 1974).

NASA sponsored a three-day symposium on parapsychology under the auspices of the American Academy of Sciences, in which I participated. The thought struck me that NASA's Apollo flights to the moon would have been ideal for expanding our research on ESP over distance, doing so on a much larger scale than our good old earth could provide (Osis, 1973). With help from engineer Martin Rudefer, I tried hard to interest NASA in allowing such an experiment to be conducted during one of their moon flights. Werner von Braun, the noted space scientist, was warm about the idea and the project was provisionally accepted by NASA with a low-priority rating. However, an outside referee organization was consulted and turned us down, giving as the reason that "ESP is not a scientific concept." There went the greatest dream I ever had.

Later, however, astronaut Edgar Mitchell (1971) simply sneaked in a small ESP experiment in his flight. I helped him evaluate his results and so did J. B. Rhine. But this small try could not give decisive results as our proposed and rejected large-scale experiment might have. So the ESP "channel," the X factor which connects the seer and the seen, is still a mystery. We do not as yet know what laws govern the ESP channel, how far this reach of mind goes, what impedes it or what may boost its efficiency. Here remains an abandoned gold mine for future researchers with vision.

Research on Phenomena Suggestive of Afterlife

Throughout recorded history, thoughtful persons have grappled with the ultimate issues of human existence. Are we a part of the physical universe or were there aspects of us that are of a nonphysical nature and that can transcend such material constraints as death? This question, of course, blends with the search for ultimate meaning, be it in life, culture, history, or in the universe at large. This quest for meaning has never achieved a uniform answer satisfactory to everyone. Instead, this quest has produced a bewildering variety of competing belief systems, expressed in religions, philosophies, and the arts and humanities.

Science, in general, researches the phenomena that seem to go reasonably well with mechanistic/materialistic world views, the views that gave rise to a philosophy nowadays called "scientism." Parapsychology, on the other hand, was originally aimed at those phenomena which seemed to call for something more—transcendental meaning in us and in the universe. While ESP and PK call for expanded views, the most obviously unfit, albeit challenging, to the scientists are phenomena pointing toward life after death: apparitions, out-of-body experiences, near-death experiences, communication with the dead, reincarnation memories, etc. Where belief systems are involved, be they religious creeds, scientism, or whatnot, do not expect only objectivity and fairness. And remember, you also have a belief system pulling you in a certain direction.

As unacceptable as the great dissidents are to the totalitarian systems, so the spirits of the dead are to the scientistic part of academia and, at times, even to devil-fearing Christians. The phenomena that point to life after death are forcefully "explained away," while positive reports are usually banished from scientific journals, conventions, and university curricula. If you are a "chicken" or if prestige and a fat pocketbook are at the top of your scale of values, stay away from the dangerous phenomena of the dead.

Fortunately I had allies who were everything but chicken. Gardner Murphy was open minded and the Carlsons were rather convinced about postmortem survival. Later, the influential psychiatrist Ian Stevenson and the economist John Wingate helped me to sustain survival-related projects at the A.S.P.R.

My first survival research project was called "Deathbed Observations by Physicians and Nurses" (1961). In the late 1950s a slim volume entitled *Death-Bed Visions* by physics professor Sir William Barrett (1926) aroused my interest. Barrett collected experiences of what patients who were very close to death "saw" or otherwise experienced that were suggestive of afterlife. Most often they described experiences of loved ones who were dead and who "came" with the reported purpose of assisting the individual's transition to postmortem existence. New survey methods were developed by Gallup and others which far surpassed those available in Barrett's time. Because of such advances I was able to use stratified random sampling of medical respondents and proceed with better interview techniques.

We systematically tried to find out what factors besides nearness to death, high temperature, pain-killing drugs, brain impairments, and such psychological variables as beliefs, expectations, and clarity of consciousness could have caused these unusual experiences. Cultural background — the cradle of religious convictions — was also taken into account. In short, I wanted clear, untainted indications for an answer to the age-old question, do the dying "see," that is, have they glimpsed postmortem existence, or do they just hallucinate their own wishes and fantasies?

My search for the best way to find reliable answers led to a forked road that parted into two basic possibilities I will describe in an oversimplified, picturesque way for those readers who are not familiar with scientific methodology. One road sign reads, "Bivariate Street," the other, "Multivariate Avenue." If one turns into Bivariate Street one will find shops offering "yes" or "no" answers. Everything is either black or white. Shopkeepers will offer their promised goods: truth from "well-controlled situations," and such answers as either "death is the end of everything," or "afterlife is the only possible interpretation." This search for an either/or answer has been going on for 100 years without delivering clear, definitive results. Somebody always comes up with another "explanation" as an alternative to the one of life after death.

On the other hand, if one turns onto the newly paved Multivariate Avenue, one finds shops of a very different kind, sporting "theoretical models" and data banks, and buzzing with computers. These models offer several overarching roofs with many things housed under them. Each "roof" symbolizes a larger overarching concept called "theory" or "metatheory." The things under each of these roofs are research findings. The better they are housed under one roof than under the others, making them integrated in one coherent whole, the more evidence is attributed to that theory. Personality theory dealing with extraversion-introversion is one example, while Darwin's ideas of evolution could be found under "metatheory."

The shopkeepers on Multivariate Avenue will not be hawking their evidence as a "final proof," although naive shoppers may be demanding they do, encouraged by the promises of the "crucial experiments" on Bivariate Street. The ideas about life after death are such roof concepts, as are personality theory and Darwin's theory of evolution: No one can prove them, but there can be *some degree of evidence* to support them that might vary from weak and declining to strong and growing. Still, the shoppers on Bivariate Street demand "proof" of postmortem survival and when the shops cannot deliver it, laments about the "stalemate" between the survival hypothesis and super-ESP (a variant of the hypothesis of destruction of the human personality at death) can be heard. To my eyes, Bivariate Street looked a bit phony, so I turned into the newer Multivariate Avenue and got busy. In retrospect, that was a bold, but necessary, turn: The shopkeepers on Bivariate never gave a hoot about what happened on Multivariate.

My first survey of deathbed observations by physicians and nurses (Osis, 1961) explored the grounds and, like bricks, provided enough coherent findings to allow me to build a model of near-death experiences. This model contrasted the two competing metatheories: death as transition, and death as the ultimate destruction of personality. It predicted how the phenomena would be in case survival was true and what to expect if the opposite was true. The model also predicted how such medical factors as brain impairments, mind-altering drugs, and such psychological factors as expectations, beliefs, stress, and clarity of consciousness affect the phenomena. The cultural backgrounds of the patients were also considered.

A new survey was then conducted in five states around New York. A cross-cultural survey was later carried out in northern India. In this phase, I was joined by Erlendur Haraldsson. All three surveys together netted more than 1,000 cases of pertinent experiences, which were computer evaluated as well as qualitatively assessed. Experiences of Christian and Hindu patients provided the main poles of contrast, while the Jewish and Moslem patients formed smaller groups. The results are presented in our book *At the Hour of Death* (Osis & Haraldsson, 1977). There was no question about how the wind blew. The survival model explained our data better than the model of death as ultimate destruction.

Our book on the deathbed surveys was well received.* However, we encountered some conceptual criticisms based on Bivariate Street–type of thinking which were not difficult to answer. No one, to my knowledge, tried to wrestle with what we really did, to employ a multivariate approach and fit our data to the model. Now that the dust has settled, this work still looks good to me. It did not result in just research findings, it also resulted in a personal gain—I now know better what to expect when I die.

I still fear a slow kind of death such as one by cancer or a stroke—who wants to be tortured or to become a burden to the family? But when it is all over and the body is buried and gone, I trust now with serenity that a new existence is in store. It will be a wonderful surprise; well beyond what I have learned from science, my own research, and religions, East and West. Our knowledge is far from complete. However, if your own world view sees no intelligent meaning in the cosmos, just the "big bang" and subsequent rushing of matter at fantastic speeds, you do not need to agree with me. There is no proof offered by the shops on Multivariate Avenue, just degrees of evidence and intelligible interpretations. The choice is yours. On my own scales the evidence for survival weighs heavier than it does for its opposite.

Suppose one assumes postmortem survival is, at least, a likely possibility. Are there not some dangers to reckon with that might mess up our transition to afterlife? We do see troubles with this-world travels such as being too late for a plane, being fogged in or in a blizzard that closes the airport, left stranded in Spain by a cheap charter flight, and so on.

Lately I have given some attention to the scattered information available about possible "transit disasters" after death. I have very few pertinent reports of near-death experiences where exceedingly self-centered individuals experience cruising in a void with no one to meet, instruct, or rescue them. While conceptions of hell and devils have made a strong comeback in American religious beliefs, most believers reserve them not for themselves but for the other guy (Gallup & Proctor, 1982), and healthy individuals do not seem to meet them in near-death experiences. In a small minority of cases individuals with personality disorders seem to experience fighting with repressed parts of themselves visualized in negative religious symbols, e.g., devils in the West and yamduts in India. Therefore such persons might "miss their flight." In one case an attending physician gathered from listening to a dying patient that she felt scared and struggled until she realized that the "bad demons" were actually

There have been two printings and 11 foreign editions. A new American edition was published in fall 1986.

good beings and brought her into a new wonderful existence. And then there are those unfortunates who appear to be hopelessly stranded in haunted houses. They might need our help.

What happens when one kills oneself? All religions are hard on suicide cases: Western religions promise damnation and Indian beliefs hold that suicides reincarnate into animal form. Near-death experiences suggest a milder outcome. I have not come across any systematic information about such "transit disasters" gathered with scientific methods and care. The clergy traditionally officiates transition in funeral rites, memorial services, etc. However, neither dead ministers and priests nor gurus show up in near-death experiences. I still have not seen a case where transgressions against organized religion, e.g., not paying dues, dropping membership, opposing or ridiculing creeds, sacraments, and rites, seem to cause difficulties "at the hour of reckoning." Most researchers seem to agree that the "other side" is mirrored in near-death experiences as much more benevolent than the Western conceptions of "judgment" and Eastern notion of Karma have portrayed it. The visions are more like the biblical parable of workers in the vineyard. Those hired at the end of the workday got the same pay as those who sweated the whole day through. This has nothing to do with the value of organized religion, institutions in which the majority of Americans trust, but it may caution us not to misperceive the church as a box-office for the afterlife. What I said there are just impressions, not certitude. But they suggest the practical relevance of survival research. At least for me, it is a much more serious quest than theoretical sparring with abstract concepts has been. If a two-thirds majority of Americans say they believe in life after death and only one-fifth oppose that concept (Gallup, 1978), why then do we not apply our resources and ingenuity to finding out more about it?

Meditation Experiences and ESP

Meditation and prayer are among the methods religions in both Eastern and Western cultures use to tune us into a spiritual side of reality; be it a personal god, "ground of being" or a totally unconceptualizable reality, like a "God-head" in Christian theology and Brahman in Hinduism. The cultural upheavals of the 1960s opened laboratory doors to research on such experiences. Scientistic philosophies of academia, however, diverted these efforts. The bulk of the research literature eclipsed what was the heart of spiritual procedures, namely, tuning into something larger than the individual. What comes out of lab efforts often are just "relaxation responses," altered states, or a new therapeutic tool. That is a far cry from what mankind has been hankering after for thousands of years: the biblical "pearl of great worth" or the "mani/jewel" of Eastern teachings.

Chester Carlson, and especially his wife, Doris, were deeply immersed in meditation procedures and found them spiritually enriching. Chet thought that meditation is a bit like an experiment; you do this and that according to "protocol," and the predicted outcome follows. Following Carlson's footsteps, I also tried and found meditation very rewarding. Then, after brainstorming with Carlson and others, an experiment was designed to test ESP and the spiritual aspects of meditation in the laboratory. Psychologists Edwin Bokert, Janet Mitchell, and Mary Lou Carlson later joined me in some phases of this research.

We developed scales (paper and pencil tests) to measure various aspects of meditation experiences. An ESP test was also designed to be dovetailed with meditation measures. It is said in prescientific meditation literature that our self-boundaries are crossed in meditation experiences, resulting in oneness or unity with the transcendental aspects of reality and with "all sentient beings." Is this oneness a totally subjective experience, or something in us that opens and truly reconnects us with other persons and reality at large? If it is a true unity then ESP should also flow more easily from one person to others during such states.

We came up with a highly technical, carefully conducted experiment. We factor analyzed our results and indeed found a factor of meditation we called "self-transcendence and openness," which reflected the idea of the unity experience. We found a significant correlation between this factor and the flow of ESP (Osis & Bokert, 1971). Of course, these were just research beginnings, but we showed that one can work with scientific methods on the spiritual core characteristics of meditation as they occur far beyond mere relaxation responses. But we stepped on the toes of many colleagues by doing this research. Scientism, the dominant philosophy of elite scientists, is too materialistic to accept such kinds of experiments. Spiritual experiences, if not explained away, were offensive, even in those days, in parapsychology. One editor who rejected our paper, which eventually was published in the *Journal of Transpersonal Psychology* (Osis, Bokert, & Carlson, 1973), told me that she found meditation outright repugnant! Nevertheless, our work was listened to; for example, our psychological scales were used by other researchers and doctoral students.

I have presented just a few examples of the ways in which parapsychology has obvious relevance to our lives and our culture. There are many more highly relevant areas on record, including practical applications of ESP such as finding natural resources, detecting murderers, and, maybe, rendering impossible a nuclear surprise attack. Perhaps one day parapsychology will step out of its puristic preoccupations with trivial experimentation, and reconnect itself in researching the true concerns of humanity.

Boggle Threshold

Dr. Pilkington requested descriptions of experiences that shattered our "boggle thresholds." Frankly, working in several of the areas I have discussed above has changed the "gauge of my eye" that measured what I considered real and what I considered illusory. However, some experiences in India further shattered my conviction that I knew the approximate limits of psi. Such convictions — usually shared by the in-group of parapsychologists — in retrospect look like wishful thinking, that we knew what we really did not know. The unknown looms much larger than I thought.

Encounters with Sri Sathya Sai Baba were particular eye-openers. When Haraldsson and I were interviewing physicians and nurses in India and their observations of deathbed experiences, we heard many wonder-stories about Sai Baba. These stories were so far beyond what I considered possible at that time that I just ignored them; they were "too good to be true," so I laughed them off. But the stories kept coming, even from the elite of India such as the vice president of a college, a governor, the highest medical official in a state with a population of 60 million, and so on. Finally, curiosity got the better of us and we traveled far south to see Sai Baba. Sai Baba is the most visible of the religious leaders in India. The assistant police commissioner of New Delhi said, in essence, that "When Baba comes here we have very severe traffic problems. The streets are jammed for hours. The crowds are second only to those which come to see Indira Gandhi."

Putaparthi is Sai Baba's birthplace. It is a dry, desolate area three hours by car on poor roads from Bangalore. His ashram was built there, we were told, to keep off the curiosity seekers. Still, huge crowds persist. Among them we could see political leaders, the very rich, middle class, and also very poor villagers. Some come for healing, some for help with their personal troubles. About one-third seemed to be primarily "spiritual seekers," as a retired dean of a large university put it. While many Westerners consider out-of-body experiences beyond their accepted scope of beliefs (Osis & McCormick, 1980), the stories about Baba's "bilocations" are much wilder and action filled. These anecdotes recount instances of healing, helping devotees in life-threatening situations, preventing suicides, and other activities.

We carefully investigated a case where Baba was said to have bilocated across the Indian continent to heal a little grade school girl, Sailaja, whom medicine could not help. Baba's "double" was described as "like a person of flesh and bone." We found ten first-hand witnesses in Kerla State, where the little girl was located. We also found records and witnesses in a palace near Madras where Baba was said to have been present in-body, in the flesh, visiting local rajas at the time he healed the girl (Haraldsson & Osis, 1976; Osis & Haraldsson, 1979).

Haraldsson and I were fortunate enough to closely observe objects appearing and disappearing in Baba's presence. This, of course, is what magicians also do. The famous stage magician Doug Henning, however, watched a film on Sai Baba in my office and commented, "I can duplicate most of it, but it does not look like he does it that way," that is, via magic tricks. There were two instances I will briefly describe that Henning said were not the types of things that magicians can do (Haraldsson & Osis, 1977; Osis & Haraldsson, 1979).

During our first visit, I challenged Baba to participate in experiments. A heated argument developed in which he scoffed at our Western meditation efforts: "I know how you Westerners meditate. You feel high up there for a while but then the next day you are where you were before, doing the same silly things again. In true meditation, life and spirit are grown together, like a double rudraksha." Haraldsson asked what a rudraksha was. Neither Baba nor his translator knew an English word for it. Haraldsson nevertheless pressed on rather aggressively until Baba grew a bit red in the face, swiftly turned his hand in small circles, and then triumphantly showed us: "This is a double rudraksha." It was a bit like two apricot stones that had grown together, but with a much more intricate and beautiful texture. We marvelled at it because it came as a response to a heated argument, not as something planned and prepared. Then Baba took it back, held it between his hands, blew on it, and handed it back to Haraldsson as a present. The double rudraksha was now encased in gold and rubies. Magicians can "materialize" only objects which they bring with them, not those decided upon on the spur of an obviously embarrassing moment. We were impressed. Haraldsson later analyzed a chip of his rudraksha. It was native grown, not artificial. Indian and British botanists told him that double rudrakshas (two grown together like double cherries) are extremely rare: very few specimens are known to exist and those are kept as very rare museum pieces.

The other thing Henning respected was the disappearance of a stone on my ring. During our first visit Baba again swung his open hand in fast little circles, closed it, and then presented me with a golden ring that had a large 1 x 1.8 cm enamel picture of himself encased in it. It was real gold and, in those days (early 1970s) was appraised at a hundred dollars. This present could have been preplanned, brought with him, so a magician's trick was a viable explanation.

A year later, I again wanted to entice Baba into an experiment. I first tried to loosen him up with a joke. I showed him the ring he had given me, which I wore on my finger, and told him that I appreciated it but that it was not enough for my colleagues in New York who said, "We can see you like your swami, but swamis have sleeves." I was implying sleight of hand. The joke misfired. Baba grew very serious, was silent, but then said, "Look at your ring." The picture of Baba that had been on the ring had disappeared. The ring had remained on my finger and my hand had been resting on my left knee as I sat cross-legged on the floor. Next to me, on my left, was Haraldsson and there was a concrete wall behind us. Baba was about six feet away from us. My mouth dropped open, which apparently satisfied the offended swami. "This was my joke," he said in a harsh voice. Later he called it "my experiment," and in a sense, it was.

I examined the notches of the ring which held the picture of Baba. None was bent. There were no traces that force had been used on it. Doug Henning respected that one, too. No one has given me a reasonable explanation of how Baba could have done this. But the event was very much beyond the boggle threshold of my colleagues. Gaither Pratt even suggested that we might have been hypnotized unbeknownst to us for three days and therefore simply could not see the stone. In that case Haraldsson's camera would also have been hypnotized, as he took a picture of the empty ring! Because of skepticism all around, I had to discontinue my work on Indian swamis. However, Haraldsson continues his research trips to India, supported by the University of Iceland where he teaches.

My "old man's advice" to future researchers is to have the courage and integrity to seek innovative truth — that is what makes life worthwhile — but be very choosey when, where, and to whom you tell it.

Way out on the boundary between the known and the unknown, people often lose their manners and objective thinking habits — scientists not excluded. We are all humans and often fall under the spell of group conformity, argumentation, and power games. It is not easy in the frontier, but I would not have missed for anything the challenge and joy of true discoveries. Parapsychology is still a frontier area, just as much so as the West once was for American pioneers. The windows to something more are still open and calling keen men and women — the future researchers. When we know the full humanity in us, we will be able to live better, even with incomplete knowledge. Trust your depth and use your own eyes to look through the still mysterious windows of psi. And do not let any intellectual juggler talk you out of your own birthright. The windows are there.

Bibliography for Karlis Osis

(1952). A test of the occurrence of a psi effect between man and cat. *Journal of Parapsychology, 16*, 233–256.

(1953). A test of relationship between ESP and PK. *Journal of Parapsychology, 17*, 298–309.

(1955). Precognition over time intervals of one to thirty-three days. *Journal of Parapsychology*, 19, 82–91.

(1956). ESP tests at long and short distances. *Journal of Parapsychology*, 20, 81–95.

(1959). The distance problem. *Journal of Parapsychology*, 23, 290.

(1960). Some methodological possibilities in spontaneous case research. *Journal of Parapsychology*, 24, 323–324.

(1961). ESP in the laboratory: Its integration and activation. *Journal of Parapsychology*, 25, 290–304.

(1961). *Deathbed Observations by Physicians and Nurses* (Parapsychological Monographs No. 3). New York: Parapsychology Foundation.

(1965). ESP over distance: A survey of experiments published in English. *Journal of the American Society for Psychical Research*, 59, 21–46.

(1966). Linkage experiments with mediums. *Journal of the American Society for Psychical Research*, 60, 92–124.

(1970). Informal methods of research in psychic phenomena for religious believers. *Pastoral Psychology*, 21.

(1978). Out-of-body research at the American Society for Psychical Research. In D. S. Rogo (ed.), *Mind Beyond the Body: The Mystery of ESP Projection* (New York: Penguin Books).

(1985). Contributions in recognition of the ASPR's centenary: The American Society for Psychical Research 1941–1985: A personal view. *Journal of the American Society for Psychical Research*, 79, 501–530.

(1971). With Bokert, E. Changed states of consciousness and ESP. In W. G. Roll, R. L. Morris, & J. D. Morris (eds.), *Proceedings of the Parapsychological Association*, 6, 1969 (Durham, N.C.: Parapsychological Association).

(1971). With Bokert, E. ESP and changed states of consciousness induced by meditation. *Journal of the American Society for Psychical Research*, 65, 17–65.

(1973). With Bokert, E., & Carlson, M. L. Dimensions of the meditative experience. *Journal of Transpersonal Psychology*, 5, 109–135.

(1972). With Carlson, M. L. The ESP channel—Open or closed? *Journal of the American Society for Psychical Research*, 66, 310–320.

(1953). With Foster, E. A test of ESP in cats. *Journal of Parapsychology*, 17, 168–186.

(1976). With Haraldsson, E. OOBE's in Indian Swamis: Sathya Sai Baba and Dadaji. In J. D. Morris, W. G. Roll, & R. L. Morris (eds.), *Research in Parapsychology 1975* (Metuchen, N.J.: Scarecrow Press), 147–150.

(1977). With Haraldsson, E. *At the Hour of Death*. New York: Avon Books.

(1980). With McCormick, D. Kinetic effects at the ostensible location of an out-of-body projection during perceptual testing. *Journal of the American Society for Psychical Research*, 74, 319–330.

(1982). With McCormick, D. A poltergeist case without an identifiable living agent. *Journal of the American Society for Psychical Research,* **76**, 23–51.

(1977). With Mitchell, J. L. Physiological correlates of reported out-of-body experiences. *Journal of the American Society for Psychical Research,* **49**, 525–536.

(1956). With Pienaar, D. ESP over a distance of seventy-five hundred miles. *Journal of Parapsychology,* **20**, 229–232.

(1968). With Turner, M. E., Jr. Distance and ESP: A transcontinental experiment. *Proceedings of the American Society for Psychical Research,* **27**, 1–48.

(1971). With Turner, M. E., Jr., & Carlson, M. L. ESP over distance: Research on the ESP channel. *Journal of the American Society for Psychical Research,* **65**, 245–288.

George Zorab

George Avetoom Marterus Zorab is the most venerable of the contributors to this volume. He was born on January 11, 1898, in Surabaya, Java (Indonesia), but has lived most of his life in the Netherlands.

His is a story of fascination with the paranormal from 8 to 88 (at the time of this writing). His parapsychological experimentation began in 1932 with spontaneous phenomena and with quantitative experiments in GESP with psychotics.

He has written numerous books and hundreds of articles on psychical research and has participated in many international conferences. Mr. Zorab has been chairman of the International Committee for the Study of Spontaneous Paranormal Phenomena, The Hague, and secretary for the First International Conference on Parapsychological Studies in Utrecht, Netherlands. He was also corresponding member of the Society for Psychical Research, London, and the Società Italiana di Parapsicologia, Rome, honorary secretary of the Netherlands Society for Psychical Research, former director of the Parapsychology Foundation's European Research Center at St. Paul de Vence, France, and European review editor of the *Indian Journal of Parapsychology*.

He is still writing and is currently an editor for the Dutch Parapsychological Society's journal, *Spiegel der Parapsychologie*, and a contributing editor for *Parapsychology Abstracts International*.

George Zorab says of himself, "I am just a man like so many other men. The only difference is that I was a very lucky one, especially with regard to what we still name love. I had a very happy marriage for 52 years" (to the late Amalia Lorch whom he married in 1925).

Frans Snel, in his contribution to a *Liber Amicorum* for Zorab (1986), tells of George and "Maaltje's" classic elopement, resulting from the bride's parents' objection to the marriage, complete with ladder, escape in George's car, and subsequent travels throughout southern Europe. During this time he acted as a scout for the Dutch tourist organization and discovered that he could earn money by writing. Thus began a long literary career.

George Zorab

Eight Decades in Parapsychology

When I was eight years old I was terrified to die. I was so afraid that I didn't dare to fall asleep, for falling asleep — so I thought — was the same as dying, which meant to me losing one's identity and sinking away into nothingness.

This fear and anxiety lasted till I was 12 years old when my problem was solved in the following manner. In those days we were living in the town of Nijmegen in the east of Holland. One day, during the summer of 1910 a married couple, relatives of my parents, visited us. When they arrived and entered our house I, too, was present to greet them. The first thing I heard them say was, "This evening we are going to have a table-lifting seance."

When I heard this I became very interested but was equally disappointed when my mother told me, "You are too young to be present at a seance, so you will go to bed at eight o'clock as usual."

When I went upstairs to my bedroom I started to make as much noise as possible, banging doors, kicking the furniture, and screaming as loud as I could. My mother came running upstairs with the intention of giving me a good scolding but after some talking I finally got my own way and so was able to attend my first seance.

It took a long time (two hours) before the table finally started to vibrate. Then, suddenly, it raised itself on two legs. The conversation between the living and the "spirits" started. About 23 deceased members of our family and friends announced themselves by spelling their names, etc.

This seance made me a very happy boy, for now I had proof that even after death I could go on being George Zorab through all eternity.

Life became very pleasant for me. I read every book and article on spiritualism I could lay my hands on and attended any lecture on the subject given in our neighborhood. I continued my studies of spiritualism and its dogmatic tenets for several years. One of these tenets was that paranormal phenomena were of a supernatural nature and therefore such phenomena cannot be produced by human beings. Only supernatural entities such as the spirits of deceased persons are able to do so.

138

Since I came into contact with the paranormal at a very early age I had no beliefs of any consequence to begin with. I never had any experiences that would have induced me to think I had done something wrong. I just went on reading about paranormal phenomena but I also was interested in learning about various theories and beliefs concerning the hereafter. I was especially interested in spontaneous cases, not in quantitative experiments such as those of Rhine and Soal.

Later I was nominated a member of the Council of the Spiritualists Association at the Hague. I also became the first editor of the Spiritualist periodicals *Life After Death (Het toekomstige leven* in Dutch) and *Know Thyself (Ken U Zelven)* during the late 1930s. However as I read books by researchers such as Aksakoff and Schrenk-Notzing and slowly came to realize that a "spirit hypothesis" was not necessary to explain psychic phenomena, my interest shifted from the problem of survival to the reality of various paranormal phenomena such as clairvoyance, precognition, psychokinesis, etc.

This interest was the reason that I became a member of the Dutch S.P.R. in 1934 and of the English S.P.R. in 1936: I was no longer a spiritualist but had chosen to be a parapsychologist. By then I was convinced that the spiritualists were wrong to believe that spirits of the dead manifested themselves at seances with the help of mediums and that this proved that survival after bodily death was a fact. What practically every spiritualist and many, especially English, parapsychologists could not understand was that a gifted medium is an excellent clairvoyant and is thus able to know all kinds of things concerning (dead) people the medium had never seen or heard about. At a seance the medium is everything, the spirit is nothing.

When I was approached by people who wanted to know whether it was true that after death we would go on existing in another world where all our deceased beloved ones would be waiting for us I would tell them that we still didn't know exactly that our personality would go on living in the hereafter but that it was certainly possible. This answer gave them hope, lessened their grief, and helped them accept their fate more easily. In truth, however, after studying parapsychology for many years I had become convinced that at death we would "fall into a black hole," so to speak, and that would be the end of everything.

I think young people should start, not with quantitative experiments, which generally produce disappointing results, but should look for a gifted medium with whom to work. I was lucky to meet Mrs. Kitty Voorzanger in the spring of 1941 when she came to The Hague. Mrs. Voorzanger had lived in Rotterdam until it was bombed by the Germans when they invaded Holland in May 1940. Mrs. Voorzanger, who was Jewish, was on the run from her persecutors and after many adventures finally found refuge in

The Hague. After the war she often visited my wife and me in our home where she insisted on reading the cards to predict our future.

In 1950 she told us that I would leave Holland and settle in the south of France because I had to organize something there with regard to my work (in parapsychology). I told her that her predicition was pure nonsense since I would never leave Holland for such work. "There is no question about it," she replied. "What is more, I see a blond girl in your neighborhood. I think she is a secretary for I see her busy looking at the kind of cards they use in archives." I told her that she was talking nonsense. But her predictions did come true. I met the girl, Miss Gerda Bos, who later became my secretary, in 1955 when she attended one of my courses in parapsychology.

In the spring of 1956 I received a letter from Mrs. Garrett asking me to go to Le Piol in the south of France to make that place a parapsychological center. She offered me a good salary but I would also have to keep an eye on the wine cellar (the best wines just disappeared) and keep the books for the restaurant and hotel. I told my wife that I would not go to Le Piol if I had to do all these things myself. If I could find a reliable secretary such as Miss Bos, who then worked as a bookkeeper with Shell, I would go. Gerda prepared to go with us to the south of France and my wife and I arrived at Le Piol in January 1958.

Mrs. Voorzanger also predicted that we were not going to stay in The Hague but would go to live in the country. She said, "When you are in your new house and look out of your window you will see a straight road with footpaths on both sides. On the footpaths little trees are planted." Several years later my wife had great difficulty in walking up and down stairs so we had to look for a house or flat with a lift. The building in which we rented a flat did not yet exist when Mrs. V. made her prediction. When we came to live in the flat in 1974 and looked out of the window we could see the straight road and the two footpaths planted with little trees. Now, in 1986, the trees are still there but have grown to a height of about 12 yards.

One of the most important contributions I made to the field of parapsychology was that I made it possible for the first parapsychological conference to be held after the end of the Second World War, the International Conference of Parapsychological Studies, to take place. The conference was organized by Eileen Garrett and sponsored by Frances Bolton. Directly after the war, in 1945, I became secretary of the Dutch S.P.R. and in 1952 the Council of this organization was approached by Mrs. Garrett's secretary, who told us that Mrs. Garrett wanted to organize a conference dealing with parapsychology to be held in Paris and that she would be very pleased if we would help her to make the conference a success. He also invited us to come to Paris and meet there with the French parapsychologists.

We spent a few happy days in Paris where we met George Amadou, the French secretary of the conference. As it turned out the conference could not be held in Paris because there were no hotels that could accommodate the more than one hundred people who were expected to attend. Therefore it was decided to have the conference at Utrecht, Holland, since Wilhelm Tenhaeff would be nominated special professor of parapsychology at the University of Utrecht in 1953.

In April 1953, Amadou and Michael Pobers came to Holland to find sufficient hotel accommodation at Utrecht. I could not accompany them as I had come down with a severe attack of flu. I heard that their mission was a failure for they could not get even one room for the conference. Mrs. Garrett had called the whole thing off.

When I was out of my sick bed I decided to go to Utrecht and have a talk with the owner of the largest and best hotel there. I asked him why he didn't want to rent his rooms to people attending the conference. He replied that he had had very bad experiences with conference attendants. Each time, a few days before the start of the conference he received a telegram that the conference was off. These incidents had caused him great financial loss. As I knew that Mrs. Garrett and Mrs. Bolton had lots of money I told him that I was prepared to deposit with him a thousand guilders. If the conference was not held at the date agreed upon the money would be his. He consented, and so the conference was held.

Then a very hectic time ensued for me: I had to do everything myself, such as hiring direct translators from Geneva, renting rooms in the University building where the conference would be held, and so on.

The conference was in many ways a great success. When it came to an end I was thanked for all the work I had done and was nominated as the chairman of the committee studying terms in parapsychology and chairman of the committee for bibliographical studies. Mrs. Garrett requested that I write a bibliography of parapsychology which was reprinted four or five times (1957).

I had now become a respected parapsychologist and a friend of many other parapsychologists such as Piero Cassoli, Eric Dingwall, Molly Goldney, Emilio Servadio, and Robert Thouless. I was also invited to many conferences on parapsychology throughout Europe and finally, I was appointed European research director of the Parapsychology Foundation in the south of France.

My other great interest, one that started as early as 1914, is genetics. In a lecture at a Parapsychology Foundation conference I pointed out the abundance of evidence that paranormal gifts are dependent on our DNA. A number of parapsychologists disliked my point of view because it implied that psi would then be of a material nature, just like the form of our noses and ears, and the color of our eyes and hair.

I was extremely pleased by the words of the S.P.R. president at the gala dinner of the Centenary-Jubilee Conference at Trinity College, Cambridge, in August 1982. I was pouring out a glass of port when I heard him say, "Thanks are due to our honorary members, Professor Robert Thouless, and George Zorab, for their contributions to parapsychology." I was so surprised that I poured the port out onto the dining table instead of into the glass.

Bibliography for George Zorab

(1940). A case for survival. *Journal of the Society for Psychical Research*, 31, 142–152.

(1949). *De Opstandingverhalen in het Licht de Parapsychologie* (The Resurrection Narratives in the Light of Parapsychology). 'S-Gravenhage: H. P. Leopold.

(1952). *Magnetiseurs en Wondergenezers* (Magnetism and Miracle Healers). Leiden: Numij.

(1954). *Wondern der Parapsychologie* (Wonders of Parapsychology). Amsterdam: G. W. Breughel.

(1957). *Bibliography of Parapsychology*. New York: Parapsychology Foundation.

(1957). ESP experiments with psychotics. *Journal of the Society for Psychical Research*, 39, 162–164.

(1958). *Parapsychologie*. 'S-Gravenhage: Universiteit voor Zelfstudie.

(1964). A further comparative analysis of some poltergeist phenomena: Cases from Continental Europe. *Journal of the American Society for Psychical Research*, 58, 105–127.

(1967). Belgium and the Netherlands. In E. J. Dingwall (ed.), *Abnormal Hypnotic Phenomena: A Survey of Nineteenth-Century Cases*, Vol. II (London: J. & A. Churchill).

(1970). Test sittings with D. D. Home at Amsterdam. *Journal of Parapsychology*, 34, 47–66.

(1973). The Sitoebondo poltergeist (Java, 1893): A firsthand account written soon after the events. *Journal of the American Society for Psychical Research*, 67, 391–406.

(1974). A tribute to Emilio Servadio on his seventieth birthday. *Parapsychology Review*, 5, 4, 7–11.

(1975). *D. D. Home the medium: A Biography and a Vindication*. Unpublished manuscript. (Pub. in Italian as *D. D. Home il Medium*, Milan: Armenia Editore, 1976).

(1980). *D. D. Home, Het Krachtigste Medium aller Tijden* (D. D. Home, The Most Powerful Medium of All Time). The Hague: Uitgeverij Leopold.

(1983). The forlorn quest. In W. G. Roll, J. Beloff, & R. H. White (eds.), *Research in Parapsychology 1982* (Metuchen, N.J.: Scarecrow Press).

(1984). *Spokenen Spookverschijnselen* (Poltergeists and Their Phenomena). Den Haag: Leopold.

For a complete bibliography of Zorab's works see:

van der Sijde, P. C. (1986). In Snel, F. W. J. J. (ed.), *In Honour of G. A. M. Zorab* (The Hague: Nederlandse Vereniging voor Parapsychologie).

Bernard Grad

Bernard Grad was born February 4, 1920, in Montreal, Canada. He received a bachelor's degree with honors in biochemistry in 1944 and his Ph.D., *magna cum laude*, in experimental morphology from McGill University in 1949.

Together with M. M. Hoffman and D. L. Wilansky, he won the CIBA Foundation's award for studies in problems in aging in 1955 and was appointed lecturer in the Gerontologic Unit of the Allan Memorial Institute of Psychiatry, McGill University, that same year. He became sssociate professor there in 1965 and associate director of biological studies in 1969. In 1972 he received appointment as associate scientist at Royal Victoria Hospital in Montreal and in 1985 became associate professor at the University of Quebec, Montreal.

Dr. Grad has been a pioneer in psychic healing research. He was the first to demonstrate under controlled laboratory conditions that the laying-on of hands by a healer was effective in speeding up the healing process in animals and, indeed, could benefit all living things. Dr. Grad discusses his own paranormal experiences, his work with Wilhelm Reich in the early 1950s, and his subsequent investigations with Oskar Estebany of "healing energy" on humans, animals, and plants. He ties together historical and current theories of "bioenergy" and emphasizes the need for scientific investigation and the dispelling of superstitious religious myths often attached to healing.

Bernard R. Grad

Experiences and Opinions of An Unconventional Scientist

How did I become involved in investigating healing by touch?

I began my studies of healing by the laying-on of hands thirty years ago and since then I have had ample time to consider what led me to become involved in such studies in the first place. This is an important question because as far as I am aware, there were no researchers in this field prior to my entry into it and indeed there are still relatively few now that the door has been opened. Such a reluctance may be due to the belief that it simply is not possible for healing to take place by such means — that is, that there is no phenomenon to be investigated here at all. Or the investigator may simply lack interest in the subject. Or in the really critical case, he may have an interest in looking at this age old practice but is put off by the difficulties in which he may find himself enmeshed once he makes any efforts in this direction. These difficulties, he will soon find, are more of a sociopolitical than scientific nature.

In 1957 when I started studies into the laying-on of hands (sometimes referred to as LH), I was well aware that I was treading in forbidden terrain, as I had already personally witnessed the imprisonment of Wilhelm Reich for his studies on the life energy. (He subsequently died in prison in the United States.) So the risks involved were very alive in my mind at that time. In this light it may appear even stranger that I should still have become involved in such studies.

I believe that there was a significant personal factor in my becoming involved with the phenomenon of LH to the degree that I did. Long before I had an intellectual interest in the question, I had a number of experiences that gave me a gut feeling about an energy present in the atmosphere around us and in some way associated with the wellbeing of my body. Some of these experiences go back to my earliest childhood while others occurred during my twenties and to some degree even later. At the present time, whenever I am challenged (or I challenge myself) as to whether I did the right thing by becoming involved in this research, I find myself returning

146

to these experiences as well as to the experiments I subsequently conducted.

One of my earliest memories of such formative experiences involved seeing a thin mist or fog or clouds moving in patches around the room on first awakening in the morning. As I lay on my back observing them, I noticed them right up to the ceiling. This was a fairly common experience in childhood for me but I have seen them also several times as an adult.

Another experience which has accompanied me throughout life is to look at the floor of any room and sense a kind of pulsatory movement between my eyes and the floor. I usually experience this motion while relaxed but alert. No sense of dizziness accompanies these sensations. Most of the time I see the floor much as everyone else does. Often I was also aware of this pulsatory activity on a much more extensive scale all around me when I walked out of the house on a fine sunny day. Often I also felt a strong sense of expansion at these times. These experiences took place on city streets but this awareness of energy was even more intense in a large city park or in the countryside.

Still another experience as a child was touching a city curbstone which had been moistened and experiencing a strong tingling sensation in the hands. In quiet moments in those years I have heard sounds of the pulsing of an ocean reminiscent of those normally heard when holding a large sea shell to the ear. Years later, as an adult I again heard these sounds under conditions which added to my feeling that I was hearing the pulsing of the energy ocean in which we are all immersed. I should like to add here that I never had ear or eye problems and I only began to wear glasses for reading when I was in my fifties.

In 1942 while lying in bed for months on end battling tuberculosis in a sanatorium, I came to experience energy as a tide, flowing in during one time of the day and flowing out later in the day. This was repeated many times, day after day, week after week.

These, and the earlier experiences, were something which I took for granted as perceptions of my body working much as one takes for granted one's breathing or the sound of one's heart beating. I felt no need for me at that time to concern myself about them, much less even discuss them with others because I assumed that everyone normally experienced such sensations at one time or other.

However, the encounter which changed all this was the one I had on August 6, 1945, the day the first atomic bomb was dropped on Hiroshima. On that day while lying down, I experienced quite suddenly and without warning a movement of "something" starting from the region of the heart down the left side of the body, down the left leg across to the right leg as if there was no physical barrier between the two legs, up the right side of the body back to the heart, only to repeat itself several times more and then suddenly stop. The sensation was as intense as if I had put my finger in an electrical outlet and it thoroughly frightened me.

In retrospect, I see this event as being a turning point in my life for no longer was I content to quietly enjoy my bioenergetic experiences as they arose. That is, whereas up to this time I just lived the experience of these phenomena without feeling the need to discuss them with anyone or trying to intellectualize about them, after the 1945 experience, I came to have an intense desire to understand them intellectually and I started searching for some written description of this subject.

This had two consequences: I began reading the psychoanalytic literature and undertook an intense self-analysis which involved the use of the free association method for an hour every day for two years. I felt that in the process of becoming a young adult I had somehow become alienated from important elements in myself. And so, I undertook the task of self-analysis because I felt it necessary to embark on a journey of the rediscovery of the self.

My feeling is that breakthroughs in some types of knowledge have as a precondition the elimination of certain blind spots in our perceptions so that we may see things more directly and freshly. I am convinced that the work of self-analysis was helpful in this direction. Moreover, I often have the feeling that those who fight parapsychologists with a special fury are in the category of those fighting some unconscious attitudes in themselves. For all their intelligence I often feel that they have no real insight into themselves nor, it seems to me, do they wish to.

In 1948 I met up with Wilhelm Reich's work on an energy associated with life. That marked the point at which I began to understand intellectually the bioenergetic nature of the experiences described earlier. At that time also I began the regular use of the orgone accumulator (ORACC), a device which Reich developed as a way of accumulating the atmospheric bioenergy and transmitting it to organisms, including humans.

While sitting in the ORACC in the period between 1948 and 1950 I repeatedly experienced bioenergetic streamings on my back, frequently heard the oceanic sounds mentioned earlier and repeatedly felt being charged up after a half hour of its use. Several times I tried staying longer than half an hour and then was forced to get out because of the feeling of being over-charged.

In 1949 I met Wilhelm Reich and began experiments with the ORACC. This included among other studies an investigation which lasted four years on the effect of the ORACC on the lymphatic leukemia of AKR mice and found that this treatment significantly lowered the incidence of this disease. That is, about 70 percent of the treated animals presented this disease at death as compared with about 90 percent of the untreated controls. As over 200 animals were used in this study, the difference in the

incidence of leukemia between the control and the treated mice was shown
to be highly significant, that is, very unlikely to be due to chance.

These and other experiments as well as my personal experiences with
the ORACC convinced me that it was not just a box. The experiments with
the ORACC marked the beginning of a pattern I have tried to follow where
possible: to test phenomena that interest me both subjectively by experiencing them directly and objectively by experimentation on animals, plants
or nonliving things. The ORACC also prepared the way for my experiments
with the healer.

In 1957 Reich was imprisoned for disobeying an injunction imposed
by the Food and Drug Administration that he no longer conduct any further
studies with the life energy, not only in humans but even in animals. In
October, 1957, I met the healer Oskar Estebany, and we began our studies
on November 2, 1957. Reich died on November 3, 1957, and I was informed
of that fact the next day.

During the first meeting with Estebany in October (I had never met
a healer before) I asked how it was possible to heal by the laying-on of
hands. He replied that he believed that in this process he transmitted
energy, not from himself, but from the atmosphere. When he made that
statement, I was immediately reminded of how the ORACC was supposed
to work and my thought at that time was that if what this man was saying
was true, then as a healer he must be functioning like a living ORACC.

Estebany also claimed to experience sensations of "something" moving
in his hands as well as vibrations and heat particularly when he placed his
hands on those places where the patient claimed to feel ill. Indeed, he
claimed that if heat developed in his hands when he placed them on a certain part of the body, then that was diagnostic of illness in that part even
if the patient was not previously aware of this.

We agreed to work in the laboratory on animals and plants. It should
be apparent that I embarked on these LH studies because of my personal
experiences with energy, my exposure to Reich's ideas of a living energy and
because of my experiments with the ORACC.

A word might be said about the term *energy* as used here. Most people
with no special training in science readily understand what is meant when
they or others say that they have energy or lack it. Everyone agrees that the
young have more energy than the old, that the strong have more energy
than the weak, and that we have more energy in health than in disease. We
all know we need to eat and to rest to restore our energy which is needed
to keep our body functioning, to help us do work, and to play. Perhaps a
better term, however, than *energy* would be *energy fields*. In any case, for
those who know the experience, the sensation of something moving in the
body, and not always in strict conformity with anatomical structures, it is
a memorable one. My view is that when we refer to the common experience

of having more or less energy under the various circumstances of life, we really mean *energy* and are not being metaphorical.

What is my most important contribution to the field?

My contribution has been in the field of healing by touch, and to understand its extent it is necessary to describe briefly the historical context in which I began my research on the laying-on of hands.

Most people in the West first become acquainted with LH by reading the Bible and particularly the stories of the healings by Jesus. However, there is evidence that LH was practiced long before the time of Jesus, and not only by the people in the eastern Mediterranean region but all over the world. Laying-on of hands was, and still is, a method of healing that arises spontaneously everywhere. Jesus used a variety of methods to heal and these were, and are, regarded by his followers as miracles. Because LH was one of the methods used by Jesus to heal, it was assumed that LH was also a miraculous method of healing. Although healing by LH was not regarded by Jesus himself as a miracle, Christians down through the centuries continued to feel that it was. And this has been the attitude of a large number of people down to our own time.

When Mesmer first came on the scene in the latter part of the 18th century, the religious attitude towards healing still predominated. For example, the Austrian priest and healer Father Gassner insisted that healing would occur only if the patient proclaimed his belief in Jesus. In a confrontation with Father Gassner, Mesmer demonstrated that making a statement of belief in Jesus was not an essential condition for healing. That is, for the first time, Mesmer demonstrated that healing by LH was essentially a natural and not a religious phenomenon. However, later, the Royal Society of Medicine in Paris rejected LH as a genuine and useful method of healing while the French Academy of Sciences rejected the reality of a healing energy, called the magnetic fluid by Mesmer. Still, one of the five commissioners of the Royal Society, the botanist de Jussieu, disagreed with the others and wrote that some real cause was operating in some of the cases treated magnetically.

The critical experiments that were the basis of the rejection of Mesmer's claims are shoddy by today's standards even though some famous names were involved in the investigations. One of these was Benjamin Franklin, American ambassador to France at the time. Franklin was considered an authority in the then young science of electricity because of his famous kite experiment by which he proved that lightning is electricity and because he invented the lightning rod.

The particular "experiment" decisive in convincing Franklin that Mesmer's animal magnetism did not exist took place as follows at Franklin's residence at Passy: Deslon, a court physician and a follower of Mesmer, touched an apricot tree in Franklin's garden, thereby presumably passing animal magnetism to it. The tree was at a considerable distance from the other trees in the garden and it was Deslon's claim that one of his patients, a boy of 12, would be able to recognize which tree was magnetized by the reactions the boy felt when he touched the magnetized tree or trees. When the boy was brought into the garden blindfolded and led to four trees in succession, he reacted to the first and fourth. However, none of these four trees was magnetized, the magnetized tree actually being 24 feet away. On this test, and only on this test, was the idea of the existence of animal magnetism rejected by Franklin. Franklin did no other experiments on this subject. The experiments on which the other members of the Academy and the Royal Society based their rejection of LH as a therapy and animal magnetism as a reality were no better than the one on which Franklin based his decision.

With the discovery of hypnosis by Mesmer's pupil, the Marquis de Puysegur, interest in the healings produced by the laying-on of hands began to recede and to be replaced with the more spectacular phenomena induced by hypnotism. Indeed, the real differences between the phenomena produced by LH and by hypnosis came to be blurred and it came to be assumed that LH was just hypnotism. As part of the process, Mesmer, and not Puysegur, was made the discoverer of hypnotism and encyclopedias and dictionaries repeatedly equate mesmerism (LH) with hypnotism.

In short, in 1957 when I started my studies on LH with Estebany, there were two main attitudes towards LH. One, held by official bodies of science and medicine, was that any effects due to LH were at best due to suggestion or hypnosis and in any case animal magnetism was a chimera. The other attitude was that held by more or less religious people in the West, namely, that the healing effects of LH were miraculous when done in the name of Jesus. Other types of healing were the work of the devil.

My contribution to the field was initiation of LH experiments not with humans but with animals, plants, and even nonliving things such as normal saline, cloth and so on (Grad, Cadoret, & Paul, 1961; Grad, 1963–1979). This was decisive in eliminating the questions of suggestion or hypnosis usually invoked when human subjects are involved. Moreover, the design of the experiments was the same in every way as if I were conducting experiments on drugs, hormones, vitamins, or other substances. That is, sufficient numbers of replicates were involved to take into consideration biological variation and to permit statistical evaluation of the data at the end of the experiment. Also, suitable controls were part of each experiment and in many of the experiments, double and multiple blinds were introduced. The only unconventional aspect of the study was the LH treatment. When LH was indeed shown to have effects on biological processes, the transmission of an energy (animal magnetism, orgone, or however it is termed) was postulated as being the agent responsible for the effects. In short, my paradigm was very close to that of Mesmer's but my experiments had the advantage of two centuries of work on experimental design and statistical methods.

To the best of my knowledge, I was the first to report studies with LH in the scientific literature. I have seen two earlier reports on attempts to heal by prayer but none of healing by LH. Reports of LH studies are also completely absent from the parapsychological literature prior to my first report in 1961, as far as I am aware. One reason for this may be because most of the researchers in parapsychology were trained as psychologists, while the methods I employed in LH required training in biology. But there may also have been some reluctance by some parapsychologists to become involved with healers who work by laying-on hands, which requires that the healer come in direct contact with the patient. Parapsychologists have difficulty enough dealing with the opposition of the scientific community for working with clairvoyants and other psychics without becoming involved with healers and so incur the additional burden of opposition by medical authorities. Despite all this, not long after my first publication in this field, reports from other parapsychologists began to appear.

There is still another point to be made here: the paradigm used in my LH studies is not the same as the ones generally accepted by the parapsychologists. In my paradigm, I assumed that the hands were a place of energy discharge from the healer's bodily energy and especially when in contact with the patient. I made that assumption because of the bioenergetic sensations reported by the healer as occurring in the hands. The expression "laying-on of hands" arose because historically, the hands were most often imposed on the patient because that was most convenient. The humor of the situation aside, one does not usually hear of laying-on of feet at least in our culture, although they may be just as effective if not more so than the hands for at least some healers. The Dutch healer Croiset stated that he could heal better with his feet than with his hands. There is an Eastern tradition which holds that the big toe of the guru carries much power, and consequently, kissing the big toe is an ancient custom known there. However, healing with feet is generally not used to any degree in the West as it certainly seems more convenient to use the hands and is probably less offensive for some.

The situation may be different again with other healers who may be able to heal with their eyes. The photos of Ted Serios could have been due to energy discharge through the eyes although healing was not involved in his case. Then again, there are those who attempt to heal by going into some alternative state in which they attempt union with the patient at a distance, long distances being no apparent impediment. With the latter we have come to the current parapsychological paradigm which implicates the centrality of mind in the healing process. It is interesting that some of those who teach healing in this way claim that LH healing may be dangerous, although there are anecdotal data over thousands of years that show otherwise. Indeed, some healers with long experience claim to heal both by LH and at a distance. There seems to be no fundamental opposition between the two methods of healing.

With the anxiety expressed by some parapsychologists, no wonder that more conventional scientists did not become involved in studies with healers. Certainly, there was, and is, no lack of healers even in the West where they are generally forced underground. In the United Kingdom, where such healing is legal, an association of healers numbers about 4500 and there is said to be several times that number outside of the association. Rational methods for deciding who really is a healer are obviously needed. Moreover, not all healers are temperamentally suited for scientific investigation but there are enough who are and would be willing to work cooperatively in scientific studies. Given the large numbers of people involved in this type of activity for millennia and given also that the experimental designs and statistical methods required to deal with these problems scientifically have been available for a long time, it is surprising that the phenomenon should have been so totally ignored by the scientific community in this century. The close identification of LH with religion may be a factor blocking an understanding that this form at least of the so-called faith healing can be studied scientifically. Conflicts of interest may also be involved.

As already mentioned, not long after the first publications of my studies, several reports by other professionally trained people appeared. The studies published so far reveal the surprising potential of one living organism to help heal another by means not hitherto suspected by the scientific community. What is even more important is that these studies show that the body has a much greater potential to heal itself than hitherto imagined by trained professionals in the field. Books on healers are appearing in considerable numbers and interest is still growing. Generally, however, people studying healing scientifically are still doing so against the powerful pressure of blind prejudice, risking their careers. Such discrimination, which is not tolerated in other aspects of life in the West, seems perfectly acceptable in this field and what is most surprising and even frightening is that the persecutors are people who have been trained to look at things objectively and to "prove all things."

It is sometimes said that it would be desirable if scientists would become more involved in politics. In general, I agree with this statement but the poor treatment of scientists with views radically different from the conventional one points to the need for checks on the political involvement of the scientific establishment. Science is beginning to come on as a kind of substitute religion and it is clear that some scientists are already lining up to become gurus. Generally, I consider scientists as a group fair and objective but some of them are still quite able to act irrationally out of unconscious prejudice.

What might I have done differently, or what beliefs of mine were changed because of my experiments?

Despite my experiences and experiments with life energy as described earlier in this chapter, I came to the study of the laying-on of hands without any knowledge about the healer phenomenon. Also, my rigorous training in biomedical research influenced me profoundly and on first undertaking the studies with the healer, it did seem to me far-fetched that objects, living and nonliving, could be affected by the simple commonplace action of bringing the hands in close contact with them. No wonder then that I responded with astonishment on seeing that LH did in fact reliably affect biological process in mice.

Since that time, I have tested a considerable number of parameters, on both living and nonliving objects, for their responsiveness to LH (many of these studies have still not been reported). The outcome is not so much that my beliefs changed but that I acquired a set of beliefs I didn't have before. Moreover, I became involved in the LH phenomenon because I was interested in bioenergy and as a result of seeing the LH phenomenon at work in widely different but interconnected realms that included the physical as well as the biological, I am convinced now more than ever that there is an energy at work not only in the biological but also in the physical realm. The nature of that energy will preoccupy us for a long time to come.

It is interesting that I emphasize the biophysical targets whereas previously those who believed that if LH had any effect at all, it was due to psychological factors operating in the recipient of the treatment. (Psychological factors operating in the healer seem definitely to be involved, however.) As the experiments of Mesmer and those who were interested in this field dealt exclusively with people, the effects of suggestion were undoubtedly substantial. But even here, effects were also observed in infants who were not hypnotizable, but opponents of the fact that there was a physical reality behind the psychological one preferred to gloss over these observations. On the other hand, I developed my convictions about the efficacy of LH by investigating the effects of LH on biophysical objects where it is not possible to invoke suggestion as a factor.

Other beliefs I have acquired since undertaking my first studies in 1957 are that healers can make a significant impact on disease and that the extent to which this is possible will vary with the healer, with the disease, and with the patient. And of course, I do not believe that healers can heal everyone of all illnesses, which is another way of saying that I do not believe that through this method of healing we have all the answers to health care.

Although precise statistics are not available as yet — these are certainly needed and funds should be made available — patterns are becoming apparent. It seems to me that one of these patterns is that there are specialists among healers just as there are among physicians; some healers are more successful with some diseases than others. One healer may be more helpful in treating goiter than another, but the latter may be more effective in kidney disease or in setting bones.

Another opinion of mine is that faith in a healer or a higher power is not essential for healing to take place in most cases, although such an attitude may certainly be helpful. If faith were essential, why then did significant changes appear in animals, plants, and even nonliving objects? On the other hand, for a patient to try too hard to believe may be detrimental as it may interfere with the patient's capacity to relax sufficiently to receive the healing. However, I feel that the really important ingredient is that the patient have an open mind about the possibility of being healed. It is certainly essential that the patient not be negative about the treatment, that is, convinced even before the laying-on of hands begins that nothing can happen under such circumstances. Negative attitudes towards conventional treatment are also counterproductive.

Since becoming involved in the LH studies, I have met a large number of people who claim to be able to heal one or another condition by LH and I feel that there is a considerable underground of such people who learn of their capacity quite spontaneously, often suddenly, and often in difficult and sometimes traumatic circumstances. The population of healers can be of very considerable help to the medical profession in the fight against disease if physicians as a group could ever surmount the difficulties, personal and professional, that stand in the way of seeing that this is so. That LH really has this potential can readily be shown, I believe, in properly designed experiments, but no one can predict when official bodies of medicine will be willing to undertake such studies and assess them as fairly and rationally as they would other potential health aids. However, important progress is being made by the introduction of therapeutic touch to the nursing profession.

In all of this, I acknowledge the primacy of a scientific approach to medicine and have not ever proposed the introduction of an irrational hocus-pocus to this field. At the risk of being repetitious, which stems from my belief that the LH phenomenon has received colossal inattention during the scientific era, I do believe that there is a rational, scientifically investigatable, objective core to the LH phenomenon. Moreover, I feel that we will learn a great deal about how the body maintains and heals itself by studying the LH phenomena and in so doing, greatly simplify medical understanding by bringing in new synthetic concepts. True, medicine today has much to be proud of but there are dangers too. These include an ever increasing cost even as new knowledge is gained and new techniques of healing are introduced.

It is not unthinkable that unless giant steps are taken to simplify present-day methods, our present system of health care will be placed in jeopardy through its sheer complexity and cost of delivery. If medical establishments continue to be insensitive to these issues, they may well find their authority seriously challenged in the future.

I also believe that healers themselves have to be very careful about how they project themselves if their acceptance by established scientific and medical bodies is ever to come about. We have often heard the expression that some doctors like to act as if they were God. Well, healers can show doctors a lesson or two in that kind of behavior. Because healing of this type has been associated for so long with Jesus, many Christian healers feel that they can heal because of their belief in Jesus. From there it is a short step for a few of them to proclaim that their power extends not only to healing but to all aspects of life. Such healers are not beyond seeing themselves as new cult figures leading the multitudes back to the Promised Land. I have drawn an extreme picture here but it has happened and may happen again. However, the vast majority of healers I have met, while religious, see themselves as ordinary people doing their best to relieve human misery without any grandiose plans in mind. It is such people that will make a rapprochement possible between natural healing methods and scientific medicine. I see an urgent need for both.

I hope that all this does not give the impression that I am antireligious. However, religion has long made so-called faith healing its prerogative and while some aspects of it, such as healing by prayer, still are, it is high time that science had a close look at the laying-on of hands phenomenon as a natural process.

Furthermore, I do not believe that healers are necessarily highly evolved spiritual beings just because of their ability to heal. Historically, some have been known to seek to take unfair advantage because of this gift. My point is that the attitude of healers and physicians should be alike in their wish to bring healing to the sick. If a patient has the potential insight to learn a spiritual lesson from his disease, he will—no matter by what method or by whom he is healed. On the other hand, proclaiming that one has a special dispensation from God because one can heal by methods poorly understood at the present time will certainly delay the day when the full power of scientific inquiry can be brought to bear on this ancient and significant method of healing.

There is another belief I acquired while investigating this type of healing. When I first began the LH studies, I had a rather naive view of the politics of science. I believed that when one did experiments carefully with the best available techniques and reported the findings, other scientists would become interested and we would engage in fruitful dialogue which would include further experimentation. Scientists in two different laboratories did repeat my plant experiments using people other than those with whom I worked (Macdonald, Hickman, & Dakin, 1976). These obtained statistically significant differences and reported their findings. Still another investigator also obtained statistically significant results using my plant model experiment but he decided not to report the findings for fear of the consequences for his career. Another (Miller, 1971–1972) used his own experimental model, showed striking differences in an experiment involving healing at a distance and reported the findings. Still other scientists extended my findings with studies on enzyme activity, salmonella, and so on (Smith, 1969, 1972, 1976a, 1976b; Rauscher, Rubik, & Gatto 1979).

But other experiences taught me how the judgment of a scientist can be influenced by the nature of the question being put to the scientific test. Such prejudices may be present in even highly prestigious scientists. Earlier, it was pointed out on what a flimsy basis Benjamin Franklin came to his opinion that animal magnetism did not exist. Most people, including most scientists, have no way of proving all things to themselves and so it is natural for them to defer to "gurus," to those whom they feel, and who often feel themselves, have a greater widsom on all matters, including those in which they may not have any direct experience. The wisdom of these "gurus" is then taken as infallible and in this way obstacles develop around even attempting investigation of certain phenomena.

Such obstacles sometimes take on the nature of taboos for which punishment is meted out when transgressed and they can be operative in society for centuries as in the case of LH phenomena and life energy. I believe that the right attitude towards any scientific issue in which one has not had direct experience, is neither acceptance nor rejection, but a holding of the question in mind until direct experience can decide the issue. Such an attitude requires detachment, patience and a low level of anxiety without which one might otherwise be impelled to act precipitously to "settle the matter" without adequate testing.

Although my studies have been mentioned in the great majority of books on healing for the lay public, the response from the biomedical community has been silence by and large. Naturally, I am disappointed but I am by no means devastated. The loss at the bottom line is that of humanity at large in its fight against illness. I have come away from this experience with the feeling that there is in many scientists a definite block to objectivity on this issue, a block that keeps them from seeing the potential for the scientific community to learn about hitherto unknown fundamental processes of healing.

I was unaware of the complexity of the issues surrounding this phenomenon when I began my studies and as this tangled situation still exists, I can't see myself doing things any differently a second time around. However, I definitely see attitudes changing everywhere in regard to holistic and alternative approaches to medicine and this may make the life of future researchers in this field more agreeable.

What unusual experiences I have had that exceeded even my "boggle threshold?"

I don't recall any such experiences, "boggling" being my limit so far. I have already mentioned that when I first saw the effect of the laying-on of hands on the healing of mice, this was quite a "boggle" experience for me. Much later, I worked with another healer who claimed to be able to mummify dead birds and fish. We eventually came to working with bananas and when I saw that soft and mushy fruit become hard as wood, I sure did some "boggling." An interesting process is involved here and further work is required to elucidate it. But by and large, this entire series of studies has been one of natural progression, though leaps are undoubtedly to be expected.

What advice would I give to young people entering the field as to what areas I feel are of utmost importance and what pitfalls to be aware of?

There are several main areas of the utmost importance in the study of healers. One involves the study of the clinical effects healers may have on humans. It is really important to get beyond the anecdotal stage and into the stage of scientific investigation with the careful documentation of case histories and the full battery of clinical, biochemical, radiological, etc., tests which would normally be applied in the study of any other agent suspected of having healing potential. This type of testing would necessarily involve the approval and full cooperation of physicians.

Another area of almost equal importance, and in which the factor of suggestion would certainly be greatly reduced, is the field of healing animals. Similar testing techniques can be applied here as with humans but in this case the cooperation of veterinarians would be necessary.

The other important field of study is the effect of LH on plants and even nonliving systems, such as water and other materials. My studies convince me that healers can have effects here where suggestion certainly cannot be said to play any role at all. To show effects in this field is of fundamental significance as it would link the LH process with chemistry and physics. I believe that naturally occurring disease triggers off their energy best of all and for that reason healers prefer to work with sick people or sick animals. It has occurred to me that this ability of one organism to heal another (and I have some evidence that some animals at least can also do this) may have an evolutionary basis, that is, it arose naturally as a way of coping with a hostile environment which certainly includes the occurrence of disease. On the other hand, studies with nonliving systems are desirable to see if an energetic process is involved. From this, it should be clear that the potential field study of LH effects is very wide and has significance for science from physics to medicine.

What are some of the ideal conditions required to exploit the rich potential of this field? An open mind; an insatiable curiosity; a tireless persistence; a rigorous training in science; a capacity for resisting indoctrination sometimes administered as part of a technical training otherwise useful; a special capacity for being able to function in the laboratory with more than one paradigm; lots of money, preferably your own, for greater freedom; a group of close friends with whom you can interact on a personal basis to overcome the isolation imposed on you by uninterested or unsympathetic scientific peers; enough stability and adaptability to survive the turmoil that not infrequently accompanies studies on life energy; no great hankering for honors or promotions to positions of influence or power. These then are some of the ideal conditions, which are hardly ever met in the real world of imperfection. Expect the unexpected because your life is bound to be full of surprises. Finally, the joys of discovery and understanding are so great in themselves that the failure to receive lesser rewards is no great loss in the end.

Bibliography for Bernard R. Grad

(1963). A telekinetic effect on plant growth. *International Journal of Parapsychology,* **5**, 117–133.

(1964). A telekinetic effect on plant growth. II. Experiments involving treatment of saline in stoppered bottles. *International Journal of Parapsychology,* **6**, 473–498.

(1965). Some biological effects of the "laying-on of hands": A review of experiments with animals and plants. *Journal of the American Society for Psychical Research,* **59**, 95–127.

(1966). The "laying-on of hands": Implications for psychotherapy and the placebo effect. *Corrective Psychiatry and Journal of Social Therapy,* **12**, 192–202.

(1967). The "laying-on of hands": Implications for psychotherapy, gentling and the placebo effect. *Journal of the American Society for Psychical Research,* **61**, 286–305.

(1970). Healing by the laying-on of hands: Review of experiments and implications. *Pastoral Psychology,* **21**, 19–26.

(1971–72). Some biological effects of the laying-on of hands: A review of an experiment with animals. *Journal of Pastoral Counseling,* **6**, 38–41.

(1976). The biological effects of the "laying-on of hands" on animals and plants: Implications for biology. In G. Schmeidler (ed.), *Parapsychology: Its Relations to Physics, Biology, Psychology and Psychiatry* (Metuchen, N.J.: Scarecrow Press).

(1977). Laboratory evidence of the "laying-on-of-hands." In N. Regush (ed.), *Frontiers of Healing* (New York: Avon Books).

(1978). Laying-on of hands: Implications for psychotherapy, gentling and the placebo effect. In M. Ebon (ed.), *The Signet Handbook of Parapsychology* (New York: New American Library).

(1979). Healing by the laying-on of hands: A review of experiments. In D. Sobel (ed.), *Ways of Health* (New York: Harcourt Brace Jovanovich).

(1980). Healing and dying. *Journal of Pastoral Counseling,* 15, 50–54.

(1981). Paranormal healing and life energy. *ASPR Newsletter,* 7, 21–22.

(1961). With Cadoret, R. J., and Paul, G. I. An unorthodox method of treatment of wound healing in mice. *International Journal of Parapsychology,* 3, 5–24.

Secondary Bibliography

Bartlett, L. E. (1978). Bernard Grad and energy. *Human Behavior,* 7, 6, 29–32.

Shubin, S. (1980). Scientific proof of psychic healing. *Fate,* December, 49–54.

Related Studies by Other Researchers

Braud, William (1984). The influence of "psychokinetically treated" saline upon the growth of rye grass seeds. Personal communication.

Fuller, J. G. (1974). *The Surgeon with the Rusty Knife.* New York: Crowell.

Heidt, P. (1981). Scientific research and therapeutic touch. In M. D. Borelli, & P. Heidt (eds.), *Therapeutic Touch: A Book of Readings* (New York: Springer).

Krieger, D. (1979). *Therapeutic Touch: How to Use Your Hands to Help or Heal.* Engelwood Cliffs, N.J.: Prentice Hall.

Krippner, S., & Villoldo, A. (1986). *The Realms of Healing,* (rev. ed.) Millbrae, Calif.: Celestial Arts.

Pleass, C. M., & Dey, N. D. (1986). Using the Dopler effect to study behavioral responses of motile algae to psi stimulus. In D. Weiner & D. Radin (eds.), *Research in Parapsychology, 1985* (Metuchen, N.J.: Scarecrow Press).

References

Akers, C. (1984). Methodological criticisms of parapsychology. In S. Krippner (ed.), *Advances in Parapsychological Research*, Vol. 4 (Jefferson, N.C.: McFarland).

Barrett, W. F. (1926). *Death-bed Visions*. London: Methuen.

Batcheldor, K. J. (1984). Contributions to the theory of PK induction from sitter-group work. *Journal of the American Society for Psychical Research*, **78**, 105–122.

Bergson, H. (1914). Presidential address to the Society for Psychical Research (1913). *Proceedings of the Society for Psychical Research*, **27**, 157–175.

Carrington, H. (1957). *The Case of Psychic Survival*. New York: Citadel.

Cavanna, R., & Servadio, E. (1964). *ESP Experiments with LSD 25 and Psilocybin: A Methodological Approach*. New York: Parapsychology Foundation.

Collins, H. M. (1985). *Changing Order: Replication and Induction in Scientific Practice*. London: Sage Publications.

Coover, J. E. (1975). *Experiments in Psychical Research at Leland Stanford Junior University*. New York: Arno Press (orig. pub. 1917).

Dunne, J. W. (1958). *An Experiment with Time*. New York: Hillary (orig. pub. 1927).

Ehrenwald, J. (1948). *Telepathy and Medical Psychology*. New York: W. W. Norton.

Ehrenwald, J. (1954). *New Dimensions of Deep Analysis*. New York: Grune and Stratton (2d ed., New York: Arno Press, 1975).

Ehrenwald, J. (1963). *Neurosis in the Family: A Study of Psychiatric Epidemiology*. New York: Harper and Row.

Ehrenwald, J. (1966). *Psychotherapy: Myth and Method, an Integrative Approach*. New York: Grune and Stratton.

Ehrenwald, J. (1966). The telepathy hypothesis and schizophrenia. *Journal of the American Academy of Psychoanalysis*, **2**, 159–169.

Ehrenwald, J. (1978). *The ESP Experience: A Psychiatric Validation*. New York: Basic Books.

Ehrenwald, J. (1978). Einstein skeptical of ESP? Postscript to a correspondence. *Journal of Parapsychology*, **2**, 137–142.

Ehrenwald, J. (1984). *Anatomy of Genius: Split Brains and Global Minds*. New York: Human Sciences Press.

Ehrenwald, J. (1984). Right- versus left-hemispheric approach to psychical research. *Journal of the American Society for Psychical Research*, **1**, 29–39.

Eisenbud, J. (1946). Telepathy and problems of psychoanalysis. *Psychoanalytic Quarterly*, **15**, 32–87. Reprinted in G. Devereux (ed.), (1953), *Psychoanalysis and the Occult* (New York: International Universities Press).

Eisenbud, J. (1947). A reply to Ellis. *Psychiatric Quarterly*, **21**, 26–40. Reprinted as The Eisenbud Findings, in G. Devereux (ed.), (1953), *Psychoanalysis and the Occult* (New York: International Universities Press).

Eisenbud, J. (1963). Psi and the nature of things. *International Journal of Parapsychology*, **5**, 245–273.

Eisenbud, J. (1967). *The World of Ted Serios*. New York: William Morrow.

Eisenbud, J. (1970). *Psi and Psychoanalysis*. New York: Grune & Stratton.

Eisenbud, J. (1982). *Paranormal Foreknowledge: Problems and Perplexities*. New York: Human Sciences Press.

Eisenbud, J. (1983). *Parapsychology and the Unconscious*. Berkeley, Calif.: North Atlantic Books.

Elkes, J. (1967). Introductory remarks to ACNP: Session on diphenylhydantoin. *International Journal of Neurospychiatry*, **3**, Supplement 2, S7–S8.

Estabrooks, G. H. (1961). A contribution to experimental telepathy. *Journal of Parapsychology*, **25**, 190–213 (orig. pub. 1927).

Fodor, N. (1938). A letter from England [blood test experiments with Eileen Garrett]. *Journal of the American Society for Psychical Research*, **32**, 6, 186–189.

Freud, S. (1933). *New Introductory Lectures on Psycho-analysis*. London: *Standard Edition*, **22**.

Gallup, G. (1978). High belief in paranormal phenomena. *Gallup Poll Release*, June 15.

Gallup, G., & Proctor, W. (1982). *Adventures in Immortality: A Look Beyond the Threshold of Death*. New York: McGraw-Hill.

Garrett, E. J. (1952). The ghost of Ash Manor. *Tomorrow*, 1, Autumn, 50–66.

Garrett, E. J. (1968). *Many Voices: The Autobiography of a Medium*. New York: Putnam.

Grad, B. (1963). A telekinetic effect on plant growth. *International Journal of Parapsychology*, **2**, 117–133.

Grad, B. (1964). A telekinetic effect on plant growth. II. Experiments involving treatment of saline in stoppered bottles. *International Journal of Parapsychology*, **4**, 473–498.

Grad, B. (1965). Some biological effects of the "laying-on of hands": A review of experiments with animals and plants. *Journal of the American Society for Psychical Research*, **59**, 95–127.

Grad, B. (1966). The "laying-on of hands": Implications for psychotherapy and the placebo effect. *Corrective Psychiatry and Journal of Social Therapy*, **2**, 192–202.

Grad, B. (1967). The "laying-on of hands": Implications for psychotherapy, gentling and the placebo effect. *Journal of the American Society for Psychical Research*, **4**, 286–305.

Grad, B. (1970). Healing by the laying-on of hands: Review of experiments and implications. *Pastoral Psychology*, **206**, 19–26.

Grad, B. (1971–72). Some biological effects of the laying-on of hands: A review of an experiment with animals. *Journal of Pastoral Counseling*, **6**, 38–41.

Grad, B. (1977). Laboratory evidence of the "laying-on of hands." In N. Regush (ed.), *Frontiers of Healing* (New York: Avon Books).

Grad, B. (1978). Laying-on of hands: Implications for psychotherapy, gentling and the placebo effect. In M. Ebon (ed.), *Signet Handbook of Parapsychology* (New York: New American Library).

Grad, B. (1979). Healing by the laying-on of hands: A review of experiments. In D. Sobel (ed.), *Ways of Health* (New York: Harcourt Brace Jovanovich).

Grad, B. R. (1976). The biological effects of the "laying-on of hands" on animals and plants: Implications for biology. In G. Schmeidler (ed.), *Parapsychology: Its Relations to Physics, Biology, Psychology and Psychiatry* (Metuchen, N.J.: Scarecrow Press).

Green, C. (1960). Analysis of spontaneous cases. *Proceedings of the Society for Psychical Research*, **53**, 97–161.

Hansel, C. E. M. (1961). A critical analysis of the Pearce-Pratt experiment. *Journal of Parapsychology*, **25**, 87–91.

Haraldsson, E., & Osis, K. (1976). OOBEs in Indian swamis: Sathya Sai Baba and Dadaji. In J. D. Morris, W. G. Roll, & R. L. Morris (eds.), *Research in Parapsychology 1975* (Metuchen, N.J.: Scarecrow Press), pp. 147–150.

Haraldsson, E., & Osis, K. (1977). The appearance and disappearance of objects in the presence of Sri Sathya Sai Baba. *Journal of the American Society for Psychical Research*, **71**, 34–43.

Hardy, A. (1966). *Gifford Lectures. Vol I: The Living Stream*. London: Collins.

Hardy, A. (1967). *Gifford Lectures. Vol. II: The Divine Flame*. London: Collins.

Haynes, E. S. P. (1925). *The Belief in Personal Immortality*, 2d ed. London: Richards (1st ed., 1913).

Haynes, R. (1970). *Philosopher King: The Humanist Pope Benedict XIV*. London: Weidenfeld.

Heywood, R. (1964). *ESP: A Personal Memoir*. New York: Dutton.

Hollós, I. (1933). Psychopathologie alltäglicher telepathischer Ercheinungen. *Imago*, **19**, 529–546. Summarized in G. Devereux (ed.), (1953), *Psychoanalysis and the Occult* (New York: International Universities Press), pp. 199–203.

Janet, P. (1930). *L' automatisme Psychologique*, 10th ed. Paris: Alcan.

Jourdain, E. F., & Moberly, C. A. (1932). *An Adventure*. London: Faber (orig. pub. 1911).

Kuhn, T. S. (1970). *The Structure of Scientific Revolutions*, 2d ed. Chicago: University of Chicago Press.

Lambert, G. W. (1955). Poltergeists, a physical theory. *Journal of the Society for Psychical Research*, **38**, 684, 49–71.

Lambertini, P. (1734, 1738) *De Servorum Dei Beatificazione et Beatorum Canonizatione*, 2 vols. Bologna.

Lang, A. (1908). *The Maid of France*. London: Longmans Green.

McConnell, R. A., Snowdon, R. J., & Powell, K. F. (1955). Wishing with dice. *Journal of Experimental Psychology*, **50**, 269–275.

Macdonald, R. G., Hickman, J. L., & Dakin, H. S. (1976). Preliminary physical measurements of psychophysical effects associated with three alleged psychic healers. San Francisco: Washington Research Center.

Miller, R. (1971–1972). The effect of thought upon the growth of remotely located plants. *Journal of Pastoral Counseling*, **6**, 61–63.

Mitchell, A. M. J., & Fisk, G. W. (1953). The application of differential scoring methods to PK tests. *Journal of the Society for Psychical Research*, **37**, 45–60.

Mitchell, E. D. (1971). An ESP test from Apollo 14. *Journal of Parapsychology*, **35**, 89–107.

Murray, M. (1921). *The Witch Cult in Western Europe*. Oxford.

Osis, K. (1952). A test of the occurence of a psi effect between man and cat. *Journal of Parapsychology*, **16**, 233–256.

Osis, K. (1956). ESP tests at long and short distances. *Journal of Parapsychology*, **20**, 81–95.

Osis, K. (1961). *Deathbed Observations by Physicians and Nurses* (Parapsychological Monographs No. 3). New York: Parapsychology Foundation.

Osis, K. (1965). ESP over distance: A survey of experiments published in English. *Journal of the American Society for Psychical Research*, **59**, 21–46.

Osis, K. (1970). ESP over long distances: In search of transmitting energy. Paper presented at the 137th Meeting of the American Association for the Advancement of Science, Chicago.

Osis, K. (1973). What can be done in space experiments that cannot be done in earth experiments? In W. G. Roll, R. L. Morris, & J. D. Morris (eds.), *Research in Parapsychology* (Metuchen, N.J.: Scarecrow Press), pp. 54–55.

Osis, K. (1974). Space, time, and consciousness in a parapsychological view. In E. Bauer (ed.), *Psi und Psyche: Festschrift für Hans Bender* (Stuttgart: Deutsche Verlagsanstalt).

Osis, K. (1976). Channel characteristics of ESP. *Proceedings of the 3rd International Conference of Computer Communications* (Toronto, Canada), pp. 23–27.

Osis, K. & Bokert, E. (1971). ESP and changed states of consciousness induced by meditation. *Journal of the American Society for Psychical Research*, **65**, 17–65.

Osis, K., Bokert, E., & Carlson, M. L. (1973). Dimensions of the meditative experience. *Journal of Transpersonal Psychology*, **5**, 109–135.

Osis, K., & Fahler, J. (1965). Space and time variables in ESP. *Journal of the American Society for Psychical Research*, **59**, 130–145.

Osis, K., & Foster, E. (1953). A test of ESP in cats. *Journal of Parapsychology*, **17**, 168–186.

Osis, K., & Haraldsson, E. (1977). *At the Hour of Death*. New York: Avon Books.

Osis, K., & Haraldsson, E. (1979). Parapsychological phenomena associated with Sri Sathya Sai Baba. *The Christian Parapsychologist*, **3**, 159–163.

Osis, K., & McCormick, D. (1980). Kinetic effects at the ostensible location of an out-of-body projection during perceptual testing. *Journal of the American Society for Psychical Research*, **74**, 319–330.

Osis, K., & Pienaar, D. (1956). ESP over a distance of seventy-five hundred miles. *Journal of Parapsychology*, **20**, 229–232.

Osis, K., & Turner, M. E., Jr. (1968). Distance and ESP: A transcontinental experiment. *Proceedings of the American Society for Psychical Research*, **27**, 1–48.

Osis, K., Turner, M. E., Jr., & Carlson, M. L. (1971). ESP over distance: Research on the ESP channel. *Journal of the American Society for Psychical Research*, **65**, 245–288.

Oteri, L. (ed.). (1975). *Quantum Physics and Parapsychology: Proceedings of an International Conference Held in Geneva, Switzerland, August 26–27, 1974.* New York: Parapsychology Foundation.

Otto, R. (1958). *The Idea of the Holy.* New York: Oxford University Press.

Palmer, J. (1978). Extrasensory perception: Research findings. In S. Krippner (ed.), *Advances in Parapsychological Research, Vol. 2* (New York: Plenum).

Parapsychological Association. (1985). Report I: Terms and methods in parapsychological research. Chapel Hill, N.C.: The Association.

Radner, D., & Radner, M. (1982). *Science and Unreason.* Belmont, Calif.: Wadsworth.

Rauscher, E. A., Rubik, B. A., & Gatto, L. (1980). Effects on motility behavior and growth rate of salmonella typhimusium in the presence of a psychic subject. In W. G. Roll (ed.), *Research in Parapsychology 1979* (Metuchen, N.J.: Scarecrow Press).

Rhine, J. B. (1934). *Extra-sensory Perception.* Boston: Boston Society for Psychical Research. (Reprinted, with a new introduction, by Branden in 1964.)

Rhine, J. B. (1934). Telepathy and clairvoyance in the normal and trance state of a "medium." *Character and Personality*, **3**, December, 92–111.

Rhine, J. B. (1947). *The Reach of the Mind.* New York: William Sloane.

Rhine, J. B., & Humphrey, B. M. (1944). The PK effect: Special evidence from hit patterns. II. Quarter distributions of the set. *Journal of Parapsychology*, **8**, 254–271. (b)

Rhine, J. B., Humphrey, B. M., & Pratt, J. G. (1945). The PK effect: Special evidence from hit patterns. III. Quarter distributions of the half-set. *Journal of Parapsychology*, **9**, 150–168.

Rhine, J. B., & Pratt, J. G. (1954). A review of the Pearce-Pratt distance series of ESP tests. *Journal of Parapsychology*, **18**, 165–177.

Rhine, J. B., & Pratt, J. G. (1961). A reply to the Hansel critique of the Pearce-Pratt series. *Journal of Parapsychology*, **25**, 92–98.

Rosenthal, R. (1966). *Experimenter Effects in Behavioral Research*. New York: Appleton-Century-Crofts.

Roy, A. (1982). Precognition—A sort of radar? In I. Grattan-Guinness (ed.), *Psychical Research: A Guide to Its History, Principles and Practices*. Wellingborough, Northamptonshire: Aquarian Press.

Rush, J. H. (1964). *New Directions in Parapsychological Research*. (Parapsychological Monographs No. 4.) New York: Parapsychology Foundation.

Rush, J. H. (1979). A non-verbal GESP study with continuous recording. In W. G. Roll (ed.), *Research in Parapsychology 1978* (Metuchen, N.J.: Scarecrow Press).

Rush, J. H. (1986). Physical and quasi-physical theories of psi. In H. L. Edge, R. L. Morris, J. Palmer, & J. H. Rush, *Foundations of Parapsychology*. London: Routledge & Kegan Paul.

Rush, J. H., & Jensen, A. (1949). A reciprocal distance GESP test with drawings. *Journal of Parapsychology*, **13**, 122–134.

Schmeidler, G. R. (1943). Predicting good and bad scores in a clairvoyance experiment: A preliminary report. *Journal of the American Society for Psychical Research*, **17**, 103–110.

Schmeidler, G. R. (1958). Analysis and evaluation of proxy sessions with Mrs. Caroline Chapman. *Journal of Parapsychology*, **22**, 137–155.

Schmeidler, G. R. (1960). *ESP in Relation to Rorschach Test Evaluation*. (Parapsychological Monographs, No. 2) New York: Parapsychology Foundation.

Schmeidler, G. R. (1961). Evidence of two kinds of telepathy. *International Journal of Parapsychology*, **3**, 5–48.

Schmeidler, G. R. (1961). Are there two kinds of telepathy? *Journal of the American Society for Psychical Research*, **55**, 87–97.

Schmeidler, G. R. (1962). ESP and tests of perception. *Journal of the American Society for Psychical Research*, **56**, 48–51.

Schmeidler, G. R. (1964). An experiment in precognitive clairvoyance. Parts I–V. *Journal of Parapsychology*, **28**, 1–27; 93–125.

Schmeidler, G. R. (1971). Mood and attitude on a pretest as predictors of ESP retest performance. *Journal of the American Society for Psychical Research*, **65**, 324–335.

Schmeidler, G. R. (1973). PK effects upon continuously recorded temperature. *Journal of the American Society for Psychical Research*, **67**, 325–340.

Schmeidler, G. R. (1974). Respice, adspice, prospice. *Proceedings of the Parapsychological Association*, **8**, 117–145.

Schmeidler, G. R. (1977). Looking ahead: A method for research on survival. *Theta*, **5**, 2–6.

Schmeidler, G. R. (1983). Psi scores and personality: Basic questions and a theory to encompass the answers. *Parapsychology Review*, **14**, 1–3.

Schmeidler, G. R. (1985). Field and stream: Background stimuli and the flow of ESP responses. *Journal of the American Society for Psychical Research*, **79**, 13–26.

Schmeidler, G. R., & Goldberg, J. (1974). Evidence for selective telepathy in group psychometry. In W. G. Roll, R. L. Morris, & J. D. Morris (eds.), *Research in Parapsychology 1973* (Metuchen, N.J.: Scarecrow Press).

Schmeidler, G. R., & Le Shan, L. (1970). An aspect of body image related to ESP scores. *Journal of the American Society for Psychical Research*, **64**, 211–218.

Schmeidler, G. R., & McConnell, R. A. (1973). *ESP and Personality Patterns*. Westport, Conn.: Greenwood Press (orig. pub. 1958).

Schmidt, H. (1969). Precognition of a quantum process. *Journal of Parapsychology*, **33**, 99–108.

Schmidt, H. (1973). PK tests with a high-speed random number generator. *Journal of Parapsychology*, **37**, 105–118.

Schmidt, H. (1976). PK action on pre-recorded targets. *Journal of the American Society for Psychical Research*, **70**, 267–292.

Schouten, S. A. (1979). Analysis of spontaneous cases as reported in *Phantasms of the Living*. *European Journal of Parapsychology*, **2**, 408–454.

Schouten, S. A. (1981). Analyzing spontaneous cases: A replication based on the Sannwald collection. *European Journal of Parapsychology*, **4**, 9–48.

Schouten, S. A. (1982). Analyzing spontaneous cases: A replication based on the Rhine collection. *European Journal of Parapsychology*, **4**, 113–158.

Schouten, S. A., and Kelly, E. F. (1978). On the experiment of Brugmans, Heymans, and Weinberg. *European Journal of Parapsychology*, **2**, 274–290.

Schwarz, B. E. (1971). *Parent-child Telepathy: A Study of the Telepathy of Everyday Life*. New York: Garrett Publications.

Servadio, E. (1935/1953). Psychoanalysis and telepathy. In G. Devereux (ed.), *Psychoanalysis and the Occult* (New York: International Universities Press; orig. pub. 1935).

Servadio, E. (1958). Telepathy and psychoanalysis. *Journal of the American Society for Psychical Research*, **52**, 127–133.

Servadio, E. (1965). *Psychology Today*. New York: Garrett Publications/Helix Press.

Servadio, E. (1977). *Passi sulla Via Initiatica* (Steps on the Way of Initiation). Rome: Edizioni Mediterranee.

Sheldrake, R. (1981). *A New Science of Life: The Hypothesis of Formative Causation*. Los Angeles: J. P. Tarcher.

Sinclair, U. (1962). *Mental Radio*. Springfield, Ill.: Charles C. Thomas (orig. pub. 1930).

Smith, M. J. (1969). Significant results on enzyme activity from healer's hands. *Newsletter of the Parapsychology Foundation*, **16**, 1, 5, 18.

Smith, M. J. (1972). Paranormal effects on enzyme activity. *Human Dimensions*, **2**, 15–19.

Smith, M. J. (1976a). Enzymes are activated by the laying on of hands. *Human Dimensions*, **5**, 1 and 2, 46–48.

Smith, M. J. (1976b). Paranormal effects on enzyme activity. *Human Dimensions*, **5**, 1 and 2, 49–51.

Spinelli, E. (1977). The effects of chronological age on GESP ability. In J. D. Morris, W. G. Roll, & R. L. Morris (eds.), *Research in Parapsychology 1976* (Metuchen, N.J.: Scarecrow Press).

Stanford, R. G., & Palmer, J. (1972). Some statistical considerations concerning process-oriented research in parapsychology. *Journal of the American Society for Psychical Research*, **66**, 166–179.

Stanford, R. G., Zenhausern, R., Taylor, A., & Dwyer, M. (1975). Psychokinesis as psi-mediated instrumental response. *Journal of the American Society for Psychical Research*, **69**, 127–133.

Tenhaeff, W. H. C. (1960). Seat experiments with Gerard Croiset. *Proceedings of the Parapsychological Institute of the State University of Utrecht*, **1**, 53–65.

Ullman, M. (1950). On the occurrence of telepathic dreams. *Journal of the American Society for Psychical Research*, **53**, 2.

Ullman, M. (1966). An experimental study of the telepathic dream. *Corrective Psychiatry and Journal of Social Therapy*, **12**, 2.

Ullman, M. (1973). A theory of vigilance and dreaming. In V. Zigmund (ed.), *The Oculomotor System and Brain Functions* (London: Butterworths).

Ullman, M. (1980). Psi communication through dream sharing. In B. Shapin & L. Coly (eds.), *Communication and Parapsychology* (New York: Parapsychological Foundation).

Ullman, M., Krippner, S., & Vaughn, A. (1973). *Dream Telepathy.* New York: Macmillan.

Vasiliev, L. L. (1963). *Experiments in Mental Suggestion.* Hampshire, England: Institute for the Study of Mental Images.

Warcollier, R. (1975). *Experimental Telepathy*, J. Gridley, trans. New York: Arno Press (orig. pub. 1938).

Zorab, G. (1957). *Bibliography of Parapsychology.* New York: Parapsychology Foundation.

Zusne, L. (1985). Magical thinking and parapsychology. In P. Kurtz (ed.), *A Skeptic's Handbook of Parapsychology.* Buffalo, N.Y.: Prometheus Books.

Index

169

170   Index